The Triple Revolution

SOCIAL PROBLEMS IN DEPTH

Robert Perrucci
Purdue University

Marc Pilisuk
University of California, Berkeley

Little, Brown and Company
Boston

LIBRARY OF CONGRESS CATALOG CARD NO. 68-18418

SIXTH PRINTING

PUBLISHED SIMULTANEOUSLY IN CANADA BY LITTLE, BROWN & COMPANY (CANADA) LIMITED

PRINTED IN THE UNITED STATES OF AMERICA

Dedicated to a generation who will use its compassionate understanding of people and social problems to build a more humane social order

PREFACE

This book was written to achieve a two-fold goal: first, to acquaint students with three significant social changes that are shaping the character of life in the 20th century, and second, to examine various solutions to problems engendered by these changes which will require fundamental shifts in American social institutions.

We have given serious consideration to the point of view that American society is in difficulty, that it is facing demands that question the very viability of our society as we know it. Rather than a society which is essentially healthy while beset by particular problems, we see a society whose very patterns of successful adjustment are causing severe and widening strains in accommodating to new and different circumstances.

We do not intend to be merely prognosticators of gloom; rather we are hopeful that in focusing a social problems text upon future and more basic problems of society, we may be helping to create those conditions from which new and more adaptive institutions will emerge.

Some elements of our approach are not typical of the field of social problems. There is no chapter specifically devoted to crime and delinquency, none on racial prejudice, none on mental illness, alcoholism, or drug addiction. Where these topics are discussed, it is in the context of more basic social trends which are precursors of such symptomatic manifestations of deeper problems.

While the organization of the book is based upon analysis of three converging revolutionary changes, the theory presented is not one clearly associated with a single discipline. We have drawn from the physical sciences and from political science, from depth psychology and urban sociology, from economic theory and strategic analysis— and more. Our sources cover this wide range because the substance of the book is defined by social problems as they are occurring right now—either in the form of human suffering or political controversy. The findings of the National Automation Report, the Moynihan controversy over the Negro family, the controlled response military doctrine, the urban riots, the plight of the migrant worker, the use of computers in social planning, the lessons of the Vietnam war, the protest movement—all are part of American life.

In our integrating text at the beginning of each section, we have tried to apply social science to these problems, rather than defining the problems within the limits of the currently existent concepts of a particular discipline. By so doing we believe that we have assembled a book of readings which will be useful in courses dealing with contemporary American society, as well as in social problems courses. Ordinarily the sociologist, psychologist, political scientist, historian, or iii social welfare specialist teaching courses concerned with contemporary problems will be able to supplement the crystallized problem statements in the selected articles with material from his own disciplinary framework, or with a more orthodox textbook on social theory. What we have tried to present is the basic substance of the problems, and the controversies over their solutions. The problems are delineated against a background which emphasizes their interrelatedness and indicates their future direction.

We would like to express our appreciation to the authors, as well as the publishers, of the readings for allowing us to reprint their works in this book. We also wish to thank Phyllis Pilisuk and Lynn Bozoki for their assistance in the selection of materials, Dena Targ and Joan Flint for their help in the preparation of the manuscript, and Carole Halpin for her careful and extensive work in obtaining the articles selected to appear in this book.

CONTENTS

v

INTRODUCTION:
Social Problems and the Triple Revolution

In March 1964 in Washington a meeting of 32 noted social critics produced a policy statement entitled "The Triple Revolution" (1964). The purpose of the statement was to call attention to changes in our society which were so revolutionary in magnitude that the society's current response to them was proving totally inadequate, and to point out that radical new measures were needed. The three revolutions— in warfare, cybernation, and human rights—were seen to reflect the theme of man's being increasingly compelled to play the servant rather than the master role in the technologies he has created. While most of the paper dealt with the cybernetic revolution and with policies appropriate to the resultant large-scale displacement of labor, the authors also presented the idea that the three problem areas were interrelated, and that the points of convergence among them exposed some of the critical foci of balance and stress in American society.

It seemed to us that the authors of the paper had hit upon a compelling theme and one that would be helpful in understanding the mass of seemingly separate and unrelated problems in our society. (An extremely negative press reaction to the proposals of that paper revealed that the analysis had cut into cherished values which were the underpinnings of the social fabric.) We felt this paper provided an excellent starting point from which to define and explore a pattern of illness which gave rise to many diverse symptoms of human distress on the American scene.

Before we can attempt to show the extent to which the umbrella of the triple revolution covers the field of contemporary problems, it is first necessary to give our own definition of a social problem and to explain the nature of the social scientist's concern with the world of problems.

SCIENCE AND SOCIAL PROBLEMS. All scientists rely on their value preferences, for these are ultimately their guides to selection of what is worthy of study. The study of social problems has provided social scientists with the particular advantage of permitting them to test the applicability of their knowledge to the resolution of human problems. There are, however, some apparent conflicts between the scholar's motivation to study people and societies and his motivation to study social problems. As an ideal (which is only approximated but, nevertheless, important) the impulse of the social scientist stems from a desire to discover principles governing the operation of social systems. He brings to this task scientific methods involving strict attention to the standards of a value-free approach to his chosen subject matter. For example, when he asserts that certain procedures at meetings are dysfunctional to the achievement of certain outcomes or that certain vii practices reduce the frequency of deviant actions, he is not passing judgment on whether efficiency in meetings, or deviant actions, should be reduced or encouraged. But as soon as that same "pure" social scientist selects a social problem as the starting point of his inquiry he is in effect saying, "Certain social conditions are 'bad' and others are 'good.' " His motivation here is to change the "bad," and extend the "good."

These two motives for the study of society have been able to flourish (without creating a major social problem in professional associations of social scientists) because of accommodations between scientific and ameliorative interests. These accommodations:

1. assert the reality of the interplay between "pure" theory and applied-practical work—theory can be advanced by practical work and much can be accomplished in problem solution by the use of established social theory;

2. maintain a commitment to the "machinery" of science such that investigations of social problems are carried out according to accepted standards of scientific research;

3. develop a definition of social problems that will isolate the subject of study without requiring individual social scientists to state their own value preferences.

An examination of many existing definitions of social problems reveals several common properties: Social problems are conditions that (1) affect a large number of people, (2) in ways that negatively affect their own value preferences, and (3) about which they think some action can and should be taken. Most of the elements in this definition can be traced to the early work of Fuller (1938) and Fuller and Myers (1941a; 1941b).

The difficulties involved in maintaining the above view of social problems have become increasingly apparent. First of all, the extreme subjectivism of this approach limits the social analyst to examining those conditions which have been found to be undesirable by consensus. Merton (1966) has raised a similar criticism in his response to Fuller and Myers' definition and has noted how considerations of power and authority enter into the process of defining a condition as a social problem. Becker (1967) has also raised questions about Fuller and Myers' conception of social problems, but he, essentially, supports the view that a defining process by certain persons or groups provides the important starting point for study.

In addition to the above-mentioned limitations there are several other factors that we believe severely limit the usefulness of current social science perspectives on social problems.

1. Different persons and groups in American society possess varying amounts of social power and prestige. Relative advantage in this connection allows some persons and groups to get items of interest placed on the social agenda (i.e., to define social problems). The differential distribution of opportunity to place items on the social agenda in-

validates the free competition of ideas notion implicit in current views, and itself represents a social problem.

2. The idea of a collectivity of concerned citizens defining social problems is much like that of participatory democracy of the pluralist society, and the pure competition of the free market. The view seems less well suited in an age of professional social problem definers, and governmental agencies whose mandate is uncovering and solving social problems. The specialization inherent in the organization of professional problem-solvers serves to fragment definitions of problems in accordance with departmental or bureau interests, and encourages the avoidance of massive attacks on social problems that cut across jurisdictional lines. (In this connection, see the article by Daniel Moynihan in Chapter 8).

3. The dominant view of citizen as definer of social problems fails to take into account the distinction between "personal problems of milieu" and "public issues of social structure" (Mills, 1959). Definitions made in terms of immediate problems of milieu are most likely to lead to solutions that are ways of *handling* or *combating* social problems rather than eliminating the social structural conditions responsible for them. Thus, city riots are handled with more portable swimming pools and anti-riot legislation; neighborhood youth gang disturbances are handled with better police protection; unemployment is handled with welfare checks.

4. Related somewhat to Point 3 above is the tendency among current social problems analysts to define in a restrictive and limiting fashion the boundaries of the social system in which problems exist; the most extensive boundaries are usually the nation state. The growing international involvement of most countries would seem to demand that domestic problems be placed within an international perspective by examining relationships between institutions in the internal system and those in the external system.

5. Current views on social problems may be especially well suited to studying how people respond to social problems *after they have become problems* (in the objective sense that their presence necessarily intrudes on people's consciousness). This may be a part of the reason why social scientists are frequently embarrassed by their failure to anticipate significant national and international events such as the civil rights movement and frequent foreign entanglements involving shooting wars. We cannot satisfactorily anticipate events if we restrict our study to problems which have already emerged full blown.

The remainder of this introduction will consider the concept of social problems that has guided the editors in this book; the concept is related to the interrelated themes of *The Triple Revolution*.

DEFINING SOCIAL PROBLEMS. The definition of a social problem reflects the norms and values of the definer. Science helps us little, for in it there are, in a sense, no troubles, pathologies, or evils; there are only ix conditions and structures which are consequences of other conditions and structures. It is as scientific for a cancerous cell to undergo growth destructive to other parts of the organism as it is scientific for other cells to undergo their more common patterns of growth. The definition of health is a normative concept dependent upon the shared values of longevity, physical capability, and upon the specific preference for normal function as dictated by the theories of medicine about healthy organs.

Our own values and preferences follow from our assumptions about a healthy human being. First, we assume that a healthy individual must be recognized to have intrinsic worth. We believe that his worth is not dependent upon particular achievements but is implicit in the fact of his birth. From this it seems that permitting a child to starve amidst plenty or the loss of a soldier in battle, no less than the assassination of a president, are social problems. This concern with the preservation of life is thrown into the forefront of our attention by the three revolutions occurring in society; particularly by the revolution in the nature of warfare. It is augmented further by a population problem radically different from any which existed previously. During our lives the number of childhood deaths has grown greater than ever before in history and the number is increasing with every year of material progress. Soldiers continue to kill and be killed; deaths of civilians are gradually outweighing those of armies. These are prima facie evidence of problems. Likewise, the possibility of nuclear war represents a social problem of unprecedented magnitude.

Next in importance to the value of life itself is our belief that an individual's worth entitles him to minimum standards of respect from other people. When police with bullwhips, or insensitive hospital personnel, or unfair voting registrars or short-tempered parents abuse the dignity of other people, then social problems are present.

A healthy individual must have resources sufficient to meet his most basic physical and psychological needs and leave him free from anxieties over deprivation or resignation to a life of scarcity. The anguish and despair which follow poverty, discrimination, and illness are also social problems.

There are psychologists who claim further that the healthy individual must maintain a measure of freedom in his choices (Rogers, 1951) and a means to actualize his potentialities (Maslow, 1954). We modify these conceptions slightly to conform to the limitations imposed on man as a member of society. People must be free and able to participate in the formation of those policy decisions which will affect their daily existence. An individual left jobless by his company's decision to move or conscripted to serve in an overseas war of which he disapproves is not living in health if his reservations about the policy concerned were not a material part of the policy decision. By this measure apathy is itself a social problem because it represents an absence of power which makes participation impossible and creates resignation and despair.

Last, a healthy society must develop individuals who will contribute to the well-being of other members of the society. In a highly interdependent society, the consequences of one group's actions have widespread repercussions. The scientist who designs methods of chemical and bacteriological warfare, the investor in a new enterprise, the city planner, the ward nurse, and the voting citizen share responsibility for the consequences of their decisions upon the well-being of others. Conscience and existential guilt are needed in human communities. A social problem exists where people do not assume responsibility for the consequences of their own action or inaction.

It should be clear that in our conception conflict, disorder, and value clashes are not by themselves social problems. Disorder could point up an underlying problem, but it could also be indicative of an adaptive attempt to improve upon bad conditions. The emphasis here is *not* upon social harmony but upon the well-being of the individual as we understand the conditions of such well-being. These are our values and the assumptions by which we define what is and what is not a social problem.

In addition to using our own values and assumptions about a healthy person and healthy society, we are also guided in our selection of problems by a notion of central and peripheral problems. When a man considers his own personality, he is prone to think of his achievements, his aspirations, and his ideals as the central and general characteristics of himself. He tends to see his more serious problems as accidents, as specific deficiencies, or as caused by someone else (if indeed he admits to seeing them at all). There is a tendency among social scientists and laymen alike to look upon their own society in much the same way. Its successes and its ideals are the permanent characterization. Its problems, when they are discovered, are accidents, specific casualties or unfortunate by-products of an otherwise healthy society. The net effect of such social perceptions is to introduce a bias into the analysis of what must be done to meet problems. Perceiving personal problems as superficial and specific permits the individual to carry on his daily activities much as usual without need for a radical and painful reappraisal of himself. Seeing social problems as separate misfortunes or as failures to achieve facile integration into the healthy mainstream of society precludes a search for the underlying pathology beneath such surface eruptions as delinquency, racial violence, bigotry, alienation, conformity, urban slums, and the high school dropout. But the effects by which we label problems are consequences rather than accidents of the social order. It is our desire to show that these and other problems can be understood as manifestations of larger difficulties which are central and even necessary features of American society as it is currently structured.

THE TRIPLE REVOLUTION. The 20th century has confronted American society with both unprecedented progress and unprecedented problems. Economic, scientific, and technological advances have brought xi material abundance, improved health standards, and a phenomenal ability to control nature and turn it to man's uses. Existing alongside all this wealth and mastery over nature are continuing states of international warfare and tension, persistent poverty and despair among millions of Americans, and a growing inability of the many to influence and control the social and political processes that so significantly affect their lives.

Efforts by many public and private groups to deal with these conditions have not yielded results that would encourage optimism. To be sure, in most approaches, war, poverty, and powerlessness are considered either as necessary evils (although not always evil, as wars are fought to preserve our freedoms) or as temporary dislocations which can be remedied. However, under the corrective responses which stem from current approaches, the conditions not only persist but they grow worse. Greater productivity and abundance for some leads to more poverty for the disadvantaged; technological advances that spark economic growth can also be measured in unemployment, worker insecurity, and alienation; and growing sophistication in military weaponry that promised supremacy and reduction of the likelihood of war seems not to have aided in keeping the United States from military involvements in the Middle East, Latin America, Africa, and Southeast Asia.

Conventional attempts to remedy these problems do not seriously question the viability of the American institutions dealing with them. Race relations, delinquency, alienation, and poverty are conceived as problems of specific sub-groups which have not yet achieved adequate integration into the larger society or into one of several interest groups providing individuals with a sense of indentification and potency. Other current conceptions assume that a problem emerges when interest groups disagree on the existence of, or solution to, some social condition. People experiencing dissatisfaction with existing arrangements, it is argued, can come together and have their views tested in the free marketplace of ideas. When groups are not powerful enough to obtain a public hearing of their complaints, it is argued that larger, more powerful forces (e.g., government, business, unions) do balance each other's interests and power in a way that contributes to the general interest.

These traditional views on the emergence and solution of social problems fail to confront the current distribution of power in American society. Established views on interest group politics, pluralism, and countervailing power do seem quite appropriate for dealing with problems that are easily absorbed by American institutions; they seem inadequate for dealing with the revolutionary changes which challenge the very nature of these institutions.

A different conception of social problems and of ways of eliminating them is required by the impact of the three revolutions upon the contemporary scene. The solutions to problems may require a basic

xii

reexamination and remodeling of our existing values and institutions. It is our belief that the revolutions that have occurred in warfare, in cybernation, and in the mobilization of demands for human rights present the society with pressures that threaten the very bases of its stability. Moreover, these revolutions reflect the increasing difficulty experienced by existing institutions in giving full expression to the simple, yet profound, principles by which American society has chosen to be known: democratic processes and the dignity of man.

The technological militarism revolution is found in the elaborate nuclear and ballistic missile technology that is having far-reaching effects upon every phase of American life. The psychological impact of nuclear capabilities may lead to "dehumanization" of certain social relationships and of persons in certain social categories. This psychological defense mechanism is one way of handling anxiety in painful situations. A second consequence is a social defense mechanism, wherein new forms of social organization are devised to handle the threats posed by international tensions. Among these forms are the shelter-centered society with a regimented populace, and the weakening of such values as individual liberty, democratic values, and a community-based society. The final consequence of an existing nuclear technology is its role in maintaining a high level of international tension which permeates many aspects of American life, and gives the military a rationale for its own continuation.

These social and psychological conditions are more than just consequences of nuclear capabilities; they also have the potential for creating greater dependence on military technology to control the fears that the technology itself has created. This process reflects one of the persistent theoretical themes of this book: certain types of technically-oriented social patterns become, with time, autonomous and impervious to attempts designed to redirect activities toward new ends.

The cybernation revolution is reflected in the combined efforts of computers and automated machinery largely though not exclusively as they are applied to the processes of production. The result has been increased productive capacity and decreased dependence upon human labor. For some, cybernation brings great material benefits and the promise of release from the degrading and unchallenging aspects of work; others see in cybernation the problems associated with reduced employment, loss of economic security, and the meaning of a life without work.

The secondary effects of cybernation which extend beyond production and employment are those which threaten to reorganize the nature of economic and social life. The emergence of "conglomerates" in American industry and their relationship to governmental power are indicative of patterns of centralization that render a citizen's participation in the affairs of his nation increasingly difficult. Moreover, cybernation technology shapes the patterns of social life through greater planning of social systems and through increased use of the xiii technology to shape and control the behavior and attitudes of citizens by government or other large organizations.

The human rights revolution is found in the growing demand for full economic, political, and social equality by millions of people in the United States and in many other countries around the globe. The demand for equality in all spheres of life reveals that established institutions have adapted to long-standing inequalities.

The three revolutions are interdependent and mutually reinforcing trends which present us with the progress-problem paradoxes described earlier. The health of a social system must be evaluated relative to the challenges which confront it. The very strengths of American institutions which provide cohesion under moderate challenges may introduce rigidities under conditions which call for a more drastic reorganization of the social order. It is our belief that American society is in serious trouble; that the revolutions wrought by the rapid changes in weaponry, in the utilization of information in cybernetic systems, and in the revolutionary demands of the impoverished around the globe cannot be met by the civilian and military institutions that have so far evolved in our society. Neither does a fair examination of these institutions reveal a capacity for adaptive changes capable of mitigating the emerging problems of centralization in decision-making, of inequitable distribution of opportunities, and of a third world war.

REFERENCES AND ADDITIONAL READING

Ad Hoc Committee, "The Triple Revolution," *Liberation*, April, 1964, 1–7.

Becker, Howard S., ed., *Social Problems: A Modern Approach*, New York: John Wiley, 1967.

Dahl, Robert, *Who Governs? Democracy and Power in an American City*, New Haven: Yale University Press, 1961.

Fuller, Richard C., "The Problem of Teaching Social Problems," *American Journal of Sociology, 44*, November, 1938, 415–435.

Fuller, Richard C. and Richard R. Myers, "Some Aspects of a Theory of Social Problems," *American Sociological Review, 6*, February, 1941, 24–32.

Fuller, Richard C. and Richard R. Myers, "The Natural History of a Social Problem," *American Sociological Review, 6*, June, 1941, 320–328.

Maslow, A. H., *Motivation and Personality*, New York: Harper, 1954.

Merton, Robert K., "Social Problems and Sociological Theory," in R. K. Merton and R. A. Nisbet, eds., *Contemporary Social Problems*, New York: Harcourt, Brace and World, Inc., 2nd edition, 1966.

Mills, C. Wright, "The Professional Ideology of Social Pathologists," *American Journal of Sociology, 49*, September, 1943, 165–180.

Mills, C. Wright, *The Sociological Imagination*, New York: Oxford University Press, 1959.

Presthus, Robert, *Men at the Top: A Study in Community Power*, New York: Oxford University Press, 1964.

Rogers, Carl R., *Client-Centered Therapy*, Boston: Houghton Mifflin, 1951.

Technological Militarism

PART ONE

Technological Militarism

ONE

SOCIAL AND PSYCHOLOGICAL CONSEQUENCES OF NUCLEAR CAPABILITIES

A revolutionary breakthrough has occurred in weapons and in their relation to the men who have created them. We have not merely increased the limits of our destructive capability but have become the first generation easily capable of terminating the complex experiment of human life on this planet. Through the organized efforts of civilized men, all of mankind must live in the shadow of the very real possibility of total destruction. A human or mechanical error, a radar team or a submarine crew acting under stress (imposed perhaps by the fact that no target on the globe is more than fifteen minutes away from a launching device) could cause a war.

How close to an intended gross nuclear attack we have come may never be known since such intentions are usually held in guarded secrecy. Several cases of accidents which have been revealed, however, came close to setting off a nuclear counter-attack in response to signals of attack which were later shown to be false. These cases raise a related question of how to determine whether a real attack is in fact an act of aggression or merely an accident. Surely the decision to launch a civilization-destroying counter-attack should require time to evaluate whether, and from which source, one has actually been attacked and whether the attack was intended. But unfortunately the speed and finality of missile delivery leaves no time for such evaluations (Livant, 1961).

The expressed purpose of technical capability in nuclear weaponry is to use the threat of annihilation to deter aggression. Society lives under this threat which is now continuous rather than merely sporadic. Threats are a form of stress which lead to certain predictable consequences in the behavior of those threatened. Since threats are psychological messages, some intended to deter war have also the capacity to incite one; such a misjudgment could bring on nuclear war. The

3

threats by rival street gangs to keep off each other's "turf" provide an illustration, on a microscopic scale, of how threats made with intention to deter serve actually to incite. This can happen when threats lack the force of an impartial legal system and must rely instead on the stubbornness or hostility of their tone if they are to be believed. The lack of impartial international jurisdiction and the self righteousness of military threats are also a part of the international scene.

The possibility of nuclear war does not come only from the reliance on threats of force by major powers. A majority of the world's population lives under conditions of severe deprivation of food, of medical care, of hope to partake in a more constructive shaping of the lives of their children. People who have long been deprived sometimes act out without fear of consequences; a sinister leader of a small power could bring on a major conflagration between large powers.

The ideas and behaviors of modern man have not kept pace with advances in military technology. It appears that people increasingly have to adjust to the realities of military weaponry but that they apparently have lost the capacity for making the technology adjust to them. One adjustment to painful reality is to deny, repress, or merely forget it. With increasing effort and cost, people struggle to achieve inadequate defenses against the weapon systems they have created. Too often the effort goes on automatically, without reflection on the dangers of such pursuits. In this first section we direct attention to the most urgent of social problems, reminding people of nuclear weaponry, and examining the ways in which people are adjusting to its existence.

The Scientists' Committee Report describes the effect of a single 20 megaton bomb exploded over a major metropolitan area. It is clear and understated in its account of expected damage. Other reports of probable target areas in the United States suggest that the first bomb would likely be accompanied by another on a second target designed specifically for neighboring military installations, with damage extending well into the region affected by the first blast. The Scientists' Committee Report emphasizes blast and incendiary damages. A fuller report of medical effects of thermonuclear attack by the Physicians for Social Responsibility (Ervin, *et al.*, 1962) indicates that radiation illness will be a severe disability and a cause of untimely death or genetic damage among the survivors. Moreover, the utter futility of a shelter program is emphasized in the physicians' report by accounts of the duration of time for decontamination of fertile soil (forty years) and the dangers inherent in a break in the delicate balance of the ecology which permits the continuation of life.

Nuclear weaponry is but one example of the application of technology to serve military purposes. The technology includes the most sophisticated design for guidance of missiles, the most insidious of airborne chemical and bacteriological agents, and the endless gimmickry of subversion, intrigue, and the covert manipulation of foreign affairs. Could this extensive armory of destruction and force be otherwise when more than half our scientists and engineers are employed in its development?

With the coming of the missile age a vast controversy emerged regarding the suitability of fallout shelters, or even underground cities, to live out the period of danger following a nuclear attack. In addition to evidence that such a program just would not work, critics reacted unfavorably to the amount of totalitarian discipline required to keep the system in operation, to the value choices involved in deciding who would be admitted and who would not and even who might have to be eaten when other sources of food were consumed, creating a rather bizarre problem of how to serve one's fellow man. Throughout the controversy it was evident that the basis upon which civil defense was founded was the belief that nuclear war is much like a natural disaster. But with this view one accepts a sense of helplessness in averting the dangerous event and rejects one's own responsibility in contributing to the very conditions which make nuclear war more likely. (Waskow and Newman, 1962; Melman, 1962)

The shelter issue provides a striking instance of the degree to which persons have come to live with the idea that war in the nuclear age is still a viable institution, that preparation for it and defense against it are inevitable parts of the human condition. The same aura of inevitability is prevalent in much of the debate over military conscription which is summarized in the review by Flacks, Howe and Lauter in Chapter Two. How men shall be conscripted to meet the military need is up for debate; whether men should automatically and unquestioningly accept the demands of the military appetite is not ordinarily considered.

The point of contention is not whether we as individuals or as a social system have grown to accept a warlike world as inevitable. What is in contention is whether such preparedness is suitable to the policy purposes for which it was intended. This question will also be discussed at length in the second chapter. The more immediate question may be asked without regard to whether the overall policy of military preparedness is wise or reasonable. We ask here what kind of people, what kind of society have we become as a result of our learning to live with the danger of total war.

The high level of military preparedness and the consequent threat of destruction are facts of modern life. Considering the utter horror of modern war, it seems remarkable that people go about their daily pursuits with only an occasional concern over such crises as the rise in radioactive fallout in milk, the Berlin blockade, the Cuban missile episode, or the Suez. This apparent calm in the face of extreme threat is similar to psychological defense mechanisms which sometimes guard the terminal patient against a full realization of the extent of his

5

illness and hence of the proper measures needed to prolong life. The patient gains, by such defense, a false and comforting security which in fact is not appropriate to the real danger. Bernard, Ottenberg, and Redl suggest the manner in which a composite psychological mechanism, dehumanization, may be affecting wide segments of American society with a similar handicap—an inappropriate adaptation to the constant threat of annihilation and the strains of mass technological society. These effects on large numbers of individuals reflect changes in the society as a whole as it also adjusts itself to the acceptance of military priorities and military values. These are the effects described in Senator J. William Fulbright's speech "The Cold War in American Life." Fulbright notes that our country's values are reflected in an appropriation of funds that does not enable the wealthiest nation on earth to meet the most basic needs of its people, thus illustrating that the pursuit of power is valued above the well being of people.

REFERENCES AND ADDITIONAL READING

Robert A. Dentler and Phillips Cutright, *Hostage America: Human Aspects of a Nuclear Attack and a Program of Prevention,* Boston, Mass.: Beacon Press, 1963.

Frank R. Ervin, *et al.,* "Human and Ecologic Effects in Massachusetts of an Assumed Thermonuclear Attack on the United States," *New England Journal of Medicine,* 266, May 31, 1962, 1127–1139.

Jerome D. Frank, "Breaking the Thought Barrier: Psychological Problems of the Nuclear Age," *Psychiatry,* 23, 1960, 245–266.

Sanford Gifford, "Death and Forever," *The Atlantic,* March, 1962, 88–92.

William P. Livant, "Attack Versus Aggression: How Can We Distinguish?," *Committee of Correspondence Newsletter,* October, 1961, 20, 22.

Seymour Melman, ed., *No Place to Hide: Fact and Fiction about Fallout Shelters,* New York: Grove Press, 1962.

Physicians for Social Responsibility Symposium: The Medical Consequences of Thermonuclear War. *New England Journal of Medicine,* 266: 1126–1155, 1174, May 31, 1962.

Stanley A. Rudin, "The Personal Price of National Glory," *Transaction,* September-October, 1965, 4–9.

Arthur Waskow, ed., *The Debate Over Thermonuclear Strategy,* Boston, Mass.: Heath, 1965.

Arthur Waskow and S. L. Newman, *America in Hiding,* New York: Ballantine, 1962.

6

Scientists' Committee for Radiation Information

The Effects of a 20-Megaton Bomb

This summary will describe in some detail what could happen to the New York metropolitan area and its residents if a single 20-megaton bomb hit Columbus Circle in midtown Manhattan.

While it is not possible to make precise predictions of damage, estimates are possible, based on evidence from test explosions, the atomic drops in Hiroshima and Nagasaki, and various published material. All estimates are derived from unclassified information, with three major sources: *Medical effects of the atomic bomb in Japan, The effects of nuclear weapons,* and *Biological and environmental effects of nuclear war.*[1]

ASSUMPTIONS

Any analysis of effects of nuclear explosion depends on the assumptions made. In this instance:

A 20-megaton bomb is assumed. Bombs of this size are generally believed to exist in substantial numbers. While there is evidence that still larger bombs exist, their effect cannot be estimated here with equal reliability. Nevertheless, one must bear in mind that the results described below could well be exceeded, and perhaps greatly exceeded.

Reprinted by permission of the publishers from *New University Thought,* Spring 1962, pp. 24–32.

[1]*Medical effects of the atomic bomb in Japan,* edited by A. W. Oughterson and S. Warren, McGraw-Hill Co., New York, 1956. *The effects of nuclear weapons,* edited by S. Glasstone and prepared by the U.S. Department of Defense, Atomic Energy Commission, Washington, 1957. U.S. Congress, Special Subcommittee on Radiation of the Joint Committee on Atomic Energy, *Report, Biological and environmental effects of nuclear war.* 86th Congress, 1st Session, June, 1959.

7

Columbus Circle is assumed as a target or hypo-center. This is a well-known landmark.

Clearly there could be a multi-bomb attack. Bombs of various sizes might be used. Target points are not entirely predictable. Considering the effect of a single bomb is helpful for illustration. But damage caused by two bombs appropriately spaced and timed can be greater than the sum of their destructive effects taken separately.

The consequences of exploding the bomb at various heights are contrasted. Particularly, destructive features are emphasized by a ground burst, a typical air burst, or a high altitude burst.

The thermal effects depend strongly on humidity and atmospheric visibility conditions. Assumed here are those conditions that would allow maximal thermal danger. This makes clear the limits of possible destruction and injury; under other conditions the thermal effects would be less severe. An attacker planning to assault a number of targets in a brief time might have limited choice of atmospheric conditions.

THE EXPLOSION AND ITS AFTERMATH

As the bomb explodes, the sky fills with a bluish-white glare. A man standing 60 miles away would see a fireball 30 times brighter than the noonday sun—a fireball hot as the center of the sun.

The fireball rapidly expands until it is 4½ miles wide. As it expands, it begins to rise, scorching an ever-widening area. Meanwhile, if the explosion was a ground *surface burst*, the fireball has sucked up a vast quantity of vaporized earth and debris.

If the bomb were exploded in the *air* on a clear day, the heat would ignite a man's clothing 21 miles away and seriously burn exposed skin at 31 miles. (A contact *surface* burst would cut the distances to 13 and 19 miles.)

The matter sucked up by the fireball in a surface burst starts to condense on reaching upper air layers, five to ten miles up. It spreads out, forming a radioactive, mushroom cloud. The material in this cloud soon begins to descend as fallout.

Meanwhile, an intense pressure wave, or shock, traveling faster than sound, spreads out from the center of the explosion, crushing almost everything in its path until it gradually loses its force.

Following the shock front comes the wind of more than 1000 miles per hour. As it moves outward, the wind diminishes; behind it a vacuum develops. Then the surrounding air rushes in, fanning the fires started by thermal radiation and initial blast damage.

Soon these fires will join and develop into a firestorm that could cover an area many miles across, destroying all that will burn—structures and living things.

The blast itself, from a surface burst, would create a hole 240 feet deep, at its deepest point, and a half mile across. Within a radius of 7.7

8

miles the destruction would be severe. Up to 15 miles the damage would still be heavy.

The population would face several distinct types of hazards, each of which must be coped with successfully for survival. The effects would vary somewhat, depending on whether the bomb drop were a contact surface burst or an air burst. Both are discussed in the report. In summary, a surface burst produces greater local blast damage, heavy local fallout. An air burst produces little local fallout, more world-wide fallout, greater danger of firestorm, and more widespread blast damage.

Seven types of hazards to be considered are as follows: (1) immediate thermal effects, (2) immediate nuclear radiation, (3) blast effects, (4) firestorm, (5) fallout, (6) economic and social disruption, and (7) long-term effects.

IMMEDIATE THERMAL EFFECTS

The fireball gives off a tremendous amount of heat, or thermal energy. One can predict the extent of heat damage by noting the number of calories (unit of heat) per square centimeter of surface a given object would receive if exposed to the flash of the bomb. If the explosion occurs within the atmosphere, the energy *required* for igniting a given material is greater the larger the total energy yield of the bomb. For example, for a 20-megaton bomb, about 7 calories per square centimeter (cal/cm^2) will ignite shredded newspaper, 13 cal/cm^2 will ignite deciduous leaves. At 23 cal/cm^2 most clothing will ignite.

Flash burns are an even more probable danger than the burning of clothing. At Hiroshima and Nagasaki, flash burn casualties were *the* major problem in medical care, accounting for more than half of all deaths.

On a clear day, a 20-megaton (MT) low air burst would produce these injuries to exposed skin:

Third-degree burns (12 cal/cm^2) 27 miles from the explosion

Second-degree burns (10 cal/cm^2) 31 miles away

First-degree burns (4 cal/cm^2) 45 miles away

For a surface burst these distances would drop by 40 per cent because there is less thermal energy to start with, and heat rays near the ground would not travel as far because they are absorbed and scattered by dust, water vapor and carbon dioxide. Unless medical supplies and facilities were somehow spared, the second- and third-degree burns would probably result in death. Such burns nearly always become infected. And radiation further reduces the chances of recovering from even minor infections.

A high altitude burst, say 20 miles up, well above most of the atmosphere, would produce even greater fire damage on earth. Atmospheric haze would reduce the range of heat damage. An explosion in clear air under a cloud layer could increase the range.

9

A person actually seeing the flash of the bomb burst would suffer a burn on the retina, which could lead to blindness. The seriousness of the burn would depend on its size and its location on the retina. For a high burst as opposed to a surface burst the flash would be seen further away. Only sparse information about retinal burns has been declassified. However, it has been disclosed that "a megaton detonation" 40 miles high produced retinal burns in rabbits 340 miles away.

IMMEDIATE NUCLEAR RADIATION

With a small bomb, say 20 kilotons (KT), immediate nuclear radiation is an important hazard; but with a large bomb, such as 20 megatons, it may be ignored because blast and heat effects of a 20-MT weapon are so great that they would far outweigh the immediate radiation danger. For example, 2.5 miles from ground zero the radiation intensity would be about 300 roentgens, a lethal dose for 3 to 18 per cent of those exposed. However, at that distance the 800-m.p.h. wind, the flying debris, and the flash heat would alone suffice to kill an exposed person.

BLAST EFFECTS

Blast damage to a building or other structure may result from one or several causes. First, the shock front squeezes everything in its path. A building may collapse because it is being blown over, or because the external pressure is suddenly so great that all four walls collapse inward.

Arriving with the shock front are the drag forces, in the form of a strong wind. Telephone poles and radio towers that may resist the squeezing effect of the shock front are quite vulnerable to being blown over. Within a few seconds, the shock wave and its accompanying winds have passed.

Following the shock front and drag forces, there is a reversal in pressure. Buildings now experience a partial vacuum and winds blowing back toward the center of the explosion. The stress is less, but it can add to damage on an already weakened structure. Also, the ground shock itself can knock a building down as an earthquake does.

A surface burst on Columbus Circle would produce a mammoth hole. It would cover a 20-block area and be deep enough to hide a 20-story building. The hole would extend from 55th to 63rd Streets and from east of Seventh Avenue to west of Columbus Avenue. The subway systems, which are interconnected in the midtown area, would be penetrated.

Any midtown 20-MT hit is likely to penetrate at least one of the subway tunnels. The deepest tunnel is the BMT 60th Street tunnel under the East River which is down 113 feet. Since all three systems are interconnected in the midtown area, the blast wave would sweep with lethal intensity through a large part of the system. Blast waves in a tunnel

10

maintain their intensity over a longer distance since they cannot spread out.

Within a 7.7-mile radius of Columbus Circle, the blast would produce severe structural damage. At the outer edge of this circle, most unreinforced brick or wood-frame houses would be completely demolished, the result of a peak over-pressure of 5 pounds per square inch (p.s.i.). Brick apartment buildings would probably still be standing, but need major repairs. However, within a 6.4-mile radius, they too would collapse. An air burst would extend the major damage radius to 10 miles.

Within a 15-mile radius, the damage would be less severe but extensive. At the edge of the circle, a wood-frame house might remain standing but need such major repairs that restoration would not be economical. The peak over-pressure at the 15-mile line would be 1.9 p.s.i. This is still enough to tear entrance doors off their hinges, breaking them into pieces, send window glass flying through the house, and dislodge window frames.

Up to 40 miles away, there would be some damage, such as window breakage, in the majority of structures. And under some atmospheric conditions, a New York City explosion could produce shattered windows in Wilmington, Delaware.

The inner circle (7.7-mile radius) of severe blast damage includes, at its outer edges, in Brooklyn, Gowanus Bay, half of Prospect Park, Ebbets Field, and the Bedford-Stuyvesant and Bushwick sections.

In Queens it would include Ridgewood, the western tip of Forest Hills, Corona, and the western edge of the Whitestone section. In the Bronx, Sound View Park, Crotona Park, and New York University. Only the tip of Manhattan above the Cloisters would not be inside this area.

In New Jersey, this zone of mass destruction would include most of Jersey City, Leonia, Ridgefield Park, Teterboro Airport, half of Kearny. The Palisade ridge would probably not provide much protection since blast waves move around such objects.

The 15-mile radius (1.9 p.s.i.) from Columbus Circle would include all of New York City, except Far Rockaway and the area beyond Staten Island Airport. In Nassau County, the eastern portion of the circle would be marked by Elmont, Floral Park, Manhasset, and Port Washington. Much of New Rochelle and of Yonkers would be within the circle. In New Jersey, these cities would be along the perimeter: Paramus, Paterson, West Orange, and Elizabeth.

It should be noted that not all brick houses would collapse within the inner circle, nor would all brick houses remain standing beyond it. There would be individual variations depending on construction differences and variations in the local behavior of the shock front.

The mass destruction of buildings and other objects would have produced an immense quantity of flying debris. It has been determined

11

that chunks of flying glass and masonry could cause casualties up to 15 miles from ground zero. (A casualty is defined as "an individual sufficiently injured to be unable to care for himself and thus becomes a burden to someone else.") It should be noted that small glass fragments lodging in the eye could produce casualties at distances much greater than those cited.

There would also be a third type of blast effect—displacement, such as picking up a man and smashing him into a wall. This, too, could occur as far away as 15 miles from ground zero. A significant number of head and skeletal injuries would occur, with the extent of the injury depending on the distance traveled prior to impact.

THE FIRESTORM

A prime threat to urban populations after a thermonuclear explosion is the firestorm. Firestorm develops when a mass of fresh air breaks into a large area with a high density of fires and replaces the hot rising air. This mass of fresh air may move with hurricane velocity. The wind causes the fires to merge and encompass the entire area.

The fires can start in two ways. First, thermal radiation would ignite trash, window curtains, dry grass, leaves and, toward the interior of the fire zone, many less flammable materials. Second, the blast would upset stoves, cause electrical short circuits, break gas lines and burst underground oil storage tanks. All of these would become ignition points.

Within the radius of 21 miles from Columbus Circle, it is probably conservative to predict an average of ten ignition points per acre in every part of the city (except for the southern part of Staten Island, which is outside this line and is partly shielded by the terrain). Since New York City covers about 200,000 acres, this would probably result in nearly 2 million fires in the city. The Fire Department could hardly cope with such a staggering number, even if it were prepared. In this case, most of the force would be unable to respond, most equipment would be unusable, water pressure would be inadequate, and many rubble-lined streets would be impassable.

In view of the density of combustible material in many parts of the city, a firestorm is probable. (The contents of a fire-proof building are combustible, even if the building is not.)

At Hiroshima, where a far smaller bomb (20 KT) was dropped, a firestorm developed and eventually covered a radius of about 1.2 miles. In Nagasaki, no firestorm developed, apparently because natural winds carried the fire into an area where there was nothing to burn. Still, all buildings in Nagasaki within 1.25 miles of ground zero were destroyed by flames.

There are, however, not enough data to justify quantitative predictions of the firestorm area.

The most complete data on firestorm casualties come from Hamburg,

12

Germany, where a firestorm occurred July 27, 1943, after pre-nuclear incendiary air raids. Some 60,000 persons were killed, almost as many as in the atomic bomb drop on Hiroshima.

Hamburg police engineers estimated that temperatures in the burning city blocks were as high as 800°C (about 1500°F). Wind velocity exceeded 150 m.p.h. Hundreds of persons were seen leaving shelters as the heat became unbearable. They ran into the streets and slowly collapsed. Days after the raids ended, as home shelters were opened, there was enough heat remaining inside for the influx of oxygen to cause the shelters to burst into flames. Many bodies had been cremated.

Death from intense heat can occur in ways other than burning or disintegration. Heat stroke can occur in a temperature of 140°F. Exterior damage can close off ventilation in a sheltered area.

Also, carbon monoxide poisoning would be one of the chief types of injuries expected. In World War II it was a common cause of death in public air raid shelters and improvised home shelters. Carbon monoxide casualties are nearly always expected in flaming buildings, where exits have been blocked by rubble. Under such conditions, a cellar protected from the blast could become a tomb. In Hamburg, it is estimated that 70 per cent of all casualties not caused by mechanical injuries or burns were brought on by carbon monoxide.

DISRUPTION OF PHYSICAL FACILITIES

Careful consideration of problems that arise from wide breakdown of physical facilities and social services in the event of a nuclear explosion is vitally important to any discussion of survival. Such consideration, however, leads beyond the competence of the Scientists' Committee for Radiation Information. At best, this segment of the report can suggest problems of physical disruption that deserve more systematic study.

In all previous American experience with large-scale disaster, relief and reconstruction assistance poured in from other communities, state, national or international agencies. It seems probable that in the event of a 20-MT nuclear explosion on New York City other major population centers in the Northeast would be attacked too. This would limit prospects for outside help in dealing with consequences of the attack.

Problems of transportation facilities: This problem may be regarded in three categories: thoroughfares, fuel, and machines. Throughout the area of the 15-mile radius from ground zero, debris would clog streets with little hope of early clearance. No vehicle could be expected to pass. It is probable that many bridges would not be serviceable and that tunnel entrances in Manhattan would be blocked. Rail and subway lines would most likely suffer commensurately. Transportation equipment remaining after blast and fire would find extremely limited fuel since local supplies would be largely consumed in mass fires. The breakdown of transportation would immediately hamper or prevent rescue, evacu-

13

ation, and emergency assistance measures. Later its impact would be felt in terms of the absence of such important products as food, medical supplies, and fuel—including fuel for central electric generators.

Problems of water supply: It seems probable that many water storage tanks, some mains, filtering and purification equipment and pumps would be destroyed or would become inoperable. There is, in addition, some risk of radioactive contamination of reservoirs. It is to be noted, however, that most of the city's water supply is in covered reservoirs and that probably 90 per cent of the fallout would be insoluble in water. The main immediate problems would likely be breakdown of pumping facilities and contamination by germs.

Problems of food supply: This question can be examined in two categories: first, that food which is stored in the city and, second, that food produced outside. Food stored under normal conditions would be subject to blast and fire. Food processing plants, storage and refrigeration facilities would also be affected by blast and fire. Metropolitan food supplies are heavily dependent on transportation. Sheltered food supplies, if available after extensive ruin, might provide sustenance for a limited period. Outside the metropolitan area the extent of damage to stock, produce and arable land would depend on fire damage and the quantity of local fallout.

Problems of housing and home fuel supplies: It is doubtful that many of New York City's approximately 2.5 million dwelling units would provide adequate shelter (in the conventional sense) for survivors, even if mass fires did not consume everything. It is more difficult to predict what would happen in suburbs. Widespread blast damage would extend in a 15-mile radius around Columbus Circle. (The firestorm, a probability within a 15-mile radius, and perhaps beyond, could create further havoc.) Those fortunate enough to have dwelling units remaining, and with a manageable radiation problem, would have a hard time during cold weather. Local supplies of fuel would probably have been destroyed and the breakdown of transportation would curtail further deliveries. Human exposure during winter months is an inevitable source of casualties.

Problems of medical facilities: It seems clear that most of the city's hospitals and related facilities would be destroyed or unusable, since virtually all of the city except the southern part of Staten Island lies within the 15-mile radius of heavy damage. The millions of dead and injured would include a sizable proportion of physicians and other trained medical personnel. Those medical centers still able to function would be faced with enormous problems arising from the general destruction, since medical services are heavily dependent on city-wide physical facilities and transportation. Few hospitals, for example, have auxiliary power sources sufficient for more than emergency periods. Destruction of city power plants and limited fuel supplies would therefore limit an important component of hospital services. Insufficient power would affect not only light, x-ray, and other machines, but also refrigeration necessary for important drugs. The failure of transportation of medical supplies and the presumed shortage of water, raising problems of general sanitation, indicate further aggravations of the health situation in event of a 20-MT nuclear explosion.

Problems of sanitation and public health: Sources of epidemic characteristically include: uncollected refuse, sewage, uncontrolled vermin, contaminated water and food supplies, and lack of medical facilities. Collection and disposal of corpses would require large numbers of workers and adequate transportation facilities. Public health problems created specifically by an extensive radioactive environment have not so far been experienced. Persons suffering from exposure to radiation, however, are particularly susceptible to infection, and a population of weakened and injured survivors, as in all comparable crises, would seem to invite epidemic.

LONG-TERM EFFECTS

The hazards discussed in earlier sections would occur largely within days, weeks and months after the explosion. There would also be longer-term radiation effects of two types: those that affect the exposed individual (somatic effects) and those that affect his descendants (genetic effects).

These effects are not fully understood by scientists. The knowledge that does exist has been exhaustively studied, but interpretations vary and are not conclusive. The uncertainties of the biology are compounded by uncertainty about radiation doses. While these effects will not be discussed in detail here, certain observations are possible.

Virtually all scientists agree that excess exposure of a population to radiation will have harmful effects on subsequent generations. The disagreements concern the relative incidence of harmful effects. These genetic effects might include miscarriages, stillbirths, neonatal deaths, congenital malformations, reduced mental and physical vigor, feeble-mindedness, and a host of physiological diseases or malfunctions, any one of which might lead to the disablement or death of an individual.

The evidence indicates that it is unlikely that long-term exposure to radiation would result in the genetic extinction of the human species, whatever the other harmful effects might be.

There is particular concern about the effects on fertility of an exposed male generation. Men exposed to a moderately high dose of radiation followed by a continuous low dose over a period of time are likely to exhibit sterility or reduced fertility for years. The gonads are among the most sensitive to radiation of all human organs.

Among other possible somatic effects are: increased incidence of leukemia and other forms of cancer, increased incidence of degenerative diseases, shortening of the life span, development of cataracts, and various adverse effects on growth and normal development, especially in embryos.

Viola W. Bernard, Perry Ottenberg, Fritz Redl

Dehumanization: A Composite Psychological Defense in Relation to Modern War

We conceive of dehumanization as a particular type of psychic defense mechanism and consider its increasing prevalence to be a social consequence of the nuclear age. By this growth it contributes, we believe, to heightening the risks of nuclear extermination.

Dehumanization as a defense against painful or overwhelming emotions entails a decrease in a person's sense of his own individuality and in his perception of the humanness of other people. The misperceiving of others ranges from viewing them *en bloc* as "subhuman" or "bad human" (a long-familiar component of group prejudice) to viewing them as "nonhuman," as though they were inanimate items or "dispensable supplies." As such, their maltreatment or even their destruction may be carried out or acquiesced in with relative freedom from the restraints of conscience or feelings of brotherhood.

In our view, dehumanization is not a wholly new mental mechanism, but rather a composite psychological defense which draws selectively on other well-known defenses, including unconscious denial, repression, depersonalization, isolation of affect, and compartmentalization (the elimination of meaning by disconnecting related mental elements and walling them off from each other). Recourse to dehumanization as a defense against stresses of inner conflict and external threat is especially

Reprinted by permission of the authors and publisher from Milton Schwebel (ed.), *Behavioral Science and Human Survival* (Palo Alto: Science and Behavior Books, Inc., 1965). Viola W. Bernard is clinical professor of psychiatry, and Director, Division of Community and Social Psychiatry, Columbia University. Perry Ottenberg is Director of the Community Psychiatry Training Program, Institute of Pennsylvania Hospital. Fritz Redl is Distinguished Professor of Behavioral Sciences, Wayne State University. (This version is a revision of the paper presented in March 1963.)

17

favored by impersonal aspects of modern social organization, along with such special technological features of nuclear weapons as their unprecedented destructive power and the distance between push button and victim.

We recognize that many adaptive, as well as maladaptive,[1] uses of self-protective dehumanization are requisite in multiple areas of contemporary life. As a maladaptive defense in relation to war, however, the freedom from fear which it achieves by apathy or blindness to implications of the threat of nuclear warfare itself increases the actuality of that threat: the masking of its true urgency inactivates motive power for an all-out effort to devise creative alternatives for resolving international conflict. Dehumanization also facilitates the tolerating of mass destruction through by-passing those psychic inhibitions against the taking of human life that have become part of civilized man. Such inhibitions cannot be called into play when those who are to be destroyed have been divested of their humanness. The magnitudes of annihilation that may be perpetrated with indifference would seem to transcend those carried out in hatred and anger. This was demonstrated by the impersonal, mechanized efficiency of extermination at the Nazi death camps.

The complex psychological phenomenon which we call dehumanization includes two distinct but interrelated series of processes: *self-directed dehumanization* relates to self-image, and denotes the diminution of an individual's sense of his own humanness; *object-directed dehumanization* refers to his perceiving others as lacking in those attributes that are considered to be most human. Despite the differences between these two in their origins and intrapsychic relationships within over-all personality development and psychodynamic functioning, both forms of dehumanization, compounded from parts of other defenses, become usable by the individual for emotional self-protection. These two forms of dehumanization are mutually reinforcing: reduction in the fullness of one's feelings for other human beings, whatever the reason for this, impoverishes one's sense of self; any lessening of the humanness of one's self-image limits one's capacity for relating to others.

It seems to us that the extensive increase of dehumanization today is causally linked to aspects of institutional changes in contemporary society and to the transformed nature of modern war. The mushrooming importance in today's world of technology, automation, urbanization, specialization, various forms of bureaucracy, mass media, and the increased influences of nationalistic, totalitarian, and other ideologies have all been widely discussed by many scholars. The net long-term implications of these processes, whether constructive or destructive, are beyond.

[1]Adaptive and maladaptive refer to a person's modes of coping with internal and external stress. The distinction hinges on the extent to which such coping is successful with respect to the optimal over-all balance of the individual's realistic interests and goals.

the scope of this paper, and we do not regard ourselves qualified to evaluate them.

We are concerned here, however, with certain of their more immediate effects on people. It would seem that, for a vast portion of the world's population, elements of these broad social changes contribute to feelings of anonymity, impersonality, separation from the decision-making processes, and a fragmented sense of one's integrated social roles, and also to pressure on the individual to constrict his affective range to some machine-like task at hand. Similarly, the average citizen feels powerless indeed with respect to control over fateful decisions about nuclear attack or its aftermath.

The consequent sense of personal unimportance and relative helplessness, socially and politically, on the part of so many people specifically inclines them to adopt dehumanization as a preferred defense against many kinds of painful, unacceptable, and unbearable feelings referable to their experiences, inclinations, and behavior. *Self-directed dehumanization* empties the individual of human emotions and passions. It is paradoxical that one of its major dynamic purposes is protection against feeling the anxieties, frustrations and conflicts associated with the "cog-in-a-big-machine" self-image into which people feel themselves pushed by socially induced pressures. Thus, it tends to fulfill the very threat that it seeks to prevent.

These pervasive reactions predispose one even more to regard other people or groups as less than human, or even nonhuman. We distinguish among several different types and gradations of *object-directed dehumanization*. Thus, the failure to recognize in others their full complement of human qualities may be either partial or relatively complete. Partial dehumanization includes the misperceiving of members of "out-groups," *en masse*, as subhuman, bad human, or superhuman; as such, it is related to the psychodynamics of group prejudice. It protects the individual from the guilt and shame he would otherwise feel from primitive or antisocial attitudes, impulses, and actions that he directs—or allows others to direct—toward those he manages to perceive in these categories: if they are sub-humans they have not yet reached full human status on the evolutionary ladder and, therefore, do not merit being treated as human; if they are bad humans, their maltreatment is justified, since their defects in human qualities are their own fault. The latter is especially true if they are seen as having superhuman qualtties as well, for it is one of the curious paradoxes of prejudice that both superhuman and debased characteristics are ascribed simultaneously to certain groups in order to justify discrimination or aggression against them. The foreigner, for instance, is seen at once as "wicked, untrustworthy, dirty," and "uncanny, powerful, and cunning." Similarly, according to the canons of race prejudice, contradictory qualities of exceptional prowess and extraordinary defect

19

—ascribed to Orientals, Negroes, Jews, or any other group—together make them a menace toward whom customary restraints on behavior do not obtain. The main conscious emotional concomitants of partial dehumanization, as with prejudice, are hostility and fear.

In its more complete form, however, object-directed dehumanization entails a perception of other people as non humans—as statistics, commodities, or interchangeable pieces in a vast "numbers game." Its predominant emotional tone is that of indifference, in contrast to the (sometimes strong) feelings of partial dehumanization, together with a sense of *non-involvement in the actual or foreseeable vicissitudes* of others. Such apathy has crucial psychosocial implications. Among these—perhaps the most important today—is its bearing on how people tolerate the risks of mass destruction by nuclear war.

Although this communication is primarily concerned with the negative and maladaptive aspects of dehumanization, we recognize that it also serves important adaptive purposes in many life situations. In this respect, it resembles other mental mechanisms of defense. Some of the ingredients of dehumanization are required for the effective mastery of many tasks in contemporary society. Thus, in crises such as natural disasters, accidents, or epidemics in which people are injured, sick, or killed, psychic mechanisms are called into play which divest the victims of their human identities, so that feelings of pity, terror, or revulsion can be overcome. Without such selective and transient dehumanization, these emotional reactions would interfere with the efficient and responsible performance of what has to be done, whether it be first aid, surgery, rescue operation, or burial.

Certain occupations in particular require such selectively dehumanized behavior.[2] Examples of these include law enforcement (police, judges, lawyers, prison officials); medicine (physicians, nurses, and ancillary personnel); and, of course, national defense (military leaders, strategists, fighting personnel). Indeed, some degree of adaptive dehumanization seems to be a basic requirement for effective participation in any institutional process. Almost every professional activity has some specific aspect that requires the capacity for appropriate detachment from full emotional responsiveness and the curtailment, at least temporarily, of those everyday human emotional exchanges that are not central to the task at hand, or which might, if present, impede it. The official at the window who stamps the passport may be by nature a warm and friendly man, but in the context of his job the emigrant's hopes or fears lie outside his emotional vision.

Margaret Bourke-White, the noted photographer, was at Buchenwald at the end of World War II as a correspondent. Her account of

[2]These occupations, therefore, carry the extra risk of their requisite dehumanization becoming maladaptive if it is carried to an extreme or used inappropriately.

herself at that time aptly describes the adaptive use of dehumanization, both self-directed and object-directed: "People often ask me how it is possible to photograph such atrocities. . . . I have to work with a veil over my mind. In photographing the murder camps, the protective veil was so tightly drawn that I hardly knew what I had taken until I saw prints of my own photographs. I believe many correspondents worked in the same self-imposed stupor. One has to or it is impossible to stand it." (1)

The only occasions to date on which nuclear bombs have been used in warfare took place when the "baby bombs" were dropped on the civilian populations of Hiroshima and Nagasaki. Lifton (2) has reported on reactions among the Hiroshima survivors, as well as his own, as investigator. His observations are particularly valuable to us since, as a research psychiatrist, he was especially qualified both to elicit and to evaluate psychodynamic data. According to the survivors whom he interviewed, at first one experienced utter horror at the sudden, strange scene of mass deaths, devastation, dreadful burns, and skin stripped from bodies. They could find no words to convey fully these initial feelings. But then each described how, before long, the horror would almost disappear. One would see terrible sights of human beings in extreme agony and yet feel nothing. The load of feeling from empathic responsiveness had become too much to endure; all one could do was to try to survive.

Lifton reports that during the first few such accounts he felt profoundly shocked, shaken, and emotionally spent. These effects gradually lessened, however, so that he became able to experience the interviews as scientific work rather than as repeated occasions of vicarious agony. For both the survivors and the investigator, the "task" provided a focus of concentration and of circumscribed activity as a means of quelling disturbing emotions.

In these instances, the immediate adaptive value of dehumanization as a defense is obvious. It remains open to question, however, whether a further, somewhat related, finding of Lifton's will in the long run prove to be adaptive or maladaptive. He learned that many people in Japan and elsewhere cannot bear to look at pictures of Hiroshima, and even avoid the museum in which they are displayed. There is avoidance and denial of the whole issue which not infrequently leads to hostility toward the A-bomb victims themselves, or toward anyone who expresses concern for these or future victims. May not *this* kind of defense reaction deflect the determination to seek ways of preventing nuclear war?

We believe that the complex mechanism of dehumanization urgently needs to be recognized and studied because its use as a defense has been stepped up so tremendously in recent times, and because of the grave risks it entails as the price for short-term relief. This paper repre-

21

sents only a preliminary delineation, with main attention to its bearing on the nuclear threat.[3]

Many people, by mobilizing this form of ego defense, manage to avoid or to lessen the emotional significance for themselves of today's kind of war. Only a very widespread and deeply rooted defense could ward off the full import of the new reality with which we live: that warfare has been transformed by modern weaponry into something mankind has never experienced before, and that in all-out nuclear war there can be no "victory" for anyone.

The extraordinary complacency with which people manage to shield themselves against fully realizing the threat of nuclear annihilation cannot be adequately explained, we think, by denial and the other well-studied psychological defense mechanisms. This is what has led us to trace out dehumanization as a composite defense, which draws upon a cluster of familiar defenses, magnifying that fraction of each which is most specifically involved with the humanness of one's self-image and the perception of others. It operates against such painful feelings as fear, inadequacy, compassion, revulsion, guilt and shame. As with other mental mechanisms of defense, its self-protective distortions of realistic perceptions occur, for the most part, outside of awareness.

The extent to which dehumanization takes place consciously or unconsciously, although of considerable interest to us, is not relevant enough to this discussion to warrant elaboration. This also holds true for questions about why dehumanization as such has not hitherto received more attention and study in clinical psychiatry.[4] At least one possible reason might be mentioned, however. Most defense mechanisms were not studied originally in relation to such issues as war and peace, national destiny or group survival. Instead, they came under scrutiny, during the course of psychotherapy, as part of the idiosyncratic pathology of individual patients. This could have obscured the recognition of their roles in widespread collective reactions.

In order to avoid confusion we should also mention that the term "dehumanization" as we are using it, refers to a concept that is different from and not connected in meaning with the words "humane" and "humanitarian." "Inhumane" cruelty causes suffering; maladaptive dehumanization, as we point out, may also lead to suffering. Yet even

---

[3]Because of this primary emphasis, we shall refrain from exploring many important facets of dehumanization which seem less directly relevant to the threat of nuclear warfare. Yet, it permeates so many aspects of modern life that, for clarity in describing it, our discussion must ramify, to some extent, beyond its war-connected context. Still we have purposely neglected areas of great interest to us, especially with regard to psychopathology, psychotherapy, and community psychiatry, which we think warrant fuller discussion elsewhere.

[4]No doubt, when the phenomenon is part of a mental disorder, it has been dealt with therapeutically, to some degree, under the names of other defense mechanisms.

these seemingly similar results are reached by very different routes; to equate them would be a mistake. A surgeon, for example, is treating his patient humanely when, by his dehumanization, he blots out feelings of either sympathy or hostility that might otherwise interfere with his surgical skill during an operation.

No one, of course, could possibly retain his mental health and carry on the business of life if he remained constantly aware of, and emphatically sensitive to, all the misery and injustice that there is in the world. But this very essentially of dehumanization, as with other defenses, makes for its greatest danger: that the constructive self-protection it achieves will cross the ever-shifting boundaries of adaptiveness and become destructive, to others as well as to the self. In combination with other social factors already mentioned, the perfection of modern techniques for automated killing on a global scale engenders a marked increase in the incidence of dehumanization. Correspondingly, there is intensified risk that this collective reaction will break through the fragile and elusive dividing line that separates healthy ego-supportive dehumanization from the maladaptive callousness and apathy that prevent people from taking those realistic actions which are within their powers to protect human rights and human lives.

A "vicious cycle" relationship would thus seem to obtain between dehumanization as a subjective phenomenon and its objective consequences. Conscience and empathy, as sources of guilt and compassion, pertain to human beings; they can be evaded if the human element in the victims of aggression is first sufficiently obscured. The aggressor is thereby freed from conscience-linked restraints, with injurious objective effects on other individuals, groups, or nations. The victims in turn respond, subjectively, by resorting even more to self-protective dehumanization, as did the Hiroshima survivors whom Lifton interviewed.

One might argue, and with some cogency, that similar conversion of enemies into pins on a military map has been part of war psychology throughout history, so are we not therefore belaboring the obvious? The answer lies in the fundamental changes, both quantitative and qualitative, that nuclear weapons have made in the meaning of war. In fact, the very term "war," with its pre-atomic connotations, has become something of an outmoded misnomer for the nuclear threat which now confronts us. "Modern war"—before Hiroshima—reflected, as a social institution, many of the social and technological developments which we have already noted as conducive to increased dehumanization. But with the possibility of instantaneously wiping out the world's population—or a very large section of it—the extent of dehumanization as well as its significance for human survival have both been abruptly and tremendously accelerated.

In part, this seems to be due to the overtaxing of our capacity really to comprehend the sudden changes in amplitudes that have become so salient. In addition to the changed factors of *distance, time,* and *magni*-

23

tude in modern technology, there is the push-button nature of today's weaponry and the *indirectness* of releasing a rocket barrage upon sites halfway around the world, all of which lie far outside our range of previous experience. When we look out of an airplane window, the earth below becomes a toy, the hills and valleys reduced to abstractions in our mental canvas; but we do not conceive of ourselves as a minute part of some moving speck in the sky—which is how we appear to people on the ground. Yet it is precisely such reciprocal awareness that is required if we are to maintain a balanced view of our actual size and vulnerability. Otherwise, perceptual confusion introduces a mechanistic and impersonal quality into our reactions.

The thinking and feeling of most people have been unable as yet to come to grips with the sheer expansion of numbers and the frightening shrinkage of space which present means of transportation and communication entail. The news of an animal run over by a car, a child stuck in a well, or the preventable death of one individual evokes an outpouring of sympathetic response and upsets the emotional equanimity of many; yet reports of six million Jews killed in Nazi death camps, or of a hundred thousand Japanese killed in Hiroshima and Nagasaki, may cause but moderate uneasiness. Arthur Koestler has put it poignantly, "Statistics don't bleed; it is the detail which counts. We are unable to embrace the total process with our awareness; we can only focus on little lumps of reality." (3)

It is this unique combination of psychosocial and situational factors that seems particularly to favor the adoption of the composite defense we have called "dehumanization"—and this in turn acts to generate more and more of the same. The new aspects of time, space magnitude, speed, automation, distance, and irreversibility are not yet "hooked up" in the psychology of man's relationships to his fellow man or to the world he inhabits. Most people feel poorly equipped, conceptually, to restructure their accustomed picture of the world, all of a sudden, in order to make it fit dimensions so alien to their lifelong learning. Anxiety aroused by this threat to one's orientation adds to the inner stress that seeks relief through the defense.

We are confronted with a *lag in our perceptual and intellectual development* so that the enormity of the new reality, with its potential for both destructive and constructive human consequences, becomes blurred in our thinking and feeling. The less elastic our capacity to comprehend meaningfully new significances, the more we cling to dehumanization, unable to challenge its fallacies through knowledge and reason. Correspondingly, the greater our reliance on dehumanization as a mechanism for coping with life, the less readily can the new facts of our existence be integrated into our full psychic functioning, since so many of its vital components, such as empathy, have been shunted aside, stifled, or obscured.

Together, in the writers opinion, these differently caused but mutual-   24 ly reinforcing cognitive and emotional deficiencies seriously intensify the nuclear risk; latent psychological barriers against the destruction of millions of people remain unmobilized, and hence ineffective, for those who feel detached from the flesh and blood implications of nuclear war. No other mechanism seems to fit so well the requirements of this unprecedented internal and external stress. Dehumanization, with its impairment of our personal involvement, allows us to "play chess with the planets."

Whether it be adaptive or maladaptive, dehumanization brings with it, as we have noted, a temporary feeling of relief, an illusion of problems solved, or at least postponed or evaded. Whatever the ultimate effects of this psychic maneuver on our destiny, however, it would seem to be a wise precaution to try to assess some of its dangerous possibilities.

Several overlapping aspects of maladaptive dehumanization may be outlined briefly and in oversimplified form, as follows:

1. *Increased emotional distance from other human beings.* Under the impact of this defense, one stops identifying with others or seeing them as essentially similar to oneself in basic human qualities. Relationships to others become stereotyped, rigid, and above all, unexpressive of mutuality. People in "out-groups" are apt to be reacted to *en bloc*; feelings of concern for them have become anesthetized.

George Orwell illustrates this aspect of dehumanization in writing of his experience as a patient (4). His account also serves as an example of the very significant hazard, already mentioned, whereby professionally adaptive uses of this defense (as in medical education and patient care) are in danger of passing that transition point beyond which they become maladaptive and so defeat their original purpose.

> Later in the day the tall, solemn, black-bearded doctor made his rounds, with an intern and a troop of students following at his heels, but there were about sixty of us in the ward and it was evident that he had other wards to attend to as well. There were many beds past which he walked day after day, sometimes followed by imploring cries. On the other hand, if you had some disease with which the students wanted to familiarize themselves you got plenty of attention of a kind. I myself, with an exceptionally fine specimen of a bronchial rattle, sometimes had as many as a dozen students queuing up to listen to my chest. It was a very queer feeling—queer, I mean, because of their intense interest in learning their job, together with a seeming lack of any perception that the patients were human beings. It is strange to relate, but sometimes as some young student stepped forward to take his turn at manipulating you, he would be actually tremulous with excitement, like a boy who has at last got his hands on some expensive piece of machinery. And then ear after ear . . . pressed against your back, relays of fingers solemnly but clumsily tapping, and not from any one of them did you get a word of conversation or a look direct

in your face. As a non-paying patient, in the uniform nightshirt, you were primarily a *specimen*, a thing I did not resent but could never quite get used to.

2. *Diminished sense of personal responsibility for the consequences of one's actions.* Ordinarily, for most people, the advocacy of or participation in the wholesale slaughter and maiming of their fellow human beings is checked by opposing feelings of guilt, shame, or horror. Immunity from these feelings may be gained, however, by a self-automatizing detachment from a sense of *personal* responsibility for the outcome of such actions, thereby making them easier to carry out. (A dramatic version of the excuse, "I was only carrying out orders," was offered by Eichmann at his trial.)

One "safe" way of dealing with such painful feelings is to focus only on one's fragmented job and ignore its many ramifications. By blocking out the ultimately destructive purpose of a military bombing action, for instance, one's component task therein may become a source of ego-acceptable gratification, as from any successful fulfillment of duty, mastery of a hard problem, or achievement of a dangerous feat. The B-29 airplane that dropped the atomic bomb on Hiroshima was named Enola Gay, after the mother of one of its crew members. This could represent the psychological defense of displacing human qualities from the population to be bombed to the machine.

One of the crew members is reported to have exclaimed: "If people knew what we were doing we could have sold tickets for $100,000!" and another is said to have commented, "Colonel, that was worth the 25¢ ride on the 'Cyclone' at Coney Island." (5) Such reactions, which may on the surface appear to be shockingly cynical, not only illustrate how cynicism may be used to conceal strong emotions (as seems quite likely in this instance); they also suggest how one may try to use cynicism to bolster one's dehumanization when that defense is not itself strong enough, even with its displacement of responsibility and its focusing on one's fragmented job, to overcome the intensity of one's inner "humanized" emotional protest against carrying out an act of such vast destructiveness.

3. *Increasing involvement with procedural problems to the detriment of human needs.* There is an overconcern with details of procedure, with impersonal deindividualized regulations, and with the formal structure of a practice, all of which result in shrinking the ability or willingness to personalize one's actions in the interests of individual human needs or special differences. This is, of course, the particular danger implicit in the trend toward bureaucracy that accompanies organizational units when they grow larger and larger. The task at hand is then apt to take precedence over the human cost: the individual is seen more as a means to an end than as an end in himself. Society, the Corporation, the Five-Year-Plan—these become overriding goals

26

in themselves, and the dehumanized man is turned into a cost item, tool, or energy-factor serving the mass-machine.

Even "scientific" studies of human behavior and development, as well as professional practices based on them, sometimes become dehumanized to a maladaptive extent (6). Such words as "communicate," "adjust," "identify," "relate," "feel," and even "love" can lose their personal meaningfulness when they are used as mere technical devices instead of being applied to specific human beings in specific life situations.[5] In response to the new hugeness of global problems, patterns of speech have emerged that additionally reflect dehumanized thinking. Segmented-fragmented concepts, such as "fallout problem," "shelter problem," "civil defense," "deterrence," "first strike," "pre-emptive attack," "overkill," and some aspects of game theory, represent a "move-countermove" type of thinking which tends to treat the potential human victim as a statistic, and to screen out the total catastrophic effect of the contemplated actions upon human lives. The content of strategy takes on an importance that is without any relation to its inevitable *results*, the defense of dehumanization having operated to block out recognition of those awesome consequences that, if they could be seen, would make the strategy unacceptable. The defense, when successful, narcotizes deeper feelings so that nuclear war, as "inevitable," may be more dispassionately contemplated and its tactical permutations assayed. In the course of this, however, almost automatic counteractions of anxiety are frequently expressed through such remarks as: "People have always lived on the brink of disaster," "You can't change human nature; there will have to be wars," and "We all have to die some day."

4. *Inability to oppose dominant group attitudes or pressures.* As the individual comes to feel more and more alienated and lonely in mass society, he finds it more and more difficult to place himself in opposition to the huge pressures of the "Organization." Fears of losing occupational security or of attacks on one's integrity, loyalty, or family are more than most people can bear. Self-directed dehumanization is resorted to as a defense against such fears and conflicts: by joining the party, organization, or club, and thus feeling himself to be an incon-

[5]Within our own discipline this is all too likely to occur when thousands of sick individuals are converted into "cases" in some of our understaffed and oversized mental hospitals. Bureaucratic hospital structure favors impersonal experience. In an enlightening study (6), Merton J. Kahne points up how this accentuation of automatic and formalized milieu propensities thwarts the specific therapeutic need of psychiatric patients for opportunities to improve their sense of involvement with people.

On another occasion we hope to enlarge on how and why maladaptive uses of dehumanization on the part of professionals, officials, and the general public hamper our collective effort as a community to instill more sensitivity to individual need into patterns of congregate care, not only in mental hospitals but also in general hospitals, children's institutions, welfare and correctional facilities, etc.

spicuous particle in some large structure, he may find relief from the difficult decisions, uncertainties, and pressures of nonconformity. He may also thereby ward off those feelings of guilt that would arise out of participating in, or failing to protest against, the injustices and cruelties perpetrated by those in power. Thus, during the Nazi regime, many usually kindhearted Germans appear to have silenced their consciences by emphasizing their own insignificance and identifying with the dehumanized values of the dictatorship. This stance permitted the detached, even dutiful, disregard of their fellow citizens, which in turn gave even freer rein to the systematic official conducting of genocide.

5. *Feelings of personal helplessness and estrangement.* The realization of one's relatively impotent position in a large organization engenders anxiety[6] which dehumanization helps to cover over. The internalized perception of the self as small, helpless, and insignificant, coupled with an externalized view of "Society" as huge, powerful, and unopposable, is expressed in such frequently heard comments as: "The government has secret information that we don't have"; or, "They know what's right, who am I to question what they are doing?"; or "What's the use? No one will listen to me. . . ."

The belief that the government or the military is either infallible or impregnable provides a tempting refuge because of its renunciation of one's own critical faculties in the name of those of the powerful and all-knowing leader. Such self-directed dehumanization has a strong appeal to the isolated and alienated citizen as a protective cloak to hide from himself his feelings of weakness, ignorance and estrangement. This is particularly relevant to the psychological attraction of certain dangerous social movements. The more inwardly frightened, lonely, helpless, and humiliated people become, the greater the susceptibility of many of them to the seductive, prejudiced promises of demagoguery: the award of spurious superiority and privilege achieved by devaluating the full humanness of some other group—racial, religious, ethnic, or political. Furthermore, as an added advantage of the dehumanization "package," self-enhancing acts of discrimination and persecution against such victim groups can be carried out without tormenting or deterrent feelings of guilt, since these are absorbed by the "rightness" of the demagogic leader.

In recent decades and in many countries, including our own, we have seen what human toll can be taken by this psychosocial configuration. It has entered into Hitlerism, Stalinism, U.S.A. "lynch-mobism." If it is extended to the international arena, against a "dehumanized" enemy instead of an oppressed national minority, atomic weapons will now empower it to inflict immeasurably more human destruction and suffering.

The indifference resulting from that form of dehumanization which

[6]This has been particularly well described in novels by Kafka and Camus.

causes one to view others as inanimate objects enables one, without conscious malice or selfishness, to write off their misery, injustices, and death as something that "just couldn't be helped." As nonhumans, they are not identified with as beings essentially similar to oneself; "their" annihilation by nuclear warfare is thus not "our" concern, despite the reality that distinctions between "they" and "we" have been rendered all the more meaningless by the mutually suicidal nature of total war.

Although this type of dehumanization is relatively complete, in the sense of perceiving others as not at all human, it may occur in an individual with selective incompleteness under certain special conditions only, while his capacity for other emotional ties is preserved. This may prove socially constructive or destructive, depending on the purposes to which it is put. Thus, we have already noted how "pulling a veil" over her mind helped Bourke-White adaptively in her socially positive job of reporting atrocities. But it was compartmentalized dehumanization that also helped many to commit those very atrocities; they were able to exterminate Jews with assembly-line efficiency as the Nazi "final solution" while still retaining access to their genuine feelings of warmth for family members, friends and associates.

These contradictory emotional qualities, often appearing side by side in the same person, are also evidenced—in the opposite direction—by outstanding deeds of heroic rescue by those who, under different circumstances, might well exhibit dehumanized behavior. Almost daily, the newspapers carry stories of exceptional altruism; individuals or whole communities devote their entire energies to the rescue of a single child, an animal, or perhaps (in wartime), a wounded enemy soldier. What accounts for the difference between this kind of response to the plight of others, and that of dehumanized callousness? How are the adaptive humanized processes released?

One research approach might consist of the detailed description and comparative analysis of sample situations of both kinds of these collective reactions, which have such opposite social effects. A case history of community apathy which could be compared in such a study with instances of group altruism already on record, was recently provided by A. M. Rosenthal, an editor of *The New York Times* (7). At first glance, perhaps, his account of dehumanization, involving but one individual and in peacetime, may not seem germane to our discussion about nuclear war. But the macrocosm is reflected in the microcosm. We agree with Mr. Rosenthal that the implications of this episode are linked with certain psychological factors that have helped pave the way for such broad social calamities as Fascism abroad and racial crises in this country, both in the North and South. It does not seem too far-fetched, therefore, to relate them to the nuclear threat as well.

For more than half an hour, one night in March, 1964, thirty-eight respectable, law-abiding citizens in a quiet middle-class neighborhood in New York City watched a killer stalk and stab a young woman in three separate attacks, close to her home. She was no stranger to these onlookers, her neighbors, who knew her as "Kitty." According to Rosenthal, "Twice the sound of their voices and the sudden glow of their bedroom lights interrupted him and frightened him off. Each time he returned, sought her out and stabbed her again. Not one person telephoned the police during the assault; one witness called after the woman was dead." Later, when these thirty-eight neighbors were asked about their baffling failure to phone for help, even though they were safe in their own homes, "the underlying attitude or explanation seemed to be fear of involvement—any kind of involvement." Their fatal apathy gains in significance precisely because, by ordinary standards, these were decent, moral people—husbands and wives attached to each other and good to their children. This is one of the forms of dehumanization that we have described, in which a reaction of massive indifference— not hostility—leads to grievous cruelty, yet all the while, in another compartment of the self, the same individual's capacity for active caring continues, at least for those within his immediate orbit.

Rosenthal describes his own reaction to this episode as a "peculiar paradoxical feeling that there is in the tale of Catherine Genovese a revelation about the human condition so appalling to contemplate that only good can come from forcing oneself to confront the truth . . . the terrible reality that only under certain situations, and only in response to certain reflexes or certain beliefs, will a man step out of his shell toward his brother. In the back of my mind . . . was the feeling that there was, that there must be some connection between [this story and] the story of the witnesses silent in the face of greater crimes—the degradation of a race, children hungering. . . . It happens from time to time in New York that the life of the city is frozen by an instant of shock. In that instant the people of the city are seized by the paralyzing realization that they are one, that each man is in some way a mirror of every other man. . . . In that instant of shock, the mirror showed quite clearly what was wrong, that the face of mankind was spotted with the disease of apathy—all mankind. But this was too frightening a thought to live with, and soon the beholders began to set boundaries for the illness, to search frantically for causes that were external and to look for the carrier."

As we strive to distinguish more clearly among the complex determinants of adaptive-maladaptive, humanized-dehumanized polarities of behavior, we recognize that stubborn impulses toward individuation are intertwined with the dehumanizing trends on which we have focused. Both humanization and dehumanization are heightened by interpenetrating social and psychological effects of current technological and institutional changes. The progress of the past hundred years has markedly furthered humanization: it has relieved much of human drudgery and strain, and helped to bring about increased leisure and a richer life for a larger part of the world's population. Despite the blurring of personal distinctiveness by excessive bureaucracy, there are now exceptional opportunities, made possible by the same technology that fosters uniformity, for the individual to make rapid contact with, and meaningful contribution to, an almost limitless number of the earth's inhabitants. The same budgets, communication networks, transportation delivery systems, and human organizations that can be used to destroy can also be turned toward the creative fulfillment of great world purposes.

Our situation today favors contradictory attitudes toward how much any individual matters in the scheme of things, both subjectively and from the standpoint of social reality. At one extreme a few individuals in key positions feel—and are generally felt to have—a hugely expanded potential for social impact. Among the vast majority there is, by contrast, an intensified sense of voiceless insignificance in the shaping of events. Objectively, too, there is now among individuals a far greater disparity in their actual power to influence crucial outcomes. More than ever before, the fate of the world depends on the judgment of a handful of heads of state and their advisers, who must make rapid decisions about actions for which there are no precedents. Ideas and events, for better or worse, can have immediate global impact.[7] A push-button can set a holocaust in motion; a transatlantic phone call can prevent one.

In spite of humanizing ingredients in modern life, and the fact that men of good will everywhere are striving ceaselessly toward goals of peace, freedom and human dignity, we nevertheless place primary emphasis, in this paper, on dehumanization because we feel that the dangers inherent in this phenomenon are particularly pervasive, insidious, and relevant to the risk of nuclear war.

From a broad biological perspective, war may be viewed as a form of aggression between members of the same species, homosapiens. The distinguished naturalist, Lorenz, has recently pointed out a difference, of great relevance to the relationship between dehumanization and nuclear warfare, in the intraspecies behavior of animals who live in two kinds of groups (8). In the one, the members live together as a crowd of strangers: there are no expressions of mutual aggression, but neither is there any evidence of mutual ties, of relationships of affection, between individuals in the group. On the other hand, some of the fiercest beasts of prey—animals whose bodily weapons are capable of killing their own kind—live in groups in which intense relationships, both *aggressive and affectionate*, exist. Among such animals, says Lorenz, the greater the intraspecies aggression, the stronger the positive mutual attachments as well. These latter develop, through evolution, out of those occasions, such as breeding, when cooperation among these

---

[7]The news of President Kennedy's assassination circled the earth with unparalleled speed, and evoked a profound worldwide emotional response.

aggressive animals becomes essential to their survival as a species.

Furthermore—and this is of the utmost importance for survival—the greater the capacity for mutual relationships, the stronger and more reliable are the *innate inhibitions* which prevent them from using the species-specific weapons of predatory aggression, fangs, claws or whatever, to maim or kill a member of their own species, no matter how strong the hostile urge of one against another. For example, when two wolves fight, according to Lorenz, the potential victor's fangs are powerfully inhibited at what would be the moment of kill, in response to the other's ritualized signal of immobile exposure to his opponent of his vulnerable jugular.

Man's weapons, by contrast, are not part of his body. They are thus not controllable by reflexes fused into his nervous system; control must depend, instead, on psychological inhibitions (which may also function through social controls of his own devising). These psychic barriers to intraspecies aggression—which can lead to our becoming extinct—are rooted in our affiliative tendencies for cooperation and personal attachment. But these are the very tendencies that, as this paper has stressed, dehumanization can so seriously undermine.

Lorenz speaks of a natural balance within a species—essential to its preservation—between the capacity for killing and inhibition. In that sense, perhaps, man jeopardizes his survival by disturbing, with his invention of nuclear bombs, such a balance as has been maintained throughout his long history of periodic "old-style" wars. Such a dire imbalance would be increased by any shift on the part of the "human animal" toward a society essentially devoid of mutual relationships. For this would vitiate the very tendencies toward emotional involvement and cooperation which are the source of our most reliable inhibitions against "over-killing." Therefore, in terms of the parallels suggested by Lorenz, in order to protect ourselves against the doom of extinction as a species, we must encourage and devise every possible means of safeguarding the "family of man" from becoming an uncaring crowd. Not merely the limiting or halting, but the reversing of maladaptive dehumanization emerges as a key to survival.

What can be done to counteract these dangers? Assuredly, there is no single or ready answer. The development of psychic antidotes of *re*-humanization must involve a multiplicity of variables, levels of discourse and sectors of human activity, commensurate in complexity with the factors that make for *de*humanization. Our attempt in this paper to identify this mental mechanism, and to alert others to its significance, its frequency and its inter-relatedness to nuclear risk, represents in itself a preliminary phase of remedial endeavor. For the very process of recognizing a psychosocial problem such as this, by marshaling, reordering and interpreting diverse sets of facts to find new significances in them, is a form of social action, and one that is especially appropriate to behavioral scientists. Beyond this initial posing of the problem, however, any chance of effectively grappling with it will require the converging efforts of those in many different professions and walks of life.

Rehumanization as a mode of neutralizing the dangerous effects that we have stressed should not be misconstrued as aiming at the reestablishment of pre-nuclear age psychology—which would be impossible in any case. We cannot set history back nostalgically to "the good old days" prior to automation and the other changes in contemporary society (nor were the conditions of those earlier days really so "good" for the self-realization of a large portion of the population.) On the contrary, the process of rehumanization means to us a way of assimilating and re-integrating, emotionally and intellectually, the profound new meanings that have been brought into our lives by our own advances, so that a much fuller conviction than ever before of our own humanity and interdependence with all mankind becomes intrinsic to our basic frame of reference.

The imperative for speeding up such a universal process of psychological change is rooted in the new and *specific* necessity to insure survival in the face of the awesome irreversibility of nuclear annihilation. The most essential approaches toward achieving this goal, however, lead us into such *general* and only seemingly unrelated issues as the degree of political freedom and social justice; our patterns of child care and child-rearing; and our philosophy of education, as well as the quality of its implementation. For the process of dehumanization, which eventuates in indifference to the suffering implicit in nuclear warfare, has its beginnings in earlier periods and other areas of the individual's life. It is through these areas that influences conducive to rehumanization must be channeled.

We need to learn more, and to make more effective use of what is already known about how to strengthen people's capacity to tolerate irreducible uncertainty, fear, and frustration without having to take refuge in illusions that cripple their potential for realistic behavior. And we urgently need to find ways of galvanizing our powers of imagination (including ways of weakening the hold of the emotionally-based mechanisms that imprison it).

Imagination and foresight are among the highest functions of the human brain, from the evolutionary standpoint, and also among the most valuable. They enable us to select and extrapolate from previously accumulated experience and knowledge, in order to create guidelines for coping with situations never before experienced, whose nature is so far unknown.

Other kinds of learning ordinarily serve us well in the complicated process of establishing behavior patterns for meeting new life situations. We are able to learn by trial and error, for example, from our firsthand experiences and from successively testing the value of alternative approaches as similar situations arise. Also, we learn

33

much by vicariously living through the reported experiences of others.

Through imagination, however, a completely new situation can be projected in the mind in its sensate and vivid entirety, so that the lessons it contains for us can be learned without the necessity of going through it in real life. This form of "future-directed" learning, which creative imagination makes possible, is therefore uniquely advantageous in dealing with the problematic issues of thermonuclear war; it permits us to arrive at more rational decisions for preventing it without having to pay the gruesome price of undergoing its actuality.

The fact is that the "once-and-for-all" character of full-scale nuclear war renders the methods of "learning through experience"—our own or others'—not only indefensible (in terms of the human cost) but also utterly unfeasible. The empirical privilege of "profiting" from an experience of that nature would have been denied to most if not all of humanity by the finality of the experience itself.

Accordingly, it would seem that whatever can quicken and extend our capacity for imagination, in both the empathic and conceptual spheres, is a vital form of "civil defense." It requires, to begin with, all the pedagogic ingenuity that we can muster to overcome the lag in our intellectual development that keeps us from fully comprehending the new dimensions of our existence. Yet, our endeavors to develop new modes of thinking can be cancelled out by the constricting and impeding effects of dehumanization. The terrible potential of this subtle mechanism to facilitate the depopulating of the earth lies in its circumventing human restraints against fratricide. We are faced, therefore, with the inescapable necessity of devising ways to increase opportunities for meaningful personal relationships and maximum social participation throughout the entire fabric of our society.

REFERENCES

1. Bourke-White, M., *Portrait of Myself*, New York, Simon and Schuster, 1963.
2. Lifton, R., "Psychological effects of the atomic bomb in Hiroshima; the theme of death," *Daedalus, Journal of the Amer. Acad. of Arts and Sciences,* 462–497, Summer, 1963.
3. Koestler, A. "On disbelieving atrocities," in *The Yogi and the Commissar*, New York, Macmillan, 1945.
4. Orwell, G. "How the poor die," in *Shooting an Elephant*, New York Harcourt, Brace, 1945.
5. *Yank, the Army Weekly,* New York, Duell, Sloane and Pearce, 1947, p. 282.
6. Kahne, M. J., "Bureaucratic Structure and Impersonal Experience in Mental Hospitals," *Psychiatry, 22,* 4, 363–375, 1959.
7. Rosenthal, A. M., *Thirty-Eight Witnesses*, New York, McGraw-Hill, 1964.
8. Lorenz, K., *Das Sogenannte Böse—Zur Naturgeschichte der Aggression*, Vienna, Dr. G. Borotha-Schoeler Verlag, 1963.

Senator J. W. Fulbright

The Cold War in American Life

The Constitution of the United States, in the words of its preamble, was established, among other reasons, in order to "provide for the common defense, promote the general welfare, and secure the blessings of liberty. . . ." In the past generation the emphasis of our public policy has been heavily weighted on measures for the common defense to the considerable neglect of programs for promoting the liberty and welfare of our people. The reason for this, of course, has been the exacting demands of two world wars and an intractable cold war, which have wrought vast changes in the character of American life.

Of all the changes in American life wrought by the cold war, the most important by far, in my opinion, has been the massive diversion of energy and resources from the creative pursuits of civilized society to the conduct of a costly and interminable struggle for world power. We have been compelled, or have felt ourselves compelled, to reverse the traditional order of our national priorities, relegating individual and community life to places on the scale below the enormously expensive military and space activities that constitute our program of national security.

This of course is not the only change in American life brought about by the cold war. There have been many others, some most welcome and constructive. Directly or indirectly, the world struggle with communism has stimulated economic and industrial expansion, accelerated the pace of intellectual inquiry and scientific discovery, broken the shell of American isolation and greatly increased public knowledge and awareness of the world outside the United States. At the same time, the continuing world conflict has cast a shadow on the tone of Ameri-

Address to the University of North Carolina, 1964 Symposium, *Arms and the Man: National Security and the Arms of a Free Society* (April 5, 1964). Reprinted here with the author's permission. J. W. Fulbright is a United States Senator and Chairman of the Senate Committee on Foreign Relations.

can life by introducing a strand of apprehension and tension into a national style which has traditionally been one of buoyant optimism. The continuing and inconclusive struggle, new in American experience, has in Walt Rostow's words "imposed a sense of limitation on the nation's old image of itself, a limitation which has been accepted with greater or less maturity and which has touched the nation's domestic life at many points with elements of escapism, with a tendency to search for scapegoats, with simple worry, and with much thoughtful, responsive effort as well."[1]

Overriding all these changes, however, good and bad, has been the massive diversion of wealth and talent from individual and community life to the increasingly complex and costly effort to maintain a minimum level of national security in a world in which no nation can be immune from the threat of sudden catastrophe. We have had to turn away from our hopes in order to concentrate on our fears and the result has been accumulating neglect of those things which bring happiness and beauty and fulfillment into our lives. The "public happiness," in August Heckscher's term, has become a luxury to be postponed to some distant day when the dangers that now beset us will have disappeared.

This, I think, is the real meaning of the cold war in American life. It has consumed money and time and talent that could otherwise be used to build schools and homes and hospitals, to remove the blight of ugliness that is spreading over the cities and highways of America, and to overcome the poverty and hopelessness that afflict the lives of one-fifth of the people in an otherwise affluent society. It has put a high premium on avoiding innovation at home because new programs involve controversy as well as expense and it is felt that we cannot afford domestic divisions at a time when external challenges require us to maintain the highest possible degree of national unity. Far more pervasively than the United Nations or the "Atlantic community" could ever do, the cold war has encroached upon our sovereignty; it has given the Russians the major voice in determining what proportion of our federal budget must be allocated to the military and what proportion, therefore, cannot be made available for domestic social and economic projects. This is the price that we have been paying for the cold war and it has been a high price indeed.

At least as striking as the inversion of priorities which the cold war has enforced upon American life is the readiness with which the American people have consented to defer programs for their welfare and happiness in favor of costly military and space programs. Indeed, if the Congress accurately reflects the temper of the country, then the American people are not only willing, they are eager, to sacrifice edu-

[1]W. W. Rostow, *The United States in the World Arena* (New York: Harper & Brothers, 1960), p. 451.

cation and urban renewal and public health programs—to say nothing of foreign aid—to the requirements of the armed forces and the space agency. There is indeed a most striking paradox in the fact that military budgets of over $50 billion are adopted by the Congress after only perfunctory debate, while domestic education and welfare programs involving sums which are mere fractions of the military budget are painstakingly examined and then either considerably reduced or rejected outright. I sometimes suspect that in its zeal for armaments at the expense of education and welfare the Congress tends to overrepresent those of our citizens who are extraordinarily agitated about national security and extraordinarily vigorous about making their agitation known.

It may be that the people and their representatives are making a carefully reasoned sacrifice of welfare to security. It may be, but I doubt it. The sacrifice is made so eagerly as to cause one to suspect that it is fairly painless, that indeed the American people prefer military rockets to public schools and flights to the moon to urban renewal. In a perverse way, we have grown rather attached to the cold war. It occupies us with a stirring and seemingly clear and simple challenge from outside and diverts us from problems here at home which many Americans would rather not try to solve, some because they find domestic problems tedious and pedestrian, others because they genuinely believe these problems to be personal rather than public, others because they are unwilling to be drawn into an abrasive national debate as to whether poverty, unemployment, and inadequate education are in fact national rather than local or individual concerns.

In the long run, the solution of our domestic problems has as vital a bearing on the success of our foreign policies as on the public happiness at home. We must therefore reassess the priorities of our public policy, with a view to redressing the disproportion between our military and space efforts on the one hand and our education and human welfare program on the other. We must distinguish between necessity and preference in our preoccupation with national security, judging our military needs by a standard which takes due account of the fact that armaments are only one aspect of national security, that military power, as Kenneth Thompson has written, "is like the fist whose force depends on the health and vitality of the body politic and the whole society."[2]

The single-minded dedication with which we Americans have committed ourselves to the struggle with communism is a manifestation of a national tendency to interpret problems in moral and absolutist terms. We are, as Louis Hartz has pointed out, a nation which was "born

[2]Kenneth W. Thompson, *Christian Ethics and the Dilemmas of Foreign Policy* (Durham, North Carolina: Duke University Press, 1959), p. 70.

free."[3] Having experienced almost none of the anguished conflict between radicalism and reaction that has characterized European politics, we have been virtually unanimous in our adherence to the basic values of liberal democracy. We have come to identify these values with the institutional forms which they take in American society and have regarded both as having moral validity not only for ourselves but for the entire world. We have therefore been greatly shocked since our emergence as a world power to find ourselves confronted with revolutionary ideologies which reject the faith in individual liberty and limited government that has served our own society so well.

Because of these predilections, the cold war has seemed to represent a profound challenge to our moral principles as well as to our security and other national interests. We have responded by treating Communist ideology itself, as distinguished from the physical power and expansionist policies of Communist states, as a grave threat to the free world. The cold war, as a result, has been a more dangerous, costly, and irreconcilable conflict than it would be if we, and the Communist states, confined it to those issues that involve the security and vital interests of the rival power blocs.

The ideological element in the cold war, reinforced by the moralist tendencies of the American people, has also had the effect of making the world conflict a much more disruptive element in American life than it would be if it were regarded primarily in terms of its effect on our national security. To an extent, the issue between the Communist and the free worlds is moral and ideological, but ideas and principles in themselves threaten no nation's vital interests except insofar as they are implemented in national policies. It is the latter, therefore, that are our proper concern. To the extent that we are able to remove the crusading spirit and the passions of ideology from the cold war, we can reduce its danger and intensity and relax its powerful hold on the minds and hearts of our people.

The fears and passions of ideological conflict have diverted the minds and energies of our people from the constructive tasks of a free society to a morbid preoccupation with the dangers of Communist aggression abroad and subversion and disloyalty at home. The problem did not end with the McCarthy era of a decade ago nor is it confined to the neurotic fantasies of today's radical right. The cold war malady affects a much broader spectrum of American society. It affects millions of sensible and intelligent citizens whose genuine concern with national security has persuaded them that the prosecution of the cold war is our only truly essential national responsibility, that missiles and nuclear armaments and space flights are so vital to the safety of the nation that it is almost unpatriotic to question their cost and their pro-

[3]Louis Hartz, *The Liberal Tradition in America* (New York: Harcourt, Brace & World, Inc.), 1955.

liferation, and that in the face of these necessities the internal requirements of the country—with respect to its schools and cities and public services—must be left for action at some remote time in the future—as if these requirements were not themselves vital to the national security, and as if, indeed, our generation is likely to know more tranquil days.

In the 1830's Alexis de Tocqueville saw America as a nation with a passion for peace, one in which the "principle of equality," which made it possible for a man to improve his status rapidly in civilian life, made it most unlikely that many Americans would ever be drawn to form a professional military caste. In 1961, President Eisenhower warned the nation of the pervasive and growing power of a "military-industrial complex." Tocqueville was quite right in his judgment that the United States was unlikely to become a *militarist* society. We have, however, as a result of worldwide involvements and responsibilities, become a great *military* power, with a vast military establishment that absorbs over half of our federal budget, profoundly influences the nation's economy, and exercises a gradually expanding influence on public attitudes and policies.

Without becoming militarist in the sense of committing themselves to the military virtues as standards of personal behavior, the American people have nonetheless come to place great—and, in my opinion, excessive—faith in military solutions to political problems. Many Americans have come to regard our defense establishment as the heart and soul of our foreign policy, rather than as one of a number of instruments of foreign policy whose effectiveness depends not only on its size and variety but also on the skill, and restraint, with which it is used.

Our faith in the military is akin to our faith in technology. We are a people more comfortable with machines than with intellectual abstractions. The military establishment is a vast and enormously complex machine, a tribute to the technological genius of the American people; foreign policy is an abstract and esoteric art, widely regarded as a highly specialized occupation of "eastern intellectuals," but not truly an "American" occupation. Our easy reliance on the military establishment as the foundation of our foreign policy is not unlike the reliance which we place on automobiles, televisions, and refrigerators: they work in a predictable and controllable manner, and on the rare occasions when they break down, any good mechanic can put them back in working order.

The trouble with the American technological bias is that it can conceal but not eliminate the ultimate importance of human judgment. Like any other piece of machinery, our military establishment can be no better than the judgment of those who control it. In a democracy control is intended to be exercised by the people and their elected rep-

39

resentatives. To a very considerable extent the American people are not now exercising effective control over the armed forces; nor indeed is the Congress, despite its primary constitutional responsibility in this field. Partly because of anxieties about the cold war, partly because of our natural technological bias, which leads us to place extraordinary faith in the ability of "technicians" to deal with matters that we ourselves find incomprehensible, and partly because of the vested interests of the "military-industrial complex," we are permitting the vast military establishment largely to run itself, to determine its own needs and to tell us what sacrifices are expected of us to sustain the national arsenal of weapons.

The abnegation of responsibility by the Congress in this field is strikingly illustrated by its debates—or, more accurately, "nondebates" —on the defense budget. When, for example, Senator McGovern of South Dakota suggested last September that defense spending might be reduced by 5 percent, the Senate, with virtually no discussion, voted the McGovern amendment down by a vote of 70 to 2 and proceeded, after an afternoon of desultory discussion, to enact the whole defense appropriation bill. When later in the fall I had the dubious honor of managing the foreign aid bill on the Senate floor through three weeks of extremely contentious debate, I could not help noting how astonishingly the forces of "economy" had picked up strength between the debate on the $50 billion defense appropriation and the $4 billion foreign aid bill.

Again this year, the Congress is speeding the enactment of the defense budget with splendid indifference to its size and content. By the end of February both Houses had enacted a military procurement authorization bill of over $17 billion. The only controversial item in the bill was an amendment authorizing $52 million for development of a new strategic manned bomber, which was adopted by both Houses despite the firm opposition of the Secretary of Defense. In the course of this debate, Senator Nelson of Wisconsin posed a most pertinent question. "I am questioning," he said, "what is apparently an established tradition—perhaps a national attitude—which holds that a bill to spend billions of dollars for the machinery of war must be rushed through the House and the Senate in a matter of hours, while a treaty to advance the cause of peace, or a program to help the underdeveloped nations of the world, or a bill to guarantee the rights of all our citizens, or a bill to advance the interests of the poor, must be scrutinized and debated and amended and thrashed over for weeks and perhaps months."[4]

"Like most other Americans . . . ," writes Julius Duscha of the *Washington Post*, "members of Congress believe that the bigger the defense

[4]*Congressional Record*, February 26, 1964, p. 3594.

budget, the safer the country. And in today's world there is no question that the United States must spend billions to keep up its defenses. But record-breaking budgets year after year do not necessarily mean a stronger nation. The bigger any government program gets, the greater are the dangers that funds will be wasted and that the goals of the program will become entangled in a morass of vested interests, venal political considerations, and the rivalries that inevitably evolve from them. And there is no better catharsis for huge government expenditures than informed, skeptical, and continued questioning of them."[5]

The ease with which defense budgets are enacted by Congress, as Mr. Duscha points out, is in no small degree due to the enormous importance of defense spending for the economy. Defense contractors and great numbers of workers all over the country have a vested interest in a high level of defense spending. It is the beneficiaries of the jobs and profits that defense spending creates, along with the generals and admirals, who constitute the formidable "military-industrial complex." And because of the jobs and profits stimulated by defense, Members of Congress have taken a benign attitude toward waste and duplication in the defense budget that is nothing less than amazing by contrast with the deeply held convictions about economy that influence their attitudes toward education, urban renewal, or foreign aid.

The truly astonishing thing about the uncritical support which the American people and their representatives give the military establishment is the apparent enthusiasm with which the sacrifice of personal and community interests is made. Goldsworthy Lowes Dickinson was, if anything, understating the matter when he wrote that "Nations are quite capable of starving every other side of life—education, sanitation, housing, public health, everything that contributes to life, physical, intellectual, moral, and spiritual, in order to maintain their armaments."[6]

Many Americans may regard huge military and space programs as the only truly urgent requirements on our national agenda, but it is difficult to believe that this enthusiasm is shared by the 4.2 million Americans who are unemployed or by the 30 million Americans who have incomes of less than $3,000 a year.

While the cold war and our enormously costly national security programs preempt so much of our time and attention and national wealth, the most important resources of our country—its human resources— are being extravagantly wasted and neglected. As the President's recently issued *Manpower Report* points out, unemployment in 1963 in-

[5]Julius Duscha, "Arms and the Big Money Men," *Harpers*, March 1964, p. 40.

[6]Goldsworthy Lowes Dickinson, *The Choice Before Us* (London: George Allen & Unwin, Ltd., 1917) pp. 200–201.

creased to 5.7 percent of the labor force despite major advancements in production and employment; unemployment of young workers, between the ages of 16 and 19, reached 17 percent in 1963 while unemployment among nonwhite Americans stood at 11 percent; despite an unemployment rate twice as high for school dropouts as for high school graduates, 30 percent of all young people continue to end their education before completing high school; despite the decline in unskilled jobs and the expanding demand for professional, technical, clerical, and service workers—for workers, that is, with at least high school education and specialized training—nearly a million young people are leaving school every year without having completed elementary or secondary school.

These are only a few of the statistics of hopelessness and deprivation that afflict the lives of millions of Americans. Unless the present trend is reversed, 7½ million of the 26 million young people between 16 and 24 who will enter the labor force during the present decade will be school dropouts. These undereducated young men and women are for the most part the children of poverty. The basic fact to be contended with, as President Johnson pointed out in his message to the Congress on poverty, is that "There are millions of Americans—one-fifth of our people—who have not shared in the abundance which has been granted to most of us, and on whom the gates of opportunity have been closed." It is one of the tragedies, and one of the great failures, of our national life that in the years between 1936 and 1964, while the total wealth and productivity of the nation grew tremendously, the number of ill-housed, ill-clothed, and ill-fed Americans dropped only to one-fifth of our population.

The statistics of poverty, though striking, are antiseptic compared to the actual misery and hopelessness of being poor. The real meaning of poverty is not just losses of learning and productivity, but thousands of angry and dispossessed teen-agers who make our city streets dangerous for "respectable" citizens; 350,000 youngsters across the nation who form what the Secretary of Labor has described as an "outlaw pack" because they have stopped looking for work, are unemployed today, and will remain so for the rest of their lives; children in a blighted mining town in eastern Kentucky who are pot-bellied and anemic from lack of food; sharecroppers, white as well as black, living in squalid shacks and working for a few dollars a day—when they can find work at all—anywhere in a crescent of rural poverty that extends from southern Virginia along the coastal plain across Georgia and Alabama into the Mississippi delta and the Ozarks.

Poverty in America has a radically different moral connotation from poverty in underdeveloped nations. The poor countries of the world have the excuse, for what it is worth, that the means of feeding, housing, and educating their people simply do not exist. In America, the means do exist; the failure is essentially one of distribution. The children who go to bed hungry in a Harlem slum or a West Virginia mining town are not being deprived because no food can be found to give them; they are going to bed hungry because, despite all our miracles of invention and production, we have not yet found a way to make the necessities of life available to all of our citizens—including those whose failure is not a lack of personal industry or initiative but only an unwise choice of parents.

What is to be done? In his poverty message to the Congress, the President made proposals for a constructive start—although only a start—toward meeting the problem of poverty in America. Under the proposed Economic Opportunity Act, a National Job Corps would undertake the social rehabilitation, through basic education, job training, and work experience, of 100,000 young men "whose background, health, and education makes them least fit for useful work"; a work-training program would provide vocation education and part-time jobs for 200,000 young men and women in projects to be developed by state and local governments and nonprofit agencies; a national work-study program would provide Federal funds for part-time jobs for 140,000 young Americans who, though qualified, would otherwise be unable to afford to go to college. In addition, the President's program would encourage and help finance local anti-poverty programs, would enlist volunteers in the war against poverty, and would undertake other financial and educational programs all to be coordinated under a new Office of Economic Opportunity.

President Johnson's program can serve as a point of departure for a full-scale national program to eliminate poverty and unemployment from American life. Such a program must be mounted through government fiscal policy, public works, and expansive economic policies, but primarily through programs of education and training. Education is not the whole solution but it is, by all available evidence, the keystone of the arch. As John Kenneth Galbraith recently wrote, "To the best of knowledge there is no place in the world where a well-educated population is really poor."[7]

Building on this premise, Professor Galbraith proposes that the hundred lowest income communities in the country be designated as "special educational districts" to be equipped with primary and secondary schools and recreational and transportation facilities of the highest quality. The schools would be staffed by an elite corps of highly qualified, highly trained, and *well-paid* teachers. Grants would be provided for food and clothing for the pupils when needed as well as counseling and medical and psychiatric services. After one year the program would be extended to another 150 or 200 areas and eventually

[7]John Kenneth Galbraith, "Let Us Begin: An Invitation to Action on Poverty," *Harpers*, March, 1964, p. 26.

CONSEQUENCES OF NUCLEAR CAPABILITIES

to cover all areas of great need. As income rises in the recipient school districts, the schools would be turned back to the localities.[8]

The Galbraith plan is an excellent one and I, for one, would welcome the submission of such a plan to the Congress, although there can be no doubt that it would generate great controversy. I think that we must face up to the need for major new legislation in the field of education regardless of the partisan divisions which it may provoke. We must do so if we truly mean to alleviate the scourge of poverty in American life. And although it is clear that there is no simple dollar for dollar relationship between savings in the defense and space budgets and Congressional willingness to appropriate money for education, it seems to me quite possible that the elimination of superfluous defense and space funds would in fact help overcome the reluctance to support education legislation of certain members of Congress whose concern with economy is genuine and strong.

As a result of the rapidly spreading automation of the American economy, the traditional mechanism of distributing purchasing power through employment and income is breaking down. In essence, our ability to generate economic demand is falling steadily behind our ability to increase the supply of purchaseable goods and services. It may be that the growing disequilibrium is so profound as to be irreversible by government policies designed to stimulate economic growth and full employment. If so, we shall eventually have to devise new ways of providing income to those who cannot be put to gainful work.

Whether truly radical measures will be required or not, there is no question that if our national war on poverty is to come anywhere near the goal of "total victory" proclaimed by President Johnson, it will require enormous public effort and a great deal of public money. To those who shrink from such a commitment in the name of economy, I would emphasize that the elimination of poverty and inadequate education are at least as important to the security of our country in the long run as the maintenance of a strong defense establishment and a good deal more important than a voyage to the moon. I commend to them the words of Edmund Burke, that "Economy is a distributive virtue, and consists not in saving but in selection. Parsimony requires no providence, no sagacity, no powers of combination, no comparison, no judgment."[9]

The cold war has diverted us from problems both quantitative and qualitative. The quantitative problem is essentially to devise ways of elevating the one-fifth of our people who live in poverty to the level of the four-fifths who live in greater material abundance than any other society in human history. The qualitative problem is to find ways of

[8]*Ibid.*
[9]Edmund Burke, *Letter to a Noble Lord* (1796).

bringing meaning and purpose and standards of excellence into the lives of a people who, because of their material affluence, are free, as no people have ever been before, to shape a spiritual and intellectual environment of their own choice.

While the attention and energy of our public policy have been focused through these postwar years on crises in Berlin and Cuba and the Far East, America, almost behind our backs, has been more and more taking on the physical appearance, and the cultural atmosphere, of a honky-tonk of continental proportions. This is not to suggest that the quest for intellectual, artistic, and scientific excellence has been abandoned in our country. On the contrary, it is being pursued by more people with more energy and more striking results than at any time in our history. But the pursuit of excellence and creativity remains the occupation of an elite segment of our society, a large and brilliant elite, to be sure, but one which is still largely isolated from the nation as a whole. The creative elements of American society are probably growing larger and are constantly reaching new levels of achievement, but they are not yet successfully communicating their standards to the generality of their countrymen.

I do not think we can avoid the conclusion that despite a broadening interest in the arts, the level of popular taste in America remains far below what it can be and ought to be. The evidences are all around us: in the mindless trivia that fill the television channels and occupy the leisure hours of tens of millions of Americans; in the paperback pornography that has become a major national industry; in the gaudy and chaotic architecture that clutters the central areas of our great cities from Manhattan to Miami and Los Angeles and in the festering slums that surround them.

It can be pointed out, and rightly, that all this is mitigated by the growing popularity of good music and good art, of the serious theater and of quality films. But this, I fear, is confined to the "other America," to the large but isolated elite who are supposed to set, or at least suggest, popular standards of taste and style but who somehow are failing to do so.

Nowhere is the vulgarization of standards more conspicuous than in the artifacts of urban America. It is difficult to judge what is the most depressing sight in New York City: the jungle of antiseptic glass towers that have taken order and humanity out of the midtown area, the sprawling slums that are never far away, or the dreary acres of identical brick housing, devoid of any charm or individuality, that constitute "urban renewal." It is equally difficult to understand how Washington, the nation's beautiful, monumental city, the living symbol of what is valued and emulated in America, should have permitted itself to be marred by stark, prison-like new Federal office buildings that suggest arid dehumanized activities within them, or by the elephantine Rayburn House Office Building, built in what has been described as the "early Mussolini" style of architecture, a building so ugly that one can only regard it as the product of an organized effort, in tastelessness and vulgarity.

I feel certain that this debasement of standards is not inevitable in contemporary America. About a half mile from the new prison-like office buildings in Washington stands the new National Geographic building, an elegant example of contemporary architecture, a structure of grace and dignity and human warmth. A half mile in another direction stands the Old Senate Office Building, a model of dignity and beauty in the classic style. This contrast symbolizes the polarization of standards between "two Americas" that constitutes a growing problem of our national life. Somehow we must strive to bring the two alienated cultures of our country together again, to make the quest for beauty and excellence a truly national endeavor.

In a recently published book of incisive text and brilliant photographs illustrating "the planned deterioration of America's landscape," Peter Blake offers the following bleak prognosis for America's cities:

> "With a very, very few exceptions, our cities seem to be headed for a grim future indeed—unless we determine to make some radical changes. That future looks something like this: first, our cities will be inhabited solely by the very poor (generally colored) and the very rich (generally white)—plus a few divisions of police to protect the latter from the former. Second, they will become *primarily* places to work in—places for office buildings and for light industry. Third, they will become totally ghettofied—not merely in terms of racial segregation, but also in terms of usage: there will be office ghettos, industrial ghettos, apartment ghettos, amusement or culture ghettos (like Manhattan's gold-plated Rockefeller ghetto, *Lincoln Center*), bureaucratic ghettos, shopping ghettos, medical-center ghettos. In other words, there will be virtually no mixed uses of streets or of neighborhoods, so that most areas of the city will be alive for mere fractions of each day or weeks, and as deserted as Wall Street on a weekend for the rest of the time."[10]

One can hope that it will not come to this, that before our cities are lost to glass palaces and slums, the suburbs to housing projects and automobile junkyards, the highways to gaudy motels, and the countryside to a solid wall of billboards, the vulgarizing trend will be arrested and reversed. If it is to be reversed, we must begin by recognizing that private property rights cannot extend to the debauching of America's landscape. An ugly city is not like a bad painting, which can be shut up in a museum out of the sight of anyone who does not wish to see it. Our cities and highways and countryside are part of our common

[10]Peter Blake, *God's Own Junkyard* (New York: Holt, Rhinehart and Winston, 1964) p. 23.

TECHNOLOGICAL MILITARISM   .

legacy. They either enrich or impoverish our lives and it cannot be left to the sole discretion of promoters and developers to determine which it will be. There is so much in the American environment that is good, so much that is both beautiful and efficient, that the widespread prevalence of disorder and decay is beyond excuse or understanding.

Obviously, we cannot impose high standards by force, as, in certain respects the Russians have—by the simple, puritanical expedient of withdrawing from their people those forms of art and recreation that are deemed to be vulgar and decadent. Only by a very limited—though still important—means can we use the law to combat ugliness and bad taste: by establishing and enforcing high architectural standards for urban construction and urban renewal; by restricting the placement of billboards on our highways; by preserving our shrinking areas of natural beauty in national parks; by revising the practice of rewarding slum landlords who allow their property to deteriorate with low tax assessments; by imposing some order on the planning of schools and housing and parks and expressways.

Beyond these limited measures of community action we must strive as individuals to bring together the "two Americas," to restore the lines of communication between the minority that value excellence and the majority that settle for mediocrity. I do not know how this is to be accomplished, but I think there is a clue in what seems to me to be one of the major sources of the postwar vulgarization of American life: the combination of widespread affluence with the intense anxieties generated by the cold war, resulting both in a fixation on foreign problems and in an almost compulsive search for release from anxiety through trivial and tasteless, but convenient and diverting, channels of popular amusement. The cold war, writes David Riesman, "is a distraction from serious thought about man's condition on the planet."[11]

If there is any validity in this analysis, then it follows that the first thing we must do toward raising the quality of American life is to turn some part of our thoughts and our creative energies away from the cold war that has engaged them for so long back in on America itself. If we do this, and then let nature take its course, we may find that the most vital resources of our nation, for its public happiness and its security as well, remain locked within our own frontiers, in our cities and in our countryside, in our work and in our leisure, in the hearts and minds of our people.

[11]David Riesman, *Abundance for What?* (Garden City, New York: Doubleday and Co., Inc., 1964) p. 98.

TWO

MILITARY IDEOLOGY
AND INFLUENCE IN SOCIETY

Students of contemporary civilization have different views about the necessity of the extensive military preparedness which characterizes the United States. The proponents of such preparedness, who are frequently found in research institutes for the study of military strategy, argue that war is one of several options which may be required by the national interest. Also the national interest may require using threats of force to deter aggressive nations from taking aggressive actions. Threats in turn require the capability to deliver or they will not be believed. A final or total threat remains unconvincing as a deterrent against relatively minor transgressions and may in fact tempt an adversary to commit minor transgressions short of those which would provoke a full-scale counterattack. Therefore, an entire series of graded threats must be made for lesser offenses than a surprise nuclear attack and these too require preparedness if they are to be credible.

The argument does not end here. Why merely react to provocations from an adversary? Why not have a graded series of offensive actions of one's own which might range from economic assistance to subversion to counterguerrilla warfare and to threats of limitless escalation? Activities like these have been studied, planned for, and carried into action in American foreign policy. The mode of thought within which such activity is not only rational but also necessary is expanded in Herman Kahn's book, *On Escalation,* which is carefully summarized in the review by Anatol Rapoport.

Rapoport's review, however, raises the important question of whether the assumptions behind such strategic analyses as these are reasonable. The underlying view that the world is made of self-interested nation states protecting or extending their national interests in a game which permits various forms of armed conflict among the moves may be quite dangerous. If the strongest nations act as if the world were an arena for competitive national advantages, the belief will likely become a self-fulfilling prophesy.

The dynamics of self-fulfilling prophesy are easily understood. If I say no one likes me, then I will react to signs of friendship with reserve and suspicion; eventually no one will like me. With nations, as with individuals, the expectation of malice serves not only to generate malice, but also to rule out attempts to change hostile motives. Even if the world did look like the interminable conflict world of the strategists, the strategic view may well preclude any opportunity to change the world, to engage in those acts of trust or good will or research into alternatives which will help to build a world more respectful of human values. The Christian admonition to "love thine enemies," while incomprehensible to the strategic view, may also have self-fulfilling properties which have not been explored.

The strategists' way of thinking has dominated American foreign policy at least since the start of the cold war. In the writings of scholars there has been a significant convergence between the intellectuals who work directly or indirectly for the Department of Defense and the "realist" school of political science thought. Both most frequently share the view of men and nations as inherently power seeking and checked in their aggrandizements only by a calculation of the costs involved. Although the work of Herman Kahn has been influential among military strategists, much of the strategy debate has been window dressing for the actual enactment of strategic policy which necessarily reflects the compromises and the preferences of those responsible for policy making. We have selected an address by former Secretary of Defense Robert McNamara as an example of strategic thinking as it occurs at the level of implementation.

The reasoning in the speech by McNamara is repeated in a host of more recent policy statements by the Departments of State and Defense. They are intended to apply a pragmatic program to the achievement of military security for this country. The most recent of these are found in the rationale for the anti-ballistic-missile program which promises a major escalation in the costs of defense. The evaluation of the effectiveness of such programs is not an easy matter. Security is a way of feeling—a psychological commodity—and no amount of expenditure on defense will necessarily purchase it. Trusting to the professional military man the judgment of just how much defense is enough is not an entirely satisfactory procedure. The preparedness of one nation provides stimulus for the preparedness of other antagonistic nations, resulting in less security for all nations. The only steady gains from self-reinforcing trends such as an arms race are in those portions of the society most closely associated with military values or with weapon production. The modest anti-ballistic-missile program currently planned in the U.S. has already had marked repercussions in Soviet society, strengthening the hard-line and militaristic

49

factions, weakening those who would seek closer accommodation with the United States. The various military establishments of the world hold symbiotic relationships to one another. They cannot survive without competitors and their growth in power and influence is dependent upon the growth, militancy and productivity of their enemies.

Policy in a large modern society does not emerge from rational debate, whether by soldiers, scholars or administration. It emerges rather from the interplay between large interest groups, public and private, jockeying for the measures most immediately beneficial to their own purposes. Pilisuk and Hayden examine the institutions which have an interest in the perpetuation of military preparedness and find them much more diverse and powerful than the old munitions makers who used to be associated with a primitive desire for the profits of war. The article raises the thesis that, right or wrong, the high level of military preparedness is no accidental policy but is rather a consistent, necessary and prominent part of the forces which keep the United States functioning in what is, at least temporarily, a stable course.

A substantial body of research exists on the question of economic consequences of disarmament. Most of this research points to a problem which is infinitely more complex than a mere reallocation of the defense dollar into one or another constructive purpose. Some industries suffer a crisis of over-specialization, leaving little margin for convertibility to civilian needs. Similarly, areas like Southern California suffer from over-concentration of governmentally subsidized defense industry. Some economic offset programs, such as retiring the national debt or drastically reducing taxes, would produce a predictable economic disaster in the country. Reallocation of money into schools, hospitals, or housing requires a high degree of planning based upon prediction of population shifts, plans in neighboring areas, the stability of industry in an area, and the economic consequences of related programs. The feeling among several economists is that the U. S., on an economic basis, could accommodate to peace, but that the political changes required for such an accommodation are not feasible (Melman, 1965). Inquiry into political changes, or shifts in power, are a relatively taboo topic among behavioral scientists. But the very absence of such inquiry reveals a society geared to retaining a status quo with a high dependence upon military machinery and a strategic conception of world affairs.

Absence of active high-level consideration characterizes the recent history of the question of whether a selective service system should exist in this country. It is around the issue of the draft, however, that heated debate is occurring at lower levels of the policy process. At issue here, as in the proposals for a National Service Corps, is the question, "Who shall decide for the individual his obligations to goals with which he is not necessarily in agreement?" This debate is discussed in the article by Flacks, Howe and Lauter. The discussion of

50

.

the draft law and its use to channel the life choice of young men into preferred occupations suggests similar forms of control over people to those discussed later in our section on Decision Control. The same basic problem recurs. In an effort to meet conditions imposed by modern technology our society has found it increasingly necessary to control the choices people are making.

The thesis of this section is that military modes of thought have contributed to an acceptance of a highly centralized social system in which the disadvantaged who get non-discriminatory job training in the military; the graduate student on a National Defense and Education Fellowship; the civilian army of scientists, engineers, industrialists, managers, and union workers who live on defense supported contracts; and the patriots who, cut off from meaningful service, substitute allegiance to nationalistic symbols all make the domestic costs of a transition to peace quite high. The very successes of the United States as a nation ready for war leaves little power in the hands of interest groups who have not yet found success or become dependent upon the dominant type of social or economic arrangement associated with military preparedness.

REFERENCES AND ADDITIONAL READING

Emile Benoit and Kenneth E. Boulding (eds.), *Disarmament and The Economy.* New York: Harper & Row, 1963.

Lewis A. Coser, "The Dysfunctions of Military Secrecy," *Social Problems,* 11, Summer 1963, 13–22.

Amitai Etzioni, *The Moon-Doggle: The Domestic and International Implications of the Space Race,* New York: Doubleday, 1964.

Morris Janowitz, "American Democracy and Military Service," *Trans-action,* March, 1967, 5-11ff.

Herman Kahn, *On Escalation: Metaphors and Scenarios,* New York: F. E. Praeger, 1965.

Herman Kahn, "The Nature and Feasibility of War Deterrence," D. Bobrow, ed., *The Components of Defense Policy,* Chicago: Rand McNally, 1965.

Seymour Melman, *Our Depleted Society,* New York: Holt, Rinehart, and Winston, 1965.

Elwin Powell, "Paradoxes of the Warfare State," *Trans-action,* March, 1964, 3–7.

Anatol Rapoport, *Strategy and Conscience,* New York: Harper & Row, 1964.

Sol Stern, "The Defense Intellectuals," *Ramparts,* 5, February, 1967, 31–37.

Anatol Rapoport

Chicken à la Kahn

The recent history of warfare is a history of applied science. No other application of science has mobilized human ingenuity on so broad a scale and in such depth. The major wars of our century have been characterized by a shift in scientific focus. Thus World War I has been called with some justification the chemists' war; World War II has been called the physicists' war. Toward its last phases, World War II was also becoming the mathematicians' war. Indeed, the electronic computer was distinctly a by-product of that war.

However, in spite of the shifting focus, it is clear that war is becoming even more a genuine co-operative enterprise among all the fields of science. The crucial role of mathematics in World War III seems definitely assured. In addition, the social sciences will surely be enlisted. Sociology and economics loom in importance as the necessity becomes apparent of preparing for social dislocations of unprecedented magnitude. One envisages also the future role of political science in creating patterns of political control concomitant with social organization required by modern war. Psychology will make its contribution not only with regard to the study of man as a link in the man-machine system but also with regard to the psychic processes of the decision maker. For these psychic processes now constitute an integral part of the new revolutionized strategic science.

It is with some aspects of the new strategic science that *On Escalation* (by Herman Kahn, Frederick A. Praeger, Inc. $6.95) is concerned. Before I undertake the discussion of the book proper, I should like to offer a few conjectures concerning its place in the history of strategic theory.

Reprinted from *The Virginia Quarterly Review*, Vol. 41, No. 3, Summer, 1965, pp. 370–389, by permission of the author and publisher. Anatol Rapoport is professor of mathematical biology and senior research mathematician at the Mental Health Research Institute, University of Michigan.

TECHNOLOGICAL MILITARISM

The art of strategy reached a peak of elegance during the eighteenth century, thanks largely to the genius of Frederick the Great of Prussia. The Napoleonic wars brought in an admixture of vulgarization, thanks to the dilution of professional armies by hordes of conscripts and volunteers. Clausewitz's classical treatise "On War" was a courageous attempt to re-establish austere standards of rationality and professionalism in the theory and practice of war. Clausewitz is justly credited with bringing into focus the cardinal principle of civilized war, namely, that war is a means, never an end in itself. By means of war, one state imposes its will upon another. Such imposition of will, namely the attainment of specific objectives, ought to be, Clausewitz argued, the one and only reason for going to war. Moreover, war ought to be conducted by competent professionals in accordance with sound and rational principles.

It goes without saying that Clausewitz would have been severely disappointed with the conduct of World War I, a war of attrition, in which it should have become immediately clear to all participants (but it didn't) that the costs of the war would far surpass the value of any of the stated objectives. What was worse, World War I was also almost devoid of strategic elegance. Nor would Clausewitz have approved of World War II for its emphasis on mystical objectives (Blood and Soil; Unconditional Surrender; the Four Freedoms). As for the rash of revolutions, civil wars, resistance movements, and the like which have erupted in our century, Clausewitz would surely have viewed this development as a degradation of a noble art, something like a spectacle of chess players hurling chess pieces at each other.

Since the end of World War II, classical Clausewitzian diplo-military principles have enjoyed a renaissance. I would venture to suggest that no small part in this renaissance was played by the introduction of nuclear weapons. At first, this seems surprising since it was thought for a while that nuclear war would destroy the rational basis of war by making all conceivable objectives prohibitively costly. Moreover, it was next to impossible to conceive of sound strategic principles relevant to the conduct of a war which would last perhaps only a few hours. These apprehensions, however, proved to have been unfounded. A new group of strategists has appeared, recruited largely from the academic rather than the military circles. These progressive thinkers brought fresh ideas to bear upon the art and science of war.

Of these new strategists, one of the most imaginative is Herman Kahn, the author of the volume under review. Mr. Kahn's earlier volume, "On Thermonuclear War," attracted attention far beyond the defense community. In it he gave full expression to the two main ideas which rescued the art of strategy from oblivion. One idea was that the art of strategy need not be confined to the battlefield but can be extended to the thrusts and parries, threats and counter-threats of mutual intimidation, which usually precede a war. The other idea was a re-

53

formulation of objectives for which wars could be fought. Granting that it is difficult to extend the notion of "victory" to any outcome of a full-scale nuclear exchange, Mr. Kahn insisted that it is still possible for one side or another to "prevail."

Both of these ideas stem from a conceptualization of war as a game of strategy. This conceptualization is already apparent in the military classics, but has come most clearly into focus against the background of recent mathematical developments known as the theory of games. Game theory includes a far-reaching taxonomy of conflict situations classified in accordance with the nature of their strategic structure. Each game is defined by a set of rules, including rules of termination, which define numerical pay-offs to each player associated with each possible outcome of the game. Hence, if we can define the pay-offs associated with various outcomes of a war, say in terms of population and material losses, as well as strategic opportunities with respect to the next war, we can surely decide which side has prevailed in any specific real or hypothetical instance by the simple expedient of keeping score.

It must be stressed that Mr. Kahn does not utilize the technical apparatus of game theory in his formulations. Indeed, his formulations are not of the sort to which formal game theory could be meaningfully applied. It is true, however, that Mr. Kahn's outlook is strongly influenced by the outlook presupposed in game theory. In game theory, it is the strategic structure of a conflict situation which constitutes the exclusive object of analysis. Thus the bulk of game theory rests on a taxonomy of games, which reveals the fundamental distinctions between two-person and N-person games, between zero-sum and non-zero-sum games, between games with solutions in terms of pure strategies and those requiring mixed strategies, et cetera. Although none of these technical questions are raised in Mr. Kahn's analysis, the spirit of his approach is quite similar. As in game theory, only the strategic structure has been abstracted from each conflict situation. As in game theory, while the magnitude of the pay-offs is relevant, the actual content of the pay-offs is not. For example, it is not legitimate to ask in the context of game theory *why* one outcome of the game is preferred to another, any more than to ask why a yard is longer than an inch. This is also the case with Mr. Kahn's analysis. His analysis always proceeds on the basis of given preference orderings. What determines the preferences and how is entirely beyond the scope of his book.

Next, the specific physical realization of the game is irrelevant to Mr. Kahn's analysis, just as it is in game theory. For example, it is quite irrelevant to the analysis of a game whether the game is played on a board with wooden pieces or on a blackboard with chalk marks or on a battle field with human bodies or as a nuclear exchange with cities as chips. Nor are the psychological processes of the players relevant except insofar as they have a bearing on strategic choices.

54

It is in this spirit that Mr. Kahn develops the science of nuclear strategy of which he is said to be an outstanding exponent. The present volume is essentially an exposition of forty-four phases of conflict (among states or power blocs), distinguished mainly by the degree of severity. Mr. Kahn calls these phases the rungs of the escalation ladder.

The simplest model of an escalation ladder has only two rungs. As such it can be formalized as the so-called game of Chicken, with which Mr. Kahn begins his exposition. The designation "Chicken" derives from the game sometimes played by American youngsters on a highway. Two cars rush headlong toward each other. The first driver to swerve from the collision course is "chicken." Thus victory goes to the bold. Consequently, Mr. Kahn points out, if the driver of one car can convey to the other that he is absolutely determined not to swerve or is drunk or has thrown the steering wheel away, he can prevail, provided the other (1) gets and understands the message; (2) is not equally determined; (3) is not drunk; (4) has not thrown away *his* steering wheel.

On Escalation is essentially an expansion of this idea. The either-or structure of Chicken is here drawn out into a large spectrum, ranging from Rungs 1, 2, and 3 (Pre-crisis Maneuvering) to Rung 44 (Spasm War). Indeed, refinement of distinctions is one of Mr. Kahn's principal contributions to strategic analysis. His recurring complaint is the crudeness of conceptualization which distinguishes only "peace" and "war" or only "conventional war" and "nuclear war." In contrast, Mr. Kahn's taxonomy of diplo-military conflict is exceedingly rich and refined. Starting with several rungs of increasingly tense inter-nation situations, he does not reach the (sporadic) shooting stage until Rung 8 (Harassing Acts of Violence), and the sustained shooting stage (Large Conventional War) until Rung 12. On the other hand, the nuclear stage is reached already at Rung 15 (Barely Nuclear War), leaving 24-29 rungs of nuclear escalation to reach the serious stages, namely, Slow Motion Counter-city War (Rung 39), Counter-value Salvo (40), Augmented Disarming Attack (41), Civilian Devastation Attack (42), Some Other Kinds of Controlled General War (43), and finally the Spasm (the 44th and last Rung).

The Spasm, that is, the all-out holocaust, is the layman's conception of nuclear war. It was shared also by John Foster Dulles, who is said by Mr. Kahn to have remarked that if war ever broke out, the State Department would be closed down.

One of Mr. Kahn's contributions to present-day thinking about war and peace is in dispelling such simplistic notions. The choice, he points out, is not between the total blessing of peace and the total curse of a spasm war. There is a wide choice of positions on the escalation ladder, along which nation states may wander up and down in the pursuit of their national interests.

The concept of escalation combines brinkmanship with measured   55 response. The former, it will be recalled, was a conception of diplomacy based upon the maximum threat. As long as war and peace were thought of in either-or terms, there seemed to be no choice open to the United States but of threatening the Soviet Union (the then Enemy Number One) with total destruction, if Communist subversion should occur anywhere in the world. The measured response theory (advanced shortly after the Soviet Union developed a nuclear capability of her own) was based on the principle of making the punishment fit the crime, i.e., retaliation was to be tailored to the provocation. The new escalation theory incorporates the best features of both. It has had some precursors. For example, it was proposed at one stage to make massive retaliation depend on a chance outcome. In this way, the threats could be properly graduated. Thus, in response to a minor provocation (say a student riot in Venezuela), the United States could threaten the Soviet Union with massive retaliation with probability .01 (that is, make the implementation of the threat dependent on an outcome of an event whose chance of occurrence was one in a hundred); while to a major provocation (for example, infiltration in South Vietnam) the response might be a threat of massive retaliation with probability .5 (e.g., making the realization dependent on the toss of a coin). Theoretically, this scheme had a great deal to recommend it, for it made the choice of strategy mathematically tractable. One could rely on a rational opponent to weigh the utilities of the possible outcomes with the respective probabilities and to act so as to maximize his utility. There is no denying, however, that the notion of "probabilistically graduated response" has an academic flavor to it, and it is not surprising that the idea did not elicit enthusiasm in practical men.

Escalation, too, embodies probabilistic ideas, but here probabilities are involved not in deliberate randomization of choices but rather in estimates which the participants make of each other's intentions. The principal feature of the game of Chicken dominates the strategic considerations of the escalation game. He who disbelieves that the opponent is willing to go the limit may thereby be enhancing his own chances of a win. For in that case, he is able to muster "resolve," and the very fact that he does so induces the credibility of *his* willingness to go the limit.

Like many great ideas, this one is simple and not particularly new. Mr. Kahn's contribution is embodied mainly in his systematic and detailed explorations of the techniques available to the participants on each rung of the escalation ladder.

The discussion of the techniques is necessarily brief (this is a survey rather than a handbook), but it is exhaustive in the sense of covering a very large number of contingencies and alternatives. Thus at Rung 2 (Political, Economic, and Diplomatic Gestures) a player may choose between refusing to facilitate negotiations, making overtures to the other side's enemies, arranging for newspaper leaks, et cetera. At Rung 4 (Hardening of Positions) one starts to "burn the bridges," i.e., to make one's own retreat impossible. At Rung 7 ("Legal" Harassment) "one may harass the opponent's prestige, property, or nationals legally." So it goes to Rung 12 (Large Conventional War), in which fighting has started in earnest, but where "quality" weapons (nuclear, bacteriological, chemical) are not yet used. As we have already mentioned, the nuclear stage is reached at Rung 15 (Barely Nuclear War). This is a delicate stage. It may be that the first use of nuclear weapons is unintentional; or it may be "unintentional," i.e., the user has used nuclear weapons deliberately but is conveying the impression that the use was accidental.

"There are at least two reasons for such deceptions," writes Mr. Kahn. "First, the mere fact that a nuclear 'accident' has occurred would indicate clearly to the opponent, and to others who could put pressure on him, that the situation was very dangerous. . . . Second, the attacker may feel that it is particularly important to destroy some key enemy installation . . . and find that he can do so only with nuclear weapons. He might destroy this installation and still hope that the opponent would accept it as an accidental and unauthorized use of a weapon. The offending side could offer to punish the guilty individuals, perhaps to provide an indemnification, or to permit a reprisal (but not really a compensating one) by the other side."

Once one has passed the "nuclear threshold," escalation becomes a tricky business. The problem is to keep it under control. Some control seems to be "built in" in the very act of "limited nuclear exchange." In one of the scenarios [a scenario is an imagined course of events, usually invoving a crisis or a part of a war. Scenarios are used in training people to think strategically, for example, to foresee the range of options open to the principals at various stages of conflict] Mr. Kahn writes:

> The Soviets . . . invade West Germany. They are advancing rapidly. The Americans might then use two or three nuclear weapons to destroy bridges in the Soviet rear . . . the purpose of the destruction is less to degrade logistics than to say, "Having used two or three nuclear weapons, are we not likely to use many more?" . . . [The Soviets] might themselves use two or three nuclear weapons . . . in order to indicate that they have not been frightened by the American use. . . . One can thus easily imagine a cease fire being called immediately after the Soviet retaliation.

On the other hand, the tit-for-tat might not end with one exchange. We read later:

> If there should come about more or less continued tit-for-tat exchanges . . . the result would be a war of almost pure resolve. . . . 57

Many strategists believe that reciprocal-reprisal wars of resolve may be a standard tactic of the future, when the balance of terror has become firm and absolute.

By the time Rung 39 is reached, the tit-for-tat exchanges are in the "city trading stage."

> This kind of war would be the most extreme and ultimate form of deliberative, selective, and controlled response—but one not necessarily or even likely to be beyond the psychological capabilities of decision makers. . . .

Each of the phases, be it noted, presents its own strategic problems and a plethora of pros and cons for escalating to the next phase. (De-escalation presents its own problems, briefly mentioned toward the end of the book.) Only the last phase (Rung 44—Spasm War) is devoid of strategic significance and hence offers no intellectual challenge. To quote Mr. Kahn once more:

> My use of the term "spasm" does not necessarily denote blind overwhelming fury, but might only mean that a response is automatic, unthinking, and uncontrolled—a function of the central nervous system, so to speak, rather than of the brain. [Possibly Mr. Kahn means here the autonomic nervous system; otherwise the end of the sentence makes no sense. The central nervous system includes the brain.]

The exposition of *On Escalation* is for the most part descriptive. The phase of escalation represented by each rung is illustrated by the diplo-military events characteristic of the phase and by the options of initiative and response open to the participants. Specific recommendations are, for the most part, not definitive, and at times include both pro and con arguments. For example, the important question of "breaching the nuclear threshold" is examined with great thoroughness. In peripheral conflicts, according to Mr. Kahn, a premium is put on the use of blackmail and threats, surprise attacks, anonymous attacks, being willing, politically and morally, to accept a high percentage of casualties, et cetera. But, he goes on, "these are precisely the desiderata in which the U. S. is most likely to be weak or incompetent." He continues, ". . . by and large the kind of war that the U. S. is most competent to fight . . . is the high explosive [thermonuclear] war." This is clearly an argument for escalation from a phase in which the United States is at a disadvantage to one where it enjoys an advantage.

There are other arguments for breaching the nuclear threshold, cited by Mr. Kahn, for example, "a world in which nuclear weapons have been used . . . purposely and effectively to punish an aggressor is a stable world." This is especially true if ". . . one or two dozen nations possess adequate stocks of nuclear weapons, [so that] no single nation or even any reasonable combination is likely to take up aggression. The process of weapon diffusion would enable any one of these nations to strike a painful and even anonymous blow against the aggressors. Such a world would clearly be discouraging for a Hitler. And it is not an improbable international political-strategic order for the future."

Admitting that this is a strong argument for nuclear use, and the consequent proliferation of nuclear weapons, Mr. Kahn nevertheless declares that he is not convinced by it, in any event "in the present climate of opinion in the U. S.—which is bitterly hostile to the proliferation of nuclear weapons." For one thing, Mr. Kahn is seriously concerned with the change in the power structure in a world in which twenty or thirty nations possess nuclear weapons—"and not all of them stable democracies." He also sees another argument against the use (and consequently the proliferation) of nuclear weapons which would not, perhaps, occur to many people: namely, the resulting accelerating arms race might act as a "spur to various kinds of ban-the-bomb movements, some wholly irresponsible, thus increasing the pressures of these groups upon democratic governments. Such groups could impair Western morale, leading to diffidence and uncertainty in the pursuit of national objectives."

On the whole, Mr. Kahn recommends prudence in the use of escalation in the pursuit of national interests: ". . . if one wishes to violate thresholds, one must be conscious of the negative effects and act in a manner that minimizes them, as well as exploits the gains that are sought."

Thus, the prescriptions to be found in *On Escalation,* are, for the most part, eclectic rather than definitive. On only one point, already mentioned above, Mr. Kahn expresses an emphatic commitment, namely, the necessity of "thinking through" all foreseeable contingencies and of preparing appropriate plans of action. He deplores the attitude which "shuts off thinking" as soon as a scenario reaches an outbreak of a thermonuclear war. He points out that such a war is (1) a distinct possibility and (2) not necessarily an unmitigated disaster. It behooves us, therefore, to extend to the hypothetical situations arising in a nuclear war the same cool, calculating demeanor that has characterized the best in diplo-military tradition. The military profession, Mr. Kahn complains, was almost ready to throw in the sponge with the advent of nuclear weapons. He notes with satisfaction that this loss of heart was only temporary. He rallies the defense community to awaken to the exciting potentialities of a new diplo-military science based on a widened range of coercive capabilities introduced by the nuclear break through.

59

My evaluation of Mr. Kahn's book will be based on the analysis of this plea and on my response to it.

Mr. Kahn supports his plea by an appeal to open-mindedness and to foresight in a rapidly changing world. I take it, then, that the investigations he pursues and encourages are motivated by intellectual curiosity and by patriotism. I assume also that Mr. Kahn is motivated, like any other professional, by pride of craftsmanship. Sophistication is the mental analogue of manual virtuosity. And so I will assume that patriotism, professional pride, and intellectual curiosity are the principal bases of Mr. Kahn's appeal for overcoming inhibitions in exploring the potentialities of escalation and nuclear war.

Let us examine patriotism first. Patriotism is a variant of loyalty, in which the object of allegiance is a nation state. Nation states have not always existed and therefore neither has patriotism. Some forms of loyalty, however, are present in all patterns of social life. For example, the basis of the serf's loyalty to the feudal lord was the power of the lord to protect the serf from marauders and from other lords. The henchman's loyalty to the gangster boss has a similar basis. Other forms of loyalty are based on sentimental attachment, for example, family, friendship, and community ties. The nation state commands loyalty primarily in two ways: first, on the basis of a belief that one's own nation state can organize life in a better way than other authorities; second, in virtue of complete and unconditional identification with the nation state. The first type of loyalty is characteristic of "popular" patriotism, for example, the sort widespread in the United States. Most Americans link their loyalty to the United States with the blessings which they believe derive from the "American way of life." The intense patriotism observed, in nascent nations, especially during their struggle for independence, also derives from expectations of benefits to be obtained from a national government; and so does the patriotism which emerges as a by-product of a social revolution, for instance, that of the French in the 1790's and of the Russians following 1917. (The distinction between patriotism and nationalism is not relevant to this discussion and is not made here.)

The second type of patriotism amounts to a replacement of one's own identity by that of the state. Psychic transformations of this sort are commonly observed in members of the military castes, the Prussian Junkers being the most commonly cited example. Junker-type patriotism, in contrast to "popular" patriotism, does not depend on current or future blessings expected from the state. It is total, unconditional, and reflex-dominated. We might note here that reflex-dominated patriotism (jingoism) has been often observed in civilian populations as well, particularly during war hysterias. However, these phenomena are usually transient. Following military defeat or an exhaustive war, mass patriotism inspired by war hysteria frequently turns into hatred directed against one's own power elite and military caste. In Russia, this reversal led to a complete liquidation of both the old power elite and of the military caste; in Germany this almost happened, but not quite, so that the military caste lived to see another war. "Antipatriotism" of varying degrees was also observed in England, in France, and even in the United States following World War I. Members of the military castes themselves, however, tend to preserve their original loyalty, sometimes even after the citadel of power to which they had owed allegiance has been destroyed.

In short, popular patriotism conceives the state as a means to an end (real or imagined), while military patriotism conceives the state as an end in itself. In a war, the man motivated by popular patriotism must constantly reassure himself that he is fighting for something of value to himself or to people with whom he identifies, or, perhaps to all people, but at any rate to *people*. Thus in World War II, the American civilian in uniform believed that he was fighting to preserve the patterns of life to which he was accustomed, or else, if he had a broader perspective, to prevent the enslavement of the world by a self-proclaimed elite. The military caste patriot does not need such reassurances. For him, the preservation of the state and the extension of its power are identical with self-preservation and with the extension of his own power. Thus military patriotism is completely compatible with the Clausewitzian view of international relations, inasmuch as the enhancement of the power of a state vis-à-vis other states is the sole aim of Clausewitzian diplo-military strategy. It is, however, questionable, whether popular patriotism is compatible with the Clausewitzian view of international relations. In particular, in the context of a nuclear war, the basis of *American* popular patriotism disappears. For it is absurd to suppose that it is possible to preserve the familiar patterns of American life on any of the upper rungs of Mr. Kahn's ladder. To be convinced, the reader need only read Mr. Kahn's description of city evacuation procedures (Rungs 17, 25, and 30). In a deeper sense, the values underlying American popular patriotism go by the wayside as soon as one accepts the very framework of thought in which Mr. Kahn develops his arguments, namely, the Clausewitzian framework and the values of the military caste. In the United States, popular support for the two world wars could be mobilized only by representing these wars as struggles *against* the Clausewitzian system, i.e., a world system dominated by power politics.

It is interesting to note that Mr. Kahn realizes the irrelevance of popular support in a World War III. He writes:

> There would probably not be any drafting, training, war mobilization, bond drives, or voting between the first and the last shots. Such a war most likely would be relatively technical, run by government

61

authorities and technicians, with little or no attention paid to the immediate problems of support from, or the morale of, the civilian population. It would probably be fought relatively coolly, and be guided by considerations of national interest little affected by propaganda or popular emotion.

Clearly, "national interest" is to be understood here in strictly Clausewitzian terms, i.e., independent of whatever might be of interest to the populations involved. World War III, like the wars of the eighteenth century, is envisaged as a war without active participation by the populations. The populations will be affected, of course, but only incidentally, as bystanders, while the professionals do their business.

Thus, if Mr. Kahn's arguments are to be supported by considerations of patriotism, we must keep in mind that only one type of patriotism is relevant in this context, namely that derived from a world view espoused by military castes and by assorted despots from Xerxes to Stalin. This view is fundamentally destructive of the values underlying the entire development of social thought which places man as the center of attention. In particular, the world view shared by Mr. Kahn is destructive of the fundamental values which underlie American political philosophy.

Once one has fathomed the sources of Mr. Kahn's patriotism, one sees also the source of his professional pride. The military caste identifies with the Clausewitzian state; Mr. Kahn identifies with the military caste. Let us not be deceived by the absence of glittering uniforms, duels, cavalry, chandelier-lit balls, and similar trappings which have kept the old European military castes in the public eye. The "defense community," to which Mr. Kahn refers, although socially inconspicuous, is nevertheless a true social organism, and so is the "analytic community" to which Mr. Kahn himself belongs, namely, the conclave of civilians, recruited largely from universities, who serve the "defense community" in the capacity of technical advisors. It is impractical to absorb these specialists into the military profession for various reasons. (For example, the military with its modest rate of professional salaries cannot compete with industry or even with academia in the recruitment of career personnel.) But the absence of military snobbism in the United States has made possible a climate of genuine fraternal solidarity between the military caste and its civilian professional corps. They share a genuine basis of common values, the Clausewitzian world view and the ideals of strategic sophistication and technical excellence.

It is characteristic of professional communities that they elicit loyalties which cut across national and ideological lines. Thus scientists and artists belong to a world community. It is more difficult for the military castes to forge a similar world community, since ostensibly at least, they are sometimes committed to each other's destruction. Nevertheless, a basis for such a community exists in the self-concept of the military professional. It is easy to trace many of Mr. Kahn's strategic arguments to assumptions of such professional solidarity. The "built-in controls" of the escalation process are supposed to be operating on the basis of mutually assumed rationality and mutually perceived common interests of the "players." In fact, the whole philosophy of escalation is based on the supposition that such controls are operating; otherwise, there is no need to distinguish the forty-four rungs between peace and the Spasm War. Without the "perception of common interests," escalation would be a purely self-catalytic, explosive process.

Now, one might ask, if "perception of common interests" can keep a nuclear war "under control" so as to limit the extent of the damage, why cannot the same "perception of common interest" prevent nuclear war altogether or, for that matter, prevent any war which results in losses to all concerned? These questions are not raised in *On Escalation*, but they were touched upon in Mr. Kahn's earlier books (for example, in connection with his discussion of disarmament). His answers to these questions were in the form of admonitions to stick to "realism." From the point of view of us bystanders, it is difficult to see why it is more realistic to agree to fight a limited nuclear war than to agree not to fight a war at all. From the point of view of the military caste, however, Mr. Kahn's conception of realism makes sense: it is not realistic for any professional community to strive for the abolition of the reason for its own existence.

Let us now examine the last and most clearly stated basis of Mr. Kahn's appeal to explore all the potentialities of nuclear warfare. As we have said, this is an appeal to openmindedness with allusions to freedom of inquiry unencumbered by fear or sentiment, the time-honored principle of scientific investigation. Mr. Kahn complains that this appeal has met with sharp hostility in some sectors of the intellectual community, and he attributes this hostility to outraged moralistic sensibilities. He has argued (or others have argued for him; cf. Raymond Aron's foreword to Herman Kahn's *Thinking about the Unthinkable*) that a detached attitude toward the genocidal by-products of modern war is no more reprehensible than a physician's detached attitude toward horrendous diseases; that a refusal to discuss the strategy and tactics of nuclear war is analogous to a prudish reluctance to discuss venereal disease, prostitution, drug addiction, and the like. An analogous argument is sometimes drawn between preparedness for natural disasters.

A reply to these arguments can be made along two lines. First, the analogy between nuclear warfare and assorted diseases, earthquakes, floods, et cetera is a false one. Diseases and natural disasters are not imposed on populations by decision makers, while wars are. Any dispassionate investigation of war *viewed as an affliction or a disaster* (which is the crux of the analogy) must inquire into the social, psy-

63

chological, or psycho-pathological determinants of war. This is not the content of Mr. Kahn's investigations. He teaches how to conduct a war and how to escalate it with a view of imposing the will of one state on another or, if this fails, with a view of inflicting maximum damage on the enemy, while minimizing damage to oneself. Now, since the "defense community" is, in a sense, a world community (as many professional communities are), Mr. Kahn's opposite numbers in other countries will be learning from him and may well improve on his ideas. Thus the results of these investigations can in no way alleviate the curse of war but can only aggravate it, as has been the case throughout the history of progress in military technology and strategy.

Against this conclusion, the defenders of Mr. Kahn's views sometimes advance the "logical consequences" argument. According to this argument, Mr. Kahn does no more than investigate the logical consequences of strategic thinking in the nuclear age. Such an investigation can serve a salubrious purpose, it is argued, for if the implications of strategic thinking are carried to their logical conclusions (as they are by Mr. Kahn), and if the results are revealed to be appalling (as they are), then the decision makers may have second thoughts in their conduct of diplo-military blackmail. If Mr. Kahn's book were truly written with this aim, I would applaud it. However, there is no evidence for this interpretation.

For one thing, the book must have been put together hastily and carelessly. The writing resembles a transcript of a brain-storming session rather than an organized exposition. There are instances of loss of contact with reality, as, for example, in the suggestion that in a "large conventional war" casualties *may* occur. There are lapses of logic, as in a statement to the effect that Khrushchev gave no sign of being *reassured* by the *possibility* that a crisis might not escalate. There are glaring inconsistencies. In discussing evacuation plans (in preparation for nuclear war), Mr. Kahn mentions the "enormous political, social, economic, and psychological problems" which these plans entail (p. 146); while on p. 201 he suggests that civilian support and morale are irrelevant to the conduct of nuclear war. At times, Mr. Kahn's discourse becomes incoherent or nearly so, as in the following passage: "Therefore, in the current situation (for purposes of damage limitation, as distinguished from deterrence only), it may be better— in several ways—to acquire additional capability for rapidly improving the posture rather than to acquire additional capability in being."

Next, the tone of the book gives the impression of being deliberately offensive. Its undercurrent of paranoia and brutality reminds one of certain standardized private-eye stories. The calculated titillation in the deliberate build-up of the war crescendo is modeled after the sex-technique books advertised in pulp magazines. The pages of the book crawl with quotation marks, which turn out to be typographical versions of giggles. Thus, Mr. Kahn sees to it that we understand what he means by "unintentional" breaches of the nuclear threshold, "justifiable" attacks, "peaceful" blockades, et cetera. Quotation marks are used also to frame Mr. Kahn's metaphors, evidently meant to liven up the detached scientific discussion. "The moment of truth" (the final confrontation) is one example.

The author of *On Escalation* is revealed not as a detached analyst, nor even as a cynically bemused observer of human folly, but rather as an enthusiastic choreographer of the dance of death. He relishes the obscene pranks he invents and the cataclysmic phantasies he invokes. Nor does the pornographic implication of his metaphors escape him. He says, for example:

> The term "spasm war" is now almost standard jargon in military and government circles and, to some degree, in journalism as well. I believe the expression originated in briefings I gave some years ago in which some war-plan proposals were referred to as "orgastic spasms of destruction." During one of these briefings, I said to the audience, "You people do not have a war plan. You have a 'war-gasm.'"

Who among us is not convinced that this gem was greeted with guffaws and slapping of thighs, an outburst of jolly fellowship among the initiated? *On Escalation*, like Mr. Kahn's earlier books, is essentially a taxonomy of Pandora's zoo, a blueprint for genocide, and a guide for the possessed. It is a recurrent symptom of a repulsive social disease, not unlike the disease to which Germany and Japan succumbed a generation ago. The disease is now incubating in our country. As this is being written (April, 1965), the United States is triumphantly climbing the escalation ladder.

Inasmuch as Mr. Kahn's exercises in "thinking about the unthinkable," as he calls them, have been in the public eye since 1960, it does not seem that they have been effective in suggesting second thoughts to the decision makers, as some defenders of Mr. Kahn hoped they would. It is barely possible, however, that Mr. Kahn's books may help ordinary people, thinking ordinary thoughts, to realize that "security through strength" has become a contradiction in terms and that our chances of escaping the unspeakable depend on whether people who think like Mr. Kahn can be removed from positions of influence.

Robert S. McNamara

Remarks Before the
Economic Club of New York

Before long this Administration will be presenting, once again, the details of a proposed national defense budget for the consideration of the Congress and the public. Given the importance of these matters, their complexities and uncertainties and the existence of real differences of opinion, a degree of controversy is inevitable, and even desirable.

Some controversies, however, reveal underlying differences in perspective that scarcely suggest the participants are living in the same world. Within the past few weeks, some critics have suggested that we have literally hundreds of times more strength than we need; others have accused us of risking the whole future of the nation by engaging in unilateral disarmament. I would like to believe that criticisms bracketing our policy in that fashion prove it to be rational and sound. But a discrepancy of that order cannot be reassuring. Rather, it indicates that we have failed to convey to some part of our audience even the broadest outlines, as we see them, of the problems that our military strategy and force structure are meant to address. I believe we should be able to move from controversy on that scale toward consensus in military affairs, not always on details or components of our policies, but at least on an appreciation of the major national security problems confronting us, on the broad alternative paths to their solution and on the dominant goals, obstacles, costs and risks affecting choice. My purpose in speaking to you this evening is to help move in this direction.

As a prelude, then, to the coming season of debate, I should like to identify and discuss some basic matters on which a considerable degree of consensus seems to me both possible and desirable, although by no means assured.

Address to the *Economic Club of New York*, Waldorf Astoria Hotel, November 18, 1963. Reprinted here with the author's permission. Robert S. McNamara is the former Secretary of Defense of the United States.

TECHNOLOGICAL MILITARISM

These include those over-all comparative strengths and weaknesses of the opposing military alliances that form the bold relief in the strategic environment. In short, they are the considerations that seem to have relatively long-term significance compared to the annual budget cycle.

Matters of that degree of permanence tend to be stamped on our minds as being unchanging and unchangeable, the unquestioned framework of daily and yearly policy-making. Yet these factors of which I shall speak do change: more swiftly and more profoundly than our picture of them tends to change. Indeed, I believe it is just the fact that over the last decade this topography has changed—while many maps have not—that accounts for some apparently irreconcilable controversies.

Let me recall the earlier period briefly, for comparison. The strategic landscape at the outset of the 'Fifties was dominated by two outstanding features. One was the practical U.S. monopoly of deliverable, strategic nuclear weapons. The other was the Soviet Union and Communist China's virtual monopoly of ground force on the continents of Europe and Asia.

Both of these determinants of Western military policy had changed considerably by the end of the Korean War. The Soviets had produced atomic explosions and had created a sizable nuclear delivery capability against Europe, while NATO ground forces had expanded rapidly, and military operations in Korea had greatly tarnished the significance of Chinese Communist superiority in numbers. But the old notions of monopoly persisted as short-cut aids to thinking on policy matters. And they were not so misleading as they came later to be. Soviet armed forces approaching five million men still heavily outweighed the NATO forces in Europe; and Soviet delivery capability against the U.S. was dwarfed by that of SAC. Moreover, tactical nuclear weapons were being heralded as a new nuclear monopoly for the West.

Even as these earlier notions of monopolies grew obsolete, ideas about the feasibility of alternative policies continued to reflect them. So did ideas about how wars might be fought. Nuclear operations, both strategic and tactical, by the U.S. in response to Soviet aggression against our allies were considered to be virtually unilateral. Hence it was supposed the problem of credibility of the U.S. response would scarcely arise, even in the case of relatively limited Soviet aggressions. Western reliance upon nuclear weapons, in particular strategic systems, both to deter and to oppose non-nuclear attack of any size seemed not only adequate but also unique in its adequacy.

That sort of situation is convenient for policy-makers. It makes policy easy to choose and easy to explain. Perhaps that is why throughout most of the 'Fifties, while the Soviets under various pressures decreased their ground forces and the NATO allies built theirs up, and while the Soviets acquired a massive nuclear threat against Europe and 67 laid the groundwork for a sizable threat against the U.S., the picture underlying most policy debate remained that appropriate to 1949. It was a picture of a Communist Goliath in conventional strength facing a Western David, almost naked of conventional arms but alone possessed of a nuclear sling.

Toward the end of that decade, the prospect that the Soviets would acquire intercontinental ballistic missiles at a time when our strategic forces consisted almost entirely of bombers focused our attention and our budget even more sharply than before upon our strategic forces. The urgency of the problem of deterring the most massive of attacks was a new reason for thinking that the West could spare neither resources nor thought to deal more specifically with lesser threats. The most urgent task was to provide for deterrence of massive aggression by assuring the survival under any attack of forces at least adequate, in the calculations of a potential attacker, to destroy his society in retaliation. It was now not the assurance of continued nuclear superiority that preempted the attention of policy-makers but, on the contrary, the struggle to maintain it.

But it is time for the maps to change by which policy is charted and justified. The old ones, which assumed a U.S. nuclear monopoly, both strategic and tactical, and a Communist monopoly of ground combat strength, are too far removed from reality to serve as even rough guides. Neither we nor our allies can afford the crudities of maps that tell us that old policies are still forced upon us, when a true picture would show important new avenues of necessity and choice.

What most needs changing is a picture of ourselves and of the Western Alliance as essentially at bay, outmanned and outgunned except for nuclear arms no longer exclusively ours. We should not think of ourselves as forced by limitations of resources to rely upon strategies of desperation and threats of vast mutual destruction, compelled to deal only with the most massive and immediate challenges, letting lesser ones go by default. It would be a striking historical phenomenon if that self-image should be justified. We are the largest member of an Alliance with a population of almost 450 million people, an aggregate annual product which is fast approaching a trillion dollars, and a modern and diverse technological base without parallel, facing the Soviet Union and its European satellites with their hundred million fewer people and an aggregate output no more than half that of the West.

And quite apart from ignoring the underlying strengths of the West, the outdated picture I have described takes no account of the military capabilities in being that our investment over the last decade, and specifically in the last few years, have bought for us. If new problems put strong claims on our attention and our resources today, it is very largely because we have come a large part of the way that is feasible toward solving some old ones.

Let me summarize the current status of the balance of strategic nuclear forces, that part of the military environment that has preoccupied our attention for so long. In strictly relative numerical terms, the situation is the familiar one. The U.S. force now contains more than 500 operational long-range ballistic missiles—ATLAS, TITAN, MINUTEMAN, POLARIS—and is planned to increase to over 1700 by 1966. There is no doubt in our minds and none in the minds of the Soviets that these missiles can penetrate to their targets. In addition, the U.S. has Strategic Air Command bombers on air alert and over 500 bombers on quick reaction ground alert. By comparison, the consensus is that today the Soviets could place about half as many bombers over North America on a first strike. The Soviets are estimated to have today only a fraction as many intercontinental missiles as we do. Furthermore, their submarine-launched ballistic missiles are short range, and generally are not comparable to our POLARIS force. The Soviets pose a very large threat against Europe, including hundreds of intermediate and medium-range ballistic missiles. This threat is today and will continue to be covered by the clear superiority of our strategic forces.

The most wishful of Soviet planners would have to calculate as a certainty that the most effective surprise attack they could launch would still leave us with the capability to destroy the attacker's society. What is equally pertinent is that the relative numbers and survivability of U.S. strategic forces would permit us to retaliate against all the urgent Soviet military targets that are subject to attack, thus contributing to the limitation of damage to ourselves and our allies.

Deterrence of deliberate, calculated attack seems as well assured as it can be, and the damage-limiting capability of our numerically superior forces is, I believe, well worth its incremental cost. It is a capability to which the smaller forces of the Soviet Union could not realistically aspire. That is one reason, among others, why I would not trade our strategic posture for that of the Soviets at any point during the coming decade.

But given the kind of force that the Soviets are building, including submarine-launched missiles beyond the reach of our offensive forces, the damage which the Soviets could inflict on us and our allies, no matter what we do to limit it, remains extremely high.

That has been true for our allies ever since the middle and late 'Fifties. Soviet acquisition of a sizable delivery capability against the U.S., and more significantly their acqustion of relatively protected forces, submarine-launched or hardened, has been long and often prematurely heralded. Its arrival at last merely dramatizes the need to recognize that strategic nuclear war would under all foreseeable circumstances be bilateral—and highly destructive to both sides.

Larger budgets for U.S. strategic forces would not change that fact. They could have only a decreasing incremental effect in limiting some-   69 what the damage that the U.S. and its allies could suffer in a general nuclear war. In short, we cannot buy the capability to make a strategic bombing campaign once again a unilateral prospect.

That must, I suggest, be accepted as one of the determinants affecting policy. Another is that the same situation confronts the Soviet leaders, in a way that is even more intensely confining. In fact, enormous increases in Soviet budgets would be required for them to achieve any significant degree of damage-limiting capability. The present Soviet leaders show no tendency to challenge the basis of the U.S. strategic deterrent posture by such expenditures.

In the last two years alone, we have increased the number of nuclear warheads in the strategic alert forces by 100%. During that period we have more than doubled the megatonnage of the strategic alert forces. The fact that further increases in strategic force size will at last encounter rapidly diminishing returns—which is largely an effect of the very large investments the U.S. has made in this area—should be reflected in future budgets. The funding for the initial introduction of missiles into our forces is nearing completion. We can anticipate that the annual expenditure on strategic forces will drop substantially, and level off well below the present rate of spending. This is not to rule out the possibility that research now in progress on possible new technological developments, including the possibility of useful ballistic missile defenses, will require major new expenditures. In any event, there will be recurring costs of modernization.

In the field of tactical nuclear weapons, the picture is in important respects similar. The U.S. at present has in stockpile or planned for stockpile tens of thousands of nuclear explosives for tactical use on the battlefield, in anti-submarine warfare and against aircraft. They include warheads for artillery, battlefield missiles, demolition munitions, bombs, depth charges, air-to-air missiles and surface-to-air missiles. The consensus is that the U.S. is presently substantially superior in design, diversity and numbers in this class of weapons.

This is an indispensable superiority, as we can readily understand if we consider how our problems of strategic choice would be altered if the tables were reversed and it were the Soviet Union which held a commanding lead in this field. Nevertheless, what we have is superiority, not monopoly, and even if tactical nuclear warfare can be limited, below some ill-defined threshold of strategic exchange, the key fact is that if the West initiates such warfare in the future it must be expected to be bilateral, in any theater which engaged the Soviet Union. Again, we cannot buy back a monopoly, or the assurance of unilateral use.

Finally, there is the area of what we call our general purpose forces. Within the last two years, we have increased the number of our combat-ready Army divisions by about 45%, from 11 to 16. There has been a 30% increase in the number of tactical air squadrons; a 75%

70

increase in airlift capabilities; and a 100% increase in ship construction and conversion to modernize the fleet.

But it is not only force size that matters. The key to the effective utilization of these forces is combat readiness and mobility.

The most recent demonstration of our ability to reinforce our troops presently stationed in Europe occurred last month in Operation BIG LIFT, the first of a series of planned large-scale, world-wide exercises. For the first time in military history, an entire division was airlifted from one continent to another. That movement could never have been accomplished without a massive increase in our airlift capability, which is still being expanded. (It will have risen 400% between 1961 and 1967.) It required the development of new techniques to preposition combat equipment, of which we have two extra division sets now in Europe. It called for new techniques in military training and administration to make sure that units are really ready to move out on a moment's notice. This exercise, in which some 16,000 airmen and soldiers and more than 350 planes took part, is directly relevant to the needs of Europe, where it brought a seventh division to join the six that are to remain in place. It is also relevant to the ability of the U.S. to fulfill its policy commitments world-wide, swiftly and in effective strength.

But, it might be asked, what is the significance of all this for the realistic security problems of the United States and its allies? To what contingencies are these forces expected to contribute, and how effective might they be, measured against the strength of opposing forces? How meaningful is it to talk of 16 or 20 or 30 divisions in opposing the ground armies of the Soviet Union and Communist China?

Such questions are often meant to be merely rhetorical, in view of the supposed masses of Communist troops. The fact is that they are serious, difficult questions, to which I shall suggest some tentative answers. But it is difficult to encourage realistic discussions of specific contingencies so long as the shadow of the Communist horde hangs unchallenged over the debate. The actual contingencies that seem to be to me most likely and most significant are not those which would involve all, or even a major part, of the Soviet Bloc or Chinese Communist armed forces, nor do they all involve Europe. Hence, aggregate figures of armed strength of NATO and the Warsaw Pact nations are not immediately relevant to them. But it is useful to make these over-all comparisons precisely because misleading or obsolete notions of these very aggregates often produce an attitude of hopelessness toward any attempt to prepare to meet Communist forces in ground combat, however limited in scope.

The announced total of Soviet armed forces for 1955 was indeed a formidable 5.75 million men. Today that figure has been cut to about 3.3 million; the Warsaw Pact total including the Soviets is only about 4.5 million. Against that, it is today the members of NATO whose active armed forces number over five million. The ground forces of NATO nations total 3.2 million, of which 2.2 million men are in Europe, as against the Soviet ground combat forces total of about 2 million men, and a Warsaw Pact total of about 3 million. Both the Soviet Union and the U.S. forces of course include units stationed in the Far East. In Central Europe, NATO has more men, and more combat troops, on the ground than does the Bloc. It has more men on the ground in West Germany than the Bloc does in East Germany. It has more and better tactical aircraft, and these planes on the average can carry twice the payload twice as far as the Soviet counterparts.

These facts are hard to reconcile with the familiar picture of the Russian Army as incomparably massive. The usual index cited to support that picture is numbers of total active divisions, and the specific number familiar from the past is 175 divisions in the Soviet Army.

This total, if true, would indeed present a paradox. The Soviet ground forces are reliably estimated to be very close to two million men, compared to about one million for the U.S. How is it that the Soviets can muster ten times the number of active, combat-ready, fully-manned divisions that the United States has manned, with only twice as many men on active duty? The answer is simply that they do not. Recent intensive investigation has shown that the number of active Soviet divisions that are maintained at manning levels anywhere close to combat readiness is less than half of the 160-175 figure.

What remains is a large number, but even that is misleading. For one thing, U.S. divisions have about twice as many men in the division unit and its immediate combat supporting units as comparable Soviet divisions. A U.S. mechanized division has far more personnel in maneuvering units, far more in armored cavalry, far more engineers, far more signals, far more light armored personnel carriers, and far more aircraft available in support than Soviet divisions. In addition to longer staying power, much of the U.S. manpower and equipment margin is muscle that would make itself felt on D-Day. If, on the other hand, we were to reorganize along Soviet lines, we could display far greater numbers of divisions comparable to those of the Soviets.

The Soviet combat-ready force remains a formidable one. Moreover, the Russians do have a powerful mobilization capability; in particular, they have a large number of lightly manned or cadre divisions to be filled out on mobilization. Still, this reality remains strikingly different from our accustomed maps of it.

I do not wish to suggest that such aggregate comparisons are by themselves a valid index to military capabilities. But they are enough to suggest the absurdity, as a picture of the prevailing military strengths on which new efforts might build, of David and Goliath notions borrowed from 1949.

None of this is to say that NATO strength on the ground in Europe

72

is adequate to turn back without nuclear weapons an all-out surprise non-nuclear attack.

But that is not in any case the contingency toward which the recent and future improvements in the mobility and capabilities of U.S. general purpose forces are primarily oriented. Aggression on that scale would mean a war about the future of Europe and, as a consequence, the future of the U.S. and the USSR. In the face of threats of that magnitude, our nuclear superiority remains highly relevant to deterrence. The Soviets know that even non-nuclear aggression at that high end of the spectrum of conflict so threatens our most vital interests that we and our allies are prepared to make whatever response may be required to defeat it, no matter how terrible the consequence for our own society.

The probability that the Soviet leaders would choose to invoke that exchange seems to me very low indeed. They know well what even the Chinese Communist leaders must recognize upon further reflection, that a nuclear war would mean destruction of everything they have built up for themselves during the last 50 years.

If we were to consider a spectrum of the possible cases of Communist aggression, then, ranging from harassment, covert aggression and indirect challenge at one end of the scale to the massive invasion of Western Europe or a full scale nuclear strike against the West at the other end, it is clear that our nuclear superiority has been and should continue to be an effective deterrent to aggression at the high end of the spectrum. It is equally clear, on the other hand, that at the very low end of the spectrum a nuclear response may not be fully credible, and that nuclear power alone cannot be an effective deterrent at this level in the future any more than it has been in the past.

The fact is that at every level of force, the Alliance in general, and the U.S. Armed Forces in particular, have greater and more effective strength than we are in the habit of thinking we have—and with reasonable continued effort we can have whatever strength we need. I have spoken already of strategic weapons, where the great superiority of the United States is the superiority also of the Alliance. In tactical nuclear weapons a parallel superiority exists—and while many of our Allies share with us in manning the systems which would use these tactical warheads in the hour of need, it is not unfair to point out that, even more than in the strategic field, the tactical nuclear strength of the Alliance is a contribution of the United States. That strength has been increased, on the ground in Europe, by more than 60% in the last two years. Today the thousands of U.S. warheads deployed on the continent for the immediate defense of Europe have a combined explosive strength more than 10,000 times the force of the nuclear weapons used to end the Second War. Tactical nuclear strength the Alliance has today, and we have provided it.

73

But neither we nor our Allies can find the detonation of such weapons—and their inevitable bilateral exchange—an easy first choice. At the lower end of the spectrum, therefore, we also need strong and ready conventional forces. We have done our part here and we continue to believe it just—and practicable—for our partners to do theirs.

The most difficult questions arise over the best means for meeting a variety of dangerous intermediate challenges in many parts of the world: those which threaten the possibility of sizable conflict while still not raising the immediate issue of the national survival of ourselves or of any member of our alliances. Conflicts might arise out of Soviet subversion and political aggression backed up by military measures in non-NATO areas in Europe, Latin America, the Middle East and Africa. There is a range of challenges that could arise from Communist China and its satellites in the Far East and in Southeast Asia. Most dangerously, approaching the upper end of the spectrum, there is the possibility of limited Soviet pressures on NATO territory itself, along the vast front running from Norway to Greece and Turkey. Both the flanks and the center contain potential targets. And always, of course, there are the contingencies that could arise in relation to Berlin.

It is difficult to say just how probable any of these circumstances might be, although they must be regarded as more likely than still larger aggressions. What one can say is that if any of these more likely contingencies should arise, they would be highly dangerous. Inaction, or weak action, could result in a serious setback, missed opportunity or even disaster. In fact, if either a nuclear exchange or a major Soviet attack should occur, it would most likely arise from a conflict on a lesser scale, which Western capabilities had failed to deter and which an inadequate Western response had failed to curb in time.

Since World War II, the expansionist impulse of the Communist Bloc is clear, but equally clear is its desire to avoid direct confrontation with the military forces of the free world. In Greece, in Berlin, and in Cuba, Communists have probed for military and political weakness but when they have encountered resistance, they have held back. Not only Communist doctrine has counselled this caution, but respect for the danger that any sizable, overt conflict would lead to nuclear war. It would follow that no deterrent would be more effective against these lesser and intermediate levels of challenge than the assurance that such moves would certainly meet prompt, effective military response by the West. That response could confront the Soviets with frustration of their purposes unless they chose themselves to escalate the conflict to a nuclear exchange, or to levels that made nuclear war highly probable—a choice they are unlikely to make in the face of our destructive power.

The basis for that particular assurance cannot be systems in development, or weapons in storage depots, or reserves that must be mobilized, trained and equipped, or troops without transport. We need the right   74 combination of forward deployment and highly mobile combat-ready ground, sea and air units, capable of prompt and effective commitment to actual combat, in short, the sort of capability we are increasingly building in our forces.

This capability requires of us—as of our Allies—a military establishment that is, in the President's words, lean and fit. We must stop and ask ourselves before deciding whether to add a new and complex weapon system to our inventory, whether it is really the most effective way to do the job under the rigorous conditions of combat. We must examine constantly the possibilities for combining functions, particularly in weapons that could be used by two or more Services. Given this tough-minded sense of reality about the requirements of combat readiness, it should be possible for the United States not only to maintain but to expand this increased strength without overall increases in our defense budget. As our national productivity and our gross national product expand, the defense budget therefore need not keep pace. Indeed, it appears likely that measured in relative—and perhaps even absolute—terms, the defense budget will level off and perhaps decline a little. At the same time, we are continuing the essential effort to reduce the impact of Defense spending on our balance of payments. We have already brought this figure down from $2.7 billion in FY 1961 to $1.7 billion for FY 1963, and we shall continue to reduce it, without reducing the combat ground forces deployed in Europe, and while strengthening our overall combat effectiveness.

And it must be our policy to continue to strengthen our combat effectiveness. I do not regard the present Communist leaders as wholly reckless in action. But recent experience, in Cuba and, on a lesser scale, in Berlin, has not persuaded me that I can predict with confidence the sorts of challenges that Communist leaders will come to think prudent and profitable. If they were again to miscalculate as dangerously as they did a year ago, it would be essential to confront them, wherever that might be, with the full consequences of their action: the certainty of meeting immediate, appropriate, and full effective military action.

All of our strengths, including our strategic and tactical nuclear forces, contributed last year, and they would contribute in similar future situations to the effectiveness of our response, by providing a basis for assurance that the Soviets would not dangerously escalate or shift the locale of the conflict. But above all, in order to fashion that response, and to promise the Soviets local defeat in case of actual ground conflict, we had to use every element of the improvements in combat readiness and mobility that had been building over the preceding year and a half, including combat divisions, air transport, and tactical air. And the last ingredient was also there: the will to use those forces against Soviet troops and equipment.

Let us not delude ourselves with obsolete images into believing that

75

our nuclear strength, great as it is, solves all of our problems of national security, or that we lack the strengths to meet those problems that it does not solve. In the contingencies that really threaten—the sort that have occurred and will occur again—we and our allies need no longer choose to live with the sense or the reality of inferiority to the Soviet Bloc in relevant, effective force. Let us be fully aware of the wide range of our military resources, and the freedom they can give us to pursue the peaceful objectives of the free world without fear of military aggression.

Marc Pilisuk and Thomas Hayden

Is There a Military-Industrial Complex Which Prevents Peace?: Consensus and Countervailing Power in Pluralistic Systems

The term "military-industrial complex" is very much in the literature. If its most sinister depictions are correct, then the peace researcher who works with the hope that his research may actually improve chances for world peace is wasting his time. A research finding, like a bit of knowledge, is always double-edged in what it portends for application. The project which tells us the surest steps to peace, tells us with equal certainty the steps which must be by-passed if peace is shunned. If there exists an omnipotent elite, committed to militarism, then there is simply no basis for hope that voices for peace have gotten, or can get, an influential channel into inner policy circles. If, on the other hand, the pluralist thesis can be said to apply in full even to basic policy directions of preparedness for war or for peace, then some influential decision makers must be eagerly awaiting the research findings on paths to peace with intentions to press for their immediate application.

Because we agree with neither of the above positions, because we believe that most research workers in this area tend either to ignore or to over-rate the potential consequences of their work to peace, and because we feel that consideration of the conditions which dictate major directions of policy is essential for an evaluation of any con-

Reprinted from *The Journal of Social Issues*, Vol. XXI, No. 3, pp. 67–117, by permission of the authors and The Society for the Psychological Study of Social Problems. Article abridged. Original reference numbers have been retained. Marc Pilisuk is associate professor of psychology at the University of California, Berkeley. Thomas Hayden is a free-lance journalist and community organizer in the Newark Community Union Project.

tribution to peace research, we are bringing the concept of the "military-industrial complex" to both the microscope and the scalpel. The implications of this inquiry point to a research approach which does have relevance to the decision process and to the most central agencies of social change, and resistance to change, within American society.

THE NEW CONCERN

Not since the 30's has there been such a rash of attention to military-industrial power as there is today. Then, as now, the President himself raised the spectre of improper military influence. FDR, on the eve of a Senate investigation of the munitions industry, said flatly that the arms race was a "grave menace . . . due in no small measure to the uncontrolled activities of the manufacturers and merchants of the engines of destruction and it must be met by the concerted action of the people of all nations." (Raymond, 1964, p. 262; also Congressional Quarterly Weekly Report, 6, 1964, pp. 265–278.) While Dwight Eisenhower did not sound as militant as Roosevelt, and while he never adopted FDR's 1932 campaign pledge to "take the profits out of war," he did resume a popular tradition with his warning about the "unwarranted influence" of the military-industrial complex. It may be a significant measure of the times that one President could make such warnings in his very first campaign for office, while the other couched it among several other going-away remarks.

The 30's serve as a prelude to the 60's, too, in the area of congressional investigation of militarism. Then it was Senator Gerald P. Nye investigating the fabulous World War I profits of U.S. Steel and Hercules Powder and discovering, with horror, the instrumental role of munitions-makers and other commercial interests in beginning the war. Nye revealed, for example, that the American ambassador in London informed President Wilson in 1917 that probably "the only way of maintaining our pre-eminent trade position and averting a panic is by declaring war on Germany" (Raymond, p. 264). As Roosevelt was more aggressive than Eisenhower, so also were Nye, Borah and other popular Senators more aggressive than their present counterparts in the 60's. But, nevertheless, similar issues are now being raised in congressional committees. The most shocking of these may be found in the hearings of Senator John McClellan's committee on *Pyramiding of Profits and Costs in the Missile Procurement Program*. This report pointed out the likely danger that the government "can be placed in the unenviable position of reluctant acquiescence to the demands and conditions set by the contractor," and that "profits were pyramided on other profits without any relationship at all to the effort being expended by those making the profit." In what might have been front page scandal in any area but national defense, the committee documented two mechanisms by which millions upon millions of dollars of excess profit have been reaped by the defense industries. The mechanisms are: a) claiming profits on work subcontracted to other firms (which in turn subcontract portions of their work to others and charge a profit on the sub-subcontracted work, too), and b) overestimating the subcontracting costs (on incentive type contracts) thereby reaping huge profit rates by undercutting the original estimates. However, the contrast with the 30's is clear; Senator McClellan only wants to improve the efficiency of what he calls "these necessary monopolies." (U.S. Senate, Committee on Government Operations, report of the Permanent Subcommittee on Investigations, *Pyramiding of Profits and Costs in the Missile Procurement Program*, March 31, 1964.) A more far-reaching investigation, under the direction of Senator Clark, deals with the convertibility of the defense empire to civilian job-creating tasks. He claims that 1) the new defense emphasis on electronics and on research and development, and the monopolization of defense by a few companies and geographic areas, considerably reduces the potential effect of defense as an economic stabilizer; and 2) that certain firms, especially those in the aerospace industry, are suffering an overcapacity crisis that spurs them to insist on more missiles than the nation needs. (U.S. Senate, Committee on Labor and Public Welfare, report of the Subcommittee on Employment and Manpower, *Convertibility of Space and Defense Resources to Civilian Needs: A Search for New Employment Potentials*, 88th Congress, 2d Session, 1964.) Senator Clark's hearings, too, are mild in contrast to the 30's. Even milder, however, was the recent survey report of Senator Hubert Humphrey, who says it is "nonsense" to believe American industry is opposed to disarmament. (U.S. Senate, Committee on Foreign Relations, Subcommittee on Disarmament, *The Economic Impact of Arms Control Agreements*, Congressional Record, October 5, 1962, pp. 2139–2194.)

Another measure of interest in military-industrial power is the number of popular and technical books dealing with the subject. In the 30's, the widely read books were Davenport's *Zaharoff, High Priest of War*, Engelbrecht and Haneghen's *Merchants of Death* and Selde's *Iron, Blood and Profits*. Two decades then passed before the work of C. Wright Mills began to attract broad attention to the subject of organized militarism. Including Mills' pioneering books, there have been at least 21 major books published in this area during the past several years. Many of them are by journalists (Cook, Coffin, Raymond, Swomley, Wise and Ross); some by economists (Benoit, Boulding, Melman, Peck, Perlo, Scherer); sociologists (Etzioni, Horowitz, Janowitz, Mills); political scientists (Meisel, Rogow); novelists (Bailey, Burdick, Knebel, Sutton); and at least one physical scientist (Lapp).

Whatever the objective referent, if any, of a "military-industrial complex" may be, it is undeniable that the concept occupies an important role in the political consciousness of many persons, on a scale without precedent since the 30's. It is a telling fact that the new literature, with the exceptions of Mills, Cook and Perlo, still lacks the bite of the old, and that the proposed solutions are quite "modest." In the 30's a typical popular solution, proposed by the Nye Committee but never implemented, was the nationalization of the munitions industries. By the 60's the reverse has happened; most military research, development, and production is done by private companies subsidized by the Federal government. The loci of military-political-industrial cooperation are so pervasive and frequent that it becomes a hair-splitting task to identify specifically any "merchants of death." Also, the scale of potential destruction has so increased, the nature of warfare strategy so changed, and the existence of the military in peacetime so accepted, that it seems quaint to associate defense contractors with bloody hands. Furthermore, the assumed threat of communist expansion has become the ultimate justification of the post-war military buildup, whereas in the past such buildups could be attributed more clearly to industrial profit and power motives. Probably reasons such as these explain both the long silence and the modest character of the current resurgence in discussion of these matters.

But these reasons account partially for the inadequacy of analysis as well. The question, "Does there exist a military-industrial complex which prevents peace?" at first seems debatable in straightforward yes-or-no terms. Indeed, it might have been answerable in the 20's or 30's but not in the post-war period. When there is permanent intermingling and coordination among military, industrial, and governmental elites, and whenever greater war-preparedness can be justified by reference to the communist movement, it becomes a much "stickier" question. Because it is sticky, the easiest conclusion to support is that a "complex" simply does not exist as an omnipresent obstacle to policy change. Indeed, this belief has become the accepted norm for "informed" discussion of interests vested in the perpetuation of military preparedness. The next most easily supported conclusion would be that we have become trapped in the hell-fires of militarism by a sinister but concealed elite of military-industrial leaders, which through its puppets, pulls the strings on every major policy decision. The latter theory is non-conformist, radical, and smacks too closely of classical conspiracy theory to be palatable to most scholars. Indeed, the dominant attitude (explicit or tacit) in most of the new literature is that there exists no military-industrial complex capable of preventing peace. It is claimed that the military-industrial complex operates as a sub-group within the limits of an essentially civilian society. In this view the complex is seen as making an interest-conscious equation of its own interests with those of the nation as a whole. But, it is argued, this tendency of power aggrandizement is checked by countervailing interest blocks in the society. Moreover, the "complex" is not seen as having a corrosive effect on democratic processes; even if it is conceded that military and technological expertise or well-financed public relations give the "complex" unusual privilege and visibility, this is no different, in principle, from certain other influental groups, all of which are limited by the web of constraints but comprise a pluralist society. Usually, it is added that the internal differences in the "complex" such as differences among the separate services or between the military and the industrial procurement sectors, tend to restrict further its ability to impose a policy "line" on the United States. These points of view appear in scattered form throughout the literature.

. . . Some important examples of this literature include *The Invisible Government* by Wise and Ross, *Power at the Pentagon* by Raymond, *Disarmament and the American Economy* edited by Benoit and Boulding, and *The Weapons Acquisition Process* by Peck and Scherer. Each points to an important power block in either the determination of foreign policies, the decision to move toward arms reduction or control, or the lobbying for increased defense expenditure. All see some impediments to change presented by the concentration of power in the group under study but none see the workings of any group sufficiently dominant to resist all forms of control or counter pressures from other segments of the society. . . .

None of these denials of irresponsible military-industrial power marshall very significant evidence to support their views. There are examples given of specific conflicts between civilian and military groups which were lost by the military (e.g., the dropping of General Walker, the refusal to be first to break the moratorium on testing). There are examples given of heated divisions between the services over what military strategy should be pursued (the arguments over conventional warfare in the late 50's and the more recent RS 70 controversy). There are sociological studies which reveal underlying diversities within single corporations, between competing corporations, and within the demographic and institutional character of each branch of the armed services.[2] And, throughout, there are citations of American pluralism as an automatic check system against any elite group.[3]

At a more general level, these fragments of evidence point toward

[2]See Janowitz for a good sociological study of interservice differences.

[3]For the thesis that a "peacefare state" counterweighs the "warfare state," see Klaus Knorr's review of Fred J. Cook in the *Journal of Conflict Resolution, VII, 4* (December, 1963). The "pluralist position," which usually is that the social system has semi-automatic checking mechanisms against tyranny, appears as basic in discussions not only of the military, but of economics and politics as well. See Robert Dahl, *Who Governs?*; John K. Galbraith, *American Capitalism*; Seymour Martin Lipset, *Political Man*; Talcott Parsons, *The Social System.*

three grounds for denying that a military-industrial complex prevents peace:

(1) it is held that the *scope* of decisions made by any interest group is quite narrow and cannot be said to govern anything so broad as foreign policy;

(2) it is held that the "complex" is not *monolithic, not self-conscious*, and *not coordinated*, the presumed attributes of a ruling elite;

(3) it is held that the military-industrial complex does not wield power if the term "power" is defined as the ability to realize its will even against the resistance of others and regardless of external conditions.

These formulations, to repeat, are made neither explicitly nor consistently in the new literature. But they crystallize the basic questions about definition which the new literature raises. Moreover, they are quite definitely the major contentions made by academic criticisms of power elite theory. The more widely read of these academic critics include Daniel Bell, Robert Dahl, and Talcott Parsons. Since their critiques are mainly directed at the work of C. Wright Mills, it is with Mills that we will begin to analyze the theories which claim there *is* a military-industrial complex blocking peace.

THE THESIS OF ELITE CONTROL

Mills is by far the most formidable exponent of the theory of a power elite. In his view, the period in America since World War II has been dominated by the ascendance of corporation and military elites to positions of institutional power. These "commanding heights" allow them to exercise control over the trends of the business cycle and international relations. The Cold War set the conditions which legitimize this ascendance, and the decline and incorporation of significant left-liberal movements, such as the CIO, symbolizes the end of opposition forces. The power elite monopolizes sovereignty, in that political initiative and control stem mainly from the top hierarchical levels of position and influence. Through the communications system the elite facilitates the growth of a politically indifferent mass society below the powerful institutions. This, according to the Mills argument, would explain why an observer finds widespread apathy. Only a small minority believes in actual participation in the larger decisions which affect their existence and only the ritual forms of "popular democracy" are practiced by the vast majority. Mills' argument addresses itself to the terms of the three basic issues we have designated, i.e., scope of decision power, awareness of common interest, and the definition of power exerted.

By *scope*, we are referring to the sphere of society over which an elite is presumed to exercise power. Mills argues that the scope of this elite is general, embracing all the decisions which in any way could be called vital (slump and boom, peace and war, etc.). He does not argue that *each* decision is directly determined, but rather that the political alternatives from which the "Deciders" choose are shaped and limited by the elite through its possession of all the large-scale institutions. By this kind of argument, Mills avoids the need to demonstrate how his elite is at work during each decision. He speaks instead in terms of institutions and resources. But the problem is that his basic evidence is of a rather negative kind. No major decisions have been made for 20 years contrary to the policies of anti-communism and corporate or military aggrandizement; *therefore* a power elite must be prevailing. Mills might have improved his claims about the scope of elite decisions by analysing a series of actual decisions in terms of the premises which were *not* debated. This could point to the mechanisms (implicit or explicit) which led to the exclusion of these premises from debate. By this and other means he might have found more satisfying evidence of the common, though perhaps tacit, presuppositions of seemingly disparate institutions. He then might have developed a framework analyzing "scope" on different levels. The scope of the Joint Chiefs of Staff, for instance, could be seen as limited, while at the same time the Joint Chiefs could be placed in a larger elite context having larger scope. Whether this could be shown awaits research of this kind. Until it is done, however, Mills theory of scope remains open to attack, but, conversely, is not subject to refutation.

Mills' theory also eludes the traditional requirements for inferring monolithic structure, i.e., consciousness of elite status, and coordination. The modern tradition of viewing elites in this way began with Mosca's *The Ruling Class* in a period when family units and inheritance systems were the basic means of conferring power. Mills departs from this influential tradition precisely because of his emphasis on institutions as the basic elements. If the military, political, and economic *institutional orders* involve a high coincidence of interest, then the groups composing the institutional orders need not be monolithic, conscious, and coordinated, yet still they can exercise elite power.[4] This means specifically that a military-industrial complex could exist as an expression of a certain fixed ideology (reflecting common institutional needs), yet be "composed" of an endless shuffle of specific groups. For instance, our tables show 82 companies have dropped out of the list of 100 top defense contractors, and only 36 "durables" have remained on the list in the years since 1940. In terms of industry, the percentage of contracts going to the automotive industry dropped from

[4]See James H. Meisel, *The Myth of the Ruling Class*, for the best available discussion of the innovation in theorizing about elites.

25 percent in World War II to 4 percent in the missile age. At the same time, the aircraft companies went from 34 to 54 percent of all contracts, and the electronics industry from 9 to 28 percent (Peck and Scherer, 1962). Mills' most central argument is that this ebb-and-flow is not necessarily evidence for the pluralists. His stress is on the unities which underlie the procession of competition and change. The decision to change the technology of warfare was one which enabled one group to "overcome" another in an overall system to which both are fundamentally committed. Moreover, the decision issued from the laboratories and planning boards of the defense establishment and only superficially involved any role for public opinion. The case studies of weapons development by Peck and Scherer, in which politics is described as a marginal ritual, would certainly buttress Mills' point of view.

Making this institution analysis enables Mills to make interesting comments on his human actors. The integration of institutions means that hundreds of individuals become familiar with several roles: General, politician, lobbyist, defense contractor. These men are the power elite, but they need not know it. They conspire, but conspiracy is not absolutely essential to their maintenance. They mix together easily, but can remain in power even if they are mostly anonymous to each other. They make decisions, big and small, sometimes with the knowledge of others and sometimes not, which ultimately control all the significant action and resources of society.

Where this approach tends to fall short, is in its unclarity about how discontinuities arise. Is the military-industrial complex a feature of American society which can disappear and still leave the general social structure intact? Horst Brand has suggested a tension between financial companies and the defense industries because of the relatively few investment markets created by defense (1962). Others are beginning to challenge the traditional view that defense spending stimulates high demand and employment. Their claim is that the concentration of contracts in a few states, the monopolization of defense and space industry by the largest 75 or 100 corporations, the low multiplier effect of the new weapons, the declining numbers of blue-collar workers required, and other factors, make the defense economy more of a drag than a stimulant (Melman et al., 1963; Etzioni, 1964). Mills died before these trends became the subject of debate, but he might have pioneered in discussion of them if his analytic categories had differentiated more finely between various industries and interest groups in his power elite. His emphasis was almost entirely on the "need" for a "permanent war economy" just when that need was being questioned even among his elite.

However, this failure does not necessarily undermine the rest of Mills' analysis. His institutional analysis is still the best means of identifying a complex without calling it monolithic, conscious and co-ordinated. Had he differentiated more exactly he might have been able to describe various degrees of commitments to an arms race, a rightist ideology constricting the arena of meaningful debate, and other characteristics of a complex. This task remains to be done, and will be discussed at a later point.

Where Mills' theory is most awkward is in his assertions that the elite can, and does, make its decisions against the will of others and regardless of external conditions. This way of looking at power is inherited by Mills, and much of modern sociology, directly from Max Weber. What is attributed to the elite is a rather fantastic quality: literal omnipotence. Conversely, any group that is *not* able to realize its will even against the resistance of others is only "influential" but not an elite. Mills attempts to defend this viewpoint but, in essence, modifies it. He says he is describing a tendency, not a finalized state of affairs. This is a helpful device in explaining cracks in the monolith—for instance, the inability of the elite to establish a full corporate state against the will of small businessmen. However, it does not change the ultimate argument—that the power elite cannot become more than a tendency, cannot realize its actual self, unless it takes on the quality of omnipotence.

When power is defined as this kind of dominance, it is easily open to critical dispute. The conception of power depicts a vital and complex social system as essentially static, as having within it a set of stable governing components, with precharted interests which infiltrate and control every outpost of decision-authority. Thereby, internal accommodation is made necessary and significant change, aside from growth, becomes impossible. This conception goes beyond the idea of social or economic determinism. In fact, it defines a "closed social system." A "closed system" may be a dramatic image, but it is a forced one as well. Its defender sees events such as the rise of the labor movement essentially as a means of rationalizing modern capitalism. But true or false as this may be, did not the labor movement also constitute a "collective will" which the elite could not resist? An accommodation was reached, probably more on the side of capital than labor, but the very term "accommodation" implies the existence of more than one independent will. On a world scale, this becomes even more obvious. Certainly the rise of communism has not been through the will of capitalists, and Mills would be the first to agree. Nor does the elite fully control technological development; surely the process of invention has some independent, even if minor, place in the process of social change.

Mills' definition of power as dominance ironically serves the pluralist argument, rather than countering it. When power is defined so extremely, it becomes rather easy to claim that such power is curbed in the contemporary United States. The pluralists can say that Mills has conjured up a bogeyman to explain his own failure to realize his will. This is indeed what has been done in review after review of Mills' writings. A leading pluralist thinker, Edward Shils, says that Mills was too much influenced by Trotsky and Kafka:

> Power, although concentrated, is not so concentrated so powerful, or so permeative as Professor Mills seems to believe. . . . There have been years in Western history, e.g., in Germany during the last years of the Weimar Republic and under the Nazis when reality approximated this picture more closely. . . . But as a picture of Western societies, and not just as an ideal type of extreme possibilities which might be realized if so much else that is vital were lacking, it will not do. (Shils, 1961)

But is Mills' definition the only suitable one here? If it is, then the pluralists have won the debate. But if there is a way to designate an irresponsible elite without giving it omnipotence, then the debate may be recast at least.

This fundamental question is not answered in the other major books which affirm the existence of a military-industrial complex. Cook's *The Warfare State* and Perlo's *Militarism and Industry* are good examples of this literature which is theoretically inferior to Mills' perplexing account.

Cook's volume has been pilloried severely by deniers of the military-industrial complex. At least it has the merit of creating discussion by being one of the few dissenting books distributed widely on a commercial basis. It suffers, however, from many of the same unclarities typical of the deniers. Its title assumes a "warfare state" while its evidence, although rich, is only a compilation of incidents, pronouncements, and trends, lacking any framework for weighing and measuring. From his writing several hypotheses can be extracted about the "face of the Warfare State," all of them suggestive but none of them conclusive: 1) the Department of Defense owns more property than any other organization in the world;[5] 2) between 60 and 70 percent of the national budget is consistently allocated to defense or defense related expenditures; 3) the Military and Big Business join in an inevitable meeting of minds over billions of dollars in contracts the one has to order and the other to fulfill; 4) the 100 top corporations monopolize three-fourths of the contracts, 85 percent of them being awarded without competition; 5) as much as one-third of all production and service indirectly depends on defense; 6) business and other conservative

---

[5]Swomley (1964) accounts for Department of Defense holdings equivalent in size to eight states of the U.S.A. Kenneth Boulding, including personnel as well as property criteria, calls the Department of Defense the world's third largest socialist state. (Personal discussion, 1963.)

groups, even though outside of the Defense establishment, benefit from the warfare emphasis because it keeps subordinate the welfare-state which is anathema to them (pages 20–24, 162–202).

Cook's work, much more than Mills' is open to the counter-argument that no monolithic semi-conspiratorial elite exists. Even his definitions of vested interests are crude and presumed. Moreover, he suffers far more than Mills from a failure to differentiate between groups. For instance, there is nothing in his book (written in 1962) which would explain the economic drag of defense spending, which Cook perceptively observed in a *Nation* article, "The Coming Politics of Disarmament," in 1963. One year he wrote that Big Business was being fattened off war contracts, but the next year the "prolonged arms race has started, at last, to commit a form of economic hara-kiri." "Hara-kiri" does not happen spontaneously; it is a culmination of long-developing abnormalities. That Cook could not diagnose them before they became common in congressional testimony illustrates the lack of refinement in his 1962 analysis. Cook's failure lies in visualizing a monolith, which obscures the strains which promote new trends and configurations.

It is in this attention to strains that Perlo's book is useful. He draws interesting connections between the largest industrial corporations and the defense economy, finding that defense accounts for 12 percent of the profits of the 25 largest firms. He adds the factor of foreign investment as one which creates a further propensity in favor of a large defense system, and he calculates that military business and foreign investments combined total 40 percent of the aggregate profits among the top 25. He draws deeper connections between companies and the major financial groups controlling their assets.

This kind of analysis begins to reveal important disunities within the business community. For instance, it can be seen that the Rockefellers are increasing their direct military investments while maintaining their largest foreign holdings in extremely volatile Middle Eastern and Latin American companies. The Morgans are involved in domestic industries of a rather easy-to-convert type, and their main foreign holdings are in the "safer" European countries, although they too have "unsafe" mining interests in Latin America and Africa. The First National City Bank, while having large holdings in Latin American sugar and fruit, has a more technical relation to its associated firms than the stock-owner relation. The Mellons have sizeable oil holdings on Kuwait, but on the whole are less involved in defense than the other groups. The DuPonts, traditionally the major munitions makers, are "diversified" into the booming aerospace and plutonium industries, but their overseas holdings are heavily in Europe. Certain other groups with financial holdings, such as Young and Eaton interests in Cleveland, have almost no profit stake in defense or foreign investments. On the other hand, some of the new wealth in Los Angeles is deeply committed to the aerospace industry.

Perlo makes several differentiations of this sort, including the use of foreign-policy statements by leading industrial groups. But he does not have a way to predict under what conditions a given company would actively support economic shifts away from the arms race. These and other gaps, however, are not nearly as grave as his lack of analysis of other components of the military-industrial complex.[6] There is no attempt to include politicians, military groups and other forces in a "map" of the military-industrial complex which Perlo believes exists. This may be partly because of the book's intent, which is to document profiteering by arms contractors, but for whatever reason, the book is not theoretically edifying about the question we are posing. Nor does it refute the pluralist case. In fact, it contains just the kind of evidence that pluralist arguments currently employ to demonstrate the absence of a monolith.

REVISING THE CRITERIA FOR INFERRING POWER

After finding fault with so many books and divergent viewpoints, the most obvious conclusion is that current social theory is currently deficient in its explanation of power. We concur with one of Mills' severest critics, Daniel Bell, who at least agrees with Mills that most current analysis concentrates on the "intermediate sectors," e.g., parties, interest groups, formal structures, without attempting to view the underlying system of "renewable power independent of any momentary group of actors" (Bell, 1964). However, we have indicated that the only formidable analysis of the underlying system of renewable power, that of Mills, has profound shortcomings because of its definition of power. Therefore, before we can offer an answer of our own to the question, "Is there a military-industrial complex which blocks peace?", it is imperative to return to the question of power itself in American society.

We have agreed essentially with the pluralist claim that ruling-group models do not "fit" the American structure. We have classified Mills' model as that of a ruling-group because of his Weberian definition of power, but we have noted also that Mills successfully went beyond two traps common to elite theories, *viz.*, that the elite is total in the scope of its decisions, and that the elite is a coordinated monolith.

But we perhaps have not stressed sufficiently that the alternative

[6]In an earlier book, *The Empire of High Finance* (1957), he documented the close relations of the major financial groups and the political executive. He did not, however, carry this analysis to congressmen and senators, nor did he offer sufficient comparative evidence to demonstrate a long-term pattern.

case for pluralism is inadequate in its claim to describe the historical dynamics of American society. The point of our dissent from pluralism is over the doctrine of "counter-vailing power." This is the modern version of Adam Smith's economics and of the Madisonian or Federalism theory of checks-and-balances, adapted to the new circumstances of large-scale organizations. Its evidence is composed of self-serving incidents and a faith in semi-mystical resources. For instance, in the sphere of political economy, it is argued that oligopoly contains automatic checking mechanisms against undue corporate growth, and that additionally, the factors of "public opinion" and "corporate conscience" are built-in limiting forces.[7] We believe that evidence in the field, however, suggests that oligopoly is a means of stabilizing an industrial sphere either through tacit agreements to follow price leadership or rigged agreements in the case of custom-made goods; that "public "opinion" tends much more to be manipulated and apathetic than independently critical; that "corporate conscience" is less suitable as a description than Reagan's terms, "corporate arrogance."

To take the more immediate example of the military sphere, the pluralist claim is that the military is subordinate to broader, civilian interests. The first problem with the statement is the ambiguity of "civilian." Is it clear that military men are more "militaristic" than civilian men? To say so would be to deny the increasing trend of "white-collar militarism." The top strategists in the Department of Defense, the Central Intelligence Agency and the key advisory positions often are Ph.D.'s. In fact, "civilians" including McGeorge Bundy, Robert Kennedy, James Rostow and Robert McNamara are mainly responsible for the development of the only remaining "heroic" form of combat: counter-insurgency operations in the jungles of the underdeveloped countries. If "militarism"[8] has permeated this deeply into the "civilian" sphere, then the distinction between the terms becomes largely nominal.

. . . The intrusion of civilian professors into the military arena has been most apparent in more than 300 universities and non-profit research institutions which supply personnel to and rely upon contracts from the Department of Defense. About half of these centers were created to do specialized strategic research. One of these, the RAND Corporation, was set up by Douglas Aviation and the Air Force to give "prestige type support for favored Air Force proposals" (Fried-

[7]For this argument, see A. A. Berle, *The Twentieth Century Capitalist Revolution* and J. K. Galbraith, *American Capitalism*. For sound criticisms, but without sound alternatives, see Mills' and Perlo's books. Also see Michael Reagan, *The Managed Economy* (1963), and Berland Nossiter, *The Mythmakers* (1964), for other refutations of the countervailing power thesis.

[8]We are defining the term as "primary reliance on coercive means, particularly violence or the threat of violence, to deal with social problems."

man, 1963). When RAND strategy experts Wohlstetter and Dinerstein discovered a mythical "missile gap" and an equally unreal preemptive war strategy in Soviet post-Sputnik policy, they paved the way for the greatest military escalation of the cold war era, the missile race.

The civilian strategists have frequently retained an exasperating measure of autonomy from the services which support them. Such conflicts reached a peak when both the Skybolt and the RS 70 projects met their demise under the "cost effectiveness" program designed by Harvard economist Charles Hitch (then with RAND, now Defense Department comptroller). (Dr. Hitch is now President of the University of California. [Ed.]) That the civilian and military planners of military policy sometimes differ does not detract from the argument. What must be stressed is that the apparent flourishing of such civilian agencies as RAND (it earned over 20 million dollars in 1962 with all the earnings going into expansion and has already spawned the non-profit Systems Development Corporation with annual earnings exceeding 50 million dollars) is no reflection of countervailing power. The doctrine of controlled response under which the RS 70 fell was one which served the general aspirations of each of the separate services; of the Polaris and Minuteman stabile deterrent factions, of the brush-fire or limited war proponents, guerilla war and paramilitary operations advocates, and of the counterforce adherents. It is a doctrine of versatility intended to leave the widest range of military options for retaliation and escalation in U.S. hands. It can hardly be claimed as victory against military thought. The fighting may have been intense but the area of consensus between military and civilian factions was great.

CONSENSUS

All that countervailing power refers to is the relationship between groups who fundamentally accept "the American system" but who compete for advantages within it. The corporate executive wants higher profits, the laborer a higher wage. The President wants the final word on military strategies, the Chairman of the Joint Chiefs does not trust him with it, Boeing wants the contract, but General Dynamics is closer at the time to the Navy Secretary and the President, and so on. What is prevented by countervailing forces is the dominance of society by a group or clique or a party. But this process suggests a profoundly important point; that *the constant pattern in American society is the rise and fall of temporarily-irresponsible groups.* By temporary we mean that, outside of the largest industrial conglomerates,[9] the groups which wield significant power to influence

[9]The term used in recent hearings by Senator Philip A. Hart refers to industrial organizations like Textron, which have holdings in every major sector of American industry.

policy decisions are not guaranteed stability. By irresponsible we mean that there are many activities within their scope which are essentially unaccountable in the democratic process. These groups are too uneven to be described with the shorthand term "class." Their personnel have many different characteristics (compare IBM executives and the Southern Dixiecrats) and their needs as groups are different enough to cause endless fights as, for example, small vs. big business. No one group or coalition of several groups can tyrannize the rest as it demonstrated, for example, in the changing status of the major financial groups, particularly the fast-rising Bank of America which has been built from the financial needs of the previously-neglected small consumer.

However, it is clear that these groups exist within consensus relationships of a more general and durable kind than their conflict relationships. This is true, first of all, of their social characteristics. The tables which follow combine data from Suzanne Keller's compilation of military, economic, political and diplomatic elite survey materials in *Beyond the Ruling Class* (1963) and from an exhaustive study of American elites contained in Warner, et al., *The American Federal Executive* (1963).

The relevant continuities represented in this data suggest an educated elite with an emphasis upon Protestant and business-oriented origins. Moreover, the data suggest inbreeding with business orientation in backgrounds likely to have been at least maintained, if not augmented, through marriage. The consistencies suggest orientations not unlike those which are to be found in examination of editorial content of major business newspapers and weeklies and in more directly sampled assessments of elite opinions.[10]

The second evidence of consensus relationships, besides attitude and background data indicating a pro-business sympathy, would come from an examination of the *practice* of decision making. By analysis of such actual behavior we can understand which consensus attitudes are reflected in decision-making. Here, in retrospect, it is possible to discover the values and assumptions which are defended recurrently. This is at least a rough means of finding the boundaries of consensus relations. Often these boundaries are invisible because of the very infrequency with which they are tested. What are visible most of the time are the parameters of conflict relationships among different groups. These conflict relationships constitute the ingredients of experience which give individuals or groups their uniqueness and varieties, while the consensus relations constitute the common underpinnings of behavior. The tendency in social science has been to study

[10]Tables on American elite characteristics are deleted here but may be found in the original article. For some interesting work bearing upon the attitudes of business and military elites see Angell, 1964; Bauer et al., 1963; Eells and Walton, 1961; and Singer, 1964.

decision-making in order to study group differences; we need to study decision-making also to understand group commonalities.

Were such studies done, our hypothesis would be that certain "core beliefs" are continuously unquestioned. One of these, undoubtedly, would be that efficacy is preferable to principle in foreign affairs. In practice, this means that violence is preferable to non-violence as a means of defense. A second is that private property is preferable to collective property. A third assumption is that the particular form of constitutional government which is practiced within the United States is preferable to any other system of government. We refer to the preferred mode as limited parliamentary democracy, a system in which institutionalized forms of direct representation are carefully retained but with fundamental limitations placed upon the prerogatives of governing. Specifically included among the areas of limitation are many matters encroaching upon corporation property and state hegemony. While adherence to this form of government is conceivably the strongest of the domestic "core values," at least among business elites, it is probably the least strongly held of the three on the international scene. American relations with, and assistance for, authoritarian and semi-feudal regimes occurs exactly in those areas where the recipient regime is evaluated primarily upon the two former assumptions and given rather extensive leeway on the latter one.

The implications of these "core beliefs" for the social system are immense, for they justify the maintenance of our largest institutional structures: the military, the corporate economy, and a system of partisan politics which protects the concept of limited democracy. These institutions, in turn, may be seen as current agencies of the more basic social structure. The "renewable basis of power" in America at the present time underlies those institutional orders linked in consensus relationships: military defense of private property and parliamentary democracy. These institutional orders are not permanently secure, by definition. Their maintenance involves a continuous coping with new conditions, such as technological innovation and with the inherent instabilities of a social structure which arbitrarily classifies persons by role, status, access to resources, and power. The myriad groups composing these orders are even less secure because of their weak ability to command "coping resources," e.g., the service branches are less stable than the institution of the military, particular companies are less stable than the institutions of corporate property, political parties are less stable than the institution of parliamentary government.

In the United States there is no ruling group. Nor is there any easily discernible ruling institutional order, so meshed have the separate sources of elite power become. But there is a social structure which is organized to create and protect power centers with only partial accountability. In this definition of power we are avoiding the Weber-Mills meaning of *omnipotence* and the contrary pluralist definition of power as consistently *diffuse*. We are describing the current system as one of overall "minimal accountability" and "minimal consent." We mean that the role of democratic review, based on genuine popular consent, is made marginal and reactive. Elite groups are minimally accountable to publics and have a substantial, though by no means maximum, freedom to shape popular attitudes. The reverse of our system would be one in which democratic participation would be the orienting demand around which the social structure is organized.

Some will counter this case by saying that we are measuring "reality" against an "ideal," a technique which permits the conclusion that the social structure is undemocratic according to its distance from our utopian values. This is a convenient apology for the present system, of course. We think it possible, at least in theory, to develop measures of the undemocratic in democratic conditions, and place given social structures along a continuum. These measures, in rough form, might include such variables as economic security, education, legal guarantees, access to information, and participatory control over systems of economy, government, and jurisprudence.

The reasons for our concern with democratic process in an article questioning the power of a purported military-industrial complex are twofold. First, just as scientific method both legitimizes and promotes change in the world of knowledge, democratic method legitimizes and promotes change in the world of social institutions. Every society, regardless of how democratic, protects its core institutions in a web of widely shared values. But if the core institutions should be dictated by the requisites of military preparedness, then restrictions on the democratic process, i.e., restrictions in either mass opinion exchange (as by voluntary or imposed news management) or in decision-making bodies (as by selection of participants in a manner guaranteeing exclusion of certain positions), then such restrictions would be critical obstacles to peace.

Second, certain elements of democratic process are inimical to features of military oriented society, and the absence of these elements offers one type of evidence for a military-industrial complex even in the absence of a ruling elite. Secretary of Defense Robert McNamara made the point amply clear in his testimony in 1961 before the Senate Armed Services Committee:

> Why should we tell Russia that the Zeus development may not be satisfactory? What we ought to be saying is that we have the most perfect anti-ICBM system that the human mind will ever devise. Instead the public domain is already full of statements that the Zeus may not

93

be satisfactory, that it has deficiencies. I think it is absurd to release that level of information. (Military Procurement Authorization Fiscal Year 1962)

Under subsequent questioning McNamara attempted to clarify his statement that he only wished to delude Russian, not American, citizens about U.S. might. Just how this might be done was not explained.

A long established tradition exists for "executive privilege" which permits the President to refuse to release information when, in his opinion, it would be damaging to the national interest. Under modern conditions responsibility for handling information of a strategic nature is shared among military, industrial, and executive agencies. The discretion regarding when to withhold what information must also be shared. Moreover, the existence of a perpetual danger makes the justification, "in this time of national crisis," suitable to every occasion in which secrecy must be justified. McNamara's statement cited above referred not to a crisis in Cuba or Viet Nam but rather to the perpetual state of cold war crisis. And since the decision about what is to be released and when, is subject to just such management the media became dependent upon the agencies for timely leaks and major stories. This not only adds an aura of omniscience to the agencies, but gives these same agencies the power to reward "good" journalists and punish the critical ones.

The issues involved in the question of news management involve more than the elements of control available to the President, the State Department, the Department of Defense, the Central Intelligence Agency, the Atomic Energy Commission or any of the major prime contractors of defense contracts. Outright control of news flow is probably less pervasive than voluntary acquiescence to the objectives of these prominent institutions of our society. Nobody has to tell the wire services when to release a story on the bearded dictator of our hemisphere or the purported brutality of Ho Chi Minh. A frequent model, the personified devil image of an enemy, has become a press tradition. In addition to a sizeable quantity of radio and television programming and spot time purchased directly by the Pentagon, an amount of service, valued at $6 million by *Variety*, is donated annually by the networks and by public relations agencies for various military shows (Swomley, 1959). Again, the pluralistic shell of an independent press or broadcasting media is left hollow by the absence of a counter-vailing social force of any significant power.

. . . Several shared premises, unquestioned by any potent locus of institutionalized power were described as:

(a) Efficacy is preferable to principle in foreign affairs (thus military means are chosen over non-violent means);

94

(b) Private property is preferable to public property; and
(c) Limited parliamentary democracy (see p. 92) is preferable to any other system of government.

At issue is the question of whether an America protecting such assumptions can exist in a world of enduring peace. Three pre-conditions of enduring peace must be held up against these premises.

The first is that enduring peace will first require or will soon generate disarmament. Offset programs for the reallocation of the defense dollar require a degree of coordinated planning for the change inconsistent with the working assumption that "private property is preferable to public property" in a corporate economy. . . .

If one pools available projections regarding the offset programs, especially regional and local offset programs, necessary to maintain economic well-being in the face of disarmament in this country, the programs will highlight two important features. One is the lag time in industrial conversion. The second is the need for coordination in the timing and spacing of programs. One cannot reinvest in new home building in an area which just been deserted by its major industry and left a ghost town. The short-term and long-term offset values of new hospitals and educational facilities will differ in the building and the utilization stages and regional offset programs have demonstrable interregional effects (Reiner, 1964). Plans requiring worker mobility on a large scale will require a central bank for storing job information and a smooth system for its dissemination. Such coordination will require a degree of centralization of controls beyond the realm which our assumption regarding primacy of private property would permit. . . . Gross intransigence has already been seen even on the contingency planning for non-defense work by single firms like Sperry Rand which have already been severely hurt by project cutbacks. And the prospect of contingency planning will not be warmly welcomed in the newer aeroframe industry (which is only 60% convertible to needs of a peace-time society) (McDonagh and Zimmerman, 1964). Private planning, by an individual firm for its own future does occur, but, without coordinated plans, the time forecast for market conditions remains smaller than the lag time for major retooling. A lag time of from six to ten years would not be atypical before plans by a somewhat over-specialized defense contractor could result in retooling for production in a peace-time market. In the meantime, technological innovations, governmental fiscal or regulatory policies, shifts in consumer preferences, or the decisions by other firms to enter that same market could well make the market vanish. Moreover, the example of defense firms which have attempted even the smaller step toward diversification presents a picture which has not been entirely promising (Fearon and Hook, 1964). Indeed, one of several reasons for the

95

failures in this endeavor has been that marketing skills necessary to compete in a private enterprise economy have been lost by those industrial giants who have been managing with a sales force of one or two retired generals to deal with the firm's only customer. Even if the path of successful conversion by some firms were to serve as the model for all individual attempts, the collective result would be poor. To avoid a financially disastrous glutting of limited markets some coordinated planning will be needed.

The intransigence regarding public or collaborative planning occurs against a backdrop of a soon-to-be increasing army of unemployed youth and aged, as well as regional armies of unemployed victims of automation. Whether one thinks of work in traditional job market terms or as anything worthwhile that a person can do with his life, work (and some means of livelihood) will have to be found for these people. There is much work to be done in community services, education, public health, and recreation, but this is people work, not product work. The lack of a countervailing force prevents the major reallocation of human and economic resources from the sector defined as preferable by the most potent institutions of society. One point must be stressed. We are not saying that limited planning to cushion the impact of arms reduction is impossible. Indeed, it is going on and with the apparent blessing of the Department of Defense (Barber, 1963). We are saying that the type of accommodation needed by a cutback of $9 billion in R & D and $16 billion in military procurement requires a type of preparation not consistent with the unchallenged assumptions.

Even the existence of facilities for coordinated planning does not, to be sure, guarantee the success of such planning. Bureaucratic institutions, designed as they may be for coordination and control, do set up internal resistance to the very coordination they seek to achieve. The mechanisms for handling these bureaucratic intransigencies usually rely upon such techniques as bringing participants into the process of formulating the decisions which will affect their own behavior. We can conceive of no system of coordinated conversion planning which could function without full and motivated cooperation from the major corporations, the larger unions, and representatives of smaller business and industry. Unfortunately, it is just as difficult to conceive of a system which would assure this necessary level of participation and cooperation. This same argument cuts deeper still when we speak of the millions of separate individuals in the "other America" whose lives would be increasingly "administered" with the type of centralized planning needed to offset a defense economy. The job assignment which requires moving, the vocational retraining program, the development of housing projects to meet minimal standards, educational enrichment programs, all of the programs which are conceived by middle-class white America for racially mixed low income groups, face the same difficulty in execution of plans. Without direct participation in the formulation of the programs, the target populations are less likely to participate in the programs and more likely to continue feelings of alienation from the social system which looks upon them as an unfortunate problem rather than as contributing members. Considering the need for active participation in real decisions, every step of coordinated planning carries with it the responsibility for an equal step in the direction of participatory democracy. This means that the voice of the unemployed urban worker may have to be heard, not only on city council meetings which discuss policy on the control of rats in his dwelling, but also on decisions about where a particular major corporation will be relocated and where the major resource allocations of the country will be invested. That such decision participation would run counter to the consensus on the items of limited parliamentary democracy and private property is exactly the point we wish to make.

Just as the theoretical offset plans can be traced to the sources of power with which they conflict, so too can the theoretical plans for international governing and peace-keeping operations be shown to conflict with the unquestioned beliefs. U.S. consent to international jurisdiction in the settlement of claims deriving from the nationalization of American overseas holdings or the removal of U.S. military installations is almost inconceivable. Moreover, the mode of American relations to less-developed countries is so much a part of the operations of those American institutions which base their existence upon interminable conflict with Communism that the contingency in which the U.S. might have to face the question of international jurisdiction in these areas seems unreal. Offers to mediate, with Cuba by Mexico, with North Viet Nam by France, are bluntly rejected. Acceptance of such offers would have called into question not one but all three of the assumptions in the core system. International jurisdictional authority could institutionalize a means to call the beliefs into question. It is for this reason (but perhaps most directly because of our preference for forceful means) that American preoccupation in those negotiations regarding the extension of international control which have taken place, deal almost exclusively with controls in the area of weaponry and police operations and not at all in the areas of political or social justice.[11]

The acceptance of complete international authority even in the area of weaponry poses certain inconsistencies with the preferred "core beliefs." Non-violent settlement of Asian-African area conflicts would be slow and ineffective in protecting American interests. The elimination, however, of military preparedness, both for projected crises and for their potential escalation, requires a faith in alternate

[11]An objective account of the major negotiations related to disarmament which have taken place may be found in Frye (1963).

means of resolution. The phasing of the American plan for general and complete disarmament is one which says in effect: prove that the alternatives are as efficient as our arms in protection of our interests and then we disarm. In the short term, however, the effectiveness of force always looks greater.

The state of world peace contains certain conditions imposed by the fact that people now compare themselves with persons who have more of the benefits of industrialization than they themselves. Such comparative reference groups serve to increase the demand for rapid change. While modern communications heighten the pressures imposed by such comparisons, the actual disparities revealed in comparison speak for violence. Population growth rates, often as high as three percent, promise population doubling within a single generation in countries least able to provide for their members. The absolute number of illiterates as well as the absolute number of persons starving is greater now than ever before in history. Foreign aid barely offsets the disparity between declining prices paid for the prime commodities exported by underdeveloped countries and rising prices paid for the finished products imported into these countries (Horowitz, 1962). All schemes for tight centralized planning employed by these countries to accrue and disperse scarce capital by rational means are blocked by the unchallenged assumptions on private property and limited parliamentary democracy. A recent restatement of the principle came in the report of General Lucius Clay's committee on foreign aid. The report stated that the U.S. should not assist foreign governments "in projects establishing government owned industrial and commercial enterprises which compete with existing private endeavors." When Congressman Broomfield's amendment on foreign aid resulted in cancellation of a U.S. promise to India to build a steel mill in Bokaro, Broomfield stated the case succinctly: "The main issue is private enterprise vs. state socialism" (*The Atlantic*, September, 1964, p. 6). Moreover, preference for forceful solutions assures that the capital now invested in preparedness will not be allocated in a gross way to the needs of underdeveloped countries. Instead, the manifest crises periodically erupting in violence justify further the need for reliance upon military preparedness.

We agree fully with an analysis by Lowi (1964) distinguishing types of decisions for which elite-like forces seem to appear and hold control (redistributive) and other types in which pluralist powers battle for their respective interests (distributive). In the latter type the pie is large and the fights are over who gets how much. Factional strife within and among military industrial and political forces in our country are largely of this nature. In redistributive decisions, the factions coalesce, for the pie itself is threatened. We have been arguing that the transition to peace is a process of redistributive decision.

Is there, then, a military-industrial complex which prevents peace? 98

The answer is inextricably imbedded into the mainstream of American institutions and mores. Our concept is not that American society contains a ruling military-industrial complex. Our concept is more nearly that American society *is* a military-industrial complex. It can accommodate a wide range of factional interests from those concerned with the production or utilization of a particular weapon to those enraptured with the mystique of optimal global strategies. It can accommodate those with rabid desires to advance toward the brink and into limitless intensification of the arms race. It can even accommodate those who wish either to prevent war or to limit the destructiveness of war through the gradual achievement of arms control and disarmament agreements. What it cannot accommodate is the type of radical departures needed to produce enduring peace.

The requirements of a social system geared to peace, as well as the requirements for making a transition to such a social system, share a pattern of resource distribution which is different from the one the world now has. Moreover, these requirements for peace are, in significant measure, inconsistent with constraints set by the more enduring convergencies among power structures in the United States. The same is true whether one speaks of allocation of material or of intellectual resources. Both are geared to the protection of the premises rather than to avenues of change. We are not saying that war is inevitable or that the changes cannot be made. We are saying that the American political, military, and industrial system operates with certain built-in stabilizers which resist a change in the system. If there is to be peace, as opposed to détente or temporary absence of war, marked changes will be needed. Whether this society can or will accommodate to such changes is a question which is fundamentally different from the questions posed by most studies conventionally grouped under the rubric of peace research. One difference which marks the question of capacity to accommodate is in the theoretical conception or model of the cold war which is assumed. And a second distinction lies in the manner in which the end product of the research may be suited to meet the social forces (as apart from the intellectual arguments) which promote long-term changes in policy.

ROLE OF THE PEACE SCHOLARS

In recent years, intellectual attention to the problem of peace has usually been directed to the problem of averting war. The context of this problem is that of the non-zero-sum game in which the players have both a joint common advantage (in averting nuclear war) and a bargaining problem in deciding upon the competitive distribution of other non-sharable advantages. Much of the intellectual attention from social scientists has been directed to problems of trust, controls, and assurances of good faith—problems relevant to protecting the common 99 advantage. Meanwhile the strategists have tended to give relatively greater emphasis to the problem of competitive advantage. There have been clashes between these two groups of intellectuals but both share, and both assume that foreign adversaries also share, the assumption that nuclear war ought to be avoided. The question is one of means to that end and of risks to be taken.

In the question of permanent peace with its contingent institutions, there is no such fundamental agreement about the desirability of the end. In fact, we have argued that there exists a large area of consensus which precludes the very set of contingent institutions which may be needed for lasting peace. Without certain shared end values, research on the part of peace protagonists cannot be used as a rational wedge in policy debate. The clash is with a social system some of whose very bases of organization run counter to the requirements of stable peace. Under such circumstances, there are zero-sum components to the conflict. Some institutions and some status positions within the society must change and some may actually have to perish if certain newer ones are to thrive. Research in this area becomes what most researchers who are justly sensitive about their scientific objectivity dread—a part of a political struggle. Dorwin Cartwright has called power "the neglected variable" in studies of interpersonal behavior (Cartwright, 1959). The scarcity of good empirical studies of the power to effect or constrain national policies shows an even greater area of neglect. Whatever the reasons for this neglect, there seems a need to follow the course once set by Freud if we are ever to learn about, and eventually make changes in, this taboo area.

Another departure intended by the type of research we shall suggest may be seen by a brief comparison with a sample of questions now being tackled by inquiry into problems of peace. Look, for example, at each of the following questions:

How will detection and punishment be regulated in the event of violations in an arms control agreement? What system of jurisdiction and policing could replace national armed forces? What institutionalized channels could be created to replace war as an expression of individual or social aggression? What sequences of events have led to escalation of conflicts in the past and how can these sequences be altered? How will the electronics industry, or Southern California, get along without defense contracts? What sequence of arms reduction and what type of inspections and controls would prevent a successful surprise attack during the disarmament process? When are unilateral gestures likely to be reciprocated?

Taken together, these questions and variations of them comprise a remarkably wide slice of the entire peace research movement (as intellectually popular as it has become on financially sparse resources). The questions are doubtlessly important ones, but they hold in common a certain format of answers. Each project seeks, and some find, as 100 an answer to its research, a scheme which—*if* it were enacted—would promote enduring peace. Why the plan is not enacted is usually not asked, or, if asked at all, then answered within the framework of basic assumptions which protect the status quo. The propensity of scholars seems often to be an equation of their own ability to understand ways to treat a problem with the actual resolution of the problem. This may have been true for smallpox but it is, so far, not true for over-population, and this understanding by itself falls many steps short of implementing the treatment for problems of war and peace. In the case of war and peace the discovery of answers could be irrelevant to their application—could be, that is, unless directed to foci of emergent power and change within the system. By and large, the efforts of the peace intellectuals have not been so directed.

We do not mean this as an indictment against the peace research movement. As an activity which institutionalizes means to support scholars who wish to devote their professional talents to the quest for peace, the movement is admirable. Moreover, it is a young movement still groping for its major task and hence capable of learning. But the nature of the current outputs by these scholars, the policy suggestions which they make as reflections of their intellectual inquiry, suggest a common denominator of difficulties.[12]

The better known among the proposals are associated with the names of Charles Osgood (GRIT), Stephan James (peace hostage exchange), Ralph Lapp and others (finite deterrence), J. David Singer (gradual accretion of U.N. custody for major weapons), John Strachey (military enforced peace through Soviet-American alliance), Morton Deutsch (suspicion-reducing and trust-building steps), Herbert Kelman (neutral international armies), Amitai Etzioni (gradual reduction of military programs to finite levels and reinvestments in economic offensives), Quincy Wright and others (building of interpersonal and organizational ties which transcend the cold war), S. I. Hayakawa (listening), Anatol Rapoport (ideological debate), Louis Sohn and others (world federal government), Jerome Frank and others (education in non-violence), Eric Fromm (major unilateral arms reduction), and so forth. Several of the authors of these and related proposals have provided us with the arguments necessary to demonstrate that each of the plans offered is "not feasible." Usually the basis for the judgment of not feasible lies in the intransigence of the very conditions which that particular plan was designed to overcome. Psycho-logic and self-fulfilling prophecy prevents as well as necessitates a reversal in the arms race. Nationalism prevents as well as necessitates the growth of international friendships, armies, and governmental agencies. Without a theoretical model of what is or is not tractable in the social sys-

[12]We wish to give credit to Philip Green's article in the *Bulletin of the Atomic Scientists*, November 1963, for a detailed critique of "peace proposals" from which we have borrowed.

tem, a marked tendency exists toward seeing the system and its basic assumptions as relatively immobile but for the cracks provided by one's own insight.

That the various proposals do not all agree on whether tensions or weapons must be first to go, or whether international institutions must precede or follow international allegiances, is not a critical problem. Each of the hypotheses presented in the plans may well be true but none may ever be tested. The specification of alternatives in the cold war is necessary. But just offering the alternatives does not serve to generate new goals for a society. Were the goals of our society appropriate to world peace all of these proposals, and many far more exotic than these, would already have been tried. Conversely, the military strategy proposals which have been either tried or subjected to serious policy consideration are not always more reasonable than the works of the peace scholars.

That the fault is not in the plans but in the absence of a market for them may be seen in a plan offered, in jest, by Anatol Rapoport which has much logical merit. Briefly, it suggests that two teams of high ranking officers of the two major powers, rather than civilian diplomats, be given the task of negotiating an agreement on general and complete disarmament. If the teams should fail, they are painlessly put to death and replaced by the next team, and so on. The plan assures a) that knowledge of the military requisites for national security will not be missing from consideration, b) that a demilitarization of society will come one way or another, and c) that those who advocate that we should be willing to die for our country would be given the opportunity to do so. What is missing here, as in each of the other plans, is the social force necessary to try the plan.[13]

[13]We have omitted reference to a number of substantial contributors among the scholars suggesting various peace policies. Some in particular bear mentioning because they have been associated with ideas which have tried to avoid the problems mentioned above. First, Seymour Melman in his emphasis upon detailed studies of industrial conversion for possible use by industrial organizations clearly intends to find a basis for breaking alliances of interest between military and industrial sectors. Second, Otto Feinstein's approach, tapping the institutional involvements in peace of such enduring groups as educators, clergy, and local political machines, is an idea with an intended market which is obvious. Third, Leo Szilard, H. S. Hughes, and others who have pioneered in the cultivation of a politically viable peace movement also have target populations in their designs. To this we must add plans for utilization of professional societies in exerting of political influence by scholars in several disciplines. Moreover, several of the very persons mentioned in the text have conscientiously sought a market for their proposals within and without government agencies. The efforts are laudable but with the possible exception of Melman, are not entirely relevant to our thesis that peace research could bear an intrinsic relationship to both the requisites of enduring peace and to the sources of power which have a stake in such a change.

What sort of research would be instrumental in the transformation of American ideologies and of the power structures in which they are encased? And where is the market for such research? We shall venture the beginnings of an answer in the suggestion of a type of research which is "politically relevant," i.e., which is related to the strategy of its own application. To do this we shall define a notion of power which determines major trends in policy. Second we shall discuss briefly the research task in identifying the potential for change in the current loci of power. And last, we shall sketch the emergence of a countervailing force, a market for the research findings.

What we have been calling the military-industrial complex is an informal and changing coalition of groups with vested psychological, moral, and material interests in the continuous development and maintenance of high levels of weaponry, in preservation of colonial markets and in military-strategic conceptions of international affairs. A survey of such a complex would probably delineate no useful boundaries except those coextensive with American society and its sphere of influence. Hence, a study of the relations of *any* group to the cold war could reveal a set of economic transactions and communication activities which give it a degree of centrality in the present consensus of power. A study of those groups with more focal positions in the power complex would reveal a particular but diverse set of institutions, each somewhat unique in internal dynamics and in the peculiarities of its participation in the cold war. The essence of such study is in differentiating among the institutions for there will certainly be varying scope and depth of commitment. Likewise, some of the institutions, and perhaps many of the key individuals, will present a picture which is psychologically, economically, and politically convertible to the needs of peace.

Convertibility has several meanings. One useful standard will be objective economic adaptability. Can the group in question *survive* a basic policy shift? Some organized social groupings within the military services and major portions of the aerospace companies may not be viable in sustained peace. If 1,800 aircraft can service all scheduled airlines in the U.S. then 33,000 aircraft and most of all aviation production facilities belonging to the U.S. armed forces could present an overabundancy crisis (Convertibility of Space and Defense Hearings, 1964). But some firms will be able to emerge unscathed and many more could probably survive with any of a wide range of governmental offset programs. Individual viability may differ sharply from that of the institution. A study of stock holdings of the officers and directors of the major defense contracting firms could reveal the types of diversification from defense orientation which has already been occurring.

A second view of convertibility is strongly social psychological but with economic underpinnings. It deals with the condition under which the desirability of shift might outweigh the positive incentives which provide psychological sustenance within the current system. We distinguish several types of incentives which research could reveal. *Profit,* of course, is one incentive which keeps some major defense contractors content but the number wholly satisfied in this manner may be shifting with the introduction of new cost-accounting devices and competitive bidding by the Pentagon. A related incentive is *foreign investment* requiring military security. Companies with holdings in Latin America, Africa, and the Near East may be "objectively adaptable" to even total loss of these holdings. However, some, like the petroleum companies, habituated to insecure holdings and high profits, may not be planning for, or willing to accept, any alternative to the military maintenance of "friendly" regimes in underdeveloped countries. The incentives of *governmental subsidy* for technological advance is often mentioned among benefits of defense contracts. Marketable civilian goods emerge as side-products of research in electronics, aviation, and machine components. Research could reveal both beneficiaries and the neglected firms in this area. Moreover, it is not clear whether similar incentives could operate to draw firms out of the current system through governmental research offerings in the areas of automated hospital, library, educational or traffic control facilities.

Approaching the more clearly psychological incentives we consider *ideological satisfaction.* The gamut ranges from a chauvinistic dedication to exorcise devils from Godly America to basic beliefs in the ultimate nature of untested assumptions of the social structure. It includes devotion to "hard nosed," masculine, competitive market-place theories of "rational" self-interest in international relations and rationalizations of special privileges which have been defended to the point of firm belief. Ideological commitment to the arms race is far from uniform. We believe that sensitive interview studies would reveal pockets of cynicism and even guilt. They might well reveal dedication to particularistic goals at the expense of other power centers (e.g., dedication to Air Force preeminence), thus indicating strains amidst the convergencies of military, political, and industrial coalitions. Further, the particular ideologies uncovered may not be consonant with the non-military goals or values of the individuals involved. This could suggest the places in which ideological transfer might occur to civilian research objectives or to the rigorous pursuit of international police operations.

A last type of incentive is *vocational satisfaction.* We know very little of the daily gratifications from the many vocational roles tied to national security. We do not know whether the lavish parties and status through personal contracts mark a peripheral or a central attraction of elite adaptations. We do not know whether the opportunities for creative intellectual effort in technology and strategy are truly basic attractions or even whether such opportunities actually exist beyond job opportunity advertisements of the electronics, missile, and Research and Development corporations. Such knowledge could suggest the possibilities for vocational convertibility in peace time. We do know, however, that in the wax and wane of success and influence within the military-industrial system, there are appearing with increasing frequency groups of individuals who are descending in position and who may be prone to such reactions as a) intensified efforts for maintaining status (and the status quo) within the society, b) nationalistic or extremist affiliations which identify scapegoats and maintain group cohesion without realistic bases, and c) defections from positions central to the complex and realignment with forces of change.

We have concentrated our discussion upon the social-psychological convertibility of economic elites. A similar study could reveal analogous information about political and military elites. Professionalization of the military holds both positive and negative omens for convertibility. Study of the psychologically reasonable retirement opportunities for officers are of obvious importance.

Studies of political elites central to the preservation of military-industrial power pose difficulties of access but also offer the promise of exposing the communication channels through which influence is exerted. Campaign contributions to congressmen and promotional efforts to obtain prime contracts in one's area are both available data. Congressional roll-call votes on cold war issues can be studied, using contract dependency in the congressman's district and reserve officer status of the congressman, as independent variables. Military and industrial lobbying activities are valid objects for study and may be found related to invitations to give testimony on pending legislation. In the executive branch, data on presidential visitors are already compiled and published regularly. Data on stock holdings, vocational histories and voluntary associations of such influential groups as the Joint Chiefs of Staff or the Council of Economic Advisors could give insight into the recruitment mechanisms which indirectly determine the agenda for questions of major resource allocations.

In some institutions, focal to decisions affecting defense policy, it may be possible to discover positive feedback mechanisms which extend militarism (as in the alleged support by certain defense contracting firms of super-patriotic "educational" programs which press the need for greater force), (Westin, 1963).

The suggested questions are neither complete nor are they a research design, but rather a part of a strategy in the use of research to promote policy change. The findings from such studies would describe institutions which are a) ripe for defection from the consensus of military orientation, b) potentially capable of accommodation to the conditions of peace, and c) completely intransigent. Depending again upon what studies of operations of influence would reveal, it may be possible to 105 classify the intransigents in accordance with their ability to constrain decisions for peace, were such decisions forthcoming. Such visibility of interests and of power relationships is itself a tool of ascendance in groups which have the most at stake in a major reallocation of American resources. . . .

REFERENCES

Angell, Robert C. A study of social values: content analysis of elite media. *The Journal of Conflict Resolution, VIII,* 1964, 4, 329–85.

Bank Holding Companies: Scope of Operations and Stock Ownership. Committee on Banking and Currency. Washington: U.S. Government Printing Office, 1963.

Barber, Arthur. Some industrial aspects of arms control. *The Journal of Conflict Resolution, VII,* 1963, 3, 491–95.

Bauer, Raymond A., Pool, I., and Dexter, L. *American business and public policy.* Alberton, New York, 1963.

Bell, Daniel. *The end of ideology.* Glencoe: Free Press, 1959.

Benoit, Emile, and Boulding, K. E. (Eds.). *Disarmament and the economy.* New York: Harper, 1963.

Berle, Adolph A. *The twentieth century capitalist revolution.* New York: Harcourt, 1954.

Bluestone, Irving. Problems of the worker in industrial conversion. *The Journal of Conflict Resolution, VII,* 1963, 3, 495–502.

Brand, Horst. Disarmament and American capitalism. *Dissent,* Summer, 1962. 236–251.

Burdick, Eugene, and Wheeler, H. *Fail-safe.* New York: McGraw, 1962.

Burton, John. *Peace theory.* New York: Knopf, 1962.

Cartwright, Dorwin. Power: a neglected variable in social psychology, in Cartwright, D. (Ed.) *Studies in social power.* Ann Arbor: Research Center for Group Dynamics, 1959.

Catton, Bruce. *The war lords of Washington.* New York: Harcourt, 1948.

Coffin, Tristran. *The passion of the hawks.* New York: Macmillan, 1964.

Cohen, Bernard, C. *The press and foreign policy.* Princeton: Princeton University Press, 1963.

Convertibility of Space and Defense Resources to Civilian Needs, 88th Congress, 2nd Session, Vol. 2, Subcommittee on Employment and Manpower. Washington: U.S. Government Printing Office, 1964.

Cook, Fred J. The coming politics of disarmament. *The Nation.* February 6, 1963.

——. *The warfare state.* New York: Macmillan, 1962.

Dahl, Robert A. *A modern political analysis.* New York: Prentice Hall, 1963.

——.*Who Governs?* New Haven: Yale University Press, 1961.

Dillon, W. *Little brother is watching.* Boston, Houghton Mifflin, 1962.

Economic impacts of disarmament. U.S. Arms Control and Disarmament Agency, Economic Series 1, Washington: U.S. Government Printing Office, 1962.

Eells, Richard, and Walton, C. *Conceptual foundations of business.* Homewood, Illinois: Irwin Press, 1961.

Etzioni, Amitai. *The hard way to peace.* New York: Collier, 1962.

———. *The moon-doggle.* Garden City, New York: Doubleday, 1964.

Fearon, H. E., and Hook, R. C., Jr. The shift from military to industrial markets. *Business Topics,* Winter, 1964, 43–52.

Feingold, Eugene and Hayden, Thomas. What happened to democracy? *New University Thought,* Summer, 1964, 1, 39–48.

Fisher, Roger (Ed.) *International conflict and behavioral science.* New York: Basic Books, 1964.

Fishman, Leslie. A note on disarmament and effective demand. *The Journal of Politcal Economy, LXX,* 1962, 2, 183–186.

Foreign Assistance Act of 1964 (Parts VI and VII), Committee on Foreign Affairs. Hearings, 88th Congress, 2nd Session. Washington: U.S. Government Printing Office, 1964.

Friedman, S. The RAND Corporation and our Policy Makers, *Atlantic Monthly,* September, 1963, 61–68.

Frye, Wm. R. Characteristics of recent arms-control proposals and agreements. In Brennan, D. G. (Ed.), *Arms control, disarmament, and national security.* New York: Braziller, 1963.

Galbraith, J. K. *American Capitalism.* Boston: Houghton Mifflin, 1956.

———. Poverty among nations. *The Atlantic Monthly,* October, 1962, 47–53.

Gans, Herbert J. Some proposals for government policy in an automating society. *The Correspondent,* 30, Jan.–Feb., 1964, 74–82.

Government Information Plans and Policies. Parts I–V, Hearings before a Subcommittee on Government Operations. 88th Congress, 1st Session, U.S. Govt. Printing Office: 1963.

Green, Philip. Alternative to overkill: dream and reality. *Bulletin of the Atomic Scientists,* November, 1963, 23–26.

Hayakawa, S. J. Formula for peace: listening. *N.Y. Times Magazine.* July 31, 1961.

Horowitz, David. *World economic disparities: the haves and the havenots.* Center for Study of Democratic Institutions: Santa Barbara, 1962.

Horowitz, I. L. *The war game: studies of the new civilian militarists.* New York: Ballantine, 1963.

Humphrey, Hubert H., *The economic impact of arms control agreements.* Congressional Record. October 5, 1962, 2139–94.

Impact of Military Supply and Service Activities on the Economy. 88th Congress, 2nd Session. Report to the Joint Economic Committee. Washington: U.S. Government Printing Office, 1963.

Isard, Walter, and Schooler, E. W. An economic analysis of local and regional impacts of reduction of military expenditures. *Papers Vol. 1, 1964 Peace Research Society International.* Chicago Conference, 1963.

107

Janowitz, Morris. Military elites and the study of war. *The Journal of Conflict Resolution, I,* 1957, 1, 9–18.

——. *The professional soldier.* Glencoe, Ill.: The Free Press, 1960.

Keller, Suzanne. *Beyond the ruling class.* New York: Random House, 1963.

Knebel, Fletcher, and Bailey, C. *Seven days in May.* New York: Harper, 1962.

Knorr, Klaus. Warfare and peacefare states and the acts of transition. *The Journal of Conflict Resolution, VII,* 1963, 4, 754–62.

Lapp, Ralph E. *Kill and overkill.* New York: Basic Books, Inc., 1962.

Larson, Arthur. *The internation rule of law.* A Report to the Committee on Research for Peace, Program of Research No. 3, Institute for International Order, 1961.

Lasswell, Harold. *Politics: Who gets what, when & how.* New York: Meridian, 1958.

Lipset, Seymour M. *Political man.* Garden City: Doubleday, 1959.

Long Island Sunday Press, The. February 23, 1964.

Lowi, Theodore J. American business, public policy, case-studies, and political theory, *World Politics,* July, 1964, 676–715.

Lumer, Hyman. *War economy and crisis.* New York: International Publishers, 1954.

Lynd, Robert S., and Merrill, Helen. *Middletown.* New York: Harcourt, 1959.

Mannheim, Karl. *Freedom, power, and democratic planning.* London: Routledge and Kegan Paul, 1956.

McDonagh, James J., and Zimmerman, Steven M. A program for civilian diversifications of the airplane industry. In *Convertibility of Space and Defense Resources to Civilian Needs.* Subcommittee on Employment and Manpower. U.S. Senate, 88th Congress. Washington: U.S. Government Printing Office, 1964.

McNamara, Robert S. Remarks of the Secretary of Defense before the Economic Club of New York. Department of Defense Office of Public Affairs, Washington, November 18, 1963.

Meisel, James H. *The fall of the republic.* Ann Arbor: University of Michigan Press, 1962.

——. *The myth of the ruling class.* Ann Arbor: University of Michigan Press, 1958.

Melman, Seymour (Ed.). *A Strategy for American Security,* New York: Lee Offset Inc., 1963.

——. *The peace race.* New York: Braziller, 1962.

Merbaum, R. RAND: technocrats and power, *New University Thought,* December–January, 1963–64, 45–57.

Michael, Donald. *Cybernation: the silent conquest.* Center for the Study of Democratic Institutions, Santa Barbara, 1962.

Milbrath, L. W. *The Washington lobbyists.* Chicago: Rand McNally, 1963.

Military Posture and Authorizing Appropriations for Aircraft, Missiles, and Naval Vessels. Hearings No. 36, 88th Congress, 2nd Session, U.S. Govt. Printing Office: 1964.

Military Procurement Authorization Fiscal Year 1962. Hearings before the Committee on Armed Services, U.S. Senate, 87th Congress, 1st Session, U.S. Govt. Printing Office: 1961.

Mills, C. Wright. *The causes of World War III.* New York: Simon & Schuster, 1958.

——. *The power elite.* New York: Oxford University Press, 1959.

Minnis, Jack. The care and feeding of power structures. *New University Thought V.* 4, Summer, 1964,1, 73–79.

Nossiter, Berland. *The Mythmakers: an essay on power and wealth.* Boston: Houghton Mifflin, 1964.

Osgood, Charles E. *An alternative to war or surrender.* Urbana: University of Illinois Press, 1962.

Parsons, Talcott. *Structure and process in modern societies.* Glencoe: Free Press, 1959.

——. *The social system.* Glencoe: Free Press, 1951.

Paul, J., and Laulicht, J. Leaders' and voters' attitudes on defense and disarmament. *In Your Opinion,* V. 1, Canadian Peace Research Inst., Clarkson, Ontario, 1963.

Peck, M. J. and Scherer, F. M. *The weapons acquisition process.* Boston: Harvard University, 1962.

Perlo, Victor. *Militarism and industry.* New York: International Publishers, 1963.

Piel, Gerard. Consumers of abundance. Center for the Study of Democratic Institutions, Santa Barbara, 1961.

Pilisuk, Marc. Dominance of the Military. *Science,* January 18, 1963, 247–48.

——. The Poor and the War on Poverty, *The Correspondent,* Summer, 1965.

Pyramiding of Profits and Costs in the Missile Procurement Program, Parts 1, 2 and 3. Committee on Government Operations, U.S. Senate. Hearings, 87th Congress, 2nd Session. Washington: U.S. Govt. Printing Office, 1962.

Pyramiding of Profits and Costs in the Missile Procurement Program, Report, 88th Congress, 2nd Session, Report No. 970. Washington: U.S. Government Printing Office, 1964.

Rapoport, Anatol. *Fights, games, and debates.* Ann Arbor: University of Michigan Press, 1960.

——. *Strategy and conscience.* New York: Harper, 1964.

Raymond, Jack. *Power at the Pentagon.* New York: Harper, 1964.

Reagan, Michael. *The Managed Economy.* New York: Oxford, 1963.

Reiner, Thomas. Spatial criteria to offset military cutbacks. Paper presented at the Univ. of Chicago Peace Research Conference, Nov. 18, 1964.

Report on the world today. *The Atlantic,* September, 1964, 4–8.

Rogow, Arnold A. *James Forrestal.* New York: Macmillan, 1963.

Satellite communications, 1964. (Part 1) Committee on Government Operations, Hearings, 88th Congress, 2nd Session. Washington: U.S. Government Printing Office, 1964.

Scherer, Frederick. *The weapons acquisition process: economic incentives.* Cambridge: Harvard Business School, 1964.

Shils, Edward. Professor Mills on the calling of sociology. *World Politics, XIII*, 1961, 4.

Singer, J. David. A study of foreign policy attitudes. *The Journal of Conflict Resolution, VIII*, 1964, 4, 424–85.

——. *Deterrence, arms control and disarmament.* Columbus: Ohio State University Press, 1962.

——. (Ed.) Weapons management in world politics. *The Journal of Conflict Resolution*, VII, No. 3, and *Journal of Arms Control*, Vol. 1, No. 4.

Stachey, John. *On the prevention of war.* New York: St. Martin's Press, 1963.

Strauss, Lewis L. *Men and decisions.* Garden City: Doubleday, 1962.

Sutton, Jefferson. *The missile lords.* New York: Dell, 1963.

Swomley, J. M., Jr. The growing power of the military. *The Progressive,* January, 1959.

——. *The military establishment.* Boston: Beacon Press, 1964.

Toward Full Employment: Proposals for a Comprehensive Employment and Manpower Policy in the U.S. A Report of the Committee on Labor and Public Welfare, United States Senate. Washington: U.S. Government Printing Office, 1964.

Toward world peace: a summary of U.S. disarmament efforts past and present. U.S. Arms Control and Disarmament Agency Publication 10: U.S. Government Printing Office, 1964.

Warner, Wm. Floyd, and Abegglen, J. D. *Big business leaders in America.* New York: Harper, 1955.

Warner, Wm. Lloyd, Van Riper, P. P., Martin, N. H., and Collins, O. F. *The American federal executive.* New Haven: Yale University Press, 1963.

Watson-Watt, Sir Robert. *Man's means to his end.* London: Heinemann, 1962.

Westin, Alan. Anti-communism and the corporations. *Commentary Magazine.* December, 1963, 479–87.

Wise, David, and Ross, Thomas. *The invisible government.* New York: Random, 1964.

Wright, Quincy, Evans, Wm., and Deutsch, Morton (Eds.). *Preventing World War III: some proposals.* New York: Simon and Schuster, 1962.

110

Richard Flacks, Florence Howe, and Paul Lauter

On the Draft

At no time in its history has the draft been opposed, evaded, defied, studied, and pronounced upon with such energy and persistence as it is today. We now have the report of a Presidential commission proposing extensive reforms, another report by a Congressional commission endorsing most of the present system, and a book presenting the case for replacing the draft altogether by a voluntary army. Yet none of these proposals really deals with the reason why the draft is now a hot political issue: the war in Vietnam.

This war, more than most wars in American history, remains unpopular even with many who do not oppose it. Yet the Administration has been able to wage the war without serious political challenge, in part because of the power to conscript. Many young Americans, still raised to value personal liberty and democratic consent, feel forced by the draft to contribute to a war which they oppose and which is certainly not of their making or liking. Among men of draft age particularly, there is a mood of anger, resistance, and cynicism, and a rapid decline of the draft's legitimacy. And for many left or liberal "doves," opposition to the war and opposition to the draft have become synonymous.

But for a much larger group, including Republicans and even some hawks, the war has served only to make visible the draft's inequities. Even now with over 400,000 American troops in Vietnam, the military needs—indeed, can use—only a minority of those eligible for the draft. Thus some men are conscripted for combat, while the majority

Reprinted by permission from *The New York Review of Books*, April 6, 1967, pp. 3–5. Copyright © 1967 by The New York Review. Richard Flacks is assistant professor of Sociology at the University of Chicago, engaged in research on student protest. Paul Lauter is associate professor, Antioch-Putney Graduate School of Education, and Project Director of the Morgan Community School, Washington, D.C. Florence Howe is assistant professor of English at Goucher College.

111

MILITARY IDEOLOGY AND INFLUENCE

remain free. Among men who are qualified—as the Marshall Commission points out—those who are white, middle class, and college-educated are likely to escape the mud and death in Southeast Asia, while those who are black, poor and "unsuitable" for college die on battlefields at a rate double that of their proportion in the population. The economic and social biases of the draft seemed intolerable during cold war; to diverse groups, for various reasons, they are a disgrace during hot war.

Speaking with a traditional American outrage about bumbling and inequality, Bruce K. Chapman documents in *The Wrong Man in Uniform*,[1] current complaints about the Selective Service System. Many abuses arise in the name of local autonomy. The bureaucratic jungle described by Chapman consists of over four thousand local draft boards which decide the fate of millions according to obscure criteria. Chapman finds great variation, from state to state, in the proportion of men who are classified as 1-F or who are, for a variety of reasons, deferred from serving. In one state, married men are vulnerable; elsewhere they are not. Peace Corps volunteers are deferred in New York, but drafted in Kansas. Illinois gives special consideration to mortuary trainees, but not Alabama. The system as a whole creaks with age, inbreeding, and inefficiency. Draft board members, the Marshall Commission documents, are all male, mostly veterans and white-collar workers, and virtually all white—only 1.3 per cent are Negro. Twenty-two per cent of board members are over seventy years old; the average age is fifty-eight. Although Congress intended that Selective Service be controlled by civilians, its top officials are heavily military in orientation and training.

Recently, the system has begun to stumble over its own manipulations. A year ago, General Hershey claimed that the 1-A pool would be exhausted shortly, and that, therefore, some students would have to lose their deferments. Draft boards began demanding reports on class standings, and hundreds of thousands of students rushed to take the Selective Service qualification test. Some were reclassified; thousands enlisted; thousands more engaged in anti-draft and "anti-ranking" sit-ins. But no manpower crisis did appear; by June, 1966, it was clear that Selective Service had simply overestimated its needs by more than a third! According to Chapman, last Spring's crisis was the result of the temporary loss—in the bureaucratic "pipelines"—of 500,000 men classified 1-A. Whether this is so or not, the entire sequence of events dramatized the draft's power to touch even the university sanctuary. General Hershey may have meant to relieve political pressure by publicizing the potential vulnerability of students. But the effect was to provoke students into opposition to the draft—

[1]Trident, 143 pp.

despite the fact that they have been among its chief beneficiaries.

A reader of Chapman's book concludes, correctly, that the present Selective Service System creates a great many absurd inequities because of decentralization as well as the deferment system itself; that it creates enormous uncertainty and unnecessary anxiety for millions; and that it is, moreover, inefficient from the military point of view, since it fails to recruit men with a stable commitment to service.

What Chapman and similar critics miss is that the Selective Service System is *designed* this way—its "flaws" are not accidental, but viewed by its administrators as necessary to its effective operation. For, over the years, General Hershey has evolved the idea that Selective Service functions not primarily for the "delivery of manpower for induction . . . . It is in dealing with the other millions of registrants that the System is heavily occupied, developing more effective human beings in the national interest."[2] Occupational and student deferments, therefore, are tools to deal with the "ever-increasing problem of how to control the service of individuals who are not in the armed services." In short, young men unfortunately desire to determine their own careers; such unreliable and unpredictable impulses can and must be disciplined and "channeled." Selective Service describes the process:

> Educators, scientists, engineers, and their professional organizations . . . have been convincing the American public that for the mentally qualified man there is a special order of patriotism other than service in uniform—that for the man having the capacity, dedicated service as a civilian in such fields as engineering, the sciences, and teaching constitutes the ultimate in their expression of patriotism. A large segment of the American public has been convinced that this is true. . . .
>
> It is in this atmosphere that the young man registers at age 18 and pressure begins to force his choice. . . .
>
> The psychological effect of this circumstantial climate depends upon the individual, his sense of good sportsmanship, his love of country and its way of life. He can obtain a sense of well-being and satisfaction that he is doing as a civilian what will help his country most. . . .
>
> In the less patriotic and more selfish individual it engenders a sense of fear, uncertainty and dissatisfaction which motivates him, nevertheless, in the same direction. He complains of the uncertainty which he must endure; he would like to be able to do as he pleases; he would

[2]These and the following quotations are taken from the *Selective Service Orientation Kit* memo on "Channeling." April, 1965, available from Chief, Public Information, Selective Service System, 1724 F Street, Washington, D.C. We are indebted to Jean Carper and Peter Henig for drawing our attention to these statements. More detailed analysis of "channeling" may be found in P. Henig, "On the Manpower Channelers," *New Left Notes,* January 20, 1967; and in a forthcoming book on the draft by Jean Casper, (*Bitter Greetings,* Grossman).

113

appreciate a certain future with no prospect of military service or civilian contribution, but he complies with the needs of the national health, safety, or interest—or is denied deferment.

Throughout his career as a student, the pressure—the threat of loss of deferment—continues. It continues with equal intensity after graduation. His local board requires periodic reports to find out what he is up to. He is impelled to pursue his skill rather than embark upon some less important enterprise and is encouraged to apply his skill in essential activity in the national interest. The loss of deferred status is the consequence for the individual who acquired the skill and either does not use it or uses it in a non-essential activity.

The psychology of granting wide choice under pressure to take action is the *American or indirect way of achieving what is done by direction in foreign countries where choice is not permitted.* [Italics added]

There it is—the lives of American men could not be better described. Are you in a state of perpetual worry about military service? Do you feel yourself pushed into a way of life against which your deeper impulses rebel? Would you rather be a poet than a graduate student in English, an organizer in the ghetto than a law student? Would you like to lumberjack or bum around Europe or "tune in and drop out" or just be free this year? Your anxieties and frustrations are not accidental; US government policy, as interpreted by General Hershey, creates them. And if you happen to rub your eyes and ask, "Tell me, again, what exactly are our objections to totalitarian collectivism?" the answer is really very simple: the American way is the indirect way.

Several years ago, some Republican congressmen began to sense the political potential in the inequitable, inefficient, and undemocratic Selective Service System, and to demand its abolition and replacement by a volunteer army. Similar proposals were urged by a few Democrats like Gaylord Nelson of Wisconsin. Barry Goldwater suggested, during the election campaign of 1964, that a volunteer army was feasible. In response to these early stirrings, President Johnson ordered a study conducted by the Department of Defense. Never fully published, the Pentagon study argued essentially in defense of the present system and against a volunteer force, primarily because of the huge sums needed to hire an army of sufficient size.

But these arguments have not silenced an increasingly articulate and cohesive Republican campaign against conscription and for a volunteer army. Chapman, a leader in the "Progressive Republican" Ripon Society, has provided ammunition for several representatives such as Thomas Curtis and Donald Rumsfeld, as Congress has moved toward a major debate on the draft this session. On this issue, liberal

114

Republicans find common ground with Goldwater conservatives. Professor Milton Friedman, Goldwater's economic advisor, judges that the price of a volunteer army would be substantially lower than Pentagon estimates; and he is supported by the economist Walter Oi, who prepared part of the Defense Department's study. Friedman argues further that men in the armed forces support much of the real cost of the draft by a hidden "direct tax" on their labor, which they are forced to contribute at a price far below its true worth. The pay of an army private, Chapman asserts, is little more than that of a Rumanian peasant on a collective farm. Housing, especially for men with families, ranges from deplorable to insipid; post amenities are primitive; social life, rigid and sterile. Give men freedom to choose, pay them a decent wage (say, $5,000 as a minimum), improve their working conditions, offer fringe benefits—in short, apply the techniques of effective business practice—and you will produce an efficient, stable military work force at a socially acceptable cost, and remove a major source of compulsion from the lives of young men.

In response to this developing Republican position, to widespread criticism of the stand-pat Pentagon report, and to growing student protest, President Johnson recently appointed the "blue-ribbon" Commission[3] headed by Burke Marshall to conduct still another study. The result is a recommendation which would essentially abolish General Hershey's channeling system. So many young men turn eighteen every year (1,800,000 now and over 2 million by 1970), that student and occupational deferments are no longer needed to ensure adequate supplies of manpower in "essential" occupations. To deal with the problem of how to select the minority of available men needed for the military, the Marshall Commission proposes what amounts to a lottery. Their system of random selection is designed to make everybody feel a lot better: it will strike only a fraction of the young, even during a war as large as the present one; it will reduce the political problems of current inequities by drawing, with equal arbitrariness, from all races, areas, economic levels. At the same time, complaints about "uncertainty" can be eliminated by drafting younger men first who, in the view of the military, are more malleable anyway.

The Commission proposes to centralize the selection system, replacing idiosyncratic local draft boards with computers that will apply uniform national standards to all registrants. In addition, the Commission recommends the creation of several hundred regional appeals boards, its members to be representative of "all elements of the public," in-

[3]*In Pursuit of Equity: Who Serves When Not All Serve?* Report of the President's National Advisory Commission on Selective Service, Burke Marshall, Chairman. U.S. Government Printing Office, 219 pp.

cluding women, and to serve for no longer than five-year terms. The Commission wants to see local boards function mainly to help registrants appeal their draft status (presumably those with hardship cases, or those wanting to avoid the draft by becoming career officers); it wants to make sure that the claims of conscientious objectors are handled expeditiously (in part, probably, because the present system can be used to stall the draft for up to two years); it wants to make sure that the public understands the working of a new, improved System. In short, the Marshall report would modernize Selective Service by making it more uniform and equitable, more impersonal in its selection, and more inclusive of a wide spectrum of society in its operation. It is a clean, almost surgical effort to eliminate the most laughable and disgusting particularities of the draft as we know it. Besides, it has the distinct virtue that most of its central proposals can be implemented by Presidential fiat and without awkward Congressional debate.

But the Marshall Commission Report implies no departure from the present goals and priorities of American society. It does not suggest how a country which devotes its public resources largely to war can deal with the fundamental problems of social inequality. Instead, it implies that military institutions can be used to patch over the effects of racism; thus, it wants the military to make special efforts to recruit and "rehabilitate" poor youths who are ordinarily rejected because they do not meet induction standards. All eighteen-year-old men would undergo physical, mental, and moral tests. "This universal testing," the Commission comments, "would meet social as well as military needs." In other words, draft registration can be used as a framework for a program of regimented social rehabilitation.

The Marshall Commission would seem to reduce government interference in the lives of young men by abolishing the privileged treatment now given to students and workers in certain occupations. But what will its impact be? The pressure now generated by America's international posture—to coordinate individual lives and careers, to plan "manpower utilization"—seems more irresistible than the Marshall commission can acknowledge. In the long run, it is unlikely that people will tolerate a system in which a fraction of the young make supreme sacrifices because they have lost a game of roulette. Waiting in the wings are proposals for vast programs of "national service," in which youth will be "expected" to serve as police cadets, teachers, job corpsmen, peace corpsmen, and so on—if they are not inducted. The Commission wants to draw sharp distinctions between military service and "national service," and seems to consider the latter politically impossible at present and of dubious constitutionality. But by reducing the vulnerability of many young men to military service, the Marshall proposal will make national service seem more desirable than ever to those who wring their hands at the individ-

TECHNOLOGICAL MILITARISM

ualism, the "lack of patriotism," and the "privatism" of young people.

One of the main hand-wringers, Margaret Mead, describes national service at work: "Every individual, including the physically handicapped, the mentally defective, the emotionally disturbed, the totally illiterate, would be registered, and every one of these, according to their needs or potentialities, would be assigned to types of rehabilitation, education, and different kind of service with different sorts of risks, benefits, and requirements." Oddly, despite this description, national service advocates persist in calling the system "voluntary." To deal with at least two-million new men annually (to say nothing of women), the system would require an enormous federal bureaucracy, fantastic expenditures for training and maintenance, and expansion of service opportunities beyond anything now imaginable. Besides, service is probably best rendered by those who freely give it.

Above all, national service—perhaps servitude is a more appropriate term—would mean an enormous jump in the degree of control by a central authority over the lives of Americans. Assignments to the military, to service, or to rehabilitation would finally be made not according to individual ability or interest, but by a centralized manpower planning commission, according to established definitions of national priorities. In this light, national service can be seen as the present draft writ large: "channeling" no longer applied "indirectly"— the "American way"—but by compulsion. The system becomes a machine, in which men are considered as a "national resource," to be developed, channeled, enriched, molded, utilized, exploited, and above all, nationalized—in the public interest, to be sure. This is a high and totalitarian price to pay for "socializing" unruly youth, controlling early marriage, and eliminating the "sense of unfairness" people feel about the draft.

The Marshall proposal is, in fact, the most suitable design for an America which intends to consolidate and extend its world-wide military power. Sophisticated strategists in the national leadership believe that continuing commitments to "stop communism" and to contain revolutions wherever these occur are militarily and technologically feasible. There is, however, the problem of how the American people will take to the role of world policeman. How will we react to fairly continuous war of one sort or another run by a huge military establishment? One danger, of course, is an outbreak of irrational and irresponsible mass jingoism, which could push toward a nuclear confrontation with the "enemy." At the opposite pole, disruptive protest and disaffection might prove embarrassing or worse. The Marshall plan meshes nicely with the "Great Society" at home: it requires no mass mobilization of the populace, and it enables the draft to affect only a random fraction of the young. A volunteer army would ac- 117 complish the same results. But the Marshall Commission rejects a voluntary system, primarily because it is not sufficiently "flexible" to meet the possibility of "crises" which require "the rapid procurement of larger numbers of men." That is, a voluntary system might inhibit escalation of wars like the one in Vietnam.

The Marshall Commission is probably right in thinking that the volunteer alternative is impossible within the context of present American foreign policy. For although it makes small-scale military operations even more simple (hardly anyone will worry if a few thousand hired hands are shipped off), it does require a somewhat smaller military force than the Pentagon has grown accustomed to having at its disposal. More important, what if escalation becomes necessary? Congress would then have to consider reinstituting conscription; public debate would then ensue; normally secure National Guardsmen and Reservists might have to be called, and months might pass before the new system got men into the field. From the perspective of the liberal establishment, which the Marshall Commission perfectly represents, the volunteer proposal combines the imperialist flavor of a mercenary army with the isolationist quest for a mechanism to restrain strong (irresponsible, interventionist) presidents. The Marshall proposals are thus the right ones, *if* one conceives that the most important problem is how to maintain a huge military force, capable of a variety of overseas activities, while keeping the American population at peace.

But for those who are opposed to American interventions and are in favor of disarmament and radical social change in countries where the US stands against it, the draft debate as it is crystallizing becomes increasingly frustrating. How can a choice be made between a system based on Russian roulette and a professional army? Both perpetuate the illusion that Pax Americana is possible. The volunteer army, its opponents say, might intensify caste barriers among the young; it could become a black and poor man's army, could increase the insulation of the military from civilian control (though we already have, in effect, a professional army—with access to conscripts). On the other hand, the volunteer army does seem to offer the slim chance of restraining the president by making mobilization more difficult and more a matter for congressional and public debate. It does remove the undemocratic effects of the draft. Furthermore it would free many men now bound to school by the channeling system to pursue their talents in their own way. It would make it possible for them to move off the campus in order to make something of the thousands of opportunities for catalyzing social change in American communities. The voluntary system is better than the Marshall Commission's draft; just as the Marshall proposal is better than continuing the present system. But 118 all of these proposals avoid the real problem, which is the nature of American foreign policy. A debate about how to raise an army cannot help but be sterile, and finally, unreal, if it evades the question of how that army is to be used.

Ignored by all these proposals, the question of fighting a dirty little war agitates young people in America, who increasingly refuse to participate in the Vietnam war. Thousands avoid the draft by subterfuge or by managing student, law, or divinity deferments. Mohammed Ali's struggles with Selective Service, chronicled on every sports page in the nation, have educated more young men on how to evade the draft than all the anti-war organizations together. Richard Paterack, a former VISTA volunteer, continues his service to Americans in Canada, where he aids hundreds of others who are also fleeing conscription. David Harris, President of Stanford University's student body said recently that going to jail "should be considered a normal part of growing up in America." Many are demonstrating the truth of Harris's statement: the "Fort Hood Three," who have refused orders to go to Vietnam; Specialist Fourth Class Harry Muir, grand-nephew of former Navy Secretary Josephus Daniels, who has refused to wear his uniform; David Miller, the first man to be jailed for burning his draft card; David Mitchell, also jailed after American judges, who established the Nuremberg precedent, rejected his defense based on it. And an increasing number of "We Won't Go" groups, some of them organized by Students for a Democratic Society, have declared their intention to resist the draft and are, in defiance of the law, organizing others to do so.

Those resisting the draft express a new mood, a different concept of heroism. It is a mood in some ways projected by John Kennedy shortly after his World War II service. "War will exist," he said, "until that distant day when the conscientious objector enjoys the same reputation and prestige that the warrior does today." The Marshall Commission has dimly perceived something of the force—and threat—of this mood:

> The majority felt that a legal recognition of selective pacifism could be disruptive to the morale and effectiveness of the armed forces. A determination of the justness or unjustness of any war could only be made within the context of that war itself. Forcing upon the individual the necessity of making that distinction—which would be the practical effect of taking away the Government's obligation of making it for him —could put a burden heretofore unknown on the man in uniform and even on the brink of combat, with results that could be disastrous to him, to his unit and to the entire military tradition.

Exactly. If individuals are free to make up their own minds about whether or not they will participate in a nation's wars, that would 119 indeed undermine the very goals the Commission's report is so carefully designed to serve.

It seems to us, then, that the issue of the draft comes down not simply and narrowly to how we raise an army. Rather, it is whether the nation will give priority to personal freedom and to building social equality, or to maintaining a policy requiring military intervention on a world scale. In trying to raise *this* issue, perhaps the self-exile, the draft-card burner, the conscientious objector, and the war resister expose what the new draft proposals mask.

THREE

PAX AMERICANA, THE AMERICAN EMPIRE AND THE THIRD WORLD

This section examines the implications of American military power and the concomitant cold war ideology upon the other areas of the world, particularly those areas which have historically been under colonial domination by the great powers. In the beginnings of British, Spanish and French colonialism, the ethical issues of exploitation of poor people were not raised. Poor people were considered neither clean nor Christian nor suited to rule themselves. Five centuries of almost invariably exploitative rule of these people and of the territories they occupy have not bettered their lot. Now they represent a majority of the world's population. They live in shoddy sections of cities surrounding foreign-owned industrial firms or, more frequently, as landless servants in their own countries. For years the poor have survived in their separate cultural settings, on a set of values more familially and community oriented than our own and less dependent upon the Western criteria of individual success in the market place. But certain factors in the lives of the poor have changed.

First and perhaps most important, the number of poor people has increased so greatly over their food productivity that malnutrition has become a fact of their daily existence and the spectre of mass starvation is imminent. There exists a delicate dependency between the continuity of human life and the manner in which man manages and allocates resources. This perspective is clearly seen in Huxley's "The Politics of Ecology." Among the most affluent countries, there exists a pattern of allocation of resources essentially incongruous with the needs for clean air, clean water, and especially for food. The misallocation of resources is so great that the precarious balance which protects the survival of regions and of races is in danger of being upset. One source of misallocation, from the ecological perspec- 121 tive, lies in the cost of warfare. Currently, the world military budget is equivalent to the entire income of the poorer half of the world's population.

In addition to the change in numbers, there is an increasing income gap between the impoverished colored majority and both their white Western neighbors and the self-serving aristocracies of their countries. While the impoverished have grown poorer or remained the same, their aristocratic enclaves have grown wealthier, as has the affluent Western world.

We do not fully understand why poverty exists, whether the basic or prime deficiency is in education or in capital for industrial investment, in agricultural productivity or in control of the size of families, in job training opportunities or in the individualistic type of motivation to achieve, excel, succeed, and save for the future. It is clear to the economist, however, that the cost of prime commodities, the exports of poorer countries, have been dropping, while the cost of manufactured goods which these countries must import has been going up. This has amounted to a form of subsidization of the rich nations by the poorer ones. Portions of the deficit are compensated for by foreign aid. However, foreign aid has been largely in the form of credits to foreign governments to purchase American-made weapons. At any rate foreign aid has not been of the type or of the scope sufficient to combat international poverty. But whatever the cause or causes of poverty, the modern revolution in communication has made the income gap highly visible and, perhaps not unexpectedly, a majority of the world's population is in a state of incipient or active revolution.

The policy of selling American arms abroad is a relic of the Dulles foreign policy which sought a "containment" of Communism through a series of military security treaties with other nations. Whatever the intention, the weapons have not deterred the formation of revolutionary Communist movements. One factor in this failure has been the very misallocation of resources away from the needed domestic production. Such allocations permit nations like India and Pakistan to face each other militarily as in the Kashmir disputes, both using American weapons and both in dire need of economic uplifting. In Jordan, which purchases Lockheed F-184 supersonic fighter bombers at approximately $2 million each, the annual per capita income is $233. The planes are said to be needed to offset the sale of American arms to Israel.

Apart from whether such major overseas suppliers as General Dynamics, Lockheed, and McDonald Aircraft could survive a change in this policy, it seems rather clear that a number of the newer countries are expending their intellectual, as well as their material, resources on weapon procurement in preference to nation development. In some instances the younger intellectual leaders of the poorer nations resent the weapons priority.

The resentment reflects yet another difference from the period of 122 unquestioning colonialism. The underdeveloped areas have evolved into nations. Their newer and more popular leaders have been influenced by the ideologies of the American revolution as well as the teachings of Marxist socialism. They have great nationalistic pride and a resentment against being used as pawns in a power struggle among larger powers. The thrust of the poorer nations to develop an identity independent of the East-West conflict has led to their common designation as "the third world."

Resentment by third-world rulers is not always visible. A large measure of the military and paramilitary assistance goes directly to aristocratic or military elites and provides them with the means to suppress revolutionary movements aimed at land reform, at nationalization of exploitative industries, at modifications in the tax structure, at domestic rule, or at the ruling elites themselves. The nature of these revolutions is described in O'Brien's article. In this article also, the theme behind the American response to such movements is described and captured in the title, "The Counterrevolutionary Reflex." O'Brien's critique assumes the viewpoint of the poorer nations. He criticizes the tacit assumption of American strategic thought, viz., that revolutions are exportable commodities which may be turned on from afar by Communist states intent upon aggrandizement through military subversion. What seems to be ignored in this formulation of the problem are the economic and social conditions which make revolutions necessary and the local support of revolutionary movements which is not only needed for their success but which, in accordance with American founding precepts of popular rule, makes them legitimate.

There have been numerous involvements by the United States in response to revolutionary movements. Some like the Dominican and Lebanon cases have involved direct and open landing of American military forces. More frequently as in Cuba, Guatemala, Indonesia, British Guinea, and probably Nigeria, the involvement has been largely through the clandestine activities of the Central Intelligence Agency and the Defense Intelligence Agency. These techniques have involved the support and training of local police, the secret subsidization of foreign students and labor unions, the bombing of foreign cities with disguised planes, the use of "black radio" employing false radio signals to coerce government officials into surrendering by making them believe their supporters had already given up, and by the careful screening of international information, not only from our adversaries but from our own press and from our own United Nations ambassador as well (Wise and Ross, 1964).

The most extensive involvement by the United States in the intervention in a revolutionary movement has occurred in Vietnam. Martin Nicolaus in "The Professor, the Policeman and the Peasant" describes the nature of the early involvement. The details of the case highlight both the assumptions and the tactics of the policy. While the costs 123 have been heavier in the Vietnam case, the strategy shows marked similarity to that of the Soviet Union at the time of the Hungarian uprisings in 1956: Support an unpopular "puppet regime" to abet one's own military posture, and fulfill "commitments" to the "legal" puppet to protect it from its own population. Hungary and Vietnam are similar also in that neither revolt began as anti-communist or as anti-western. Both were nationalistic in objectives. Both were said to be sparked by alien agitators, who were said to be solely responsible for the unrest. Yet suppression has left a legacy of extreme anti-Soviet feeling among the Hungarian refugees even now after many objectives of the revolt have been conceded. Similarly anti-Americanism in Vietnam has become very prevalent and will endure beyond the period of fighting. It is through such reactions that force as a technique of international relations comes frequently to beget further force, and the war to end wars becomes mythology.

In a later article in *Viet Report,* Nicolaus (1966) describes what the involvement in secret, counter-insurgency work has meant to the academic standards of the university and to the participants themselves. However, the consequences for the domestic character of the United States, as the global counter-revolutionary policeman go beyond the involvement of small numbers of academicians on specific "classified" projects. The early detection of a revolt, which can be defused, controlled or managed before it gains momentum, requires a far greater mobilization of domestic energies. Horowitz' article on Project Camelot describes one attempt at a greater mobilization. The extent of this centralized enterprise raises complex issues: Who should decide what is to be studied by the social sciences? What is to be the nature of a trusting relationship between an academic researcher and the people he is studying? Has there been a reversal of functions such that Defense sets the purposes of projects and the State and the Executive merely monitor certain instrumentalities as civilian fronts for paramilitary endeavors? In any event, the article is illustrative of the rifts in our own society which follow from attempts to control the directions of an impoverished and struggling world under the directives of an enforced "pax Americana."

REFERENCES AND ADDITIONAL READING

Kenneth Boulding, "After Civilization, What?," *Bulletin of the Atomic Scientists*, October, 1962, 2–6.

Editors of Ramparts, "3 Tales of the CIA," *Ramparts*, April, 1967, 15–28.

John Kenneth Galbraith, "The Poverty of Nations," *The Atlantic*, March, 1962, 47–54.

Eugene J. McCarthy, "The U. S.: Supplier of Weapons to the World," *Saturday Review*, July 9, 1966, 13–16.

John McDermott, "Two Programs for South Vietnam," *Viet Report*, 2, February, 1966, 3–10.

Martin Nicolaus, "The Professor, the Policeman, and the Peasant,—II," *Viet Report*, March-April, 1966, 3–8ff.

Abdus Salam, "Diseases of the Rich and Diseases of the Poor," *Bulletin of the Atomic Scientists,* April, 1963, 3ff.

David Wise and Thomas B. Ross, *The Invisible Government,* New York: Random House, 1964.

Aldous Huxley

The Politics of Ecology

In politics, the central and fundamental problem is the problem of power. Who is to exercise power? And by what means, by what authority, with what purpose in view, and under what controls? Yes, under what controls? For, as history has made it abundantly clear, to possess power is *ipso facto* to be tempted to abuse it. In mere self-preservation we must create and maintain institutions that make it difficult for the powerful to be led into those temptations which, succumbed to, transform them into tyrants at home and imperialists abroad.

For this purpose what kind of institutions are effective? And, having created them, how can we guarantee them against obsolescence? Circumstances change, and as they change, the old, the once so admirably effective devices for controlling power cease to be adequate. What then? Specifically, when advancing science and acceleratingly progressive technology alter man's long-established relationship with the planet on which he lives, revolutionize his societies, and at the same time equip his rulers with new and immensely more powerful instruments of domination, what ought we to do? What *can* we do?

Very briefly let us review the situation in which we now find ourselves and, in the light of present facts, hazard a few guesses about the future.

On the biological level, advancing science and technology have set going a revolutionary process that seems to be destined for the next century at least, perhaps for much longer, to exercise a decisive influence upon the destinies of all human societies and their individual

Reprinted by permission of the Center for the Study of Democratic Institutions (Santa Barbara, California, 1963). Aldous Huxley, who died in 1965, was a distinguished author of many notable works, including *Brave New World* in 1932.

members. In the course of the last fifty years extremely effective methods for lowering the prevailing rates of infant and adult mortality were developed by Western scientists. These methods were very simple and could be applied with the expenditure of very little money by very small numbers of not very highly trained technicians. For these reasons, and because everyone regards life as intrinsically good and death as intrinsically bad, they were in fact applied on a worldwide scale. The results were spectacular. In the past, high birth rates were balanced by high death rates. Thanks to science, death rates have been halved but, except in the most highly industrialized, contraceptive-using countries, birth rates remain as high as ever. An enormous and accelerating increase in human numbers has been the inevitable consequence.

At the beginning of the Christian era, so demographers assure us, our planet supported a human population of about two hundred and fifty millions. When the Pilgrim Fathers stepped ashore, the figure had risen to about five hundred millions. We see, then, that in the relatively recent past it took sixteen hundred years for the human species to double its numbers. Today world population stands at three thousand millions. By the year 2000, unless something appallingly bad or miraculously good should happen in the interval, six thousand million of us will be sitting down to breakfast every morning. In a word, twelve times as many people are destined to double their numbers in one-fortieth of the time.

This is not the whole story. In many areas of the world human numbers are increasing at a rate much higher than the average for the whole species. In India, for example, the rate of increase is now 2.3 per cent per annum. By 1990 its four hundred and fifty million inhabitants will have become nine hundred million inhabitants. A comparable rate of increase will raise the population of China to the billion mark by 1980. In Ceylon, in Egypt, in many of the countries of South and Central America, human numbers are increasing at an annual rate of 3 per cent. The result will be a doubling of their present populations in approximately twenty-three years.

On the social, political, and economic levels, what is likely to happen in an underdeveloped country whose people double themselves in a single generation, or even less? An underdeveloped society is a society without adequate capital resources (for capital is what is left over after primary needs have been satisfied, and in underdeveloped countries most people never satisfy their primary needs); a society without a sufficient force of trained teachers, administrators, and technicians; a society with few or no industries and few or no developed sources of industrial power; a society, finally, with enormous arrears to be made good in food production, education, road building, housing, and sanitation. A quarter of a century from now, when there will be twice as many of them as there are today, what is the likeli- 127 hood that the members of such a society will be better fed, housed, clothed, and schooled than at present? And what are the chances in such a society for the maintenance, if they already exist, or the creation, if they do not exist, of democratic institutions?

Not long ago Mr. Eugene Black, the former president of the World Bank, expressed the opinion that it would be extremely difficult, perhaps even impossible, for an underdeveloped country with a very rapid rate of population increase to achieve full industrialization. All its resources, he pointed out, would be absorbed year by year in the task of supplying, or not quite supplying, the primary needs of its new members. Merely to stand still, to maintain its current subhumanly inadequate standard of living, will require hard work and the expenditure of all the nation's available capital. Available capital may be increased by loans and gifts from abroad; but in a world where the industrialized nations are involved in power politics and an increasingly expensive armament race, there will never be enough foreign aid to make much difference. And even if the loans and gifts to underdeveloped countries were to be substantially increased, any resulting gains would be largely nullified by the uncontrolled population explosion.

The situation of these nations with such rapidly increasing populations reminds one of Lewis Carroll's parable in *Through the Looking Glass,* where Alice and the Red Queen start running at full speed and run for a long time until Alice is completely out of breath. When they stop, Alice is amazed to see that they are still at their starting point. In the looking glass world, if you wish to retain your present position, you must run as fast as you can. If you wish to get ahead, you must run at least twice as fast as you can.

If Mr. Black is correct (and there are plenty of economists and demographers who share his opinion), the outlook for most of the world's newly independent and economically non-viable nations is gloomy indeed. To those that have shall be given. Within the next ten or twenty years, if war can be avoided, poverty will almost have disappeared from the highly industrialized and contraceptive-using societies of the West. Meanwhile, in the underdeveloped and uncontrolledly breeding societies of Asia, Africa, and Latin America the condition of the masses (twice as numerous, a generation from now, as they are today) will have become no better and may even be decidedly worse than it is at present. Such a decline is foreshadowed by current statistics of the Food and Agriculture Organization of the United Nations. In some underdeveloped regions of the world, we are told, people are somewhat less adequately fed, clothed, and housed than were their parents and grandparents thirty and forty years ago. And what of elementary education? UNESCO recently provided an answer. Since the end of World War II heroic efforts have been made to teach the whole world how to read. The population explosion 128 has largely stultified these efforts. The absolute number of illiterates is greater now than at any time.

The contraceptive revolution which, thanks to advancing science and technology, has made it possible for the highly developed societies of the West to offset the consequences of death by a planned control of births, has had as yet no effect upon the family life of people in underdeveloped countries. This is not surprising. Death control, as I have already remarked, is easy, cheap, and can be carried out by a small force of technicians. Birth control, on the other hand, is rather expensive, involves the whole adult population, and demands of those who practice it a good deal of forethought and directed willpower. To persuade hundreds of millions of men and women to abandon their tradition-hallowed views of sexual morality, then to distribute and teach them to make use of contraceptive devices or fertility-controlling drugs—this is a huge and difficult task, so huge and so difficult that it seems very unlikely that it can be successfully carried out, within a sufficiently short space of time, in any of the countries where control of the birth rate is most urgently needed.

Extreme poverty, when combined with ignorance, breeds that lack of desire for better things which has been called "wantlessness"—the resigned acceptance of a subhuman lot. But extreme poverty, when it is combined with the knowledge that some societies are affluent, breeds envious desires and the expectation that these desires must of necessity, and very soon, be satisfied. By means of the mass media (those easily exportable products of advancing science and technology) some knowledge of what life is like in affluent societies has been widely disseminated throughout the world's underdeveloped regions. But, alas, the science and technology which have given the industrial West its cars, refrigerators, and contraceptives have given the people of Asia, Africa, and Latin America only movies and radio broadcasts, which they are too simple-minded to be able to criticize, together with a population explosion, which they are still too poor and too tradition-bound to be able to control by deliberate family planning.

In the context of a 3, or even of a mere 2 per cent annual increase in numbers, high expectations are fore-doomed to disappointment. From disappointment, through resentful frustration, to widespread social unrest the road is short. Shorter still is the road from social unrest, through chaos, to dictatorship, possibly of the Communist party, more probably of generals and colonels. It would seem, then, that for two-thirds of the human race now suffering from the consequences of uncontrolled breeding in a context of industrial backwardness, poverty, and illiteracy, the prospects for democracy, during the next ten or twenty years, are very poor.

From underdeveloped societies and the probable political consequences of their explosive increase in numbers we now pass to the 129 prospect for democracy in the fully industrialized, contraceptive-using societies of Europe and North America.

It used to be assumed that political freedom was a necessary precondition of scientific research. Ideological dogmatism and dictatorial institutions were supposed to be incompatible with the open-mindedness and the freedom of experimental action, in the absence of which discovery and invention are impossible. Recent history has proved these comforting assumptions to be completely unfounded. It was under Stalin that Russian scientists developed the A-bomb and, a few years later, the H-bomb. And it is under a more-than-Stalinist dictatorship that Chinese scientists are now in process of performing the same feat.

Another disquieting lesson of recent history is that, in a developing society, science and technology can be used exclusively for the enhancement of military power, not at all for the benefit of the masses. Russia has demonstrated, and China is now doing its best to demonstrate, that poverty and primitive conditions of life for the overwhelming majority of the population are perfectly compatible with the wholesale production of the most advanced and sophisticated military hardware. Indeed, it is by deliberately imposing poverty on the masses that the rulers of developing industrial nations are able to create the capital necessary for building an armament industry and maintaining a well equipped army, with which to play their parts in the suicidal game of international power politics.

We see, then, that democratic institutions and libertarian traditions are not at all necessary to the progress of science and technology, and that such progress does not of itself make for human betterment at home and peace abroad. Only where democratic institutions already exist, only where the masses can vote their rulers out of office and so compel them to pay attention to the popular will, are science and technology used for the benefit of the majority as well as for increasing the power of the State. Most human beings prefer peace to war, and practically all of them would rather be alive than dead. But in every part of the world men and women have been brought up to regard nationalism as axiomatic and war between nations as something cosmically ordained by the Nature of Things. Prisoners of their culture, the masses, even when they are free to vote, are inhibited by the fundamental postulates of the frame of reference within which they do their thinking and their feeling from decreeing an end to the collective paranoia that governs international relations. As for the world's ruling minorities, by the very fact of their power they are chained even more closely to the current system of ideas and the prevailing political customs; for this reason they are even less capable than their subjects of expressing the simple human preference for life and peace.

Some day, let us hope, rulers and ruled will break out of the cultural prison in which they are now confined. Some day. . . . And may that day come soon! For, thanks to our rapidly advancing science 130 and technology, we have very little time at our disposal. The river of change flows ever faster, and somewhere downstream, perhaps only a few years ahead, we shall come to the rapids, shall hear, louder and ever louder, the roaring of a cataract.

Modern war is a product of advancing science and technology. Conversely, advancing science and technology are products of modern war. It was in order to wage war more effectively that first the United States, then Britain and the USSR, financed the crash programs that resulted so quickly in the harnessing of atomic forces. Again, it was primarily for military purposes that the techniques of automation, which are now in process of revolutionizing industrial production and the whole system of administrative and bureaucratic control, were first developed. "During World War II," writes Mr. John Diebold, "the theory and use of feedback was studied in great detail by a number of scientists both in this country and in Britain. The introduction of rapidly moving aircraft very quickly made traditional gun-laying techniques of anti-aircraft warfare obsolete. As a result, a large part of scientific manpower in this country was directed towards the development of self-regulating devices and systems to control our military equipment. It is out of this work that the technology of automation as we understand it today has developed."

The headlong rapidity with which scientific and technological changes, with all their disturbing consequences in the fields of politics and social relations, are taking place is due in large measure to the fact that, both in the USA and the USSR, research in pure and applied science is lavishly financed by military planners whose first concern is in the development of bigger and better weapons in the shortest possible time. In the frantic effort, on one side of the Iron Curtain, to keep up with the Joneses—on the other, to keep up with the Ivanovs—these military planners spend gigantic sums on research and development. The military revolution advances under forced draft, and as it goes forward it initiates an uninterrupted succession of industrial, social, and political revolutions. It is against this background of chronic upheaval that the members of a species, biologically and historically adapted to a slowly changing environment, must now live out their bewildered lives.

Old-fashioned war was incompatible, while it was being waged, with democracy. Nuclear war, if it is ever waged, will prove in all likelihood to be incompatible with civilization, perhaps with human survival. Meanwhile, what of the preparations for nuclear war? If certain physicists and military planners had their way, democracy, where it exists, would be replaced by a system of regimentation centered upon the bomb shelter. The entire population would have to be systematically drilled in the ticklish operation of going underground at a moment's notice, systematically exercised in the art of living troglodytically 131 under conditions resembling those in the hold of an eighteenth-century slave ship. The notion fills most of us with horror. But if we fail to break out of the ideological prison of our nationalistic and militaristic culture, we may find ourselves compelled by the military consequences of our science and technology to descend into the steel and concrete dungeons of total and totalitarian civil defense.

In the past, one of the most effective guarantees of liberty was governmental inefficiency. The spirit of tyranny was always willing; but its technical and organizational flesh was weak. Today the flesh is as strong as the spirit. Governmental organization is a fine art, based upon scientific principles and disposing of marvelously efficient equipment. Fifty years ago an armed revolution still had some chance of success. In the context of modern weaponry a popular uprising is foredoomed. Crowds armed with rifles and home-made grenades are no match for tanks. And it is not only to its armament that a modern government owes its overwhelming power. It also possesses the strength of superior knowledge derived from its communication systems, its stores of accumulated data, its batteries of computers, its network of inspection and administration.

Where democratic institutions exist and the masses can vote their rulers out of office, the enormous powers with which science, technology, and the arts of organization have endowed the ruling minority are used with discretion and a decent regard for civil and political liberty. Where the masses can exercise no control over their rulers, these powers are used without compunction to enforce ideological orthodoxy and to strengthen the dictatorial state. The nature of science and technology is such that it is peculiarly easy for a dictatorial government to use them for its own purposes. Well financed, equipped and organized, an astonishingly small number of scientists and technologists can achieve prodigious results. The crash program that produced the A-bomb and ushered in a new historical era was planned and directed by some four thousand theoreticians, experimenters, and engineers. To parody the words of Winston Churchill, never have so many been so completely at the mercy of so few.

Throughout the nineteenth century the State was relatively feeble, and its interest in, and influence upon, scientific research were negligible. In our day the State is everywhere exceedingly powerful and a lavish patron of basic and *ad hoc* research. In Western Europe and North America the relations between the State and its scientists on the one hand and individual citizens, professional organizations, and industrial, commercial, and educational institutions on the other are fairly satisfactory. Advancing science, the population explosion, the armament race, and the steady increase and centralization of political and economic power are still compatible, in countries that have a libertarian tradition, with democratic forms of government. To maintain 132 this compatability in a rapidly changing world, bearing less and less resemblance to the world in which these democratic institutions were developed—this, quite obviously, is going to be increasingly difficult.

A rapid and accelerating population increase that will nullify the best efforts of underdeveloped societies to better their lot and will keep two-thirds of the human race in a condition of misery in anarchy or of misery under dictatorship, and the intensive preparations for a new kind of war that, if it breaks out, may bring irretrievable ruin to the one-third of the human race now living prosperously in highly indus-trialized societies—these are the two main threats to democracy now confronting us. Can these threats be eliminated? Or, if not eliminated, at least reduced?

My own view is that only by shifting our collective attention from the merely political to the basic biological aspects of the human situa-tion can we hope to mitigate and shorten the time of troubles into which it would seem, we are now moving. We cannot do without politics; but we can no longer afford to indulge in bad, unrealistic politics. To work for the survival of the species as a whole and for the actualization in the greatest possible number of individual men and women of their potentialities for good will, intelligence, and creativity —this, in the world of today, is good, realistic politics. To cultivate the religion of idolatrous nationalism, to subordinate the interests of the species and its individual members to the interests of a single na-tional state and its ruling minority—in the context of the population explosion, missiles, and atomic warheads, this is bad and thoroughly unrealistic politics. Unfortunately, it is to bad and unrealistic politics that our rulers are now committed.

Ecology is the science of the mutual relations of organisms with their environment and with one another. Only when we get it into our collective head that the basic problem confronting twentieth-century man is an ecological problem will our politics improve and become realistic. How does the human race propose to survive and, if possible, improve the lot and intrinsic quality of its individual mem-bers? Do we propose to live on this planet in symbiotic harmony with our environment? Or, preferring to be wantonly stupid, shall we choose to live like murderous parasites that kill their host and so destroy themselves?

Committing that sin of overweening bumptiousness, which the Greeks called *hubris,* we behave as though we were not members of earth's ecological community, as though we were privileged and, in some sort, supernatural beings and could throw our weight around like gods. But in fact we are, among other things, animals—emergent parts of the natural order. If our politicians were realists, they would think rather less about missiles and the problem of landing a couple of astronauts 133 on the moon, rather more about hunger and moral squalor and the problem of enabling three billion men, women, and children, who will soon be six billions, to lead a tolerably human existence without, in the process, ruining and befouling their planetary environment. Animals have no souls; therefore, according to the most authoritative Christian theologians, they may be treated as though they were things. The truth, as we are now beginning to realize, is that even things ought not to be treated as *mere* things. They should be treated as though they were parts of a vast living organism. "Do as you would be done by." The Golden Rule applies to our dealings with nature no less than to our dealings with our fellow-men. If we hope to be well treated by nature, we must stop talking about "mere things" and start treating our planet with intelligence and consideration.

Power politics in the context of nationalism raises problems that, except by war, are practically insoluble. The problems of ecology, on the other hand, admit of a rational solution and can be tackled without the arousal of those violent passions always associated with dogmatic ideology and nationalistic idolatry. There may be arguments about the best way of raising wheat in a cold climate or of re-foresting a denuded mountain. But such arguments never lead to organized slaughter. Organized slaughter is the result of arguments about such questions as the following. Which is the best nation? The best religion? The best political theory? The best form of government? Why are other people so stupid and wicked? Why can't they see how good and intelligent *we* are? Why do they resist our beneficient efforts to bring them under our control and make them like ourselves?

To questions of this kind the final answer has always been war. "War," said Clausewitz, "is not merely a political act, but also a political instrument, a continuation of political relationships, a carrying out of the same by other means." This was true enough in the eighteen thirties, when Clausewitz published his famous treatise and it continued to be true until 1945. Now, pretty obviously, nuclear weapons, long-range rockets, nerve gases, bacterial aerosols, and the "Laser" (that highly promising, latest addition to the world's military arsenal) have given the lie to Clausewitz. All-out war with modern weapons is no longer a continuation of previous policy; it is a complete and irreversible break with previous policy.

Power politics, nationalism, and dogmatic ideology are luxuries that the human race can no longer afford. Nor, as a species, can we afford the luxury of ignoring man's ecological situation. By shifting our attention from the now completely irrelevant and anachronistic politics of nationalism and military power to the problems of the human species and the still inchoate politics of human ecology we shall be killing two birds with one stone—reducing the threat of sudden destruction by scientific war and at the same time reducing the threat of more gradual biological disaster.

134

The beginnings of ecological politics are to be found in the special services of the United Nations Organization. UNESCO, the Food and Agriculture Organization, the World Health Organization, the various Technical Aid Services—all these are, partially or completely, concerned with the ecological problems of the human species. In a world where political problems are thought of and worked upon within a frame of reference whose coordinates are nationalism and military power, these ecology-oriented organizations are regarded as peripheral. If the problems of humanity could be thought about and acted upon within a frame of reference that has survival for the species, the well-being of individuals, and the actualization of man's desirable potentialities as its coordinates, these peripheral organizations would become central. The subordinate politics of survival, happiness, and personal fulfillment would take the place now occupied by the politics of power, ideology, nationalistic idolatry, and unrelieved misery.

In the process of reaching this kind of politics we shall find, no doubt, that we have done something, in President Wilson's prematurely optimistic words, "to make the world safe for democracy."

Conor Cruise O'Brien

The Counterrevolutionary Reflex

It is widely asserted, and believed, that social revolution can be peacefully accomplished. I can accept this as a reasonable hypothesis when applied to the so-called pockets of poverty in this country and other rich countries, where available resources are large in relation to the scale of the problem, where there is a relatively alert and far-seeing ruling class, and where social changes of the magnitude required may well be consistent with the interests of the ruling class. Even in rich countries, an increase in sporadic violence seems likely, but it seems highly unlikely that the relation of violence to change will be such as to deserve the name revolution in anything but the rhetorical or declamatory sense.

In the poor world, or the poor part of the third world, the situation is qualitatively different. Throughout most of the area the oppressed are not minorities but the masses, and they are confronted by ruling classes that cling avidly to their traditional large share of scarce resources. The interests of the ruling classes are simply not consistent with any social change in the interests of the people as a whole. The landowners, usurers, sweat-shop owners, corrupt political bosses, and parasitic bureaucrats who now control in varying combinations most governments of the third world are precisely those people who must be deprived of their *raison d'être* if there is to be a social revolution. Why should these people allow themselves to be peacefully ousted as long as they have the money to pay others to defend their interests? Such defense need not always be as obvious as the employment of white mercenaries by the government of the Congo. Rulers of most

Reprinted by permission of the author and publisher from *Columbia University FORUM*, Spring 1966, Volume IX, Number 2. Copyright © 1966 by the Trustees of Columbia University in the City of New York. Conor Cruise O'Brien is Regents Professor and Schweitzer Professor of Humanities at New York University.

poor countries, by reason of that very poverty, can recruit mercenaries from among their own people. This method is less conspicuous than the Congolese method, but it is also less reliable because the danger of defection and mutiny is inescapable when national forces are used in a revolutionary situation. This danger, in turn, can give rise to a demand for extra-national counterrevolutionary forces—Belgian regular troops in the nominally independent Congo, French troops in nominally independent Gabon, U.S. regular troops in nominally independent Santo Domingo and South Vietnam.

If this line of reasoning is correct, and recent history seems to support it, then it is not likely that social revolution will occur without political revolution; political revolution will be opposed by force, and cannot prevail without greater force. The forms that political revolutions take and the relations they bear to social change vary according to the widely differing social realities of the regions covered. What seems certain, however, is that change of the dimensions implied by the term "social revolution" is not accomplished without political change of corresponding dimensions—that is, without political revolution. Even Japan, sometimes cited as an example of social revolution without political revolution, actually went through two political revolutions, one in the last century and one in this.

Ruling classes, about to be overwhelmed in their own country, will look outside their country for military help, or will actually receive that help, without looking for it, from outsiders who either have important interests of their own in the country concerned, or judge their general network of international interests threatened by the combination of political and social revolution in any country. The former was the case of Belgium in the Congo, and France in Gabon; the latter has become the established position of the government of the United States.

At a given moment then, social revolution in any country, having taken political form, provokes the use of violence, first national and then—if successful—probably international. When violence threatens to cross national boundaries, the United Nations comes into the matter, at least in theory, for the purpose of that organization, in the words of the first line of the first article of the Charter, is "to maintain international peace and security." However, what the UN does or can do in places where social revolution threatens international peace depends largely on the international posture of the United States. This country is not only the greatest and richest of world powers, with widespread economic, financial, diplomatic and military influence, but it is also the major contributor to the UN budget, and as such exercises a predominant influence over UN policies, decisions and—most important—interpretation of policies at the level of the Secretariat. This situation is widely recognized in the world at large—not only

137

in the Communist world, but also in Western Europe, Latin America and elsewhere. Only in this country does the illusion persist that the UN is an organization run by Africans for the purpose of thwarting and tormenting Uncle Sam. It is an illusion that has its uses especially when, as so often happens, resolutions favorable to U.S. purposes are extorted from this putatively reluctant body.

The position of the U.S. Government, as far as it can be deduced from its actions and statements, is as follows: It is in favor of social revolution, verbally, provided this takes place peacefully, and it exhorts parasitic ruling classes to inculcate social revolution, just as it exhorts Dr. Verwoerd to abandon apartheid. And with the same degree of success. Failing peaceful social revolution, it favors no revolution—combined with continued exhortation.

When, nonetheless, social revolutionary pressures lead to political revolutions, the government of the United States claims to be a better judge than the people of the country concerned as to whether that revolution best serves their interests. This judgment is variously exercised, and normally we learn little about its workings. Occasionally, however, we get glimpses: the expert, for example, on what form a revolution in Cuba should take is not Fidel Castro but Arthur M. Schlesinger, Jr., who, among others, discovered it had been betrayed. Mr. Schlesinger, a connoisseur it seems not merely of revolution but of counterrevolution, has told us in *A Thousand Days* that when the Bay of Pigs operation was under way, the unfortunate Cubans who were supposed to be leading the insurrection drew up a manifesto for distribution in Cuba. The manifesto was aimed, not surprisingly, at eliciting the support of people who had lost money in the revolution, and was apparently judged insufficiently Cuban and revolutionary by Mr. Schlesinger and his colleagues in Washington. So they sent it to two Harvard Latin American experts who rewrote it, putting in a lot of nice liberal notions about Negroes and the like, and in this form it was put out in the name of the corrected Cubans. How the improved manifesto sounded in Havana I don't know, but it certainly sounded a lot better at Harvard, and that was the point. In the lapidary words of the celebrated discoverer of Parkinson's Law, "All propaganda begins, and ends, at home."

In publicly assessing whether a given political revolution is or is not in the interests of the people concerned, the sole criterion now regularly and explicitly applied by the government of the U.S. is whether Communists are associated with the revolution. As Communists are by definition revolutionaries, it is overwhelmingly probable that in any country any political revolution aiming at social revolution will have Communists associated with it. It follows logically that the United States is committed, contrary to its professions, to opposing social revolution throughout the world. This will be done by force, if 138 practicable, as in the case of Santo Domingo. In that case, the United States violated the Charter of the United Nations quite as clearly as the Soviet Union had in the case of Hungary in 1956. In neither case did the UN take any effective action—as it could have in theory under the Uniting for Peace procedure. In the case of Hungary, however, the General Assembly condemned the Soviet action; in the case of Santo Domingo it refused to condemn the United States. This does not mean that the "moral conscience" of the world made any distinction between the two actions: it just means that the U.S., unlike the Soviet Union, has sufficient influence on the General Assembly to block any resolutions aimed against it.

It follows, therefore, that wherever and whenever social revolutionary pressures encounter the counterrevolutionary power of the United States and threaten, or break, international peace, the United Nations is not only unable to act, but even unable to speak, in defense of its own Charter. More than this, the United Nations can actually be used as an instrument of U.S. policy, as demonstrated by the history of the UN operation in the Congo. This situation, grim as it is, does not mean that the UN should be abandoned as entirely futile. It continues to provide valuable services, especially in situations where *both* sides are frightened and neither wishes to lose face. When it cannot help is when one great power intervenes against a small one and the other great power does not regard its interests as directly involved. And since most outbreaks of social revolution fall into that category, to ask that the UN *do* something is usually a snare and a delusion, or sometimes a way of shedding responsibility.

The American citizen is not in a position to promote social revolution in other people's countries, or to decide how they should be conducted, or whether they are being betrayed. What he is in a position to do is to consider this country's policies and to exert what influence he can in favor of saner ones.

Do the vital interests of the United States really require it to ensure that no country in the alleged free world adopts, by whatever means, a Communist form of government? If that assumption remains unchallenged then the present U.S. involvement in the internal policies of scores of countries can be justified; the war in Vietnam can be justified; the Bay of Pigs can be justified; the destruction of Lumumba can be justified; the invasion of Santo Domingo can be justified; justified also can be as many plots and counterplots, lies, murders, and aggressive acts as the intelligence and military establishments may find necessary to arrest the spread of communism.

I challenge the assumption that it is necessary for the U.S. to stop the spread of Communism. I do so on the following grounds:

The old assumption on which anti-Communism policy was devised 139 no longer holds. There is no longer a monolithic Communist empire whose power can be thought of as increased by every new country that "goes Communist."

Active hostility to the U.S. is not a necessary permanent attribute of every Communist country. The richest and most powerful country in the world must expect to attract considerable ill-feeling in capitalist as well as Communist countries. Policy should seek, however, to prevent ill-feeling from passing over into active hostility. Active hostility is fanned by U.S. anti-Communist actions such as in Vietnam. If Asian communism is today bitterly anti-American—as it is—this is a resultant of American anti-Communist activity in Asia.

Where it may be thought U.S. interests are menaced by the spread of communism there are nonideological means of defending those interests. The Truman Doctrine, to the extent that it provided against the territorial expansion of Russian military power was nonideological. The principle expressed in Eisenhower's formula of "checking indirect aggression" is ideological, involving an indefinitely extended series of political judgments, and of actions based on such judgments, about the internal affairs of other countries. Once it is the business of the United States to prevent Communists from coming to power in a given country, then everything in that country comes under permanent U.S. surveillance, which may, in certain circumstances turn into U.S. tutelage. The result is an incalculable extension of this country's commitments. A doctrine against offensive weapons or bases, or soldiers, in this hemisphere would make more sense and involve fewer risks than the present policy against future Castros. Similarly, economic measures damaging to U.S. interests could be met by appropriate countermeasures. The doctrine of containment could be interpreted to mean that the extension of Russian or Chinese power *by force* would be damaging to U.S. interests and would involve risks of retaliation.

Such positions would be unambiguous, clearly defensive and respected. They would release the U.S. from a role I believe most of its citizens would reject if they understood it—the role of ideological policeman of the world, ready in every part of the world to meet the spread of an idea with armed force. If the U.S. were to relinquish this role, the peace-keeping function of the UN could be strengthened. At present that organization falls far short of the moral strength which, for the sake of our common survival, it should possess. When—in the interests of the U.S. anti-Communist policy—UN officials help to destroy the government of a country that invited the UN in, or when at the behest of the U.S., in pursuit of the same anti-Communist policy, the General Assembly persists in seating a U.S. satellite delegation as representing China, what suffers is not communism but the reputation and influence of the United Nations itself.

I believe there is no more urgent task in the world than the dis- 140 intoxication of the public opinion of this country; the correction of those dangerous reflexes which past events and past propaganda have conditioned in Americans, and which make them think of communism as incarnate evil, instead of as a set of ideas in which human beings believe and which, like other important human beliefs, have led to great achievements as well as great crimes. Neither the achievements nor the crimes are all on one side. The problem of our age is not how to stop, fight, or eradicate communism. It is how to cope with its challenges and its appeals in such a way that the competing systems on the planet may produce more benefits to mankind than threats and suffering.

Martin Nicolaus

The Professor, the Policeman
and the Peasant

On a day in April 1960 in a small town in South Vietnam, the following event took place: an American professor interviewed the chief of
the local police in the latter's headquarters, while (according to the
professor's report) "curled up on a mat in the corner was a twenty-
year-old peasant in tattered clothes. His feet were in manacles, the left
side of his face was swollen and his eye and cheek were bruised." The
youth was "suspected of Vietcong membership."[1] He had been interro-
gated by the secret police chief. The professor, who was doing basic
research under contract to the U.S. government and to the Saigon
government, noted these facts but asked no further questions about the
peasant. Neither the police chief nor the professor indicated that the
peasant's presence disturbed them or struck them as strange.

Yet it does seem strange for an American professor to have an
amiable interview with a secret police chief in the latter's interrogation
center, and even more strange that the interview took place while a
young man who had been convicted of no crime lay bruised and manacled in the corner. A closer examination of the event yields even more
alien facts: the interrogation room had been paid for, and the police
chief's equipment, including the manacles that held the peasant, had
been supplied by an American university,—the same university that
paid the professor's salary. The professor, the policeman and the
peasant were here assembled in exactly their intended roles, playing
the parts the university had designed for them: the professor researching, the policeman interrogating, the peasant silent, bruised. This indeed

Reprinted by permission of the author and publisher from *Viet-Report*,
February 1966, pp. 16–21. Martin Nicolaus is Secretary-Treasurer of Viet
Report, Inc.

[1] Joseph Zasloff, *A Study of Administration in Binh Minh District*, MSUG,
Saigon, October 1961 (mimeo), p. 25.

142

seems like an extraordinary episode in the annals of American academia. And the fact that the professor did not think the event was worth special comment—that seems inexplicable, inexcusable, scandalous.

Nevertheless, it happened, and it happened regularly. Not that the professors regularly encountered manacled peasants in their interviews; that was not a typical event. Still, this encounter in April 1960 is like a microcosm of the larger drama that had been unfolding since 1950 and ended only in 1962. The peasant lying manacled in a corner of the room symbolizes, perhaps in an exaggerated way, perhaps not, the predicament of a great many South Vietnamese peasants: they were all being bound, beaten or manacled in one way or another, although not all of them took it as silently as this one, as the professors well knew. The secret police chief was also playing a typical role—getting information out of peasants was his job. The professor, too, was doing his job: asking some questions, not asking other questions, writing down the responses, and not expressing opinions outside his field of professional competence. And the manacles, together with related equipment, were supplied to the police by the university on a regular schedule; there was nothing extraordinary about it. This one event expresses Michigan State University's Vietnam Project in a nutshell.

Nor, for that matter, is the episode an isolated instance in American intellectual history. Certainly the majority of university projects overseas do not involve such collaboration with the secret police—American or foreign—and they do follow a stricter definition of what is "technical" assistance. But the needs which the Michigan State project was designed to serve exist now, or are growing into existence, in many parts of the world. The conditions that made it possible to use American professors as they were used in Vietnam persist. The Michigan State University Group (MSUG) was not an unrepeatable event. More and more it appears as the prototype, the pilot model of a growing family of overseas "research projects" of which the controversial Project Camelot in Latin America was the latest member, but not the last. The MSU project reflects not only a few individual professors, not just one particular university, not merely an especially dark period of American history—although these things were at work too; its roots go back further and deeper into the "normal," the established and enduring life of American professors, universities, and American foreign policy in general.

A STRANGE BEGINNING

Credit for being the first to piece together and publish the outlines of the MSUG story belongs to *Ramparts* magazine's staff writer and some-time foreign correspondent Robert Scheer. Since the publication 143 of Scheer's booklet, *How the United States Got Involved in Vietnam,*[2] in which Scheer made several allegations that disturbed Michigan State University, new evidence has come to light[3] which makes it possible for the first time to substantiate some of these charges with a solid network of proof. This is how the Vietnam project began:

In Tokyo in July 1950, Ngo Dinh Diem, then one of many exiled Vietnamese politicians, met Wesley Fishel, who had just accepted a position as assistant professor of political science at Michigan State University (then called Michigan State College).[4] The circumstances surrounding the meeting are obscure, but it was hardly accidental. Diem had been a frequent guest at American consulates-general in Asia since 1946, and it was rumored that certain elements of the American government—the CIA most frequently mentioned in this regard—were in fact grooming him for the job of eventually replacing Bao Dai, the playboy emperor of Vietnam.[5] Nor is it likely that Wesley Fishel was simply another young Ph.D. off on a lark in Japan, and just happened to run into Diem in a tearoom. In any case, this meeting proved to be an extraordinarily fortunate coincidence for both men. The two exchanged letters when Fishel returned to the United States, and a bare seven months later their friendship had blossomed to the point where Fishel had Diem made a "consultant" to Michigan State's "Governmental Research Bureau."[6] How a mere assistant professor in his first year at MSU was able to pull such strings for his friend is one of the several little mysteries that surround the MSU project and the person of Wesley Fishel. Only one and a half years after their initial meeting in Tokyo, Diem and Fishel—both without any overt official standing—were engaging in international diplomacy on behalf of the U.S. government. In 1952, Diem "asked the French to permit Michigan State College to furnish technical aid to the Vietnamese government, the cost of which would be borne by the United States government, but the French refused."[7] After that, Diem moved his base of operations from MSU's East Lansing campus eastward into Cardinal Spellman's territory, and began the series of publicity triumphs (recounted in Scheer's booklet) which catapulted him into power in Saigon in mid-1954. Less than two months later, his friend Wesley Fishel hurried to Saigon as Diem's special advisor and as a member of U.S. Special Ambassador Lawton Collin's personal staff.[8] "Not surprisingly," in

[2]Available from the Center for the Study of Democratic Institutions, Santa Barbara, California.

[3]Robert Scigliano and Guy H. Fox, *Technical Assistance in Vietnam, The Michigan State University Experience*, Prager Special Studies, 1965.

[4]Scigliano & Fox, p. 1.

[5]Georges Chaffard, *L'Indochine—dix ans d'indépendance*, Calmann-Levy, Paris, 1964, pp. 24, 27, 53.

[6]Scigliano & Fox, p. 1.

[7]*ibid.*

[8]*ibid*; also Scheer.

144

the words of Professors Scigliano and Fox, both of whom were high-ranking members of the MSU project, Fishel's discussions with Diem led to a request that Michigan State "undertake to help Vietnam in its current difficulties."[9] A team of four officials from the East Lansing Campus, headed by Arthur Brandstatter, chief of MSU's School of Police Administration, made a whirlwind, two-week tour of Vietnam and returned in early October 1954 with a recommendation that MSU undertake a huge project of technical assistance to the Diem government.[10] During subsequent negotiations between Diem, Fishel, MSU, and the U.S. Foreign Operations Administration (now called, less candidly, Agency for International Development), the size of the project was somewhat reduced, but its scope remained broad. Its purpose was to give the Diem government assistance in strengthening nearly all aspects of its functioning, with particular emphasis on the economy, the civil service, and the police.[11]

However, in early 1955, the Diem government was so near collapse that the MSU project almost died stillborn. The majority of Diem's cabinet deserted him, the army was in near revolt, and the city was under virtual siege by one of the armed sects, the Binh Xuyen. Even Special Ambassador Collins sent a pessimistic note to Eisenhower, suggesting that a new man can be found to replace Diem. However, firm support for Diem came from the CIA's ubiquitous Colonel Lansdale, and (via CIA chief Allen Dulles to his brother, John Foster, to Eisenhower) Collins was overruled, and Diem's future was assured.[12] The persons in Saigon who did the most to keep Diem in power during this crisis, according to the French journalist Georges Chaffard, were certain American military counsellors and unnamed "activists" from Michigan State University.[13] Their efforts were successful; Diem rode out the crisis, and in the spring of 1955 the U.S. National Security Council formally endorsed Diem. According to Scheer, who says he got it from Fishel, at this time "no less a personage than Vice-President Nixon called John Hannah, the president of Michigan State, to elicit his support."[14] Hannah, an important figure in the GOP and a former Assistant Secretary of Defense, was told (according to Scheer quoting Fishel) that it was "in the national interest for his university to become involved."[15] According to Hannah, however, there was no request from Nixon. Hannah claims that the request came from "authority even

[9]*ibid.*

[10]Scigliano & Fox, pp. 2, 75.

[11]Scigliano & Fox, p. 3.

[12]See, for example, Wise & Ross, *The Invisible Government*, Random House, 1964, pp. 157-158.

[13]Chaffard, pp. 75, 82.

[14]Scheer, quoted in *Viet Nam*, ed. Marvin Gettleman, Fawcett, 1965, p. 249.

[15]*ibid.*

higher than Nixon's."[16] However that may be, Michigan State's interests, Diem's interests, and the national interest were already thoroughly intertwined before this phone call to Hannah took place.

According to Scheer, the MSU project filled a special need of American foreign policy at this time. "The Geneva Accords had prohibited increases in the strength of either side through the introduction of 'all types of arms' or buildups in troop strength. The presence of the International Control Commission . . . offered the prospect of unfavorable publicity to the United States if its Military Assistance and Advisory Group, United States Operations Mission, or CIA agents operated openly. The Michigan group would serve as 'cover'."[17] It is true that the Geneva accords (Article 17a) forbad arms increases and it is a fact that the International Control Commission could have created heavily damaging publicity. But whether or not the Michigan group served as "cover" is a question that should be suspended for the moment, waiting until more of the evidence is in.

In May 1955, the Michigan State University Group was officially born with the signing of two contracts, one between MSU and the Diem government, the other between MSU and the U.S. government. The contracts were for two years, and were renewed with modifications in 1957 and 1959.[18] The first MSUG advisors under the contract arrived at the end of May, 1955.[19] For a project of its size, it was prepared in a remarkably short time. Actually "the team of MSU professors," as one is tempted to call the group, were neither predominantly from MSU nor were most of them professors. It was an academic program neither in numbers nor in purpose, only in publicity. From 1955 to 1962, the term of the project, MSUG had 104 American staff members altogether, who served various lengths of time. Of these 104, 32 were clerical or administrative personnel. Only 72 were full-fledged MSUG advisors. Of these 72 advisors, 33 were in the police division, 34 in the Public Administration Division, and 5 were short-term consultants. Of the 33 police advisors, only 4 came from the MSU campus, the remainder being recruited from law enforcement and other agencies. Of the 34 non-police advisors, only 11 were from the MSU campus. Only 25 of all 72 advisors were actually professors, and almost all of these were in the non-police division. The only reason to call the group the "MSU professors" is that all five of the Chief Advisors were political science professors at Michigan State, and Michigan State faculty held all other controlling positions in the project. But professors from Yale, Pittsburgh, UCLA,[20] and

[16]Quoted in "Deny MSU Fronted for CIA in Vietnam," *The Detroit News*, Sunday, Nov. 28, 1965.

[17]Scheer, p. 249.

[18]*Final Report*, MSUG, Saigon, June 1962 (mimeo), p. 1.

[19]*Final Report*, pp. 61, 62.

[20]Scigliano & Fox, pp. 40–41.

146

other universities also took part. While Michigan State lent its name and its respectability to the project and acted as coordinating agency, the real direction of the program came from the U.S. government and from the Saigon government. In doing its utmost to cooperate with these powers, MSU did no more than many other American universities would have done, and are doing.

Compared to the cost of a jet fighter-bomber, MSUG was a trivial operation, but compared to the cost of most "research" projects even in the physical sciences, MSUG was a behemoth. The cost of salaries, transportation, and overhead for the American staff alone was $5.3 *million,* and the equivalent of an additional $5.1 million in Vietnamese piastres was spent on the staff of about 200 Vietnamese scholars, translators, typists, chauffeurs, and security guards. To this tidy subtotal of $10.4 million must be added another $15 million more, according to the estimate of Scigliano and Fox. This amount approximately represents equipment and material aid funds controlled and disbursed by MSUG.[21] Nearly all of this amount was spent by the Police Division, but there is no way of knowing by how much the estimate is too low, since certain activities of the Police Division were never formally reported to MSUG's Chief Advisors.[22] But if the estimate is anywhere near accuracy, it means that MSUG spent the neat sum of about $25 million, or about two dollars for every man, woman and child in the country. The entire cost, of course, was borne by the U.S. government.

Wesley Fishel became MSUG Chief Advisor in early 1956. Scheer quotes Fishel as having said ". . . I surfaced—to use a CIA term—to become head of the MSUG program,"[23] but Fishel denies that he ever used such language.[24] In any case, it was not a bad job for a man who had begun academic life as an assistant professor only six years before.

All these factors are worth keeping in mind when asking the question whether MSUG acted as "cover" for the CIA.

AN URGENT REQUEST

The first MSUG advisors to arrive in Saigon were police experts, and the first task undertaken by MSUG was a police project, so it seems fair to begin to describe the behemoth here. MSUG was divided into two Divisions: Police and Public Administration, with the Chief Advisor responsible for both. As the project became organized the two Divisions worked quite separately from one another and the Chief

[21]*ibid.,* p. 4.
[22]*ibid.,* p. 21.
[23]Scheer, p. 249.
[24]*The Detroit News, loc. cit.*

Advisor acted as the only channel of information between them, at least formally; but in the first few months the two groups worked together. Throughout 1955 much of Saigon was in ruins from the pitched street battles; frequent plastic bomb explosions rocked the residential districts, and some MSUG members happened to be living in a hotel that was raided during a riot, and suffered considerable property damage.[25] In the midst of this atmosphere of crisis and chaos came an "urgent request" from the American Embassy in Saigon that MSUG devote all its energies to strengthening the police and security organizations, particularly the *Sureté* and the Civil Guard, and to reorganizing the refugee commissariat.[26] Since the first advisors on the scene happened to be a secret police specialist and a civil guard specialist, MSUG readily acceded to the request. The first real professors who arrived were assigned to the refugees.

The Vietnamese secret police was nothing more or less than a branch of the French *Sureté,* a name that means to Vietnamese approximately what Okhrana meant to the Bolsheviks and Gestapo meant to German Jews. When the French abandoned Vietnam in 1954-1955, the Saigon government inherited the organization lock, stock and barrel, and set about patching its war wounds. The first step was to abolish the dreaded name *Sureté* and replace it with something more suited to a brave new nation. The MSUG advisors had the answer: the secret police was henceforth called the Vietnamese Bureau of Investigation, or VBI.[27] They then devoted a great part of their energies to increasing the organization's efficiency. Its scattered facilities and records were consolidated and expanded in a former French army camp which was later renovated for the purpose. Here, under MSUG guidance and with MSUG-supplied funds, the VBI built an interrogation center, detention center, laboratory, records and identification center, and communications headquarters.[28] They undertook to modernize the *Sureté's* fingerprint files by reclassifying them from the French to the American system. After a year of work, they had reclassified 600,000 files in the "criminal and subversive" section, and expected the job to take another two years, which gives an idea of how many people the *Sureté* had its eyes on—perhaps from ten to twenty per cent of the population; not bad for an antiquated outfit, but not good enough by American standards.[29]

In order to improve on this percentage, the University Group in 1959 took charge of the national identity card program, designed to furnish every South Vietnamese over 21, for a small fee, with an obligatory, nearly indestructible plastic-laminated ID card bearing his

[25]*Final Report*, p. 2. Scigliano & Fox, p. 5.
[26]Scigliano & Fox, pp. 6, 66.
[27]Scheer, p. 251; also *Final Report,* p. 61.
[28]*Final Report*, p. 48.
[29]*ibid.*, my projections.

148

photograph and thumbprint. MSUG imported specially-designed laminating machines and portable photography studios, and it trained, equipped, and advised the heavily-armed identification teams which sought unsuccessfully, to dogtag every peasant in the country. After a number of identification teams were ambushed, the program was abandoned.[30]

MSUG established a special training school under the jurisdiction of the VBI high command, in which the Americans gave instruction in subjects ranging from jeep driving to the use of different types of tear gas. They wrote or had translated manuals on weapons maintenance, riot control, and related subjects.[31] They gave advice on all aspects of the VBI's operations, including the location of training camps and the so-called detention centers.[32] However, despite the advisors' best efforts, when the project ended in 1962, the VBI (in the words of MSUG's Final Report) "still fell far short of the revised set-up which had been recommended."[33]

The U.S. Embassy's urgent request for help with the Civil Guard was a matter of special importance, but MSUG was less helpful here. The Civil Guard, an ill-equipped body of about 50,000 men staffed with military officers, quartered in army encampments and under control of the province chiefs, played a key role in Diem's strategy for seizing power in a largely hostile countryside. Regular units of the Civil Guard would sweep through an area to soften it up and to overcome whatever resistance was encountered, and then remained, using the old French forts to keep the area pacified. The MSUG advisors wanted to reduce the organization in size and to convert it into a rural police force, to take it out of military control and base it in the villages, somewhat on the model of Franco's *Guardia Civil*. USOM and MAAG, on the other hand, wanted the Guard to be "organized into company, battalion, and regimental groups, and armed with rifles, automatic rifles, and machine guns."[34] As a result of this conflict, which was won by USOM and MAAG in 1959, MSUG's role in the Civil Guard was confined to some training and some supply activities.[35]

MSUG advisors also trained and supplied the municipal police; reorganized traffic patterns in Saigon; gave training in pistol marksmanship to the palace guard and to other "special groups"; and advised the government on counter-insurgency.[36]

But all these training and advisory activities paled in importance compared to what Scigliano and Fox call "the core of the police pro-

---

[30]*ibid.*, p. 49.
[31]*ibid.*, p. 45.
[32]Scigliano & Fox, p. 6.
[33]*Final Report*, p. 47.
[34]Scigliano & Fox, pp. 17, 23.
[35]Scigliano & Fox, pp. 17, 19. *Final Report*, p. 48.
[36]*Final Report*, 45–51. On the palace guard, Scigliano & Fox, p. 18.

gram," the provision of "material aid."[37] From 1955 to 1959, according to Scigliano and Fox, the University Group was for all practical purposes the sole supplier of weapons, ammunition, vehicles, and equipment to the entire South Vietnamese secret police, municipal police, Civil Guard, and palace guard.[38] Scigliano and Fox state that "the major items, some of which came from local stocks of American material that had been given to the French Expeditionary Corps, were revolvers, riot guns, ammunition, tear gas, jeeps and other vehicles, handcuffs, office equipment, traffic lights, and communications equipment."[39] Even MSUG's Final Report, available on request from MSU, admits these facts: "The Division arranged to supply, wherever possible, motor vehicles, small arms weapons and tear gas. . . . Schedules of distribution of weapons to patrolmen and maintenance of training was also established."[40] But "patrolmen" is a characteristic euphemism. The most substantial portion of these supplies and funds went to the secret police directly; and even more, indirectly, in the name of Michigan State University.[41]

The weapons supply program was the biggest and most successful part of the entire MSU project. It received the lion's share of the project's cost, and the greatest number of man-hours were devoted to it. Most of all of the Police Division's training programs centered around the weapons and equipment supplied by MSUG; Scigliano and Fox note that the Vietnamese were eager to be instructed in the handling of riot guns but turned a deaf ear to attempts to instruct them in the rules of evidence or the rights of prisoners. Americans refrained from trying to impose their cultural values in these matters on the Vietnamese, although some instructors were "guilty" of the attempt.[42] Even when the training programs had been largely completed in 1958, the Police Division still found it necessary to maintain a staff of more than 20 advisors to handle the distribution schedules.[43] During the peak period of MSUG's operations, mid-1957 to mid-1959, the Police Division staff outnumbered the Public Administration staff—despite the latter's much wider range of tasks—by a ratio of about 5 to 3, and the Public Administration Division never had as many advisors in it at any time.[44] If one did not know that the program was sponsored by a respectable American university, one could easily come to the conclusion that MSUG was primarily a para-military aid program with a research bureau thinly spread over it, like icing on the cake.

[37]Scigliano & Fox, p. 15.
[38]*ibid.*
[39]*ibid.*, p. 16.
[40]*Final Report*, p. 47.
[41]Scigliano & Fox, pp. 16, 21; *Final Report*, p. 47.
[42]Scigliano & Fox, p. 19.
[43]Scigliano & Fox, p. 18; *Final Report,* p. 66.
[44]*Final Report*, pp. 65–67.

Finally, the accusation that MSUG acted as a cover for the CIA can now be regarded as definitely proven. Although both MSU and Wesley Fishel have denied Robert Scheer's allegations to this effect,[45] —Scheer lacked decisive evidence, after all—recent testimony by three top-ranking MSUG members makes these denials extremely dubious. Ralph Smuckler, MSUG Chief Advisor from April 1958 to December 1959 (immediately after Fishel's tenure), stated in a newspaper interview that "a few" of the Police Division's "borrowed helpers were from the CIA." But, he continued, "these were cloak and dagger operations, and the use of CIA agents was a drop in the bucket compared to the overall project."[46] Smuckler is presently Acting Dean of International Programs at MSU. MSU political science professors Robert Scigliano (Assistant to Chief Advisor, July 1957 to September 1959—covering most of Fishel's term) and Guy Fox (Chief Advisor, May 1961 to June 1962), both colleagues of Fishel, have this to say in their recently-published book: "The non-professional advisors in the police program were overwhelmingly from state and municipal law enforcement agencies, although there was also a group of CIA agents."[47] Further: "Lack of adequate information makes it impossible to assess the work that several persons conducted with a special internal security unit of the *Surete* between 1955 and 1959. Although attached to MSUG, these persons were members of the CIA and reported only to the American Embassy in Saigon."[48] Scigliano and Fox also complain that MSUG's intimate involvement with police work "blurred for too many persons, including its own staff, its primary mission as an educational institution. The last point applies with even greater force to MSUG's somewhat forced hospitality as an organizational cover for certain intelligence functions of the American government until mid-1959. Not only was the cover quite transparent, but what it did not conceal tended to bring the whole MSU endeavor under suspicion."[49] What the rather vague phrase "somewhat forced hospitality" refers to is not clear; but what is clear is that MSUG's function as a cover for the CIA unit was written into MSUG's original contract. In mid-1959, after reviewing its progress, the group "refused to provide cover for this unit in the new contract period."[50] At that time the CIA unit moved from MSUG to under the wings of USOM, which also absorbed the weapons distribution program.[51] As soon as these transfers had been accomplished, the Police Division staff

[45]*The Detroit News, ibid.*
[46]*ibid.*
[47]Scigliano & Fox, p. 41.
[48]*ibid.,* p. 21.
[49]*ibid.,* p. 60.
[50]*ibid.,* p. 11.
[51]*ibid.*

dwindled rapidly to the vanishing point; its mission had been success-fully accomplished.[52] In the light of these circumstances, MSU's pro-testations of innocence and ignorance are simply not credible.

It is a fact that article 17(a) of the Geneva Agreements prohibits the introduction into Vietnam of all types of arms and munitions, and it is another fact that from 1954 to 1957 the United States maintained an official posture of strict respect for the Agreements, even while supporting the Diem government's refusal to honor them by holding the 1956 national reunification elections. During Eisenhower's second term the official line changed to open disregard for the Agreements, and about a year later the International Control Commission began growing increasingly ineffectual because of an irreconcilable split be-tween the Canadian and the Polish delegations, so that the Com-mission no longer represented a publicity threat. Could these facts be related to the fact that the CIA and USOM-MAAG shed their pro-fessorial cloaks and began to distribute daggers openly at about the same time? Then, too, by 1957, the manacled peasant had begun his flight from Diem's repression into the *maquis*[53]; for the peasant, his urban sympathizers, together with the sects and certain ethnic minori-ties, and for the Diem regime, the gloves were off.

[52]*Final Report*, pp. 65–67.
[53]See Philippe Devillers, "The Struggle for Unification," *China Quarterly,* January-March 1962.

Irving Louis Horowitz

The Life and Death
Of Project Camelot

In June of this year—in the midst of the crisis over the Dominican Republic—the United States Ambassador to Chile sent an urgent and angry cable to the State Department. Ambassador Ralph Dungan was confronted with a growing outburst of anti-Americanism from Chilean newspapers and intellectuals. Further, left-wing members of the Chilean Senate had accused the United States of espionage.

The anti-American attacks that agitated Dungan had no direct connection with sending US troops to Santo Domingo. Their target was a mysterious and cloudy American research program called Project Camelot.

Dungan wanted to know from the State Department what Project Camelot was all about. Further, whatever Camelot was, he wanted it stopped because it was fast becoming a *cause célèbre* in Chile (as it soon would throughout capitals of Latin America and in Washington) and Dungan had not been told anything about it—even though it was sponsored by the US Army and involved the tinderbox subjects of counter-revolution and counter-insurgency in Latin America.

Within a few weeks Project Camelot created repercussions from Capitol Hill to the White House. Senator J. William Fulbright, chairman of the Foreign Relations Committee, registered his personal concern about such projects as Camelot because of their "reactionary, backward-looking policy opposed to change. Implicit in Camelot, as in the concept of 'counter-insurgency,' is an assumption that revolutionary movements are dangerous to the interests of the United States and that the United States must be prepared to assist, if not actually to participate in, measures to repress them."

Reprinted by permission of the author and publisher from *Trans-action* Magazine (Washington University, St. Louis, Missouri), Vol. III, No. 1, November 1965, pp. 3–7. Irving L. Horowitz is professor of sociology at Washington University in St. Louis.

By mid-June the State Department and Defense Department— which had created and funded Camelot—were in open contention over the project and the jurisdiction each department should have over certain foreign policy operations.

On July 8, Project Camelot was killed by Defense Secretary Robert McNamara's office which has a veto power over the military budget. The decision had been made under the President's direction.

On the same day, the director of Camelot's parent body, the Special Operations Research Organization, told a Congressional committee that the research project on revolution and counter-insurgency had taken its name from King Arthur's mythical domain because "It connotes the right sort of things—development of a stable society with peace and justice for all." Whatever Camelot's outcome, there should be no mistaking the deep sincerity behind this appeal for an applied social science pertinent to current policy.

However, Camelot left a horizon of disarray in its wake: an open dispute between State and Defense; fuel for the anti-American fires in Latin America; a cut in US Army research appropriations. In addition, serious and perhaps ominous implications for social science research, bordering on censorship, have been raised by the heated reaction of the executive branch of government.

GLOBAL COUNTER-INSURGENCY

What was Project Camelot? Basically, it was a project for measuring and forecasting the causes of revolutions and insurgency in underdeveloped areas of the world. It also aimed to find ways of eliminating the causes, or coping with the revolutions and insurgencies. Camelot was sponsored by the US Army on a four to six million dollar contract, spaced out over three to four years, with the Special Operations Research Organization (SORO). This agency is nominally under the aegis of American University in Washington, D.C., and does a variety of research for the Army. This includes making analytical surveys of foreign areas; keeping up-to-date information on the military, political, and social complexes of those areas; and maintaining a "rapid response" file for getting immediate information, upon Army request, on any situation deemed militarily important.

Latin America was the first area chosen for concentrated study, but countries on Camelot's four-year list included some in Asia, Africa, and Europe. In a working paper issued on December 5, 1964, at the request of the Office of the Chief of Research and Development, Department of the Army, it was recommended that "comparative historical studies" be made in these countries:

(Latin America) Argentina, Bolivia, Brazil, Colombia, Cuba, Dominican Republic, El Salvador, Guatemala, Mexico, Paraguay, Peru, Venezuela.

154

(Middle East) Egypt, Iran, Turkey.

(Far East) Korea, Indonesia, Malaysia, Thailand.

(Others) France, Greece, Nigeria.

"Survey research and other field studies" were recommended for Bolivia, Colombia, Ecuador, Paraguay, Peru, Venezuela, Iran, Thailand. Preliminary consideration was also being given to a study of the separatist movement in French Canada. It, too, had a code name: Project Revolt.

In a recruiting letter sent to selected scholars all over the world at the end of 1964, Project Camelot's aims were defined as a study to "make it possible to predict and influence politically significant aspects of social change in the developing nations of the world." This would include devising procedures for "assessing the potential for internal war within national societies" and "identify(ing) with increased degrees of confidence, those actions which a government might take to relieve conditions which are assessed as giving rise to a potential for internal war." The letter further stated:

> The US Army has an important mission in the positive and constructive aspects of nation-building in less developed countries as well as a responsibility to assist friendly governments in dealing with active insurgency problems.

Such activities by the US Army were described as "insurgency prophylaxis" rather than the "sometimes misleading label of counterinsurgency."

Project Camelot was conceived in late 1963 by a group of high-ranking Army officers connected with the Army Research Office of the Department of Defense. They were concerned about new types of warfare springing up around the world. Revolutions in Cuba and Yemen and insurgency movements in Vietnam and the Congo were a far cry from the battles of World War II and also different from the envisioned—and planned for—apocalypse of nuclear war. For the first time in modern warfare, military establishments were not in a position to use the immense arsenals at their disposal—but were, instead, compelled by force of a geopolitical stalemate to increasingly engage in primitive forms of armed combat. The questions of moment for the Army were: Why can't the "hardware" be used? And what alternatives can social science "software" provide?

A well-known Latin American area specialist, Rex Hopper, was chosen as director of Project Camelot. Hopper was a professor of sociology and chairman of the department at Brooklyn College. He had been to Latin America many times over a thirty-year span on research projects and lecture tours, including some under government sponsorship. He was highly recommended for the position by his professional associates in Washington and elsewhere. Hopper had a long- 155 standing interest in problems of revolution and saw in this multi-million dollar contract the possible realization of a life-long scientific ambition.

THE CHILEAN DEBACLE

How did this social science research project create a foreign policy furore? And, at another level, how did such high intentions result in so disastrous an outcome?

The answers involve a network spreading from a professor of anthropology at the University of Pittsburgh, to a professor of sociology at the University of Oslo, and yet a third professor of sociology at the University of Chile in Santiago, Chile. The "showdown" took place in Chile, first within the confines of the university, next on the floor of the Chilean Senate, then in the popular press of Santiago, and finally, behind US embassy walls.

It was ironic that Chile was the scene of wild newspaper tales of spying and academic outrage at scholars being recruited for "spying missions." For the working papers of Project Camelot stipulated as a criterion for study that a country "should show promise of high pay-offs in terms of the kinds of data required." Chile did not meet these requirements—it is not on the preliminary list of nations specified as prospects.

How then did Chile become involved in Project Camelot's affairs? The answer requires consideration of the position of Hugo G. Nutini, assistant professor of anthropology at Pittsburgh, citizen of the United States and former citizen of Chile. His presence in Santiago as a self-identified Camelot representative triggered the climactic chain of events.

Nutini, who inquired about an appointment in Camelot's beginning stages, never was given a regular Camelot appointment. Because he was planning a trip to Chile in April of this year—on other academic business—he was asked to prepare a report concerning possibilities of cooperation from Chilean scholars. In general, it was the kind of survey which has mild results and a modest honorarium attached to it (Nutini was offered $750). But Nutini had an obviously different notion of his role. Despite the limitations and precautions which Rex Hopper placed on his trip, especially Hopper's insistence on its informal nature, Nutini managed to convey the impression of being an official of Project Camelot with the authority to make proposals to prospective Chilean participants. Here was an opportunity to link the country of his birth with the country of his choice.

At about the same time, Johan Galtung, a Norwegian sociologist famous for his research on conflict and conflict resolution in under-developed areas, especially in Latin America, entered the picture. Galtung, who was in Chile at the time and associated with the Latin American Faculty of Social Science (FLACSO), received an invitation to participate in a Camelot planning conference scheduled for Washington, D.C., in August 1965. The fee to social scientists attending the conference would be $2,000 for four weeks. Galtung turned down the invitation. He gave several reasons. He could not accept the role of the US Army as a sponsoring agent in a study of counter-insurgency. He could not accept the notion of the Army as an agency of national development; he saw the Army as managing conflict and even promoting conflict. Finally, he could not accept the asymmetry of the project—he found it difficult to understand why there would be studies of counter-insurgency in Latin-America, but no studies of "counter-intervention" (conditions under which Latin American nations might intervene in the affairs of the United States). Galtung was also deeply concerned about the possibility of European scholars being frozen out of Latin American studies by an inundation of sociologists from the United States. Furthermore, he expressed fears that the scale of Camelot honoraria would completely destroy the social science labor market in Latin America.

Galtung had spoken to others in Oslo, Santiago, and throughout Latin America about the project, and he had shown the memorandum of December 1964 to many of his colleagues.

Soon after Nutini arrived in Santiago, he had a conference with Vice-Chancellor Alvaro Bunster of the University of Chile to discuss the character of Project Camelot. Their second meeting, arranged by the vice-chancellor, was also attended by Professor Eduardo Fuenzalida, a sociologist. After a half-hour of exposition by Nutini, Fuenzalida asked him pointblank to specify the ultimate aims of the project, its sponsors, and its military implications. Before Nutini could reply, Professor Fuenzalida, apparently with some drama, pulled a copy of the December 4 circular letter from his briefcase and read a prepared Spanish translation. Simultaneously, the authorities at FLACSO turned over the matter to their associates in the Chilean Senate and in the left-wing Chilean press.

In Washington, under the political pressures of State Department officials and Congressional reaction, Project Camelot was halted in midstream, or more precisely, before it ever really got under way. When the ambassador's communication reached Washington, there was already considerable official ferment about Project Camelot. Senators Fulbright, Morse, and McCarthy soon asked for hearings by the Senate Foreign Relations Committee. Only an agreement between Secretary of Defense McNamara and Secretary of State Rusk to settle their differences on future overseas research projects forestalled Senate action. But in the House of Representatives, a hearing was conducted by the Foreign Affairs Committee on July 8, The SORO director, Theodore Vallance, was questioned by committee members on the worth of Camelot and the matter of military intrusion into foreign policy areas.

157

That morning, even before Vallance was sworn in as a witness—and without his knowledge—the Defense Department issued a terse announcement terminating Project Camelot. President Johnson had decided the issue in favor of the State Department. In a memo to Secretary Rusk on August 5 the President stipulated that "no government sponsorship of foreign area research should be undertaken which in the judgment of the Secretary of State would adversely affect United States foreign relations."

The State Department has recently established machinery to screen and judge all federally-financed research projects overseas. The policy and research consequences of the Presidential directive will be discussed later.

What effect will the cancellation of Camelot have on the continuing rivalry between Defense and State departments for primacy in foreign policy? How will government sponsorship of future social science research be affected? And was Project Camelot a scholarly protective cover for US Army planning—or a legitimate research operation on a valid research subject independent of sponsorship?

Let us begin with a collective self-portrait of Camelot as the social scientists who directed the project perceived it. There seems to be general consensus on seven points.

First, the men who went to work for Camelot felt the need for a large-scale, "big picture" project in social science. They wanted to create a sociology of contemporary relevance which would not suffer from the parochial narrowness of vision to which their own professional backgrounds had generally conditioned them. Most of the men viewed Camelot as a bona fide opportunity to do fundamental research with relatively unlimited funds at their disposal. (No social science project ever before had up to $6,000,000 available.) Under such optimal conditions, these scholars tended not to look a gift horse in the mouth. As one of them put it, there was no desire to inquire too deeply as to the source of the funds of the ultimate purpose of the project.

Second, most social scientists affiliated with Camelot felt that there was actually more freedom to do fundamental research under military sponsorship than at a university or college. One man noted that during the 1950's there was far more freedom to do fundamental research in the RAND corporation (an Air Force research organization) than on any campus in America. Indeed, once the protective covering of RAND was adopted, it was almost viewed as a society of Platonist elites or "knowers" permitted to search for truth on behalf of the powerful. In a neoplatonic definition of their situation, the Camelot men hoped that their ideas would be taken seriously by the wielders of power (although, conversely, they were convinced that the armed forces would not accept their preliminary recommendations).

Third, many of the Camelot associates felt distinctly uncomfortable with military sponsorship, especially given the present United States 158 military posture. But their reaction to this discomfort was that "the Army has to be educated." This view was sometimes cast in Freudian terms: the Army's bent toward violence ought to be sublimated. Underlying this theme was the notion of the armed forces as an agency for potential social good—the discipline and the order embodied by an army could be channeled into the process of economic and social development in the United States as well as in Latin America.

Fourth, there was a profound conviction in the perfectibility of mankind; particularly in the possibility of the military establishment performing a major role in the general process of growth. They sought to correct the intellectual paternalism and parochialism under which Pentagon generals, State Department diplomats, and Defense Department planners seemed to operate.

Fifth, a major long-range purpose of Camelot, at least for some of its policy-makers, was to prevent another revolutionary holocaust on a grand scale, such as occurred in Cuba. At the very least, there was a shared belief that *Pax Americana* was severely threatened and its future could be bolstered.

Sixth, none of them viewed their role on the project as spying for the United States government, or for anyone else.

Seventh, the men on Project Camelot felt that they made heavy sacrifices for social science. Their personal and professional risks were much higher than those taken by university academics. Government work, while well-compensated, remains professionally marginal. It can be terminated abruptly (as indeed was the case) and its project directors are subject to a public scrutiny not customary behind the walls of ivy.

In the main, there was perhaps a keener desire on the part of the directing members of Camelot not to "sell out" than there is among social scientists with regular academic appointments. This concern with the ethics of social science research seemed to be due largely to daily confrontation of the problems of betrayal, treason, secrecy, and abuse of data, in a critical situation. In contrast, even though a university position may be created by federally-sponsored research, the connection with policy matters is often too remote to cause any *crise de conscience*.

THE INSIDERS REPORT

Were the men on Camelot critical of any aspects of the project?

Some had doubts from the outset about the character of the work they would be doing, and about the conditions under which it would be done. It was pointed out, for example, that the US Army tends to exercise a far more stringent intellectual control of research findings than does the US Air Force. As evidence for this, it was stated that SORO generally had fewer "free-wheeling" aspects to its research 159 designs than did RAND (the Air Force-supported research organization). One critic inside SORO went so far as to say that he knew of no SORO research which had a "playful" or unregimented quality, such as one finds at RAND (where for example, computers are used to plan invasions but also to play chess). One staff member said that "the self-conscious seriousness gets to you after a while." "It was all grim stuff," said another.

Another line of criticism was that pressures on the "reformers" (as the men engaged in Camelot research spoke of themselves) to come up with ideas were much stronger than the pressures on the military to actually bring off any policy changes recommended. The social scientists were expected to be social reformers, while the military adjutants were expected to be conservative. It was further felt that the relationship between sponsors and researchers was not one of equals, but rather one of superordinate military needs and subordinate academic roles. On the other hand, some officials were impressed by the disinterestedness of the military, and thought that far from exercising undue influence, the Army personnel were loath to offer opinions.

Another objection was that if one had to work on policy matters—if research is to have international ramifications—it might better be conducted under conventional State Department sponsorship. "After all," one man said, "they are at least nominally committed to civilian political norms." In other words, there was a considerable reluctance to believe that the Defense Department, despite its superior organization, greater financial affluence, and executive influence, would actually improve upon State Department styles of work, or accept recommendations at variance with Pentagon policies.

There seemed to be few, if any, expressions of disrespect for the intrinsic merit for the work contemplated by Camelot, or of disdain for policy-oriented work in general. The scholars engaged in the Camelot effort used two distinct vocabularies. The various Camelot documents reveal a military vocabulary provided with an array of military justifications; often followed (within the same document) by a social science vocabulary offering social science justifications and rationalizations. The dilemma in the Camelot literature from the preliminary report issued in August 1964 until the more advanced document issued in April 1965, is the same: an incomplete amalgamation of the military and sociological vocabularies. (At an early date the project had the code name SPEARPOINT.)

POLICY CONFLICTS OVER CAMELOT

The directors of SORO are concerned that the cancellation of Camelot might mean the end of SORO as well in a wholesale slash of research funds. For a while over $1,000,000 was allotted to Camelot each year, the annual budget of SORO, its parent organization, is a good deal 160 less. Although no such action has taken place, SORO's future is being examined. For example, the Senate and House Appropriations Committee blocked a move by the Army to transfer unused Camelot funds to SORO.

However, the end of Project Camelot does not necessarily imply the end of the Special Operations Research Office, nor does it imply an end to research designs which are similar in character to Project Camelot. In fact, the termination of the contract does not even imply an intellectual change of heart on the part of the originating sponsors or key figures of the project.

One of the characteristics of Project Camelot was the number of antagonistic forces it set in motion on grounds of strategy and timing rather than from what may be called considerations of scientific principles.

The State Department grounded its opposition to Camelot on the basis of the ultimate authority it has in the area of foreign affairs. There is no published report showing serious criticism of the projected research itself.

Congressional opposition seemed to be generated by a concern not to rock any foreign alliances, especially in Latin America. Again, there was no statement about the project's scientific or intellectual grounds.

A third group of skeptics, academic social scientists, generally thought that Project Camelot, and studies of the processes of revolution and war in general, were better left in the control of major university centers, and in this way, kept free of direct military supervision.

The Army, creator of the project, did nothing to contradict McNamara's order cancelling Project Camelot. Army influentials did not only feel that they had to execute the Defense Department's orders, but they are traditionally dubious of the value of "software" research to support "hardware" systems.

Let us take a closer look at each of these groups which voiced opposition to Project Camelot. A number of issues did not so much hinge upon, as swim about, Project Camelot. In particular, the "jurisdictional" dispute between Defense and State loomed largest.

STATE VS. DEFENSE. In substance, the debate between the Defense Department and the State Department is not unlike that between electricians and bricklayers in the construction of a new apartment house. What "union" is responsible for which processes? Less generously, the issue is: who controls what? At the policy level, Camelot was a tool tossed about in a larger power struggle which has been going on in government circles since the end of World War II, when the Defense Department emerged as a competitor for honors as the most powerful bureau of the administrative branch of government.

In some sense, the divisions between Defense and State are outcomes of the rise of ambiguous conflicts such as Korea and Vietnam, 161 in contrast to the more precise and diplomatically controlled "classical" world wars. What are the lines dividing political policy from military posture? Who is the most important representative of the United States abroad: the ambassador or the military attaché in charge of the military mission? When soldiers from foreign lands are sent to the United States for political orientation, should such orientation be within the province of the State Department or of the Defense Department? When undercover activities are conducted, should the direction of such activities belong to military or political authorities? Each of these is a strategic question with little pragmatic or historic precedent. Each of these was entwined in the Project Camelot explosion.

It should be plain therefore that the State Department was not simply responding to the recommendations of Chilean left-wingers in urging the cancellation of Camelot. It merely employed the Chilean hostility to "interventionist" projects as an opportunity to redefine the balance of forces and power with the Defense Department. What is clear from this resistance to such projects is not so much a defense of the sovereignty of the nations where ambassadors are stationed, as it is a contention that conventional political channels are sufficient to yield the information desired or deemed necessary.

CONGRESS. In the main, congressional reaction seems to be that Project Camelot was bad because it rocked the diplomatic boat in a sensitive area. Underlying most congressional criticisms is the plain fact that most congressmen are more sympathetic to State Department control of foreign affairs than they are to Defense Department control. In other words, despite military sponsored world junkets, National Guard and State Guard pressures from the home State, and military training in the backgrounds of many congressmen, the sentiment for political rather than military control is greater. In addition, there is a mounting suspicion in Congress of varying kinds of behavioral science research stemming from hearings into such matters as wiretapping, uses of lie detectors, and truth-in-packaging.

SOCIAL SCIENTISTS. One reason for the violent response to Project Camelot, especially among Latin American scholars, is its sponsorship by the Department of Defense. The fact is that Latin Americans have become quite accustomed to State Department involvements in the internal affairs of various nations. The Defense Department is a newcomer, a dangerous one, inside the Latin American orbit. The train of thought connected to its activities is in terms of international warfare, spying missions, military manipulations, etc. The State Department, for its part, is often a consultative party to shifts in government, and has played an enormous part in either fending off or bringing about *coups d'état*. This State Department role has by now been accepted and even taken for granted. Not so the Defense Department's role. But it is interesting to conjecture on how matter-of-factly 162

Camelot might have been accepted if it had State Department sponsorship.

Social scientists in the United States have, for the most part, been publicly silent on the matter of Camelot. The reasons for this are not hard to find. First, many "giants of the field" are involved in government contract work in one capacity or another. And few souls are in a position to tamper with the gods. Second, most information on Project Camelot has thus far been of a newspaper variety; and professional men are not in a habit of criticizing colleagues on the basis of such information. Third, many social scientists doubtless see nothing wrong or immoral in the Project Camelot designs. And they are therefore more likely to be either confused or angered at the Latin American response than at the directors of Project Camelot. (At the time of the blowup, Camelot people spoke about the "Chilean mess" rather than the "Camelot mess.")

The directors of Project Camelot did not "classify" research materials, so that there would be no stigma of secrecy. And they also tried to hire, and even hired away from academic positions, people well known and respected for their independence of mind. The difficulty is that even though the stigma of secrecy was formally erased, it remained in the attitudes of many of the employees and would-be employees of Project Camelot. They unfortunately thought in terms of secrecy, clearance, missions, and the rest of the professional nonsense that so powerfully afflicts the Washington scientific as well as political ambience.

Further, it is apparent that Project Camelot had much greater difficulty hiring a full-time staff of high professional competence, than in getting part-time, summertime, weekend, and sundry assistance. Few established figures in academic life were willing to surrender the advantages of their positions for the risks of the project.

One of the cloudiest aspects to Project Camelot is the role of American University. Its actual supervision of the contract appears to have begun and ended with the 25 percent overhead on those parts of the contract that a university receives on most federal grants. Thus, while there can be no question as to the "concern and disappointment" of President Hurst R. Anderson of the American University over the demise of Project Camelot, the reasons for this regret do not seem to extend beyond the formal and the financial. No official at American University appears to have been willing to make any statement of responsibility, support, chagrin, opposition, or anything else related to the project. The issues are indeed momentous, and must be faced by all universities at which government sponsored research is conducted: the amount of control a university has over contract work; the role of university officials in the distribution of funds from grants; the relationships that ought to be established once a grant is issued. 163

There is also a major question concerning project directors: are they members of the faculty, and if so, do they have necessary teaching responsibilities and opportunities for tenure as do other faculty members.

The difficulty with American University is that it seems to be remarkably unlike other universities in its permissiveness. The Special Operations Research Office received neither guidance nor support from university officials. From the outset, there seems to have been a "gentleman's agreement" not to inquire or interfere in Project Camelot, but simply to serve as some sort of camouflage. If American University were genuinely autonomous it might have been able to lend highly supportive aid to Project Camelot during the crisis months. As it is, American University maintained an official silence which preserved it from more congressional or executive criticism. This points up some serious flaws in its administrative and financial policies.

The relationship of Camelot to SORO represented a similarly muddled organizational picture. The director of Project Camelot was nominally autonomous and in charge of an organization surpassing in size and importance the overall SORO operation. Yet at the critical point the organizational blueprint served to protect SORO and sacrifice what nominally was its limb. That Camelot happened to be a vital organ may have hurt, especially when Congress blocked the transfer of unused Camelot funds to SORO.

MILITARY. Military reaction to the cancellation of Camelot varied. It should be borne in mind that expenditures on Camelot were minimal in the Army's overall budget and most military leaders are skeptical, to begin with, about the worth of social science research. So there was no open protest about the demise of Camelot. Those officers who have a positive attitude toward social science materials, or are themselves trained in the social sciences, were dismayed. Some had hoped to find "software" alternatives to the "hardware systems" approach applied by the Secretary of Defense to every military-political contingency. These officers saw the attack on Camelot as a double attack —on their role as officers and on their professional standards. But the Army was so clearly treading in new waters that it could scarcely jeopardize the entire structure of military research to preserve one project. This very inability or impotence to preserve Camelot—a situation threatening to other governmental contracts with social scientists —no doubt impressed many armed forces officers.

The claim is made by the Camelot staff (and various military aides) that the critics of the project played into the hands of those sections of other military predisposed to veto any social science recommendations. Then why did the military offer such a huge support to a social science project to begin with? Because $6,000,000 is actually a trifling sum for the Army in an age of multi-billion dollar military establish-   164 ment. The amount is significantly more important for the social sciences, where such contract awards remain relatively scarce. Thus, there were differing perspectives of the importance of Camelot: an Army view which considered the contract as one of several forms of "software" investment; a social science perception of Project Camelot as the equivalent of the Manhattan Project.

WAS PROJECT CAMELOT WORKABLE?

While most public opposition to Project Camelot focused on its strategy and timing, a considerable amount of private opposition centered on more basic, though theoretical, questions: was Camelot scientifically feasible and ethically correct? No public document or statement contested the possibility that, given the successful completion of the data gathering, Camelot could have, indeed, established basic criteria for measuring the level and potential for internal war in a given nation. Thus, by never challenging the feasibility of the work, the political critics of Project Camelot were providing back-handed compliments to the efficacy of the project.

But much more than political considerations are involved. It is clear that some of the most critical problems presented by Project Camelot are scientific. Although for an extensive analysis of Camelot, the reader would, in fairness, have to be familiar with all of its documents, salient general criticisms can be made without a full reading.

The research design of Camelot was from the outset plagued by ambiguities. It was never quite settled whether the purpose was to study counter-insurgency possibilities, or the revolutionary process. Similarly, it was difficult to determine whether it was to be a study of comparative social structures, a set of case studies of single nations "in depth," or a study of social structure with particular emphasis on the military. In addition, there was a lack of treatment of what indicators were to be used, and whether a given social system in Nation A could be as stable in Nation B.

In one Camelot document there is a general critique of social science for failing to deal with social conflict and social control. While this in itself is admirable, the tenor and context of Camelot's documents make it plain that a "stable society" is considered the norm no less than the desired outcome. The "breakdown of social order" is spoken of accusatively. Stabilizing agencies in developing areas are presumed to be absent. There is no critique of US Army policy in developing areas because the Army is presumed to be a stabilizing agency. The research formulations always assume the legitimacy of Army tasks— "if the US Army is to perform effectively its parts in the US mission of counter-insurgency it must recognize that insurgency represents a breakdown of social order. . . ." But such a proposition has never been doubted—by Army officials or anyone else. The issue is whether such breakdowns are in the nature of the existing system or a product of conspiratorial movements.

The use of hygienic language disguises the anti-revolutionary assumptions under a cloud of powder puff recommended "because trends in this situation (the Stroessner regime) may also render it 'unique' when analyzed in terms of the transition from 'dictatorship' to political stability." But to speak about changes from dictatorship to stability is an obvious ruse. In this case, it is a tactic to disguise the fact that Paraguay is one of the most vicious, undemocratic (and like most dictatorships, stable) societies in the Western Hemisphere.

These typify the sort of hygienic sociological premises that do not have scientific purposes. They illustrate the confusion of commitments within Project Camelot. Indeed the very absence of emotive words such as revolutionary masses, communism, socialism, and capitalism only serves to intensify the discomfort one must feel on examination of the documents—since the abstract vocabulary disguises, rather than resolves, the problems of international revolution. To have used clearly political rather than military language would not "justify" governmental support. Furthermore, shabby assumptions of academic conventionalism replaced innovative orientations. By adopting a systems approach, the problematic, open-ended aspects of the study of revolutions were largely omitted; and the design of the study became an oppressive curb on the study of the problems inspected.

This points up a critical implication for Camelot (as well as other projects). The importance of the subject being researched does not *per se* determine the importance of the project. A sociology of large-scale relevance and reference is all to the good. It is important that scholars be willing to risk something of their shaky reputations in helping resolve major world social problems. But it is no less urgent that in the process of addressing major problems, the autonomous character of the social science disciplines—their own criteria of worthwhile scholarship—should not be abandoned. Project Camelot lost sight of this "autonomous" social science character.

It never seemed to occur to its personnel to inquire into the desirability for successful revolution. This is just as solid a line of inquiry as the one stressed—the conditions under which revolutionary movements will be able to overthrow a government. Furthermore, they seem not to have thought about inquiring into the role of the United States in these countries. This points up the lack of symmetry. The problem should have been phrased to include the study of "us" as well as "them." It is not possible to make a decent analysis of a situation unless one takes into account the role of all the different people and groups involved in it; and there was no room in the design for such contingency analysis.

In discussing the policy impact on a social science research project, we should not overlook the difference between "contract" work and "grants." Project Camelot commenced with the US Army; that is to say, it was initiated for a practical purpose determined by the client. This differs markedly from the typical academic grant in that its sponsorship had "built-in" ends. The scholar usually *seeks* a grant; in this case the donor, the Army, promoted its own aims. In some measure, the hostility for Project Camelot may be an unconscious reflection of this distinction—a dim feeling that there was something "non-academic," and certainly not disinterested, about Project Camelot, irrespective of the quality of the scholars associated with it.

THE ETHICS OF POLICY RESEARCH

The issue of "scientific rights" versus "social myths" is perennial. Some maintain that the scientist ought not penetrate beyond legally or morally sanctioned limits and others argue that such limits cannot exist for science. In treading on the sensitive issue of national sovereignty, Project Camelot reflects the generalized dilemma. In deference to intelligent researchers, in recognition of them as scholars, they should have been invited by Camelot to air their misgivings and qualms about government (and especially Army sponsored) research—to declare their moral conscience. Instead, they were mistakenly approached as skillful, useful potential employees of a higher body, subject to an authority higher than their scientific calling.

What is central is not the political motives of the sponsor. For social scientists were not being enlisted in an intelligence system for "spying" purposes. But given their professional standing, their great sense of intellectual honor and pride, they could not be "employed" without proper deference for their stature. Professional authority should have prevailed from beginning to end with complete command of the right to thrash out the moral and political dilemmas as researchers saw them. The Army, however respectful and protective of free expression, was "hiring help" and not openly and honestly submitting a problem to the higher professional and scientific authority of social science.

The propriety of the Army to define and delimit all questions, which Camelot should have had a right to examine, was never placed in doubt. This is a tragic precedent; it reflects the arrogance of a consumer of intellectual merchandise. And this relationship of inequality corrupted the lines of authority, and profoundly limited the autonomy of the social scientists involved. It became clear that the social scientist savant was not so much functioning as an applied social scientist as he was supplying information to a powerful client.

The question of who sponsors research is not nearly so decisive as the question of ultimate use of such information. The sponsorship of a project, whether by the United States Army or by the Boy Scouts of 167

America, is by itself neither good nor bad. Sponsorship is good or bad only insofar as the intended outcomes can be pre-determined and the parameters of those intended outcomes tailored to the sponsor's expectations. Those social scientists critical of the project never really denied its freedom and independence, but questioned instead the purpose and character of its intended results.

It would be a gross oversimplification, if not an outright error, to assume that the theoretical problems of Project Camelot derive from any reactionary character of the project designers. The director went far and wide to select a group of men for the advisory board, the core planning group, the summer study group, and the various conference groupings, who in fact were more liberal in their orientations than any random sampling of the sociological profession would likely turn up.

However, in nearly every page of the various working papers, there are assertions which clearly derive from American military policy objectives rather than scientific method. The steady assumption that internal warfare is damaging disregards the possibility that a government may not be in a position to take actions either to relieve or improve mass conditions, or that such actions as are contemplated may be more concerned with reducing conflict than with improving conditions. The added statements about the United States Army and its "important mission in the positive and constructive aspects of nation building . . ." assumes the reality of such a function in an utterly unquestioning and unconvincing form. The first rule of the scientific game is not to make assumptions about friends and enemies in such a way as to promote the use of different criteria for the former and the latter.

The story of Project Camelot was not a confrontation of good versus evil. Obviously, not all men behaved with equal fidelity or with equal civility. Some men were weaker than others, some more callous, and some more stupid. But all of this is extrinsic to the heart of the problem of Camelot: what are and are not the legitimate functions of a scientist?

In conclusion, two important points must be clearly kept in mind and clearly apart. First, Project Camelot was intellectually, and from my own perspective, ideologically unsound. However, and more significantly, Camelot was not cancelled because of its faulty intellectual approaches. Instead, its cancellation came as an act of government censorship, and an expression of the contempt for social science so prevalent among those who need it most. Thus it was political expedience, rather than its lack of scientific merit, that led to the demise of Camelot because it threatened to rock State Department relations with Latin America.

Second, giving the State Department the right to screen and approve government-funded social science research projects on other countries, as the President has ordered, is a supreme act of censorship. Among the agencies that grant funds for such research are the National Institutes of Mental Health, the National Science Foundation, the National Aeronautics and Space Agency, and the Office of Education. Why should the State Department have veto power over the scientific pursuits of men and projects funded by these and other agencies in order to satisfy the policy needs—or policy failures—of the moment? President Johnson's directive is a gross violation of the autonomous nature of science.

We must be careful not to allow social science projects with which we may vociferously disagree on political and ideological grounds to be decimated or dismantled by government fiat. Across the ideological divide is a common social science understanding that the contemporary expression of reason in politics today is applied social science, and that the cancellation of Camelot, however pleasing it may be on political grounds to advocates of a civilian solution to Latin American affairs, represents a decisive setback for social science research.

PART TWO

Cybernation

FOUR

AUTOMATION: PROCESSES AND POLICIES

One of the most visible trends in America during the 20th century has been the rapidly changing occupational structure. Professional and managerial occupations have grown in significance, along with other lower white-collar occupations. In the blue-collar ranks there have been a growing need for skilled workers and service workers, and a sharp decline in farm occupations and unskilled occupations. Such trends are often viewed as a natural outgrowth of a healthy industrial society, reflecting great advances in technology which would relieve man from burdensome work, thereby freeing him for more creative employment.

The pace of change in the occupational structure was made more rapid by the introduction of systems of production that could be carried out without human intervention. Automation in many production areas had the potential for eliminating tens of thousands of jobs, especially those in large-scale manufacturing industries. The efficiencies of these working machine-systems soon spread to those occupations that process paper rather than produce products; the lower white-collar clerical employee as well as the middle management could no longer compete with the speed, accuracy, and dependability of information processing systems (Ginberg, 1964). A rapid extension of these trends suggests a future with a three class occupational structure: professionals, technicians, and service workers.

The questions and issues raised by the automation-produced occupational structure fall into two main areas: (1) how to maintain employment; and (2) how to reduce unemployment. Virtually all observers of the impact of automation agree that unemployment is one of the most immediate consequences of automation. There is considerable disagreement, however, concerning the manner in which unemployment due to job dislocation can be remedied. One view—the

173

so-called aggregate-demand view—maintains that displacements due to automation are temporary, and can be reduced by a stimulated economy. The structuralist approach to unemployment from automation views job dislocation as permanent, since the people being displaced have little education and available skill to bring to a new occupation. Those with little skill or education will find it increasingly difficult to find a place in the occupational structure except in the third-class service occupations referred to earlier.

The structuralist view of automation-produced unemployment has also led to such proposals as the guaranteed annual income (Theobold, 1967). Starting with the assumption that the technological capability does exist for a very small proportion of the labor force to produce enough for the entire country, the guaranteed income is necessary for allowing the displaced worker to maintain a decent standard of living.

The full significance of automation is not only that it may eliminate some jobs, but also that it eliminates an entire class of jobs, leaving the displaced worker without a place in the occupational structure. This clearly points to the close connection between the processes of automation and the revolution in human rights presented in Part Three of this book. For example many of the ameliorative programs of job retraining, or reducing high-school dropout rates, often result in preparing people for occupations that are being rapidly eliminated. One result of this situation is that programs designed to deal with poverty and unemployment are ineffective because they are unrealistically connected to the economic system.

Lekachman's paper, "The Automation Report," contains a discussion of the Report of the National Commission on Technology, Automation, and Economic Progress which offered a number of solutions for dealing with the connection between automation and poverty. Lekachman criticizes the National Commission Report for its seeming to hold the view that the technological problem of automation is best solved by technological means. In fact, most of the solutions offered by the Commission to the question, "what can our society have, how can it get what it wants?" are again technological solutions. The author's answer to the question posed by the Commission deals with political rather than technological solutions.

The tendency to solve social ills with technical means, as in the case of automation, is a consequence of trying to reduce certain social ills to manageable dimensions in order that precise solutions might be applied. This results in thinking about automation as "the problem" and "manpower planning and retraining" as the technological solution. What is overlooked, however, is the possibility that the solutions are themselves an intimate part of the problem. Automation is only the visible part of that iceberg called the cybernetic revolution. What is less visible is the emergence of large-scale planned systems in the 174 social, political and economic realms. A recent experiment in forecasting the future undertaken by the RAND Corporation (Gordon and Helmer, 1964) suggests that there will be major efforts in the years ahead in (1) the establishment of large-scale systems in developing, controlling and using our energy and natural resources; (2) continued development of automated manufacturing industries and the emergence of manufactured food to meet the needs of an expanding world population; (3) development of rapid transportation systems for land, sea, and air; (4) the development of bio-social systems concerned not only with medical advances, housing, community development, and pollution control, but in the coordination of these advances into large-scale social systems such as the design of cities; and (5) the expansion of space programs and military defense systems.

The tendency toward planned and controlled systems has raised questions of whether the operation of a computerized government will render the average citizen ineffective in influencing policy, partly through ignorance, and increasingly through apathy (Michael, 1962). One is tempted to conclude from these arguments that while the strengths of a computerized government are in seeking the "best" solutions to national problems, the technology itself leads to an avoidance of certain problems and questions that are not amenable to the techniques. In such a situation there is the possibility that both the definition of problems and the effective solutions will be made within the constraints of the problem-solving technology. Thus, the reliance on cybernetic technology minimizes the average citizen's ability to affect national policy, while at the same time limiting consideration of alternatives in national policy to those that are amenable to the problem-solving tools that are available.

Michael's article, "Some Speculations on the Social Impact of Technology," covers a wide range of technological changes which have influenced warfare, genetic control, invasion of privacy, leisure, urban growth, and concentration of power. The key issue posed by these changes in biological technology, cybernation, and social engineering is that they have both positive and negative consequences for man and society. How are we to estimate the particular balance between these consequences? How can the institutions of society be changed fast enough to deal with technological change?

Technology, then, can be viewed as one of the constraints in choosing among alternative solutions to national problems. The problem posed in this area is reflected in the efforts of many groups to include certain conditions on the list of national problems or national "needs." Further difficulty stems from the fact that even among the subgroups who are able to get their needs represented on the national agenda, there is considerable disagreement concerning the needs which should have priority. Melman's article, "American Needs and Limits on Resources: The Priorities Problem," presents a discussion of America's 175 needs in housing, health services, education, transportation, natural resource development, water, waste and pollution. His main point is that the pursuit of the above-stated needs is seriously hampered by the priority given to military programs and military expenditures, and that there is in fact a priorities problem that is often unrecognized. Within the framework of the popular "guns and butter" debate, the arguments center about whether or not there is a priorities problem, for if there is no need to choose between guns and butter, special group interests are not being slighted by national policy decisions. This is part of the meaning of a "consensual society," where significant national debate is made unnecessary by the fact that all needs are being satisfied.

Assuming, however, that American society must make choices in allocating its resources, it is of vital importance to learn how those who make decisions on behalf of the people learn about the people's needs. Some observers of the cybernetic revolution such as Michael (mentioned above) envision a future where it will become increasingly difficult for the average citizen to make his voice heard on matters related to his interests. A less pessimistic view recognizes the growing complexity of society which makes direct individual participation in government increasingly difficult, but sees the needs and interests of the average citizen being represented through the federal government. This view is often expressed under the theory of "countervailing power," wherein the citizen copes with "big business" through his "big government" and "big unions."

The relevance of the countervailing power thesis requires close inspection at a time when the nation's defense establishment has become one of industry's best customers, awarding defense contracts approaching 40 billion dollars. It is the increasingly close association between government and business that is the focus of Barber's paper entitled "The New Partnership: Big Government and Big Business"; the emergence of the so-called "conglomerates" in American industry (as one consequence of cybernation) and their relationship to the seats of governmental power becomes one of the major constraints on the policy alternatives for dealing with the consequences of cybernation. Under such conditions of centralization of economic power, government's ability and willingness to protect the "public interest" is severely restricted.

REFERENCES AND ADDITIONAL READING

John G. Burke, ed., *The New Technology and Human Values,* Belmont, California: Wadsworth, 1967.

Jacques Ellul, *The Technological Society,* New York: Knopf, 1964.

John K. Galbraith, *The New Industrial State,* Boston: Houghton-Mifflin, 1967.

176

Paul Ginberg, "Computers: How They're Remaking Companies," *Business Week,* Special Report, February 29, 1964.

T. J. Gordon and O. Helmer, *Report on a Long-Range Forecasting Study,* Santa Monica, California: RAND Corporation, September, 1964.

Edward D. Kalachek, "Automation and Full Employment," *Transaction,* March, 1967, 24–29.

Donald Michael, *Cybernation: The Silent Conquest,* Santa Barbara, California: Center for the Study of Democratic Institutions, 1962.

Robert Theobold, *The Guaranteed Income,* New York: Doubleday, 1967.

Norbert Weiner, "Some Moral and Technical Consequences of Automation," *Science,* 131, May, 1960, 1355–1358.

Robert Lekachman

The Automation Report

As a public document, the Report of the National Commission on Technology, Automation, and Economic Progress possesses rare virtue. The search for consensus by distinguished academics like Daniel Bell and Robert Solow, labor leaders like Walter Reuther and Joseph Bierne, and businessmen like Philip Sporn and Thomas J. Watson, Jr. has not been permitted to blunt an unusually vigorous intellectual thrust toward sharp diagnosis and effective remedy.

In order to appreciate the full value of the Report, it is wise to recall something of the context in which the Commission began its short life. The Commission was the federal government's response to the general sense of uneasiness and apprehension which has accompanied the rapid introduction into factories and offices of the computers and automatic control devices usually grouped together under the name of automation. At about the same time as the members of the group received their Presidential appointments (December 1964), the Ad Hoc Committee on the Triple Revolution issued its apocalyptic diagnosis of a forthcoming condition in which much or most work (as work is currently defined) would be rendered otiose by the new computer technology. The portion of the Ad Hoc Committee's recommendations which received the most public attention was a guaranteed minimum income payable to all members of the population either unemployed, unemployable, or earning sums below a decent minimum. Closely related to this proposal was an extreme position in the argument that has been raging for some years among economists, sociologists, and public officials—a controversy over the actual rate at which technological change has been occurring and the actual numbers of men

Reprinted from *Commentary*, May 1966, Volume 41, No. 5, by permission of the author and publisher; copyright © 1966 by the American Jewish Committee. Robert Lekachman is chairman of the economics department of the State University of New York at Stony Brook.

and women who either have already been displaced by automation or are likely in the near future to be displaced.

In the sluggish economy of the 1950's, attempts at explaining American rates of unemployment—rates which were uniquely high for that decade among industrial nations—focused upon either structural deficiencies in our national arrangements, or deficiencies in aggregate demand caused by the fiscal and monetary primitivism of an unenlightened national administration. The structuralists tended to argue that the pace of technological change had indeed accelerated and that one of the consequences of the acceleration was the permanent displacement of those individuals who possessed no readily transferable skills, particularly blue-collar workers. If this were true, it followed that simply stimulating the economy was no adequate remedy for the situation of workers who lacked education, skill, or aptitude for the new jobs created by the new technology: extensive programs of reeducation and retraining were necessary. Conservative structuralists hoped that such programs would take care of most of the new unemployed; extreme structuralists more pessimistically postulated a large number of the permanently displaced.

For its part, the aggregate-demand school argued that the pace of technical change in the 1950's was perfectly consistent with the statistical trend of the past half century, and that unemployment was largely a consequence not of automation but of the defective fiscal and monetary policies of the Eisenhower administration. It followed from this diagnosis that the remedy lay in policies of the variety by now banal among economists brought up on Keynes—stimulation of the economy either by a substantial increase in public spending or by a sharp tax reduction. Indeed, insofar as the 1960 Presidential campaign developed a substantial issue between Nixon and Kennedy, it turned on the question of whether or not two Republican administrations had been culpable in permitting the United States to finish next to last (ahead only of Great Britain) in the international growth sweepstakes. Reinforcing the Democratic position was the fact that the year of John Kennedy's inauguration was part of the *third* recession the United States had experienced in less than eight years—a record equaled by no other country.

At least in his first year as President, it was the structuralist rather than the aggregate-demand approach which exerted a greater appeal on Kennedy as a way of dealing with our lagging economy. In part, this preference was shaped by a difficult balance-of-payments situation, and in part by the genuine fiscal conservatism of a politician with direct experience of a New England economy whose ailments seemed mostly structural. No doubt the politics of the Eisenhower aftermath also implied a structuralist program, for eight years of Eisenhower timidity, caution, and emphasis upon the heroic qualities of budget-balancing made it difficult to persuade Congress that either large spend-

179

ing programs or substantial tax cuts were advantageous. For reasons of this sort, what the President asked of Congress in 1961 was mostly a series of rather inexpensive measures designed to effect at least a marginal improvement in the situation of particular groups and localities. Congress had made several feints at the issue before, but it was only in 1961 that it finally passed the Area Redevelopment Act. A ragbag of policies, including a small retraining program, the measure was soon converted into another pork-barrel, open to Congressional raiding even for the benefit of districts not very depressed. In 1961, too, the Manpower Retraining and Development Act was passed. This bill was also based on the structuralist premise that long-term unemployment was caused above all by the deficiencies of skill, education, and motivation of the unemployed themselves. Indeed, Kennedy's single deliberate concession to the aggregate-demand school was the investment tax credit (the first of several tax benefits offered by Kennedy and Johnson). In effect, this tax credit amounted to a 7 per cent reduction in the price of all the machines, tools, equipment, and factory structures which business decided to purchase. In Keynesian theory, a stimulant to investment is twice blessed, since it increases national income immediately by the amount of the new investment and, through the "multiplier" impact of the investment, also enlarges personal income and personal consumption by a still greater amount. Such was the oddity of the political climate in 1961 that the business community had to be argued into accepting a measure so obviously beneficial to investment and profit.

The sensible, modest, tentative initial steps toward a coherent economic policy for a changing industrial society which Kennedy sought and received from Congress were all too evidently no more than that—sensible, modest, and tentative. To be sure, the economy did begin to expand in 1961, but it was an exceedingly dilatory expansion, so majestic in its pace as to hold out very little hope of reaching the so-called interim unemployment target of 4 per cent in Kennedy's first term. In fact, it was not until the very end of 1965 that this figure—itself far from a condition of full employment—was finally recorded.

The economy's unsatisfactory response to 1961 policies combined with Walter Heller's and Paul Samuelson's patient tuition to persuade Kennedy that the time had come to try other, bolder devices. In 1962 and 1963, the choice lay between a dramatic rise in public spending on the order of $10 billion and a tax cut of the same size. The first alternative included a social bonus: an increase in the importance of the public sector. The second contained a political bonus: the support, in Congress and out, of everyone who wanted to enlarge the sphere of private choice.

Although Kennedy plumped for a major tax reduction as the centerpiece of his 1963 program, it was not until February 1964 that Congress enacted the measure. As a way of stimulating the economy, there is no question that the Tax Act of 1964 has been a success. Its effects began to be felt from the moment the proposal was introduced in January 1963, as businessmen and consumers made an upward revision in their expectations of income, sales, and profits. The economic expansion begun in 1961 and accelerated in 1963 still continues, and provides as vivid a testimonial as one could wish to the efficacy of Keynesian public finance.

Thus, we are brought to our current situation. During the year or so of the deliberations of the Commission on Technology, Automation, and Economic Progress, unemployment has steadily declined. The decline—and still more the likelihood of a further drop in 1966—explains an important feature of the Report: the fact that it begins as an investigation of unemployment and ends as a major essay on social policy.

II

One of the virtues of the Report is a well-argued resolution of the automation controversy. As the Commission interprets present rates of productivity change, the United States is not trembling on the "verge of a glut of productivity sufficient to make our economic institutions and the notion of gainful employment obsolete"—the central claim of the Triple Revolutionaries. Nevertheless, "the pace of technological change has increased in recent decades, and may increase in the future, but a sharp break in the continuity of technical progress has not occurred, nor is it likely to occur in the next decade." To this conclusion is attached an important qualification. The present acceleration in annual per capita productivity gains (excluding agriculture) from 2.0 per cent before World War II to 2.5 per cent since World War II, entails a doubling of total output in 28 years instead of in 36 years as in the past. The shortened time scale, judges the Report, "is quite enough to justify the feeling of continuous change that is so much a part of the contemporary environment." And, one might add, is a political fact of considerable significance.

All the Report's predictions are for the next decade only, but it is plain that the Commission is skeptical about the possibility that major technological novelties (either now in development or in earlier stages of evolution) will significantly alter present rates of technical change even beyond the next decade. Studies made for the Commission indicate that, in spite of an acceleration in the rate at which novelties are diffused, it still takes some fourteen years before inventions are translated into consumer or producer goods and a further 1-15 years before as many as half of the firms in an industry emulate the innovating leader. The inference drawn is this: "It seems safe to conclude that most major technological discoveries which will have a significant 181 economic impact within the next decade are already at least in an identifiable stage of commercial development."

On this critical issue the Commission's argument is convincing. The Report thus reinforces the confidence of most economists in the efficacy of federal stimulation of aggregate demand as the best way to reduce unemployment. Although 4 per cent is still a high rate of unemployment, it is a rate that compares favorably with the 5-7 per cent range of the 1950's and early 1960's. Moreover, unemployment in 1966 may well descend to 3 per cent—a figure which is very close to most definitions of full employment. During the last five years, "automation" has indeed displaced workers, and quite probably at the 20,000-per-week clip so often cited in alarm, but most of those displaced have secured other jobs. The Commission has a point when it says that "the basic fact is that technology eliminates jobs, not work," at least when sensible public policy directs itself to the maintenance of high levels of aggregate demand.

This out of the way, the Report turns to the issues involved in managing social and economic policy in such a manner as to make full use of gains in productivity and full provision for a decent existence for all members of the community. What the Commission recommends to start with is familiar enough to readers of Kennedy-Johnson messages to Congress and the *Economic Reports* of the Council of Economic Advisers. Above all, it is essential that budgetary and interest-rate policy be directed toward the support at high levels of the total spending of consumers, businessmen, and public bodies. In a glancing reference to current discussions, the Commission affirms its disbelief in the idea that the "toleration of unnecessary unemployment is an acceptable way to relieve inflationary pressure." In a time of incipient inflationary pressure, what is appropriate instead is an intensification of efforts to retrain displaced workers, upgrade the semi-literate, encourage the shift of workers from less productive to more productive occupations—in short, a commitment to those elements of manpower policy which have already demonstrated their worth even according to the newly-fashionable criteria of cost-benefit analysis. "Manpower policy," the Commission assures us, "is triply productive as it enriches the prospects of the disadvantaged, adds to the productive capacity of the nation, and helps relieve inflationary pressures.

As the Commission sees it, a sensible, enlightened manpower policy would facilitate desirable shifts in the occupational and the geographic job structure—movements from farms to cities, South to North, blue-collar to white-collar production of goods to production of services. It would meet the special national obligation to diminish the dangerously high rate of unemployment among the young. It would undertake a serious national mission to tackle Negro unemployment. Here the Commission makes one projection which deserves wide attention: "If non-whites continue to hold the same proportion of jobs in each oc-

182

cupation as in 1964, the non-white unemployment rate in 1975 will be more than five times that for the labor force as a whole." The moral could not be plainer: ". . . non-whites must gain access to the rapidly-growing higher skilled and white-collar occupations at a faster rate than in the past eight years if their unemployment rate is to be brought down to the common level." This is possible in a buoyant economy, but only if manpower measures do their job, as an indispensable supplement to aggregate measures.

All this is forthcoming and convincing, but still little more than an expression of the conventional wisdom of the 1960's, a brew which even though infinitely preferable to the insipid beverages of the Eisenhower era, is still rather low-proof. But the Report does pass beyond these fiscal, monetary, and manpower recommendations in its advocacy of two major new policies. The first emerges from the recognition that there are some people whose skills and aptitudes are simply insufficient, even after training, to enable them to compete successfully in contemporary labor markets even when these markets operate within a prosperous economy. For such unfortunates, the Commission quietly proposes that the federal government turn itself into an employer of last resort. A striking set of numbers estimates the jobs which need to be filled in order to bring public services up to *present* levels of acceptable operation. Here are the Commission's estimates:

Potential Sources of New Jobs
through Public Service Employment

Source of Employment	Job Potential
Medical institutions & health services	1,200,000
Educational institutions	1,100,000
National beautification	1,300,000
Welfare and home care	700,000
Public protection	350,000
Urban renewal and sanitation	650,000
Total	5,300,000

For the most part, these are jobs which require the simplest variety of manual skill. They are the custodial, personal-service, and public-improvement jobs, the scamping of which in our society has much to do with the filth of the cities, the inhumanity of the hospitals, the limited hours during which museums are open, and the lack of amenity that characterizes our public places. There is a refreshing simplicity in the combination of unfilled national needs and unwanted human beings. With admirable aplomb, the Commission suggests an initial appropriation of $2-billion, enough to support possibly 500,000 additional full-time jobs.

There is a group still more unfortunate than the candidates for public-service employment. Of the 20 million people who in the fiscal year 1964-65 received $28 billion in welfare benefits, perhaps half subsist below the poverty line. They include the widowed, the disabled, the elderly, the totally incapacitated. For the genuinely needy, our welfare arrangements are woefully inadequate. As Nathan Glazer has recently emphasized, insofar as the assault on poverty is intended to raise incomes, it is in large part misdirected. We could drastically reduce the number of individuals who fall below the poverty line simply by reconstructing and enlarging our welfare benefits.

For some of the unemployed, there is at least the hope of a job sometimes. But consider the size of the average payment per person under the aid to dependent children program (ADC): it is $34 per month. As the Report summarizes the entire welfare situation: "Less than one-quarter of the 35 million people now living in poverty receive any type of public assistance payment and less than one-third of the 15 million children living in poverty benefit from public assistance." Such as it is, all assistance is administered under the most humiliating conditions, complete with means tests, detailed regulations, invasions of privacy, and incessant surveillance. The social workers, who in a more rational society might assist their clients, instead spend the bulk of their time checking up on them and filling out the endless forms which are the testimonials to their diligence, if not the mark of their own servitude.

To its great credit, the Commission proposes *not* a patching of the system alone but a negative income tax, whereby those whose income falls below a certain level would receive supplementary payments from the government. The tax is not designed as a substitute for all social-welfare programs—as Professor Milton Friedman, one of the tax's proponents, hopes—but as a valuable income supplement to the rehabilitation and sympathetic support of a better social-welfare program. For a mere $5-8 billion, it is possible to go 50 per cent of the way toward the elimination of poverty-level incomes. Employing existing income-tax mechanisms, it is easy to adjust rates for negative as well as positive returns. The Commission proposal is coupled with a useful note of amplification from the labor members: federal standards should be established to prevent the more ungenerous states from seizing the opportunity to reduce their already exiguous welfare payments.

For accepting unrhetorically in a matter-of-fact manner both income maintenance and expanded government employment, the Commission deserves the very highest praise. In particular, the negative income tax, promoted by this Report and aided by the unusual concurrence (for different reasons) of liberal economists like James Tobin and conservative economists like Milton Friedman, may stand a real chance of enactment within the next five or ten years, particularly if the Vietnam war contracts in scale. At the least, the Commission has 184 set in motion two proposals which not so very long ago had a most radical aspect to them. If it helps achieve public familiarity and then public acceptance of these proposals, the Report will deserve an honorable place as an important document of American social progress.

After saying this much, is there any reason to do other than dismiss the members of the Commission with thanks for a job far better performed than one could reasonably have anticipated of a semi-public body representing diverse interests? The answer, I think, is yes, and I shall devote the remainder of this essay to saying why.

The Report's shortcomings are closely related to its objectives, and these in turn are *not* comprehended by the fiscal, monetary, manpower, welfare, and income-maintenance programs which I have already discussed. There is no question that a society which pursued these policies and adopted these programs would be a considerably more humane society than the United States in 1966; oddly enough, it would also be a much more efficient society. Nevertheless, the thrust of the Commission's argument stretches far beyond a mere transformation of existing economic policy and social care. In the Commission's words and italics, ". . . we are being asked, *what can our society have, how can it get what it wants?* In short, we are being asked to deal with the quality of human life in the years ahead." It is according to the adequacy of the Commission's answers to its own questions that one can appropriately evaluate its work.

The Report approaches the issue of the shape of a better society in a special manner, by asking whether any means are available to us for identifying human and community needs. To this question, the Reports returns a negative answer. We lack the rational mechanisms we require to tell us what is wrong with ourselves. Social policy is generally made "piecemeal." It is distorted by "vested interests" which often use their power to "obtain unjust shares." There are at hand "few mechanisms" of the kind which are necessary "to see the range of alternatives and thus enable us to choose with a comprehension of the consequences of our choice."

If we accept the Commission's reasoning, much of the explanation for the critical weaknesses of our social decisions is to be found in the division of economic goods between public and private production. For the latter, free markets are the means by which preference scales are organized. Where competition is even reasonably effective, producers who sense the tastes and inclinations of their customers flourish; those who do not, falter and fail. Thus the pattern of output corresponds broadly to the preferences of individual consumers. Not so with public goods. For "we cannot individually buy in the market-place our share of unpolluted air," or, for that matter, our share of national defense or space exploration. If we limited higher education to those families able to purchase it for their children, we should frustrate the talents of many young people and deny the fruits of these talents to the community. Hence nobody would apply unqualified market tests to government output. Nevertheless, public production requires some acceptable justification, and it is a deficiency of our society that we lack "an effective social calculus to give us true valuations of the entire costs and benefits of individual and social purchases." So long as we lack the calculus, we cannot tell with any assurance just what the optimum combination of private consumption and public services is.

It is possible to quarrel with the Report's statement of the condition. As economists have known for a long time, private production often entails some unregistered costs. For example, Consolidated Edison's pollution of the metropolitan air raises expenditures for window cleaning, building rehabilitation, dry cleaning, medical attendance, and hospital care: in short, electrical energy costs more than the bill from the utility declares it does. And there are people who seriously question the efficiency of a private sector in which oligopoly, monopoly, and the conscientious distortion of consumer tastes by advertising are so prominent. To be really certain of the rational consequences of private markets, we should fragmentize giant corporations, ban advertising, and destroy trade unions—not a program for tomorrow.

However, for purposes of orderly exposition, let us accept the Commission's position and see where we are taken next. The Commission wants above all to improve the rationality of public choice and public expenditure. With that goal in mind, it makes three suggestions. The first is research into community needs: "For example, a research effort which resulted in a new, integrated concept of water supply, desalination, and waste disposal might prompt political action, just as the potential space and rocketry research resulted in the decision to embark on the man-to-the-moon project." (In America, the Commission seems to say, what *can* be done, soon gets done.) A second suggestion goes to the heart of the problem of estimating costs. "Efforts should be made to improve our capability to recognize and evaluate social costs and social benefits more adequately and to supply better information to the public and to political leaders on cost-benefit relationships." Finally, the Report, in an ominous throwback to the Eisenhower Commission on National Goals, recommends a commission "of high prestige and distinction which would engage in the study of national goals and in the evaluation of our national performance in relation to such goals."

On the issues raised by these proposals, the Report has much to say that is interesting and a good deal that is novel. Thus, in a discussion of health care, the Commission sees possibilities in automated multiphasic screens, diagnosing the condition of hundreds of patients each hour, and in regional health computer centers capable of storing the medical histories of 12-20 million persons; it also advances more conventional proposals for expanded training of doctors, nurses, and ancillary personnel. When it approaches the massive difficulties of creating an attractive urban environment out of our traffic-dogged, dirt-covered, and slum-defaced cities, the Commission concentrates on transportation, air and water pollution, and housing. It is convinced that federal support of a "systems research program directed toward particular multi-state regions" holds the largest promise of success. Since information about the causes of air and water pollution, and particularly about the costs of its control and prevention, is comparatively meager, the Commission is led to "urge an enlargement of current research," and more quickly a fee system designed to promote the construction of waste-disposal systems and the federal creation of river-basin authorities on a regional basis.

As for housing, the Commission regards it as the most recalcitrant of urban problems, the most antique in its techniques, the most afflicted by racial prejudice (both in construction and sale), and the most corrupted by special alliances (of contractors, unions, and politicians). Even more than usual, the Report relies here on federal action as the catalyst. The role of the federal government is crucial as the patron of basic research, the market for experimental housing, the standard-setter in its own housing programs, the leader in the modernization of obsolete building codes, and the natural promoter of a new industry centered upon mass-production techniques and massive urban reconstruction.

We have, says the Commission, the technology to do almost anything we collectively decide we want to do to improve the quality of our common environment. We simply lack the knowledge about how best to apply the technology. In social affairs, as in rocketry and military weapons systems, knowledge leads to action, even if sometimes a technology-infatuated culture does not pause to ask the consequences of the action. But just as Robert McNamara has used cost effectiveness and program budgets to rationalize the $50-60 billion which the Department of Defense annually expends, we can apply cost-benefit and systems-analysis to the programming of social spending.

As a proposition, this is exceedingly seductive. It amounts to a recipe for cool research rather than hot politics, orderly university training rather than untidy street demonstrations, and the forging of a consensus out of rational thought rather than out of conflicts of ideologies and interests. Even if the picture misrepresents reality, one would like to believe that its central premise can be turned into a creative social myth of the sort which persuades people to behave in new ways.

This is why it is a pity that so little in our recent experience or   187 our immediate prospects lends plausibility to such a vision of orderly social change. As it happens, our technology has been quite adequate for a long time to achieve certain social goals—and without any help from systems analysis. We do not need systems analysis to send larger checks to welfare clients; nor are there any technical obstacles in the way of liberalizing training allowances, educational grants to the talented sons and daughters of poor families, and unemployment compensation payments. No advance in cost-benefit analysis is required to extend the protection of workmen's compensation, unemployment insurance, and old-age benefits to migrant farm laborers. Or, to return to the shortage of health facilities: granted that computer diagnosis and sophisticated computer retrieval methods can generate vast economies in medical care, these potential gains still do not explain why in 1966 we have too few doctors. After all, we know how to train them; it is a profession endowed with high prestige: why then don't youngsters flock into medical schools, some years later to staff hospitals now largely served by foreign interns and residents? Everybody knows the familiar answers—the trade-union attitudes of the American Medical Association, the vast cost of training facilities, and the inadequate scholarship aid available for medical students. What impedes expansion is existing institutional interests and existing inequities of income distribution.

A similar observation applies to urban slums. The disgrace of their existence will persist even if building technology is modernized, craft-union sabotage defeated, and ancient building codes discarded. Given the racial prejudice which has prevented public construction of low-income housing in the suburbs and which has confined growing numbers of Negroes and Puerto Ricans to central city ghettos, not even six thousand computers deployed in serried array can bring decent housing to minorities.

What these comments imply about the Commission's approach to social change is simple enough. Change takes place either when the interests of politically potent groups are allied to change, or when such groups accept change in preference to riot and revolt. In the 1960's, the triumph of Keynesian public finance was the consequence of the belated perception by a not-very-bright business community of the benefits that government-supported prosperity offered the businessman in his search for sales and profits. Support for federal aid to higher education grew with the ascent of college tuition charges. The conservative middle classes saw their interest in higher quality education only when its costs hit them personally.

Thus, it is quite possible that in the next decade there will be general public support for federal auto-safety standards, meaningful control of pesticides, and genuine assaults upon water and air pollution. These are environmental hazards which afflict everybody. It is here, no doubt, that systems analysis, computer science, and cost-   188 benefit analysis stand their best chance of influencing events. But it should be plain that not all the measures which the Commission supports coincide so obviously with the interests of the large prosperous majority of Americans whose incomes place them far above the poverty line and whose skin color protects them against the continuing discriminations which their less fortunately pigmented fellow-citizens continue to encounter.

The most massive evidence of the familiar human reluctance to set the public good above personal advantage is the obvious national preference in 1963, 1964, and 1965 for general tax reductions over large social-welfare expenditures. In the last five years, federal taxes have been slashed something like $20 billion. This sum, available each year, could easily have paid for the $2 billion public-employment program the Commission recommends, and a generous negative income tax into the bargain. The tax-cut choice had very little to do with social valuations and a great deal to do with the political force and influence of the businessmen and middle- and upper-income families —who derived the bulk of the gains—as against the relative lack of such force and influence among the poor and the unemployed—who benefited only slightly from the successive tax slashes.

The remedies of poverty, like its causes, are in substantial degree political and not technical. Public transportation is more likely to become available in Watts because of last year's riots than because of the generalized good will—a chancy emotion—of more affluent Californians. Negro schools in the South will be integrated more rapidly as Negroes become a political force to be reckoned with. As Saul Alinsky has repeatedly demonstrated, militancy on the part of the poor improves garbage collection, housing inspection, school services, even police manners. It is no accident that the Community Action Program of the War on Poverty has run into so much trouble. The dimmest mayor realizes that when the poor organize they are bound to ask for a great many inconvenient things.

It does not detract from the general intellectual value of systems and cost-benefit analysis to point out that political pressures and political choices will determine the sphere of application of the techniques. Indeed, even when these instruments of rational choice are employed, we should be wary of the results. Cost-benefit analysis can help compare the relative virtues of various job-training programs, various approaches to pollution control, or even various ways of expanding the supply of low-cost housing. But cost-benefit analysis is most unlikely to demonstrate persuasively that it is better to raise taxes than to reduce social-welfare expenditures (one of 1966's possible issues), and it is even less likely to explain just how to distribute the pains of tax increases or the pleasures of tax cuts. One wonders just how useful to Mayor Lindsay a cost-benefit 189 analysis of commuter payments and receipts would be. Would the triumphant conclusion that the commuters are paying less than their fair share toward city services (which everybody knows anyway) really persuade them to accept a city income tax with good grace? It is not cynical to conclude that they would continue to resist such a tax to the full extent of their political power and personal influence.

Thus at its center, the Report is flawed. Implicitly, its authors assume a basic harmony of interests among the major orders of American society. We know that this harmony has severe limits which are defined by self- and group-interest. The Report evinces a lingering confidence in the appeal to authority, here personified by "some national body of distinguished private citizens representing diverse interests and constituencies and devoted to a continuing discussion of national goals." From such a body, the Commission expects a "monitoring" of social change, an identification of "possible social trends," and a suggestion of "policy alternatives to deal with them." What it is likely to receive are either the windy platitudes of Eisenhower study groups or a series of minority reports.

Worst of all is the Commission's excessive dependence upon technique and method as the solvents of social change. Here, it seems to me, the Commission has things the wrong way around: it is not so much that social needs can be fulfilled when the technical prerequisites to their fulfillment are present; it is rather that urgently-enough felt social needs will produce the technical tools required to relieve them. This is the lesson of military technology. The commitment to social change precedes the methods by which change can be rationally evaluated; it does not follow them.

In sum, this Report deserves general gratitude and respect for what it has recommended and for the platitudes it has refrained from emitting. One hopes that it will be widely read and discussed. Its very merits entitle it to criticism for its neglect of the politics of social change, and for the optimism which leads to the hope that important social changes can be the result of amicable discussion and intelligent measurement. Even in America, even in the 1960's, significant alteration in the way we conduct our lives seems mainly to come about through social and political conflict, extra-legal action, riots in the streets, and the death of martyrs.

Donald N. Michael

Some Speculations on the Social Impact of Technology

I want to draw your attention to what I think are the important aspects of the social impact of technology that we have so far ignored or attended to only in passing. I do not intend to convince anyone of anything: I am not sure what the questions are in this area—much less what the answers might be. Rather, I want to sketch a variety of perspectives and circumstances that I think merit attention, so that you may determine whether or not these are significant issues for scholars and actionists concerned with the impact of technology on society on more than an occasional basis. These are issues that we ought to be concerned with at least as much as we have been with productivity, investment policies, employment, and so on.

Let me begin by making clear that I am not asserting that technology is a villain, or that technology is a saviour. The problem is not that simple. The positive and negative interplay between technology and social processes is much too complicated to comprehend if only one aspect, technology, rather than technology in the context of society as a whole is dealt with. In no sense am I insensitive to or unappreciative of the great opportunities implicit in technology, particularly in the new technologies. Nor may the odds on adverse consequences from these technologies be any higher than on favorable ones. But I believe that the consequences themselves, favorable or unfavorable, are of such magnitude that if they are negative, they will bring upon us much more serious trouble than we would have had in the past, in simpler days, when technologies had fewer derivative implications,

Reprinted by permission of the publisher from D. Morse and A. Warner (eds.), *Technical Innovations in Society* (Columbia University Press, 1966) pp. 118–154. Donald Michael is Program Director of the Center for Research on Utilization of Scientific Knowledge at the University of Michigan.

and affected fewer people in a smaller area over a longer period of time. Let me also make clear that I do not believe that the solutions to the problems we will discuss are to be found, by and large, in a moratorium on technological development. Such is the social environment technology has already produced that, unless we are to change our value system and way of life totally, we must use more technology to make an adequate environment out of the circumstances technology has already brought about. I fully expect the technologies to help deal with the problems the technologies produce. I also fully expect that unless we take a larger and deeper view of the social implications of technology than we have so far, we will not use our technologies or other resources sufficiently to protect us from the enormous potential for social disruption and disaster implicit in these technologies. Hence, I am going to emphasize aspects of the social impact of technology that I believe present problems which must be solved if we are to enjoy the advantages the technologies can provide. I think we can expect in our type of society, and in a society as rich as ours, that the opportunities will take care of themselves. Put another way, the opportunities do not need to be optimized, but the dangers, I think, must be minimized.

Sketchy and impressionistic as these observations will be, I have tried to organize them into three general categories. First I shall make some observations on the general considerations that should be applied to any estimate of the present and contemplated social impact of technology. Then, I want to mention three technologies which I expect will have a wide social impact in the next two decades or so, and which by their characteristics imply a far broader range of social impact than we have felt so far, certainly than we have studied so far. And finally, I will set out some examples of aspects of social impact that should be studied intensively now, if we are to be prepared to use the results of such studies for guiding the felicitous integration of technology and society in the years ahead.

Let me say something else by way of introduction. In many ways I will be implying that the methods and knowledge of our various disciplines are inadequate or nonexistent and, therefore, cannot help us understand what is happening to society vis-à-vis technology. I hope I will be able to imply convincingly that many, probably most, of what may be the significant issues are *not* being explored effectively and on a scale and with the attention they deserve. If I "get to you" I will thereby, inevitably, threaten our various senses of self and status and purpose; I will question who we are, what we do, why we are what we are, and how important we are to ourselves and to others.

There are typical ways to defend oneself against such threats: by "not hearing" or misunderstanding the speaker's choice of points of emphasis and context of qualifying remarks; by translating and transforming what he emphasizes into a problem or a syntax with which the auditor is comfortable and familiar, thereby shifting the plane of discourse; by attending to the speaker's mood rather than to what he says, and so on. Inevitably, these defenses will operate here just as they do throughout the community of persons and institutions whose favored perspectives and, thereby, senses of self, are challenged by the interplay of technology and society which makes obsolete or inadequate the conventional techniques for perceiving the society and dealing with it. Indeed, this type of threat to self and these responses to it, produced by a changed and changing world, conveyed from one person to another through the different perspectives of those involved, are in themselves important social impacts of technology about which we know too little, and which we need to understand much better.

With this forewarning, let me now turn to some general considerations on understanding the relationship between technology and society, which I think are too seldom appreciated or made central to the context when specific issues are explored.

1. It is important to remember that some of the significant impacts of technology derive from the accumulated effects of technological changes that have been under way for some time. Let me remind you of three examples: the population explosion, a direct product of medical technology initiated some years ago; the urban chaos that has been fundamentally exacerbated by transportation technology in the form of the private car; and the distortion and disruption of ecology in local areas and, probably, in much larger areas by the wholesale application of pesticides and fungicides, to say nothing of the continental pollution of the ecology by the waste products of many technologies. In the future some of these accumulated consequences will become more emphatic and complex, when the new technologies contribute their consequences too. The technologies we have to be concerned with thus include some older ones as well as the new ones. This is important: we do not have to wait for the new technologies in order to improve our concepts and methods for understanding their impact. All we have to do is recognize our ignorance and indifference regarding the present social impact—and do something about it.

2. A major purpose of our preoccupation with technology and social change is to prepare for the future. But doing so is going to be very difficult. There are some social consequences of technology for which we should have begun to prepare yesterday. For example, the type of education appropriate for a rapidly changing work force and for substantial increases in leisure probably requires fundamentally different attitudes and approaches by the teachers in primary and secondary schools than the present ones. But recruiting the teachers and teaching the teachers requires changes at least in the schools of   193

education and in teachers colleges, and all such sequential changes take time to introduce. The upshot is that most of those teaching today's youngsters and imbuing them with the values and attitudes they will carry into their lives tomorrow are probably conveying the wrong things, because the teachers were wrongly trained and perhaps, in part, wrongly selected. Similarly, problem-solving investigations in the area of urban affairs must be undertaken long in advance of the actual reconstruction and reorganization of our cities. The riots in Los Angeles and the water shortage in New York may be mild precursors of the potential disasters that may otherwise overtake us.

In general, we do not understand and appreciate, and thereby tend to overlook, the nature of the time lag between recognition of a problem and the development of techniques for dealing with it.

We do not allow for—often we do not know how to allow for—the needed intervening period to accumulate knowledge and understanding. I suspect that over the next couple of decades or so, this gap between problem recognition and the development of solutions, or approximate solutions, is going to become increasingly serious: problems will confront us before we are able to deal with them knowledgeably. The integration of technology with other social processes and the felicitous sequencing of contingent social actions to accomplish the integration is going to be much more difficult than it has been in the past.

3. Value conflicts, and tensions between generations will very likely increase, especially between the new generation that is moving into political and professional power and is using new types of operational and substantive expertise, and the older generations already occupying the field. These conflicts and their various expressions in differing values and operating techniques will mean that both the pressures and the innibitions to make the kind of social and technological changes that we are going to need are certain to be very great. As the distinguished public servant, systems theorist, and student of decision processes, Sir Geoffrey Vickers, puts it:

> In the transitional period from the conditions of free fall to those of regulation (at whatsoever level), political and social life is bound, I think, to become much more collectivist or much more anarchic or—almost certainly—both. Communities national, subnational and even supranational will become more closely knit insofar as they can handle the political social and psychological problems involved and more violent in their mutual rejections insofar as they cannot. The loyalties we accept will impose wider obligations and more comprehensive acceptance. The loyalties we reject will separate us by wider gulfs from those who accept them and will involve us in fiercer and more unqualified struggles.[1]

[1]"The End of Free Fall," p. 21. Mimeographed article (Fall, 1964).

What the resolution or stalemate will be between the old and new approaches to the uses of knowledge and power via technology remains to be seen, but an understanding of this conflict in approaches will be prerequisite to an understanding of the social impact of technology.

4. Under what circumstances does an issue become significant or critical? What determines when small percents, such as the unemployment rate for example, become sufficiently large in absolute numbers to become a major issue? When does indifference become transformed into action, as for example, in the poverty program? When does the ability to extrapolate trends begin to carry real significance in terms of program implementation, as, for example, in the moon program, where the ability to use computer technology to predict whether we could succeed was an important factor in the decision to go ahead.

Understanding the general principles of when, or how, or why issues become important and become recognized as issues, would be essential for estimating the seriousness of or coping with, among other things, the gap between posing a problem about and finding a solution to an impact of technology on society.

5. Often interpretations of the past are called upon to help interpret the present and to suggest solutions to expected problems in the future. By and large I think these interpretations have been inadequate. First of all, there is often only a surface similarity: the presumed analogy is based on a partial or on a misunderstood picture of the past. A prime example of this is the frequent submission of the Periclean age of Greece as evidence of what our future leisure patterns should or could be. That the "leisured" society of Greece numbered only in the tens of thousands, that it spent much of its time warring or doing those political tasks we have professionalized, that no women were involved, that the system lasted only a couple of generations and then decayed, all such considerations are left out of the supposed apt and happy analogy.

Or consider the argument that since we mastered the first Industrial Revolution, we will not have any enduring trouble with the second industrial revolution that the new technologies represent. But we have not mastered the first Industrial Revolution. Let me mention three social consequences of the first Industrial Revolution that are increasingly acute. While other factors have contributed to them and while in some form or another they may have existed previous to the first Industrial Revolution, undoubtedly our inability to deal with the consequences of that revolution have enormously exacerbated these conditions. The first is the increasing gap between the developed nations and the have-not nations that was widened by the technological prowess of the developed nations, and by their inability to share their technology with the underdeveloped nations. The second example is the persistence—the growth, in some cases—of slums and poverty. This peculiar type of degrading, enclaved existence was the direct result of the first Industrial Revolution's concentration of factory technology, and the resulting transfer of manpower from the farms to the factories. The third example is the alienation from and breakdown of earlier, more stable, systems of value and faith. There are very few students of this problem who feel that the Industrial Revolution has not contributed enormously to the complexity and persistence of the problem.

Another inadequacy in appealing to the past is that even if there is more than a surface similarity in the particular social processes involved, there usually are differences in the surrounding social or physical circumstances, which imply very different consequences than those occurring in the past. Two very important examples of such differences are worth mentioning.

First, never before in history has any nation had such a complex technology combined with a population as large as that of the U.S., now and as it will be—230 million around 1975, 250 million around 1980. Those who assert that because thus and such a technological consequence was coped with in the past, or that a specific social consequence is not new and neither, by implication, are its future consequences, have to consider whether the multiple social and physical consequences of a population of such huge size carry significantly different implications for the future.

The second difference, which we tend to overlook, is that today there very probably are different expectations than there were in the past of what the implications of technology on society will be. Because people are different today, they expect different things to happen to them as a result of technology than people did in the past. It does not help to say, "Their beliefs do not really jibe with the facts." (Especially since we probably do not know the facts). If they think, for example, that technological change is galloping along at a rate never before equalled, then this results in various reactions by business executives, scientists, pundits, and government officials—to say nothing of the man in the street. These reactions, very likely, are significantly different from those in the past, when this kind of issue did not cross most people's minds. For example, I strongly suspect (but we have not bothered to find out) that a recent major social consequence of the interaction of several technologies is that more types of people are concerned about the future social impact of technology, and more different viewpoints have arisen regarding it, and that these in turn are initiating other social consequences.

Let me now turn to three technologies, biological technology, cybernation, and social engineering. I expect these will, over the next two decades, have very great implications for the nature of society and for the place of the individual in it. I want to emphasize those implications that go beyond those we have tended to preoccupy our-

196

selves with, not because I think they have been unimportant, but because I believe the ones I want to mention are equally important, perhaps more so. Let me again make clear that I recognize that many of the impacts will not be new in kind. However, I do believe that it is likely that the scale and scope, the potency, of their impact, as they interact with an already huge and enormously complex society will be of an unprecedented order of magnitude. In that potency of impact lie many exciting opportunities, and some very profound problems having to do with the place the individual has in a democratic society, and the way we conduct our lives. Again, I will emphasize problems not because I am certain that they will outrun the opportunities, but rather because I feel that if the problems are not dealt with effectively, the consequences may be so disastrous that we shall never enjoy the opportunities—at least not within the format of presently preferred values. (Of course, a different set of values may be all right or even better than the present ones. But what I want to emphasize is the kind of confrontations these technologies are to our present values, if only to indicate the necessity for understanding the social impact of technology better, so that we may invent or respond to a more appropriate set of values).

Perhaps the fundamental question that the potency of these technologies raises is how do we deliberately decide how we are going to balance the social costs and social benefits; obviously I mean infinitely more here than the dollar costs and benefits. I think we must do much more than hope for the best or retreat behind some inhuman "averaging out" philosophy. But what do we do if, as I believe they will, the consequences of these technologies will be upon us before we accumulate the understanding needed to establish such a balance—if we ever can accumulate such understanding?

In the application of biological technology—the engineering of man's biological self and his biological environment—we will face moral, ethical, psychological, and political issues, which will make those faced by the atomic scientists look like child's play. Biological and chemical warfare will very likely be used much more in local wars, even perhaps in the pacification activities of international police forces. But whether it is used to kill, hurt, nauseate, paralyze, cause hallucination, or to terrify military personnel and civilians, the systematic use of biological and chemical warfare will require the resolution of major moral and ethical problems—especially since the most likely victims will be nonwhites in Asia and Africa.

Psychopharmacology is another aspect of biological technology already beginning to confront us with interesting issues. What is to be the role of hallucinogenic chemicals in society? There are two schools of thought on this—even the theologians seem to have taken sides. One is that these chemicals represent sin and corruption; the other, that they are exciting means for enlarging emotional or aesthetic or re- 197 ligious experience. Moreover, new drugs will permit many people, who otherwise would be in mental institutions, to walk the streets and to engage in regular social activities. Questions arise about the "nature" of the individual. How do we judge the extent to which a person is "responsible" for himself in such circumstances? For, while the chemical affects the individual, the person is significant to himself and to society in his *social* context—at work, at home, at play. The consequences are social consequences. In deciding how to deal with such alterers of the ego and of experience (and consequently alterers of the personality after the experience), and in deciding how to deal with the "changed" human beings, we will have to face new questions such as, "Who am I?" "When am I who?" "Who are *they* in relation to me?"

As far as the hallucinogenic agents are concerned, how will we judge whether people, just because they want it, are entitled to a risky if richer emotional experience than that provided by their everyday life? Are these decisions to be left to the individual, like skiing or surfboarding, or will they need legal restrictions like homosexual liaisons or the present use of nonhabitforming marijuana? In general, will "multiple" personalities and increasing amounts of idiosyncratic behavior simply be absorbed into the already proliferating scale of novelties, sensations, and leisure-time pursuits, or will they have to be controlled to facilitate the functioning of a stable society? Whatever way is chosen, what are the ethical, legal, political, and psychological considerations needed to help us understand the implications of such altered egos and their control?

A related aspect of biological technology merits mention here: with the increasing dissemination of birth control information and technology, we can expect the pressures on the poor to limit family size to become greater. Though such pressure already exists, in the form of inadequate housing for large, poor families, the pressure may well become more explicit as the "excuses" for having large families inadvertently are eliminated by the pervasive availability of birth control methods. If our laws and ways of operating come to condone this invasion of the right of couples to choose the number of children they want, then a new ethical issue will arise and it will reverberate into other areas of private affairs, conduct, and choice.

A third area in biological technology has to do with organ transplants. Some top research people in this area are convinced that in a few years techniques will have improved substantially. The problem then arises, Who is entitled to what transplant under what criteria of priority? We will have to do better than "women and children first." This situation already exists on a tiny scale with regard to the use of scarce kidney-substitute machines. Difficult as the decisions are now, they will become more difficult and more socially consequential when more people compete for more organs. 198

Though it is unlikely that organ transplantation will be available to such an extent as to increase substantially the number of people who will live longer, it is likely that developments in the technology of preventing and treating malignant diseases, will mean that there will be still more older people in this society, which has not yet learned to deal humanely with the older population it now has. Thus, developments in biological technology, combined with those from cybernation, in particular, will add to the numbers and to the social problems of older people. The accumulated social impact on our political system, and thereby on our social priorities, will undoubtedly be substantial as the old become a larger proportion of the voting public. Here, too, our understanding of the situation is much too slight at present to give us the knowledge we need to plan effectively for this growing population.

Finally, there is the question of genetic engineering: the deliberate controlled alteration of human inheritance. Late in the next couple of decades, either the capability to do so will exist or almost certainly it will become clear that soon thereafter the capability will exist. Indeed, there are already expressions of exuberant optimism, as well as sober concern, about the possibilities this presents. The optimists, typically, are concerned with technological manipulation, pointing out that maybe we could give everybody an IQ of 140 and eliminate all inherited human "inadequacies." The concerned, typically, look at the looming social and ethical issues that arise from such actions. For example, what are the psychological and, therefore, social consequences of producing a generation of adults who, as youngsters, shared little with their parents because their IQs were so much higher? And who is to decide when an inherited "inadequacy" is one that should be eliminated by genetic engineering? Who will decide where the line is to be drawn on the definition of "inadequacy"? Fundamentally, who will make what decisions about which human beings are to be changed before they are born, and in what way? Or, for that matter, who will determine that we will not use the technology wtih its implicit potentialities for improving the race?

Cybernation—the application of automation to material processes and the application of computers to symbols—is the second technology I want to mention. I shall not dwell on the usual questions about cybernation's impact on employment: they have been discussed amply enough to demonstrate our awareness of the matter as a social impact —even if we are unclear on what the impact is, much less what it will be. (Indeed, I suspect we put so much of our emphasis on the employment effects of cybernation simply because, having some figures and concepts available, it is psychologically more comfortable to emphasize this narrow aspect of the issue than to struggle with the clear evidence of our wider ignorance.) However, two aspects of cybernation's effects on employment should be mentioned here to broaden the picture.

Substantial numbers of the relatively skilled, including the middle-level manager and the middle-level engineer, are going to be displaced; *Business Week, Newsweek,* and *Time* a little late—acknowledge this.[2] The competences that have made these people economically valuable in the past will increasingly be made obsolete, either because cybernation, particularly computers, can do the job better, or because the process of rationalizing the overall activity in which they were involved will eliminate, or substantially reduce, the need for humans to do the tasks. Here we have members of a career-oriented, affluent segment of society, who were brought up to believe they possessed all the credentials for a lifetime of advancement, now forced to find another job, or to go back to school and learn something new. They are now perpetually under the threat of being displaced by younger men and by more sophisticated machines. Many of these people are already anxious and insecure personalities—as well as substantially in debt. It is likely, then, that they and their families will suffer considerable disruption as they revise their images of themselves; who they are, what they might become, and how others see them. What will happen to these ex-cynosures, to their aspirations, and to their way of living? And what political action will they take in response to the threats to their status and security?

There is another economic and emotional problem that cybernation's impact on employment level and employment changes will pose: What is to be the future of unskilled women in the work force? In the work force, of which one-third are women, about eighty percent are no more than semiskilled; many of them do the clerical and routine service jobs, which cybernation will replace as its application is accelerated by the increasing size of organizations responding to the increasing population. Now, about sixty percent of the $9,000 to $15,000 a year incomes in this country are those of families in which both spouses work. If the unskilled women lose their jobs, there will be less family income, less consumption. And there is also the question of psychic income; many women work for other reasons than to earn money. What will provide this psychic income?

Doubtless, many jobs could be invented, particularly in the human services area, which trained women could fill and which, because of the interpersonal nature of the task, no machine could do. As it now stands, however, and the poverty program demonstrates this, we are neither seriously inventing these jobs nor making the elaborate effort needed to motivate young women so that we can retrain them,

[2]"Computers: How they're Remaking Companies," *Business Week* (Feb. 29, 1964); "The Challenge of Automation," *Newsweek* (Jan. 25, 1965); "The Cybernated Generation," *Time* (April 2, 1965).

and older women, for such jobs. It is likely that this problem will be upon us before techniques for job-producing, motivating, recruiting, and training are sufficiently developed, in which case there will be serious social consequences. But if we do develop such techniques, society will become significantly different from today's, because the roles of so many women will be so different from what they traditionally have been.

This leads me to the third technology: social engineering. I yield to no one in my reservations about the ability of the behavioral sciences to deal with complex issues at the present time, but the evidence to date indicates that this situation will very likely change dramatically in the next two decades. The combination of large research funds and the computer provides the social scientist with both the incentive and the technique to do two things he has always needed to do and never been able to do in order to develop a deep understanding of and technology for the manipulation of social processes.

On the one hand, the computer provides the means for combining in complex models as many variables as the social scientist wants in order to simulate the behavior of men and institutions. In the past, the behavioral scientist simply could not deal with all the many important variables that would help him understand and predict human behavior. Now he can. (This is not to say that everything that is important about the human condition can be so formulated, but much that is important can be put in these terms; almost certainly enough to bring about substantial improvements in our ability to understand and predict behavior). And then the social scientist can test these models against conditions representing "real life." For, on the other hand, the computer has a unique capacity for collecting and processing enormous amounts of data about the state of individuals and of society today—not that of ten years ago. Thus, the behavioral scientist not only can know the state of society *now* as represented by these data, but he can use them to test and refine his theoretical models. The convergence of government programs and the computer is of critical importance; it will result in an efflorescence of longitudinal studies of individual and institutional change as functions of the changes in the social and physical environment. Such knowledge, now essentially nonexistent, will inevitably increase our ability to effect social change. And given the convergence of the powerful technologies and our already enormously complex and huge society, it would seem that social manipulation will be necessary if we are to introduce appropriate changes in society at the appropriate times. The problem, of course, is: Who is to decide who is to be manipulated and for what ends?

Let me now turn to some general questions regarding the social impact of technology—questions that to some extent refer to circumstances already with us, and which seem to me to be greatly in need of serious and extensive study. Let me hasten to add that I am certain that in many cases we do not at present know how to study these problems, but if we do not start now to try to invent means for doing so, we shall be in a far worse position when the time comes for us to understand these issues better. Again, the time-lag problem bedevils us.

What happens to the sense of self in a world of giant and pervasive man-made events, especially when, at the same time, we insist on emphasizing the autonomy of the individual? We talk about the importance of the individual and of the wealth of options this world offers him. Yet we have surrounded him with pollution, radiation, megalopolis, etc., which, though man-made, may appear to many people to be of such power and scale as to dominate them like "acts of God." How does a man see himself in relation to his espoused ideal of individual autonomy when he also sees other *men* and man-made circumstances, as awesome and implacable and often as impersonal as "acts of God," framing his destiny?

What kind of personalities live most fully in the midst of multiple and simultaneous change? Daniel Bell has pointed out that we are experiencing the end of the rational vision, that events today (and more so tomorrow) do not have simple cause-and-effect sequences, that, instead, events all happen at once and in circular and probabilistic ways.[3] What kind of person can live meaningfully in that type of world, and can keep in touch with it?

I suspect three kinds of responses will have increasing social implications as technology alters the scale of events that define the individual to himself—and thereby the ways in which he responds to the world.

One response is that of "selective involvement." People pick the issues and things they are going to respond to and be responsible about, and ignore the rest. We know people do this now, deliberately or, more often, unconsciously: there are limits to the amount of information humans can process in a given amount of time.

Therefore, it behooves us to examine carefully the degree of validity, as measured by actual behavior, of the statement that a benefit of technology will be to increase the number of options and alternatives the individual can choose from. In principle, it could; in fact, the individual may use any number of psychological devices to avoid the discomfort of information overload, and thereby keep the range of alternatives to which he responds much narrower than that which technology in principle makes available to him.

[3]Daniel Bell, "The Post-Industrial Society," in *Technology and Social Change*, ed. by Eli Ginzberg (New York: Columbia University Press, 1964), pp. 58–59.

Another type of response, now evident among returned Peace Corps volunteers, college students, and some executives, is withdrawal—pulling out of the big system, looking for environments in which one can have face-to-face relationships in a simple, less technologized more direct world.

A third response, protest, is exemplified by such things as the urban race riots and the Berkeley demonstrations. Here, the individual responds to overwhelming complexity by sidestepping the legal or ethical constraints that sustain or are at least associated with the complexity. (It is worth noting that a battle cry in the Berkeley protests was "Put your body where your punch card is!" It was one of the chief reasons for the sit-in in Sproul Hall). I suspect that these attempts, these experiments, to simplify an increasingly complex world will have very important social consequences, produced, in part, by a proliferating technology. If these responses are important in the future, we need to know much more about them, at least as responses to technology, than we do now.

Another way to look at the implications of technology for the individual is to consider the roles he plays. Two examples typify the unanswered and, for the most part, unstudied, questions in this area. The psychiatrist Robert Rieff has suggested that to the extent that tomorrow's society is service-oriented (material productivity becoming increasingly cybernated), many men will play roles which traditionally, in our society, have been women's roles, i.e., person-to-person helping roles. What, then, happens to the image and conduct of men? What happens to the relation between the sexes, as the hard-won pattern of women competing with men for "male" jobs is reversed and men begin to compete with women for "female" jobs?

A second role implication: as society puts more and more emphasis on rationalization, logic, science, and technology, and as our educational system reflects this emphasis from the lower grades on, what will be the role of the mother—the female—in preserving the ineffable, the intuitive, and the aesthetic in the basic learning experiences of the young? This, traditionally, has been what we expect of women, but traditionally we have deprecated those contributions, at least out of one side of our mouth. Will we come to appreciate this contribution more? Will we insist that women fulfill this role more effectively, or will we further deprecate its utility in a society oriented toward technology? And what effect will our choice have on our way of life and on societal goals?

The opportunities and problems that increased leisure—resulting from the increased productivity of the new technologies—provides, to help individuals find themselves or to extend the means by which they lose themselves, have been commented on extensively and, to my mind, unimaginatively and unperceptively. I will not explore 203 the issue here. A couple of observations, however, are in order.

An increasing number of theologians and religious denominations are becoming concerned with this problem. Their theologies assert that it is through work that man gains his salvation and fulfills himself. If work is to be a much less significant part of life for more people, what are the revisions in theology and the revisions in religious bureaucracies required to cope with this? On the other hand, the Protestant ethic, in its original form, may not be as pervasive as we have surmised, or at least its modes of implementation may be changing. Instead of leisure being a reward for hard work, we "travel first and pay later"—which may mean, of course, that work is now a "punishment" for taking the leisure first. Or, of course, it may mean that many people no longer need the justification of work in order to comfortably enjoy a vacation.

We can assume that leisure should have meaning in addition to that associated with recreation and hobbies, as is now taught. But it is hard to see how the state of mind required for this is to be conveyed to young people in an educational system stressing efficiency, and by adults who themselves are products of the Protestant ethic. Tranquility, contemplation, loafing, the cultivation of self, require a different school and different teachers. Just how real or serious would be the variety of social consequences implicit in these observations remains to be seen. Again we have not studied and again we have not tried to lay out the implications in a sufficiently elaborate social and technological context.

What *is* to be the relationship between the churches and an increasingly rationalized and technologized society? In a society preoccupied with dealing with the average, with the mass of the population, with grandiose schemes for remaking man and his environment (often accompanied by an arrogance indistinguishable from *hubris*), will it be the role of the churches to insist on another set of values for judging the direction and purpose of man, in order to protect the ideal of the individual and the validity of extralogical and transcendent motives and experiences? Here, indeed, a profound confrontation between two cultures *may* occur or, perhaps, one may absorb the other. Whatever the case may be, the consequences of the new technologies for the churches are bound to be great.

Consider the changing role of the scientist and the scientist-engineer. The symbiosis between science and technology has, as we all know, evolved into big science and big technology, and these two, in turn, are dependent on big money, which inevitably means big politics. The result, as a Report of the Committee on Science in the Promotion of Human Welfare of the American Association for the Advancement of Science argues, is that the integrity of science has been eroded and that in the absence of procedures (which have not been invented, much 204 less implemented) the erosion of the integrity of science will very likely increase in the future.[4] In part, this is because in the future still bigger technological investments in science and engineering will be needed. Hence, still more funds will have to be raised, and political methods will have to be used still more often to mediate between the needs of technology, the other needs of society, and the needs of competing groups within the science and engineering communities. Inevitably, there will be persistent, very likely increasing, confusion between the political and rhetorical validity and utility of scientific knowledge and its inherent scientific validity and utility. For not only will scientists and engineers turn to politics to get the technology they want in the first place, but they will use politics to praise, apologize for, or criticize the social consequences of that technology when they happen.

> [The] combination of esoteric knowledge and political power alters the function and character of the scientific elites. They no longer merely advise on the basis of expert knowledge, but they are also the champions of policies promoted with unrivaled authority and frequently determined by virtue of it. In the eyes of both of the political authorities and the public at large, the scientific elites appear as the guardians of the *arcana imperii,* the secret remedies for public ills.
>
> As the nature and importance of scientific knowledge transform the nature and functions of the scientific elites, the availability of democratic control becomes extinguished. Scientific knowledge is by its very nature esoteric knowledge; since it is inaccessible to the public at large, it is bound to be secret. The public finds itself in the same position vis-à-vis scientific advice as do the political authorities: unable to retrace the arguments underlying the scientific advice, it must take that advice on faith.[5]

The growing potency of social engineering will become a crucial ethical issue for the behavioral scientist. Whether he is working for the government, for business, for Madison Avenue, for the CIA, for the Poverty Program, or is doing basic research, the results of his work are going to be used to "guide," "stimulate," "motivate," and "manipulate" society. Again, it is the potency of the technology, its capacity to do wonderful good or monstrous evil, that will make the situation in the future different from the past.

This ethical problem: whether to assist in the growth of social engineering, is going to become ever more serious as the potency of

[4]*The Integrity of Science* (Washington, D.C., American Association for the Advancement of Science, 1964).

[5]Hans J. Morgenthau, "Modern Science and Political Power," *Columbia Law Review,* CLIV (1964), 1402.

social engineering increases. And right now we have no ethical or scientific models for dealing with this problem. One example of this dilemma: The Job Corps trainees will have very elaborate computerized reports prepared about them, to cover their whole social and psychological background, their experience in the Job Corps, and what happens to them for several years after they have left the Job Corps. The reason for these records is a very good one—they will improve the selection and training techniques. However, such a record also means that the Job Corps trainee will no longer have a private life: once recorded, his life history will always be available in this form. The dilemma that faces the social scientist is that on the one hand he needs this kind of information to improve the Job Corps, and that, on the other hand, so much personal information made available to as yet unspecified people, may completely undermine the conventional privilege and social advantages of privacy.

Underlying these issues is the profoundly important one: what are the implications, for the form and conduct of democratic political processes, of the complex social issues that technology generates and of the esoteric methods technology provides, for dealing with these complex issues? The increasing complexity of social problems and of the techniques for dealing with them will mean that the average well-educated person—to say nothing of the man in the street—will no longer be able to understand what the issues and the alternatives are.

This will be partly a matter of the complexity of the issues and of the technologies for defining, interpreting, planning for, and then dealing with, them. It will be partly a matter of the partial availability of knowledge. Often the issues will be politically sensitive and, as now, the interested parties will release only what they wish to release. Moreover, laymen able to use the knowledge, if they did have it, would need reasoning abilities which most people now lack. They would have to understand that the world picture is in most critical cases a statistical one, not black or white. These laymen would have to be comfortable dealing with multivariable problems operating in multiple feedback processes, where cause and effect are inextricably intermixed, and where it is often meaningless to try to differentiate one from the other. And they would have to be comfortable with making judgments based on a much longer time perspective than most people are used to now. They would have to be able to think ahead ten and twenty years, and make their judgments accordingly. These are not characteristics we are going to find in large numbers in our population: our educational system simply does not mass-produce such people—and evidently will not do so for some years to come. But if we are to operate a democracy, the need for such reasoning abilities will be upon us sooner than that. Indeed, it is already upon us. The political scientist and pundit, Joseph Kraft, recently observed:

206

To apply common sense to what is visible on the surface is to be almost always wrong; it produces about as good an idea of how the world goes around as that afforded by the Ptolemaic system. A true grasp of even the slightest transaction requires special knowledge and the ability to use abstractions which, like the Copernican system, are at odds with common-sense impressions. Without this kind of knowledge, it is difficult to know what to think about even such prominent matters as the United Nations financing problem, or the bombing of North Vietnam, or the farm program, or the federal Budget— which is one reason that most people don't know what they think about these questions. The simple fact is that the stuff of public life eludes the grasp of the ordinary man. Events have become professionalized.[6]

Moreover, the problems, whether they be urban renewal, air pollution, education for the new age, Medicare, international development programs, the exploitation of the oceans, assigning technology development priorities, etc., will be too complicated to be dealt with effectively by the techniques that have characterized our society to date. And the issues will be too critical, the potentials for and scale of disaster too great to stake our social survival upon conventional approaches— even when they are undertaken (as they rarely are) with the best of disinterested goodwill. All we have to do is to look at the looming disaster our cities represent, to recognize that we are going to have to do much better.

The tasks we face, then, will require the full use of whatever rationalized techniques we have, and these techniques will proliferate in the years ahead with advances in the social sciences, with increasing use of computers, data banks, simulation, system analyses, operations research, and so on.

In consequence, planners and decision makers will be confronted with a set of circumstances that will also suggest important changes in the democratic process. The competing demands for human and physical resources, necessarily expended over long periods of time, will require the development of ways to assign priorities and to revise costly efforts, even if it is politically uncomfortable and institutionally disruptive. At present we have neither the priority scheme nor the means for efficiently and reliably transcending conventional and institutional restraints. Yet, obviously, we will have to be able to choose between major technological and social developments, and we will have to be able to maintain or alter these decisions more in the light of their real accomplishments, rather than in the light of political commitments. Furthermore, because of the massive needs of the society, there will be a tendency to respond to average human and

[6]"The Politics of the Washington Press Corps," *Harper's Magazine* (June, 1965), pp. 101–2.

social requirements, rather than to the needs of the individual qua individual. This tendency will be exacerbated by the inherent characteristics of technologies, of systems analysis, and of operations research and computer simulation. The pressures to value those things most about the society that can be described and dealt with in terms of the techniques available, and the pressures to deal with the massive needs of the society will make it especially difficult for the policy maker and decision maker to preserve a sensitivity for and responsibility toward the idea of the idiosyncratic and extrarational needs of the individual.

If, then, we are to preserve the ideal of the cherished individual, we will need wise men more than we will need technically skilled men, though obviously we will need the technically skilled men too. As it is, we do not know how to produce wise men, and we do not know how to provide them with an environment that will encourage their wisdom to blossom and act. Yet without wise men, the chances are that the democratic concept and the Judeo-Christian tradition built around the obligations and rights of the individual will be lost under the crush of the vast needs of the society and the enormous potency of the technologies put into operation in a massive society to meet those needs. How shall we prepare for and invent the new forms of democracy and the new roles to be played by citizen and leader in such a system?

Above, I implied the need for the ability to change institutions rapidly. This, too, is a consequence of the impact of technologies on society, for through their effects technologies make the mandates of institutions, and the validity of the operating styles within the mandates obsolete. Yet institutions persist and change only slowly and usually reluctantly—barring some kind of disaster. Some observers have pointed out the potentialities for society if we apply our technologies. They then bemoan the apathy of the public and the ineffectualness of institutions because they do not take advantage of the technologies. The usual interpretation of this state of affairs is that we lack "leadership." But this is a naive solution and a premature definition of the problem. The question really is how to change institutions so that leadership arises in a given situation and then acts. Here our formal knowledge, limited as it is, makes it clear that this is an extremely difficult condition to deal with expeditiously.

As institutions produce and use the new technologies, they inevitably will have to change at a rate concomitant with the changes produced in the society by the very technologies they have encouraged and applied. But getting institutions or, rather, the people in them, to shift their perspectives radically as technology radically alters reality; getting the members of institutions to risk statuses, self-images, empires, in order to prepare for future needs, is an enormously difficult task, usually only successfully accomplished after a major institutional disaster has occurred. Over the years we can expect that the social sciences will provide us with more knowledge about how to make these changes quickly (or perhaps provide us with an understanding of why, if we want to preserve a humanitarian set of values, institutions cannot be changed quickly). But even if we assume the former, there are still many years ahead in which institutions will lag behind in their ability to respond to the real environment as it is altered by technologies, and this lag will become increasingly dangerous. What we do now and in the long run about this impact of technology is a matter that I believe deserves intensive attention.

Perhaps we might do well to spend some significant portion of our professional time stockpiling solutions to social problems, which we cannot hope to get into our social system now, but which we can reasonably expect to apply if some of these problems back up on us to the point where we cannot cope with them within the present social format. It is after disasters that institutions can most easily be changed.

Let me close with some comments on the special social impact on scholars or action-oriented professionals of the very *question* of the social impact of technology. One direct effect of the new technologies is to challenge deeply the adequacy of our academic disciplines for dealing with the kind of world they are producing. We sit here and talk learnedly about economic and social processes—rates of change, institutional process, etc.,—but my impression is that few of our disciplines or techniques are now really adequate. Even in the well-studied area of productivity and technological change we cannot be sanguine about our methods. As Solomon Fabricant recently said,

> The problem of measurement has not yet been solved . . . There are competing and widely differing measurements of technological change . . . I'm afraid that people talk about both the past and the future . . . with more confidence than is warranted by the available knowledge about technological change.[7]

In the few cases where our techniques are adequate, they are not being used broadly or intensively enough to deal with the multiple issues that must be understood if we are going to secure the advantages these new technologies possess.

If my impression is accurate, we face some very uncomfortable questions, which, as scholars and professionals, we are morally bound to wrestle with far more than we have until now. What about our research techniques? What must we do—and what must we abandon of what we now take status and comfort in—to get methods that adequately tackle the issues? We must find out what we should really be studying, even if it means breaking down cherished disciplinary

[7] *Measurement of Technological Change* (Washington, D.C., Manpower Administration, U.S. Department of Labor, 1965), p. 3.

barriers and repudiating the importance of the issues we have studied up to now? Over the next few decades many of our techniques are likely to become much more adequate, but what is our role until then? It seems to me that we belong to one of the institutions of society whose members and operating styles need to be shaken up quickly— we need to have our awareness of reality enlarged and refined and revised if we are to make our contribution in good conscience and with significant effect.

One might decide, of course, that even with all these conflicts and changes and even without the participation of the scholars, some kind of accommodation will be worked out. Probably so, but there is the possibility that the accommodation will be one we will not like. And there is also the possibility that there will be no accommodation. Certainly ours would not be the first society that disappeared because it could not find a way to accommodate in time to changes generated within it by its own momentum and style.

Seymour Melman

American Needs and Limits On Resources: The Priorities Problem

A nation's "needs" are given workable meaning by a plausible, socially validated shopping list of goods and services, set against the production capability of the nation. In terms of these criteria it is possible to define the following set of American needs:[1]

About seven million American families live in *dwellings* that are substandard in terms of minimal requirements of health and decency. The replacement of this housing on a nationwide basis will require an annual outlay of not less than $15 billion per year, over a period of five years.

In order to raise the level of *health services* to a reasonable standard, additional outlays of $8 billion per year are required in the nation.

In order to conduct *education,* from the nursery school to the university at an acceptable (not gold-plated) standard, the United States requires additional education outlays of $25 billion per year.

In order to assure an adequate supply of clean *drinking water* the nation requires additional outlays of $4 to $5 billion per year to develop new water resources.

Many aspects of *transportation* in the nation require substantial investment for acceptable performance. The railroads of the nation can be brought up to a modern standard of performance with capital investment of $1.5 billion per year over the present level of investment.

The conservation of *natural resources,* including soil for agriculture, forests, restoration of eroded or strip-mined land, and the care of

Reprinted by permission of the publisher from *New University Thought,* Special Issue, 1966–67, pp. 3–8. Seymour Melman is professor of industrial engineering at Columbia University.

[1]These estimates are drawn mainly from *Our Depleted Society* by Seymour Melman, Holt, Rinehart and Winston, New York, N. Y., Chapter 10. The original estimates have been modified for updating.

211

beach areas requires additional investment by the nation of $2 billion per year.

Major *water and hydroelectric power* developments that would restore and improve these resources for the whole North American continent require an annual capital outlay of $5 billion per year.

Technological and allied renewal of many *depleted civilian industries* like merchant ship building and many machinery producing industries, requires incremental investment of about $10 billion per year.

For the great cities of the United States *sewer, water, and waste disposal* systems require annual capital outlays of $4.5 billion per year.

All told, this partial agenda of America's investment needs amounts to $76 billions per year.

None of these estimates takes into account major upgrading of acceptable standards in the several spheres involved. Many classes of public outlays are not included: air pollution reduction will require major investments in every large city, and these will appear increasingly urgent as the public health impact of air pollution is more widely understood; regional economic development in several parts of the United States will require major investments over a long period; upgrading the nation's poor into participation in an equal opportunity (choice availability) system will need special occupational, medical, educational and allied investments. The omission of these and other areas of need from the present national estimates defines the figure of $76 billion per year as a minimal agenda of social investments.

These investments that could be made in American society would substantially improve our present depleted human and community resources, raising them to an acceptable American standard. The largest part of these new investments clearly belong in the public sector, and must therefore come from the tax revenue of federal and local governments. In the immediate future the present allocation of taxing power means that local governments will not have the capability for making investments of these magnitudes. New York City alone, for example, needs $4.3 billion each year for the next ten years if it is to do a serious job of replacing its abominable slum dwellings. Bringing education and health care in the city up to a reasonable standard will surely cost at least $1 billion more per year. In 1966-67 the whole city budget amounts to $4.5 billion. So New York City alone needs $5 billion more per year for the most essential needs of its people.[2]

The federal government now has the largest single block of tax revenue—about $110 billion per year. This is the primary capital reservoir whose allocation could have a controlling effect on the ability of the United States to fulfill a plausible set of national needs.

It is significant that principal federal officials have announced that

[2] New York City taxpayers now pay about $15 billion each year in taxes to the federal government.

the nation does not have a priorities problem. During 1966, Dr. Gardner Ackley, Chairman of the President's Council of Economic Advisors told us that there is no need to choose between guns and butter as a result of the war in Vietnam. Defense Secretary Robert McNamara placed the prestige of his office behind the public declaration that the United States is an affluent society and can afford as much defense and space spending as it wishes to have.

By January 1966 an unfamiliar drama was being enacted in Washington. It was budget time, and the President, with his aides, was seeking ways of reducing non-military expenditures so that the priority military budget and Vietnam war operations could be funded at expected levels. The main casualty of the budget pruning was the whole gamut of social investments for human betterment, from the "war on poverty" to fulfillment of the so-called "Great Society" program.

The Administration requests for housing, health care, and education did not even meet by as much as 10 percent the additional national expenditures needed to bring the work in these areas up to decent standards. New research projects in the biological and physical sciences were scheduled for a cut of about one-third. The budget cutting extended to the school milk program, where the White House ordered (and the Congress restored!) an 80 percent cut from last year's spending of about $110 million. Lyndon Johnson literally tried to finance a part of his war in Vietnam by taking milk out of the mouths of children!

What was the reason for this unprecedented zeal by the federal government for cutting civilian spending? The principal clue is given in the following brief summary of the main Great Society budget priorities. The ordinary military budget for the next year is to be about $50 billion. The Vietnam war is approaching a cost of $24 billion a year. The space race to the moon now requires $5 billion per year. These budget items total $79 billion a year—more than three-fourths of our tax payments—and leaves very little for everything else.

The U. S. Gross National Product (GNP) is now somewhat more than $725 billion a year. Nevertheless, while the United States is rich, it is not infinitely rich. The size of our enormous GNP tends to overshadow the fact that an important part of this money is payment for economically parasitic activity rather than for productive growth. *Military and space work is paid for, but yields a result which cannot be used either for further production or as part of the current level of living.* By this functional test, military work is parasitic, since it only uses up manpower and materials. The contrast is productive growth: producing goods or services that can be used for further production or for the present level of living. A printing press multiplies its worth many times over in its products. An atomic weapon does not.   213

Americans have become hypnotized by the spectacle of a constantly growing Gross National Product, measured in money units. We have tended to ignore the fact that the nature of the monetary unit places no constraints on the quantity that is created. Thus the quantity of money may be enlarged, indefinitely, by government decision to issue currency, by the decision of bankers to issue credit, and by the decision of citizens to write checks and make loans.

Manpower, especially skilled manpower, is finite in quantity during meaningful periods of time. The number of people available to do skilled work of any sort is therefore restricted in quantity by those already trained and by the number who are capable of receiving such training—and by the availability of facilities and incentives to do so. *The stock of skilled manpower and its allocation to varied types of work is the final constraint on the production capability of American society.* The present allocation of skilled manpower gives us important clues about the limitation on the ability of America to meet the needs of its people.

Between one-half and two-thirds of the present engineering-science research and development manpower of the nation is now devoted to military work. These proportions are not implied by the 10 percent of the Gross National Product that is now being consumed for military purposes. For that 10 percent is not an average 10 percent of a homogeneous mix of American economic resources. Included in the 10 percent of Gross National Product used up for military purposes is a large proportion of the highly trained manpower of the society. The essential fact is this: the man engaged in the design of military products cannot also be a designer of commercial ships, of apartment buildings, of medical schools, or of modern equipment for railroads, water treatment and waste disposal. Entire industries in the United States now operate without the benefit of meaningful research and development facilities of any sort. Some Americans are prepared to understand or justify these gaps in our productive process on the grounds that these sectors are primarily the proper sphere of private enterprise and therefore are not deserving of the government's economic attention. It is evident, however, that where the public interest is understood to be present from the standpoint, say, of the operation of a military establishment, then public funds and public decisions are made to build up the technological and allied capability of the industry in question. This is the story of the principal industries producing military material.

As the finite stock of technological brain power has been allocated with priority to the military sphere over a long period of time, crumbs from the table, and often nothing at all, has been left as the share of a great array of civilian industries and activities. This technological underdevelopment in the civilian sphere has played an important part in generating other defects. For example: the private house-building industry is now incapable of investing in and constructing multiple dwellings for the lowest quartile of rent payers in American cities. This fact is not rooted in laws of nature. This limitation on the capability of the apartment house construction industry is closely related on the one hand to the virtual absence of any research and development on apartment house construction toward producing a quality product at low cost; and on the other hand, the present deficiency is strongly affected by limitations on capital (meaning materials and manpower) that are available for apartment house construction work because of present military priorities.

In the enumeration of American needs that I outlined above, I have not applied in any case an unusual, in the sense of a culturally unacceptable, standard. In the case of medical service I have assumed, for example, that the ratio of physicians in private practice to citizens should not be allowed to decline further, as it has from 1950 to 1963 when physicians in practice dropped from 109 doctors per 100,000 population to 97 per 100,000. On the basis of plausible estimates of population growth and a standard of physician availability in some of our states, I have calculated that the nation needs a average of three new medical schools per state, or about 150 new medical schools by 1975. These estimates also assume that it is unreasonable for one out of four nursing posts in the nation to be vacant.

ALTERNATIVE POLICY SYSTEMS

The entire discussion of national needs and possible alternative priorities assumes that alternative policy systems (and budgets) can be formulated for the conduct of the nation's business at home and abroad. Starting with the assignment of great importance to personal and political freedom and a high level of material well-being for our own people and for others in the world, it is feasible to design alternative policy strategies for the pursuit of these ends. In December, 1963 I formulated a statement of seven alternative national security strategies for the United States and circulated this statement to Members of Congress and to senior officers of the Executive branch of the government. This analysis of "The Structure of Alternative Security Policies and Budgets" now appears as Appendix B in my book, *Our Depleted Society*. Examination of this schedule of alternative policies discloses that these imply a range of alternative *priority* policies.

Whatever one's judgment may be as to preferred policies within this spectrum of alternatives, this much is clear: it is not possible to implement all of these priority systems at once. This essential point is contradicted by a body of doctrine that has been built into the understanding of many Americans during the last years. I think it is useful to enumerate some of the propositions which have supported the idea that a priorities choice need not be made in American society. (1) The

United States is indefinitely wealthy and is able to afford as much defense and space activity as it desires while also implementing "Great Society" type programs at a meaningful rate. (2) The growth of the nation's Gross National Product is so great that the annual increments, measured in money, are enough to finance major new investments for American needs. (3) Military and allied spending bolsters the economy by putting money into circulation. (4) The concentration of technical brain power in the military and related sphere is partly justified by the spillover of technical knowledge from military purposes that can be applied to civilian uses. (5) If the Congress didn't vote the money as it now does then it probably wouldn't spend it for civilian needs anyhow. Therefore, on the grounds of putting money into circulation it is just as well that the funds are spent as they are.

Every one of these propositions is found to be substantially defective when contrasted with reality.

Economists have not even begun to make an appropriate measure of the cost to the nation of the sustained high level of military and allied activity. At least a two-fold cost is involved: the resources actually consumed for these purposes; and second, the value of the goods and services whose production is foregone because of the present priorities.

Neither the administrators of the nation's expenditures nor those sections of the academic community concerned with these policy areas have attempted an assessment of the full cost of the present military-first priority system to American society. No attempt has been made to assess the meaning of the qualitative changes in American society that are produced by long range concentration on present priorities.

The big cities of the United States, for example, where two out of three Americans live, are concentration points of physical deterioration and pressing race problems. In order to repair this urban decay and to bring equal economic opportunity to all our people, the investment agenda that I described at the beginning of this paper is a minimum requirement. Failing such a program of social expenditures, and given a continuation of the present neglect of our massive social needs, the quality of American society may well begin to deteriorate in a way that would be very hard to repair or reverse.

While depletion in society owing to concentration on military priority has had material as well as social effects, it is the latter which are most distressing and damaging to the quality of life, and least amenable to repair in a short period of time. We must give the closest attention to the warning that was addressed to the nation in 1965 by John McCone and his colleagues in their report on "Violence in the City: An End or A Beginning," following the riots in Watts, Los Angeles. The McCone report concluded that "As a Commission we are seriously concerned that the existing breach, if allowed to persist could in time

216

split our society irretrievably. So serious and so explosive is the situation that, unless it is checked, the August riots may seem by comparison only a curtain raiser for what could blow up one day in the future."

It is time to examine afresh the dominant American priorities system. It is incontestable that choices of priorities must be made—even in the wealthiest nation on earth. In public life cost-effectiveness has been accepted as a desirable pattern of behavior. We have yet to introduce policy-effectiveness: explicit choice of priorities—in terms of our country's needs and capabilities.

Richard J. Barber

The New Partnership
BIG GOVERNMENT AND BIG BUSINESS

Big business is getting bigger. This year more than a thousand corporations will be consolidated into larger financial enterprises in the greatest merger wave in the country's history. As a result the character of US industry is being radically transformed and the typical corporation of the 1970's is very likely to bear a disturbingly close resemblance to the General Motors Corporation of the mid-1960's. With 735,000 employees, 1.3 million shareholders in more than 80 countries, plants in 24 countries, and a line of products that includes autos, refrigerators, earth-moving equipment, locomotives, jet engines, and missile guidance systems, GM's 1965 net profit (after taxes) of $2.1 billion was greater than the general revenue of 48 states and its sales of $21 billion exceeded the GNP of all except nine foreign nations. Though its proportions are truly massive, GM is by no means exceptional, even now. Many other companies also are sharply increasing their sales (60 US companies reported revenue last year of at least $1 billion), enlarging their profits (82 manufacturers had net earnings of $50 million or more in 1965), and expanding their international commitments (American firms are increasing their overseas investments at a rate of more than $10 million each day). Simply put, the era of the huge, diversified, international company is here.

Just as fundamental changes are taking place in industry, so too are traditional government-business relationships being markedly altered. New economic forces are threatening to outmode the classic American antipathy to bigness. "From this country's beginning," Justice Hugo Black said a few weeks ago in a Supreme Court opinion, "there has been an abiding and widespread fear of the evils which

Reprinted by permission of the author and *The New Republic* from *The New Republic*, August 13, 1966, pp. 17–22. Copyright 1966, Harrison-Blaine of New Jersey, Inc. Richard J. Barber works for the United States Senate Sub-committee on Antitrust and Monopoly.

218

flow from monopoly—that is, the concentration of economic power in the hands of a few." But that attitude, however meritorious, conflicts squarely with what is going on in the economy and with present government policy. In consonance with the prevailing Administration consensus philosophy, the federal government—relinquishing its customary role as a foe of corporate size—is in fact now forging a New Partnership with big business. Naturally this has many troublesome implications, but certainly it means that one no longer can be confident that government will keep the exercise of private economic power within reasonable bounds.

At the moment 200 corporations (out of a total of approximately 200,000) control nearly 60 per cent of the country's manufacturing wealth and occupy commanding positions in virtually all principal markets. Just 10 companies, with General Motors at the head of the list, reported profits in 1965 equal to the total profits of the next 490 largest firms. Already far larger than modern technology requires, these industrial titans, through internal growth and merger, are certain to increase their relative position even more in the immediate future. Internationally their power will be no less than it is domestically. In the past seven years US firms have more than doubled their overseas investment—it now totals more than $50 billion—with the result that the foreign sales of Standard Oil of New Jersey, Burroughs, Colgate-Palmolive, Mobil, and National Cash Register, among many others, often exceed half their total income. Within a decade a group of 200 American companies plus another 50 to 100 large foreign enterprises will possess most of the world's manufacturing assets and make the great preponderance of sales and profits, having as tight a grip on global industry as our big companies now have at home.

Last year a thousand companies disappeared through merger in the US, and in 1966 they will be joined in the graveyard by an estimated 1,300. Not only is the absolute number of mergers high by any standard of comparison (fewer than 200 firms a year vanished a decade ago), but a great many large firms are involved. In 1965 Pure Oil (with assets of $750 million), Richfield Oil (assets: $500 million), Consolidation Coal (assets: $465 million), and ABC-Paramount were acquired by, respectively, Union Oil, Atlantic Refining, Continental Oil, and ITT. Between 1948 and 1965 more than 800 companies with assets of at least $10 million each were assimilated into larger empires, mostly those ruled by the 200 biggest manufacturing corporations. At this rate Art Buchwald may well be right in thinking that "the whole country will soon be merged into one large company."

The sheer volume of mergers, important though it is, must not obscure the most striking fact of all: their changing character. At one time most mergers involved direct competitors, or suppliers and their customers. This is no longer true. Today more than 70 percent of all mergers are of the conglomerate variety, bringing together entirely 219 unrelated firms. Horizontal—direct competitor—consolidations currently make up only 12 percent of all mergers, down from more than 30 percent in the early 1950's.

A NEW KIND OF COMPANY

Conglomerate acquisitions have carried many firms into widely diversified product or geographic markets. Borden, usually thought of as a dairy company, is heavily engaged in chemicals. Lipton Tea (a subsidiary of Unilever, the English-Dutch colossus) controls Good Humor. Hershey Chocolate has just entered the macaroni business. R. J. Reynolds, commonly associated with cigarettes, sells poultry, canned soups, catsup, and soft drinks. These and hundreds of other well-established firms have been broadening their product base through the acquisition of going concerns.

An excellent example of the conglomerate is International Telephone & Telegraph. For years engaged in the communications business outside the US (it still is, with 150,000 employees in its foreign manufacturing plants alone), ITT has acquired an odd assortment of enterprises, well described by some of their names: Hayes Furnace Co., Aetna Finance, Great International Life Insurance, Hamilton Management Co. (a $400 million mutual fund), Avis Rent-a-Car, ABC-Paramount (itself diversified, with broadcasting, theatre, phonograph record, and publishing assets), and Airport Parking (with parking facilities at air terminals in 59 of the nation's largest cities).

ITT is only one of an expanding breed of conglomerates. Gulf & Western Industries (from auto parts manufacture it has broadly expanded into mining and chemicals and soon will acquire Paramount Pictures), Litton Industries (which sells more than a hundred different products, ranging from adding machines to nuclear submarines), Textron, the FMC Corporation, and Olin have similar attributes. A few months ago the US Rubber Company changed its name to Uniroyal, explaining that fewer than half the things it now makes have anything to do with rubber.

Under the pressure of conglomerate mergers many industries are losing their distinctive characteristics. Electronics firms are aggressively moving into the publishing and educational product fields, as signified by RCA's acquisition of Random House (which previously had swallowed Knopf), the sale of D. C. Heath to Raytheon, Xerox's purchase of Wesleyan University Press (rumors now suggest possible merger with Harcourt-Brace), and IBM's absorption of Science Research Associates. From their strong base the computer companies will no doubt continue to diversify, subsuming publishing and educational hardware, and perhaps entertainment and broadcasting (CBS's purchase of the New York Yankees and its interests in Broadway musicals notably *My Fair Lady*, is suggestive of future trends) in a single 220 amorphous industry—one that does not yield well to traditional tools of economic analysis.

Many factors have helped bring about the conglomerate merger explosion, but one key explanation has been a rising stock market which has permitted mergers to be made on highly advantageous terms. Since most acquisitions take the form of an exchange of stock (usually tax-free), companies whose securities trade in the market at high price-earning ratios have found it particularly easy to purchase lower price-earning companies at relatively small cost. If, for instance, two companies, X and Y, have earnings of $1.00 per share but the X shares sell for $20 and the Y shares for only $10, a merger can easily be arranged that is mutually attractive. Y shareholders might, as one possibility, exchange each of their shares for X shares having a market value of, say, $11 (this gain in value is usually free of tax). With Y's earnings added to their previous profits, X shareholders could also reasonably expect their own holdings to rise in price in view of the market's tendency to capitalize their corporation's earnings at a higher rate. Exactly this kind of swap is involved in Consolidated Food's proposed purchase of United Artists, the nation's most successful film distributor. Under comparable conditions Litton, ITT, and other firms have made many acquisitions on highly advantageous terms in the last few years.

Although the largest corporations have lately been substantially increasing their already tight hold on the country's manufacturing wealth, primarily through conglomerate mergers, the federal government has provided little in the way of an antidote. Antitrust enforcement has served to check mergers between competitors (the merger of Bethlehem and Youngstown Steel was barred, for instance) but no such attention has been given to conglomerate acquisitions. Despite the fact that they are now the most common form of merger (nearly 1,000 will be carried out this year) and can seriously lessen competition at the same time they increase concentration, fewer than one percent have been formally protested by the federal antitrust enforcement agencies. The green light is on and the race to diversify by acquisition is well underway. The government's unwillingness to challenge conglomerate merger is matched by its refusal to test the legality of established oligopolistic positions. The word is technical but all it refers to are those industries in which a few big companies account for most of the sales. In autos GM, Ford and Chrysler make 95 percent of the country's new cars; similarly, Alcoa, Reynolds, and Kaiser control about 90 percent of the aluminum market; US Steel, Bethlehem, and Republic produce almost 60 percent of the steel; Anaconda, Kennecott, American Smelting, and Phelps Dodge refine virtually all of the copper. In the same fashion a handful of corporations dominate many other manufacturing industries, with four firms accounting for at least 75 percent of the output of synthetic fibers, 221 soap, salt, flat glass, metal cans, electric bulbs, and computers, to cite only a few specific cases.

Statistics aside, the basic economic significance is that in oligopolistic markets the big sellers come to recognize that it is more profitable not to compete in price. A classic illustration took place in 1956. That year the Ford Motor Company initially announced an average price increase on its 1957 models of 2.9 percent. Two weeks later, however, when GM increased its 1957 model prices by an average 6.1 percent, Ford promptly revised its prices upward to match the GM prices almost dollar for dollar (and Chrysler soon followed suit). Ten years have brought about no change in the situation. Prices for 1966 cars show the same intimate relationship, with dealers' base prices differing by only pennies on comparable Ford, GM, and Chrysler models. This kind of coordinated pricing occurs regularly in the highly concentrated industries. Official government reports reveal the receipt from supposed competitors of hundreds of sealed bids that are identical to the fourth decimal place in the purchase of steel, aluminum, electrical, and other products. The result is the same as if the producers conspired to fix their prices, but while this does occur from time to time, generally it is not necessary. As Chief Justice Warren put it, "an industry which does not have a competitive structure will not have competitive behavior." Yet no steps have been taken to bring about a less concentrated structure.

Quite understandably smaller businessmen feel they are being discriminated against in favor of the giants when it comes to antitrust enforcement. Last May, for instance, the merger of two foodstore chains that together accounted for about 7.5 percent of sales in Los Angeles was held unlawful. Promptly after the decision was handed down, Donald F. Turner, head of the Antitrust Division, announced that he would challenge any merger between competitors having eight percent or more of any given market. While this may represent sound policy, if it is unaccompanied by action taken against already dominant firms, it means that other companies are forbidden to join forces at the same time that General Motors, US Steel, Goodyear, General Electric, Anaconda, and others of the top 200 are tacitly immunized from antitrust prosecution that would seriously curb or reduce their power.

The government's failure to take steps through antitrust action to block the growth of conglomerate firms and to deconcentrate those industries in which a few companies occupy commanding positions is attributable to a number of factors. First, the myth persists that enterprises become more efficient as they get bigger. To break up General Motors, General Electric, or US Steel thus would run counter to the public interest by destroying their supposed efficiencies of scale. Similarly, while it may not be desirable to let two direct 222 competitors merge, it is thought that there is nothing wrong—quite the contrary—with the formation via merger of a sprawling conglomerate. The entry of Litton or ITT into a new market, so the argument goes, is likely to increase efficiency by bringing in aggressive management, adding capital, and letting in the fresh breezes of modern research. While these arguments are familiar to just about everyone who reads the *Wall Street Journal* or *Fortune,* let alone the *Harvard Business Review,* they are not generally backed up by empirical evidence.

LACK OF ANTITRUST ACTIVITY

Many studies have shown that small and medium-sized firms, specializing in a single product line, are typically more efficient, more innovative (the great bulk of important inventions still are made, not in corporate laboratories, but by individual inventors or small research organizations), and quicker to offer new products and adopt new marketing techniques than their largest rivals. In the steel industry, for example, the two most important technological advances in recent years—the basic oxygen process (it cuts the time needed to make a ton of steel to less than a quarter of that required in an open hearth) and continuous casting—were first used in the United States, not by the steel giants, but by the industry's smaller firms. Nonetheless, many people continue to believe that massive, conglomerate enterprises somehow contribute to greater efficiency. Clearly this attitude, however inaccurate, seriously inhibits antitrust enforcement.

A second reason for the lack of really meaningful antitrust activity is that existing legislation is less than ideally designed to deal with oligopolistic industries and conglomerate mergers. Neither the Sherman Act (passed in 1890) nor the Clayton Act (last amended in 1950), though broad in their coverage, specifically was tailored to cope either with markets in which a small group of firms controls prices or with diversification mergers. As a result, while existing legislation can be used to reach these situations, it makes antitrust enforcement difficult and cumbersome, offering another excuse for the failure to bring the kind of cases that might have made major economic impact.

There is still a third factor and it is probably the most important of all for it places the issue in its political perspective. What is happening is that within the government there is a growing acceptance of business bigness as positively beneficial. Viewed in this light, the disinclination to use antitrust to deal with established dominant positions or to interfere with conglomerate mergers is only one incident of the New Partnership which is being formed by government and big business. This "new interdependence," as *Fortune* calls it, is the product of several forces, economic and political. 223

For one thing, business has prospered immensely under recent Democratic Administrations and has come to accept government as a useful ally. Stimulated by a consciously expansionary fiscal policy, the economy has grown rapidly since 1961, sending corporate sales and profits to record heights. Corporate after-tax profits for 1965 totaled $45 billion (up from $27 billion in 1960), equal to a return of 13 percent on net worth—the highest profit rate in history. And based on figures for the first quarter of 1966, corporate profits could go even higher this year. A booming economy, lower tax rates, provisions for larger depreciation allowances, and a generous tax credit have helped show that Democratic government can be great for business.

Billion-dollar expenditures for defense, space, and the Great Society provide additional reason for business' growing appreciation of government. This year defense procurement alone will exceed $23 billion. The cost of putting a man on the moon (and certainly we will not stop there) will be near the $30 billion mark, and most of the money will go to private companies like North American Aviation, Boeing, and McDonnell Aircraft. The Atomic Energy Commission continues to fund large amounts of nuclear research ($1.9 billion in fiscal 1967), much of it done by General Electric and Westinghouse, the world's leading suppliers of nuclear reactors. As well, key AEC installations, such as the Oak Ridge Laboratory, are managed, for a sizable fee, by Union Carbide and other concerns. No one knows for sure how much revenue the government's defense-space-nuclear programs generate for the nation's businesses, but for many industries, government contracts are essential to survival.

How crucial government's support can be is starkly revealed by the aircraft industry. When World War II ended the sales of the big military plane builders abruptly halted. At this point a benevolent defense establishment, in the fashion of the WPA, created enough work to keep them alive. Thus, in 1946, the Air Force—in a then-secret guideline (it was not declassified until 1960)—directed that "contracts [be] parceled out among the old established manufacturers on an equitable basis so that they may be assured enough business to perpetuate their existence." Given this kind of cordial treatment, firms like Boeing, North American, Douglas, and Lockheed were able to survive until they entered the golden days of the 1950's when highly lucrative contracts for aircraft and missiles became commonplace.

Although the large defense-space contractors currently rank among the largest of all manufacturers, they continue to be so closely tied to the government that they still cannot realistically be viewed as private enterprises. Most of the major aircraft corporations—like Lockheed, North America, and Aerojet-General—are engaged in very

224

little non-government work. For these companies defense-space sales account for close to 100 percent of their total income. Moreover, they often use government-owned plants and machines in carrying out production contracts. In a fairly typical case a defense firm will be supplied with more than 50 percent of its fixed capital and with as much as 90 percent of its working capital. Actual investment, therefore, is relatively small, with the result that profit rates can be unusually high (in 1965 Boeing's profits came to 21 percent of net worth, and Lockheed 19 percent—more than 50 percent higher than the profit rate for the 500 largest manufacturers.) So intimate is their association with the defense establishment that the big aircraft-missile concerns can most sensibly be viewed as government appendages, with roughly the same status as the Post Office Department. Given this relationship nothing could be more natural than for Air Force and Navy officers to put the supersonic experimental bomber, the XB-70, and other aircraft at the disposal of General Electric as part of the company's ill-fated public relations stunt earlier this year. The XB-70 and one other military aircraft collided in mid-air and crashed with the death of two pilots and the destruction of the $1.2 billion bomber. Answering criticism that the planes should never have been made available to the company, military officials argue that GE—an important defense supplier—is simply a member of the defense family, and in many ways they are right.

Government's essential role in many defense industries is matched by the large part it plays in the nation's research. The federal government today supports nearly 70 percent of all research done in the United States. With annual expenditures of about $16 billion (more than it spent for all purposes during the entire nineteenth century), the government—especially the Defense Department, NASA, AEC, and the National Institutes of Health—subsidizes most of the research done by the universities and the thousands of nonprofit organizations as well as private industry. For all practical purposes American science has been nationalized and government participation is routinely expected. To cite an instance, when the development of a Mach-3 Supersonic Transport (SST) was proposed, it was considered perfectly normal for the government to offer initially to pay 75 percent of the minimum $1 billion cost—now the government is expected to contribute at least 90 percent.

More is in the government cornucopia, however, than funds for defense and space. The fulfillment of Great Society domestic objectives creates nearly unlimited additional business opportunities. The renewal of our cities ($10 billion a year is a reasonable price tag), urban mass transit (the new rapid transit system in San Francisco will cost $1 billion), improved intercity rail transportation (estimated cost: $15 billion), the alleviation of air and water pollution (the latter alone could call for expenditures of $75 billion over 15 years), better medical care, greater educational opportunities, job training (ITT's Federal Electric subsidiary manages the Kilmer Job Corps Center, for an $11.5 million fee): all of this means billions in sales and profits.

Sensing the economic significance of government defense and domestic programs, big business has now swung its support behind the Democratic Party. In 1964 "Democrats became the party of the 'fat cats'," observes Herbert J. Alexander in his extensive study of campaign spending. Sixty-nine percent of individual contributions received by national Democratic campaign committees was in sums of $500 or more; only 28 percent of individual Republican contributions came in such large amounts.

The key element in the support of Democratic candidates—explaining the large percentage of big contributors—is business. Members of the President's Club, almost all of whom were company executives or their advisers, contributed at least $4 million in aid of President Johnson's campaign. Of the 4,000 1964 Club members 532 were in California, home of the biggest defense-space contractors and the state which accounts for about a third of all contract awards. In addition to individual gifts, the Democrats sold 93 full-page advertisements to corporations in their 1964 Official Convention Program, yielding another $1.5 million. Among the takers were several of the biggest defense contractors. If allowance also is made for the sums which came from corporations whose lobbyists bought, with cash, tickets at $25 to $100 per plate luncheons and dinners, business picked up at least three-fourths of the tab for President Johnson's election. And Democratic Senators and Representatives—and their Republican colleagues—have like cause to be grateful.

In return for its support, big business has received appropriate recognition. Within days after his 1965 inauguration the President held a dinner for a group of business leaders, most of whom were members of the Business Council. The Council, which rose to prominence under President Eisenhower and then fell into disfavor in the early days of the Kennedy Administration (ties were reestablished in September 1961), has once more been extended a cordial greeting at the White House. Its roster is a veritable Who's Who of big business (of its four officers, three are presidents of corporations ranked among the largest 100 manufacturers; the fourth is the head of the country's biggest railroad). With 65 executives comprising its active membership, the Council meets regularly with top government officials in and near Washington.

SCIENCE OF MANAGEMENT

These contacts are strengthened by a steady two-way exchange of personnel. As did its predecessors, the Johnson Administration has drawn heavily on big business and its advisers (the Wall Street and   226

Washington law firms in particular) to fill important policy-making positions at both cabinet and subordinate levels. One example is the Foreign Intelligence Advisory Board, created in 1961 by President Kennedy to monitor the intelligence community. So great is its authority that it is informed in detail about the CIA's plans and methods of operation, precisely the information which will not be given to any Senator or Congressman who does not sit on the existing oversight subcommittees. Yet, with the present composition of the Board, such details are regularly disclosed to executives of AT&T, the Polaroid Corporation, and Corning Glass. Much other valuable information reaches Robert Kintner, a high White House staff aide and former president of NBC.

The flow of personnel between big business and government is not one-way, of course, and many important executives in private industry can point to earlier public service. Retiring State Department diplomats or AID officials find homes in the companies with extensive international operations. Generals and admirals, by the hundreds, are hired by major contractors anxious to maintain good contacts with the services (Admiral William F. Raborn, former CIA director, is expected to return soon to Aerojet-General). These are well-known instances, but industry has also tapped government for experts in other fields, such as education. Francis Keppel, former US Commissioner of Education, now heads General Learning Corporation, a General Electric-Time, Inc. venture.

In the face of these various indicia of the growing intimacy between government and business—as reflected in procurement contracts, political contributions, and exchanges of key personnel—their old hostility is fast coming to an end. A new breed of corporate executive is on the scene, professionally trained and more oriented to the science of management than to the perpetuation of an ideology which looks upon government as intrinsically evil. The modern company officer accepts government (much like he accepts the labor union) and works actively with it, seeking to take full advantage of the opportunities it offers and striving to influence the policies it adopts. This new attitude toward government comes as a shock to the old conservatives. Barry Goldwater, no doubt reflecting the opinion of many small businessmen, sarcastically views big business leaders as "money manipulators" who are "willing to do almost anything for the dollar."

CHECKING CORPORATE POWER

No assessment of the New Partnership would be complete, however, without an effort to identify some of its larger implications. One thing should be clear: if not restrained, the giant corporations, which, under prevailing circumstances, are likely to tighten even more the control they exert over large segments of the American economy, can act in 227 a manner distinctly contrary to the public interest. Through the manipulation of prices, free from traditional competitive inhibitions, they can levy a monopoly toll on the consumer.

During the last several months big business has been implored on several occasions to exercise restraint in its pricing practices. In each case the White House has met at best only very limited success, demonstrating that the enunciation of guidelines, backed up by no more than jaw-bone diplomacy, is insufficient to insure that the benefits of increasing productivity are passed along to the consumer. With labor productivity in many industries climbing more rapidly than in the economy generally (meaning that fewer manhours are required for a given amount of output), prices should be *reduced,* not just held at the existing level. Yet the best the Administration has been able to do—as in copper, aluminum, and molybdenum—is to block further price *increases.* (And in cigarettes, chemicals, and steel it has not even been able to accomplish that much.) A good example is provided by the auto industry. Last fall the car makers increased prices on the 1966 models even though labor productivity was rising so rapidly in the industry that the companies could have cut prices, with full allowances made for higher labor compensation and for the cost of installation of previously optional equipment. With continuing high prices and declining costs it is no wonder that GM and Ford profits rose steeply in 1965. Much the same situation is true of molybdenum. Under government pressure, American Metal Climax, on July 13, rescinded a proposed five percent price hike; nevertheless, prices remain high enough to give the corporation an estimated 30 percent return on its molybdenum investment (and an overall profit rate of 17 percent).

Recent price behavior in the major manufacturing industries shows that while the executives of powerful companies like to be regarded as part of the Great Society consensus, generally they give first priority to their own corporate well-being when making decisions about prices and other matters. To curtail the undesirable exercise of their power demands much stronger instruments of control than verbal admonition.

The problem of corporate power could be dealt with at its source by initiating a strong antitrust program that would check further economic concentration (the mere filing of a few cases against conglomerate mergers would alone be insufficient) and weaken the hold of the firms which presently dominate most of our major industries. But can an Administration that is wedded to big business undertake this kind of action when it would unquestionably be regarded by industry as a ground for divorce? If it cannot, and there is much evidence to suggest that is the case, the antitrust laws no longer can be regarded as a central instrument of economic policy.

The principal alternative means of checking corporate power is some sort of direct regulation. The possible techniques range from a 228 system that would require big companies in concentrated industries to give formal advance notice of price increases and to provide evidence of justification, but that would leave them free to hike their prices if they wished (bills embodying this approach have been introduced in the 89th Congress by Representatives Celler and Reuss) to utility-like regulation that would call for detailed government control of prices. These proposals naturally raise many interesting questions, but any detailed examination would only be academic since the very thought of regulation is anathema to an Administration that is anxious to please business. It has steadfastly refused even to acknowledge the possibility that some day it might have to seek explicit statutory authority to back up its wage-price guidelines.

In the process of forming a New Partnership with big business, the harsh fact is that the present Administration has surrendered much of its ability to select the means that will protect the public from concentrated economic power. In effect, through adherence to the consensus phiolsophy it has become less a partner than a captive of big business. For the foreseeable future, therefore, the American corporate giants will be able to expand their position, at home and abroad, with considerable freedom, and to exert their power much as they wish. Without government protection the best the public can hope for is that big business will be charitable.

229

FIVE

THE DEPERSONALIZED

As the American economy has climbed to unprecedented levels of productivity and national prosperity, it has moved so swiftly that millions of Americans have been left behind. Automated and mechanized industries produce more with fewer people, a trend which has not yet reached a stable equilibrium. Many of the technological changes have displaced those who do not have the necessary skills and education to find jobs that will provide a decent living and some security.

While automation can bring a release from the drudgery of work and an opportunity for more creative uses of human talent, such statements may have little meaning for the condition of life faced by the agricultural poor, the poorly educated and the unskilled industrial rejects. It is only these highly selected segments of the population that have felt the effects of technological unemployment.

The urban poor who have been displaced by technological change are the 20 million Americans that Harrington (1963) has called the "rejects." Occupations requiring little skill and education represent the only types of work left for industrial rejects; these are jobs in the "economic underworld" such as domestic workers, hotel employees, kitchen help, and busboys. An added burden of workers in marginal occupations is that they are unprotected by any organization that has their interests in mind; they neither work in large scale organizations with wage programs, sick leave, and health plans, nor are they in a unionized occupation.

The rural poor live in chronic low-income areas and have high rates of unemployment and underemployment. The far-reaching technological, occupational and educational changes of the last fifty years have left these areas with a larger supply of human resources than the land and capital resources require to maintain a decent level of productivity. The result has been a marked reduction in farms and farm 230 occupations with large numbers of unemployed who are unsuited for non-farm occupations even if they should be available in the area.

Most solutions to the problems of the rural poor have not been able to deal with the central issues behind rural poverty, and in many cases solutions have seemed only to exacerbate the problems. Technological-economic solutions have focused upon more intensive and "rational" use of existing resources (i.e., by changing machinery, crops, or land use); however, farms in low-income areas operate with such restricted resources that the usual federal farm programs have little effect upon farm income. Similarly, suggestions to combine smaller farms into larger units with intensive mechanization have the short-run effect of reducing farm occupations. Another solution offered, which is in accord with the aggregate-demand approach to unemployment, has to do with encouraging the rural poor to move into other jobs and other regions. Given the limited education and skills of the rural poor, moving out of farm occupations would mean movement into un-skilled non-farm positions that have their own form of instability and insecurity. The ultimate effect of such job changes might simply be that unemployment is transferred from the rural area to the city, where it may be more difficult to cope with the problems of poverty (Perrucci and Iwamoto, 1966).

The displacement of workers in many industries represents one form of depersonalization. A sense of identification depends on a particular kind of work, and the American criterion for status depends upon job level, suggesting how an entire way of life can be disrupted by the loss of occupation. Thus, when one comes into contact with society through a low-status job, or the police, or hospital, or a social-work contact, the experience further reinforces the feelings of worth-lessness.

The essay by Swados raises the question of depersonalization as a part of the very nature of work itself. Writing about the degrading nature of work in assembly-line type of jobs, he challenges popular arguments that workers are essentially middle class. Although workers may vote, dress, dream and consume like the middle class, they still work like workers. Swados also suggests the possibility that the mind-lessness of working-class occupations also seems to be found in white-collar positions, thereby extending the boundaries of depersonal-ization.

Another form of depersonalization may be found in organizations whose official purpose is to serve the needs of clients, but in the day-to-day operations, the organization and its members' needs and interests take priority over clients. The article by Morris explores this form of depersonalization as it confronts women in a maternity ward. The intimate and highly personal experience of childbirth is placed within the impersonal hospital setting which transfers mothers and children

231

into objects to be processed, studied, and ignored as human beings. The critical hypothesis offered by Morris is that this impersonal experience, in which the new mother bears and faces her child, affects the mother's response to her child. It is possible that we find here the beginnings of a cycle of pathology that manifests itself in adolescence and adulthood, and is again transmitted across the generations: early rejection, less secure in self-help, less easily helped by existing education and welfare, and more subject to become part of a culture of rejects likely to seek status through gang memberships and narcotics.

The situation described in the Morris essay is most likely to be found among lower-income families and mothers who are on welfare rolls; all of which suggest that medical services in general, and hospital organization in particular, have not adapted their services to the values and life styles of the poor (Strauss, 1967).

The final paper by Caudill presents a detailed case of how automated and mechanized coal mining has displaced thousands of workers in eastern Kentucky. In addition to describing the nation's indifference to the needs of these workers, Caudill has also described the inadequacy of government programs to deal with the mass displacement of man by machines. Programs that do exist are mainly concerned with providing food-stamp benefits and welfare checks, while hoping that displaced miners will be absorbed by new industries.

In writing this essay in 1964, Caudill soberly warned of the revolutionary potential of a situation where once prosperous Americans "find themselves slipping inexorably into an economic mire that breeds poverty, despair, (and) dependency. . . ." A *New York Times* news story on March 27, 1967 described the growing militancy in the Appalachian region which has replaced the apathy, that formerly characterized the residents of the region. The article attributed the "rural revolution" to the activities of young workers of the Appalachian Volunteers, and Volunteers in Service to America (VISTA). The views of the workers in some antipoverty programs are similar to those expressed in Part Four by representatives of the Fourth Revolution.

The relevance of depersonalization for the cybernetic revolution is that it reflects a tendency of the society to act like a coordinated production machine with the social value of "progress" used to justify moving a man out of his job while economic theories tell us that he will be absorbed by the economy somewhere else. It also reflects a tendency to use large numbers of people as unimportant cogs in psychologically meaningless work, to reject them entirely from the production machine and relegate them to a category of problems rather than the category of people.

232

REFERENCES AND ADDITIONAL READING

Michael Harrington, *The Other America,* Baltimore: Penguin Books, 1963.

Mirra Kamarovsky, "The Long Arm of the Job," in her *Blue Collar Marriage,* New York: Random House, 1962.

Robert Perrucci and Kichiro K. Iwamoto, "Work, Family, and Community in a Rural Depressed Area," in H. Meissner, ed., *Poverty in the Affluent Society*, New York: Harper & Row, 1966.

Anselm L. Strauss, "Medical Ghettos," *Trans-action,* May, 1967, 7–15.

233

THE DEPERSONALIZED

Harvey Swados

The Myth of the Happy Worker

"From where we sit in the company," says one of the best personnel men in the country, "we have to look at only the aspects of
work that cut across all sorts of jobs—administration and human
relations. Now these are aspects of work, abstractions, but it's easy
for personnel people to get so hipped on their importance that they
look on the specific tasks of making things and selling them as
secondary . . ."

—William H. Whyte, Jr., The Organization Man

The personnel man who made this remark to Mr. Whyte differed from
his brothers only in that he had a moment of insight. Actually, "the
specific tasks of making things" are now not only regarded by his
white-collar fellows as "secondary," but as irrelevant to the vaguer but
more "challenging" tasks of the man at the desk. This is true not just
of the personnel man, who places workers, replaces them, displaces
them—in brief, manipulates them. The union leader also, who represents workers and sometimes manipulates them, seems increasingly to
regard what his workers do as merely subsidiary to the job he himself is doing in the larger community. This job may be building the
Red Cross or the Community Chest, or it may sometimes be—as the
Senate hearings suggest—participating in such communal endeavors as
gambling, prostitution, and improving the breed. In any case, the impression is left that the problems of the workers in the background
(or underground) have been stabilized, if not permanently solved.

With the personnel man and the union leader, both of whom presumably see the worker from day to day, growing so far away from
him, it is hardly to be wondered at that the middle class in general,
and articulate middle-class intellectuals in particular, see the worker
vaguely, as through a cloud. One gets the impression that when they

234

do consider him, they operate from one of two unspoken assumptions: (1) The worker has died out like the passenger pigeon, or is dying out, or becoming accultured, like the Navajo. (2) If he *is* still around, he is just like the rest of us—fat, satisfied, smug, a little restless, but hardly distinguishable from his fellow TV-viewers of the middle class.

Lest it be thought that (1) is somewhat exaggerated, I hasten to quote from a recently published article apparently dedicated to the laudable task of urging slothful middle-class intellectuals to wake up and live: "The old-style sweatshop crippled mainly the working people. Now there are no workers left in America; we are almost all middle-class as to income and expectations." I do not believe the writer meant to state—although he comes perilously close to it—that nobody works any more. If I understand him correctly, he is referring to the fact that the worker's rise in real income over the last decade, plus the diffusion of middle-class tastes and values throughout a large part of the underlying population, have made it increasingly difficult to tell blue-collar from white-collar worker without a program. In short, if the worker earns like the middle class, votes like the middle class, dresses like the middle class, dreams like the middle class, then he ceases to exist as a worker.

But there is one thing that the worker doesn't do like the middle class: he works like a worker. The steel-mill puddler does not yet sort memos, the coal miner does not yet sit in conferences, the cotton mill-hand does not yet sip martinis from his lunchbox. The worker's attitude toward his work is generally compounded of hatred, shame, and resignation.

Before I spell out what I think this means, I should like first to examine some of the implications of the widely held belief that "we are almost all middle-class as to income and expectations." I am neither economist, sociologist, nor politician, and I hold in my hand no doctored statistics to be haggled over. I have had occasion to work in factories at various times during the Thirties, Forties, and Fifties. The following observations are simply impressions based on my last period of factory servitude, in 1956.

The average automobile worker gets a little better than two dollars an hour. As such he is one of the best-paid factory workers in the country. After twenty years of militant struggle led by the union that I believe to be one of the finest and most democratic labor organizations in the United States, he is earning less than the starting salaries offered to inexperienced and often semiliterate college graduates without dependents. After compulsory deductions for taxes, social security, old-age insurance and union dues, and optional deductions for hospitalization and assorted charities, his pay check for forty hours of work is going to be closer to seventy than to eighty dollars a week. Does this make him middle-class as to income? Does it rate with the weekly take of a dentist, an accountant, a salesman, a drafts- 235 man, a journalist? Surely it would be more to the point to ask how a family man can get by in the Fifties on that kind of income. I know how he does it, and I should think the answers would be a little disconcerting to those who wax glib on the satisfactory status of the "formerly" underprivileged.

For one thing, he works a lot longer than forty hours a week—when he can. Since no automobile company is as yet in a position to guarantee its workers anything like fifty weeks of steady forty-hour pay checks, the auto worker knows he has to make it while he can. During peak production periods he therefore puts in nine, ten, eleven, and often twelve hours a day on the assembly line for weeks on end. And that's not all. If he has dependents, as like as not he also holds down a "spare-time" job. I have worked on the line with men who doubled as mechanics, repairmen, salesmen, contractors, builders, farmers, cab-drivers, lumberyard workers, countermen. I would guess that there are many more of these than show up in the official statistics: often a man will work for less if he can be paid under the counter with tax-free dollars.

Nor is that all. The factory worker with dependents cannot carry the debt load he now shoulders—the middle-class debt load, if you like, of nagging payments on car, washer, dryer, TV, clothing, house itself—without family help. Even if he puts in fifty, sixty, or seventy hours a week at one or two jobs, he has to count on his wife's pay check, or his son's, his daughter's, his brother-in-law's; or on his mother's social security, or his father's veteran's pension. The working-class family today is not typically held together by the male wage-earner, but by multiple wage-earners often of several generations who club together to get the things they want and need—or are pressured into believing they must have. It is at best a precarious arrangement; as for its toll on the physical organism and the psyche, that is a question perhaps worthy of further investigation by those who currently pronounce themselves bored with Utopia Unlimited in the Fat Fifties.

But what of the worker's middle-class expectations? I had been under the impression that this was the rock on which socialist agitation had foundered for generations: it proved useless to tell the proletarian that he had a world to win when he was reasonably certain that with a few breaks he could have his own gas station. If these expectations have changed at all in recent years, they would seem to have narrowed rather than expanded, leaving a psychological increment of resignation rather than of unbounded optimism (except among the very young —and even among them the optimism focuses more often on better-paying opportunities elsewhere in the labor market than on illusory hopes of swift status advancement). The worker's expectations are for better pay, more humane working conditions, more job security. As long as he feels that he is going to achieve them through an exten-   236 sion of existing conditions, for that long he is going to continue to be a middle-class conservative in temper. But only for that long.

I suspect that what middle-class writers mean by the worker's middle-class expectations are his cravings for commodities—his determination to have not only fintailed cars and single-unit washer-dryers, but butterfly chairs in the rumpus room, African masks on the wall, and power boats in the garage. Before the middle-class intellectuals condemn these expectations too harshly, let them consider, first, who has been utilizing every known technique of suasion and propaganda to convert luxuries into necessities, and second, at what cost these new necessities are acquired by the American working-class family.

Now I should like to return to the second image of the American worker: satisfied, doped by TV, essentially middle-class in outlook. This is an image bred not of communication with workers (except as mediated by hired interviewers sent "into the field" like anthropologists or entomologists), but of contempt for people, based perhaps on self-contempt and on a feeling among intellectuals that the worker has let them down. In order to see this clearly we have to place it against the intellectual's changing attitudes toward the worker since the Thirties.

At the time of the organization of the CIO, the middle-class intellectual saw the proletarian as society's figure of virtue—heroic, magnanimous, bearing in his loins the seeds of a better future; he would have found ludicrous the suggestion that a sit-down striker might harbor anti-Semitic feelings. After Pearl Harbor, the glamorization of the worker was taken over as a function of government. Then, however, he was no longer the builder of the future good society; instead he was second only to the fighting man as the vital winner of the war. Many intellectuals, as government employees, found themselves helping to create this new portrait of the worker as patriot.

But in the decade following the war intellectuals have discovered that workers are no longer either building socialism or forging the tools of victory. All they are doing is making the things that other people buy. That, and participating in the great commodity scramble. The disillusionment, it would seem, is almost too terrible to bear. Word has gotten around among the highbrows that the worker is not heroic or idealistic; public-opinion polls prove that he wants barbecue pits more than foreign aid and air-conditioning more than desegregation, that he doesn't particularly want to go on strike, that he is reluctant to form a Labor Party, that he votes for Stevenson and often even for Eisenhower and Nixon—that he is, in short, animated by the same aspirations as drive the middle-class onward and upward in suburbia.

There is of course a certain admixture of self-delusion in the middle-class attitude that workers are now the same as everybody 237 else. For me it was expressed most precisely last year in the dismay and sympathy with which middle-class friends greeted the news that I had gone back to work in a factory. If workers are now full-fledged members of the middle class, why the dismay? What difference whether one sits in an office or stands in a shop? The answer is so obvious that one feels shame at laboring the point. But I have news for my friends among the intellectuals. The answer is obvious to workers, too.

They know that there is a difference between working with your back and working with your behind (I do not make the distinction between handwork and brainwork, since we are all learning that white-collar work is becoming less and less brainwork). They know that they work harder than the middle class for less money. Nor is it simply a question of status, that magic word so dear to the hearts of the sociologues, the new anatomizers of the American corpus. It is not simply status-hunger that makes a man hate work which pays *less* than other work he knows about, if *more* than any other work he has been trained for (the only reason my fellow workers stayed on the assembly line, they told me again and again). It is not simply status-hunger that makes a man hate work that is mindless, endless, stupefying, sweaty, filthy, noisy, exhausting, insecure in its prospects, and practically without hope of advancement.

The plain truth is that factory work is degrading. It is degrading to any man who ever dreams of doing something worthwhile with his life; and it is about time we faced the fact. The more a man is exposed to middle-class values, the more sophisticated he becomes and the more production-line work is degrading to him. The immigrant who slaved in the poorly lighted, foul, vermin-ridden sweatshop found his work less degrading than the native-born high school graduate who reads "Judge Parker," "Rex Morgan, M.D.," and "Judd Saxon, Business Executive," in the funnies, and works in a fluorescent factory with ticker-tape production-control machines. For the immigrant laborer, even the one who did not dream of socialism, his long hours were going to buy his freedom. For the factory worker of the Fifties, his long hours are going to buy him commodities . . . and maybe reduce a few of his debts.

Almost without exception, the men with whom I worked on the assembly line last year felt like trapped animals. Depending on their age and personal circumstances, they were either resigned to their fate, furiously angry at *themselves* for what they were doing, or desperately hunting other work that would pay as well and in addition offer some variety, some prospect of change and betterment. They were sick of being pushed around by harried foremen (themselves more pitied than hated), sick of working like blinkered donkeys, sick of being dependent for their livelihood on a maniacal production-merchandising setup, sick of working in a place where there was no

238

spot to relax during the twelve-minute rest period. (Someday—let us hope—we will marvel that production was still so worshiped in the Fifties that new factories could be built with every splendid facility for the storage and movement of essential parts, but with no place for a resting worker to sit down for a moment but on a fireplug, the edge of a packing case, or the sputum- and oil-stained stairway of a toilet.)

The older men stay put and wait for their vacations. But since the assembly line demands young blood (you will have a hard time getting hired if you are over thirty-five), the factory in which I worked was aswarm with new faces every day; labor turnover was so fantastic and absenteeism so rampant, with the young men knocking off a day or two every week to hunt up other jobs, that the company was forced to overhire in order to have sufficient workers on hand at the starting siren.

To those who will object—fortified by their readings in C. Wright Mills and A. C. Spectorsky—that the white-collar commuter, too, dislikes his work, accepts it only because it buys his family commodities, and is constantly on the prowl for other work, I can only reply that for me at any rate this is proof not of the disappearance of the working class but of the proletarianization of the middle class. Perhaps it is not taking place quite in the way that Marx envisaged it, but the alienation of the white-collar man (like that of the laborer) from both his tools and whatever he produces, the slavery that chains the exurbanite to the commuting timetable (as the worker is still chained to the time clock), the anxiety that sends the white-collar man home with his briefcase for an evening's work (as it degrades the working-man into pleading for long hours of overtime), the displacement of the white-collar slum from the wrong side of the tracks to the suburbs (just as the working-class slum is moved from old-law tenements to skyscraper barracks)—all these mean to me that the white-collar man is entering (though his arms may be loaded with commodities) the gray world of the working man.

Three quotations from men with whom I worked may help to bring my view into focus:

Before starting work: "Come on, suckers, they say the Foundation wants to give away *more* than half a billion this year. Let's do and die for the old Foundation."

During rest period: "Ever stop to think how we crawl here bumper to bumper, and crawl home bumper to bumper, and we've got to turn out more every minute to keep our jobs, when there isn't even any room for them on the highways?"

At quitting time (this from older foremen, whose job is not only to keep things moving, but by extension to serve as company spokesmen): "You're smart to get out of here. . . . I curse the day I ever started, now I'm stuck: any man with brains that stays here ought 239 to have his head examined. This is no place for an intelligent human being."

Such is the attitude toward the work. And toward the product? On the one hand it is admired and desired as a symbol of freedom, almost a substitute for freedom, not because the worker participated in making it, but because our whole culture is dedicated to the proposition that the automobile is both necessary and beautiful. On the other hand it is hated and despised—so much that if your new car smells bad it may be due to a banana peel crammed down its gullet and sealed up thereafter, so much so that if your dealer can't locate the rattle in your new car you might ask him to open the welds on one of those tail fins and vacuum out the nuts and bolts thrown in by workers sabotaging their own product.

Sooner or later, if we want a decent society—by which I do not mean a society glutted with commodities or one maintained in precarious equilibrium by overbuying and forced premature obsolescence —we are going to have to come face to face with the problem of work. Apparently the Russians have committed themselves to the replenishment of their labor force through automatic recruitment of those intellectually incapable of keeping up with severe scholastic requirements in the public educational system. Apparently we, too, are heading in the same direction: although our economy is not directed, and although college education is as yet far from free, we seem to be operating in this capitalist economy on the totalitarian assumption that we can funnel the underprivileged, undereducated, or just plain underequipped, into the factory, where we can proceed to forget about them once we have posted the minimum fair labor standards on the factory wall.

If this is what we want, let's be honest enough to say so. If we conclude that there is nothing noble about repetitive work, but that it is nevertheless good enough for the lower orders, let's say that, too, so we will at least know where we stand. But if we cling to the belief that other men are our brothers, not just Egyptians, or Israelis, or Hungarians, but *all* men, including millions of Americans who grind their lives away on an insane treadmill, then we will have to start thinking about how their work and their lives can be made meaningful. That is what I assume the Hungarians, both workers and intellectuals, have been thinking about. Since no one has been ordering us what to think, since no one has been forbidding our intellectuals to fraternize with our workers, shouldn't it be a little easier for us to admit, first, that our problems exist, then to state them, and then to see if we can resolve them?

Marian Gennaria Morris

Psychological Miscarriage:
An End to Mother Love

Not long ago a mother in the Midwest, while giving her baby its bath, held its head underwater until it drowned. She said that there was something wrong with the child. Its smell was strange and unpleasant; it drooled; it seemed dull and listless. It reminded her of a retarded relative, and the thought of having to spend the rest of her life caring for such a person terrified her. Her husband was out of work, and she was pregnant again. She said she "felt the walls closing in." When, in her confused and ignorant way, she had asked her husband, a neighbor, and a doctor for help, she got promises, preachments, and evasions. So she drowned the baby.

This mother said she had felt "so all alone." But, unfortunately, she had plenty of company. Many thousands of American women do not love or want their babies. Although few actually kill their infants, the crippling effects of early maternal rejection on children can hardly be exaggerated—or glossed over. The number directly involved is large. The social harm, for everybody, is great. An idea of the size of the problem can be gained from the following figures, taken from federal, state, and local sources:

> 50-70,000 children neglected, battered, exploited annually;
> 150,000 children in foster homes for these reasons;

Reprinted by permission of the author and publisher from *Trans-action*, a publication of the Community Leadership Project (Washington University, St. Louis, Missouri), January 1966, pp. 8–13. Marian Gennaria Morris is Director of Social Work for Comprehensive Pediatric Care for Children and Youth, Woman's Medical College of Pennsylvania.

THE DEPERSONALIZED

over 300,000 children in foster care altogether;

8 to 10 percent of all school children in one twenty-county study in need of psychiatric examination and some type of treatment for their problems.

But even these figures can hardly begin to describe the violence, deprivation, and dehumanization involved.

Recently we concluded a study of thirty rejecting mothers and their children who can serve as examples. Our findings are supported by a number of other studies of parents and their children who have various physical and psychological disorders. Although the poor are hardest hit by family and emotional problems it should be noted that the majority of these families were not poverty-stricken. Psychological miscarriage of motherhood attacks all classes and levels.

Twenty-one of the thirty mothers demonstrated clearly from the time of delivery that they could not properly mother or care for their babies—could not even meet their basic needs. Yet no one who had had contact with them—neither doctors, nurses, nor social workers—had apparently been able to help, effectively, any one of them, nor even seemed aware that severe problems existed.

The entire population of mothers was characterized by old troubles and hopelessness, stretching back to the previous generation—and in one-third of the cases, back to the third generation. Half the children were illegitimate, or conceived before marriage. Sixty per cent of the families had been in juvenile, criminal or domestic courts at some earlier time. Two-thirds of the children were either first-borns, or first-borns of their sex—and lack of experience with children increased their mothers' insecurities.

All thirty children needed intensive psychiatric treatment. Only two of the thirty were "well" enough—from homes that were "stable" enough—for out-patient care to even be considered. The remaining twenty-eight were headed for institutions. Their prognoses are grave, their chances doubtful. They will cost us a great deal in the years to come, and their problems will be with us a long time. Some will never walk the streets as free men and women.

Actually, the children were so disturbed that they could not be diagnosed with great accuracy. For instance, it was impossible to tell how intelligent most really were because they were in such emotional turmoil that they could not function properly on tests, and seemed retarded. A fifth of them had been so beaten around the head that it is quite possible their brains were damaged. (One baby had been thrown across the room and allowed to stay where it fell.) Women who feel neglected and less than human in turn neglect their children and treat them as less than human.

242

In our supposedly interdependent society, we are close together in violence, but apathetic to each other's needs. But apathy to their needs constitutes a violence to women facing labor, delivery, and the early and bewildering adjustments of motherhood. And it is in these days and weeks that psychological miscarriage occurs.

During pregnancy, labor, and delivery the basic fears of childhood —mutilation, abandonment, and loss of love—are vividly revived for a woman, and with double force—for herself and the baby. Nor are these fears simply fantasies: mothers *are* frequently cut, torn, and injured, babies *are* born with congenital defects.

The entire pregnancy period, with its lowering of defenses, makes the mother more capable of loving and feeling for her baby. But whether she finds his needs pleasing or threatening depends on what happened to her in the past, and the support she gets in the present.

After delivery, still in physical and emotional stress, under great pressure, she must make the most important, difficult adjustments of all. She must "claim" her baby. That is, she must make it, emotionally, part of herself again; identify it with the qualities and values in herself and her life that she finds good, safe, reassuring, and rewarding. After all the dreams and fears of pregnancy, she now must face and cope with the reality—the baby and his needs. If she miscarries now and rejects the child as something bad that cannot be accepted, then the child cannot grow to be normal. Nor can its society be normal, since the mothers must hand down to each generation the values by which society survives.

In older days, when most women had their babies at home, these adjustments were made in familiar surroundings, with such family support as was available. Now they are made largely in the hospital. What actually happens to mothers in today's hospitals?

Childbirth, once a magnificent shared experience, has increasingly become a technical event. Administrative and physical needs get priority. Emotional needs and personalities tend to get in the way of efficiency. Administrators and medical personnel, like everyone else, respond most readily to those pressures which affect them. Since they are in charge, they pass them down to the patient, whether they help the patient or not.

The mothers of the poor in particular arrive faceless, knowing no one on the ward, with little personal, human contact from before birth until they leave. Increasingly, they arrive already in labor, so that the hospitals cannot turn them away. They also come at this late stage so that they can avoid the constant procession of doctors and the three and four-hour clinic waits, during which they are called "mother" because their names have been lost in the impersonal 243

THE DEPERSONALIZED .

clinic protocols. In the wards, they may be referred to simply by their bed numbers.

Birth itself may be subordinated to the schedule: some doctors schedule their deliveries, and induce labor to keep them on time. Even "natural" labor may be slowed down or speeded up by drugs for convenience.

A PUBLIC EVENT

Mothers say that they are allowed little dignity or modesty. Doctors strange to them may, and do, examine them intimately, with little attempt at privacy. They say that without their permission they are often used as live lecture material, giving birth before interested audiences of young interns and students while the obstetrician meticulously describes each step and tissue. How apathetic we have become to the routine dehumanization of mothers is well illustrated by the story of an upper-middle-class woman I know. She was in labor, almost hidden by drapes preparatory to vaginal examination, light flooding her perineum (but not her face). Approached by a nurse and gloved physician she suddenly sat up in her short-tailed hospital gown and said, "I don't know who *you* are, doctor, but *I* am Mrs. Mullahy." Good for Mrs. Mullahy! She has a strong sense of personal identity, and is determined to preserve it.

Mothers say they are isolated and humiliated. They say that in addition to their own anxieties they must worry about what their doctors think, and be careful to please and propitiate the staff members, who may have power of life and death over them and their babies.

They say that they are kept in stirrups for hours—shackled in what reduces them to something sub-human—yet afraid to complain.

Is it increasingly true, as mothers say, that babies are not presented to them for from four to twelve hours after birth? Social histories show that prompt presentation is necessary for the mental health of the mothers; studies of other mammals indicate that such delay interrupts mothering impulses and may bring on rejection of the young. Is this happening to human mothers and babies? How necessary, medically, is such a delay? Is it worth the price?

Many women become deeply depressed after childbirth. Is this at least partly a reaction to hospital experiences? Is it an early distress signal of psychological miscarriage? There is very little research that attempts to assess early maternal adaptation, and we need such research badly. Are the violent mothers, so brutal to their children, violent at least in part because of our faceless and impersonal birth practices? Clinical studies show that the less sense of identity and personal worth a mother has, the more easily she displaces her aggressions onto others—*any* others. Are we scapegoating our children?

244

To a mother, the birth of her baby is not a technical event. It starts in intimate contact with the father, and has deep roots in her feelings for and relationship with him, whether positive or negative. It reflects her personality, her state of maturity, the experiences of her most intimate anxieties and special hopes, and her associations with the adults who have had most influence on her. She enters the hospital prey to childhood insecurities, and stripped alike of defenses and clothes. Attitudes and cues from the hospital personnel, and from others, strongly affect her self respect and her feelings about her own and her baby's worth.

It is difficult to observe most normal claiming behavior in a hospital. But some of it can be observed. Most mothers, for example, do find ways to make contact with their babies' bodies—touching and examining them all over delightedly, even to the tiny spaces between fingers and toes—cooing and listening to them, inhaling their odors, nuzzling and kissing them.

Socially, a major way to claim a child is to name it. Names suggest protective good magic; they establish identity and suggest personality; they emphasize masculinity or femininity; they affirm family continuity and the child's place in it.

Nevertheless, it is usually difficult to follow claiming behavior for two reasons. First, because hospital routines and tasks interfere. To the staff, the process of mothers becoming acquainted with infants is seen as merely cute, amusing, or inconvenient. Babies are presented briefly, pinned and blanketed tightly, making intimate fondling—for women who have carried these infants for months—difficult and sometimes even guilt-producing.

The second reason is related to the nature of normal motherhood. The well-adjusted mother is secure within herself, content to confine her communications mostly to her baby, rather than project them outward. As Tolstoy said of marriage, all happy ones tend to be happy in the same way, and relatively quiet. But the unhappy ones are different and dramatic—and it is by observing unhappy mothers that the pathological breakdown of maternal claiming can be most easily traced.

Let us consider a few examples:

Tim—Breakdown in Early Infancy. When Tim's mother first felt him move in her, and realized then that all evasion and doubt about her pregnancy was past, she blacked out (she said) and fell down a flight of stairs.

Tim was her second child. Her first pregnancy was difficult and lonely and, she had been told, both she and the baby had almost died during delivery. She suffered from migraine headaches, and was terrified of a second delivery.

245

THE DEPERSONALIZED

For the first four months of Tim's life, she complained that he had virulent diarrhea and an ugly odor, and took him from doctor to doctor. Assured by each one that there was nothing wrong with the child (in the hospital the diarrhea cleared up in one day), she took this to mean that there was something wrong with *her*—so she sought another doctor. She took out thirteen different kinds of cancer insurance on Tim.

During an interview, she told a woman social worker that it was too bad that doctors could not look inside a baby and know he was *all* O.K.

The social worker decided to probe deeper: "You would have a hard time convincing me that you *deliberately* threw yourself down those stairs."

"Who, me? Why I told my mother all along that I would never *willingly* hurt a hair of one of my children's heads."

"But suppose you had, unwillingly. Would you blame someone else for doing it, under the circumstances?"

"No! I was sick and don't even know how it happened."

After that, the demon that had haunted her was in the open, and recovery began. She had felt that she was both criminal and victim, with the child as the instrument of her punishment. (Only a "good" mother deserves a good baby; a "bad" mother deserves a "bad"— damaged or sick—baby.) The implied criticisms of her mother and doctor had aggravated these feelings. She identified Tim not with the good in her but the "evil"—he was something faulty, something to be shunned.

Under treatment she learned to accept herself and regain her role of mother. She was not really the bad little girl her critical mother and doctor had implied; neither, therefore, was Tim bad—she could accept him. It was no longer dangerous to identify with her. She let Tim see her face; she held him comfortably for the first time; she did not mention his "ugly" smell; she stayed by his bed instead of restlessly patrolling the corridors. She referred to our hospital as the place she had "got him *at,*" instead of the hospital, ninety miles away, where he had actually been born.

Jack—Effects on an Older Child. Shortly after Jack was born, his mother asked her obstetrician whether Jack's head was all right. Gently touching the forceps marks, he said, *"These* will clear up." Thinking that she had been told delicately that she had a defective child, she did not talk to Jack for five-and-a-half years—did not believe he could understand speech.

At five-and-a-half, approaching school, he had never spoken. A psychologist, thinking that the child was not essentially retarded, referred the mother to a child guidance clinic, where the social worker asked whether she had ever found out if the obstetrician

246

had meant the *inside* of Jack's head. For the first time in all the years it occurred to her that there might have been a misunderstanding. Three months later Jack was talking—though many more months of treatment were still necessary before he could function adequately for his age.

Behind this, of course, was much more than a misunderstanding. Behind it was Jack's mother's feelings of guilt for having caused her own mother's death. Guilt went back many years. During an auto ride long ago, she had an accident in which her mother suffered a mild blow on the head. In the early months of pregnancy with Jack, she had found her mother dead in the tub. The cause was cancer, which had nothing to do with the bump. But deep down she could not believe this, and she developed the fear that Jack's head, too, was damaged—a fitting punishment for a woman who feared she had killed her mother. When her obstetrician seemed to confirm it, she did not question further.

For almost six years Jack was not so much an infant or child as a damaged head. Like her mother he was silent—from "brain injury." It was only under treatment that she accepted the possibility that she might have "misunderstood."

Babs—Hell Revisited. Babs was fourteen months old when she was flown to our hospital from South America, physically ill with diarrhea and dehydration, and emotionally badly withdrawn. In South America, her mother had trouble getting proper drugs and talking effectively with Spanish-speaking doctors—and when she had had to face Bab's pleading eyes with little relief to offer, she had gone into acute panic. She hadn't been able to comfort her child, but had drawn away and could hardly look at her or touch her. From this rejection Babs had in turn withdrawn, and a mutual vicious cycle of rebuff and retreat had come about.

The mother felt that she had lived through all this before in her own childhood. When she was five, she had had a little brother, aged three. Her sick mother often left him in her charge. ("He was *my* baby.") One day both ate sprayed peaches from a tree. Both came down with severe diarrhea. She survived. She remembers vividly seeing him in "his little white coffin."

The pregnancy period with Babs had been stormy, full of family crises; she felt guilty about "not feeding Babs right." She could not accept the reassurances of her obstetrician. After Babs was born she was over-meticulous about cleaning her after bowel movements.

During treatment she shook visibly when asked whether Babs resembled her in any way. But when asked: "Could you have been Jim's *real* mother when you were only five?" she relaxed, and grew radiant. Later she said: "I know *now* that I couldn't have known that the peaches were poisoned."

247

"Nor that Babs would get sick with diarrhea if you went to South America to live with your husband?"

"No. I know now that the *place* is not good for any of us. I didn't know that before."

In a few days she was admiring in Babs the very qualities she had said she admired in herself—her sense of fun, and her determination. The positive identification between them had been made.

CLUES TO MATERNAL HAZARDS IN MOTHERING

There are several criteria that can be used to assess the adequacy of a mother's behavior during the early weeks of an infant's life. Mother-infant unity can be said to be *satisfactory* when a mother can: find pleasure in her infant and in tasks for and with him; understand his emotional states and comfort him; read his cues for new experience, sense his fatigue points.

For example she can receive his eye contact with pleasure; can promote his new learnings through use of her face, hands and objects; does not overstimulate him for her own pleasure.

In contrast, there are specific signs that mothers give when they are *not adapting* to their infants:

> See their infants as ugly or unattractive.
> Perceive the odor of their infants as revolting.
> Are disgusted by their drooling and sucking sounds.
> Become upset by vomiting, but seem fascinated by it.
> Are revolted by any of the infants' body fluids which touch them, or which they touch.
> Show annoyance at having to clean up infants' stools.
> Become preoccupied with the odor, consistency and number of infants' stools.
> Let infants' heads dangle, without support or concern.
> Hold infants away from their own bodies.
> Pick up infants without warning by touch or speech.
> Juggle and play with infants, roughly, after feeding, even though they often vomit at this behavior.
> Think infants' natural motor activity is unnatural.
> Worry about infant's relaxation following feeding.
> Avoid eye contact with infants, or stare fixedly into their eyes.
> Do not coo or talk with infants.
> Think that their infants do not love them.
> Believe their infants expose them as unlovable, unloving parents.
> Think of their infants as judging them and their efforts as an adult would.
> Perceive their infants' natural dependent needs as dangerous.
> Fear death at appearance of mild diarrhea or cold.
> Are convinced that infants have defects, in spite of repeated physical examinations which prove negative.

248

Often fear that infants have diseases connected with "eating", leukemia, or one of the other malignancies; diabetes; cystic fibrosis.

Constantly demand reassurance that no defect or disease exists, cannot believe relieving facts when they are given.

Demand that feared defects be found and relieved.

Cannot find in their infants any physical or psychological attribute which they value in themselves.

Cannot discriminate between infant signals of hunger, fatigue, need for soothing or stimulating speech, comforting body contact, or for eye contact.

Develop inappropriate responses to infant needs: over or under-feed; over or under-hold; tickle or bounce the baby when he is fatigued; talk too much, too little, and at the wrong time; force eye contact, or refuse it; leave infant alone in room; leave infant in noisy room and ignore him.

Develop paradoxical attitudes and behaviors.

MOTHERS AS PATIENTS

How can we prevent such psychological miscarriages—and how can we limit their ravages once they have already occurred?

The dynamics of maternal rejection are not completely known—we need far more research, far more detailed and orderly observation of early maternal behavior. Nevertheless, enough is known already about the symptoms for us to be able to work up a reliable profile of the kind of woman who is most likely to suffer damage, and to take steps to make sure that help is offered in time. After all, the ultimate cause of maladaptation is lack of human sympathy, contact, and support, even though the roots may go back for more than one generation. We must, therefore, offer that support. We may not be able completely to heal old, festering wounds, but we can palliate their worst effects, and keep them from infecting new babies.

Mothers in our study identified the periods of greatest danger as just before and after delivery. It is then—and swiftly—that intervention by a psychiatric team should occur. What can be done?

We must have early recognition of trouble. Early signs of maternal maladaptation are evident in the mutual aversion of mother and child. But these signs have to be watched for—they cannot be ignored because of hospital routine that is "more important."

Let the mother have enough time to see and become acquainted with the hospital personnel with whom she will experience birth. Length of hospital stay is geared to technical requirements—five days for middle-class mothers, down (in some places) to twenty-four hours or less for the poor. Therefore, acquaintance should start before birth, at least with the physician, so that when delivery comes the mother will not be faced with a stranger in cap and gown, but a human being she already knows. Nurses and social workers should also be 249 included. (The Hahnemann Medical College and Hospital in Philadelphia already assigns resident physicians to the pre-natal clinics to provide this continuity.)

Mothers of young infants suffer from geographical and psychological isolation. Services should work toward reducing both of these isolations. Ideally such services should come from a team, including not only the doctor and nurses, but a sympathetic pediatrician, psychiatric and medical social workers, of both sexes, who could also act as substitute parents. This help should be as available to the middle-class as to the poor (middle-class patients are sometimes denied hospital social services).

Help should carry over into home care. *Make sure that each mother has someone to care for her at home.* After their too brief hospital stay, poverty-stricken women, many without husband or family, are often more helpless and lost at home than in the hospital.

Mothers should not be left alone for long periods, whether under sedation or not. Schedules should and must be modified to allow them to have normal family support as long as possible. If they have none, substitutes—volunteers—should be found. Isolated mothers, cut off from support or even contact with their physicians, and treated as objects, much too often displace their loneliness, depression, resentment, bitterness, humiliation, rage, and pain onto their babies.

Get rid of the stirrups—and the practice of using them to hang mothers' legs in the air for hours! Find some other way to hold women on the delivery table until the last moments. Women often spend months recovering from backaches caused by stirrups.

Present the baby as soon as possible. The most frequent comment from mothers who remain conscious in the delivery room is, "The doctor gave him to me." This is psychologically very sound; when the father-image (doctor) presents the baby with the obvious approval of the mother-image (nurse), latent feelings of guilt about having a baby and about the acceptability of the baby—and of motherhood —are lulled and dispelled. Too often, however, the nurse is cast, or casts herself, in the role of unwilling, stingy, critical giver of the baby —in fact the whole institution lends itself to this. Presentation should precede and not depend on feeding; it should be made gladly and willingly; it should allow time and ease of access for the mother to examine her baby's body.

Doctors, nurses, and aides should understand and come to know pregnancy, labor, delivery, and early growth as a continuing process, rather than in bits and pieces, a series of techniques. They need to understand and see it from the mothers' viewpoint, as well as in terms of bottles, diapers, rooms, instruments, and procedures.

Reassure mothers about their infants. This includes understanding the real meanings of their questions. If a mother continually discounts good reports, rejection may be underway, and psychological miscarriage imminent.

250

First-born children, and the first-borns of each sex, are the ones most commonly rejected; their mothers need special care—as do the mothers of the poor and those without family, husband, or outside human supports.

None of these proposals are radical—even administratively. Most are quite simple, and could be done directly in the wards and the private rooms.

Overall, we need more research. We do not know enough about the earliest signals of psychological miscarriage; we have not trained ourselves, nor taken the trouble, to watch for these early signs. Nor do we know enough about the long-term effects of maladaptation. Are the older children completely lost? Is the process irreversible? Cannot something be done to bring them back to productive life?

There is nothing more important in a maternity pavilion, nor in a home, than the experiences with which life begins. We must stop the dehumanization of mothers. We must give all children a chance for life.

Harry M. Caudill

The Permanent Poor
THE LESSON OF EASTERN KENTUCKY

The Cumberland Plateau of Kentucky is one of the great natural resource regions of the American continent. Industrialists bought up its great wealth three quarters of a century ago and soon after 1900 commenced the large-scale extraction of its timber and minerals. When the development of the eastern Kentucky coalfields began, mining was largely a manual pursuit. Mining machines were displacing mules and ponies, and electricity was making it possible to do an increasing number of tasks with electric power rather than muscle power. Nevertheless, some of the undercutting of coal, much of the drilling, and practically all of the loading into cars were done by armies of grit-blackened miners. Industrial wages enticed thousands of mountaineers to turn from the plow and hoe to the pick and shovel. Hordes of Negroes were induced away from the cotton rows of Georgia, the Carolinas, Tennessee, Mississippi, and Alabama and forsook plantation life for the mines. Shiploads of Europeans were brought to the southern coalfield. The extraction of the region's mineral wealth was undertaken in the atmosphere of a tremendous industrial boom.

The Depression destroyed the coalfield's prosperity, but the Second World War revived it, and for a few years the boom returned and the miner was again a useful and honored citizen. The coal industry depended upon his skill and courage, and steel production, electric-power generation, and other basic industries were dependent upon coal. The collapse of the war and of the post-war boom is now history, and we have an opportunity to reflect upon the social, political, and

Reprinted by permission of the author and publisher from *The Atlantic Monthly*, June 1964, pp. 49–53. Copyright © 1964, by The Atlantic Monthly Company (Boston, Massachusetts). Harry M. Caudill, an attorney in Whiteburg, Kentucky, is author of *Night Comes to the Cumberlands*.

252

economic consequences that result when a modernized industry is able to cast aside three quarters of its workmen within the span of a decade.

In the post-war years technologists were able to design and manufacture machines of remarkable power and efficiency. Their genius was nowhere better demonstrated than in the coal industry. Devices were developed for boring directly back into the face of the coal seam, and chewing out immense quantities of the mineral, thus eliminating the need to undercut or blast the seam. Simultaneously, the conveyor belt displaced the tracks, mining locomotives, and strings of cars in many mines. Roof bolting made its appearance. This method of supporting the roof eliminated the need for wooden props and proved most effective. A single mechanical loading machine could load more coal than two dozen hardworking shovelers.

Machines were costly, but investment capital was plentiful. The mine operators borrowed from the banks and mechanized and automated the mines and tipples to a remarkable degree. Big, amply financed operations bought up their small competitors. Many inefficient and nearly worked-out pits suspended operations altogether. Thus in a few years the fragmented and archaic coal industry became surprisingly modern and technologically advanced. The operators were delighted. Corporations that were bankrupt only a few years before now basked in a sustained new prosperity. For example, Consolidation Coal Company, which had been in receivership, paid off all its obligations and acquired a controlling interest in Chrysler Corporation.

While a new optimism pervaded the officer of the automated and mechanized companies, disaster befell thousands of the men who had depended for so long upon the old industry. By the thousands they found the scrip offices and payroll windows closed in their faces. Mining companies for which they and their fathers had worked, in some instances for two generations, simply vanished altogether. Some three fourths of eastern Kentucky's miners found themselves without work. They had become the victims of a materialistic social order which venerates efficiency and wealth above all other things and largely disregards social and human consequences. When they were no longer needed, their employers dropped them as a coal miner might have thrown away the scrip coins of a bankrupt company.

The legions of industrial outcasts were left with three choices. They could leave the area and find work elsewhere if employment of any kind could be found. Many thousands followed this course, and the population of the mining counties subsided dramatically. A third of the people fled from the shadow of starvation.

They could remain within the region and attempt to live by mining coal from the thin seams not monopolized by the big and highly efficient operations. These men could operate small "doghole" mines 253 with little equipment and trifling capital, pitting their arms and backs against the tireless machines of their big competitors. They were goaded to desperation by the fact that in a camp house or a creek shanty a wife and five to ten children depended upon them for clothes and bread. They had been educated for the mines at a time when little formal education was required for that calling. Thus, in the contest with the big coal corporations they could contribute little except their muscles and their will. Thousands entered these small mines, often "gang-working" as partners and sharing the meager profits at paydays.

In the third situation was the miner who for one reason or another could not or would not leave the area, and found that however hard he toiled in the small mines his income was too meager to provide for the needs of his household. He and his family became charges of the government. Federal and state agencies came to his relief with a wide variety of cash and commodity doles. He was confined to a kind of dull, bleak reservation-existence reminiscent of that imposed by military fiat on the reservation Indians of the Western plains.

Living by welfare, without work and without purpose save existence, these numerous mountaineers settled down to while away the years and await developments.

The men who left the region for the great cities of the North and Middle West did not always find smooth sailing. The rapid process of industrial modernization which had first, and so dramatically, waved its wand across the eastern Kentucky coalfield had penetrated into the immense industrial complexes of the nation's cities. Assembly lines which had traditionally required hundreds of swarming workmen were reorganized, and wonderfully efficient machines were introduced into the automobile and other great manufacturing industries. In many instances, these machines were guided by sensitive electronic masters which, with belts of punched plastic and electric current, could impose unerring and immediate obedience.

In some respects, to be sure, eastern Kentucky is unique. Its people were dependent for fifty years on but a single industry, and, remarkably, they were an industrial people living in a rural rather than an urban setting. The coal industry, like extractive industries generally, invested little of its profits back in the region and allowed its communities to maintain schools of only the most rudimentary sort. It created an environment which left its workmen almost totally dependent upon their employers for bread and leadership, then provided only a small measure of the former and practically none of the latter. Nevertheless, the collapse of coal as a mass hirer of men left in the Kentucky mountains a splendid case study of the social and political implications arising from the displacement of men by machines.

Government at all levels was wholly unprepared for the dramatic 254 developments that ensued. To be sure, these developments were a logical outgrowth of the continuing industrial revolution, which, once set in motion, appears to be destined to carry us inevitably toward a day when a few people and many machines will do the work for a leisurely population of consumers. But between the first spinning jenny and the distant utopia lie many pitfalls, some of which yawn before us today.

In short, government in our democratic society proved practically bankrupt of ideas when confronted with this new challenge. Hoping against hope that expansion in other industries would eventually absorb the displaced miners, government agencies waited. When the stranded miner had exhausted his unemployment insurance benefits and his savings, when he had come to the ragged edge of starvation and was cloaked in bewilderment and frustration, government came to his rescue with the dole. It arranged to give him a bag of cheese, rice, cornmeal, beef, butter, and dried milk solids at intervals, and in most instances to send him a small check. Having thus contrived to keep the miner and his family alive, the government lost interest in him. Appropriations were made from time to time for his sustenance, but little thought was given to his spirit, his character, his manhood. He was left to dry-rot in the vast paleface reservation created for his perpetuation in his native hills.

And, inevitably, he fell prey to the politicians who dispense the bread and money by which he lives. Coal mining and thirty years of subservience to the scrip window had already done much to impair the mountaineer's ability to adapt well to rapidly changing circumstances. He had dwelt too long as a kind of industrial serf in company-owned houses, on company-owned streets, in company-owned towns. For too long the company had buffered him from the swift-flowing social and economic tides swirling in the world outside his narrow valleys. When his employers cast him aside, he still possessed only a single valuable remnant of his birthright—the ballot. He was essential to the politicians because he could vote, so he was placed in a sort of suspended animation in which he came fully to life only at election time. He became increasingly dependent upon the political machines that ran his counties. He accepted the food doles and the welfare checks and ratified the arrangement by voting for the men and women who thus sustained him. The politicians expanded their operations into other fields where public funds could make the difference between life and death. In all too many counties they captured the school systems, thereby acquiring large new sums to be dispensed as patronage. The positions of schoolteacher, bus driver, lunchroom director, truant officer, and a multitude of others were treated as so many plums to be dispensed to the acquiescent, the obedient, and the meek. The union of school politics and welfare politics resulted in a formidable prodigy indeed. Its power was quickly recognized at Frankfort and Washington. New political pacts were made, and a wide range of state jobs 255 were placed at the disposal of the local overlords. Thus their power became virtually complete.

Today in many eastern Kentucky counties political machines of remarkable efficiency are to be found. Their effectiveness surpasses Tammany Hall at its best. In a typical county the school board and state agencies control the biggest payrolls. The politicians who run them can also reach and influence the many small merchants, automobile dealers, and service-station operators with whom they do business. Thus they are masters of the majority of those who still work for a living.

The state and federal governments act as tax-collecting enterprises, which funnel vast sums into the hands of merciless and amoral local political dynasties. The county machines dispense the funds so as to perpetuate themselves and their allies at Frankfort and Washington. Increasingly, these omniscient organizations manage to gather into their hands funds and gifts from private charities, including even the American Red Cross. Taxpayers in fifty states, oblivious to what their dollars buy, pay little heed to this ominous course of events.

These developments raise a disquieting question which Americans have never confronted before:

How fares the American concept of government of the people, by the people, and for the people when a clear majority become permanently dependent upon and subservient to their elected leaders?

Indeed, can democratic government survive at all in such a setting?

The situation in eastern Kentucky is new to the American scene, but much of the pattern is as old as Rome.

In ancient Italy the social order was remarkably healthy so long as the populace consisted, in the main, of freeholding farmers and self-employed artisans and artificers. The scene darkened when Roman armies conquered distant territories and sent home multitudes of captives. The rich bought up the small plots of farmers and cultivated the resultant plantations with the labor of slaves. Other slaves were set to work in mass manufactories. Because of their great numbers, their carefully planned organization, and their specialization, they were able to produce far more cheaply than their self-employed, free competitors. The corporations that ran these huge enterprises provided grain, leather goods, cloth, and weapons for the empire. The free men and women flocked to the towns and cities to cluster in slums. To keep them orderly the government fed them, clothed them, and entertained them with games. An astoundingly complex system of doles and subsidies was perfected to sustain the idled millions of Roman citizens. In idleness the Roman decayed. He became bitter, vengeful, irresponsible, and bloodthirsty. The mutterings of Roman mobs came to speak more loudly than the voice of Caesar. Rome withered within, long before alien armies crashed through her walls.

These ancient events cast shadows of portent for us today. The machine is a far more profitable servant than any slave. It is untiring, wears out slowly, and requires no food or medication. Technological progress is inexorable and moves toward perfection. What will be the final consequences of it all for the American ideals of equality, liberty, and justice?

We are in the throes of a rapidly quickening new technological revolution. Fifty years ago 700,000 American coal miners were able to mine less coal than 140,000 dig today. Experts tell us that coal production may double by 1980 without any increase in the number of miners. Automobile production increases year by year, but the number of workmen declines. In every field of manufacturing, sensitive, accurate, unfailing steel monsters crowd men and women from workbench and turning lathe, from well and mine. On the land the number of farmers decreases as farms are consolidated into giant tracts. Tractors and mechanical cotton pickers and threshers have rendered the farm laborer as obsolete as the coal miner of 1945.

New turns of the technological wheel are in sight. In twenty years nuclear power may render all fossil fuels obsolete, valued only for their chemical derivatives. If this occurs, new legions of workmen will follow the coal miner into abrupt obsolescence.

On the material side, this revolution undoubtedly represents only progress. It brings us more and more goods for less and less work, thus bringing to fruition one of mankind's ancient dreams.

But what of man's social, spiritual, and political aspects? Is it possible we are moving rapidly forward on the one hand and going backward to barbarism on the other?

What is to become of the jobless miner who takes his family to a Chicago housing development, there to press in upon a onetime automobile assembler from Detroit and a discarded tool and die maker from Pittsburgh? What results when these men and their wives and children are joined by a Negro from Mississippi whose job as a cotton picker was taken over by a machine, or by a white hill-farmer from Tennessee whose ninety acres could not produce corn in competition with the splendidly mechanized farms of Iowa? Are the mushrooming housing developments of the great cities to become the habitations of millions of permanently idled people, supported by a welfare program as ruinous as the one devised by the Caesars? Are whole segments of American citizenry to be consigned to lifetimes of vexatious idleness, resentment, and bitterness? Are these centers to become vast new slums out of which will issue the ominous rumblings of titanic new mobs?

And what torrents of new bitterness will be added to the nation's bloodstream when computers send multitudes of white-collar workers into abrupt idleness in the mortgaged houses of suburbia?

257

In my opinion these questions pose the foremost issue of our time.

It strikes me that our scientists may develop the explosive power to send a few Americans to Mars while, simultaneously, our society prepares a vastly greater explosive power among disillusioned millions of Americans who remain behind on our own battered planet.

The industrialists who run the eastern Kentucky coalfield laid careful plans for the creation and use of mining machines but cast aside their mining men as lightheartedly as one might discard a banana peel. Most of the victims of this callous treatment accepted their fate resignedly. Some did not, however, and in the winter of 1962–1963 the hills in four eastern Kentucky counties resounded with gunfire and nocturnal explosions. For several months a situation bordering on anarchy prevailed across a wide region. Tipples and mines were blasted. Automobiles, power lines, and mining machines were destroyed. Such acts were committed by desperate men seeking to strike at a social and economic order which had rejected them.

Today the challenge of eastern Kentucky is a great national challenge. If we can triumph over it, the solutions we find will offer hope to the entire nation. Increasingly, the agony of eastern Kentucky is but a part of the misery that afflicts great cities, mill towns, and mining regions everywhere. The pain grows out of the evil paradox of mass idleness in the midst of booming production.

Liberty, like a chain, is no stronger than its weakest part. If the freedom and well-being of a part of the people are lost, the freedom and well-being of all are mortally imperiled. If the nation writes off our southern highlands as unworthy of rescue and rehabilitation, then the nation as a whole is unworthy of survival. As an optimist and a liberal I believe that the nation will rise to the challenge of the depressed and backward Appalachian region, and that in so doing, it will find many of the answers that democracy requires for survival throughout the nation.

A population equivalent to the present population of New York State is being added to the nation every four or five years. Technology eliminates some 40,000 jobs each week. These facts tell us that we must successfully master new frontiers of social justice, and do so in a hurry, or become another nation of regimented serfs.

A social and political crisis of the first magnitude will confront America before the end of another decade. Substitutes for such presently accepted goals as full employment will have to be found. Fresh definitions of the concepts of work, leisure, abundance, and scarcity are imperatively needed. Economic theories adequate to an infant industrial revolution are wholly unsatisfactory when applied to a full-fledged scientific revolution such as that which now engulfs us. The complexity and interdependence of the scientific-industrial nation call for national planning and action. Government must and will intervene more and more in the nation's industrial life. The destiny toward which we move is a national economy under the law. A radical change in public attitude toward law and government is necessary if the general welfare is to be achieved without the total sacrifice of of individual liberty. Having bargained for the benefits of technology on all fronts, law is our only means of assuring that it serves the common good.

In 1963 the American economy brought unprecedented prosperity to some 80 percent of the people. Simultaneously, a segment of the population as numerous as the inhabitants of Poland consisted of paupers, and 5.5 percent of the nation's bread-winners were without jobs. Clearly a new tack must be taken soon unless America the Beautiful is to become a crazy quilt of bustle and sloth, brilliance and ignorance, magnificence and squalor.

For more than a dozen years the prevailing political ideology has implemented a *de facto* return to the Articles of Confederation. This doctrine holds that action at the state or local level is admirable while any direct effort by Washington to deal with social or economic malaise is un-American and dangerous. The result is a growing paralysis of the national government as an instrumentality of the public will. This reasoning has brought tremendous outpouring of federal grants-in-aid to states and communities, under circumstances which entail much waste and, often, minimal benefits.

In eastern Kentucky, and in many other depressed areas, the state government will not act effectively to combat poverty and economic decline because it is allied to or controlled by the interests that produced the problems. Thus, state officials talk piously about reform but strenuously oppose any real effort to attack the status quo. They respond to the political machines nurtured by welfare grants and founded on impoverished and dependent citizens. It is not too much to expect that, as matters now stand, federal funds trickling through state treasuries will finance the rebuilding of new political machines in practically every state—machines more odious than those once bossed by Crump, Pendergast, and Hague.

Common sense and past experience argue strongly for a system of federally administered public works. Only in America are able-bodied men permitted to loaf in idleness amid a profusion of unperformed tasks. Should not the thousands of jobless Kentucky coal miners be set to work reforesting the wasted hills, building decent consolidated schoolhouses and roads, and providing decent housing in lieu of the dreadful shacks that now dot every creek and hollow? And why not a modernized version of TVA—a Southern Mountain Authority— to develop the immense hydro- and thermal-power potential of the Appalachian South for the benefit of the entire nation, and to stop the hideous waste of the land now being wrought by the strip- and 259 auger-mining industries? What of the possibility of an educational Peace Corps to break the old cycle of poor schools, poor job preparation, poor pay, and poor people?

Unless the nation can profit from the terrible lesson eastern Kentucky so poignantly teaches, new multitudes of once prosperous Americans may find themselves slipping inexorably into an economic mire that breeds poverty, despair, dependency, and, eventually, revolution.

SIX

PEOPLE AND PLANNED COMMUNITIES

Where and how a person lives in American society is a factor of considerable importance influencing many other aspects of social life. The place of residence can become invested with status and prestige considerations, making the home an extension of the self, testifying to or validating social position. The home also has strong cultural and traditional meanings which represent such cherished values as family and private property.

Yet one's home has more than just symbolic meaning which affects psychological well-being by enhancing status or reinforcing cultural values. There is a very direct connection between residence and such life chances as quality education, police protection, decent health services, integrated schools, recreational centers, and cultural activities. It is often recognized that the vicious cycles of poverty and segregation are maintained by patterns of residential segregation.

An awareness of the importance of home and neighborhood is reflected in such large-scale programs as low-cost housing projects, urban renewal, and controlled urban growth. They are designed to allow people on marginal incomes to have decent homes, and to remove the slums that breed despair and pathology among their residents.

In the development of planned communities there has been a tendency to see most of the problems as "technical," and to focus upon these rather than upon the human problems. An extreme example of the application of technology to social problems is the recent experiment in New York City whereby an entire apartment building was completely renovated in a 72-hour period. The roof was removed from the building and totally-assembled rooms were lowered into the building to replace the old rooms. And all this was accomplished while the residents were displaced for only three days.

This is truly an amazing technical accomplishment which can in fact provide better living conditions for each resident. Still it is probably 261 true that the low-income apartments which were built 20 years ago were also viewed as amazing technical accomplishments; they provided a large number of dwelling units at very low cost to the public and to the residents. Today many of these technical feats called public housing are nothing more than high-rise slums. It should also be noted that the preoccupation with the technical-economic features of public housing fails to deal with the feelings of those who are to reside in public housing projects. A very vivid passage by James Baldwin (1961, p. 61) attempts to describe the nature of the project dwellers' response to their housing and the reasons for this response.

> They began hating it at about the time people began moving out of their condemned houses to make room for this additional proof of how thoroughly the white world despised them. And they had scarcely moved in, naturally, before they began smashing windows, defacing walls, urinating in the elevators, and fornicating in the playgrounds. Liberals, both white and black, were appalled at the spectacle. I was appalled by the liberal innocence—or cynicism, which comes out in practice as much the same thing. Other people were delighted to be able to point to proof positive that nothing could be done to better the lot of the colored people. They were, and are, right in one respect: that nothing can be done as long as they are treated like colored people.

Technical solutions, without the human or political ones, will not produce anything lasting. They do provide immediate responses which give the impression that progress is being made. Supporters of federal housing programs can point to the existence of the programs with pride, while opponents can point to the deterioration of older projects as evidence that public housing is a failure. The only one who doesn't profit from all this is the low-income resident.

The full complexity of the problems of planned communities is described in the essay by Gans. He points out how urban renewal projects often accomplish little more than to displace the slum dweller and force him to relocate in a new slum, or to overcrowd a marginal area and turn it into a slum. The issues of public development of housing as compared to the private market are also presented as part of the political debate over current and proposed programs. Gans raises the question of federal rent subsidy for low-income families to allow them to choose private housing without suffering the stigma of public housing. This solution, however, raises all the latent issues of communities that will be more mixed economically and ethnically.

The Weissbourd essay tends to be somewhat pessimistic about solutions that will allow more residents to flee the city for the suburbs. Proposals to encourage development of low-density regions outside of the city (similar to Gans' proposals) are viewed by Weissbourd as failure to confront the problems of the city. The author points to the 262 resources that the federal government has at its disposal to reshape the character of the city. Once again, the solution offered must confront the political issues associated with federal intervention, and the social issues associated with interracial communities.

The final essay by Oscar Lewis reveals how the meaning of a move from a slum to a middle-class housing project is much more than simply a matter of changing physical surroundings. Living in the slums produces many adaptations which become part of a pattern of living and which do not work in the middle-class project. Although Lewis' essay is based upon a family's experience in San Juan, Puerto Rico, the universality of the situation is quite clear.

One of the critical issues that must be faced with respect to planned communities—an issue which goes beyond the question of greater federal involvement in public housing—is inherent in the process of planning itself. This issue is the "gap" that develops between the "planners" and the "planned for." The lack of communication, the detachment that comes from not being in on the planning in a responsible way, may be one of the reasons why planned communities do not meet the needs of the people involved.

REFERENCES AND ADDITIONAL READING

James Baldwin, *Nobody Knows My Name*, New York: Dell Books, 1961.

Andrew Kopkind, "The Future-Planners," *The New Republic,* February 25, 1967, 19–24.

Morton Rubin, "Resident Response to Urban Rehabilitation in a Negro Working Class Neighborhood," in A.B. Shostak and W. Gomberg, eds., *Blue-Collar World,* Englewood Cliffs, New Jersey: Prentice-Hall, 1964.

"Social Goals and Indicators for American Society, Volume 1," *The Annals*, 371, May, 1967, entire issue.

Herbert J. Gans

The Failure of Urban Renewal
A CRITIQUE AND SOME PROPOSALS

Suppose that the government decided that jalopies were a menace to public safety and a blight on the beauty of our highways, and therefore took them away from their drivers. Suppose, then, that to replenish the supply of automobiles, it gave these drivers a hundred dollars each to buy a good used car and also made special grants to General Motors, Ford, and Chrysler to lower the cost—although not necessarily the price—of Cadillacs, Lincolns, and Imperials by a few hundred dollars. Absurd as this may sound, change the jalopies to slum housing, and I have described, with only slight poetic license, the first fifteen years of a federal program called urban renewal.

Since 1949, this program has provided local renewal agencies with federal funds and the power of eminent domain to condemn slum neighborhoods, tear down the buildings, and resell the cleared land to private developers at a reduced price. In addition to relocating the slum dwellers in "decent, safe, and sanitary" housing, the program was intended to stimulate large-scale private rebuilding, add new tax revenues to the dwindling coffers of the cities, revitalize their downtown areas, and halt the exodus of middle-class whites to the suburbs.

For some time now, a few city planners and housing experts have been pointing out that urban renewal was not achieving its general aims, and social scientists have produced a number of critical studies of individual renewal projects. These critiques, however, have mostly appeared in academic books and journals; otherwise there has been remarkably little public discussion of the federal program. Slum-dwellers whose homes were to be torn down have indeed protested

Reprinted from *Commentary*, April 1965, Volume 39, Number 4, pp. 29–37, by permission of the author and publisher. Copyright © 1965 by the American Jewish Committee. Herbert J. Gans is Senior Research Sociologist, Center for Urban Education, and Adjunct Professor of Sociology and Education, Teachers College, Columbia University.

bitterly, but their outcries have been limited to particular projects; and because such outcries have rarely been supported by the local press, they have been easily brushed aside by the political power of the supporters of the projects in question. In the last few years, the civil rights movement has backed protesting slum-dwellers, though again only at the local level, while rightists have opposed the use of eminent domain to take private property from one owner in order to give it to another (especially when the new one is likely to be from out-of-town and financed by New York capital).

Slum clearance has also come under fire from several prominent architectural and social critics, led by Jane Jacobs, who have been struggling to preserve neighborhoods like Greenwich Village, with their brownstones, lofts, and small apartment houses, against the encroachment of the large, high-rise projects built for the luxury market and the poor alike. But these efforts have been directed mainly at private clearance outside the federal program, and their intent has been to save the city for people (intellectuals and artists, for example) who, like tourists, want jumbled diversity, antique "charm," and narrow streets for visual adventure and aesthetic pleasure. (Norman Mailer carried such thinking to its farthest point in his recent attack in the *New York Times Magazine* on the physical and social sterility of high-rise housing; Mailer's attack was also accompanied by an entirely reasonable suggestion—in fact the only viable one that could be made in this context—that the advantages of brownstone living be incorporated into skyscraper projects.)

But if criticism of the urban renewal program has in the past been spotty and sporadic, there are signs that the program as a whole is now beginning to be seriously and tellingly evaluated. At least two comprehensive studies, by Charles Abrams and Scott Greer, are nearing publication, and one highly negative analysis—by an ultra-conservative economist and often irresponsible polemicist—has already appeared: Martin Anderson's *The Federal Bulldozer*.[1] Ironically enough, Anderson's data are based largely on statistics collected by the Urban Renewal Administration. What, according to these and other data, has the program accomplished? It has cleared slums to make room for many luxury-housing and a few middle-income projects, and it has also provided inexpensive land for the expansion of colleges, hospitals, libraries, shopping areas, and other such institutions located in slum areas. As of March 1961, 126,000 dwelling units had been demolished and about 28,000 new ones built. The median monthly rental of all those erected during 1960 came to $158, and in 1962, to $192—a staggering figure for any area outside of Manhattan.

Needless to say, none of the slum-dwellers who were dispossessed

[1] M.I.T. Press, 272 pp., $5.95.

in the process could afford to move into these new apartments. Local renewal agencies were supposed to relocate the dispossessed tenants in "standard" housing within their means before demolition began, but such vacant housing is scarce in most cities, and altogether unavailable in some. And since the agencies were under strong pressure to clear the land and get renewal projects going, the relocation of the tenants was impatiently, if not ruthlessly, handled. Thus, a 1961 study of renewal projects in 41 cities showed that 60 per cent of the dispossessed tenants were merely relocated in other slums; and in big cities, the proportion was even higher (over 70 per cent in Philadelphia, according to a 1958 study). Renewal sometimes even created new slums by pushing relocatees into areas and buildings which then became overcrowded and deteriorated rapidly. This has principally been the case with Negroes who, both for economic and racial reasons, have been forced to double up in other ghettos. Indeed, because almost two-thirds of the cleared slum units have been occupied by Negroes, the urban renewal program has often been characterized as Negro clearance, and in too many cities, this has been its intent.

Moreover, those dispossessed tenants who found better housing usually had to pay more rent than they could afford. In his careful study of relocation in Boston's heavily Italian West End,[2] Chester Hartman shows that 41 per cent of the West Enders lived in good housing in this so-called slum (thus suggesting that much of it should not have been torn down) and that 73 per cent were relocated in good housing—thanks in part to the fact that the West Enders were white. This improvement was achieved at a heavy price, however, for median rents rose from $41 to $71 per month after the move.

According to renewal officials, 80 per cent of all persons relocated now live in good housing, and rent increases were justified because many had been paying unduly low rent before. Hartman's study was the first to compare these official statistics with housing realities, and his figure of 73 per cent challenges the official claim that 97 per cent of the Boston West Enders were properly re-housed. This discrepancy may arise from the fact that renewal officials collected their data after the poorest of the uprooted tenants had fled in panic to other slums, and that officials also tended toward a rather lenient evaluation of the relocation housing of those actually studied in order to make a good record for their agency. (On the other hand, when they were certifying areas for clearance, these officials often exaggerated the degree of "blight" in order to prove their case.)

As for the substandard rents paid by slum-dwellers, this is true in only a small proportion of cases, and then mostly among whites.

[2]See the November 1964 issue of the *Journal of the American Institute of Planners*. The article also reviews all other relocation research and is a more reliable study of the consequences of renewal than Anderson's.

266

Real-estate economists argue that families should pay at least 20 per cent of their income for housing, but what is manageable for middle-income people is a burden to those with low incomes who pay a higher share of their earnings for food and other necessities. Yet even so, Negroes generally have to devote about 30 per cent of their income to housing, and a Chicago study cited by Hartman reports that among non-white families earning less than $3,000 a year, median rent rose from 35 per cent of income before relocation to 46 per cent afterward.

To compound the failure of urban renewal to help the poor, many clearance areas (Boston's West End is an example) were chosen, as Anderson points out, not because they had the worst slums, but because they offered the best sites for luxury housing—housing which would have been built whether the urban renewal program existed or not. Since public funds were used to clear the slums and to make the land available to private builders at reduced costs, the low-income population was in effect subsidizing its own removal for the benefit of the wealthy. What was done for the slum-dwellers in return is starkly suggested by the following statistic: *only one-half of one per cent* of all federal expenditures for urban renewal between 1949 and 1964 was spent on relocation of families and individuals; and 2 per cent if payments are included.

Finally, because the policy has been to clear a district of all slums at once in order to assemble large sites to attract private developers, entire neighborhoods have frequently been destroyed, uprooting people who had lived there for decades, closing down their institutions, ruining small businesses by the hundreds, and scattering families and friends all over the city. By removing the structure of social and emotional support provided by the neighborhood, and by forcing people to rebuild their lives separately and amid strangers elsewhere, slum clearance has often come at a serious psychological as well as financial cost to its supposed beneficiaries. Marc Fried, a clinical psychologist who studied the West Enders after relocation, reported that 46 per cent of the women and 38 per cent of the men "give evidence of a fairly severe grief reaction or worse" in response to questions about leaving their tight-knit community. Far from "adjusting" eventually to this trauma, 26 per cent of the women remained sad or depressed even two years after they had been pushed out of the West End.[3]

People like the Italians or the Puerto Ricans who live in an intensely group-centered way among three-generation "extended families" and ethnic peers have naturally suffered greatly from the clearance of entire neighborhoods. It may well be, however, that slum clearance has in-

[3]See "Grieving for a Lost Home," in *The Urban Condition,* edited by Leonard Duhl.

flicted yet graver emotional burdens on Negroes, despite the fact that they generally live in less cohesive and often disorganized neighborhoods. In fact, I suspect that Negroes who lack a stable family life and have trouble finding neighbors, shopkeepers, and institutions they can trust may have been hurt even more by forcible removal to new areas. This suspicion is supported by another of Fried's findings—that the socially marginal West Enders were more injured by relocation than those who had been integral members of the old neighborhood. Admittedly, some Negroes move very often on their own, but then they at least do so voluntarily, and not in consequence of a public policy which is supposed to help them in the first place. Admittedly also, relocation has made it possible for social workers to help slumdwellers whom they could not reach until renewal brought them out in the open, so to speak. But then only a few cities have so far used social workers to make relocation a more humane process.

These high financial, social, and emotional costs paid by the slumdwellers have generally been written off as an unavoidable by-product of "progress," the price of helping cities to collect more taxes, bring back the middle class, make better use of downtown land, stimulate private investment, and restore civic pride. But as Anderson shows, urban renewal has hardly justified these claims either. For one thing, urban renewal is a slow process: the average project has taken twelve years to complete. Moreover, while the few areas suitable for luxury housing were quickly rebuilt, less desirable cleared land might lie vacant for many years because developers were—and are—unwilling to risk putting up high- and middle-class income housing in areas still surrounded by slums. Frequently, they can be attracted only by promises of tax write-offs, which absorb the increased revenues that renewal is supposed to create for the city. Anderson reports that, instead of the anticipated four dollars for every public dollar, private investments have only just matched the public subsidies, and even the money for luxury housing has come forth largely because of federal subsidies. Thus, all too few of the new projects have produced tax gains and returned suburbanites, or generated the magic rebuilding boom.

Anderson goes on to argue that during the fifteen years of the federal urban renewal program, the private housing market has achieved what urban renewal has failed to do. Between 1950 and 1960, twelve million new dwelling units were built, and fully six million substandard ones disappeared—all without government action. The proportion of substandard housing in the total housing supply was reduced from 37 to 19 per cent, and even among the dwelling units occupied by non-whites, the proportion of substandard units has dropped from 72 to 44 per cent. This comparison leads Anderson to the conclusion that the private market is much more effective than government action in removing slums and supplying new 268 housing, and that the urban renewal program ought to be repealed.

It would appear that Anderson's findings and those of the other studies I have cited make an excellent case for doing so. However, a less biased anaylsis of the figures and a less tendentious mode of evaluating them than Anderson's leads to a different conclusion. To begin with, Anderson's use of nationwide statistics misses the few good renewal projects, those which have helped both the slum-dwellers and the cities, or those which brought in enough new taxes to finance other city services for the poor. Such projects can be found in small cities and especially in those where high vacancy rates assured sufficient relocation housing of standard quality. More important, all the studies I have mentioned deal with projects carried out during the 1950's, and fail to take account of the improvements in urban renewal practice under the Kennedy and Johnson administrations. Although Anderson's study supposedly covers the period up to 1963, much of his data go no further than 1960. Since then, the federal bulldozer has moved into fewer neighborhoods, and the concept of rehabilitating rather than clearing blighted neighborhoods is more and more being underwritten by subsidized loans. A new housing subsidy program—known as 221(d) (3)—for families above the income ceiling for public housing has also been launched, and in 1964, Congress passed legislation for assistance to relocatees who cannot afford their new rents.

None of this is to say that Anderson would have had to revise his findings drastically if he had taken the pains to update them. These recent innovations have so far been small in scope—only 13,000 units were financed under 221 (d) (3) in the first two years—and they still do not provide subsidies sufficient to bring better housing within the price range of the slum residents. In addition, rehabilitation unaccompanied by new construction is nearly useless because it does not eliminate overcrowding. And finally, some cities are still scheduling projects to clear away the non-white poor who stand in the path of the progress of private enterprise. Unfortunately, many cities pay little attention to federal pleas to improve the program, using the local initiative granted them by urban renewal legislation to perpetuate the practices of the 1950's. Yet even with the legislation of the 1960's, the basic error in the original design of urban renewal remains: it is still a method for eliminating the slums in order to "renew" the city, rather than a program for properly rehousing slum-dwellers.

Before going into this crucial distinction, we first need to be clear that private housing is not going to solve our slum problems. In the first place, Anderson conveniently ignores the fact that if urban renewal has benefited anyone, it is private enterprise. Bending to the pressure of the real-estate lobby, the legislation that launched urban renewal in effect required that private developers do the rebuilding, and most projects could therefore get off the drawing board only if they appeared to be financially attractive to a developer. Thus, his choice of a site and 269 his rebuilding plans inevitably took priority over the needs of the slum-dwellers.

It is true that Anderson is not defending private enterprise *per se* but the free market, although he forgets that it only exists today as a concept in reactionary minds and dated economics texts. The costs of land, capital, and construction have long since made it impossible for private developers to build for anyone but the rich, and some form of subsidy is needed to house everyone else. The building boom of the 1950's which Anderson credits to the free market was subsidized by income-tax deductions to homeowners and by F.H.A. 2nd V.A. mortgage insurance, not to mention the federal highway programs that have made the suburbs possible.

To be sure, these supports enabled private builders to put up a great deal of housing for middle-class whites. This in turn permitted well-employed workers, including some non-whites, to improve their own situation by moving into the vacated neighborhoods. Anderson is quite right in arguing that if people earn good wages, they can obtain better housing more easily and cheaply in the not-quite-private market than through urban renewal. But this market is of little help to those employed at low or even factory wages, or the unemployed, or most Negroes who, whatever their earnings, cannot live in the suburbs. In consequence, 44 per cent of all housing occupied by non-whites in 1960 was still substandard, and even with present subsidies, private enterprise can do nothing for these people. As for laissez faire, it played a major role in creating the slums in the first place.

The solution, then, is not to repeal urban renewal, but to transform it from a program of slum clearance and rehabilitation into a program of urban rehousing. This means, first, building low- and moderate-cost housing on vacant land in cities, suburbs, and new towns beyond the suburbs, and also helping slum-dwellers to move into existing housing outside the slums; and then, *after* a portion of the urban low-income population has left the slums, clearing and rehabilitating them through urban renewal. This approach is commonplace in many European countries, which have long since realized that private enterprise can no more house the population and eliminate slums than it can run the post office.

Of course, governments in Europe have a much easier task than ours in developing decent low-income projects. Because they take it for granted that housing is a national rather than a local responsibility, the government agencies are not hampered by the kind of real-estate and construction lobbies which can defeat or subvert American programs by charges of socialism. Moreover, their municipalities own a great deal of the vacant land, and have greater control over the use of private land than do American cities. But perhaps their main advantage is the lack of popular opposition to moving the poor out of the slums and into the midst of the more affluent residents. Not only 270 is housing desperately short for all income groups, but the European class structure, even in Western socialist countries, is still rigid enough so that low- and middle-income groups can live near each other if not next to each other, and still "know their place."

In America, on the other hand, one's house and address are major signs of social status, and no one who has any say in the matter wants people of lower income or status in his neighborhood. Middle-class homeowners use zoning as a way of keeping out cheaper or less prestigious housing, while working-class communities employ less subtle forms of exclusion. Consequently, low-income groups, whatever their creed or color, have been forced to live in slums or near-slums, and to wait until they could acquire the means to move as a group, taking over better neighborhoods when the older occupants were ready to move on themselves.

For many years now, the only source of new housing for such people, and their only hope of escaping the worst slums, has been public housing. But this is no longer a practical alternative. Initiated during the Depression, public housing has always been a politically embattled program; its opponents, among whom the real-estate lobby looms large, first saddled it with restrictions and then effectively crippled it. Congress now permits only 35,000 units a year to be built in the entire country.

The irony is that public housing has declined because, intended only for the poor, it faithfully carried out its mandate. Originally, sites were obtained by slum clearance; after the war, however, in order to increase the supply of low-cost housing, cities sought to build public housing on vacant land. But limited as it was to low-income tenants and thus labeled and stigmatized as an institution of the dependent poor, public housing was kept out of vacant land in the better neighborhoods. This, plus the high cost of land and construction, left housing officials with no other choice but to build high-rise projects on whatever vacant land they could obtain, often next to factories or along railroad yards. Because tenants of public housing are ruled by a set of strict regulations—sometimes necessary, sometimes politically inspired, but always degrading—anyone who could afford housing in the private market shunned the public projects. During the early years of the program, when fewer citizens had that choice, public housing became respectable shelter for the working class and even for the unemployed middle class. After the war, federal officials decided, and rightly so, that public housing ought to be reserved for those who had no other alternative, and therefore set income limits that admitted only the really poor. Today, public housing is home for the underclass—families who earn less than $3000-$4000 annually, many with unstable jobs or none at all, and most of them non-white.

Meanwhile the enthusiasm for public housing has been steadily 271 dwindling and with it, badly needed political support. Newspaper reports reinforce the popular image of public-housing projects as huge nests of crime and delinquency—despite clear evidence to the contrary —and as the domicile of unregenerate and undeserving families whose children urinate only in the elevators. The position of public housing, particularly among liberal intellectuals, has also been weakened by the slurs of the social and architectural aesthetes who condemn the projects' poor exterior designs as "sterile," "monotonous," and "dehumanizing," often in ignorance of the fact that the tightly restricted funds have been allocated mainly to make the apartments themselves as spacious and livable as possible, and that the waiting lists among slum-dwellers who want these apartments remain long. Be that as it may, suburban communities and urban neighborhoods with vacant land are as hostile to public housing as ever, and their opposition is partly responsible for the program's having been cut down to its present minuscule size.

The net result is that low-income people today cannot get out of the slums, either because they cannot afford the subsidized private market, or because the project they could afford cannot be built on vacant land. There is only one way to break through this impasse, and that is to permit them equal access to new subsidized, privately built housing by adding another subsidy to make up the difference between the actual rent and what they can reasonably be expected to pay. Such a plan, giving them a chance to choose housing like all other citizens, would help to remove the stigma of poverty and inferiority placed on them by public housing. Many forms of rent subsidy have been proposed, but the best one, now being tried in New York, is to put low- and middle-income people in the same middle-income project with the former getting the same apartments at smaller rentals.

Admittedly, this approach assumes that the poor can live with the middle class and that their presence and behavior will not threaten their neighbors' security or status. No one knows whether this is really possible, but experiments in education, job training, and social-welfare programs do show that many low-income people when once offered *genuine* opportunities to improve their lives and given help in making use of them, are able to shake off the hold of the culture of poverty. Despite the popular stereotype, the proportion of those whom Hylan Lewis calls the clinical poor, too ravaged emotionally by poverty and deprivation to adapt to new opportunities, seems to be small. As for the rest, they only reject programs offering spurious opportunities, like job-training schemes for non-existent jobs. Further, anyone who has lived in a slum neighborhood can testify that whatever the condition of the building most women keep their apartments clean by expenditures of time and effort inconceivable to the middle-class housewife. Moving to a better apartment would require little basic cultural change from these women, and re-housing is thus a type of new opportunity   272 that stands a better chance of succeeding than, say, a program to inculcate new child-rearing techniques.

We have no way of telling how many slum-dwellers would be willing to participate in such a plan. However poor the condition of the flat, the slum is home, and for many it provides the support of neighboring relatives and friends, and a cultural milieu in which everyone has the same problems and is therefore willing to overlook occasional disreputable behavior. A middle-income project cannot help but have a middle-class ethos, and some lower-class people may be fearful of risking what little stability they have achieved where they are now in exchange for something new, strange, demanding, and potentially hostile. It would be hard to imagine an unwed Negro mother moving her household to a middle-income project full of married couples and far removed from the mother, sisters, and aunts who play such an important role in the female-centered life of lower-class Negroes. However, there are today a large number of stable two-parent families who live in the slums only because income and race exclude them from the better housing that is available. Families like these would surely be only too willing to leave the Harlems and Black Belts. They would have to be helped with loans to make the move, and perhaps even with grants to buy new furniture so as not to feel ashamed in their new surroundings. They might be further encouraged by being offered income-tax relief for giving up the slums, just as we now offer such relief to people who give up being renters to become home-owners.

Undoubtedly there would be friction between the classes, and the more affluent residents would likely want to segregate themselves and their children from neighbors who did not toe the middle-class line, especially with respect to child-rearing. The new housing would therefore have to be planned to allow some voluntary social segregation for both groups, if only to make sure that enough middle-income families would move in (especially in cities where there was no shortage of housing for them). The proportion of middle- and low-income tenants would have to be regulated not only to minimize the status fears of the former, but also to give the latter enough peers to keep them from feeling socially isolated and without emotional support when problems arise. Fortunately, non-profit and limited dividend institutions, which do not have to worry about showing an immediate profit, are now being encouraged to build moderate-income housing; they can do a more careful job of planning the physical and social details of this approach than speculative private builders.

If the slums are really to be emptied and their residents properly housed elsewhere, the rehousing program will have to be extended beyond the city limits, for the simple reason that that is where most 273 of the vacant land is located. This means admitting the low-income population to the suburbs; it also means creating new towns—self-contained communities with their own industry which would not, like the suburbs, be dependent on the city for employment opportunities, and could therefore be situated in presently rural areas. Federal support for the construction of new towns was requested as part of the 1964 Housing Act, and although Congress refused to pass it, the legislation will come up again in 1965[4]

To be sure, white middle-class suburbanites and rural residents are not likely to welcome non-white low-income people into their communities even if the latter are no longer clearly labeled as poor. The opposition to be expected in city neighborhoods chosen for mixed-income projects would be multiplied a hundredfold in outlying areas. Being politically autonomous, and having constituencies who are not about to support measures that will threaten their security or status in the slightest, the suburbs possess the political power to keep the rehousing program out of their own vacant lots, even if they cannot stop the federal legislation that would initiate it. On the other hand, experience with the federal highway program and with urban renewal itself has demonstrated that few communities can afford to turn down large amounts of federal money. For instance, New York City is likely to build a Lower Manhattan Expressway in the teeth of considerable local opposition, if only because the federal government will pay 90 per cent of the cost and thus bring a huge sum into the city coffers. If the rehousing program were sufficiently large to put a sizable mixed-income project in every community, and if the federal government were to pick up at least 90 per cent of the tab, while also strengthening the appeal of the program by helping to solve present transportation, school, and tax problems in the suburbs, enough political support might be generated to overcome the objections of segregationist and class-conscious whites.

Yet even if the outlying areas could be persuaded to cooperate, it is not at all certain that slum-dwellers would leave the city. Urban renewal experience has shown that for many slum-dwellers, there are more urgent needs than good housing. One is employment, and most of the opportunities for unskilled or semi-skilled work are in the city. Another is money, and some New York City slum residents recently refused to let the government inspect—much less repair their buildings because they would lose the rent reductions they had received previously. If leaving the city meant higher rents, more limited access to job possibilities, and also separation from people and institutions which

[4]Meanwhile, several private developers are planning new towns (for example, James Rouse who is building Columbia near Baltimore, and Robert Simon who has already begun Reston, outside Washington) in which they propose to house some low-income people.

274

give them stability, some slum residents might very well choose over-crowding and dilapidation as the lesser of two evils.

These problems would have to be considered in planning a rehousing program beyond the city limits. The current exodus of industry from the city would of course make jobs available to the new suburbanites. The trouble is that the industries now going into the suburbs, or those that would probably be attracted to the new towns, are often precisely the ones which use the most modern machinery and the fewest unskilled workers. Thus, our rehousing plan comes up against the same obstacle—the shortage of jobs—that has frustrated other programs to help the low-income population and that will surely defeat the War on Poverty in its present form. Like so many other programs, rehousing is finally seen to depend on a step that American society is as yet unwilling to take: the deliberate creation of new jobs by government action. The building of new towns especially would have to be coordinated with measures aimed at attracting private industry to employ the prospective residents, at creating other job opportunities, and at offering intensive training for the unskilled after they have been hired. If they are not sure of a job before they leave the city, they simply will not leave.

The same social and cultural inhibitions that make slum residents hesitant to move into a mixed-income project in the city would, of course, be even stronger when it came to moving out of the city. These inhibitions might be relaxed by moving small groups of slum residents en masse, or by getting those who move first to encourage their neighbors to follow. In any case, new social institutions and community facilities would have to be developed to help the erstwhile slum-dweller feel comfortable in his new community, yet without labeling him as poor.

Despite its many virtues, a rehousing program based on the use of vacant land on either side of the city limits would not immediately clear the slums. Given suburban opposition and the occupational and social restraints on the slum-dwellers themselves, it can be predicted that if such a program were set into motion it would be small in size, and that it would pull out only the upwardly mobile—particularly the young people with stable families and incomes—who are at best a sizable minority among the poor. What can be done now to help the rest leave the slums?

The best solution is a public effort to encourage their moving into existing neighborhoods within the city and in older suburbs just beyond the city limits. Indeed, a direct rent subsidy like that now given to relocatees could enable people to obtain decent housing in these areas. This approach has several advantages. It would allow low-income people to be close to jobs and to move in groups, and it would prob- 275 ably attract the unwed mother who wanted to give her children a better chance in life. It would also be cheaper than building new housing, although the subsidies would have to be large enough to discourage low-income families from overcrowding—and thus deteriorating—the units in order to save on rent.

There are, however, some obvious disadvantages as well. For one thing, because non-white low-income people would be moving into presently white or partially integrated areas, the government would in effect be encouraging racial invasion. This approach would thus have the effect of pushing the white and middle-income people further toward the outer edge of the city or into the suburbs. Although some whites might decide to stay, many would surely want to move, and not all would be able to afford to do so. It would be necessary to help them with rent subsidies as well; indeed, they might become prospective middle-income tenants for rehousing projects on vacant land.

Undoubtedly, all this would bring us closer to the all-black city that has already been predicted. For this reason alone, a scheme that pushes the whites further out can only be justified when combined with a rehousing program on vacant land that would begin to integrate the suburbs. But even that could not prevent a further racial imbalance between cities and suburbs.

Yet would the predominantly non-white city really be so bad? It might be for the middle class which needs the jobs, shops, and culture that the city provides. Of course, the greater the suburban exodus, the more likely it would become that middle-class culture would also move to the suburbs. This is already happening in most American cities— obvious testimony to the fact that culture (at least of the middlebrow kind represented by tent theaters and art movie-houses) does not need the city in order to flourish; and the artists who create high culture seem not to mind living among the poor even now.

Non-white low-income people might feel more positive about a city in which they were the majority, for if they had the votes, municipal services would be more attuned to their priorities than is now the case. To be sure, if poor people (of any color) were to dominate the city, its tax revenues would decrease even further, and cities would be less able than ever to supply the high quality public services that the low-income population needs so much more urgently than the middle class. Consequently, new sources of municipal income not dependent on the property tax would have to be found; federal and state grants to cities (like those already paying half the public-school costs in several states) would probably be the principal form. Even under present conditions, in fact, new sources of municipal income must soon be located if the cities are not to collapse financially.

If non-whites were to leave the slums en masse, new ghettos would eventually form in the areas to which they would move. Although this 276 is undesirable by conventional liberal standards, the fact is that many low-income Negroes are not yet very enthusiastic about living among white neighbors. They do not favor segregation, of course; what they want is a free choice and then the ability to select predominantly non-white areas that are in better shape than the ones they live in now. If the suburbs were opened to non-whites—to the upwardly mobile ones who want integration now—free choice would become available. If the new ghettos were decent neighborhoods with good schools, and if their occupants had jobs and other opportunities to bring stability into their lives, they would be training their children to want integration a generation hence.

In short, then, a workable rehousing scheme must provide new housing on both sides of the city limits for the upwardly mobile minority, and encouragement to move into older areas for the remainder. If, in these ways, enough slum-dwellers could be enabled and induced to leave the slums, it would then be possible to clear or rehabilitate the remaining slums. Once slum areas were less crowded, and empty apartments were going begging, their profitability and market value would be reduced, and urban renewal could take place far more cheaply, and far more quickly. Relocation would be less of a problem, and with land values down, rebuilding and rehabilitation could be carried out to fit the resources of the low-income people who needed or wanted to remain in the city. A semi-suburban style of living that would be attractive to the upper-middle class could also be provided.

At this point, it would be possible to begin to remake the inner city into what it must eventually become—the hub of a vast metropolitan complex of urban neighborhoods, suburbs, and new towns, in which those institutions and functions that have to be at the center—the specialized business districts, the civil and cultural facilities, and the great hospital complexes and university campuses—would be located.

Even in such a city, there would be slums—for people who wanted to live in them, for the clinical poor who would be unable to make it elsewhere, and for rural newcomers who would become urbanized in them before moving on. But it might also be possible to relocate many of these in a new kind of public housing in which quasi-communities would be established to help those whose problems were soluble and to provide at least decent shelter for those who cannot be helped except by letting them live without harassment until we learn how to cure mental illness, addiction, and other forms of self-destructive behavior.

This massive program has much to recommend it, but we must clearly understand that moving the low-income population out of the slums would not eliminate poverty or the other problems that stem from it. A standard dwelling unit can make life more comfortable, and a decent neighborhood can discourage some anti-social behavior, 277 but by themselves, neither can effect radical transformations. What poor people need most are decent incomes, proper jobs, better schools, and freedom from racial and class discrimination. Indeed, if the choice were between a program solely dedicated to rehousing, and a program that kept the low-income population in the city slums for another generation but provided for these needs, the latter would be preferable, for it would produce people who were able to leave the slums under their own steam. Obviously, the ideal approach is one that coordinates the elimination of slums with the reduction of poverty.

As I have been indicating, an adequate rehousing program would be extremely costly and very difficult to carry out. Both its complexity and expense can be justified, however, on several grounds. Morally, it can be argued that no one in the Great Society should have to live in a slum, at least not involuntarily.

From a political point of view, it is urgently necessary to begin integrating the suburbs and to improve housing conditions in the city before the latter becomes an ominous ghetto of poor and increasingly angry Negroes and Puerto Ricans, and the suburbs become enclaves of affluent whites who commute fearfully to a downtown bastion of stores and offices. If the visible group tensions of recent years are allowed to expand and sharpen, another decade may very well see the beginning of open and often violent class and race warfare.

But the most persuasive argument for a rehousing program is economic. Between 50 and 60 percent of building costs go into wages and create work for the unskilled who are now increasingly unemployable elsewhere. A dwelling unit that costs $15,000 would thus provide as much as $9000 in wages—one-and-a-half years of respectably paid employment for a single worker. Adding four-and-a-half million new low-cost housing units to rehouse half of those in substandard units in 1960 would provide almost seven million man-years of work, and the subsequent renewal of these and other substandard units yet more. Many additional jobs would also be created by the construction and operation of new shopping centers, schools, and other community facilities, as well as the highways and public transit systems that would be needed to serve the new suburbs and towns. If precedent must be cited for using a housing program to create jobs, it should be recalled that public housing was started in the Depression for precisely this reason.

The residential building industry (and the real-estate lobby) would have to be persuaded to give up their stubborn resistance to government housing programs, but the danger of future underemployment, and the opportunity of participating profitably in the rehousing scheme, should either convert present builders or attract new ones into the industry. As for the building trades unions, they have always supported government housing programs, but they have been unwilling to admit non-whites to membership. If, however, the rehousing effort

278

were sizable enough to require many more workers than are now in the unions, the sheer demand for labor—and the enforcement of federal non-discriminatory hiring policies for public works—would probably break down the color barriers without much difficulty.

While the federal government is tooling up to change the urban renewal program into a rehousing scheme, it should also make immediate changes in current renewal practices to remove their economic and social cost from the shoulders of the slum-dwellers. Future projects should be directed at the clearance of *really harmful* slums, instead of taking units that are *run down but not demonstrably harmful* out of the supply of low-cost housing, especially for downtown revitalization and other less pressing community improvement schemes. Occupants of harmful slums, moreover, ought to be rehoused in decent units they can afford. For this purpose, more public housing and 221 (d) (3) projects must be built, and relocation and rent assistance payments should be increased to eliminate the expense of moving for the slum-dweller. Indeed, the simplest way out of the relocation impasse is to give every relocatee a sizable grant, like the five-hundred dollars to one thousand dollars paid by private builders in New York City to get tenants out of existing structures quickly and painlessly. Such a grant is not only a real incentive to relocatees but a means of reducing opposition to urban renewal. By itself, however, it cannot reduce the shortage of relocation housing. Where such housing now exists in plentiful supply, renewal ought to move ahead more quickly, but where there is a shortage that cannot be appreciably reduced, it would be wise to eliminate or postpone clearance and rehabilitation projects that require a large amount of relocation.

Nothing is easier than to suggest radical new programs to the overworked and relatively powerless officials of federal and local renewal agencies who must carry out the present law, badly written or not, and who are constantly pressured by influential private interests to make decisions in their favor. Many of these officials are as unhappy with what urban renewal has wrought as their armchair critics and would change the program if they could—that is, if they received encouragement from the White House, effective support in getting new legislation through Congress, and, equally important, political help at city halls to incorporate these innovations into local programs. But it should be noted that little of what I have suggested is very radical, for none of the proposals involves conflict with the entrenched American practice of subsidizing private enterprise to carry out public works at a reasonable profit. The proposals are radical only in demanding an end to our no less entrenched practice of punishing the poor. Yet they also make sure that middle-class communities are rewarded financially for whatever discomfort they may have to endure.

Nor are these suggestions very new. Indeed, only last month Presi- 279 dent Johnson sent a housing message to Congress which proposes the payment of rent subsidies as the principal method for improving housing conditions. It also requests federal financing of municipal services for tax-starved communities, and aid toward the building of new towns. These represent bold and desirable steps toward the evolution of a federal rehousing program. Unfortunately, however, the message offers little help to those who need it most. Slum-dwellers may be pleased that there will be no increase in urban renewal activity and that relocation housing subsidies and other grants are being stepped up. But no expansion of public housing is being requested, and to make matters worse, the new rent subsidies will be available only to households above the income limits for public housing. Thus, the President's message offers no escape for the mass of the non-white low-income population from the ghetto slums; in fact it threatens to widen the gap between such people and the lower-middle-income population which will be eligible for rent subsidies.

On the other hand, as in the case of the War on Poverty, a new principle of government responsibility in housing is being established, and evidently the President's strategy is to obtain legislative approval for the principle by combining it with a minimal and a minimally controversial program for the first year. Once the principle has been accepted, however, the program must change quickly. It may have taken fifteen years for urban renewal even to begin providing some relief to the mass of slum-dwellers, but it cannot take that long again to become a rehousing scheme that will give them significant help. The evolution of federal policies can no longer proceed in the leisurely fashion to which politicians, bureaucrats, and middle-class voters have become accustomed, for unemployment, racial discrimination, and the condition of our cities are becoming ever more critical problems, and those who suffer from them are now considerably less patient than they have been in the past.

Bernard Weissbourd

Segregation, Subsidies, and Megalopolis

From 55,000,000 to 60,000,000 *more* people will be living in metropolitan areas in 1980 than were living there in 1960. How will we manage? Already our cities are decaying faster than they can be rebuilt. Parking is a universal problem. The tax base of the city is eroding as industry moves to the suburbs. A significant part of the white population is also moving to the suburbs, while the cores of our cities are filling with Negroes as the migration from the South steadily rises. The cost to the cities of trying to adjust the migrants to a new kind of existence imposes additional burdens upon the city's tax base.

Taxes are also rising in the suburbs to pay for the high cost of municipal services spread out over areas of low population density. Open space is being consumed at a terrifying rate, so that suburbs once in open country are now surrounded. Travel time to the city has multiplied as the expressways get clogged during rush hours.

Some experts do not find these problems of city decay and suburban sprawl unduly alarming. They maintain that the continuing dispersal that present trends indicate for the future is inevitable, and not necessarily undesirable. I believe the opposite.

Suburban sprawl and urban decay have *not* come about solely because people have made a free choice in a free enterprise market. That choice has been influenced by federal housing subsidies, which, purporting to be neutral, have in fact subsidized low-density middle-

Reprinted by permission of the author and the Center for the Study of Democratic Institutions (Santa Barbara, California, 1964). Bernard Weissbourd is President of Metropolitan Structures, Inc., and is engaged in the construction and development of apartments, hotels, and office buildings in Chicago, Baltimore, Newark, and other cities in the East and Midwest. He also was a chemist and worked on the Manhattan Project at the University of Chicago.

281

income living in the suburbs and have thereby financed the flight of white population from the city. Another factor affecting this dispersal has been our segregation practices within the city.

The lack of public discussion about the influence of housing segregation and federal housing subsidies upon urban growth patterns has been a barrier to understanding the problems of the city and suburbs and has created a feeling of hopelessness about the future of America's cities. It is my purpose here to show that it is possible to deal constructively with the problems of the metropolitan region if these important factors are not ignored.

THE LOW-DENSITY URBAN REGION

Compared to the time span of Western civilization the modern urban complex, sometimes called megalopolis, is a new, young phenomenon. Some people are confident that a new technology of communication and transportation will solve many of the most intractable problems of the metropolitan region and that, in time, the region of the future will emerge.[1] "The spatial patterns of American settlements," it is now believed, will "be considerably more dispersed, varied and space consuming than they ever were in the past. . . ."[2] One author envisions "continuous low density urban belts stretching from Maine to Virginia, from Toronto and Pittsburgh to Milwaukee, and from Amsterdam to Frankfort and Mannheim. . . . However, there seems to be no reason why, properly organized and interlaced with greenbelts, freeways, natural reservations and sites of historic interest, and accented vertically by occasional high-rise elements, these low-density urban regions of tomorrow should not be more livable and effective in satisfying the totality of human values than the transitional urban forms of today."[3]

Acceptance of low-density regional development as the pattern for the future is encouraged by the lack of genuine popular support for a massive attack on the problems of the city and the region. To most suburban residents their experience "seems not one of personal retrogression but of continuous improvement. By moving out of the slag heaps of the worked-out city they have improved their surroundings sufficient for a generation."[4]

While no businessman whose offices must be located in the central business district, and no dweller in the city slums, can accept the decline of the city with equanimity, it is quite likely that if we do

[1]Webber, "Order in Diversity: Community Without Propinquity," in *Cities and Space, The Future Use of Urban Land,* 1963, 43.

[2]Id., 23.

[3]Tunnard and Pushkarev, *Man-Made America: Chaos or Control,* 1963, 443.

[4]Vernon, *The Myth and Reality of Our Urban Problems,* 1961, 30–31.

nothing to alter present trends the low-density urban region will be the pattern of the future. The New York metropolitan region, for example, has grown outward along major transportation arteries. The axis of growth extended five miles in 1900, twenty-five miles in 1960, and may become fifty miles by 1985. Under existing zoning patterns of low-density development twice the amount of land will be developed in the next twenty-five years as in the entire history of the New York region.[5] A similar pattern emerges for every metropolitan region in the United States as a projected 45,000,000 to 50,000,000 *more* people are added to suburbia by 1980.

Acceptance of low-density regional growth also implies a curtailment of mass transportation, for mass transportation works well only in highly concentrated areas where trip origins and destinations are clustered and not where they are widely dispersed. Conversely, the automobile, which functions so efficiently for decentralized traffic, becomes highly inefficient under conditions of intense demand. Suburban sprawl will thus bring about a further decline in mass transportation, as increasing reliance on the automobile brings more congestion to the central districts.

THE DECLINE OF THE CITY

Each new expressway not only undercuts the market for mass transportation but accelerates the movement of industry away from the central cities. The truck and the car have given the manufacturer new opportunities to select sites in outlying areas. The movement of industry from central city locations to outlying suburban locations has created a new phenomenon—out-commuting. "The movement each morning of people from homes in the center portions of the urban areas to jobs on the periphery is growing fast. The spectacle of groups of blue-collar workers traveling outward by car pool against the flow of incoming traffic is now a common sight on the roads of many large cities. In fact the spotty and fragmentary information on this phenomenon suggests that it may be one of the fastest-growing streams of traffic among the complex currents of our urban areas."[6]

Nor have the results of the federal programs for slum clearance, urban renewal, and public housing so far given any reason to expect that the trend toward city decline and low-density regional settlement will be reversed. Slums in the cities are growing faster than we can clear them. Even in New York City, which has had the largest slum clearance and rebuilding program of any city in the United States, the rate of deterioration of housing units has been as great as the

[5]Tankel, "Importance of Open Space in the Urban Patterns," in *Cities and Space, The Future Use of Urban Land,* 1963, 53.

[6]Vernon, *The Myth and Reality of Our Urban Problems,* 1961, 6.

rate at which new housing has been constructed. We should not expect urban renewal to work so long as there is no place for persons evacuated from the slums to live. People displaced by urban renewal and by the new expressways have created new slums.

The new luxury apartment buildings constructed since the end of World War II have not prevented the exodus of middle-income white families to the suburbs. It was thought that upper-income families would move into these expensive apartments and people in the next income level would move into the apartments thus vacated. Instead, the vacated apartments were converted for occupancy by lower-income people. Middle-income families who could not afford private schools for their children moved to the suburbs, leaving behind in the cities people without children, upper-income families, and low-income families who had no choice. The problem was compounded by the impact of segregation practices. Apartment buildings vacated by those who moved into new luxury accommodations were converted into slums overnight. The "trickle-down" approach failed as the trickle became a torrent.

Moreover, no one is satisfied with public housing. By rejecting all those whose incomes exceeded the prescribed limits public housing has developed a concentration of those members of society who are not able to support themselves. Coupled with the fact that most cities have followed a deliberate program of segregation in public housing, the result has been to create in many places an environment lacking in all of the positive attributes of urban life. The second generation of many public housing occupants is now coming to maturity and it is already clear that many of them will never become viable members of society.

Urban renewal programs aimed at aiding the central business district show greater promise of long-range success, probably because there is considerable strength in the central business district to begin with. New office buildings in the central areas of each of the metropolitan regions demonstrate that financial and commercial institutions, public utilities, newspapers and magazines, and government, together with the lawyers, accountants, stock brokers, and others involved in serving these institutions, require a centralized location.[7] Most cities in the United States have only one business district. The fact that Los Angeles now has several scattered clusters of office buildings does not indicate a decentralization of office activities. The diffusion may make doing business in Los Angeles a little more difficult than in Chicago or Baltimore, for example, but the clusters of office buildings in the California city are still reasonably close together in relation to the

[7]Id., 42. Also see Edwards, "Central Business Districts," 4 *Journal of Housing*, 186.

region as a whole. It is certainly not possible for the office activities of Manhattan Island to be spread out over suburbia. Even most of the retail stores in the central business districts, which declined for a while because of the competition of suburban shopping centers, have begun to revive.

Thus, although a sizable number of people and industries has moved out of the central city, there has been far less movement of office activities to outlying areas than some reports would lead us to believe.

THE EXPLODING POPULATION

The movement of white population to suburban areas and the concentration of Negro population in the central city will be intensified during the next fifteen years if present trends continue.

In 1960 about 63 per cent of the total population of the United States or about 112,000,000 persons lived in what are known statistically as "standard metropolitan areas."[8] Between 1970 and 1980 as much as 73 per cent of the total population will reside within the urban complex. If the post-war birth rate continues, the total population will have increased between 1950 and 1980 from 150,000,000 to 260,-000,000, an increase of 110,000,000 people in thirty years (a single human generation).[9] More than two-thirds of these 110,000,000 people will have settled in megalopolis, if events do not alter present trends.

Population projections beyond the year 2000 begin to reach astronomical numbers. It is not necessary, however, to look that far ahead. The children are already born who will be forming households in 1980, only sixteen years from now. It is becoming clear that the new dwellings, transportation, offices, and factories that these people will require will either contribute further to city decay and suburban sprawl or provide the opportunity for creating a new regional environment.

Since the end of World War II the Negro population has been increasing even faster than the white population. Philip Hauser points out that the decline of the non-white death rate together with the increase in their birth rate has resulted in a rate of growth for non-whites 60 per cent higher than for whites.[10] This great national rise is dwarfed by an even more explosive increase of non-whites in metropolitan areas.[11] By 1990 about 2,500,000 Negroes are expected to be living in the Chicago metropolitan area, about 1,500,000 more than in 1960. "At that time there would still be a slight majority of whites in the city of Chicago and one-fourth of the entire consolidated area

[8]Hauser, *Population Perspectives*, 1960, 72.
[9]Id., 35.
[10]Id., 58.
[11]Id., 59.

285

population would be non-white."[12] These projections assume accelerated suburbanization of non-whites in the future. However, "if the exact trends of the 1950 to 1960 decade were to be extrapolated into the future they would show a majority of non-whites in the city of Chicago by 1975 and a substantially higher proportion of non-whites for the total consolidated areas."[13]

The migration to the cities of rural Negroes and Southern whites and Puerto Ricans has already imposed heavy tax burdens on the city. In 1959, for example, New York City spent $50,000,000 for remedial programs for its Puerto Rican newcomers, more than it spent on all its parks, libraries, zoos, and museums in that year.[14] In its 1959-60 budget New York City assigned 23 per cent to public hospitalization, health, and welfare and 20 per cent to education.[15] The great growth rate of the Negro population in New York, through continued migration as well as natural increase during the next fifteen years, will tend to increase even further the city's costs for welfare, health, and education.

The picture that emerges from these forecasts is far from salutary. Low-density regional settlements in which industry and the white population spread out over the countryside without adequate mass transportation contrasts with the concentrated Negro occupancy of the center city, whose tax base has diminished by the flight of industry and whose expenses have increased for the care of its immigrants. Moreover, a growing number of the center-city population will be commuting to jobs in the suburbs while many of the suburban whites will continue to travel to jobs in a still strong central business district.

The waste of human resources and money in this increased commuting, the inability of the automobile and the expressways to handle the traffic, the changing character of the city largely occupied by a financial and business community and a segregated Negro population, the financing of public services for a migrant population in the face of disappearing industry and lost taxes, the interdependence of the financial and commercial life of the suburbs and the city—these are all reasons for not allowing present trends to continue.

But are there alternatives? As we have noted, there are many who doubt whether the trends are reversible. I believe the pattern can be changed, but first it is necessary to say something about the federal housing subsidies, because they are both one of the causes of suburban growth and one of the possible tools for creating a different picture for the future.

[12]Bogue and Dandekar, *Population Trends and Prospects for the Chicago-Northeastern Indiana Consolidated Metropolitan Area: 1960–1990,* 1952, 28.
[13]Id., 28.
[14]Higby, *The Squeeze,* 1960, 38.
[15]Id., 42.

286

It is important to understand that dispersal of the urban population in the United States has not come about solely as a result of a free and open market. Government inducements to buy in the suburbs have been substantial and have brought about a remarkable increase in home ownership since the war. In 1957, of the total mortgage debt of $107,000,000,000 on one- to four-family non-farm homes, $47,200,000,000 were FHA-insured or VA-guaranteed.[16] Of the balance, so-called conventional loans, a substantial portion was held by savings and loan associations.[17] The funds involved in the federal encouragement of home ownership are thus enormous compared to the amounts involved for rental housing in the city. Inducements for home ownership, of course, have been of little or no value to the city, since land has not been available in most of America's major cities for single-family homes.

The success of the federal housing program in suburbia results from the availability of mortgage funds that have not had to measure up to the usual free-market considerations of risk and competitive yield of other investments. Guarantees and insurance by the United States provide money for suburban home ownership at interest rates lower than the market over longer periods of time.

A subsidy is also involved in the activities of federal and state savings and loan associations. Because law restricts the investments of these associations largely to home mortgages,[18] the flow of capital has been directed artificially to suburbia, and money has been made available for houses at rates lower than those which would have been available if the home owner had had to compete for the funds with other sources of investment of comparable risk. To the extent that deposits in savings and loan associations are insured by the federal government under the Federal Home Loan Bank System, capital is attracted that *must* be invested in home mortgages. The federal insurance, then, constitutes an indirect subsidy.[19]

Another heavily subsidized federal housing program—public housing—has also contributed to the condition of our cities. Public housing

[16]Haar, *Federal Credit and Private Housing,* 1960, 132. Mr. Haar deliberately excluded the role of the savings and loan associations from an otherwise excellent book.

[17]Id., 138.

[18]12 USCA Sec. 1464(c). See also Ch. 32 Ill. Rev. Stat. 791.

[19]The special tax treatment under the Internal Revenue Code for state and federal savings and loan associations also requires that a certain portion of their funds be invested in "residential real property containing 4 or fewer family units." 1954 Internal Revenue Code, Subtitle F, Ch. 79, Sec. 7701(a) 19. See, also, Internal Revenue Code, Subtitle A, Ch. 1H, Part II. Secs. 591–593.

287

has been the prisoner of its opponents, who have largely determined its character. Locating public housing projects in the inner city has contributed to keeping lower-income people in the city and has strengthened the patterns of segregation, except in a few cases where careful planning has been able to achieve successfully integrated projects.[20] One arm of the federal housing program has financed housing for middle-income families in the suburbs. The question may well be asked: Why should not the opposite program have been adopted?

Other federal subsidies have also had their influence. The disproportionate amount of the federal budget allotted to agriculture[21] has helped bring about the mechanization of the farm and speeded up the migration of both Negro and white farm labor to the city. Similarly, the federal defense highway program has represented an enormous subsidy to the automobile at the expense of mass transportation. Whether these subsidies have been beneficial or detrimental is not pertinent here; what they indicate is that the condition of our metropolitan regions is not the result of "natural" forces alone. The federal government has played a major role in contributing to the shape and character of urban America.

The goals of the federal housing program originated in the New Deal attempt to house the one-third of the nation that was ill-housed. Attention was focused on home ownership for the middle class and public housing for the needy. The impact of these programs on the physical and economic aspects of the city and region was not considered. Moreover, the acute housing shortage of the post-World War II period obscured the need for a national long-term housing program. In more recent years social goals have been subordinated to stimulate the construction industry in order to minimize unemployment. It is impossible to predict what the shape and character of city and region might have been if the United States had had a national long-range program designed to provide housing for middle-income workers in the city and sites for industry and lower-income industrial workers in outlying areas. Surely, if the country had decided in 1948 that it wanted to subsidize higher-density apartment development in the suburbs rather than lower-density home ownership, and mass transportation rather than expressways, it is unlikely that all of the forecasts would point to suburban sprawl as the pattern of the future.

Catherine Bauer, in noting "the general past trend, however imperfectly realized, toward Everyone in His Place, in a standardized one-class, one-age-group, and one-color district, devoted wholly to residence" has pointed out that "this was not, however, the result of any conscious

[20]Mayer and Stein, "Public Housing as Community," *Architectural Record*, April 1964, 169.
[21]Statement by Senator Harrison A. Williams, Jr. is particularly pertinent. 11 *Journal of Housing* 609.

288

over-all plan or public decision to encourage maximum social segregation. It came about more or less by accident, as a side result of forces and policies employed for quite different and often distinctly progressive or idealistic ends, and because we were reluctant to assume any conscious collective responsibility whatsoever for the social pattern. . . . What we failed to recognize was that the powerful tools employed for civic development and home production *also* predetermine social structure to such an extent that there is little room left for free personal choice or flexible adjustment. The big social decisions are all made in advance, inherent in the planning and building process. And if these decisions are not made responsibly and democratically, then they are made irresponsibly by the accidents of technology, the myths of property interest, or the blindness and prejudice of a reactionary minority."[22]

TOWARD RENEWAL AND NEW DEVELOPMENT

To avoid the implications of present trends America will have to assume some responsibility for its overall social patterns and use the "powerful tools employed for civic development and home production" to reshape the areas of "free personal choice."

The forces at work in the city and region are cumulative. They all move together toward making the city a more desirable or less desirable place to live. The federal subsidies that have encouraged highway construction instead of mass commuter transportation and thus drawn industry out of the city have reduced the city's tax base. A lower tax base means less money for education and for the adjustment of rural migrants to urban life. Poor schools and changing neighborhoods encourage middle-class white families to move to the suburbs. Higher welfare costs increase the tax rate and thus encourage industry to relocate in outlying areas. All these factors are interrelated. If they can be altered, it might be possible to reverse the cycle of urban decay and deterioration and move the forces of the market-place toward renewal and reconstruction.

A total program is needed that recognizes the interdependence of city and suburbs. The creation of new communities on the outskirts of suburbia is a necessary element in the restoration of the inner city. The vitality of the city is, in turn, important for all of the inhabitants of the region. A total program must be able to differentiate between which of the forces must be shaped by government action in a private enterprise system and which may not.

[22]Bauer, "Social Questions in Housing and Community Planning," 7 *Journal of Social Issues* 21-3. Cf. Miss Bauer's "The Form and Structure of the Future Urban Complex," in *Cities and Space, The Future Use of Urban Land*, 1963, 73.

We cannot, for example, prevent those industries which do not require a central location from moving to less expensive land in outlying areas. However, through a regional open-space plan, we can limit the areas in which these industries may choose to locate. We cannot prevent middle-class white families from leaving the cities because their children are not being educated in accordance with middle-class standards. But we can induce middle-class families to live within the city if we can create areas large enough to establish a genuine community with good schools. We can find the land for these communities by clearing industrial as well as residential slum property, provided that we undertake to relieve the city of part of its tax burden or change the methods by which it collects taxes.

"New towns" are already being created in areas beyond suburbia to accommodate an exploding population, but these "new towns" may become exclusive suburbs, which in time will be engulfed by suburban sprawl.

I am suggesting a different kind of "new town" program. We should attempt to create "new towns" pursuant to regional open space and transportation plans. These towns will also accommodate industrial workers and industries displaced by an intensified residential and industrial slum clearance program in the core areas of our major cities. At the same time, on the land within the cities made available by slum clearance, new communities can be established for middle-income families.

This program would make both the central city and the "new towns" more heterogeneous in social composition, reduce travel distances to work and thus diminish the transportation problem, and, finally, bring suburban sprawl under control by regional planning of open spaces and mass transportation.

SEGREGATION

Present segregation practices are a serious obstacle to this kind of program; at the same time they provide an additional reason why a program designed to create heterogeneous communities both within the city and beyond the suburbs has become imperative. If there were no racial problem in the United States, we might have begun long ago to shape our policies toward moving industry and industrial workers to outlying locations and restoring the city to city workers.

Not only is the Negro population of our cities increasing in numbers but housing for Negroes is becoming increasingly segregated. The question of segregation is always present when the character and location of public housing and urban renewal projects are being determined. An unwillingness to face up to it has paralyzed city planning. It is necessary to deal with the question not only for the sake of civil rights for Negroes but in order to free city planning from some unspoken assumptions that underlie almost everything that happens about housing in our cities.

Juvenile delinquency and adult crime, school drop-outs and unemployment, the spread of slums and the cost of welfare, are all related to segregation in the cores of our cities. The social and economic costs of these problem areas both to the Negro and to the community as a whole are enormous.

Some sociologists compare the urbanization of the migrant Negro from the rural South to the Americanization of the earlier waves of immigrants from Europe.[23] It is true that each new immigrant group settled at the center of our cities, often in slums, becoming part of the labor pool. Each worked its way up toward social and economic success despite the discrimination practiced by older and more established members of the community. It is true that the same cycle is also going on in the Negro community. But the process is slow, the numbers involved are large, and the rising discontent of the Negro people will not permit patterns of segregation to continue without increasingly severe upheaval.

Migrants from the rural South, whether they are Negro or white, come from a culture very different from that of urban America. The problems of educating their children so that they will be equipped to work in the modern world of science and automation are enormously compounded by cultural segregation. And because the ghetto has become so large, the problem has changed in character. Some of the students in Chicago high schools located in the midst of Negro neighborhoods have never been "downtown." Some have never seen a suburb. Their contact with the urban culture of the metropolis is limited to school and to television. Their culture is that of the rural Negro living in the city, a culture that cannot interact with the urban culture unless the two can come in contact. Under these circumstances education for Negro children is of primary importance. Yet the segregated school pattern will be very difficult to change wherever there is a substantial segregated Negro population within the boundaries of the city.[24] In Chicago, just as one example, more than 50 per cent of the children in the public grade schools are non-white.

The Negro ghettos will not dissolve of themselves. The middle-class Negro family has had great difficulty in finding suitable housing outside of the segregated lower-income neighborhoods; only very recently has housing for these and higher-income Negroes begun to open up. A policy of non-discrimination in rentals or sales can help, but the

[23]Handlin, *The Newcomers*, 1959. Cf. Silberman, *Crises in Black and White*, 1954, 36–58.

[24]See Hauser, in *Chicago Perspective*, June 1964, 36.

ghettos are still so large that only a major plan to induce a substantial part of the Negro working population to live in outlying "new towns" can bring about a more uniform and just distribution of these people among the population as a whole.

We should not underestimate the difficulties of creating interracial communities. Experience shows, however, that it is possible to create interracial housing in stable communities where the housing is sufficiently subsidized. New York's state-subsidized housing program has produced a number of interracial projects. Prairie Shores in Chicago, a successfully integrated housing project, demonstrates that racial antagonism recedes if the accommodations are "a bargain." It is easier to establish integrated housing in new developments than in areas that are already either all-white or all-Negro, but it is not necessary for every neighborhood in a "new town" to be interracial. If there is no policy of segregation, neighborhoods can develop by choice, as has happened in ethnic communities created by second-generation European immigrants.

The existence of heterogeneous communities in outlying areas will make it more possible for the Negro to relate to the urban culture. Schools in a smaller community, for example, can be so located that even if there are neighborhoods within the community that are predominantly white or predominantly Negro all of the children can attend the same schools. So many industrial workers are Negro that any program for creating outlying "new towns" for industry and industrial workers must aim for heterogeneity. As for the cities, where Negroes are already established, a program to bring back middle-income white families must encompass the creation of interracial middle-income neighborhoods. If America is not prepared to accept interracial communities, there is little hope of arresting the decline of the city.

THE VALUE OF CITY LAND

There has been a tendency to assume that the flight to the suburbs means that people prefer a suburban home to a city home. But the ability to make a choice has not been possible since the 1920's when most of the land within the borders of every American city was built upon; the choice ever since has been between apartment living in the city and a house in the suburbs.

Land values are perhaps the best measure of what people prefer. The fact that residential land values in the city are everywhere substantially higher than in the suburbs shows how desirable central location is to most people. The amount of new construction of high-rise apartment buildings in the city indicates that some people with means 292 are willing to pay more for apartments built at higher cost on more expensive land in the city than for houses built at lower cost on less expensive land in outlying areas, even if their choice means sending their children to private schools. Moreover, the current boom in suburban garden apartment developments suggests that when close-in suburban land for homes is scarce many people choose close-in sub-urban apartments rather than outlying homesites despite the subsidies available for the latter.

Central location still retains great economic value, and this is the best evidence that the city can be restored. Land value, in the end, is the measure of economic potential. Favorable economic forces do exist in the city, and therefore the restoration of middle-income com-munities in the city becomes a possibility. The task of restoring the city also becomes easier because large areas of relatively inexpensive industrial land are available in virtually every American city.[25] Most of these areas are centrally located, having been the sites of the early industries around which the city clustered. They are now often used for very low economic purposes, such as coal and lumber storage and no-longer-functional railroad yards. Many of the buildings in these industrial slums are dilapidated; some are abandoned. Several square miles of this type of land exist in Chicago along the south branch of the Chicago River and in the railroad yards south of the Loop. In Baltimore, the Baltimore & Ohio Railroad owns more than 150 acres of such land south of the Camden Station within a stone's throw of downtown. If new outlying communities are created, thereby increas-ing the total housing supply for people now living in city slums, the values of both residential and industrial slum property will decline and thus reduce the cost of acquiring this ill-used land for urban renewal.

FEDERAL SUBSIDIES REDIRECTED

Only a slight extension of the tools already in hand is needed to foster the development of middle-income communities within the city and of "new towns" on the outskirts of suburbia. The Housing Community Development Act of 1964 (which was not enacted into law) proposed for the first time that the Federal Housing Administration insure mortgages for the purchase of land leading to the development of new communities. The Administration thus proposed to finance "new town" developments, although the result may well have been that under such a program the "new towns" would have become exclusive suburbs like many "new towns" now being built with private financing.

Assume, however, that FHA and VA financing were abandoned

[25]Vernon, *The Myth and Reality of Our Urban Problems*, 1961, 45–46.   293

except in urban renewal areas in the city and in "new town" developments. In addition, assume that a regional open space and transportation plan were required before this financing is made available. Assume, further, that the regulations governing savings and loan associations were amended to allow them to allocate a substantial portion of their funds to financing mortgages for multiple dwellings, and to limit financing of either homes or multiple dwellings to established suburban areas, to the cities, or to "new towns," in regions where an open space and transportation plan exists. Moreover, suppose that the VA and FHA regulations prohibiting discrimination because of race were also applied to savings and loan associations. Suppose, in addition, that the FHA programs for middle-income housing (Section 221d3) were made available in the "new towns," so that the goal of an economically heterogeneous community would be vigorously pursued. Suppose, finally, that each "new town" were required to provide some minimum of public housing and housing for the elderly in order to be eligible for federal financing.

These federal tools, almost all of them readily adaptable, would be powerful inducements for the creation of heterogeneous "new towns" in which individuals and industry displaced from the city, together with some of the 80,000,000 new people to be housed between now and 1980, could be accommodated. Moreover, federal incentives could be geared to the creation of "new towns" of higher density so that effective mass transportation between them and the center city could be developed.

Assume that the federal urban renewal programs for clearing residential slums and renewing central business districts were extended to permit the clearance of industrial slums. And assume that the federal government were prepared to finance the construction of industrial facilities in "new town" industrial parks. Can there be any doubt that such a program would have enormous impact in hastening the creation of "new town" developments and in clearing land within the city for the construction of middle-income communities?

The large subsidies involved in public housing might also be used to encourage these developments. From the beginning public housing in the United States has always been intimately associated with welfare, but more than thirty years have now passed without any examination of this underlying premise. The question today might well be: Why should public housing subsidies be associated with welfare at all?

The defects of the public housing program result largely from the segregation practices of most cities and from the income limitations on the occupants. The result in most large cities has been to concentrate the lowest-income Negroes in these central city projects. As soon as a family exceeds the income limits, it is evicted. But if the income is still inadequate for a middle-class dwelling, the family often has to 294 move into a slum dwelling. As long as our cities are not free from slums, the question may properly be asked whether the slums should be occupied by employed lower-income families or by people on public welfare.

This is not the place for a full exposition of the problems associated with public housing. The questions are raised, however, to show that if we were to make welfare payments for rent to persons needing shelter, and use the public housing program to build housing for industrial workers in "new town" developments, the resulting housing would be more in keeping with the needs of the city and the region.

LONDON'S "NEW TOWNS"

An approach similar to the one proposed here has been undertaken in England. The enormous urban population growth that is now occurring in the United States was anticipated in England some thirty years ago. London was the capital of an empire and its population crossed the million mark about 1800. The trend to the suburbs was already well under way in the 1920's; in the two decades before World War II the smaller ring around London gained 1,700,000 residents and the regional ring gained 5,900,000, while the county of London lost population.[26]

London's answer was the creation of "new towns." They were built beyond the greenbelt that had been established outside the suburban ring. Occupants of the East End and industry resettled there. The program has been the subject of controversy, but it is now generally conceded that, on the whole, it has been successful; current criticism centers about errors in planning, lack of culture in the new towns, and other faults not directly pertinent here.[27] Although conditions in the United States are very different from those in England, and London's program cannot be imitated here, the establishment of "new towns" to accommodate economic expansion, population growth, and what the English call "over-spill" from the areas being cleared inside the city is a sound idea.

REGIONAL PLANNING

It should be clear by now that I am proposing regional planning only in a most restricted sense. It is not necessary for public agencies to provide comprehensive master plans for each region, leaving no room

[26]Foley, *Controlling London's Growth,* 1964, 9–10.
[27]Madge, "The New Towns Program in Britain," *Journal of the American Institute of Planners,* Vol. XXVIII, No. 4, Nov. 1962, 208.

for diversity created by private choices. Some planning, however, is necessary, particularly by the agencies responsible for water, sewer, and transportation because they must be able to project the future needs for public services of an ever-expanding population. In many places these agencies plan independently of each other, and the federal agencies that subsidize housing do no planning at all. What each region now needs is a plan covering all of the agencies already involved in the expenditure of public funds, which states where and when the public will spend its money for water systems, sanitary and storm sewers, highways and rapid mass transportation, and in what areas subsidies will be available for housing. Regional growth can thus be controlled, with private enterprise left to develop variety within the over-all framework of the plan.

The agencies that decide on the location of public buildings, such as federal office buildings and state college campuses, should also be involved in this planning, because where these buildings are placed greatly influences the direction of regional growth. The General Services Administration of the federal government, for example, has been seeking a site for a new United States Patent Office, to be built on the outskirts of Baltimore. The Urban Renewal Administration, on the other hand, has spent a great deal of federal money in renewing the central business district of Baltimore. It apparently had not occurred to anyone that building the Patent Office in downtown Baltimore might substantially help the downtown renewal process and that land might be available there. Fortunately, the situation may yet be rectified since the Baltimore & Ohio Railroad has offered a free site for the Patent Office on the undeveloped industrial land that it owns within a stone's throw of downtown Baltimore and of the commuter station between Baltimore and Washington. The location would have many advantages both for the Patent Office and for Baltimore's renewal process.

REAL ESTATE TAXES

An essential part of this program is the clearance of industrial slums at the cores of most of America's cities. One of the major obstacles to this has been the reluctance of cities to lose industry for fear of further jeopardizing their real estate tax base. But industry is moving to the suburbs anyway, and the real estate tax structure of the city will have to be revised in any event. Real estate taxes in most places have already reached the limits of economic feasibility, representing 18 to 25 per cent of the gross rentals of residential properties. Assessments against property are still the major means by which cities collect taxes, and they have fallen behind in their share of the total tax dollar. In 1932 all cities collected $2,600,000,000 in taxes, all states collected

$2,300,000,000, and the federal government collected only $2,000,-000,000. By 1959 the cities had become poor relatives and collected only $11,000,000,000 compared to $20,000,000,000 by the states and $73,000,000,000 by the federal government.[28]

A case can be made that the wealth produced by the cities has been drained out by federal taxes and re-distributed first to agriculture, second to suburbia, and third to the cities. At the same time the welfare costs of the cities have increased their tax rates, so that what the federal government has contributed in the form of urban renewal has been taken away by the costs of municipal services. The cities must revise the methods by which they raise revenues, and a greater share of the cost of health, welfare, and education must be allocated to the federal government. The migration to the cities of rural Negroes, Southern whites, and Puerto Ricans is a national problem; the federal government should bear the tax burdens this has created.

Before state as well as federal power becomes available to solve the problems of real estate tax revision and regional planning, the now rural-dominated state legislatures must develop greater sympathy than they have exhibited for the problems of the city and region. The recent decisions of the United States Supreme Court on reapportionment give some hope that city and suburb may soon have more influence upon state legislatures in their dealings with urban problems.

CONCLUSION

Obviously, each city or each region has unique problems that require more specific solutions than a generalized paper like this can provide. Nevertheless, these proposals are not offered just as a panacea. We should bring suburban sprawl under control so that we can get better transportation, water and sewer control, and more open space, but a regional plan will not necessarily produce a beautiful region. There is still much to learn about "new town" development, about the creation of communities in which the citizens can govern themselves and in which life is pleasant and interesting. Similarly, the restoration of middle-income families to the city does not automatically solve the financial problems of the city, nor will troubles in race relations disappear even if all communities are racially heterogeneous. We should not try to control too much. At best, we can give direction to economic and social forces already at work and seek to provide better communities in which people can create a variety of environments appropriate to their way of life.

It is possible to shape the character of our urban environment. The population explosion provides the opportunity and existing federal

[28]Higby, *The Squeeze*, 1960, 31.   297

subsidies provide a means. If we deal realistically with segregation and with the sources of city revenues, we can create a more livable community. Public thinking and discussion can clarify what we value about urban life. If we know what kind of urban environment we want, the power and the tools to create it are at our disposal.

Oscar Lewis

Even the Saints Cry

"You cannot take people out of an old-fashioned slum, where reality has been giving them a grim, distorted education for years, place them in a project, and expect them to exhibit all kinds of gentle, middle-class virtues."

Michael Harrington

This article describes the experiences of a young Puerto Rican mother, Cruz Rios, who moved from La Esmeralda—one of the oldest slums in San Juan only a short distance from the governor's palace—about four miles east to Villa Hermosa, a new government housing project in a middle-class section of Rio Piedras. Cruz' story illustrates the difficult problems of adjustment in her new environment and helps us understand why, in spite of the efforts of well-intentioned governments and the spending of huge sums of money on public housing, the positive effects hoped for by social planners are not always forthcoming.

When I began my study of Cruz in 1963, she was just 17 and living alone on relief with her two children. She lived in a small, dark, one-room apartment for which she paid a rental of eight dollars a month. Her kitchen was a tiny corner alcove equipped with a three-burner kerosene stove and a water faucet jutting out from the wall. She shared a run-down hall toilet with two other families and paid a

From *La Vida*, by Oscar Lewis. © Copyright 1965, 1966 by Oscar Lewis. Reprinted by permission of Random House, Inc. Oscar Lewis is professor of anthropology at the University of Illinois. This article is drawn from his book *La Vida, Puerto Rican Family in the Culture of Poverty; San Juan and New York*, Random House, 1966.

neighbor $1.50 a month for the privilege of an extension cord which supplied her with electricity.

Cruz, a crippled, mulatto girl with reddish brown kinky hair and a pretty face, was lame since early childhood. She left school after the fifth grade, set up house with her sweetheart at 14 and gave birth to her first child at 15. Two years later, before the birth of her second child, she separated from her husband, Emilio, who refused to recognize the baby as his own.

Part I gives the reader a glimpse of living conditions in the slum; part II, recorded five months after Cruz had moved, gives her reactions to the housing project. (Names of all places and people in this tape-recorded narrative have been changed to guarantee the anonymity of the narrator.)

I

Here in La Esmeralda, the only thing that disturbs me are the rats. Lice, bedbugs, and rats have always been a problem in my room. When I moved in here a year ago, the first thing I found were little baby rats. "Kill them!" my friend Gloria said. "*Ay Bendito!* I can't do it. Poor little things—they look like children," I said, and I left them there in a hole. The next day they were gone. I didn't kill them, they just disappeared. I cleaned up the house and about a month later they were going back and forth through the room from one hole to another, with me just looking at them.

When Alejandro was living with me, more rats came because there was a hen with eggs under the house. A rat had given birth and had eaten some of the chicks. The owner took the hen and 29 chicks out of there because there were baby rats underneath the hen too. The man threw them out but a week later they came back and were all over the place, even getting into the pan with the baby's milk and eating up whatever I left around.

One Sunday my *mamá* said, "Let's buy a rat trap and see if we can't get rid of some of them." Well, we tried it and that day between us and the next-door neighbor we caught 29 little rats. After a while, more came. Anita used to chase them across the room to see if she could catch them, and the boys who came to the house would say, "Look, a rat."

I would tell them, "Let it be, it's one of the family. They keep me company, now that I'm all by myself. I'm raising them for soup."

So I left them alone, but before I knew it, there were great big rats here. One Sunday I said to Catín, who had just eaten a breaded cutlet, "Catín, you'd better go bathe or the rats will eat you up." Then I forgot about it and she lay down. Later I took a bath and went to bed. About midnight, Catín screamed, "*Ay, ay, ay,* it bit me!" The first thing that came to my mind was that it was a snake or a scorpion. "What bit you?" I asked and when I turned on the light, she said, "Look, look!" and I could see a rat running way.

She had been bitten on the arm and I could see the little teeth marks. I squeezed out the blood and smeared urine and bay rum on it.

Then I said, "Catín, you'd better come into my bed with me. God knows whether it was because the crib is dirty or you are dirty." I was wearing only panties, Chuito and Anita were naked, but Catín was wearing a jacket and pants. Well, later that same rat came and bit her again on the other arm. I sprinkled bay rum all over the bed where she was sleeping and rubbed it on her and nothing else happened that night.

The next day I went to the church and told the Sister that the girl had been bitten by a rat. She told me that if Catín didn't start running a fever, to leave her alone, and if she did, to take her to the hospital. Then I said to Catín, "You see? That's what happens when you don't bathe." She took a bath every day after that.

At the end of the year, Anita got a rat bite on the lip. I squeezed it out for her and it dried up and she didn't get a fever or anything. A few days after that, I was sitting in a chair with my arm hanging down when a rat came and *pra!* it tried to take off my finger. It wanted human flesh. I lifted my hand, and the rat ran to a hole and disappeared.

Then I said to myself, "These rats have to be finished off. I can't live like this with so many blessed rats. There are more rats than people." And I bought a trap from the man next door. I fixed the bacon myself and put it in the trap. First I caught a real big rat, then another and another. Three in all that same night. But there were still more left.

The next morning, I heard screams coming from Rosa Maria's room up above. I said, "Rosa, what's wrong?" Her little boy was crying and shaking his hand, with a rat hanging from it. "Kill it," I said, but he answered, "I can't. Its teeth are stuck in my finger." Finally he got it off by dragging it along the floor. Rosa Maria attended him but the next day the child had a fever which kept going up. The doctor said that the boy was getting tetanus and had to go to the hospital.

The people upstairs leave a lot of rotting clothes piled there, and cans of food and rice. If they don't get rid of that filth, the rats won't leave. I asked the landlord to cover the holes because the rats keep coming in and out as if they were in a bus terminal. He said he didn't live here and I should do it myself.

There are lots of cockroaches in my room too. And new fleas have come in, I don't know from where, except probably from the rats themselves. There are also crickets and lizards. These houses are hollow   301 underneath, and below the floor there's a lot of old boards and filth and all kinds of garbage that has accumulated, and at night the animals come crawling up.

I've noticed that it's on Thursday nights that the rats give us the most trouble. Every other Thursday, before the social worker comes, I clean my house from top to bottom so there are no crumbs on the floor for the rats to eat and no dirty dishes for them to clean. I've learned that unless I leave something for them, the rats come closer and closer to us. When the house is clean, we are in more danger of getting bitten.

The social worker told me it would be a good idea to get the children out of La Esmeralda because there's so much delinquency there. My moving to the housing project was practically her idea; she insisted and insisted. Finally one day she came to me and said, "Tomorrow you have to move to the *caserío* in Villa Hermosa." I didn't want to upset her because she's been good to me, so I said okay.

You should have seen this place when I moved in. It was bursting with garbage and smelling of shit, pure shit. Imagine, when the social worker opened the door that first day, a breeze happened to blow her way. She stepped back and said, "Wait, I can't go in. This is barbarous." I had to go outside with her. I tell you, the people who lived here before me were dirtier than the dirtiest pig. When I moved out of my little room in La Esmeralda, I scrubbed it so clean you could have eaten off the floor. Whoever moved in could see that a decent person had lived there. And then I came here and found this pig-sty, and the place looked so big I felt too little and weak to get it clean. So, fool that I am, instead of sending out for a mop and getting right down to work, I just stood in a corner and cried. I locked the door and stayed in all day, weeping. I cried floods.

And this place isn't like La Esmeralda, you know, where there's so much liveliness and noise and something is always going on. Here you never see any movement on the street, not one little domino or card game or anything. The place is dead. People act as if they're angry or in mourning. Either they don't know how to live or they're afraid to. And yet it's full of shameless good-for-nothings. It's true what the proverb says, "May God deliver me from quiet places; I can defend myself in the wild ones."

Everything was so strange to me when I first moved here that I was scared to death. I hated to go out because it's hard to find your way back to this place even if you know the address. The first couple of times I got lost, and I didn't dare ask anybody the way for fear they would fall on me and beat me. If anyone knocked on my door I thought four times before deciding to open it. Then when I did, I took a knife along. But I'm not like that any more. I've made my decision: if someone wants to kill me, let him. I can't live shut in like that. And if anybody interferes with me it will be the worse for them. I have a couple of tricks up my sleeve and can really fuck things up for anybody when I want to.

After a few days, I finally started cleaning up the place. I scrubbed the floors and put everything in order. I even painted the whole apartment, although I had to fight tooth and nail with the man in charge of the buildings in order to get the paint. That old man wanted to get something from me in return, but I wouldn't give it to him. I never have been attracted to old men.

The apartment is a good one. I have a living room, bedroom, kitchen, porch and my own private bathroom. That's something I never had in La Esmeralda. I clean it every morning and when the children use it I go and pull the chain right away.

I never had a kitchen sink in La Esmeralda either, and here I have a brand new one. It's easy to wash the dishes in these double sinks because they're so wide and comfortable. The only trouble is the water, because sometimes it goes off and the electricity, too—three times since I've been here.

I still don't have an ice-box or refrigerator but the stove here is the first electric one I've ever had in my life. I didn't know how to light it the day I move in. I tried everything I could think of, backward and forward. Luckily, the social worker came and she lit it for me, but even so I didn't learn and Nanda had to show me again that afternoon. She has worked for rich people so long that she knows all those things. I really miss my own little kerosene stove, but Nanda wanted it, so what could I do? She's my *mamá* and if she hankered after a star I would climb up to heaven to get it for her if I could.

The main advantage of the electric stove is that when I have a lot of work to do and it gets to be ten or eleven o'clock, I just connect the stove and have lunch ready in no time. In La Esmeralda I had to wait for the kerosene to light up well before I could even start to cook. And this stove doesn't smoke and leave soot all over the place, either. Still, if the power fails again or is cut off because I don't pay my bill, the kids will just have to go hungry. I won't even be able to heat a cup of milk for them. In La Esmeralda, whenever I didn't have a quarter to buy a full gallon of kerosene, I got ten cents worth. But who's going to sell you five or ten cents worth of electricity?

I haven't seen any rats here, just one tiny little mouse. It doesn't bother me much because it lives down below, in a hole at the bottom of the stairs. There's no lack of company anywhere, I guess—rats in La Esmeralda and lots of little cockroaches here.

This apartment is so big that I don't have to knock myself out keeping it in order. There's plenty of room for my junk. I even have closets here, and lots of shelves. I have so many shelves and so few dishes that

303

I have to put a dish here and a dish there just to keep each shelf from being completely empty. All the counters and things are no use at all to me, because I just cook a bit of oatmeal for the children and let them sit anywhere to eat it since I have no dishes with which to set a table. Half of my plates broke on the way from La Esmeralda. I guess they wanted to stay back there where they weren't so lonely.

Here even my saints cry! They look so sad. They think I am punishing them. This house is so big I had to separate the saints and hang them up in different places just to cover the empty walls. In La Esmeralda I kept them all together to form a little altar, and I lit candles for them. In La Esmeralda they helped me, but here I ask until I'm tired of asking and they don't help me at all. They are punishing me.

In La Esmeralda I never seemed to need as many things as here. I think it is because we all had about the same, so we didn't need any more. But here, when you go to other people's apartment and see all their things. . . . It's not that I'm jealous. God forbid! I don't want anyone to have less than they have. It's only that I would like to have things of my own too.

What does bother me is the way people here come into my apartment and furnish the place with their mouths. They start saying, "Oh, here's where the set of furniture should go; you need a TV set in that corner and this one is just right for a record-player." And so on. I bite my tongue to keep from swearing at them because, damn it, I have good taste too. I know a TV set would look fine in that corner, but if I don't have the money to buy one, how can I put it there? That's what I like about La Esmeralda—if people there could help someone, they did; if not, they kept their mouths shut.

I really would like a TV though, because they don't have public sets here, the way they do in La Esmeralda. I filled in some blanks for that program, Queen for a Day, to see if I can get one as a gift. It was Nanda's idea and she's so lucky that maybe I will get it. If I do, then at least I could spend the holidays looking at TV. And the children might stay home instead of wandering around the neighborhood so much.

The traffic here really scares me. That's the main reason I don't like this place. Cars scud by like clouds in a high wind and, I'm telling you, I'm always afraid a car will hit the children. If something should happen to my little penguins, I'd go mad, I swear I would. My kids are little devils, and when I bring them in through the front door, they slip out again by climbing over the porch railing. Back in La Esmeralda, where our house was so small, they had to play out in the street whenever people came over, but here there is plenty of room to run around indoors.

Maybe I was better off in La Esmeralda. You certainly have to pay for the comforts you have here! Listen, I'm jittery, really nervous, be-

304

cause if you fail to pay the rent even once here, the following month you're thrown out. I hardly ever got behind on my payments in La Esmeralda, but if I did, I knew that they wouldn't put me out on the street. It's true that my rent is only $6.50 a month here while I paid $11.50 in La Esmeralda, but there I didn't have a water bill and I paid only $1.50 a month for electricity. Here I have already had to pay $3.50 for electricity and if I use more than the minimum they allow in water, I'll have to pay for that too. And I do so much washing!

It's a fact that as long as I lived in La Esmeralda I could always scare up some money, but here I'm always broke. I've gone as much as two days without eating. I don't play the races at El Comandante any more. I can't afford to. And I can't sell *bolita* numbers here because several cops live in this *caserío* and the place is full of detectives. Only the other day I almost sold a number to one of them, but luckily I was warned in time. I don't want to be arrested for anything in the world, not because I'm scared of being in jail but because of the children.

Since I can't sell numbers here, I sell Avon cosmetics. I like the pretty sets of china they give away, and I'm trying to sell a lot so that they'll give me one. But there's hardly any profit in it for me.

In La Esmeralda I could get an old man now and then to give me five dollars for sleeping with him. But here I haven't found anything like that at all. The truth is, if a man comes here and tries to strike up a conversation I usually slam the door in his face. So, well, I have this beautiful, clean apartment, but what good does it do me? Where am I to get money? I can't dig for it.

In La Esmeralda we used to buy things cheap from thieves. They stole from people who lived far away and then they came to La Esmeralda through one of the side entrances to sell. And who the hell is going to go looking for his things down there? Not a chance! You hardly ever saw a rich person in La Esmeralda. We didn't like them, and we scared them off. But so far as I can tell, these dopes around here always steal from the *blanquitos,* the rich people, nearby. Suppose one of them took it into his head to come here to look for the missing stuff? What then?

Since I've moved I'm worse off than I have ever been before, because, before now I realize all the things I lack and, besides, the rich people around here are always wanting everything for themselves. In La Esmeralda you can bum a nickel from anyone. But with these people, the more they have, the more they want. It's everything for themselves. If you ask them for work, they'll find something for you to do fast enough, but when it's time to pay you'd think it hurt them to pull a dollar out of their pocket.

Listen, to get a few beans from some people who live in a house near here I had to help pick and shell them. People here are real 305 hard and stingy. What's worse, they take advantage of you. The other day I ironed all day long for a woman and all I got for it was two dollars and my dinner. I felt like throwing the money in her face but I just calmly took it. I would have been paid six dollars at the very least for a whole day's ironing in La Esmeralda. At another lady's house near here I cooked, washed the dishes, even scrubbed the floor, and for all that she just gave me one of her old dresses, which I can't even wear because it's too big for me.

Right now, I don't have a cent. The lady next door lets me charge the food for breakfast at her husband's *kiosko*. She's become so fond of me, you can't imagine. Her husband won't sell on credit to anybody, but there's nothing impossible for the person who is really interested in helping you out. She trusts me, so she lets me write down what I take and keep the account myself.

I buy most of my food at the Villa Hermosa grocery. It's a long way from here and I have to walk it on foot every time I need something, like rice or tomato sauce. It's a supermarket, so they don't give credit, but everything is cheaper there, much cheaper. A can of tomato sauce costs seven cents there and 10 cents in La Esmeralda. Ten pounds of rice costs $1.25 in La Esmeralda and 99 cents here. The small bottles of King Pine that cost 15 cents each in La Esmeralda are two for a quarter here.

Sometimes Public Welfare gives me food, but not always, and I don't like most of the things they give. That long-grained rice doesn't taste like anything. It's like eating hay. The meat they give has fat on top and it comes in a can and it's real dark. They say it's corned beef but I don't know. The same goes for that powdered milk. Who could drink the stuff? In La Esmeralda I saved it until I was really hard up and then I sold it to anybody who was willing to shell out a quarter for it to feed it to their animals or something. But I don't dare do that here because it's federal government food, and it's against the law to sell it. I could get into trouble that way in a place like this, where I don't know anybody. I might try to sell that stuff to a detective without realizing who he was and I'd land in jail.

I haven't been to La Esmeralda often since I moved here, because I can't afford it. Every trip costs 40 cents, 20 cents each way. I want to pay off all my debts in La Esmeralda so that I can hold my head high and proud when I go there. I want people to think I've bettered myself because one can't be screwed all one's life. Even now when I visit, still owing money as I do, I put on my best clothes and always try to carry a little cash. I do this so Minerva, Emilio's aunt, won't get the idea I'm starving or anything like that. She really suffers when she sees me in La Esmeralda, and I do all that just to bother her. I dress up the kids real nice and take them to call on everybody except her.

When I first moved out of La Esmeralda, nobody knew that I was leaving, in the first place because it made me sad and in the second place because that old Minerva had gone around telling everybody she hoped I'd clear out. She even said it to my face. I'd yell back at her, "What right do you have to say that? Did you buy La Esmeralda or something?"

Another reason why I hardly ever go to La Esmeralda is because Emilio spies on me. He has come after me in the *caserío* just the way he did in La Esmeralda, though not as often. He likes to use the shower in my new apartment when he comes. When I start home after visiting La Esmeralda, he gets into his car and drives along behind me, offering to give me a lift. But, listen, I wouldn't get into that car even if I had to walk all the way from San Juan to Villa Hermosa. I put a curse on that car, such a tremendous curse that I'm just waiting to see it strike. I did it one day when Anita had asthma and I had no money to take her to the hospital. I happened to glance out of the window and I saw Emilio stretched out in his car, relaxed as could be, as if he deserved nothing but the best. I let go and yelled with all the breath in my chest, "I hope to God someday you'll wear that car as a hat. I hope it turns to dust with you all fucked up inside it." Now I can't ride in the car, because I'm afraid the curse will come true some time when both of us are in it.

You can't imagine how lonely I feel here. I have friends, but they're sort of artificial, pasted-on friends. I couldn't confide in them at all. For example, I got pregnant a little while ago, and I had to have an abortion. I nearly went crazy thinking about it. Having a baby is nothing, it's the burden you have to take on afterwards, especially with a cowardly husband like mine who takes the easiest way out, denying that the child is his. So there I was, pregnant and, you know, I was ashamed. I was already out of La Esmeralda, see? Well, I know that my womb is weak, so I took two doses of Epsom salts with quinine and out came the kid. You can't imagine how unpleasant that is. In La Esmeralda you can tell everybody about it, and that sort of eases your heart. But here I didn't tell anybody. These girls I know here are *señoritas,* mere children, and something like that . . . *ay bendito!*

But, to tell you the truth, I don't know what they call a *señorita* here in Villa Hermosa. The way it is in La Esmeralda, a girl and boy fall in love. For a few months they control themselves. Then they can't any more, and the boy does what he has to do to the girl. The hole is bigger than the full moon and that's that. They tell everybody and become husband and wife in the eyes of all the world. There's no trying to hide it. But here you see girls, who by rights should already have had a couple of kids, trying to keep from being found out. They'll go to a hotel with their sweethearts and let them stick their pricks into every hole in their body except the right one. And then they're so brazen as to come out of that hotel claiming they're still *señoritas*. It's plain shameless.

307

There are some policemen here who make love like this to some girls I know. Well, the policeman who did it to my friend Mimi came and told me that if I loaned him my bed for a little while he would give me three pesos. As that money wouldn't be bad at all and as he wasn't going to do it to me, I rented him the bed and grabbed the three pesos. Let them go screw! They locked themselves in the bedroom for a little while and then they went away. It was none of my business. If they didn't do it here, they would go do it somewhere else. And she didn't lose her virginity or anything here. So my hands are clean.

Sometimes I want to go back to La Esmeralda to live and other times I don't. It's not that I miss my family so much. On the contrary, relatives can be very bothersome. But you do need them in case you get sick because then you can dump the children on them. Sometimes I cry for loneliness here. Sometimes I'm bored to death. There's more neighborliness in La Esmeralda. I was used to having good friends stop by my house all the time. I haven't seen much of this neighborhood because I never go out. There's a Catholic church nearby but I've never been there. And I haven't been to the movies once since I've been living here. In La Esmeralda I used to go now and then. And in La Esmeralda, when nothing else was going on, you could at least hear the sea.

In La Esmeralda nobody ever made fun of my lameness. On the contrary, it was an advantage because everyone went out of his way to help me: "Let me help the lame girl. Let me buy *bolita* numbers from Lame Crucita, because cripples bring luck." But it isn't like that here, where people just laugh. That's why I'd like to live in La Esmeralda again or have Nanda move in here with me.

The social worker told me that I could go to the hospital and have an operation to fix my back. But who could I leave my little baby crows with? And suppose what they do is take my guts out in order to make me look right? Still, now that I live in a place like Villa Hermosa, I would like to have an operation to make me straight.

SEVEN

DECISION CONTROL

The fabric of social life is heavily dependent upon the existence of control techniques and influence processes. Man continually tries to influence or control the behavior of others by manipulating his own behavior and various other resources which he can make available or withhold from others. In fact, social life is only possible to the extent that culture operates as a coercive force influencing members of a society to think and behave in accord with established traditions. As one social scientist has noted, each generation faces the threat that it will be overcome by a wave of barbarians. These barbarians are, of course, the new generation of children—those who as yet are unfamiliar with the patterns of living of the society into which they are born.

Advances in scientific and technological knowledge over the last several decades have increased the current use and future potential of *planned, consciously applied control* techniques on human behavior. We are experiencing, on a scale never thought possible, the application of many techniques and practices, the uses of which have not been fully explored. Centralized data banks bringing together a lifetime of information on every citizen are now in limited use and have been proposed on a very large scale. Drug therapies and psychological analysis have been widely applied to problems ranging from treating mental illness to selling mouthwash. Highly sensitive and unobtrusive electronic devices for "picking up" and recording sound are now standard equipment available to all.

The existence of this new technology raises serious questions concerning the net balance of consequences (favorable and unfavorable) in their use. Certainly, computerized and centralized record systems developed by the federal government would greatly facilitate the activities of many branches of government in serving the people. Yet such centralized data also increase the totalitarian potential of a society as it slowly encroaches on the private world of every citizen.

There is another sense, however, in which the new technology goes far beyond simply value-based disagreements in the uses and consequences of technology. There is the distinct possibility that centralized and computerized decision-making systems make the issues of value disagreement over uses and consequences an irrelevant one. Many of the new technological advances create problems of removing decision-making from the people so that value disagreements do not even occur. This is the real issue behind what is called decision control. The technology itself can become self-perpetuating and self-validating.

This tendency toward the emergence of decision-making systems which are impervious to external validation or control has a well-established home in bureaucracy, whether or not there is an elaborate surveillance technology. This can be seen in the operation of government employment programs which subject prospective employees to testing on such personal matters as sex, politics, associations, and beliefs for the purpose of screening security risks. Once such programs are established they are often found to be used for employees in nonsensitive positions (Ridgeway, 1964).

Similar examples are found in the recent controversy on wiretapping between the Attorney General's office and the Federal Bureau of Investigation (Cipes, 1966). The federal government makes a distinction between the use of electronic devices to overhear a conversation ("bugging") and the interception of a telephone communication (wiretapping). Bugging is not prohibited by federal statute and is used in matters related to national security and high level organized crime. Wiretapping is prohibited by federal law, but has been used in situations involving intelligence activities and national security. In such cases wiretapping must be carried out with the approval and supervision of the Attorney General.

What many court cases concerning the legality of wiretapping and bugging clearly indicate is the difficulty involved in trying to restrain law enforcement agencies from full-scale use of the surveillance technology. This is quite understandable, for it is the law enforcement agent's job to collect information bearing on a certain case whether or not that evidence is admissable in a court of law. Often they may hope that the illegal use of wiretapping may reveal information about a suspect which can be pursued with legal approval.

Such incidents clearly reflect a situation where the technology itself cannot be adequately restrained. There are also a small but growing number of incidents reported in the press where surveillance technology is used in industry for protection of industrial secrets or the pursuit of a competitor's secrets. The most popularized incident of an attempt by private industry to protect its interests through surveillance techniques is that concerning the author Ralph Nader (*Unsafe at Any Speed*) and General Motors. Nader, who was researching the auto 310 industry for a book on safety standards among auto manufacturers, was faced with an inquiry into his personal and professional life by private investigators in the employ of auto firms. Such investigations can be very effective means of intimidation, as few people can subject their lives to a detailed investigation which would not reveal the elements of an incriminating dossier. Nor should people have to subject themselves to such investigations, which leave the traditional rights to privacy guaranteed only by the discretion of those organizations large and powerful enough to determine whom they wish to have shadowed and for what purposes.

The papers in this section describe the capabilities and potentialities for control by government or other large organizations of the behavior and attitudes of the public. Starting first with the specific potentialities for control (as with bugging and wiretapping discussed above), the Packard article focuses upon the uses of behavioral technology in creating artificial consumption patterns and conditioning buyers to be dissatisfied with last year's models. In the face of this technology, the average consumer finds that his needs are manipulated, his self-estimate is dependent upon consumption behavior, and that he suffers from the sense of relative deprivation that is inherent in the patterns of planned obsolescence of products.

An extreme case of the potential of behavioral technology is found in the article by Szasz which is a review of Valeriy Tarsis' *Ward 7,* a book which describes the use of psychiatric definitions of illness and psychiatric controls to prevent political controversy in the Soviet Union. The review also deals with the application of similar techniques in the United States.

The Szasz article reflects an extreme application of the study of psychological illness and health to the control over people. A more common application exists in the use of human adjustment techniques in industry. The beneficial use of such methods lies in their ability to help people find some interpersonally rewarding aspects in their work and to increase opportunity for democratic participation in decisions affecting their work. The sinister aspect of these methods is that people can be dissuaded from expressing genuine conflicts of interests, over wages or pensions let us say, through the manipulation of feigned or half-hearted interest in their problems or in the frustrations of their work by a psychiatrically-oriented personnel manager. Hence the technical field of human relations is frequently abused as a money-saving or trouble-saving substitute for facing genuine conflicts of interests in large organizations. Like the situation of forced hospitalization of deviants, the abuse of human relations techniques is particularly frightening because it goes on within a framework in which those with power to control tend to believe that the exercise of their techniques is in the best interests of those controlled. This orientation frequently comes to be shared by those whose behavior is being con-

311

trolled, hence creating superficial consensus which prevents necessary work on issues of difference. Social systems which preclude expression of conflicting interests are totalitarian, even when the populace is apparently supportive of the contrived consensus.

The increased use of control through techniques developed in the behavioral sciences parallels an increase in the ability of large agencies to "manage" the news by withholding information or by exercising sanctions against "uncooperative" reporters or television studios. The process is generally subtle with news going through successive rewrites which filter out much criticism of dominant streams of thought. The process can also be more coercive; for example, an important information officer of the Defense Department threatened reporters who presented news from Viet Nam inconsistent with American objectives there.

The three remaining articles deal with the broader context of the new technology, with special emphasis upon who is to use this technology and for what ends. The Skinner-Rogers debate is concerned with the frequently unexamined issues in the use of behavioral science knowledge in controlling human behavior. The capabilities of the scientist's knowledge and the applicability of his own values are of central importance in these essays.

Boguslaw opens up a new dimension of decision control in his examination of the way in which system designers create decision-making organizations which are incapable of revising their implicit values or being redirected by their members. Since these new systems are based upon efficiency values rather than humanitarian values, much of the diversity and conflict that characterizes social life is reduced to "manageable" alternative actions where decisions are made by fiat. The emergence of what Boguslaw has called "the new utopians" also suggests a significant shift in power and control away from the public and elected representatives to system specialists.

Finally, we have a description of a most elaborate form of decision control; Stern describes how the Central Intelligence Agency infiltrates and seeks to control a private domestic institution, the National Student Association. The issues raised by such events are similar to those involving the more limited control techniques like wiretapping: In the name of national security, domestic institutions vital for free debate and representative democracy are subverted by agencies whose activities are a matter of great secrecy to the people and to their elected representatives, and whose objectives are not subject to public debate.

REFERENCES AND ADDITIONAL READING

Anonymous, "Deep Therapy on the Assembly Line," *Ammunition*, 7, April, 1949, 47–51.

Robert M. Cipes, "The Wiretap War," *The New Republic,* December 24, 1966, 16–22.

Donald N. Michael, "Speculation on the Relation of the Computer to Individual Freedom and the Right to Privacy," *George Washington Law Review,* 33, October, 1964, 270–286.

James Ridgeway, "The Snoops: Private Lives and Public Service," *The New Republic,* December 19, 1964, 13–17.

Morley Safer, "Television Covers the War," *War-Peace Report,* June-July, 1966, 9–11.

Thomas S. Szasz, *Law, Liberty and Psychiatry,* New York: Macmillan, 1966.

Vance Packard

The Waste Makers

The people of the United States are in a sense becoming a nation on a tiger. They must learn to consume more and more or, they are warned, their magnificent economic machine may turn and devour them. They must be induced to step up their individual consumption higher and higher whether they have any pressing need for the goods or not. Their ever-expanding economy demands it.

Where are the Americans drifting under the pressure to make them more wasteful, imprudent, and carefree in their consuming habits? What is the impact of all this pressure toward wastefulness on the nation and on the behavior and character of its people?

In a good-humored forecast of things to come, the senior editor of *Sales Management* asserted on May 6, 1960: "If we Americans are to buy and consume everything that automated manufacture, sock-o-selling and all-out advertising can thrust upon us, each of our mounting millions must have extra ears and eyes and other senses—as well as extra income. Indeed, the only sure way to meet all the demands may be to create a brand new breed of super customers."

Some marketing experts have been announcing that the average citizen will have to step up his buying by nearly 50 per cent in the next dozen years, or the economy will sicken. In a mere decade United States citizens will have to improve their level of consumption as much as their forebears had managed to do in the two hundred years from Colonial times to 1939.

The challenge of finding significant improvements that can be made in existing products, however, is becoming more difficult each year.

When the Appliance Technical Conference was held in Chicago in 1958, the vice-president of engineering for Whirlpool Corporation made a notably candid statement. He said: "The industry has wrung the last possible ounce of research out of the present appliance products. We can only offer prettier equipment." He urged the industry to start basic research in the properties of clothing and meats in order to come up with radically new products.

All this is not to suggest that genuine technological improvements are not being made—or in prospect of being made—in some products. The pushbutton and long-distance dialing telephone and the jet passenger airplane are improvements that have produced considerable enchantment among consumers. There is the probability that Americans soon will be offered improvements in home products that will produce a degree of enchantment in some circles: refrigerators with no moving parts, ultrasonic dishwashers that reportedly will remove fried egg from plates, remote-control stoves, lighting based on electroluminescent phosphors for ceiling or wall panels.

But how much should we rejoice when General Electric introduces a toaster with nine buttons, which make it possible to obtain a piece of toast in any of nine shades? How much should we rejoice when another company introduces a mechanical martini-stirring spoon, which relieves the person stirring from the labor of twisting his wrist? And what American housewife is dreaming of the day when she can prepare breakfast by simply flicking a bedside switch, which will turn on an electronic recipe maker coded on punch cards?

The recession in the late fifties served as a sharp reminder to many of the developing dilemma posed by the need for ever-greater production. Recessions were nothing new. But this one was the most severe of the three postwar recessions. In many industries, companies found themselves with heavy inventories of goods and began cutting back production. The public was still buying, but not fast enough.

Marketers reacted to the challenge of coping with mounting glut during the recession by shifting to the really hard sell. In Flint, Michigan, sales executives began firing a cannon every time a motorcar was sold. Citizens across the land were admonished by industrialists and Government leaders of all stripes to begin buying for their own good. At a press conference, President Eisenhower was asked what the people should do to make the recession recede. Here is the dialogue that followed:

"A.—Buy."
"Q.—Buy what?"
"A.—Anything."

The President was advised that this was possibly an over-simplified response in view of the fact that his own Secretary of the Treasury was then urging people to put their money in Government bonds. The President then said the public should buy only what it needs and "wants." An appliance store in Killingsley, Connecticut, immediately 315 responded by putting this sign in its window: "Okay Ike, we're doing our part!"

Thus the challenge was to develop a public that would always have an appetite as voracious as its machines. The emerging philosophy was most fervently and bluntly stated perhaps in two long articles in *The Journal of Retailing* during the mid-fifties. The author was Marketing Consultant Victor Lebow. He made a forthright plea for "forced consumption":

"Our enormously productive economy . . . demands that we make consumption our way of life, that we convert the buying and use of goods into rituals, that we seek our spiritual satisfactions, or ego satisfactions, in consumption. . . . We need things consumed, burned up, worn out, replaced, and discarded at an ever increasing rate."

At other points he spoke of the "consumption requirements of our productive capacity" and of the "obligation" of retailers "to push more goods across their counters."

Old-fashioned selling methods based on offering goods to fill an obvious need in a straightforward manner were no longer enough. Even the use of status appeals and sly appeals to the subconscious needs and anxieties of the public—which I have examined in earlier works—would not move goods in the mountainous dimensions desired.

What was needed were strategies that would make Americans in large numbers into voracious, wasteful, compulsive consumers—and strategies that would provide products assuring such wastefulness. Even where wastefulness was not involved strategies were needed that would induce the public to consume at ever-higher levels.

As the marketing experts groped for ways to keep sales soaring in the face of mounting saturation, one of the first thoughts that struck them was that each consumer should be induced to buy more of each product than he had been buying. The way to end glut was to produce gluttons.

The makers of one deodorant introduced a he-she kit for husbands and wives, so that they could get two applicators rather than one in each master bathroom. Men previously had tended to use their wives' applicator rather than buy their own.

Hosiery manufacturers began trying to sell more pairs of stockings to each American woman by introducing colored stockings. Women were told that their stockings should match whatever costume or accessories they would be wearing. This concept of more-sales-through-matching took hold in a number of fields. A spokesman for Revlon, Inc., the cosmetics firm, explained that one of the secrets of the company's fabulous success during the late fifties was that it "taught women to match their nail enamel to their moods and occasions, so that they bought more."

One of the Big Four swim-suit producers, Catalina, began promoting

316

the idea of having one suit for the morning sun, one for the noonday sun, and a third for the evening sun. And another of the Big Four, Rose Marie Reid, began urging that women use one suit for swimming, one for sunning, and one for "psychology."

SAFETY AND STYLE

Makers of eyeglasses set their sights on the goal of selling more spectacles per head. The Optical Wholesalers National Association began promoting the notion that every person wearing glasses needs more than one pair. A spokesman explained: "We want glass wearers to own several pairs now—not only for safety but for style as well."

The concept of color "matching" in order to broaden sales was also used in promoting home accessories. A spokesman for *Kleenex* tissue announced over a television network that "there's a color for every room in your home." And the Bell System sought to get more telephone extensions in each home by the same there's-a-different-color-for-every-room approach. American Telegraph and Telephone urged, in fact, that families install a second, entirely new line into the house for extra convenience. A Midwestern telephone company official told me of a study made in motels that showed that telephoning could be increased about 20 per cent by the use of phones in a color other than the conventional black. Apparently bright colors promote an impulse to call someone just for the heck of it.

A campaign by the world's largest manufacturer of wedding rings to popularize the "double ring" ceremony greatly increased the sale of gold wedding rings. Several hundred radio commentators and society editors began making special note of the fact if the groom, as well as the bride, wore a nuptial ring.

The makers of a number of products for the home concluded that no home was really a home if it did not have doubles in the products they were promoting. The president of Servel, Inc., announced that the American standard of living now called for "two refrigerators in every home." The chief of the washer division of American Home Laundry Manufacturers Association declared that a well-equipped home should have two washers and two dryers. Meanwhile, the Plumbing Fixture Manufacturers Association began promoting the "privazone" home. In a privazone home, each member of the family has his own private water closet. Radio manufacturers disclosed with pride that they had succeeded in selling an average of three radios to every family in the land.

TWO HOMES FOR EVERY FAMILY

Perhaps the ultimate of this two-or-more-of-a-kind concept—which began so humbly in the twenties with the political promise of two 317

DECISION CONTROL .

chickens in every pot—was the promotion of the idea of two homes for every family. Home builders began pressing the idea. Others joined in. Building suppliers, appliance manufacturers, and advertising agencies excitedly grasped the potentialities inherent in spreading the idea that every family needed a town house and a country house, or a work house and play house. The marketing possibilities were spelled out by an official of the plywood association in these terms: "The second home is going to . . . provide tremendous markets for everybody in the building-materials field, for appliance manufacturers, builders, and developers, lending agencies, etc. We in the plywood industry are leading the parade."

Another leader of the two-house parade was the J. Walter Thompson advertising agency, which began pointing out in business journals the inviting potentialities of the two-house family. "With the two-house famly," it said, "America has clearly entered a new age of consumption for household equipment." It pointed out that the two-house family is likely to have: three or four bathrooms, two to four television sets, two fully equipped kitchens, four to twelve beds, multiples of furniture, linens, rugs, china, etc.

J. Walter Thompson called for an "aggressive advertising and selling" campaign to overcome the public's "habit lag" in sticking with one car when two cars were obviously needed for modern living. One attempt at aggressive reeducation was conducted by the Chevrolet company. Its announcer on the Dinah Shore program began talking of those deprived citizens who were victims of "one-car captivity." The essence of the message, as television critic John Crosby assimilated it, was that, "You peasants who own only one car . . . are chained to the land like serfs in the Middle Ages."

Another tack that the marketers took was to try to induce Americans to demand more with each product bought. It should be either bigger or more complex, or both, in order to be appropriate for modern living. The goal was to justify a higher price tag. Victor Lebow in his blueprint for "forced consumption" put this imperative of a higher price tag in these words: "The second essential is what we might call 'expensive consumption.' "

The lawn mower offers an excellent illustration of the strategy of upgrading the nation's concept of what is appropriate. A simple-minded, intensely rational person might assume that hand mowers would be increasingly popular today and that power mowers would be almost impossible to sell. After all, lawns are getting smaller all the time. And adult males are feeling more and more the need for physical exercise as they spend more time in sedentary, short-week jobs. They come home from the office beating their chests and growling for exercise. The situation that has developed, however, shows how dangerous it has become to try to anticipate consumer behavior by 318 the application of humorless logic, and ignoring the role marketing strategies may play.

The lawn-mower industry was able to convince American males that it was somehow shameful to be seen pushing a hand mower. And power mowers were promoted as a wonderful new gadget. Power-mowers sales rose seventeen-fold in fifteen years! By 1960, more than nine out of every ten lawn mowers sold were powered. Such powered mowers cost three to five times as much as hand mowers. Further-more, having a mere motor on your mower was not enough in some neighborhoods. You also needed a seat on it. Hundreds of thousands of American males began buying power mowers with seats. These, of course, cost ten times as much as a hand mower.

Another general tack the marketers took was to try to induce people to get rid of the products they already owned. In its broadest form this took the form of encouraging people to throw things away.

In the hair-raising utopia, "Brave New World," that Mr. Aldous Huxley projected in the 1930's for six centuries hence, babies come in bottles and the zombie-like citizens move about in doped-up bliss. To keep the industrial machines humming, each citizen is "compelled to consume so much a year." To that end, newness as a trait is cherished. And sleep teachers stress love of newness because they have the responsibility of "adapting future demand to future industrial supply." The dictator of the utopia, Mustapha Mond, at one point explains: "We don't want people to be attracted by old things. We want them to like the new ones."

When Huxley wrote his book in 1932, he was visualizing what might come about in the distant future. But within a quarter of a century the people of the United States, without any help from dictators or out-and-out sleep teachers, were exhibiting a throwaway mood that would tickle even Mustapha Mond. Much of this was deliberately encouraged. The voice of the television announcer—in 1960—chanted, "You use it once and throw it away. . . . You use it once and throw it away." This specific chant was used to promote the sale of a deo-dorant pad.

DISCARD, USE UP, DESTROY, WASTE

Residents of the United States were discarding, using up, destroying, and wasting products at a rate that offered considerable encourage-ment to those charged with achieving ever-higher levels of consump-tion for their products. A business writer for *Time* magazine related, as the sixties were about to begin: "The force that gives the U.S. economy its pep is being generated more and more in the teeming aisles of the nation's stores. . . . U.S. consumers no longer hold on to suits, coats, and dresses as if they were heirlooms. . . . Furniture, re-

319

DECISION CONTROL .

frigerators, rugs—all once bought to last for years or life—are now replaced with register-tingling regularity."

The new mood of the disposable era was reflected in the pages of the *Engineering News Record,* which observed: "Nowhere in the world except in the U.S. would a skyscraper office building in sound condition be torn down merely to be replaced by another one."

Dennis Brogan has characterized modern Americans as a people "who go away and leave things." The voluptuous wastefulness of modern Americans could be seen not only in their littered parks but in market surveys. The industrial-design firm, Harley Earl Associates of Detroit, reported: "In most households we found there were two to five rolls of Scotch tape—but no one could locate any of them."

Americans had developed their own democratic version of sleep indoctrination of the young. There were the soft, insistent commercials the youngsters heard during their weekly twenty-odd hours of television watching. And there were the breakable plastic toys, which taught them at an early age that everything in this world is replaceable.

All the efforts to keep consumption rising—when taken together—amount to an unprecedented saturation of American life with pleas, hints, and other inducements to buy. The sheer dimensions of the current and contemplated selling efforts are becoming a national problem. Commercialization is becoming so all-pervasive that at times it seems to be getting into the air the public breathes.

"Advertising must mass-produce customers just as factories mass-produce products in a growing economy," stated the publisher of *Printers' Ink.* He suggested that outlays for advertising might reach twenty-five billion dollars by 1965. That meant more than doubling the amount being spent to create want and discontent within a few years.

An official of General Foods reported that a typical American family is exposed to 1518 selling messages in the course of an average day. And this does not include the material stuffed into the nation's mailboxes: a total of sixteen billion pieces a year, or four times the amount found in mailboxes a decade earlier.

Members of this average family, for example, are exposed to 117 television and radio commercials a day. Other studies have shown that on television alone members of an average family are subjected to nearly an hour of commercials a day. This growth of messages beamed at the public over the airways is worth special note because airborne messages are hard to ignore and because the public presumably controls the airways in its own interest.

THE "PRESSURE-COOKER" LIFE

The increase in commercials has complicated the life of television writers, directors, and performers as they have tried to sustain their 320 moods of gaiety, tragedy, or suspense. In the spring of 1959, Peter Lind Hayes gave up his ABC daytime show because of the "pressure-cooker existence" the network proposed to inaugurate by cutting his hour-long show to a half hour. He explained: "When you figure the number of commercials we have to give, it actually takes an hour to do a half-hour show. Can you imagine half a dozen commercial interruptions in thirty minutes? That is what it would amount to." Garry Moore revealed that he left daytime television "because frankly, I couldn't cope with the number of commercials we had to accommodate." And, in 1960, he won a singular battle for his nighttime show by successfully demanding that commercial interruptions of his hour-long show be limited to four rather than the then-prevailing seven interruptions.

The tastefulness of television and radio commercials likewise has shown signs of deterioration as the pressure to sell has mounted. Selling messages for "intimately personal products" such as feminine-hygiene products and hemorrhoid treatments are beamed into many living rooms. At this writing, more than 140 television stations accept commercials for the hemorrhoid treatment *Preparation H*.

One might speculate also on what it does to a people's sense of values—especially their children's—when discussions of significant events are followed on television by announcers who in often louder and more solemn voices announce a great new discovery for a hair bleach. Or, to consider another kind of juxtaposition, a broadcast appeal to aid hungry children in mid-1960 was followed immediately by a dog-food commercial.

Certain of the magazines, too, showed the impact of commercialism as their publishers sought to create an editorial climate attractive to advertisers. In some cases, articles appeared which, while possibly appealing to readers, were most certainly gratifying to advertisers and potential advertisers. One of the mass women's magazines with a primarily working-class audience carried an article called "What's the Big Attraction?" in early 1960. Its illustration showed an attractive girl surrounded by six handsome men. The article purported to show the secrets of the Feminine Girl who is irresistible with the Water Cooler Set. Before you were eight hundred words into this revealing article, you were aware that she relied upon "hand lotions," "moisture creams," "cleaning fluid," "scarves," "fresh glove supply," "bath salts," "bath oil," "special foot lotion," "creamy depilatory," "silky body lotion," "anti-perspirant," "cologne," "cosmetics," "shampoos," "astringent-saturated cotton balls," "nail enamels," "make-up shades," and "lipstick."

Advertising messages have begun appearing in places where heretofore they have been banned, usually on grounds of taste or public policy. Enterpreneurs and public officials are proving to be willing to let down the bars in order to gain extra revenue. For the first time

321

in half a century, thousands of buses in New York have been carrying advertising posters on their exteriors. Many railroad terminals are so crowded with billboards and commerial displays that it is difficult for a traveler to find the announcement of departures. A New York television station has begun beaming its programs into more than four hundred supermarkets and into three hundred self-service laundries. In the stores the housewife finds herself exposed to as many as eight television screens and to about twenty commercials in the course of her average shopping trip.

So pervasive have billboards become along many stretches of highway in the United States, that even an outdoor advertising expert publicly lamented that a journey he and his wife took to Florida had been "ruined" because "hundreds" of miles of what would have been beautiful highways had been lined with signboards. Lobbyists for the outdoor advertisers have been charged by a New York state legislator with keeping state legislators in their debt—to forestall restrictive legislation—by giving them free sign space, or space at reduced rates, at election time. An investigator for *The Reader's Digest* concluded that the new 41,000-mile federal highway system would become "a billboard slum" unless state legislators acted to prevent it.

In order to cope with situations that arise when states do outlaw billboards along highways, an enterprising signmaker developed a lightweight sign so gargantuan it can be seen from hundreds of yards away.

A still more ingenious entrepreneur has begun offering admen the chance to plant their messages against clouds and mountaintops. Unexcelled Chemical Corporation has been inviting advertisers to use its giant magic lantern called Skyjector. It is capable of beaming an advertisement one-half mile wide against a cloud five miles away. And the company expects that within a year it will be able to create its own clouds if there are none handy. Columnist Inez Robb commented: "It opens up the prospect of a horizon-to-horizon gray-flannel world with the sky . . . available to nature lovers only in rainy weather."

People who wish to stroll along a few public beaches of Florida's Gold Coast are not able to let their fancies roam too far off the notion of consumption. Every hour or so old biplanes roar along just offshore, hauling hundred-foot-long sky billboards. And on the backs of hundreds of ocean-front benches are tacked small billboards. Advertising men offered to install benches in many downtown areas of Philadelphia—and pay the city in addition $15 a month for each bench if they could merely plaster the backs with ads. The offer was rejected.

Some paperback book publishers have begun accepting paid advertisements in their books. One book on child care has been carrying more than a dozen full-page advertisements scattered through the book. 322

A final price that must be considered in assessing the implications of the current drift of American society under the impact of an economy based on ever-mounting consumption is the change it may be producing in the character of the people involved.

What is the impact on the human spirit of all these pressures to consume?

Business Week made a report on the many subtle and adroit persuasion techniques being developed to encourage Americans to be more zestful consumers and commented: ". . . it looks as though all of our business forces are bent on getting everyone to . . . Borrow. Spend. Buy. Waste."

It is unrealistic to assume that all such pressures are not producing changes at a deeper level than mere consumption habits. For example, a person who finds himself induced to spend beyond his income habitually does not wish to feel guilty about his excesses and welcomes a system of morality that condones such habits. Much of the average American's consumption has been channeled into frivolous or playful or whimsical outlets, which also requires rationalizing. United States residents have been spending more on smoking, drinking, and gambling than they have on education. They have been spending more on admission tickets to pastimes than they have on foreign economic aid. They have been spending more on jewelry and watches than they have on either books or basic research. Further, they spend more for greeting cards than they do for medical research.

In earlier years, economists pondering the controls necessary to keep the seller-buyer relationship in fair balance concluded that ordinary human prudence would protect the buyer from being exploited or overwhelmed. *Caveat emptor,* they intoned.

Letting the buyer beware was thought to be no real problem because the buyer was assumed to hold the whip hand since the money was in his pocket. The consumer was assumed to be sovereign. And marketers and merchandisers still like to flatter the consuming public by referring to it as "king."

Marketers in the mid-twentieth century, however, have been subjecting the consumer to a barrage of selling strategies that has rarely heretofore been matched in variety, intensity, or ingenuity. Millions of consumers are manipulated, razzle-dazzled, indoctrinated, mood-conditioned, and flimflammed. They are conditioned to be discontented with last year's models, and they are conditioned to accept flimsily built products.

The attitude of all too many marketers was revealed in the January 29, 1960, issue of *Printer's Ink*—"The Weekly Magazine of Advertising and Marketing"—when it earnestly reported efforts being made by

323

DECISION CONTROL

marketing researchers to understand how people acquire and retain information and attitudes. It stated: "Perhaps most important of all [the researchers] are edging toward that ultimate question for advertising: How can the consumer, like Pavlov's dog, be taught the habit of buying a specific brand?"

If that truly is the "ultimate question" for advertising, then the industry had better search its soul. And consumers had better take to the barricades.

In the face of all these pressures, the lone consumer of ordinary intelligence and impulsiveness is usually no match for the subtle and massive onslaughts aimed at him. Today, the consumer is far from sovereign. To restore the consumer to any real sovereignty, there needs to be a return on a large scale to pride in prudent buying and informative support for that prudence.

Thomas S. Szasz

Toward the Therapeutic State

Valeriy Tarsis is a literary critic, translator, and writer. In 1960 he sent an English publisher a manuscript which was highly critical of life in Khrushchev's Russia. This work, *The Blue-bottle,* appeared in England in October, 1962, under the pseudonym Ivan Valeriy. Actually, Tarsis had opposed the use of a pseudonym and made no secret in Russia of having sent his book abroad. In August, 1962, two months before the appearance of *The Blue-bottle* in London, Tarsis was arrested and committed to the Koshchenko psychiatric hospital in Moscow. News of his fate soon reached the West and an article about it by the British journalist Edward Crankshaw appeared in *The Observer* for February, 1963. In March, Tarsis was released.

Ward 7[1] is Tarsis' account of what happened to him in the "mental hospital." It was written shortly after his release and smuggled to England in the summer of 1964. In this autobiographical novel, Valentine Alamazov, a Russian writer, is arrested and incarcerated in a psychiatric institution for the same offense as Tarsis had been; he is held in the notorious Russian insane asylum, the "Villat Kanatchikov," the nickname in Moscow for the Koshchenko Hospital; and he is released after protests from the West.

This, in bare outline, is the plot of *Ward 7* and the story of the events behind it. The question is: What shall we make of it?

I have seen many English and American comments on this book;

Reprinted by permission of the author and *The New Republic* from *The New Republic,* December 11, 1965. © 1965, Harrison-Blaine of New Jersey, Inc. Thomas S. Szasz, M.D., is a practicing psychoanalyst and professor of psychiatry at the State University of New York Upstate Medical Center at Syracuse.

[1] *Ward 7, An Autobiographical Novel,* by Valeriy Tarsis, translated by Katya Brown (Dutton).

325

all deal with it as political criticism. Nearly a year before the book's American publication, such an interpretation was offered by Mr. C. L. Sulzberger, in *The New York Times* for October 28, 1964:

> Khrushchev . . . conducted a running battle with writers who felt sufficiently revitalized by his reforms to fight for total freedom. Khrushchev struck back by restraining some of the boldest of these spirits—not in prisons or concentration camps, but in mental homes and sanatoriums.

After briefly reviewing the book, and noting that "The material conditions of Ward 7 are not too bad. . . . All they (the 'patients') lack is freedom," Mr. Sulzberger concluded:

> When contemplating this strange book one cannot but wonder if in any way the system that invented *Ward 7* under Khrushchev as a halfway house to prison might now be affecting Khrushchev himself. In Stalin's day, political disgrace terminated in torture cells, execution cellars or Siberian barbed wire enclaves. Khrushchev, to his enduring credit, virtually did away with all that. . . .

The supposition that *Ward 7* should be read as political commentary on contemporary Soviet society is further borne out by Mr. Elliot Graham of E. P. Dutton & Co. Tarsis was eager to have *Ward 7* published in the West, writes Mr. Graham, "because although the Soviet government claims that there are no political prisoners in the Soviet Union, the practice of putting inconvenient citizens into lunatic asylums seems to have become fairly widespread and is all the more shocking because this can be done without putting them on trial and because the term of their detention is indefinite."

These comments do not, in my opinion, penetrate to the significant lessons in this book. Approached as a piece on psychiatric hospitalization—as an exposé, as it were, of the Soviet mental hospital system—what do we find? The same claim—that they have been incarcerated improperly and unjustly—is made by people in mental hospitals all over the world. How do we judge whether such a claim is valid or not?

The irony of *Ward 7* will elude those who do not mentally substitute a German, a Frenchman, or an American for Valeriy Tarsis. Suppose an American poet were committed to a mental hospital and were to claim that he is sane; who would believe him? Valeriy Tarsis was confined for 6 months; Ezra Pound, for 13 years.

Our logic concerning involuntary mental hospitalization is evidently this: If a Russian is committed as insane, it is because he is sane but loves liberty too much; if an American is committed as insane, it is because he is insane but loves liberty so little that by depriving him 326 of it we provide him with a "therapeutic milieu." "This is the only court," said a judge in Chicago, "where the defendant always wins. If he is released, it means he is well. If he is committed, it is for his own good." Pity the poor Russians, deprived of such guarantees of the "civil rights of mentally ill."

Actually, Tarsis' comments about psychiatry and psychiatrists are far more detailed and damaging than his observations about Soviet society or the Soviet political system. Here are a few examples:

The hero, Alamazov, has been taken to the hospital by force: "In the morning Alamazov was examined by the head city psychiatrist, exactly as a prisoner is examined by a magistrate. He was brought to Dr. Yanushkevich's consulting room under guard. The doctor made no attempt to treat him as a patient; illness was never mentioned. Pink and smug, he seemed to take his role as prosecutor for granted."

Alamazov's view of the situation is this: "I don't regard you as a doctor. You call this a hospital, I call it a prison to which, in a typically fascist way, I have been sent without trial. So now, let's get everything straight. I am your prisoner, you are my jailer, and there isn't going to be any nonsense about my health or relations, or about examination and treatment. . . ." Clearly, Alamazov has no insight into his condition: the poor fellow does not even realize he is sick!

Then there is this revealing exchange between Alamazov and Professor Stein, one of the nastier psychiatric types in the hospital:

> [Stein] "We shall get acquainted, Valentine Ivanovich. . . . Tell us why you are here—what are your symptoms?"—Alamazov glared at him with such contempt that Stein looked uncomfortable. "I have not the slightest wish to get acquainted with you, but evidently I must. The reason I am here is that I was brought in by the police. My health is excellent. It's your job to make me ill. But I warn you, you won't succeed."—"How you actually got here is irrelevant. The point you should keep in mind is that healthy people are not in hospitals."—"That's exactly what the Cheka interrogators used to say to their victims: 'Innocent people are not in prison. You say you are innocent, that means you are anti-Soviet, so prison is the place for you.' The only difference is that now it's the madhouse,"—"I see. . . . You don't sound exactly sane!"

It would be a grave mistake to believe that *Ward 7* is populated only by political dissenters. Many of the inmates are ordinary people, like the elderly husband who stood in the way of his wife's fuller sexual life. This is Tatyana speaking to her friend Anna:

> "It's quite simple. You write to the clinic. You tell them that your husband, who is much older than you are and beginning to be impotent, is insanely jealous and has been threatening your life."—"It's true. He said 'I'll kill you'."

327

I was intrigued, and pleased, by the views Tarsis put in the mouth of Professor Nezhevsky. Nezhevsky is an elderly psychiatrist, at odds with the police methods of his Soviet colleagues. In a conversation with a French psychiatrist, René Gillard, Nezhevsky says: "I told them at the Ministry that you avoid drugs, . . . your staff are forbidden to talk about 'illness,' the patients . . . are free to come and go. . . ." Replies Gillard: "So you stick to happiness pills?" "Yes, exactly," says Nezhevsky. "Happiness pills. Andaxin, aminodin, and the rest of the muck—our doctors think the world of it." And so on, until at the end, Gillard says: "I must say, the idea of compulsory treatment really revolts me. We'd never stand for it."

On the day I write this—responding partly to CORE demonstrations and draft-card burning by a Syracuse youth—Mayor William F. Walsh of Syracuse offered a "six-point legislative program beamed at reducing youthful crime and *civil disobedience*. . . ." Walsh asked that "a treatment and research center for juvenile delinquents be included in the new multi-million-dollar *mental health center* to be built here."

No, *Ward 7* is not only in Moscow. Nor is *Ward 7* a recent phenomenon. Psychiatric sanctions have been with us for centuries. Successors to the witch hunts, they are one of the manifestations of a passage, in Western societies, from theological to secular, and from magical to "scientific," methods of *social control*. However, only through the creation of vast psychiatric bureaucracies in modern mass societies has involuntary mental hospitalization become a major force in the police powers of the state. To attribute this evil to Communism, or to Capitalism, would thus be both an oversimplification and an evasion.

Indeed, by alluding to Chekhov's *Ward No. 6*, Tarsis admits that he knows this. Chekhov, himself a physician, had as his protagonist not a patient, but a psychiatrist—Dr. Andrei Yefimich. The psychiatrist is honest and soon cannot tolerate the task he has unwittingly assumed. He then commits the fatal mistake of actually engaging a patient in *conversation*—as if such a thing were possible with one who is insane! The dramatic end follows swiftly: the psychiatrist is declared insane, is commited to the hospital, and following a near-fatal beating by an attendant, dies of a stroke. Before he is declared insane, Chekhov's psychiatrist has this to say:

> I am serving an evil cause, and receive my salary from people whom I dupe; I am not honest. But then I, by myself, am nothing; I am but a particle of necessary social evil: all the district bureaucrats are harmful and receive their salaries for nothing. Therefore it is not I who am to blame for my dishonesty but the times.

It is necessary to be absolutely clear about two points, lest *Ward 7* be misread: 1. Neither involuntary mental hospitalization as such, nor its political uses and abuses, was discovered by the Soviets. 2. The   328 fundamental logic behind commitment has been accepted throughout the world for several centuries, and is still widely accepted today: according to it, it is "humane" and "helpful" to deprive a person of his *liberty*—a right second only to his right to his life—on the ground of "mental illness" (or because such "illness" renders him "dangerous to himself and others"); if so, the only question is to define and determine what mental illness is or who is mentally ill.

Thus, Tarsis explains, it is "assumed, by doctors and politicians, writers and ideologists, that anyone dissatisfied with the socialist paradise must be a lunatic. . . ." Every one of the modern nation-states has, in the course of the last century-and-a-half, produced its own definitions and theories of lunacy. It is in this way that both a political and a psychiatric analysis of *Ward 7* must come to the same thing: a better understanding of secular society, its bureaucracies, and its methods of social control—among them, institutional psychiatry.

The list of famous persons deprived of liberty by means of psychiatric incarceration would run to several pages; for example, Secretary of State Forrestal, Governor Earl Long, General Edwin Walker, Ezra Pound, Norman Mailer, and Mary Todd Lincoln in the United States; in Germany—Marga Krupp, the wife of Fritz Krupp, committed by the Kaiser for making a nuisance of herself with complaints about her husband's homosexual orgies; and, in Austria-Hungary, Ignaz Semmelweiss, discoverer of childbed fever, for upsetting his colleagues and the public with the view that the disease was caused by the doctors' dirty hands.

Only a short time ago, men believed that slavery was a good institution, so long as only the proper people were enslaved: in historical order, the proper persons were the enemy vanquished in battle, the heathen, and the Negro. At long last, mankind concluded that slavery was a basic human wrong, regardless of who was placed in the class of slaves or why. I consider involuntary mental hospitalization also a basic human wrong. No adult should ever be cast in the sick role through the power of the state. The only deviance of which a person should be accused by the government is law-breaking; and once so charged, he should, of course, enjoy all the protection of the Constitution.

Many years ago, Lord Russell predicted that the Communist East and the Free West will, under the pressure of the forces of collectivism, drift ever closer together until the differences between the two will be indistinguishable. Years later, Orwell warned of the same dismal future in *Animal Farm*. The concluding paragraph reads thus: "Twelve voices were shouting . . . and they were all alike. No question, now, what had happened to the faces of the pigs. The creatures outside looked from pig to man, and from man to pig, and pig to man again; but already it was impossible to say which was which."

The nature of the "machine" that homogenizes man and pig now seems clear: it is the modern state, regardless of whether it is the 329 police state of the East or the bureaucratic state of the West. By substituting "private happiness" for "public happiness," all modern societies tend to wean the individual from the *polis,* and thus deprive him of a voice in the decision of all but his most trivial interests. The result is depoliticized man. It is small wonder, then, that the "Psychological Man" of today is more interested in mental health than in liberty. Thus it is inevitable that the individual seems less a citizen and more a patient.

But not only is the nature of modern bureaucratic mass society as a depoliticizing apparatus clear. It is also clear that institutional psychiatry is an important cog in it: the Russians call it Ward 7 and Villat Kanatchikov; we call it the state hospital and the community mental health center. Totalitarian tyranny and popular (non-constitutional) democracy thus rush to meet each other in the Therapeutic State.

Carl R. Rogers and B. F. Skinner

Some issues concerning
the control of human behavior:
A symposium

I—SKINNER

Science is steadily increasing our power to influence, change, mold—
in a word, control—human behavior. It has extended our "understanding" (whatever that may be) so that we deal more successfully
with people in nonscientific ways, but it has also identified conditions
or variables which can be used to predict and control behavior in a
new, and increasingly rigorous, technology. The broad disciplines of
government and economics offer examples of this, but there is special
cogency in those contributions of anthropology, sociology, and psychology which deal with individual behavior. Carl Rogers has listed
some of the achievements to date in a recent paper (1956). Those of
his examples which show or imply the control of the single organism
are primarily due, as we should expect, to psychology. It is the experimental study of behavior which carries us beyond awkward or
inaccessible "principles," "factors," and so on, to variables which can
be directly manipulated.

It is also, and for more or less the same reasons, the conception of
human behavior emerging from an experimental analysis which most
directly challenges traditional views. Psychologists themselves often do
not seem to be aware of how far they have moved in this direction.
But the change is not passing unnoticed by others. Until only recently
it was customary to deny the possibility of a rigorous science of human
behavior by arguing, either that a lawful science was impossible be-

Reprinted by permission of the author and publisher from *Science*, Vol.
124, November 30, 1956, pp. 1057–1066. Carl Rogers is resident fellow,
Western Behavioral Science Institute in LaJolla, California. B. F. Skinner
is professor of psychology at Harvard University.

cause man was a free agent, or that merely statistical predictions would always leave room for personal freedom. But those who used to take this line have become most vociferous in expressing their alarm at the way these obstacles are being surmounted.

Now, the control of human behavior has always been unpopular. Any undisguised effort to control usually arouses emotional reactions. We hesitate to admit, even to ourselves, that we are engaged in control, and we may refuse to control, even when this would be helpful, for fear of criticism. Those who have explicitly avowed an interest in control have been roughly treated by history. Machiavelli is the great prototype. As Macaulay said of him, "Out of his surname they coined an epithet for a knave and out of his Christian name a synonym for the devil." There were obvious reasons. The control that Machiavelli analyzed and recommended, like most political control, used techniques that were aversive to the controllee. The threats and punishments of the bully, like those of the government operating on the same plan, are not designed—whatever their success—to endear themselves to those who are controlled. Even when the techniques themselves are not aversive, control is usually exercised for the selfish purposes of the controller and, hence, has indirectly punishing effects upon others.

Man's natural inclination to revolt against selfish control has been exploited to good purpose in what we call the philosophy and literature of democracy. The doctrine of the rights of man has been effective in arousing individuals to concerted action against governmental and religious tyranny. The literature which has had this effect has greatly extended the number of terms in our language which express reactions to the control of men. But the ubiquity and ease of expression of this attitude spells trouble for any science which may give birth to a powerful technology of behavior. Intelligent men and women, dominated by the humanistic philosophy of the past two centuries, cannot view with equanimity what Andrew Hacker has called "the specter of predictable man" (1954). Even the statistical or actuarial prediction of human events, such as the number of fatalities to be expected on a holiday weekend, strikes many people as uncanny and evil, while the prediction and control of individual behavior is regarded as little less than the work of the devil. I am not so much concerned here with the political or economic consequences for psychology, although research following certain channels may well suffer harmful effects. We ourselves, as intelligent men and women, and as exponents of Western thought, share these attitudes. They have already interfered with the free exercise of a scientific analysis, and their influence threatens to assume more serious proportions.

Three broad areas of human behavior supply good examples. The first of these—*personal control*—may be taken to include person-to-person relationships in the family, among friends, in social and work groups, and in counseling and psychotherapy. Other fields are *education* and *government*. A few examples from each will show how nonscientific preconceptions are affecting our current thinking about human behavior.

Personal Control. People living together in groups come to control one another with a technique which is not inappropriately called "ethical." When an individual behaves in a fashion acceptable to the group, he receives admiration, approval, affection, and many other reinforcements which increase the likelihood that he will continue to behave in that fashion. When his behavior is not acceptable, he is criticized, censured, blamed, or otherwise punished. In the first case the group calls him "good"; in the second, "bad." This practice is so thoroughly ingrained in our culture that we often fail to see that it is a technique of control. Yet we are almost always engaged in such control, even though the reinforcements and punishments are often subtle.

The practice of admiration is an important part of a culture, because behavior which is otherwise inclined to be weak can be set up and maintained with its help. The individual is especially likely to be praised, admired, or loved when he acts for the group in the face of great danger, for example, or sacrifices himself or his possessions, or submits to prolonged hardship, or suffers martyrdom. These actions are not admirable in any absolute sense, but they require admiration if they are to be strong. Similarly, we admire people who behave in original or exceptional ways, not because such behavior is itself admirable, but because we do not know how to encourage original or exceptional behavior in any other way. The group acclaims independent, unaided behavior in part because it is easier to reinforce than to help.

As long as this technique of control is misunderstood, we cannot judge correctly an environment in which there is less need for heroism, hardship, or independent action. We are likely to argue that such an environment is itself less admirable or produces less admirable people. In the old days, for example, young scholars often lived in undesirable quarters, ate unappetizing or inadequate food, performed unprofitable tasks for a living or to pay for necessary books and materials or publication. Older scholars and other members of the group offered compensating reinforcement in the form of approval and admiration for these sacrifices. When the modern graduate student receives a generous scholarship, enjoys good living conditions, and has his research and publication subsidized, the grounds for evaluation seem to be pulled from under us. Such a student no longer *needs* admiration to carry him over a series of obstacles (no matter how much he may need it for other reasons), and, in missing certain familiar objects of admiration, we are likely to conclude that such *conditions* are less 333 admirable. Obstacles to scholarly work may serve as a useful measure of motivation—and we may go wrong unless some substitute is found —but we can scarcely defend a deliberate harassment of the student for this purpose. The productivity of any set of conditions can be evaluated only when we have freed ourselves of the attitudes which have been generated in us as members of an ethical group.

A similar difficulty arises from our use of punishment in the form of censure or blame. The concept of responsibility and the related concept of foreknowledge and choice are used to justify techniques of control using punishment. Was So-and-So aware of the probable consequences of his action, and was the action deliberate? If so, we are justified in punishing him. But what does this mean? It appears to be a question concerning the efficacy of the contingent relations between behavior and punishing consequences. We punish behavior because it is objectionable to us or the group, but in a minor refinement of rather recent origin we have come to withhold punishment when it cannot be expected to have any effect. If the objectionable consequences of an act were accidental and not likely to occur again, there is no point in punishing. We say that the individual was not "aware of the consequences of his action" or that the consequences were not "intentional." If the action could not have been avoided—if the individual "had no choice"—punishment is also withheld, as it is if the individual is incapable of being changed by punishment because he is of "unsound mind." In all these cases—different as they are—the individual is held "not responsible" and goes unpunished.

Just as we say that it is "not fair" to punish a man for something he could not help doing, so we call it "unfair" when one is rewarded beyond his due or for something he could not help doing. In other words, we also object to wasting *reinforcers* where they are not needed or will do no good. We make the same point with the words *just* and *right*. Thus we have no right to punish the irresponsible, and a man has no right to reinforcers he does not earn or deserve. But concepts of choice, responsibility, justice, and so on, provide a most inadequate analysis of efficient reinforcing and punishing contingencies because they carry a heavy semantic cargo of a quite different sort, which obscures any attempt to clarify controlling practices or to improve techniques. In particular, they fail to prepare us for techniques based on other than aversive techniques of control. Most people would object to forcing prisoners to serve as subjects of dangerous medical experiments, but few object when they are induced to serve by the offer of return privileges—even when the reinforcing effect of these privileges has been created by forcible deprivation. In the traditional scheme the right to refuse guarantees the individual against coercion or an unfair bargain. But to what extent *can* a prisoner refuse under such circumstances?

We need not go so far afield to make the point. We can observe

334

our own attitude toward personal freedom in the way we resent any interference with what we want to do. Suppose we want to buy a car of a particular sort. Then we may object, for example, if our wife urges us to buy a less expensive model and to put the difference into a new refrigerator. Or we may resent it if our neighbor questions our need for such a car or our ability to pay for it. We would certainly resent it if it were illegal to buy such a car (remember Prohibition); and if we find we cannot actually afford it, we may resent governmental control of the price through tariffs and taxes. We resent it if we discover that we cannot get the car because the manufacturer is holding the model in deliberately short supply in order to push a model we do not want. In all this we assert our democratic right to buy the car of our choice. We are well prepared to do so and to resent any restriction on our freedom.

But why do we not ask *why* it is the car of our choice and resent the forces which made it so? Perhaps our favorite toy as a child was a car, of a very different model, but nevertheless bearing the name of the car we now want. Perhaps our favorite TV program is sponsored by the manufacturer of that car. Perhaps we have seen pictures of many beautiful or prestigeful persons driving it—in pleasant or glamorous places. Perhaps the car has been designed with respect to our motivational patterns: the device on the hood is a phallic symbol; or the horsepower has been stepped up to please our competitive spirit in enabling us to pass other cars swiftly (or, as the advertisements say, "safely"). The concept of freedom that has emerged as part of the cultural practice of our group makes little or no provision for recognizing or dealing with these kinds of control. Concepts like "responsibility" and "rights" are scarcely applicable. We are prepared to deal with coercive measures, but we have no traditional recourse with respect to other measures which in the long run (and especially with the help of science) may be much more powerful and dangerous.

Education. The techniques of education were once frankly aversive. The teacher was usually older and stronger than his pupils and was able to "make them learn." This meant that they were not actually taught but were surrounded by a threatening world from which they could escape only by learning. Usually they were left to their own resources in discovering how to do so. Claude Coleman has published a grimly amusing reminder of these older practices (1953). He tells of a school-teacher who published a careful account of his services during 51 years of teaching, during which he administered: ". . . 911,527 blows with a cane; 124,010 with a rod; 20,989 with a ruler; 136,715 with the hand; 10,295 over the mouth; 7,905 boxes on the ear; [and] 1,115,800 slaps on the head. . . ."

Progressive education was a humanitarian effort to substitute positive reinforcement for such aversive measures, but in the search for useful   335 human values in the classroom it has never fully replaced the variables it abandoned. Viewed as a branch of behavioral technology, education remains relatively inefficient. We supplement it, and rationalize it, by admiring the pupil who learns *for himself*; and we often attribute the learning process, or knowledge itself, to something *inside* the individual. We admire behavior which seems to have inner sources. Thus we admire one who *recites* a poem more than one who simply *reads* it. We admire one who *knows* the answer more than one who *knows where to look it up*. We admire the *writer* rather than the *reader*. We admire the arithmetician who can do a problem in his head rather than with a slide rule or calculating machine, or in "original" ways rather than by a strict application of rules. In general we feel that any aid or "crutch"—except those aids to which we are now thoroughly accustomed—reduces the credit due. In Plato's *Phaedrus,* Thamus, the king, attacks the invention of the alphabet on similar grounds! He is afraid "it will produce forgetfulness in the minds of those who learn to use it, because they will not practice their memories. . . ." In other words, he holds it more admirable to remember than to use a memorandum. He also objects that pupils "will read many things without instruction . . . [and] will therefore seem to know many things when they are for the most part ignorant." In the same vein we are today sometimes contemptuous of book learning, but, as educators, we can scarcely afford to adopt this view without reservation.

By admiring the student for knowledge and blaming him for ignorance, we escape some of the responsibility of teaching him. We resist any analysis of the educational process which threatens the notion of inner wisdom or questions the contention that the fault of ignorance lies with the student. More powerful techniques which bring about the same changes in behavior by manipulating *external* variables are decried as brainwashing or thought control. We are quite unprepared to judge *effective* educational measures. As long as only a few pupils learn much of what is taught, we do not worry about uniformity or regimentation. We do not fear the feeble technique; but we should view with dismay a system under which every student learned everything listed in a syllabus—although such a condition is far from unthinkable. Similarly, we do not fear a system which is so defective that the student must *work* for an education; but we are loath to give credit for anything learned without effort— although this could well be taken as an ideal result—and we flatly refuse to give credit if the student already knows what a school teaches.

A world in which people are wise and good without trying, without "having to be," without "choosing to be," could conceivably be a far better world for everyone. In such a world we should not have to "give anyone credit"—we should not need to admire anyone—for being wise and good. From our present point of view we cannot believe that such a world would be admirable. We do not even permit ourselves to imagine what it would be like.

Government. Government has always been the special field of aversive control. The state is frequently defined in terms of the power to punish, and jurisprudence leans heavily upon the associated notion of personal responsibility. Yet it is becoming increasingly difficult to reconcile current practice and theory with these earlier views. In criminology, for example, there is a strong tendency to drop the notion of responsibility in favor of some such alternative as capacity or controllability. But no matter how strongly the facts, or even practical expedience, support such a change, it is difficult to make the change in a legal system designed on a different plan. When governments resort to other techniques (for example, positive reinforcement), the concept of responsibility is no longer relevant and the theory of government is no longer applicable.

The conflict is illustrated by two decisions of the Supreme Court in the 1930's which dealt with, and disagreed on, the definition of control or coercion (Freund, *et al.,* 1954, p. 233). The Agricultural Adjustment Act proposed that the Secretary of Agriculture make "rental or benefit payments" to those farmers who agreed to reduce production. The government agreed that the Act would be unconstitutional if the farmer had been *compelled* to reduce production but was not, since he was merely *invited* to do so. Justice Roberts expressed the contrary majority view of the court that "The power to confer or withhold unlimited benefits is the power to coerce or destroy." This recognition of positive reinforcement was withdrawn a few years later in another case in which Justice Cardozo (Freund, *et al.,* 1954, p. 244) wrote "To hold that motive or temptation is equivalent to coercion is to plunge the law in endless difficulties." We may agree with him, without implying that the proposition is therefore wrong. Sooner or later the law must be prepared to deal with all possible techniques of governmental control.

The uneasiness with which we view government (in the broadest possible sense) when it does not use punishment is shown by the reception of my utopian novel, *Walden Two* (Skinner, 1948b). This was essentially a proposal to apply a behavioral technology to the construction of a workable, effective, and productive pattern of government. It was greeted with wrathful violence. *Life* magazine called it "a travesty on the good life," and "a menace . . . a triumph of mortmain or the dead hand not envisaged since the days of Sparta . . . a slur upon a name, a corruption of an impulse." Joseph Wood Krutch devoted a substantial part of his book, *The Measure of Man* (1954), to attacking my views and those of the protagonist, Frazier, in the same vein, and Morris Viteles has recently criticized the book

337

in a similar manner in *Science* (1955). Perhaps the reaction is best expressed in a quotation from *The Quest for Utopia* by Negley and Patrick (1952):

> "Halfway through this contemporary utopia, the reader may feel sure, as we did, that this is a beautifully ironic satire on what has been called 'behavioral engineering.' The longer one stays in this better world of the psychologist, however, the plainer it becomes that the inspiration is not satiric, but messianic. This is indeed the behaviorally engineered society, and while it was to be expected that sooner or later the principle of psychological conditioning would be made the basis of a serious construction of utopia—Brown anticipated it in *Limanora*—yet not even the effective satire of Huxley is adequate preparation for the shocking horror of the idea when positively presented. Of all the dictatorships espoused by utopists, this is the most profound, and incipient dictators might well find in this utopia a guidebook of political practice."

One would scarcely guess that the authors are talking about a world in which there is food, clothing, and shelter for all, where everyone chooses his own work and works on the average only 4 hours a day, where music and the arts flourish, where personal relationships develop under the most favorable circumstances, where education prepares every child for the social and intellectual life which lies before him, where—in short—people are truly happy, secure, productive, creative, and forward-looking. What is wrong with it? Only one thing: someone "planned it that way." If these critics had come upon a society in some remote corner of the world which boasted similar advantages, they would undoubtedly have hailed it as providing a pattern we all might well follow—provided that it was clearly the result of a natural process of cultural evolution. Any evidence that intelligence had been used in arriving at this version of the good life would, in their eyes, be a serious flaw. No matter if the planner of *Walden Two* diverts none of the proceeds of the community to his own use, no matter if he has no current control or is, indeed, unknown to most of the other members of the community (he planned that, too), somewhere back of it all he occupies the position of prime mover. And this, to the child of the democratic tradition, spoils it all.

The dangers inherent in the control of human behavior are very real. The possibility of the misuse of scientific knowledge must always be faced. We cannot escape by denying the power of a science of behavior or arresting its development. It is no help to cling to familiar philosophies of human behavior simply because they are more reassuring. As I have pointed out elsewhere (Skinner, 1955), the new techniques emerging from a science of behavior must be subject to the explicit countercontrol which has already been applied to earlier and cruder forms. Brute force and deception, for example, are now

338

fairly generally suppressed by ethical practices and by explicit governmental and religious agencies. A similar countercontrol of scientific knowledge in the interests of the group is a feasible and promising possibility. Although we cannot say how devious the course of its evolution may be, a cultural pattern of control and countercontrol will presumably emerge which will be most widely supported because it is most widely reinforcing.

If we cannot foresee all the details of this (as we obviously cannot), it is important to remember that this is true of the critics of science as well. The dire consequences of new techniques of control, the hidden menace in original cultural designs—these need some proof. It is only another example of my present point that the need for proof is so often overlooked. Man has got himself into some pretty fixes, and it is easy to believe that he will do so again. But there is a more optimistic possibility. The slow growth of the method of science, now for the first time being applied to human affairs, *may* mean a new and exciting phase of human life to which historical analogies will not apply and in which earlier political slogans will not be appropriate. If we are to use the knowledge that a science of behavior is now making available with any hope of success, we must look at human nature as it is brought into focus through the methods of science rather than as it has been presented to us in a series of historical accidents.

If the advent of a powerful science of behavior causes trouble, it will not be because science itself is inimical to human welfare but because older conceptions have not yielded easily or gracefully. We expect resistance to new techniques of control from those who have heavy investments in the old, but we have no reason to help them preserve a series of principles that are not ends in themselves but rather outmoded means to an end. What is needed is a new conception of human behavior which is compatible with the implications of a scientific analysis. All men control and are controlled. The question of government in the broadest possible sense is not how freedom is to be preserved but what kinds of control are to be used and to what ends. Control must be analyzed and considered in its proper proportions. No one, I am sure, wishes to develop new master-slave relationships or bend the will of the people to despotic rulers in new ways. These are patterns of control appropriate to a world without science. They may well be the first to go when the experimental analysis of behavior comes into its own in the design of cultural practices.

II—ROGERS

There are, I believe, a number of matters in connection with this important topic on which the authors of this article, and probably a large majority of psychologists, are in agreement. These matters then 339 are not issues as far as we are concerned, and I should like to mention them briefly in order to put them to one side.

Points of Agreement. I am sure we agree that men—as individuals and as societies—have always endeavored to understand, predict, influence, and control human behavior—their own behavior and that of others.

I believe we agree that the behavioral sciences are making and will continue to make increasingly rapid progress in the understanding of behavior, and that as a consequence the capacity to predict and to control behavior is developing with equal rapidity.

I believe we agree that to deny these advances, or to claim that man's behavior cannot be a field of science, is unrealistic. Even though this is not an issue for us, we should recognize that many intelligent men still hold strongly to the view that the actions of men are free in some sense such that scientific knowledge of man's behavior is impossible. Thus Reinhold Niebuhr, the noted theologian, heaps scorn on the concept of psychology as a science of man's behavior and even says, "In any event, no scientific investigation of past behavior can become the basis of predictions of future behavior." (1955, p. 47). So, while this is not an issue for psychologists, we should at least notice in passing that it is an issue for many people.

I believe we are in agreement that the tremendous potential power of a science which permits the prediction and control of behavior may be misused, and that the possibility of such misuse constitutes a serious threat.

Consequently Skinner and I are in agreement that the whole question of the scientific control of human behavior is a matter with which psychologists and the general public should concern themselves. As Robert Oppenheimer told the American Psychological Association last year (1956a) the problems that psychologists will pose for society by their growing ability to control behavior will be much more grave than the problems posed by the ability of physicists to control the reactions of matter. I am not sure whether psychologists generally recognize this. My impression is that by and large they hold a laissez-faire attitude. Obviously Skinner and I do not hold this laissez-faire view, or we would not have written this article.

Points of Issue. With these several points of basic and important agreement, are there then any issues that remain on which there are differences? I believe there are. They can be stated very briefly: Who will be controlled? Who will exercise control? What type of control will be exercised? Most important of all, toward what end or what purpose, or in the pursuit of what value, will control be exercised?

It is on questions of this sort that there exist ambiguities, misunderstandings, and probably deep differences. These differences exist 340 among psychologists, among members of the general public in this country, and among various world cultures. Without any hope of achieving a final resolution of these questions, we can, I believe, put these issues in clearer form.

Some Meanings. To avoid ambiguity and faulty communication. I would like to clarify the meanings of some of the terms we are using.

Behavioral science is a term that might be defined from several angles but in the context of this discussion it refers primarily to knowledge that the existence of certain describable conditions in the human being and/or in his environment is followed by certain describable consequences in his actions.

Prediction means the prior identification of behaviors which then occur. Because it is important in some things I wish to say later, I would point out that one may predict a highly specific behavior, such as an eye blink, or one may predict a class of behaviors. One might correctly predict "avoidant behavior," for example, without being able to specify whether the individual will run away or simply close his eyes.

The word *control* is a very slippery one, which can be used with any one of several meanings. I would like to specify three that seem most important for our present purposes. *Control* may mean: (i) The setting of conditions by B for A, A having no voice in the matter, such that certain predictable behaviors then occur in A. I refer to this as external control. (ii) The setting of conditions by B for A, A giving some degree of consent to these conditions, such that certain predictable behaviors then occur in A. I refer to this as the influence of B on A. (iii) The setting of conditions by A such that certain predictable behaviors then occur in himself. I refer to this as internal control. It will be noted that Skinner lumps together the first two meanings, external control and influence, under the concept of control. I find this confusing.

Usual Concept of Control of Human Behavior. With the underbrush thus cleared away (I hope), let us review very briefly the various elements that are involved in the usual concept of the control of human behavior as mediated by the behavioral sciences. I am drawing here on the previous writings of Skinner, on his present statements, on the writings of others who have considered in either friendly or antagonistic fashion the meanings that would be involved in such control. I have not excluded the science fiction writers, as reported recently by Vandenberg (1956), since they often show an awareness of the issues involved, even though the methods described are as yet fictional. These then are the elements that seem common to these different concepts of the application of science to human behavior.

(1) There must first be some sort of decision about goals. Usually 341

desirable goals are assumed, but sometimes, as in George Orwell's book *1984*, the goal that is selected is an aggrandizement of individual power with which most of us would disagree. In a recent paper Skinner suggests that one possible set of goals to be assigned to the behavioral technology is this: "Let men be happy, informed, skillful, well-behaved and productive." (1955–1956) In the first draft of his part of this article, which he was kind enough to show me, he did not mention such definite goals as these, but desired "improved" educational practices, "wiser" use of knowledge in government, and the like. In the final version of his article he avoids even these value-laden terms, and his implicit goal is the very general one that scientific control of behavior is desirable, because it would perhaps bring "a far better world for everyone."

Thus the first step in thinking about the control of human behavior is the choice of goals, whether specific or general. It is necessary to come to terms in some way with the issue, "For what purpose?"

(2) A second element is that, whether the end selected is highly specific or is a very general one such as wanting "a better world," we proceed by the methods of science to discover the means to these ends. We continue through further experimentation and investigation to discover more effective means. The method of science is self-correcting in thus arriving at increasingly effective ways of achieving the purpose we have in mind.

(3) The third aspect of such control is that as the conditions or methods are discovered by which to reach the goal, some person or some group establishes these conditions and uses these methods, having in one way or another obtained the power to do so.

(4) The fourth element is the exposure of individuals to the prescribed conditions, and this leads, with a high degree of probability, to behavior which is in line with the goals desired. Individuals are now happy, if that has been the goal, or well-behaved, or submissive, or whatever it has been decided to make them.

(5) The fifth element is that if the process I have described is put in motion then there is a continuing social organization which will continue to produce the types of behavior that have been valued.

Some Flaws. Are there any flaws in this way of viewing the control of human behavior? I believe there are. In fact the only element in this description with which I find myself in agreement is the second. It seems to me quite incontrovertibly true that the scientific method is an excellent way to discover the means by which to achieve our goals. Beyond that, I feel many sharp differences, which I will try to spell out.

I believe that in Skinner's presentation here and in his previous writings, there is a serious underestimation of the problem of power. To hope that the power which is being made available by the behav- 342 ioral sciences will be exercised by the scientists, or by a benevolent group, seems to me a hope little supported by either recent or distant history. It seems far more likely that behavioral scientists, holding their present attitudes, will be in the position of the German rocket scientists specializing in guided missiles. First they worked devotedly for Hitler to destroy the U.S.S.R. and the United States. Now, depending on who captured them, they work devotedly for the U.S.S.R. in the interest of destroying the United States, or devotedly for the United States in the interest of destroying the U.S.S.R. If behavioral scientists are concerned solely with advancing their science, it seems most probable that they will serve the purposes of whatever individual or group has the power.

But the major flaw I see in this review of what is involved in the scientific control of human behavior is the denial, misunderstanding, or gross underestimation of the place of ends, goals or values in their relationship to science. This error (as it seems to me) has so many implications that I would like to devote some space to it.

Ends and Values in Relation to Science. In sharp contradiction to some views that have been advanced, I would like to propose a two-pronged thesis: (i) In any scientific endeavor—whether "pure" or applied science—there is a prior subjective choice of the purpose or value which that scientific work is perceived as serving. (ii) This subjective value choice which brings that scientific endeavor into being must always lie outside of that endeavor and can never become a part of the science involved in that endeavor.

Let me illustrate the first point from Skinner himself. It is clear that in his earlier writing (1955–1956) it is recognized that a prior value choice is necessary, and it is specified as the goal that men are to become happy, well-behaved, productive, and so on. I am pleased that Skinner has retreated from the goals he then chose, because to me they seem to be stultifying values. I can only feel that he was choosing these goals for others, not for himself. I would hate to see Skinner become "well-behaved," as that term would be defined for him by behavioral scientists. His recent article in the *American Psychologist* (1956) shows that he certainly does not want to be "productive" as that value is defined by most psychologists. And the most awful fate I can imagine for him would be to have him constantly "happy." It is the fact that he is very unhappy about many things which makes me prize him.

In the first draft of his part of this article, he also included such prior value choices, saying for example, "We must decide how we are to use the knowledge which a science of human behavior is now making available." Now he has dropped all mention of such choices, and if I understand him correctly, he believes that science can proceed without them. He has suggested this view in another recent paper, 343 stating that "We must continue to experiment in cultural design . . . testing the consequences as we go. Eventually the practices which make for the greatest biological and psychological strength of the group will presumably survive" (Skinner, 1955, p. 549).

I would point out, however, that to choose to experiment is a value choice. Even to move in the direction of perfectly random experimentation is a value choice. To test the consequences of an experiment is possible only if we have first made a subjective choice of a criterion value. And implicit in his statement is a valuing of biological and psychological strength. So even when trying to avoid such choice, it seems inescapable that a prior subjective value choice is necessary for any scientific endeavor, or for any application of scientific knowledge.

I wish to make clear that I am not saying that values cannot be included as a subject of science. It is not true that science deals only with certain classes of "facts" and that these classes do not include values. It is a bit more complex than that, as a simple illustration or two may make clear.

If I value knowledge of the "three R's" as a goal of education, the methods of science can give me increasingly accurate information on how this goal may be achieved. If I value problem-solving ability as a goal of education, the scientific method can give me the same kind of help.

Now, if I wish to determine whether problem-solving ability is "better" than knowledge of the three R's, then scientific method can also study those two values but *only*—and this is very important— in terms of some other value which I have subjectively chosen. I may value college success. Then I can determine whether problem-solving ability or knowldge of the three R's is most closely associated with that value. I may value personal integration or vocational success or responsible citizenship. I can determine whether problem-solving ability or knowledge of the three R's is most closely associated with one of these values. But the value or purpose that gives meaning to a particular scientific endeavor must always lie outside of that endeavor.

Although our concern in this symposium is largely with applied science, what I have been saying seems equally true of so-called "pure" science. In pure science the usual prior subjective value choice is the discovery of truth. But this is a subjective choice, and science can never say whether it is the best choice, save in the light of some other value. Geneticists in the U.S.S.R., for example, had to make a subjective choice of whether it was better to pursue truth or to discover facts which upheld a governmental dogma. Which choice is "better"? We could make a scientific investigation of those alternatives but only in the light of some other subjectively chosen value. If, for example, 344 we value the survival of a culture, then we could begin to investigate with the methods of science the question of whether pursuit of truth or support of governmental dogma is most closely associated with cultural survival.

My point then is that any endeavor in science, pure or applied, is carried on in the pursuit of a purpose or value that is subjectively chosen by persons. It is important that this choice be made explicit, since the particular value which is being sought can never be tested or evaluated, confirmed or denied, by the scientific endeavor to which it gives birth. The initial purpose or value always and necessarily lies outside the scope of the scientific effort which it sets in motion.

Among other things this means that if we choose some particular goal or series of goals for human beings and then set out on a large scale to control human behavior to the end of achieving those goals, we are locked in the rigidity of our initial choice, because such a scientific endeavor can never transcend itself to select new goals. Only subjective human persons can do that. Thus if we chose as our goal the state of happiness for human beings (a goal deservedly ridiculed by Aldous Huxley in *Brave New World*), and if we involved all of society in a successful scientific program by which people became happy, we would be locked in a colossal rigidity in which no one would be free to question this goal, because our scientific operations could not transcend themselves to question their guiding purposes. And without laboring this point, I would remark that colossal rigidity, whether in dinosaurs, or dictatorships, has a very poor record of evolutionary survival.

If, however, a part of our scheme is to set free some "planners" who do not have to be happy, who are not controlled, and who are therefore free to choose other values, this has several meanings. It means that the purpose we have chosen as our goal is not a sufficient and a satisfying one for human beings but must be supplemented. It also means that if it is necessary to set up an elite group which is free, then this shows all too clearly that the great majority are only the slaves—no matter by what high-sounding name we call them—of those who select the goals.

Perhaps, however, the thought is that a continuing scientific endeavor will evolve its own goals; that the initial findings will alter the directions, and subsequent findings will alter them still further, and that science somehow develops its own purpose. Although he does not clearly say so, this appears to be the pattern Skinner has in mind. It is surely a reasonable description, but it overlooks one element in this continuing development, which is that subjective personal choice enters in at every point at which the direction changes. The findings of a science, the results of an experiment, do not and never can tell us what next scientific purpose to pursue. Even in the purest of science, the scientist must decide what the findings mean and must subjectively choose what next step will be most profitable in the pursuit of his purpose. And if we are speaking of the application of scientific knowledge, then it is distressingly clear that the increasing scientific knowledge of the structure of the atom carries with it no necessary choice as to the purpose to which this knowledge will be put. This is a subjective personal choice which must be made by many individuals.

Thus I return to the proposition with which I began this section of my remarks—and which I now repeat in different words. Science has its meaning as the objective pursuit of a purpose which has been subjectively chosen by a person or persons. This purpose or value can never be investigated by the particular scientific experiment or investigation to which it has given birth and meaning. Consequently, any discussion of the control of human beings by the behavioral sciences must first and most deeply concern itself with the subjectively chosen purposes which such an application of science is intended to implement.

Is the Situation Hopeless? The thoughtful reader may recognize that, although my remarks up to this point have introduced some modifications in the conception of the processes by which human behavior will be controlled, these remarks may have made such control seem, if anything, even more inevitable. We might sum it up this way: Behavioral science is clearly moving forward; the increasing power for control which it gives will be held by someone or some group; such an individual or group will surely choose the values or goals to be achieved; and most of us will then be increasingly controlled by means so subtle that we will not even be aware of them as controls. Thus, whether a council of wise psychologists (if this is not a contradiction in terms), or a Stalin, or a Big Brother has the power, and whether the goal is happiness, or productivity, or resolution of the Oedipus complex, or submission, or love of Big Brother, we will inevitably find ourselves moving toward the chosen goal and probably thinking that we ourselves desire it. Thus, if this line of reasoning is correct, it appears that some form of *Walden Two* or of *1984* (and at a deep philosophic level they seem indistinguishable) is coming. The fact that it would surely arrive piecemeal, rather than all at once, does not greatly change the fundamental issues. In any event, as Skinner has indicated in his writings, we would then look back upon the concepts of human freedom, the capacity for choice, the responsibility for choice, and the worth of the human individual as historical curiosities which once existed by cultural accident as values in a prescientific civilization.

I believe that any person observant of trends must regard something like the foregoing sequence as a real possibility. It is not simply 346 a fantasy. Something of that sort may even be the most likely future. But is it an inevitable future? I want to devote the remainder of my remarks to an alternative possibility.

Alternative Set of Values. Suppose we start with a set of ends, values, purposes, quite different from the type of goals we have been considering. Suppose we do this quite openly, setting them forth as a possible value choice to be accepted or rejected. Suppose we select a set of values that focuses on fluid elements of process rather than static attributes. We might then value: man as a process of becoming, as a process of achieving worth and dignity through the development of his potentialities; the individual human being as a self-actualizing process, moving on to more challenging and enriching experiences; the process by which the individual creatively adapts to an ever-new and changing world; the process by which knowledge transcends itself, as, for example, the theory of relativity transcended Newtonian physics, itself to be transcended in some future day by a new perception.

If we select values such as these we turn to our science and technology of behavior with a very different set of questions. We will want to know such things as these: Can science aid in the discovery of new modes of richly rewarding living? more meaningful and satisfying modes of interpersonal relationships? Can science inform us on how the human race can become a more intelligent participant in its own evolution—its physical, psychological and social evolution? Can science inform us on ways of releasing the creative capacity of individuals, which seems so necessary if we are to survive in this fantastically expanding atomic age? Oppenheimer has pointed out (1956b) that knowledge, which used to double in millennia or centuries, now doubles in a generation or a decade. It appears that we must discover the utmost in release of creativity if we are to be able to adapt effectively. In short, can science discover the methods by which man can most readily become a continually developing and self-transcending process, in his behavior, his thinking, his knowledge? Can science predict and release an essentially "unpredictable" freedom?

It is one of the virtues of science as a method that it is as able to advance and implement goals and purposes of this sort as it is to serve static values, such as states of being well-informed, happy, obedient. Indeed we have some evidence of this.

Small Example. I will perhaps be forgiven if I document some of the possibilities along this line by turning to psychotherapy, the field I know best.

Psychotherapy, as Meerloo (1955) and others have pointed out, can be one of the most subtle tools for the control of *A* by *B*. The therapist can subtly mold individuals in imitation of himself. He can cause an individual to become a submissive and conforming being. 347

When certain therapeutic principles are used in extreme fashion, we call it brainwashing, an instance of the disintegration of the personality and a reformulation of the person along lines desired by the controlling individual. So the principles of therapy can be used as an effective means of external control of human personality and behavior. Can psychotherapy be anything else?

Here I find the developments going on in client-centered psychotherapy (Rogers, 1951) an exciting hint of what a behavioral science can do in achieving the kinds of values I have stated. Quite aside from being a somewhat new orientation in psychotherapy, this development has important implications regarding the relation of a behavioral science to the control of human behavior. Let me describe our experience as it relates to the issues of this discussion.

In client-centered therapy, we are deeply engaged in the prediction and influencing of behavior, or even the control of behavior. As therapists we institute certain attitudinal conditions, and the client has relatively little voice in the establishment of these conditions. We predict that if these conditions are instituted, certain behavioral consequences will ensue in the client. Up to this point this is largely external control, no different from what Skinner has described, and no different from what I have discussed in the preceding sections of this article. But here the similarity ceases.

The conditions we have chosen to establish predict such behavioral consequences as these: that the client will become self-directing, less rigid, more open to the evidence of his senses, better organized and integrated, more similar to the ideal which he has chosen for himself. In other words, we have established by external control conditions which we predict will be followed by internal control by the individual, in pursuit of internally chosen goals. We have set the conditions which predict various classes of behaviors—self-directing behaviors, sensitivity to realities within and without, flexible adaptiveness—which are by their very nature unpredictable in their specifics. Our recent research (Rogers and Dymond, 1954) indicates that our predictions are to a significant degree corroborated, and our commitment to the scientific method causes us to believe that more effective means of achieving these goals may be realized.

Research exists in other fields—industry, education, group dynamics—which seems to support our own findings. I believe it may be conservatively stated that scientific progress has been made in identifying those conditions in an interpersonal relationship which, if they exist in B, are followed in A by greater maturity in behavior, less dependence on others, an increase in expressiveness as a person, an increase in variability, flexibility and effectiveness of adaptation, an increase in self-responsibility and self-direction. And, quite in contrast to the concern expressed by some, we do not find that the creatively 348 adaptive behavior which results from such self-directed variability of expression is a "happy accident" which occurs in "chaos." Rather, the individual who is open to his experience, and self-directing, is harmonious not chaotic, ingenious rather than random, as he orders his responses imaginatively toward the achievement of his own purposes. His creative actions are no more a "happy accident" than was Einstein's development of the theory of relativity.

Thus we find ourselves in fundamental agreement with John Dewey's statement: "Science has made its way by releasing, not by suppressing, the elements of variation, of invention and innovation, of novel creation in individuals." (Ratner, 1939, p. 359). Progress in personal life and in group living is, we believe, made in the same way.

Possible Concept of the Control of Human Behavior. It is quite clear that the point of view I am expressing is in sharp contrast to the usual conception of the relationship of the behavioral sciences to the control of human behavior. In order to make this contrast even more blunt, I will state this possibility in paragraphs parallel to those used before.

(1) It is possible for us to choose to value man as a self-actualizing process of becoming; to value creativity, and the process by which knowledge becomes self-transcending.

(2) We can proceed, by the methods of science, to discover the conditions which necessarily precede these processes and, through continuing experimentation, to discover better means of achieving these purposes.

(3) It is possible for individuals or groups to set these conditions, with a minimum of power or control. According to present knowledge, the only authority necessary is the authority to establish certain qualities of interpersonal relationship.

(4) Exposed to these conditions, present knowledge suggests that individuals become more self-responsible, make progress in self-actualization, become more flexible, and become more creatively adaptive.

(5) Thus such an initial choice would inaugurate the beginnings of a social system or subsystem in which values, knowledge, adaptive skills, and even the concept of science would be continually changing and self-transcending. The emphasis would be upon man as a process of becoming.

I believe it is clear that such a view as I have been describing does not lead to any definable utopia. It would be impossible to predict its final outcome. It involves a step-by-step development, based on a continuing subjective choice of purposes, which are implemented by the behavioral sciences. It is the direction of the "open society," as that term has been defined by Popper (1945), where individuals 349 carry responsibility for personal decisions. It is at the opposite pole from his concept of the closed society, of which *Walden Two* would be an example.

I trust it is also evident that the whole emphasis is on process, not on end-states of being. I am suggesting that it is by choosing to value certain qualitative elements of the process of becoming that we can find a pathway toward the open society.

The Choice. It is my hope that we have helped to clarify the range of choice which will lie before us and our children in regard to the behavioral sciences. We can choose to use our growing knowledge to enslave people in ways never dreamed of before, depersonalizing them, controlling them by means so carefully selected that they will perhaps never be aware of their loss of personhood. We can choose to utilize our scientific knowledge to make men happy, well-behaved, and productive, as Skinner earlier suggested. Or we can insure that each person learns all the syllabus which we select and set before him, as Skinner now suggests. Or at the other end of the spectrum or choice we can choose to use the behavioral sciences in ways which will free, not control; which will bring about constructive variability, not conformity; which will develop creativity, not contentment; which will facilitate each person in his self-directed process of becoming; which will aid individuals, groups, and even the concept of science to become self-transcending in freshly adaptive ways of meeting life and its problems. The choice is up to us, and, the human race being what it is, we are likely to stumble about, making at times some nearly disastrous value choices and at other times highly constructive ones.

I am aware that to some, this setting forth of a choice is unrealistic, because a choice of values is regarded as not possible. Skinner has stated:

> "Man's vaunted creative powers . . . his capacity to choose and our right to hold him responsible for his choice—none of these is conspicuous in this new self-portrait (provided by science). Man, we once believed, was free to express himself in art, music, and literature, to inquire into nature, to seek salvation in his own way. He could initiate action and make spontaneous and capricious changes of course. . . . But science insists that action is initiated by forces impinging upon the individual, and that caprice is only another name for behavior for which we have not yet found a cause." (1955–1956, pp. 52–53).

I can understand this point of view, but I believe that it avoids looking at the great paradox of behavioral science. Behavior, when it is examined scientifically, is surely best understood as determined by prior causation. This is one great fact of science. But responsible 350 personal choice, which is the most essential element in being a person, which is the core experience in psychotherapy, which exists prior to any scientific endeavor, is an equally prominent fact in our lives. To deny the experience of responsible choice is, to me, as restricted a view as to deny the possibility of a behavioral science. That these two important elements of our experience appear to be in contradiction has perhaps the same significance as the contradiction between the wave theory and the corpuscular theory of light, both of which can be shown to be true, even though incompatible. We cannot profitably deny our subjective life, any more than we can deny the objective description of that life.

In conclusion then, it is my contention that science cannot come into being without a personal choice of the values we wish to achieve. And these values we choose to implement will forever lie outside of the science which implements them; the goals we select, the purposes we wish to follow, must always be outside of the science which achieves them. To me this has the encouraging meaning that the human person, with his capacity of subjective choice, can and will always exist, separate from and prior to any of his scientific undertakings. Unless as individuals and groups we choose to relinquish our capacity of subjective choice, we will always remain persons, not simply pawns of a self-created science.

III—SKINNER

I cannot quite agree that the practice of science *requires* a prior decision about goals or a prior choice of values. The metallurgist can study the properties of steel and the engineer can design a bridge without raising the question of whether a bridge is to be built. But such questions are certainly frequently raised and tentatively answered. Rogers wants to call the answers "subjective choices of values." To me, such an expression suggests that we have had to abandon more rigorous scientific practices in order to talk about our own behavior. In the experimental analysis of other organisms I would use other terms, and I shall try to do so here. Any list of values is a list of reinforcers—conditioned or otherwise. We are so constituted that under certain circumstances food, water, sexual contact, and so on, will make any behavior which produces them more likely to occur again. Other things may acquire this power. We do not need to say than an organism chooses to eat rather than to starve. If you answer that it is a very different thing when a man chooses to starve, I am only too happy to agree. If it were not so, we should have cleared up the question of choice long ago. An organism can be reinforced by —can be made to "choose"—almost any given state of affairs.

Rogers is concerned with choices that involve multiple and usually conflicting consequenes. I have dealt with some of these elsewhere   351

(Skinner, 1953) in an analysis of self-control. Shall I eat these delicious strawberries today if I will then suffer an annoying rash tomorrow? The decision I am to make used to be assigned to the province of ethics. But we are now studying similar combinations of positive and negative consequences, as well as collateral conditions which affect the result in a laboratory. Even a pigeon can be taught some measure of self-control! And this work helps us to understand the operation of certain formulas—among them value judgments—which folk-wisdom, religion, and psychotherapy have advanced in the interests of self-discipline. The observable effect of any statement of value is to alter the relative effectiveness of reinforcers. We may no longer enjoy the strawberries for thinking about the rash. If rashes are made sufficiently shameful, illegal, sinful, maladjusted, or unwise, we may glow with satisfaction as we push the strawberries aside in a grandiose avoidance response which would bring a smile to the lips of Murray Sidman.

People behave in ways which as we say, conform to ethical, governmental, or religious patterns because they are reinforced for doing so. The resulting behavior may have far-reaching consequences for the survival of the pattern to which it conforms. And whether we like it or not, survival is the ultimate criterion. This is where, it seems to me, science can help—not in choosing a goal, but in enabling us to predict the survival value of cultural practices. Man has too long tried to get the kind of world he wants by glorifying some brand of immediate reinforcement. As science points up more and more of the remoter consequences, he may begin to work to strengthen behavior, not in slavish devotion to a chosen value, but with respect to the ultimate survival of mankind. Do not ask me why I want mankind to survive. I can tell you why only in the sense in which the physiologist can tell you why I want to breathe. Once the relation between a given step and the survival of my group has been pointed out, I will take that step. And it is the business of science to point out just such relations.

The values I have occasionally recommended (and Rogers has not led me to recant) are transitional. Other things being equal, I am betting on the group whose practices make for healthy, happy, secure, productive, and creative people. And I insist that the values recommended by Rogers are transitional, too, for I can ask him the same kind of question. Man as a process of becoming—*what?* Self-actualization—for what? Inner control is no more a goal than external.

What Rogers seems to me to be proposing both here and elsewhere (Rogers, 1956), is this: Let us use our increasing power of control to create individuals who will not need and perhaps will no longer respond to control. Let us solve the problem of our power by renouncing it. At first blush this seems as implausible as a benevolent despot. Yet power has occasionally been foresworn. A nation has 352 burned its Reichstag, rich men have given away their wealth, beautiful women have become ugly hermits in the desert, and psychotherapists have become nondirective. When this happens. I look to other possible reinforcements for a plausible explanation. A people relinquish democratic power when a tyrant promises them the earth. Rich men give away wealth to escape the accusing finger of their fellowmen. A woman destroys her beauty in the hope of salvation. And a psychotherapist relinquishes control because he can thus help his client more effectively.

The solution that Rogers is suggesting is thus understandable. But is he correctly interpreting the result? What evidence is there that a client ever becomes truly *self*-directing? What evidence is there that he ever makes a truly *inner* choice of ideal or goal? Even though the therapist does not do the choosing, even though he encourages "self-actualization"—he is not out of control as long as he holds himself ready to step in when occasion demands—when, for example, the client chooses the goal of becoming a more accomplished liar or murdering his boss. But supposing the therapist does withdraw completely or is no longer necessary—what about all the other forces acting upon the client? Is the self-chosen goal independent of his early ethical and religious training? of the folk-wisdom of his group? of the opinions and attitudes of others who are important to him? Surely not. The therapeutic situation is only a small part of the world of the client. From the therapist's point of view it may appear to be possible to relinquish control. But the control passes not to a "self," but to forces in other parts of the client's world. The solution of the therapist's problem of power cannot be *our* solution, for we must consider *all* the forces acting upon the individual.

The child who must be prodded and nagged is something less than a fully developed human being. We want to see him hurrying to his appointment, not because each step is taken in response to verbal reminders from his mother, but because certain temporal contingencies, in which dawdling has been punished and hurrying reinforced, have worked a change in his behavior. Call this a state of better organization, a greater sensitivity to reality, or what you will. The plain fact is that the child passes from a temporary verbal control exercised by his parents to control by certain inexorable features of the environment. I should suppose that something of the same sort happens in successful psychotherapy. Rogers seems to me to be saying this: Let us put an end, as quickly as possible, to any pattern of master-and-slave, to any direct obedience to command, to the submissive following of suggestions. Let the individual be free to adjust himself to more rewarding features of the world about him. In the end, let his teachers and counselors "wither away," like the Marxist state. I not only agree with this as a useful ideal, I have constructed a fanciful world to demonstrate its advantages. It saddens me to hear 353

Rogers say that "at a deep philosophic level" *Walden Two* and George Orwell's *1984* "seem indistinguishable." They could scarcely be more unlike—at any level. The book *1984* is a picture of immediate aversive control for vicious selfish purposes. The founder of *Walden Two*, on the other hand, has built a community in which neither he nor any other person exerts any *current* control. His achievement lay in his original *plan*, and when he boasts of this ("It is enough to satisfy the thirstiest tyrant") we do not fear him but only pity him for his weakness.

Another critic of *Walden Two*, Andrew Hacker (1955), has discussed this point in considering the bearing of mass conditioning upon the liberal notion of autonomous man. In drawing certain parallels between the Grand Inquisition passage in Dostoevsky's *Brothers Karamazov*, Huxley's *Brave New World*, and *Walden Two*, he attempts to set up a distinction to be drawn in any society between conditioners and conditioned. He assumes that "the conditioner can be said to be autonomous in the traditional liberal sense." But then he notes: "Of course the conditioner has been conditioned. But he has not been conditioned by the conscious manipulation of another *person*." But how does this affect the resulting behavior? Can we not soon forget the origins of the "artificial" diamond which is identical with the real thing? Whether it is an "accidental" cultural pattern, such as is said to have produced the founder of *Walden Two*, or the engineered environment which is about to produce his successors, we are dealing with sets of conditions generating human behavior which will ultimately be measured by their contribution to the strength of the group. We look to the future, not the past, for the test of "goodness" or acceptability.

If we are worthy of our democratic heritage we shall, of course, be ready to resist any tyrannical use of science for immediate or selfish purposes. But if we value the achievements and goals of democracy we must not refuse to apply science to the design and construction of cultural patterns, even though we may then find ourselves in some sense in the position of controllers. Fear of control, generalized beyond any warrant, has led to a misinterpretation of valid practices and the blind rejection of intelligent planning for a better way of life. In terms which I trust Rogers will approve, in conquering this fear we shall become more mature and better organized and shall, thus, more fully actualize ourselves as human beings.

REFERENCES AND NOTES

Coleman, C. The hickory stick. *Bull. Amer. Ass. univ. Professors,* 1953, 39, 457–473.

Freund, P. A., *et al. Constitutional law: Cases and other problems.* Vol. 1. Boston: Little, Brown, 1954.

Hacker, A. The specter of predictable man. *Antioch Rev.*, 1954, 14, 195–207.

Hacker, A. Dostoevsky's disciples: Man and sheep in political theory. *J. Politics*, 1955, 17, 590–613.

Krutch, J. W. *The measure of man.* New York: Bobbs-Merrill, 1954.

Meerloo, J. A. M. Medication into submission: danger of therapeutic coercion. *J. nerv. ment. Dis.*, 1955, 122, 353–360.

Negley, G., and Patrick, J. M. *The quest for utopia.* New York: Schuman, 1952.

Niebuhr, R. *The self and the dramas of history.* New York: Scribners, 1955.

Oppenheimer, J. R. Analogy in science. *Amer. Psychologist*, 1956a, 11, 127–135.

Oppenheimer, J. R. Science and our times. *Roosevelt U. occasional Papers*, 1956b, No. 2.

Popper, K. R. *The open society and its enemies.* London: Routledge & Kegan Paul, 1945.

Ratner, J. (Ed.) *Intelligence in the modern world: John Dewey's philosophy.* New York: Modern Library, 1939.

Rogers, C. R. Implications of recent advances in prediction and control of behavior. *Teachers coll. Rec.*, 1951, 57, 316–322.

Rogers, C. R., and Dymond, R. (Eds.) *Psychotherapy and personality change.* Chicago: U. of Chicago Press, 1954.

Skinner, B. F. *Walden two.* New York: Macmillan, 1948.

Skinner, B. F. *Science and human behavior.* New York: Macmillan, 1953.

Skinner, B. F. The control of human behavior. *Trans. N. Y. Acad. Sci.*, 1955, 17, 547–551.

Skinner, B. F. Freedom and the control of men. *Amer. Scholar*, Winter, 1955–1956, 25, special issue, 47–65.

Skinner, B. F. A case history in scientific method. *Amer. Psychologist*, 1956, 11, 221–233.

Vandenberg, S. G. Great expectations or the future of psychology (as seen in science fiction). *Amer. Psychologist*, 1956, 11, 339–342.

Viteles, M. S. The new utopia. *Science*, 1955, 122, 1167–1171.

Robert Boguslaw

The Power of Systems and Systems of Power

One of the more popular pastimes developed in the wake of a rapidly burgeoning high-speed computer technology has been the game of "let's play you think computers are bad and I think they are good." In one reported encounter, the protagonists were Norbert Wiener (the father of cybernetics) and Arthur L. Samuel (one of IBM's bright sons). Wiener stated as his thesis that "machines can and do transcend some of the limitations of their designers, and that in doing so they may be both effective and dangerous."[1] Samuel, invoking the familiar argument that "most, if not all, of man's inventions are instrumentalities which may be employed by both saints and sinners,"[2] concluded that "the modern digital computer is a modality whose value is overwhelmingly on the side of the good."[3]

History does not record a score for this particular contest, but one is tempted to question whether the game was played in the right ballpark. The Wiener thesis seems to proceed from a perspective that sees the computer as something like a bow and arrow contraption possessing more or less indeterminate, boomeranglike performance characteristics. Samuel seems to see his product essentially as a better mousetrap (and who wants to be on the side of the rats)?

From Robert Boguslaw, *The New Utopians: A Study of System Design and Social Change,* © 1965. Reprinted by permission of Prentice-Hall, Inc., Englewood Cliffs, New Jersey. Robert Boguslaw is professor of sociology at Washington University in St. Louis.

[1]Norbert Wiener, "Some Moral and Technical Consequences of Automation," *Automation Implications for the Future,* ed. Morris Philipson (New York: Random House, 1962), p. 163.

[2]Arthur L. Samuel, "Some Moral and Technical Consequences of Automation—A Refutation," *ibid.,* p. 179.

[3]*Ibid.*

There is, of course, at least one additional perspective from which we may contemplate the computer. This is the perspective that helps us to see it as an integral part of a larger, more encompassing social structure. Computers are not found in nature. They have to be built. And they must take their places within a framework of existing social systems. A decision to place them within a framework redefines existing system arrangements in significant ways. Indeed, as computer complexes assume functions previously performed by bureaucratic hierarchies or disparate units or unorganized work groups, they almost invariably lead to the redesign of existing systems. Specifically, this means changes in information organization (with the aid of computers or other physical equipment), formalized work procedures (that is, customs, computer programs, organizational directives, and so forth), and people.

The process of engaging in this redesign inevitably raises issues about how various system "functions" are to be accomplished. Without becoming embroiled in the intricacies of several hoary controversies among anthropologists and sociologists about the precise meaning of function and the usefulness of "functional analysis," we may note a formulation that defines function as the contribution an activity within a system makes to the whole.[4] This definition points up the importance of "specifying precisely both the part and the whole to which a functional statement refers. A practice which is functional within one social region need not be functional in one which is more (or less) inclusive."[5]

The credo of an engineer designing systems composed exclusively of physical or "hardware" components includes the assumption that all functions performed by the components will be *manifest* (that is, "intended and recognized" by the designer).[6] *Latent* functions (those that are neither intended nor recognized) are hopefully omitted. The same credo is held by designers of classical utopias.

The difficulties that arise when computerized systems are designed *without* deviating from this credo have become legend among sophisticates. Suppose, for example, you wish to "automate" the communication functions carried on within a large system. A preliminary step must consist of a detailed specification of the various classes of information currently being communicated. To obtain such a specification, one might examine messages transmitted in the past, and perhaps codify the information normally transmitted over telephone or tele-

[4]Harold Fallding, "Functional Analysis in Sociology," *American Sociological Review*, XXVIII, No. 1 (February 1963).
[5]*Ibid.*, p. 6.
[6]Robert K. Merton, "Manifest and Latent Functions," *Social Theory and Social Structure*, rev. ed. (New York: Free Press of Glencoe, Inc., 1957), p. 51.

357

graph lines, and so on. In the process of conducting such an examination, it is all too easy for the neophyte to overlook classes of information characteristically transmitted, let us say, during coffee breaks. Ignoring the latent communicative function of the coffee break can result in a highly complex computerized system that has no way of dealing with some of its most crucial categories of system information.

As Robert K. Merton expressed it many years ago, "any attempt to eliminate an existing social structure without providing adequate alternative structures for fulfilling the functions previously fulfilled by the abolished organization is doomed to failure."[7]

Now one of the most pervasive characteristics of all social structures is the fact of social differentiation. This, in itself, does not seem very startling. We are accustomed to the notion that some people are old and some young, some female, some male, and so forth. Social differentiation becomes a matter for controversy only after it is used as a basis for social stratification: the distribution of unequal rewards among the various participants in a social system.

Many years ago, two sociologists (Kingsley Davis and Wilbert E. Moore) tried to explain these differences essentially on the basis that "*if* the more important, highly skilled, and physically and psychologically demanding positions in a complex division of labor are to be adequately filled both from the standpoint of numbers and of minimally efficient performance, *then* there must be *some* unequal rewards favoring these positions over others."[8]

It seems clear that the particular scale of unequal rewards existing in a society tends to be self-perpetuating. People become accustomed to the allocation of certain differences in reward and tend to resist drastic changes.[9] A president of an industrial firm makes more money than a charwoman—this is considered appropriate and fair; and anyone who suggested a reversal in the reward system for our society would encounter serious resistance, not only from presidents, but from most "reasonable" people—including charwomen.

In designing a computerized system on the site of a previously existing "manual" social structure, one inevitably must deal with the effects the new system will have on previously existing roles and their incumbents. When the role incumbents are unskilled or semiskilled workers whose more or less routinized jobs are assumed by the computerized installation, this takes the form of concern with "technological displacement" and consideration of the consequences of "auto-

[7]*Ibid.*, p. 81.
[8]Cf. Dennis H. Wrong, "The Functional Theory of Stratification: Some Neglected Considerations," *American Sociological Review*, XXIV, No. 6 (December 1959), 774.
[9]*Ibid.*

mation." The dialogue may proceed along lines of "these displaced workers must be trained for new skills—like computer programming; however, some people are untrainable and they constitute the core of the social problem accompanying automation. This is something like what happened when the automobile replaced the horse and buggy— new jobs will emerge for which people can be trained—the black-smiths will simply have to face reality, and so forth."

In terms of social stratification, the human, low-skilled workers are simply eliminated. They are not just placed at the bottom of the status and economic-reward ladder; they are removed from it.

But this removal inevitably has direct consequences for those who remain. The middle-level bureaucrat whose value consisted primarily of the uncodified information in his desk, file, or head now finds that he has been asked to furnish all relevant information to a central repository. Much of the prior basis of his unequal reward has been removed. The second- or third-level executive whose value consisted of an ability to analyze large quantities of data and come up with significant policy recommendations now finds his data analysis can be done more effectively according to predetermined analytical schemes. The highly skilled and psychologically demanding positions become those relating to operations of the computer and the formula-tion of computer programs.

All this, of course, shakes the foundations of existing stratification realities. Former "key decision makers" begin to feel, and indeed are regarded, as anachronistic hangers-on. Experienced computer experts have many techniques for dealing with this problem. One approach is to point out that the locus of decision making still rests with the former executive or manager. This, of course, is not really true. Disbelievers see the light when they ask for a given set of figures or ask that a pet procedure be implemented.

The answer, all too frequently, becomes "but the program can't handle it." Or, "We can't do that just yet, but in about six months, after these immediate problems are ironed out, I'm sure we can get that for you." Or, "This set of figures will cover about 98 per cent of all the cases you could possibly be interested in; it just wouldn't be economical to try to get 100 per cent of all the cases," and so on.

To an executive accustomed to getting his own way from human employees, even if they have to work overtime or develop ulcers in the process, this may all sound like an unpardonable affront to man-agerial prerogatives. He is thus inexorably driven to the next step in the process—the "I want a computer course" step. The feeling seems to be: "If I could only learn a little about computer programming, I could keep those snotty kids from being in a position to tell me how to run my business."

But, unfortunately, computer courses for executives seldom provide 359 enduring solutions. At best, the executive learns to deal with his frustrations by accepting the frame of reference of the computer expert and adjusting his sights accordingly. The exercise of power, which formerly was mediated through conventions of law, custom, "what the union will stand still for," or "principles of human relations" —now must be mediated through the current state of computer technology.

To proceed in this fashion (that is, through technology-screened power) is to adopt an orientation that is essentially formalist in nature (although the work of Newell, Simon, and Shaw in the area of heuristic programming provides the promise of creative alternatives). The specification of future and current system states within this orientation characteristically requires an insistence upon a uniformity of perspective, a standardization of language, and a consensus of values that is characteristic of highly authoritarian social structures. Nonconforming perspectives, language, and values can be and, indeed, must be excluded as system elements.

All this is a familiar pattern in classical utopias. Although the inhabitants of utopian societies were frequently prepared to deal with external threats, internal dissension was almost invariably taboo. The tradition of specifying functions within computer-based systems enhances the points of structural correspondence of these systems and classical utopias. In this connection, Ralf Dahrendorf's summary of the structural features of utopian societies provides some useful insights. He points out that: 1) Utopias do not grow out of familiar reality or follow realistic patterns of development. 2) Utopias characteristically have universal consensus on values and institutional arrangements; that is, they are highly uniform throughout. 3) Utopias are characterized by an absence of internal conflict; that is, they are characterized by social harmony, which helps to account for their stability. 4) All processes within utopian societies follow recurrent patterns and occur as part of the design of the whole. 5) Utopias are characteristically isolated in time and space from other parts of the world.[10]

The simple fact of the matter seems to be that classically designed computer-based systems, like classical utopias, resolve problems of conflict, consensus, and reality by simple fiat. But these old problems do not thereby simply fade away. Environments change. Internal conditions change. Systems and utopias alike must be ready and able to change if they are to survive. But crucial types of change originate *within* systems—out of the contradictions and conflicts existing between

[10]Cf. Ralf Dahrendorf, "Out of Utopia: Toward a Reorientation of Sociological Analysis," *The American Journal of Sociology,* LXIV, No. 2 (September 1958), 116–117.

two or more opposing sets of values, ideologies, roles, institutions, or groups.[11]

To insist that social structures must always be shaped and controlled from "topside," is to reinforce maladaptive tendencies in systems and to help to insure their ultimate collapse. A façade of value homogeneity cannot resolve the internal stresses, conflicts, and dilemmas that arise in any system designed to cope effectively with the fact of change.

POWER AND BUREAUCRACY

The problem of understanding what it is that makes human societies "stick together" or cohere has been studied by philosophers and social theorists for thousands of years. In general, two different kinds of explanation are offered. The first of these emphasizes the role of *consensus*—the existence of a general agreement on values within the society. The second explanation emphasizes the role of *coercion*—the use of force and constraint to hold a society together.[12]

One of the interesting limitations of traditional utopias is the relative lack of detailed concern they reflect about the composition of the glue used to hold things together.

In the *consensus* formula for social glue, people with common values voluntarily associate to help insure more effective cooperation. In the *coercion* formula, positions within the system are defined to insure effective application of force and constraints.[13] To understand the operation of any system, it is crucial to understand the distribution of authority and power within it. Differences in system design may, in the last analysis, involve little more than different allocations of power and authority throughout the system. Indeed, alternate arguments about the merits of different system design formats may well involve little beyond implicit rationalizations for alternate modes of power distribution.

Each of these formulas is based upon a set of assumptions about the nature of society or social systems. The consensus formula assumes that society is a relatively stable and well-integrated structure of elements, each of which has a well-defined function. Throughout the system itself, there exists a consensus of values among its various members. The coercion formula assumes that every society is at every point subject to both processes of change and social conflict. It further

[11]Cf. Pierre L. Van Den Berghe, "Dialectic and Functionalism: Toward a Theoretical Synthesis," *American Sociological Review,* XXVIII, No. 5 (October 1963), 699.

[12]Ralf Dahrendorf, *Class and Class Conflict in Industrial Society* (Stanford, Calif.: Stanford University Press, 1959), pp. 157–159.

[13]Cf. *ibid.,* p. 169.

361

assumes that every element in a society contributes to the system's disintegration and change. And finally, the coercion formula assumes that every society is based on the coercion of some of its members by others. . . .[14]

The point to be stressed here, however, is the importance of specifying the exact nature of the particular glue to be used in a specific system design. Perhaps the easiest error to make is the one that assumes that a consensus glue exists, when in point of fact the design either requires, or has surreptitiously imposed, a coercion formula.

To clarify this somewhat, it may be helpful to note how power, in the sociological sense, is differentiated from force on the one hand and authority on the other.

Force, in this context, refers to the reduction, limitation, closure, or total elimination of alternatives to the social action of one person or group by another person or group. For example, "Your money or your life," symbolizes a situation in which the alternatives have been reduced to two. Hanging a convicted criminal exemplifies the total elimination of alternatives. Dismissal or demotion of personnel in an organization illustrates the closure of alternatives. An army may successively place limitations upon the social action of its enemy until only two alternatives remain—to surrender or die.[16]

Power refers to the ability to apply force, rather than to its actual application. It is the "predisposition or prior capacity which makes the application of force possible."[17]

Authority refers to institutionalized power. In an idealized organization, power and authority become equivalent to each other. The right to use force is attached to certain statuses within the organization. "It is . . . authority in virtue of which persons in an association exercise command or control over other persons in the same association."[18] Examples of the use of authority include: the bishop who transfers a priest from his parish, the commanding officer who assigns a subordinate to a post of duty, a baseball team manager who changes a pitcher in the middle of an inning, and a factory superintendent who requires that an employee complete a task by a given time.[19]

"Your money or your life," constitutes what in the computer trade would be called a binary choice. If the alternatives available were extended to include, let us say, "the twenty-dollar bill you now have in your pocket," "room and board at your home for two days," "a serviceable overcoat," "the three bottles of scotch you have in your

[14]Cf. *ibid.*, pp. 161–162.
[16]Cf. Robert Bierstedt, "An Analysis of Social Power," *American Sociological Review,* XV, No. 6 (December 1950), 733.
[17]*Ibid.*
[18]*Ibid.,* 734.
[19]*Ibid.*

closet," or "a friendly chat over a good meal," then the intensity of of the force being applied might be seen as somewhat diminished. This is simply another way of noting that the exercise of force is related to the range of action alternatives made available. The person with the ability to specify the alternatives—in this case, the person with the gun —is the one who possesses power.

And so it is that a designer of systems, who has the de facto prerogative to specify the range of phenomena that his system will distinguish, clearly is in possession of enormous degrees of power (depending, of course, upon the nature of the system being designed). It is by no means necessary that this power be formalized through the allocation of specific authority to wield nightsticks or guns.

The strength of high-speed computers lies precisely in their capacity to process binary choice data rapidly. But to process these data, the world of reality must at some point in time be reduced to binary form. This occurs initially through operational specifications handed to a computer programmer. These specifications serve as the basis for more detailed reductions to binary choices. The range of possibilities is ultimately set by the circuitry of the computer, which places finite limits on alternatives for data storage and processing. The structure of the language used to communicate with the computer places additional restrictions on the range of alternatives. The programmer himself, through the specific sets of data he uses in his solution to a programming problem and the specific techniques he uses for his solution, places a final set of restrictions on action alternatives available within a computer-based system.

It is in this sense that computer programmers, the designers of computer equipment, and the developers of computer languages possess power. To the extent that decisions made by each of these participants in the design process serve to reduce, limit, or totally eliminate action alternatives, they are applying force and wielding power in the precise sociological meaning of these terms. . . .

As computer-based systems become increasingly more significant in shaping the realistic terms of existence in contemporary society, it becomes increasingly more relevant to inquire about the implications contained for expression of individual values. The process of obtaining representation for individual values is one of the specific notions contained in popular conceptions of democracy. However, the central idea of democracy has been penetratingly described as "one particular way in which the authority to govern is acquired and held."[33] Thus, "A man may be said to hold authority democratically when he has been freely chosen to hold such authority by those who must live

[33]Charles Frankel, "Bureaucracy & Democracy in the New Europe," *Daedalus* (Proceedings of the American Academy of Arts and Sciences), XCIII, No. 1 (Winter 1964), 476.

under it, when they have had, and will have, the alternative of choosing somebody else, and when he is accountable to them for the way in which he exercises this authority."[34]

It is, of course, clear that there are limits on the democratic principle and that legal and institutional safeguards must exist to protect values other than those of democracy itself. It is equally clear that at best the democratic principle can be only approximated. No one in our society seriously suggests that every person must be absolutely equal to every other person in power and influence.[35] But, "the working touchstone of a 'democratic' system of authority is simply the degree to which it gives individuals legitimate instruments for reaching those who make the decisions that affect them, and for bringing influence to bear upon them. A system is more or less 'democratic' depending on the number, availability, and effectiveness of these instruments, and on the proportion of the population entitled and able to use them."[36]

Now, whether the "masses" are denied legitimate access to decision makers by reason of despotism, bureaucratic deviousness, or simple technical obfuscation, the resultant erosion of democratic process can be much the same. To the extent that decisions made by equipment manufacturers, computer programmers, or system designers are enshrouded in the mystery of "technical" detail, the persons most affected by these decisions (including customers, publics, and employees) will be denied the opportunity to participate or react to the decision made. The spectrum of values represented in the new decision-making order can and is being increasingly more circumscribed by fiat disguised as technological necessity. The paramount issues to be raised in connection with the design of our new computerized utopias are not technological—they are issues of values and the power through which these values become translated into action.

[34]*Ibid.*
[35]Cf. *ibid.,* 476–477.
[36]*Ibid.,* 477.

Sol Stern

NSA and the CIA

A SHORT ACCOUNT OF INTERNATIONAL STUDENT POLITICS & THE COLD WAR WITH PARTICULAR REFERENCE TO THE NSA, CIA, ETC.

I. SOME NECESSARY BACKGROUND

The chill of the cold war was already in the air in August of 1946, when some 300 students from 38 countries assembled in the flag-bedecked Artists' Hall in Prague for the first World Student Congress. Among the delegates were 24 American students, many of them World War II veterans, representing various youth and student organizations and ten prominent universities. The communists were in the majority at the Congress, and disputes arose as to the proper role of international student organizations. Still, the Congress ended on an amicable note, with a call for further cooperation and the building of a truly representative international student organization—which came into existence shortly afterwards, and was named the International Union of Students (IUS). The American delegates, who came to be known as the Prague 25, returned home, fully convinced that a new, truly representative *national* organization had to be created which could fittingly represent the U.S. student community in the international student world.

Establishing themselves as an organizing committee, the Prague 25 issued a call for a national conference of student leaders to organize a new national union of students. They were remarkably successful. In the summer of 1947, a new body known as the United States National Student Association (NSA) held its Constitutional Convention in Madison, Wisconsin. By the time of this convention, the atmosphere

Reprinted by permission of the author and publisher from *Ramparts*, March 1967, pp. 29–37. © Ramparts Magazine, Inc., March 1967. Sol Stern is assistant managing editor of *Ramparts*.

365

of the IUS had become even more openly pro-communist than it had been in Prague. However, it was not until the communist coup had taken place in Czechoslovakia in 1948 and the IUS had failed to condemn the communists' mishandling of Czech students that the break between NSA and IUS became official.

Finally, in 1950, NSA met in Stockholm with 18 other national student groups to form a new international student body which was ultimately called the International Student Conference (ISC). During the first meetings, the overwhelming majority of the delegates were opposed to the conception of the ISC as a "rival," set up to fight the IUS and international communism. The delegates to the first ISC wanted to avoid controversial political questions and any further schism of the international student world.

The new international organization grew quickly and impressively. By the middle '50s, over 55 national student unions were participating, more than half of which were from the underdeveloped "Third World," and the ISC had a huge budget providing for many programs of technical assistance, education and student exchanges. The ISC became the pacesetter for international student politics and NSA was on its way to becoming the most powerful force within the new international organization.

As the ISC grew, the students of the underdeveloped world pressed the hardest for it to take political stands on controversial issues such as colonialism and racism. And as the "Third World" student unions started to press political issues in the ISC, it was usually the NSA delegation that played the moderating role, trying to keep the ISC focused on the problems of "students as students."

In a sense, the very growth of the ISC engendered its problems. Most student unions, originally attracted to the organization out of resentment against the strictures imposed by the IUS, became alienated from it when, partly under NSA's prodding, the ISC began to set forth its own tight Cold War positions. By the 1960's, the situation had begun to reverse itself: the IUS was making gestures for consultations that might lead to a reunification of the world student movement, while the ISC—with NSA in the lead—kept to a rigid Cold War line and put off most of these overtures.

At its peak in 1960, over 400 schools were affiliated with NSA. Its staff operations and budget grew every year. Though there was little income from the dues of its constituent members, NSA picked up financial support for its operations from a number of foundations. Most of this went entirely to NSA's international operations. NSA was able to sponsor yearly international relations seminars, foreign student leadership training projects, scholarships for foreign students, and still maintain a large travel budget for its international commission staff and its overseas representatives.

366

Despite the formal democracy in NSA, there was little relationship between its overseas operations and its on-campus base. NSA Congresses were massive affairs attended mostly by students sent as delegates from the student governments of NSA's member schools. They had little knowledge of NSA's year-round staff operations. International affairs and the operations of NSA's international staff were debated by a select few who could usually move the rest of the Congress on the basis of their esoteric expertise. Overseas representatives of NSA and delegates to the ISC were never elected by the NSA Congress.

NSA has always shown two faces. Its domestic programs, its Congresses and its regional meetings have always been open and spontaneous. If NSA national leaders were occasionally over-cautious, they still moved with the liberal currents of opinion among American students. In the '50s, NSA took even more liberal stands than the prevailing apathy among students might have suggested. And in the '60s, NSA responded to the new militant protest mood on the campuses. It supported students against the draft, opposed the war in Vietnam, and participated in civil rights struggles. It played a crucial role in the formation of the Student Nonviolent Coordinating Committee and was one of its staunchest supporters, a position which cost it the affiliation of many schools in 1961.

Yet NSA's overseas image has been very different. Despite its liberal rhetoric, NSA-ers abroad seemed more like professional diplomats than students; there was something tough and secretive about them that was out of keeping with their openness and spontaneity back home.

In the light of all this, it is not surprising that a number of NSA's critics have pointed a suspicious finger at its international operations. Nor is it a shock to discover that some people in the left wing of NSA, like Paul Potter, who was elected national affairs vice president in 1961 and went on to become president of Students for a Democratic Society, revealed that they had always suspected NSA's international operations of being tightly tied in with the State Department. Very few ever seriously raised the more sinister spectre of CIA involvement.

II. SOME FANCY FINANCING

It is widely known that the CIA has a number of foundations which serve as direct fronts or as secret "conduits" that channel money from the CIA to preferred organizations. An intimation of the scope of this financial web was afforded the public on August 31, 1964, when Texas Congressman Wright Patman, in the course of an investigation into the use of foundations for tax dodges, announced that the J. M. Kaplan Fund of New York was serving as a secret conduit for CIA funds. As soon as Patman made his announcement, representatives of 367 the CIA and Internal Revenue came scurrying to his office for a hasty conference. Patman apparently was satisfied with the results. Without retracting his allegations about the Kaplan Fund he announced: ". . . The CIA does not belong in this foundation investigation."

Before bringing down the curtain of secrecy, he did, at least, reveal one fact of substance. It turned out that a number of other foundations had contributed to the Kaplan Fund during the crucial years of 1961-63 when the Fund had been serving the CIA. Five of these foundations were not even on the Internal Revenue Service's list of tax-exempt foundations. They were the Borden Trust, the Price Fund, the Edsel Fund, the Beacon Fund and the Kentfield Fund. The implication was clear that some or all of these were the channel through which the CIA money passed into the Kaplan foundation coffers.

Ramparts was provided with an unusual insight into the manner in which the CIA uses legitimate foundations with liberal interests, such as the Kaplan Fund, in a recent conversation with the president of a prominent New England foundation who asked tø remain anonymous: "I didn't want my foundation dragged through the CIA mud." In 1965 he was approached by what he described as "two nice middle-aged Irish cop types who flashed CIA cards at me." The men asked the foundation president if they could look over the list of organizations that his foundation supports. He volunteered the list to them and after looking it over, the agents said that there were organizations on the list that they would also be willing to support. The CIA men explained, "We are trying to pose an alternative to communism and want to back third-force programs, which we could not do if it was known that this support comes from a government source."

The agents then proposed to support some of the organizations already on the foundation's list as well as suggesting new prospective recipients. The agents promised that if this arrangement was accepted, they would be able to channel CIA money into the foundation without it ever being traced back to the CIA. They said that they were very skilled at these manipulations.

The president, however, took the proposal directly to the board which rejected it by a vote of four to one, out of what the foundation president called "a 19th century sense of morality. We just did not like the secrecy of it."

The CIA-Suspect Funds mentioned in the Patman investigation are a key to understanding part of NSA's finances. Conveniently, they are spread all over the country (Borden in Philadelphia, Price in New York, Beacon in Boston, Kenfield in Dallas and Edsel, whose last known address was in San Francisco). When a Ramparts reporter checked out the addresses officially listed by the foundations, he usually found himself in a law office where no one was willing to talk about the Funds.

368

.

Two foundations that have supported the international programs of NSA—the J. Frederick Brown Foundation and the Independence Foundation—have received regular contributions from four of these CIA-linked Funds: Price, Borden, Kentfield, and Edsel. Both the J. Frederick Brown and the Independence Foundations list the same address, 60 State Street, Boston, which is also the address of the prestigious law firm of Hale and Dorr. Paul F. Hellmuth, a well-known Boston attorney and a member of Hale and Dorr, and David B. Stone, a Boston businessman and philanthropist, are the trustees of the Independence Foundation. Hellmuth alone is the trustee of the J. Frederick Brown Foundation.

Of the two, J. Frederick Brown is less important as a source of NSA funds. It made only $3300 in contributions to NSA, in 1963. It also made contributions to the American Friends of the Middle East, among other organizations with overseas interests. In an article in the May 9, 1966 issue of The Nation, Robert G. Sherrill implied that the American Friends had CIA ties. No official of the organization denied the allegations.

As far as NSA is concerned, the Independence Foundation is the more important of Mr. Hellmuth's two interests. Independence got its tax-exempt status in 1960. Since then, most of its funds have come from other trusts and foundations. In 1962, for example, the Independence Foundation received a total of $247,000, of which only $18,500 came from individuals or corporations; all the rest came from other foundations. Of the total, the four Funds cited in the Patman investigation gave $100,000.

Between 1962 and 1965, NSA received $256,483.33 in grants for its international programs from Independence. Much of that sum went to pay for NSA's International Student Relations Seminars, yearly extravaganzas which served as effective training grounds for future NSA international leaders.

NSA is still coasting on Independence's largesse. The building which houses NSA's present headquarters is occupied under a 15-year rent-free agreement with the Independence Foundation. Originally, NSA purchased the building with a down payment and a yearly mortgage payment to be secured from Independence. But Independence suddenly changed its mind and bought the property back from NSA. Deeds on file with the clerk of the District of Columbia reveal that NSA sold the property on October 20th, 1965, to the First National Bank, but that the bank was acting as a "trustee under an undisclosed trust." The undisclosed party is Paul Hellmuth, who secured the property, and leased it to the Independence Foundation which turned it over to NSA for the 15-year free rent agreement.

Shortly after NSA moved into its new, plush Washington offices in the fall of 1965, a reporter from the Washington Post, who was doing a feature article on NSA, asked NSA President Phil Sherburne who 369 was paying the rent on the building. Shelburne refused to divulge this information. This secrecy in protecting the names of NSA's benefactors was not unusual. In fact, NSA has never made a full financial accounting to its own Congresses.

The Independence Foundation has served NSA's overseas operations in other indirect ways. It has provided a number of scholarships for former NSA officers, usually in the neighborhood of $3000 per year. The purpose of these scholarships was to enable former NSA officers to function as overseas representatives where they were free to make contacts with foreign student unions and roam as free operatives for NSA, sending back periodic reports. Ostensibly, the overseas representatives were supposed to be in overseas universities, but this was entirely pro forma.

Independence has not restricted its largesse exclusively to NSA. In the period between 1961 and 1965 it spent $180,000 in financing an interesting operation known as the Independent Research Service (IRS). This was the organization that made life so miserable for the organizers of the communist-leaning world youth festivals in Vienna in 1959, and in Helsinki in 1962. The Independent Research Service actively recruited a delegation of hundreds of young Americans to attend the festivals in order to actively oppose the communists. The travel expenses of all the delegates were fully paid for and the bill was footed as well for a jazz group, an exhibition of famous American painters and a daily newspaper printed in five languages, all of which accompanied the delegates.

Although the official position of the NSA Congress was not to participate in the youth festivals, important NSA officers and ex-officers were very active in the Independent Research Service activities in Vienna and Helsinki. The director of the IRS during the Helsinki Youth Festival was Dennis Shaul, who was elected NSA president shortly thereafter. Shaul has also been the recipient of one of the Independence Foundation's "scholarships" in 1964.

When questioned by a Ramparts reporter about some of the activities and sources of funds for his Independence Foundation, Mr. Hellmuth, a normally outgoing man, became guarded and curt. He refused to divulge the addresses or any other information about the money which had been donated to both of his foundations. However, he was quite voluble about his close friendship with the officers of NSA.

Still another foundation which has given to NSA is the Sidney and Esther Rabb Charitable Foundation of Boston. The similarities between the Rabb Foundation and the J. M. Kaplan Fund are striking. Rabb, like Kaplan, is a Jewish businessman, prominent in liberal democratic circles. The records show that up until 1963 the Rabb Foundation's only source of income was from Rabb himself. And 370 up to that year, the Rabb Foundation's contributions were minimal and only to local charities.

Then, in 1963, two contributions to the Rabb Foundation flowed in from the Price Fund of New York—one of the Funds named in the Patman investigation, and a contributor to the J. Frederick Brown and Independence Foundations. The contributions were for $25,000 and $15,000 respectively. Strikingly, in the same year, the Rabb Foundation itself made two unusual and large contributions in precisely the same amounts—one for $25,000 to Operations and Policy Research Incorporated, a Cold War-oriented strategy organization; and $15,000 to the Fairfield Foundation. Fairfield, in its turn, has been a frequent contributor to the Congress for Cultural Freedom, previously identified in The New York Times as having received CIA funds.

During 1964, the Rabb Foundation again received unusual contributions, from three Funds, and also made three matching disbursements. It received $25,000 from the Tower Fund, and turned over the exact sum of $25,000 as a grant to the International Development Foundation which has been engaged in organizing anti-communist peasant unions in Latin America. It was particularly active in the Dominican Republic during that country's period of revolution and American intervention. The Rabb Foundation also received a $20,000 contribution from the Appalachian Fund, and during that year made a disbursement of $20,000 to the American Society of African Culture. Finally, the Rabb Foundation received $6000 from the ubiquitous Price Fund, and during the same year it turned over—would you believe—$6000 to the United States National Student Association to help retire an NSA deficit. Rabb made at least one other contribution to NSA in 1965 in the amount of $5000.

It is not always easy to obtain information on the foundations which have sustained NSA's international operations. Take the San Jacinto Foundation, for example. In the past, San Jacinto has not only funded important portions of NSA's international program, but it has also given huge sums of money to the program budget of the ISC. In particular, it has been overly generous in supporting The Student, an ISC publication printed in five languages and distributed all over the world as an anti-communist weapon.

One other interesting fact about the San Jacinto Foundation is that, like the J. Frederick Brown Foundation, it has contributed to the CIA-suspect American Friends of the Middle East. No one at NSA, or ISC for that matter, appears to have the vaguest notion of what the San Jacinto Foundation is, who is on its board of directors or where its money comes from. San Jacinto has also apparently managed to avoid the reporting procedures required by law of all tax-exempt foundations. No records for it have been entered at the district office 371 of the Internal Revenue Service in Austin, or with the secretary of the State of Texas, or with the county clerk.

San Jacinto's mailing address is the offices of F. G. O'Conner in the San Jacinto Building in downtown Houston. Mr. O'Conner is the secretary of the foundation. When asked by Ramparts' peripatetic reporter for some information about the foundation, Mr. O'Conner, a graying, distinguished-looking man in his sixties replied, "It is a private, closed foundation, never had any publicity and doesn't want any."

As far back as anyone can remember, the mainstay of NSA's overseas operations has been the Foundation for Youth and Student Affairs of New York City, founded in 1952. In contrast to the likes of Independence and San Jacinto, FYSA has a for-real office, a full-time staff and an eminently respectable board of directors.

In recent years, FYSA annually pumped hundreds of thousands of dollars per year in to NSA's treasury. The figure for October 1965 to October 1966 was $292,753.60. It provided a general administrative grant of up to $120,000 per year and funded projects such as NSA's magazine, The American Student, foreign student participation at NSA Congresses, technical assistance projects; and its funds paid NSA's dues to the ISC. In addition, FYSA could be relied upon to pick up any operating deficit that NSA incurred during the year, and FYSA gives "scholarships" to ex-NSA officers for overseas study.

FYSA has also been the chief U.S. source for channeling money overseas to national unions of students favored by the NSA leadership. And FYSA has been practically the only external source of support, except for the mysterious San Jacinto Foundation, of the programs of the ISC. Between 1962-1964, ISC records show that these two foundations provided over 90 per cent of ISC's program budget (most of it from FYSA)—a gargantuan total of $1,826,000 in grants completed or in progress. The ISC would be literally impotent as an international organization without the support of FYSA, having been unable to establish any sizable alternative sources of funding.

The executive secretary of FYSA is Harry Lunn, a tall, ruddy-faced, balding man in his middle thirties, himself a past president of NSA, who used to make applications for grants to the foundation which he now directs. Lunn vehemently denied the suggestion that his foundation might be channeling CIA money for NSA, although he would not release a financial statement to this magazine.

After his presidency of NSA (1954-55) had terminated, Lunn became a member of an ISC delegation to Southeast Asia. Then, following a short stint in the Army, he went to the Department of Defense as a research analyst. From there he went on up the ladder to the political desk of the American embassy in Paris and then on up to the Agency for International Development, where he worked on the Alliance for Progress. It was from this last position that Lunn came 372 to FYSA in 1965. Lunn also took part in the activities of the militantly anti-communist Independent Research Service at the Vienna Youth Festival in 1959, while he was attached to the Department of Defense.

Lunn's career is a case study in the intimate relationship between NSA, international student politics and the Cold War. It is living documentation of a slogan that used to hang in NSA's old Philadelphia headquarters: "The student leader of today is the student leader of tomorrow."

III. AN EXTRAORDINARY CONVERSATION

The scene was the Sirloin and Saddle, a plush, dimly-lit, continental style restaurant on Washington, D.C.'s Connecticut Avenue. It was lunchtime, the third week of March 1966, and over a table an earnest conversation was taking place that eventually resulted in the exposure of the CIA's 15-year infiltration of the National Student Association.

There were two people there that day. One of them was Phil Sherburne, NSA president for 1965–1966. Athletic-looking, blond self-possessed, his NSA post was his latest stop in a meteoric career in student politics.

Sherburne's luncheon companion that eventful day was 23-year-old Michael Wood, NSA's director of development, or fund raising chief. Wood, too, had risen rapidly in student politics. He left Pomona College during his senior year to become a civil rights worker in Watts, where one of his projects had caught the eye of an NSA officer. He became an NSA consultant in the spring of 1965, and was soon promoted to the post of director of development. Besides raising money for NSA, he helped Sherburne work out new programs, and had even been consulted by the White House staff on possible Presidential proposals about the draft and the lowering of the voting age. He had received a letter from Douglass Cater, special assistant to the President, commending him for his excellent reports.

Wood was talking to Sherburne because he was troubled. He had been running into irritating roadblocks in trying to raise money for NSA. He had encountered a curious lack of concern among other members of the Association's international staff about the rigorous preparation usually required for foundation fund raising. The amount of money needed often ran into hundreds of thousands of dollars, yet the proposals being submitted to the foundations funding the international program were ill-prepared, perfunctory and brief. Furthermore, President Sherburne was negotiating with the foundations without Wood's participation.

After six months of this confusion, Wood told Sherburne, with whom he had grown quite close, that he either had to be given full responsibility for the fund raising program or he would have to resign. It was at this time that Sherburne invited him to a heart-to-heart 373 lunch conference. The following is Wood's account of what transpired during this and subsequent conversations:

Sherburne began by telling Wood that NSA had "certain relationships with certain government agencies engaged in international relations" which Wood didn't know about. This, explained Sherburne, was why Wood couldn't have full responsibility for NSA's fund raising. Wood was astonished. "You mean the CIA?" he asked. Sherburne nodded yes. Sherburne then told Wood that he was supposed to have been informed of the CIA relationship after he was appointed director of development, but that other NSA staff members and CIA contacts had decided he was politically unreliable. As well as having been a civil rights worker, Wood had gained a reputation as something of a radical. Because he couldn't be told of the CIA relationship, it was necessary to keep him in the dark about certain aspects of NSA funding.

Sherburne told Wood he hoped that everything said over lunch that day would be kept secret. He was divulging the information only because he did not want Wood to leave NSA. Later he explained that he wanted a friend he could trust with whom to discuss the CIA relationship, other than staffers who were already involved.

The CIA, said Sherburne, had managed to inject itself into the Association's international operations in the early 1950's. Since that time, virtually every president and international affairs vice president of the organization had been aware of the CIA relationship and had cooperated.

Sherburne went on to say that most of the foundations that had funded NSA's international operations were merely passing along CIA money. Moreover, some of them had made up NSA's yearly deficits, and had financed the purchase and renovation of NSA's new offices in Washington. This explained the mystery surrounding the acquisition and the rent for NSA's new national offices.

Among the CIA-front foundations specifically mentioned, according to Wood, were the Independence Foundation, the San Jacinto Foundation, the Foundation for Youth and Student Affairs, the Sidney and Esther Rabb Foundation, and the J. Frederick Brown Foundation. To the best of Sherburne's knowledge, CIA money did not pass through the Ford Foundation, the Rockefeller Foundation, the Asia Foundation, and other groups which had also funded NSA international programs in the past.

Sherburne presented the Agency's involvement in international student politics as a *fait accompli*; he argued that the CIA's vast supply of money was absolutely essential. Although he had serious doubts about the desirability of the relationship, he felt that NSA could not get as much money from any other source; moreover, the Agency had supported many worthwhile and liberal overseas programs. In 374 any event, Sherburne felt that a sudden termination of the relationship would leave NSA in disastrous financial straits.

The CIA was interested almost exclusively in NSA's international programs. Over the years no staff member who worked exclusively on NSA's national program was involved in a CIA relationship, and few, if any, even knew about it. Keeping the CIA connection secret was made easier by the fact that NSA's national and international departments were in different cities from 1947-1960.

During their frequent conversations, Sherburne gave Wood a partial glossary of "black" language that was used by NSA's CIA operatives whenever they discussed the relationship in a semi-public place. They referred to the CIA as the "firm" and not the Agency; people were not described as operatives or agents but as being "witty"; those who worked inside the Agency bureaucracy were referred to as the "fellas" or the "boys." Frequently, important NSA-ers were given code names for their contacts with the Agency. Sherburne's code name was "Mr. Grants" (based on his facility for fund raising).

Sherburne told Wood that normal procedure involved a careful evaluation by former NSA international officers of international staff members for their reliability—as well as a full national security check by the CIA. If a member passed the test, he was made "witty."

The prospective "witty" staff member would usually be taken out to lunch by another already "witty" staff member, and a representative of the CIA. NSA's dealings were with Covert Action Division No. Five of the CIA's Plans Division, and the personnel they dealt with there were themselves former NSA officers. Thus, when the new officer was taken to lunch, he at first assumed that he was merely going out with another staff member and an NSA alumnus. The prospective "witty" staff member was told at lunch that there was information relating to work on the international staff which affected national security and which he should know about, but which required him to sign a national security oath. If he signed the oath, which pledged him to keep secret any information that was then divulged, he was then told about the CIA relationship and asked to cooperate.

The implication was clear that if the international staff member ever divulged any of the information about the relationship, there could be severe legal penalties. Thus the international officers were placed in a position in which they could not acknowledge the existence of the relationship, even to other "non-witty" NSA-ers. Sherburne made the first breach in a 15-year wall of secrecy.

The typical "witty" international staff member would first consult with an Agency representative about his overseas programs. Grants for international programs, travel allowances and expense accounts for NSA members going to overseas student conferences, would then all be supplied by CIA front foundations. 375

So intimately was the CIA involved in NSA's international program, that it treated NSA as an arm of U.S. foreign policy. The point is illustrated by a story that Sherburne told Wood. At one point during his tenure in office, Sherburne was to attend the International Student Travel Conference in Istanbul. There had already been much talk in NSA circles of opening up some bilateral contact with student unions in Soviet-bloc countries. Sherburne felt his trip to Turkey would provide a good opportunity to meet with Soviet students and discuss possible student exchanges. Sherburne sent off a cable to the Soviet National Union of Students saying that he would be in Istanbul and requesting permission to travel on to Moscow for a meeting with the Soviet student organization. But the CIA got wind of Sherburne's cable and admonished him for doing such things without first consulting the Agency. A CIA agent explained to Sherburne that since KGB (the Soviet "CIA") assumed that NSA took its cues from the U.S. government, Sherburne's gesture might be interpreted as an official change in CIA policy on bilateral student contacts. Sherburne, even though he was president of the United States National Student Association, was enjoined against making such diplomatic overtures without first requesting permission from the Agency.

The Soviet Union has always spent a good deal of money working with student and youth groups, especially in underdeveloped countries. The CIA's instrument for countering Soviet efforts was NSA, working through the International Student Conference. Former "witty" NSA staffers were always in the Secretariat of the ISC.

And NSA, with the CIA's aid, was able to play a major role in cooperating with favored national unions of students all over the world. No other union of students in the Western world has the kind of financial backing as NSA. The Canadian Union of Students, for example, operates on a budget of about $14,000 a year for its international programs, all of which comes from the dues of member schools. NSA, with its almost unlimited funds, was able to conduct a full program of foreign diplomacy.

Of course, the CIA was also interested in intelligence. "Witty" NSA international staff members would pass along reports on foreign student leaders directly to the Agency. This information helped the CIA in evaluating the political tendencies of prospective political leaders in critical areas of the world.

One of the lures the CIA dangled before NSA was the assurance that this intelligence gathering role did not seem to require NSA to violate its foreign policy principles. The CIA is interested in alternatives to communism in the underdeveloped world, even if the only alternative is a moderate left. "Witty" staff members were told that, in working with the CIA, they would be providing the information that would help get a more enlightened foreign policy presented in high Washington circles.

376

Thus an NSA international staffer, while on an overseas assignment cleared with the CIA, visited student groups in Spain that were militantly protesting against the Franco dictatorship's suppression of free student unions. This NSA-er, a genuine supporter of the Spanish students, joined a protest meeting and was roughed up by the Spanish police, jailed, and held incommunicado for three days. The same staff member had previously gone to the Dominican Republic shortly after the American intervention there. He brought back a report on his contacts with university students who had participated in the civil war on the side of the constitutionalists.

To NSA the CIA relationship was a comfortable one. It meant lots of money, a sense of doing important work, overseas travel, and, perhaps most important of all, very little feeling of having sold out one's political convictions. The CIA relationship meant something more personal, too. For years elected (and appointed) officials and staffers of NSA have been getting draft deferments. The deferment given for having an "occupation vital to the national interest" would last as long as the member worked for NSA; it was then possible for him to go on to graduate school and receive a student deferment again.

The standard practice was for the president of NSA to send a letter to the local draft board stating that the staff member's services were required in an area that affected the national interest. Always included was a Cold War paragraph about how NSA was combatting communism. In what had become almost a form letter, the NSA president, asking for an occupational deferment for his staff member, wrote: "NSA is largely responsible for the creation and maintenance of the International Student Conference, which was established in 1950 to combat the communist-controlled International Union of Students. More than 50 countries—almost every state with a national union this side of the Iron Curtain—now participate in the International Student Conference."

During 1965-66 the war in Vietnam escalated, and a panic developed in the NSA office when staff members suddenly found themselves re-classified I-A under the impact of the increased draft quotas. Sherburne took the matter of the office staff's status to the Selective Service Presidential Review Board, and also went directly to General Hershey. No NSA staff members, "witty" or "non-witty," were drafted. The Agency looks after its own.

IV. THE PRESIDENT REBELS

When the CIA made Phil Sherburne "witty" it got more than it bargained for. Sherburne has a tough-minded, gritty independence that soon led him into conflict with those who were paying NSA's bills. Not only did Sherburne break the CIA cult of secrecy, but he also began fighting for NSA autonomy in international programming.

Sherburne's initial attitude to the Agency was friendly but reserved. He was willing to take CIA money for NSA projects and to consult with the Agency on matters of common interest, but he was the first NSA president who demanded full control of international programs. Previously, international programs—scholarships, student exchanges, conferences and the like—had all been worked out by NSA staff members and their CIA contacts.

But the Agency resisted Sherburne's reforms and applied pressure through their foundations. For the first time in years there were delays in the granting of funds from foundations such as FYSA and San Jacinto. But Sherburne fought back. He refused to release the funds (paid for by FYSA) that would have paid the dues of NSA to the International Student Conference. Finally, most of the money was released to NSA and a *modus vivendi* of sorts was reached. Eventually, Sherburne told Wood, Covert Action Division No. Five became so upset at its errant child, it considered severing ties with the NSA altogether.

Sherburne's effort at establishing some independence left its financial marks. Previously, any year-end operating deficits were quickly picked up by FYSA or some other foundation. In 1962-63 NSA had blundered into a disastrous financial venture with a book cooperative and wound up with approximately a $70,000 deficit. After NSA made a pro forma appeal to alumni that brought in practically nil, several key CIA foundations and individuals came through with the cash and the debt was miraculously retired in two years. The cost of NSA's move from Philadelphia and at least $35,000 worth of furniture and renovations for the new Washington offices were just as easily absorbed. Among others, FYSA put up $15,000 and two men, Thomas Millbank and George Baker, put up $10,000 and $5,000 respectively. Millbank and Baker are both well-established New York corporate executives and fellow members of the Racquet and Tennis Club. These two men once joined with FYSA in making an $18,000 grant to the ISC for a Latin American student conference. When asked about his interest in NSA and international student politics by this magazine, Mr. Millbank, once an assistant naval attache in Cairo, said: "It is none of your business," and promptly hung up the phone.

At the end of a year of relative independence, Sherburne was faced with approximately a $35,000 deficit that no one picked up. The deficit has remained, despite staff cutbacks. The "firm" doesn't like rebellious children.

By the end of a year of wrangling with the CIA, Sherburne was convinced that it was impossible to maintain an independent but friendly relationship. In an attempt to find new funds that would free NSA of its financial dependence on the CIA, Sherburne went to see Vice President Humphrey in July of 1966. Humphrey had

378

been friendly to NSA, had addressed its National Congress in 1965, and had met Sherburne once previously.

Sherburne told the Vice President about the CIA ties and NSA's financial predicament. Humphrey promised to help NSA get other, independent sources of financing.

Humphrey kept his word and wrote to Roger Blough, Chairman of the Board of U.S. Steel, David Rockefeller of the Chase Manhattan Bank, and Henry Ford, among others. In a typical letter (the one to Roger Blough), Humphrey said:

> I have been very much impressed by the work done over the past few years by the National Student Association. I know the officers of the Association well.
>
> As with other such groups the NSA has had a continuing financial difficulty.
>
> I believe that this organization should be able to find support in the private sector, which will enable it to continue its work independently and in the best spirit of private initiative.

Despite Humphrey's entreaties, only a few hundred dollars rolled in from "the private sector." Thus NSA went to its 1966 Congress, the deficit still on its back, and its relationship with the CIA badly damaged. Sherburne continued to resist Wood's suggestions that he make a thoughtful public statement about the relationship and have it openly discussed as a public issue.

Yet what Sherburne had accomplished was considerable. For the first time in years, new national officers were elected without apparent commitments to the CIA relationship. The only problems bothering the new officers were their knowledge of the past, and the large financial deficit—for it appeared that Humphrey's friends in the "private sector" were not as interested in supporting NSA as a rather un-public part of the "public sector" had been.

V. EPITAPH TO A CAPER

Phil Sherburne finally went to Harvard Law School after his year of escapades with the CIA. He was in Cambridge when Ramparts called him early last month to get his reaction to Mike Wood's revelations. In a subdued voice he said: "I think I would prefer not to say anything until I have had a chance to look at the article pretty carefully. . . . I think the article should be discussed by the current administration of NSA, and that anything that I would say would be resolved in discussions with them."

Then he was asked, "Did you sign a national security oath?" Sherburne paused a few moments and said, "At this point I don't want to make any comment."

Sherburne was under enormous pressure, not only out of a remaining loyalty to NSA, but also from the CIA. That "enlightened"   379 organization had viciously turned on him for talking to Wood, and was trying hard to intimidate him into publicly denying Wood's story.

Sometime in the middle of January, the NSA officers and Sherburne heard that Michael Wood had passed his information along to Ramparts. Sherburne called Wood and asked him to fly to Boston, where Sherburne pleaded with him for an entire day to retract his story. Then they both flew to Washington for four more days of intense and harrowing discussion with two of the current NSA national officers, an NSA staff member, and a former national affairs vice president.

In the Washington conversations with Wood, the officers of NSA desperately tried to dissuade him from giving the information to this magazine. Wood refused and instead urged the officers to affirm the story publicly, which would be the only way of salvaging NSA's dignity. The officers would not commit themselves.

There followed two weeks of hectic caucusing and emergency meetings at NSA headquarters. NSA officers visited a number of well-known NSA alumni, including Douglass Cater of the White House staff, to ask their advice. At least one of the officers also went straight to the Agency. The current CIA operative whom he contacted is a former NSA president. He is officially employed by the Agency for International Development in Washington.

At one point the officers assembled the staff, told them of the impending story and flatly denied that it was true. They suggested that Wood was making up the story to revenge NSA for having lost his job as director of development. Finally, another staff meeting was called and it was admitted that the story was true.

Meanwhile, on the west coast, two Ramparts editors were talking to Ed Schwartz, NSA's current national affairs vice president. Schwartz, talkative and quick-witted, had been the leader of the liberal caucus in NSA. He was in Berkeley, working as a behind-the-scenes student political advisor-negotiator during the University of California campus crisis precipitated by the firing of Clark Kerr.

It seems a direct, ironic result of Cold War politics that Schwartz had to drop his liberal Berkeley activities and cross the Bay to discuss his organization's cooperation with the CIA. Through a long and tiring discussion that lasted most of one night, Schwartz did not deny NSA's relationship to the CIA. Instead, he pleaded that great damage would be done to the good works of NSA by the revelation of this relationship. As the discussion ended, he muttered something about losing his draft deferment.

A few days later, in Washington, D.C., a Ramparts editor had an almost identical conversation with two other NSA officers. The talk began in NSA's national headquarters, a four-story colonial-style brick building in a quiet residential section. On the desk in President Gene Groves' office there was an autographed picture of Hubert 380

Humphrey. With Groves was Rick Stearns, the international affairs vice president.

During the conversation neither Stearns nor Groves denied NSA's CIA connections in the past but stated that "all of our current financing comes from legitimate sources which observe the normal legitimate reporting procedures." And yet NSA's current budget records grants totaling $56,673.30 from FYSA. Stearns was asked, "Will you flatly say you have had no contact with the CIA during your time in office?" He shook his head.

Stearns and Groves pleaded that disclosure of the CIA relationship would be disastrous for NSA. It would put them in an awful political predicament. If they publicly admitted past CIA connections, it would tarnish NSA's image badly at home and abroad, and hurt its chances of receiving grants from other government agencies. NSA staff members also feared CIA retaliation, especially the loss of their draft deferments.

Having kept quiet about the CIA since their election, the officers now went into action to minimize the effects of the forthcoming disclosures. NSA President Gene Groves flew off to Leiden, Holland for an emergency Summit meeting with the leaders of the ISC. Groves came back convinced that NSA must make some acknowledgment of the CIA relationship—but at the urging of his colleagues in Leiden there would be as few details as possible admitted.

If older Americans have been a little put off by the style of the draft card burners or the Mario Savios, there has always been somewhat of a consensus about the good works of the young men and women of the United States National Student Association. The NSA seemed to mix the idealism of the community organizers, the FSM activists and the Peace Corps with the buttoned-down practicality of young junior executives.

The quality which rank and file NSA-ers have cherished most about themselves is independence, especially independence from government controls. It was this quality that was supposed to distinguish their organization from national unions of students in the communist world. The quality for the most part was genuine, for the rank and file never knew of the CIA connection.

There were many arguments put forward by NSA's current officers as to why the CIA-NSA relationship should be kept secret, and many similar arguments desperately made to Mike Wood as to why he should not have given the information to anyone. Of all the reasons given —by Stearns and Groves to Ramparts' editor in Washington, and by others who pleaded with Wood—the most pathetic, which appeared again and again, was this: exposing the story would not only hurt NSA, it would hurt the CIA. Covert Action Division No. Five, after all, was not in the business of assassinating Latin American leftists, it was supporting liberal groups like NSA, groups with international

381

programs in the best tradition of cultural exchanges between countries. NSA might be anti-communist, but certainly no one could ever argue that its anti-communism was more militant or more narrow-minded than that of the average American. Rather, it was less so. Thus the exposure of the NSA-CIA tie would deeply hurt the enlightened, liberal, internationalist wing of the CIA. Conservative congressmen, such as L. Mendell Rivers of the House Armed Services Committee, would cut off Agency funds for these purposes, and the hardliners in CIA's "core" would be proven right in their contentions that the Agency shouldn't give large sums of money to support liberal students, no matter what intelligence it was getting in return.

The twisted sickness of this Orwellian argument should speak for itself. Yet it is extraordinary, and frightening, that it could be so easily made by the talented young liberals at the head of NSA. One would think the idea of "an enlightened wing of the CIA" would be an obvious contradiction in terms. But the idea's acceptance and support by a generation of student leaders indicates how deeply the corruption of means for ends has become ingrained in our society, and how much dishonesty is tolerated in the name of the Cold War.

PART THREE

Human Rights

EIGHT

POVERTY AND INEQUALITY

Estimates of the number of poor in the United States range from a low of 20 million to a high of 40 million persons. The great variation in these estimates is due almost entirely to the definitions that are used to classify an individual or family above or below the poverty line. This reflects the relative nature of poverty (or luxury for that matter) and illustrates an important point: persons classified as poor are done so relative to other persons and to a standard of living that is currently accepted as statistically normal. Failure to understand this basic fact often leads to efforts to show how America's "poor" earn more than the vast majority of persons in the rest of the world, or that the "poor" have television sets, cars and other "luxuries." Such comparisons do not make use of some basic understandings concerning the *social* definitions of poverty.

In 1963 the Department of Health, Education and Welfare found that there were some 34½ million persons in the United States with incomes below a minimum budget; the budget is based upon a minimum level of living for families and persons living alone (Miller, 1966). About 5 million of the poor lived alone, and 30 million, one-half of these being children, lived in families. Many of those families below the poverty line are not there because of unemployment. About one-half of the families are headed by males who had full-time employment at some point throughout the year. This indicates that many of the poverty families are working families with poor incomes and with little chance to improve their incomes because of limited skills and education.

A substantial number of the poor are the older persons in our society. There are approximately 8,000,000 Americans over sixty-five with incomes below the poverty line, with about 1,500,000 of these who live alone on an income of less than $500 a year. The plight of the aged poor is described in the following account of a man on a pension. 385

Mr. MacIntosh depended on hard-boiled eggs because his hotel room has no refrigerator and he can't afford to eat out. He is trying to live on his $50-a-month Social Security check. Room rent is $38.50 a month, which provides a room with clean linen every two weeks and clean towels every day. The remainder goes for food and chewing tobacco. Every week friends on the same floor buy him two dozen eggs, seven small cans of V-8 juice, two cans of Spam, a carton of dry cereal (because the box says, "Minimum daily requirement of vitamins") and his tobacco. He boils his eggs at once and eats them morning and evening. He stretches a can of Spam for three days or so. It has cost him violent nausea to discover that hard-boiled eggs and opened Spam need refrigeration in warm weather. (Bagdikian, 1966)

The impact of poverty upon the poor has been well documented. The sense of despair, alienation and hopelessness combine to produce limited aspirations and a sense of powerlessness among the young. It is in the *adaptations* to poverty that these conditions are maintained and transmitted intergenerationally. Poverty does breed poverty! Other adaptations to poverty which have become part of the life style of the poor are often responded to as if they were the causes of the problems of the poor. Claude Brown (1965) in his personal account of growing up in Harlem illustrates how the role of the "hustler" is simply one of many deviant occupations providing the outward symbols of success that is available to ghetto youth. Similarly, Gertrude Samuels' (1959) description of New York youth gangs reveals how gangs function to provide that sense of security and personal worth that they cannot obtain in socially acceptable ways.

Yet we must be careful not to place too great an emphasis upon the psychological impact of poverty which leads to self-defeating personal and cultural patterns. For to do so would turn our attention away from the more basic causes of poverty which are to be found in existing social institutions in American society. Moreover, an over emphasis upon the pathological aspects of poverty leads us to neglect the stable patterns of social organization that are to be found in ghettos and low-income areas. In seeking out such existing strengths we may come to understand that there are many viable patterns of social life in American society in addition to the dominant middle-class patterns. In other words, the poor should not have to be required to be "totally transformed" in order to enjoy a decent standard of living and equal access to the rights guaranteed to all citizens.

Many of the issues raised here have been brought into very sharp focus within the context of the civil rights movement. Black men have been given legal equality as many of the unequal-treatment laws have been declared unconstitutional and new legislation has provided guarantees of equality in education and voting. Yet while there have been great strides toward legal equality, the Negro has been denied the

386

economic and political power which is necessary for social equality. It is hardly likely that Negroes derive any great satisfaction from knowing that racist explanations for his inferiority have been replaced by economic and political ones.

The papers in this section deal with many of these questions. The emphasis, however, is clearly upon the facts of inequality and injustice that are associated with poverty. The articles will attempt to present the scope of the problem as it is found in the North as well as the South. They will also illustrate the nature of the disagreements concerning the causes of poverty, its consequences, and the programs needed to help eradicate it.

The South has been the traditional setting in which the Negroes' quest for equality has taken place. The civil rights movement as an organizational weapon had its greatest impact with the early boycotts and sit-ins. The nationally televised accounts of beating, police dogs, gas, and cattle prods as the southern communities' response to the awakened Negro was sufficient to raise a national clamor for much of the civil rights legislation currently in effect. The article by Peter Weiss describes a voter registration project in Mississippi. It reveals the difficulty in voter registration of poor Negroes and whites after the years of subordination (for the Negro) that have left them apathetic or fearful, with little knowledge of their rights as citizens.

The white northerner's support of the civil rights movement *in the South* was often accompanied by a smug complacency that the North was civilized and aware of human decency and the law of the land. The response of the white northerners to the civil rights movement was seen in Cicero, Illinois, and Milwaukee, Wisconsin, as Negroes sought to move into white working-class neighborhoods; it was seen in the support received by George Wallace in Democratic primaries in Wisconsin and Indiana; it was seen in the repeal of an open housing law by the voters of California. As the civil rights movement attempted to deal with problems in the North, the moral superiority of the white northerner over the white southerner vanished. The comforting belief that racist America was only found in the South was shattered.

The article by Robert Coles describes the special problems experienced by the white northerner regarding the civil rights movement. The author suggests that the northerner may be more sensitive to the demands of the Negro, and he attempts to link the problems of the poor Negro in achieving full equality with the more general problem of poverty and insecurity in American society. Unsure of his own economic and social status, and feeling his own opportunities for middle-class status restricted by technological change, the working-class white is both envious and resentful of the attention being given to the Negro at a time when no one seems concerned with his own plight.

Much of the difficulty in dealing with poverty among various sub- 387 groups in American society resides in the inability of existing social institutions to adapt to the patterns of life in the disadvantaged groups. Residents of urban ghettos are limited in their contacts with legal and welfare institutions to the policeman and social worker who come into their area but are not from their area. There is often little opportunity for the ghetto resident to make legal and welfare services more adaptable to his needs. The low-status client without power has great difficulty in influencing the professionals who come into the ghetto to serve him. The article by Truman Moore deals with the plight of the 2,000,000 migrants who move about the country harvesting crops. For not only are the migrants without the power needed to influence state and federal agencies, but they are also transients who do not remain in an area long enough to be eligible to use existing services or to make agencies feel obligated to provide such services.

Moore indicates the failure of existing agencies at the state and national levels in providing minimum wage protection, decent housing, health services, and schooling for children. The economic interests of the corporate farms that employ migrants are clearly of greater importance to those who make legislation than are the interests of the migrant. The vulnerability of an unprotected economically-disadvantaged group is probably found in more extreme form among migrants than among urban poor who at least have the *potential* for group power through their more stable residence patterns.

The question raised earlier in this introduction regarding whether one chooses to emphasize the barriers to full equality that reside within the disadvantaged group, or to emphasize the barriers that exist in the institutional structure which fails to adapt to the needs of the poor is illustrated most clearly in the articles by Daniel Moynihan and Laura Carper. The Moynihan paper deals with the controversial Department of Labor report entitled *The Negro Family: The Case for National Action* written by Daniel P. Moynihan with the assistance of Paul Barton and Ellen Broderich (the report is most often referred to as the "Moynihan Report"). The essential argument of the Moynihan Report was that the government efforts to lift the legal barriers in the area of discrimination would not lead to full equality for the Negro. Moynihan reasoned that the history of slavery and subordination had such a marked impact upon the Negro social structure (particularly the family) that many Negroes would be unable to take advantage of the new opportunities that were made available to them. As it was stated in the Report: "at the heart of the deterioration of the fabric of Negro society is the deterioration of the Negro family." Moynihan used this argument to urge the establishment of a national family policy designed to enhance "the stability and resources of the Negro American family."

Controversy in government circles, the civil rights movement, the press, and among academic social scientists followed this report. Many of the reactions to the report have been collected in a single volume by Rainwater and Yancey (1967).

Moynihan's article in this chapter restates the position of the Department of Labor Report and then proceeds to re-examine the controversy surrounding the report. What emerges is an interpretation of the reasons for the criticism from within the government bureaucracy, segments of the civil rights movement, and the "liberal left."

As a political document, then, the Moynihan Report attempted to encourage a particular national policy. The controversy over the objectives of the Report is less pronounced than the controversy over the Report's emphasis upon the pathology of the ghetto and the breakdown of the Negro family. The article by Laura Carper questions the Moynihan Report's central arguments and suggests that the Report is more ideology than science. Contrary to Moynihan, she chooses to emphasize the defective features of American society that have failed to provide full equality for the Negro. In effect, Carper believes that white America is the social problem, not the Negro family.

As the legal barriers to equality have been steadily eliminated, progress toward social equality has been hampered by an occupational structure that is incapable of providing the poorly educated with a decent income. The combination of rising expectations and limited real opportunities has increased the discontent in the Negro community. The summer of 1967 saw riots in over thirty cities in the United States, almost all in the predominantly Negro low-income areas of the city. This was an increase over the eighteen riots in 1966 and two riots in 1965. Some have chosen to view these riots as expressions of lawlessness by criminal elements and youthful gangs. Such interpretations have led to quick responses at the federal and state level for anti-riot bills, riot control training for law enforcement agencies, and the hot pursuit of militant Negroes charged with "stirring up" the Negro community. Others have chosen to view the riots as uprisings or rebellions, and direct expressions of the discontent among Negroes. Those holding such views have pointed out that participants in the riot activities are the better educated upwardly mobile Negroes, and not the aimless criminal elements in the community.

The final article in this chapter, by Bayard Rustin, discusses the riots that took place in Watts in August of 1966, and the McCone Report, written by a select committee of citizens charged with investigating the causes of the Watts riots and the steps that should be taken to prevent future riots. The author's reactions to the McCone Report is reminiscent of some of the criticisms of the Moynihan Report, and serves to illustrate again that there are important differences concerning the viability of existing social institutions for solving some societal problems. He contends, first of all, that Watts was a rebellion and not a riot, citing as evidence the particular pattern of the looting and destruction. 389

The solutions offered in the McCone Report for dealing with the conditions of life in the Negro ghetto are those which produce the least disruption of existing social institutions. Improving the quality of education and increasing the motivation of young Negroes are solutions that Rustin views as least disruptive. The McCone Report, however, provides few answers for dealing with existing rates of unemployment, and with de facto segregation in schools and housing. Without more far-reaching solutions, Rustin contends, the deprivations of the Negro may continue to find expression in violence.

REFERENCES AND ADDITIONAL READING

Ben H. Bagdikian, "Ed MacIntosh: Man on a Pension," in H. P. Miller, ed., *Poverty, American Style*, Belmont, California: Wadsworth Publishing Co., 1966.

Claude Brown, *Manchild in the Promised Land*, New York: Macmillan, 1965.

Louis A. Ferman, Joyce L. Kornbluh, and Alan Haber (eds.), *Poverty in America*, Ann Arbor: Univ. of Michigan Press, 1965.

Michael Harrington, *The Other America*, Baltimore, Maryland: Penguin Books, 1962.

Herman P. Miller, "Facts about Poverty, Revised," in H. P. Miller, ed., *Poverty, American Style,* Belmont, California: Wadsworth Publishing Co., 1966.

The Negro Family: The Case for National Action, (Moynihan Report), Washington D. C.: U. S. Government Printing Office, March, 1965.

Lee Rainwater and William L. Yancey, *The Moynihan Report and The Politics of Controversy,* Cambridge, Mass.: M. I. T. Press, 1967.

Gertrude Samuels, "Why 'The Assassins' Can't Be 'Punks,'" *New York Times Magazine,* August 16, 1959, 13 ff.

Peter Weiss

Nightmare in Mississippi

In Mississippi this summer, against the background of the jack-booted terror of official and unofficial reprisals, one could not avoid being startled by the success of the Summer Project, an educational and voter registration program sponsored by the Council of Federated Organizations (COFO), and by the enthusiasm and concentration of the young civil rights volunteers working on it. It has split Mississippi wide open and revealed to the nation a social order so rotten and corrupt that it defies comprehension. The student volunteers who came here from middle-class Northern homes early in the summer are already veterans, as hardened to their battle as any soldiers can be, and the likelihood of frightening them away has all but disappeared from the mind of white Mississippi.

The war on racism is a serious one, and these student volunteers have moved constantly in the shadow of violence and death. But the words *"freedom now"* burn in their stomachs, and they have learned to live with their fear and perpetual concern about safety. In doing so, they have implicated all of us and revealed that had we thought of the Negroes as people we would have been implicated long ago.

Such courage born of purpose is still hard for us to believe. In Jackson, I met a tall, soft spoken, tow-headed Stanford University student who had just been bombed out of the Freedom House in McComb and was recuperating from his injuries. His ear drums had been split, and he had a mild concussion and cuts from glass. He was frightened and at first spoke little (the night before he had awakened screaming in a thunderstorm).

Reprinted by permission of the author and publisher from *The Progressive*, September 1964, pp. 19–22 (The Progressive Magazine, Madison, Wisconsin). Peter Weiss, a psychologist, is director of the county mental hospital project at The Psychiatric Institute of The University of Wisconsin. 391

He told me that he was on his way back to McComb to help with repairs and to continue canvassing for voters. He explained that McComb was a new project (in the dangerous southwest hill country where the Klan has been very active) and that in time the community would become more tolerant. "When they see that we mean to stay, then they will slow up." He said this less than twenty-four hours after he had left McComb and after a wild chase given by carloads of armed whites up the highway to Jackson.

Again, in a church in Meridian, I witnessed a similar display of courage in a young Negro member of the Congress of Racial Equality (CORE), who was planning to go back into Neshoba County, a death trap for civil rights workers and the place where the bodies of the three young volunteers, James Chaney, Andrew Goodman, and Michael Schwerner, who "disappeared" in June, have now been found: "I will go up there on Saturday with Lilly (a local volunteer) and stay the weekend. Then on Monday we'll move in." They would go there armed only with pencils and sample registration forms and a deep commitment to non-violence. "God help this boy," a woman jumped up and cried, "He's going there for you and me and I haven't the nerve to go with him. He is going up there to die for us just like James Chaney and the other boys did."

Courage such as this is already legendary in the young movement of nearly 1,000 volunteers recruited by the Student Nonviolent Coordinating Committee, CORE, and other civil rights groups. There is hardly an SNCC staff member around who hasn't been clubbed, beaten, and drenched in his own blood by the police and the young hoods that serve them. What is overpowering about the Summer Project and the COFO organization is not the program, which is startling enough, but the people in it. They reveal the passion that is their youth, and they are armed with the ideals of Christ and Patrick Henry and Jefferson and Gandhi. The righteous raging at the "student volunteers—the beatniks, the wild-eyed, left-wing nuts, the unshaven and unwashed trash . . ." reveals a desperate need among the local racists to create as much social distance from the students as possible, lest they see too closely the broken promise of their own youth.

Thus, while the white citizens don their sheets and tough sheriffs go around looking for someone to "knock the fire out of," COFO has been nailing its message to the door of Mississippi. Biracial teams have fanned out daily into Negro neighborhoods to plead with the people there to "go down and register." They have met the apathy and resignation that constitute the Mississippi Negro, and they have read the fear that has been laminated into his hide.

This work is discouraging, often infuriating, but mostly humbling, because on those fearful black faces is the searing truth about tyranny: 392

So many of the subjects have collapsed before the king and are cooperating in their own beheading. "And when," puzzled one Project youth, "they ask us, 'What you goin' to do when they knock my head off, if I go down to register?' what can we say?" There is nothing that can be said, but the Negroes do see these COFO workers risking life and limb, and they, like the whites, cannot help but be impressed. The Summer Project is moving a civilization just by its very existence, and the paltry returns from the voter registrar's office do not detract from this.

If Negroes cannot be placed on the regular voting rolls then COFO will register them on its own freedom rolls. Thousands are being registered this way, allowing them to vote, even if it is not legally recognized. What cannot be done within the racist political structure of Mississippi is being done outside it and within the structure of the new Freedom Democratic Party (FDP). This political move has an uncertain future, but as an experiment in political education it is already a stunning success.

At a church meeting one night the breathtaking truth of this was revealed when a young Negro COFO worker staged a mock election. With the sensitivity and finesse of King Solomon, he drew shy and retiring people into a contrived precinct meeting and assigned them participating roles. He explained to them the meaning of an election and what a precinct was and told them of the coming county FDP convention. He explained how they were to elect a chairman for their group.

Then they tried it. A woman nominated herself for chairman. Someone had to second the nomination, and the COFO worker showed them how. They did it over again. They squirmed, and someone stood up and complained that she didn't know what was going on. The worker patiently went through the process again, and you could feel the tension and the impatience and the frustration they felt in their ignorance, in front of white people who were in the audience.

These Mississippians were enacting fundamental democratic roles which the caste system has forced them to ignore. They were full grown adults who were participating, for the first time in their restricted lives, in the basic process of a free society. The light of pride in their faces showed through their embarrassment. Moreover, as they became absorbed in this process, they began to function on a new level. They elected a committee to seek the use of the courthouse for the FDP county convention. The subjects of the king had declared themselves citizens of the republic.

It is difficult for a subjugated people to take advantage of such an opportunity merely by having it presented to them. The cost of political interest is so high for the Mississippi Negro, and he has learned so well to avoid it, that in many ways citizenship is not yet 393 a psychological possibility. Education, here, is thus not the mere acquisition of skills but also the process of developing an awareness of self and learning the significance of one's own life experience.

The crushing effects of the caste system in Mississippi, as elsewhere, have left the Negro so severely depressed that he walks in a haze, never knowing who he is and never understanding the real meaning of his trying life. His education has been a preparation for an adjustment to a white world that does not recognize him. It is an education —what there is of it—for a life of servitude, turning him away from opportunities that are not his and teaching him not to see them. COFO is trying to supplement this thin diet with its voter registration drive, with its encompassing mass-meeting workshops, and, more pointedly, in the establishment of freedom schools with their enriched curriculum of Negro history and contemporary problems.

These schools have functioned all over Mississippi this summer in the hope of providing Negro teenagers with some awareness of their past and its significance in terms of their present life situation. The courses in Negro history, English language expression, art, and other subjects are all designed to encourage these young people to get into the freedom movement and to work for social change. The social renewal of a broken people is a complex task and cannot rest solely on voting. In Mississippi an enlightened local leadership needs to be developed, and people need to be awakened.

For similar reasons community centers are being established not only as a resource for recreational, educational, and welfare activities but also to validate the need for people to express varied aims in life so that they can advance beyond working and bearing slave children. As with the freedom schools, these centers also provide Negro children with an opportunity to see the possibilities of an integrated world and to learn something about people beyond their being dangerous or safe. The program is undermining some of the intense hatreds that otherwise would inevitably consume these children when they grow up, and is providing them with some new meanings about freedom that have to do with an inner sense of belonging to this world.

All this has sparked the summer outrage of white Mississippi, and the violence of its reprisals has left its people spent of their energy for cooperation. White Mississippi lacks heart and courage, but most of all it lacks perspective. It is choking on its own lynch-rope and pulling the knot tighter and tighter around its own neck. Here are the *white* victims of the caste system and its racial mythology that keeps them entranced in a state of dysphoric excitement.

The COFO program in its entirety is open to white Mississippi on a segregated basis if need be. The response from whites has been less than enthusiastic, and the rare inquiries that are made make COFO news. On July 5 in Ruleville a local white man came into the community center to inquire of the activities there and to engage in a critical but friendly dialogue (the beginning of enlightenment). He was arrested. More often such dialogues with COFO take place from the window of a pick-up truck, guns blazing with buckshot to scatter "them nigger lovers."

This is Mississippi's ruthless reply to the COFO peace corps. To date this state has an almost unblemished record of lawlessness, which is supported by the limitless patience of the Justice Department. The present restraint of official violence against the COFO volunteers, however encouraging, is misleading, because local Negroes suffer the reprisals. Bombings, burnings, whippings, shootings, and job dismissals continue to occur with unfaltering regularity. It is appalling to find them appearing in the Northern press as "scattered incidents."

To the Negroes of Mississippi and to the COFO staff, these incidents are a nightmare reality that faces them daily. I cannot recall an instant of my visit in Mississippi that I was not afraid. And you don't have to be a civil rights worker or a COFO supporter to get hurt. If you are black, you might still get killed in a night's "funnin'," and be dumped half and half into the river.

Those who catch the worst of this terror are the Negro civil rights workers, especially those from SNCC who are frequently faced with being beaten by the police in the jailhouse while "resisting arrest." Somehow personal dignity and nonviolence combine to terrorize the authorities and sorely try their already limited capacity for restraint. The record is full of incidents such as this one:

On June 8, five SNCC workers were passing through Columbus, Mississippi, enroute to a staff meeting in Atlanta. They were stopped by the state highway patrol. (Governor Paul Johnson relies heavily on the patrol in his struggle with the county sheriffs for the control of Mississippi.) The patrolman walked up to the car and said, "You goddamn niggers want to change our way of life." (This to my knowledge is not a traffic problem.) He then ordered the five out of the car and searched it, finding Summer Project literature and Fanny Lou Hamer (a Negro candidate for Congress sponsored by COFO) campaign posters. He called the sheriff of Lowndes County and searched each one of the five young men. The sheriff arrived and took four of them, handcuffed, to jail. The fifth went with the highway patrolman to a spot about a mile from where the car had been stopped. The affidavit dated June 8, 1964, and signed by James Black, age seventeen, reads:

"He told me to get out of the car; I refused to get out. So he pulled me out. He started hitting me with his fists, and after about twenty blows he got out his blackjack and hit me one time with it and knocked me down. Then he told me to get back in the car. While he was beating me, he asked if any white folks had ever treated me bad; I told him yes, and he hit me again. He asked me again had   395 any white folks in Mississippi treated me bad, and I told him no. At that point he helped me back into the car.

"Then he took me to the county jail (Lowndes) where I was questioned by the sheriff. The sheriff asked for my driver's license and to take everything out of my pockets . . . I had a friend's I.D. card in my pocket and he asked me if my friend was a Negro or a nigger. I told him a Negro. The same highway patrolman was there, and took out his blackjack and again asked if my friend was a Negro or a nigger. He started to hit me with the blackjack, and I told him my friend was a nigger."

The four other young men were questioned similarly throughout the night and finally charged with reckless driving. James Black was tried, convicted, and fined the following day in court. All were released, after paying $4 each for their night in jail.

This is a common occurrence in Mississippi. In it the cry of "Jew! Jew! Jew!" echoes from the Nazi past amid the thumping cadence of blows to the head and groin, only to be thinly covered up by the barest formalities of the judicial process. And people say, as they once said, "We didn't know."

In its deep commitment to the safety of its volunteers, COFO has covered Mississippi with a security network that would make the Central Intelligence Agency envious. COFO knows when you are out and where you will be and the route you will take and your time of arrival. If at any point in this process a person "disappears," the Federal Bureau of Investigation is notified, and search parties set out immediately. Sometimes the sheriffs get coy and start shifting a prisoner around in order to foul up the search. In one case the sheriff's wife took the jailhouse telephone off the hook to prevent the location of a COFO prisoner. None of this has so far succeeded.

The three young students who "disappeared" in June were not "sacrificed," as was cynically claimed, to bring Federal pressure on Mississippi. Federal attention to the constitutional rights of the student volunteers is what it was from the start—minimal. In a statement to the press July 10 in Jackson, J. Edgar Hoover stated that the FBI does not "and will not give protection to the civil rights workers . . ." And, indeed, the FBI has not. The opening of a permanent FBI office in Jackson and the addition of fifty agents in Mississippi were not very encouraging to the civil rights workers, since the existing contingent of one hundred did not allow itself to become overworked.

The catalogue of official and unofficial violations of Federal law, especially interference with voter registration work in the first month of the Summer Project, covers eight legal-size pages of single spaced type. The FBI arrested three people in one case. It has been called repeatedly for help and has done little if anything. When Chaney, Goodman, and Schwerner disappeared on June 21, the FBI was notified at 10 p.m. It entered the case twenty hours later, after sixteen calls had been made to the FBI and to the Justice Department. This is usual. It leaves the impression that the FBI, this summer in Mississippi, had been little more than a telephone answering service for the Federal government.

The FBI is not entirely to blame, however. Its activity depends on Federal policy. Hoover's televised gesture of solidarity with Mississippi officials was a *tour de force*. They looked as if they were getting married as they upheld the rule of law and order and exchanged vows of allegiance to it. But of the flagrant and systematic violations of the state and Federal constitutions in the denial of due process to U.S. citizens in Mississippi, nothing was said.

The problem of anarchy—the lawlessness of Mississippi law enforcement—seems to have been referred once again to the local authorities. The Federal government is not enforcing the law. Its failure to do so has encouraged local indifference to it in Mississippi. If a Federal judge, hearing a voter registration case in the name of the United States, refers from the bench to the applicants as "a bunch of niggers who are acting like a bunch of chimpanzees," then what can be expected from a county sheriff in the discharge of his duties?

Here is the alarming frustration of the civil rights movement. You fight your way past the bottles and curses to the courthouse. Then you fight your way through a gauntlet of billy clubs up the steps to the registrar's office only to find that you cannot exercise your birthright as an American citizen. Then you fight your way back home again through the same mob. That night your house is bombed, and you stumble dazed and deaf into the front yard where a policeman stands spitting on your grass, trying to conceal his glee. Mississippi, 1964, is Germany, 1936, revisited.

Robert Coles, M.D.

The White Northerner
PRIDE AND PREJUDICE

For decades a steady trek of Negroes from the South has increasingly confronted the North and the Far West with race as a local, volatile problem. But it is only recently that the North has had to face its white problem, in contrast with that of a Negro one. The historical and political pressures working to liberate the Negro have not been confined to the South. Negroes everywhere in America are awakened. No longer do they stay quietly in their bulging neighborhoods, out of everyone's way but their own. Aroused Negroes in the South have had a clear direction to travel; there were—and even with new laws still are—voting polls to enter, restaurants to frequent, schools to claim as theirs too. Negroes in the North have the complaints of the poor. Even to lodge those complaints, and certainly to make sure that those complaints lead to changes, requires not a struggle for political rights supposedly every American's by birth, but a direct assault on our complicated, ambiguous, not always equitable social and economic system.

Yet Negroes are not the only ones struggling for money and position in America. In the South they alone have been excluded from a wide variety of places and privileges, though there—and elsewhere, too—there are millions whose white skin gives them precious little more than the Negro has. In the North such people have not even had what is any Southern white man's consolation. "I'm poor," a fiercely segregationist farmer in Alabama once told me, "but I'm proud of my race, and I'd as soon die as see it contaminated." I can still see his home, a cabin really, "two rooms and a pathway." His farm is small, and so is his income. His children are getting neither the quality of food nor the education this country can well afford for everyone. His wife is a tired but determined woman. Once, a few years ago, they left their farm for the city; but there, too, they saw hardship, and a kind of impersonal living they could not bear. "So we're back here. At least we can grow some food; and the niggers aren't creeping in on us." As long as Negroes were niggers, and niggers tightly kept in their place, the farmer was at least that much a man of property. Millions of blacks were his.

I spent a number of years in the South, trying to comprehend the feelings and attitudes of hard-pressed yeomen like that man, as well as those of Negroes no longer willing to sacrifice their lives and livelihood to the emotional security of such white people. More recently I have returned North, now to learn how Negro and white children manage under the desegregation, by busing, of so-called de facto segregated schools. Beyond that, however, I am trying to gain some sense of how their parents, and others like them, feel, not only about particular problems, like the value of the neighborhood school or of busing, but the more general matter of their racial feelings, their attitudes toward whites or Negroes, as the case may be.

In the case of the Negro families I have come to know, there is, frankly, little new to be heard and seen. All over the country, Negroes are waging a similar struggle, and though the Southern sector of the battle is harder, the Northern one is no easy game either. What Negroes in both sections share is their long-subdued rage, their finally acknowledged, freely proclaimed frustration. They are on the march, everywhere on the march. This is their historical moment, and it is a binding one for large numbers of them in every region. "Every time we make a gain, anywhere, I feel it," a twelve-year-old boy from Boston told me recently. Two years ago I heard words like that almost daily from Negro children in Georgia and Louisiana. Even Negroes who still feel terribly cornered, or beyond that, dazed by years of hunger, uselessness, and joblessness, manage to say what I heard from one old man in a Northern ghetto, "It's all over for me, and a lot of others; but one thing makes me glad, every time I think of it: it'll never be as bad again for us. It just can't be. That's what civil rights means to me."

For whites the civil rights movement has supplied no such reassurance, confidence, or new comradery. Quite the contrary, in both North and South there has been characteristic but quite differently expressed confusion. The white Southerner has found himself less and less that; more and more he is a Southerner, with all the special problems every region has, who happens to be white. "The nigras, we have to get them to cooperate with us, like everybody else, if we're going to get more industry here and keep the city booming." Once a convinced segregationist, in two years he had yielded one way of thinking for another, 399 and seemed not the slightest troubled or hurt for the exchange. In point of fact he was only confused by his own resiliency, by an occasional twinge of memory: "How can you say 'never' one year, then 'yes' the next? It wasn't just that we obeyed the law. I guess it was really because we finally got it through our heads that it was in our own best interests to do it."

In the North and the West the issues have not been so clear-cut. It is not a matter of swinging into line with the rest of the nation so that its laws are obeyed, its customs followed. The rest of the nation *is* the North and the West, and from Harlem to Watts, uneasy, suspicious millions present themselves, newly aroused and aware, to the rest of us. What they demand cannot be satisfied by compliant voting registrars or the fresh hospitality of restaurant owners. Very poor, and long scorned, they are asking for money and power. In so doing they stand alongside others, who have their own reasons to feel shaky, apprehensive, and needy.

Recently in Boston some Negro children were bused into neighborhood schools serving white children, not by the city, but upon the initiative of individual Negro parents. Indignation spread through the area. The people became aroused, and in unusually large numbers registered their sentiments at the polls. There is uneasy talk about a so-called "white backlash vote," waiting in the wings to single out and dismiss summarily anyone trying to give special favor to Negroes, most particularly by encouraging them to live and go to school in white neighborhoods.

Here are the words of a thirty-year-old woman, the mother of six. She is Irish. Her husband works in the repair shop of a utility company. They live in a mixed Irish and Italian neighborhood in Boston where homes vary, some modestly comfortable and well kept, others in obvious decline. Her young children now have several Negro children in classes with them, and though the two young boys and the little girl do not seem to mind, their mother is quite upset.

> Why do they do it? I don't understand them at all. They have their own people, just as we do, but suddenly they're not happy together. They want to go here and there, and send their children everywhere. All you hear these days is news about them. You'd think Negroes were the only people in America that have a tough time. What about the rest of us? Who comes here asking us how we get by, or how we feel about what *we* had to go through?
>
> My father couldn't find a job either, not a steady one, anyway. I remember my mother telling us how he walked and walked, practically begging for work. She said he would almost offer to work for nothing rather than sit around home doing nothing. The day he applied for relief was the saddest day of his life. It broke him. He hated himself ever after. He was always against taking charity, and

400

to have to ask for it was too much for him. When the war came he got steady work again, but my mother said he never was the same. He was always nervous, worried about losing his job, like in the thirties. He became very tight with his money; he even hoarded pennies in a bank. . . . He was plain scared for the rest of his life. To be truthful, I think he died happy. It was like a relief for him. He was very religious. He went to Mass every morning. He died with a smile on his face, and our mother, she said he had been waiting for that day for a long time. He used to say to her that whether it was heaven or hell the good Lord chose for him, it would be better than the worry and the trying to make ends meet of this world.

That's the trouble, though, with Negroes. They're a superstitious lot. They have no real faith, except all that shouting they do, and they only know how to ask, not go out and earn. I know they had it bad here, but so did we all, my father and everyone else practically, except for the rich. And it's the rich, out there in the suburbs, who keep on telling us what we should do. They preach at us to take them here and let them live there, and act this way to them, and that, and so on until you get sick hearing it all. Suddenly they're so kind, the suburban crowd. They stepped all over us, and kept us out of everything, the Yankees and the college people over there at Harvard did. Now they're so good. They're all excited and worried about people, but only the Negroes get their sympathy, only them. Talking about prejudice, that's what we face, prejudice against *us*. I think we should start suing in all the courts, and marching down those streets, like the Negroes. Maybe if we had done that a long time ago, we wouldn't still be so up against it now.

In nearly every interview, I hear in one way or another certain common themes: we all have it rough, the Negro being only one of many in that regard; what the Negro calls the civil rights movement in the North is in fact an attempt to crowd out others, from schools, jobs, and opportunities of one sort or another; no one is entitled to anything "special," not when others have to sit by and get little or nothing; somehow the Negro is rather devious and clever, as well as half-witted and immoral, because he has managed to exact both sympathy and consistent help from people—the well born, the well educated—who have ignored the misery of other people for decades.

In the South the Negro can be lived with by the white man, at very close quarters, too. Even the poorest white man can keep company with Negroes, share jokes and general talk with them. The white child can play with Negroes; while growing up he can eat from their hands; as an adult he works with them every day. The Negro's general position helps the white man feel on sure ground, above the uncertain social and economic waters that threaten most of us at one time or another with feelings of worthlessness or insecurity. In the particular situations of daily life, however, a given Negro can be depended upon, 401 even though, as a race, they can be excluded or looked down upon.

In the North, for many white people the Negro, perhaps pitied in the past, is now a constant topic of news and conversation. He comes upon a scene where his presence is new. He comes upon a region with its own history of religious prejudices and racial antagonisms, at times cloaked perhaps, but no less grim and brutal than those the South has lived with so defiantly. While he has aroused the concern, even the devotion, of many, to others his arrival and the widespread solicitous response to his arrival only confirm a number of existing fears and suspicions. Life is indeed harshly competitive; another group is coming, and at a time when jobs may be scarce. Moreover, those who favor the Negro and want so earnestly to aid him are the very people who care not at all about the poor (and white) people who have been living in the cities and towns of the North for generations, or at the least before the Negro came to stake out his claim.

A young lawyer—an aspiring politician—in an extremely poor section of Boston spoke as follows:

> This is a slum . . . but it's a white slum, so no one cares about it. There's no glamour in white slums, only Negro ones. The suburban housewives and the Ivy League students, they've gone poor-crazy, but only for the colored poor. They've been pushing us around all these years before the Negroes started coming up from the South, and now they have someone to do it for them. They do a good job, too, the Negroes do. They act as if they own the world, just like their friends out there in the suburbs. It's contagious, you see. The ministers and the students come on Saturdays to tutor the Negro kids and take them to the park. They drive right by this neighborhood without blinking an eye. We have overcrowded schools. We have rotten buildings that should have been torn down years ago. We have lousy parks that aren't half the size they should be. A lot of the people here have jobs that barely give them enough to get by; and the others, I'll tell you, are on relief or unemployment checks or veterans' checks, or something. We have our delinquents and our dropouts—the works. Who cares, though? Who has ever cared about this neighborhood? If we have some alcoholics here, or people in the rackets, that shows how no good we are. If the Negroes pull a switchblade on you and rob and steal you to the poorhouse, that means they've been persecuted, and we have to overlook everything they do and treat them as if they were God's gift to America. It's a two-faced business, if you ask me, and it's becoming worse now that they talk about juggling our kids around so that they're "integrated." That's when you'll get the explosion here, when they try to move our kids across the city, or bring all those little darkies here. We've got enough, enough of our own troubles.

His voice was strong, sometimes strident. At first I didn't know whether he meant everything he said, or whether he confused me with 402 an audience in one of his campaigns. After a few months he relaxed some with me, and though he never really changed his views, he did become more philosophical:

> I don't hate Negroes. A lot of people in this district do, but it's a recent thing, and I agree that the real trouble isn't the Negroes, though they sure manage to irritate people. I think a lot of this trouble between Negroes and whites will last until the whole setup in the cities changes. Probably it's true the race issue has made it better in the long run for the poor white man as well as the Negro. You can't sit here and see others demanding jobs without . . . wondering why you don't have one either, or if you do, why it pays so little, or gives you nothing if you're fired or retire.
>
> I don't think we'll get through it without trouble, though. My people really are sensitive to this thing now, and unless the whole country changes, and we get as good a break as every Negro seems to think he's entitled to, then there will be resentment, and you'll have what they call the "backlash."
>
> I admit a politician is in a bind over this. He can try to lead his people, try to make them realize what's really going on; or he can ride with the tide, and make sure he wins every time; or he can really work the race thing up into something, so that he makes it worse, but wins bigger and bigger each time. I think most politicians are in the business of winning elections, so they're not going to do the first. But most of them aren't rabble-rousers, either. They just want to get elected; so it's the second choice they take, just like everyone else does, usually. They try to steer a middle ground, not too much one way or the other.

Through talks with people like him I think I have a fairly good sense of how cheated and nervous many white people in Northern cities feel; cheated out of the most ordinary comforts and opportunities, and nervous about losing what they do have in the one war, the poverty program, which is being waged on their home territory.

In many ways the poor and lower-middle-class white people in our Northern cities are going through a kind of experience precisely opposite to that of Negroes. At this time in history Negroes are being affirmed, while these white people feel increasingly deserted and alone. The Negro's excuse for his present condition is everywhere made known: it was not his fault, but ours. We carried him here by force and kept him in bondage for three centuries. He was not simply poor, but singled out for a very particular form of exploitation. The brutality and exclusion that he experienced have now become our national problem, because the price once exacted for the Negro's compliance lives on in the illiteracy and fearfulness we encouraged in him for so long.

In the Northern cities a white man who is poor has no such past   403 history to justify his condition. He is poor, or uneasily not-poor, but no more than that. Even our expanding middle class has its definite limitations. Those limitations are now shifting in character, but by no means disappearing. While it is true that educational opportunity and the money to secure it are much more available than ever before, we are also facing severe technological problems, as machines replace not only men but other machines. It no longer is fatuous to predict an astonishing productivity harnessed to a relative handful of workers.

Meanwhile, we stubbornly cling to an ethic that prefers to reward only those who can find work, while consigning all the rest to charity, and not a little contempt. Through no fault of their own, not improvidence, not ignorance, not apathy, many people simply cannot obtain the regular work they want and need. Others may have reasonably secure jobs, but they are jobs that hardly pay enough to guarantee much security against an inflationary economy. "Who can keep up with it?" a mother who was barely able to make ends meet said to me in an aside during a talk we were having on racial tensions in Boston.

> The Negroes say they have nothing. Well, we have more, that's true. My husband works, and it's a steady job. We're Irish, so in this city there's no trouble there, I'll have to admit. But it's as hard as can be just living and staying even with everything. My husband has to work extra just to pay the bills. We don't have any money put away. The kids always want something. All the television does is tell you to buy, buy, buy. A few years ago my husband didn't have a job, and we didn't know where our next penny was coming from. Now he has the job all right, but it's even harder in a way. Any raise he gets means nothing compared to what happens to the cost of everything. You have to be an owner of something or a professional man to have an easy mind today.

On another occasion I found her directly envious of Negroes. They were on the bottom, and at least had somewhere to go. She didn't think there was much room "up there" for her family. Moreover, the Negro gets an enormous amount of sympathy and attention, and from people and institutions she feels possessive about. As a matter of fact, in one of the bluntest conversations I have had, she said to me:

> They may be poorer than a lot of white people, but not by very much. Anyway, what they don't get in money they more than gain in popularity these days. The papers have suddenly decided that the Negro is teacher's pet. Whatever he does good is wonderful, and we should clap. But if he does anything bad, it's our fault. I can't read the papers anymore when they talk about the race thing. I'm sick of their editorials. All of a sudden they start giving us a lecture every day on how bad we are. They never used to care about anything, the Negro or anything else. Now they're so worried. And the 404

same goes with the Church. I'm as devout a Catholic as you'll find around. My brother is a priest, and I do more than go to Church once a week. But I just can't take what some of our priests are saying these days. They're talking as if we did something wrong for being white. I don't understand it at all. Priests never used to talk about the Negro when I was a child. Now they talk to my kids about them all the time. I thought the Church is supposed to stand for religion, and eternal things. They shouldn't get themselves into every little fight that comes along. The same goes with the schools. I went to school here in Boston, and nobody was talking about Negroes and busing us around. The Negroes were there in Roxbury and we were here.

Everybody can't live with you, can they? Everybody likes his own. But now even the school people tell us we have to have our kids with this kind and that kind of person, or else they will be hurt, or something. Now how am I supposed to believe everything all these people say? They weren't talking that way a few years ago. The governor wasn't either. Nor the mayor. They're all just like cattle stampeding to sound like one another. The same with those people out in the suburbs. Suddenly they're interested in the Negro. They worked and worked to get away from him, of course, and get away from us, too. That's why they moved so far, instead of staying here, where they *can* do something, if they mean so well. But no. They moved and now they're all ready to come back—but only to drive a few Negro kids out for a Sunday picnic. Who has to live with all this, and pay for it in taxes and everything? Whose kids are pushed around? And who gets called "prejudiced" and all the other sneery words? I've had enough of it. It's hypocrisy, right down the line. And we're the ones who get it; the final buck gets passed to us.

Can we really solve the racial problem in this country without coming to terms with the worries and fears of this woman? There is an unnerving thread of truth that runs through her remarks. She and her husband do indeed have cause to worry about jobs and money, even as Negroes do. It is quite true that our newspapers, our churches, our political leaders have changed recently. Because they have learned new social concerns does not mean that the people who for years followed their leadership can fall in line easily, particularly when there are no concrete, persuasive reasons for them to do so. Moreover, the rivalrous and envious observations made by the people I have quoted ring sadly and ironically true: there is a certain snobbish and faddish "interest" in Negroes from people who would not think of concerning themselves with those many white families who share with Negroes slums, poor schools, uncertain employment—the parade of crippling events that make up what "we" so easily call "poverty" or "cultural disadvantages."

Many of the poor white people I know in both the South and the North envy not merely the attention the Negro is now getting, or even 405 the help he so badly needs. While most of them are not aware of it—I have met a few who are exquisitely aware of it—they also envy the Negro his success at finding a viable protest movement. *They* need one too; though likely as not they don't know they do, or don't know how to achieve it. They are stymied at the complexity of our social and economic system; it is easier to hate than to think up a way to make more and better-paying jobs available, or make a minimum income for every family the law, and ethical principle, of the land.

If such people are frustrated, then so are we—the comfortable, well-educated, and secure. This nation has yet to settle upon a policy that would aim to distribute fairly our astonishing wealth, including all its surpluses and potential productive capacities. Do we need wars and military spending to keep our economy going, or can it be harnessed to provide the schools, houses, hospitals, and just plain food and clothing that millions of us need and don't have? Until such problems are solved, the bitterness and resentment we see between whites and Negroes will continue, and perhaps increase—a reminder of man's devious ability to conceal his real struggles, and thus remain at their mercy.

Truman Moore

Slaves for Rent
THE SHAME OF AMERICAN FARMING

Each year when the harvest begins, thousands of buses haul thousands of crews to fields across America as millions of migrant workers hit the road. They ride in flatbed trucks or old condemned school buses patched together for just one more season. They go by car: Hudson bombers with engines knocking, laying a smoke screen of oil; pre-war Fords packed with bags, bundles, pots and pans, children crying. They go in pickups made into mobile tents—a home for the season. They ride the rods of the "friendly" Southern Pacific.

They come from farms in the Black Belt, from closed mines in the mountains of Kentucky and West Virginia, from wherever men are desperate for work. They come by whatever means they can find. These are the migrants—the gasoline gypsies, the rubber tramps— crossing and recrossing America, scouring the countryside in a land where the season never ends. There's always a harvest somewhere.

From Florida to Oregon the fruit tramp pursues the orchards. From Texas to Michigan the berry migrants work from field to field. Two million men, women, and children invade every state of the Union to pick fruit, to chop cotton, to scrap beans, to top onions, to bunch carrots, to pull corn, to fill their hampers with the richest harvest earth ever yielded to man.

The circus and the college house parties leave Florida after Easter. The first week of April, the major league clubs wind up their spring training and go home to play ball. The snowbirds start back to the cities of the north with their tans. And the migrants form crews and follow the sun. Sometimes a single bus will carry a crew; sometimes they pass in ragged convoys as the migrant battalions rumble out of Florida and up the Eastern seaboard.

The invasion hits South Carolina in May, North Carolina and Virginia by June. By late summer they have passed through Pennsylvania into New Jersey and New York State. Some go into Delaware and Maryland, others to Long Island, and a few on to Maine. By October the upstate crops are in, and the migrant tide flows back to the southern tip of Florida.

The workers find little to do in November. It is after a lean Thanksgiving and a bleak Christmas that hands are needed again in the fields and groves of the winter gardens.

From Texas the pattern is much the same. This is the home base of the largest migrant group. The exodus begins in early spring. Storekeepers close down for the season as the little towns depopulate. Everyone who can bend and stoop starts for the great corporate farms of the North and the West. From the steaming valleys of Arizona and California to the great Pacific Northwest comes a string of harvests. There is no crop in the world that can't be grown on the Pacific coast, and relatively few that aren't. Where once was a vast desert wasteland, there are now the rich irrigated valleys, principally the Imperial and the San Joaquin. In steady sun and several inches of water, crop after crop is produced with factorylike precision.

Into all these fields, through state after state, the migrants cut a footpath across America. But in spite of their mobility, the migrants are shut off in their own world. Migrant America is a network of side roads, of farm towns and labor camps and riverbanks, of fields and packing sheds. The famous cities are not New York, Boston, and San Francisco, but the capitals of the agricultural empire of the big growers: Homestead and Belle Glade in Florida; Stockton in California; Riverhead on Long Island; and Benton Harbor in Michigan. For the migrants, no roadside motel or tavern offers a neon welcome. The host community sees them not as a potential payroll but as a blight to the community's health and a threat to the relief rolls. Businessmen, dance bands, and tourists making their way across the country find many services and comforts at their disposal. The migrant can hope at most for good weather, a grassy bank, and a filling station that will permit him to use the rest room.

There is always blood on the harvest moon. No one knows how many luckless migrants have died on their way to gather the harvest. Only a few of the more spectacular crashes make their way to America's breakfast table by way of the local newspaper. A few years ago, a half-ton truck left Texas for the sugar-beet fields of Wyoming. In it were fifty-four migrant workers. As the truck neared the outskirts of Agate, Colorado, the driver suddenly hit the brakes. The truck spun 408 around and turned over twice, scattering workers across the highway. There was one death, a baby who died in a Denver hospital shortly after the accident. In October, 1963, not three miles from the spot in Fayetteville, North Carolina, where a truckload of migrants died in 1957, a truck carrying twenty-four bean-pickers turned over when a tire blew out, strewing its human cargo like a handful of oats. Fortunately no one was killed.

When the ICC was considering regulation of migrant transportation in 1957, a representative of the "jolly" Green Giant Company complained that restriction of travel between 8 P.M. and 6 A.M. was a hardship on the workers and the employers. "It has been our experience," said the company's man, "that these trucks can complete the trip from Texas to Wisconsin in from fifty to sixty hours with stops only for meals, gasoline, and general stretching."

A vegetable packer said that it was practically impossible to attach seats securely and still use the trucks to haul produce. He did not advance this as an argument against carrying workers in produce trucks, but against using seats. Many crew leaders use trucks because of the extra money they can make hauling the crops from the fields to the processors. Jon Misner, the director of migrant labor at Stokely-Van Camp in Indianapolis, said he knew crew leaders who made $15,000 hauling vegetables—in an eight-week season.

THE CREW LEADER

Little Jim was a good crew leader. His bus, the Bean-picker Special, was a bit run-down, and the tires were slick. But the driver was sober and careful. The camps that Little Jim found for his crew while they were on the road were not always what he had promised them, but he could hardly help that. He couldn't demand that the grower put the crew up in the Holiday Inn.

The crew went hungry before the crop came in, but Little Jim never told them he was going to feed them. If he lent them money to buy food before they got work, he charged them no more than the going rates, just as a bank would. And he had not been greedy about the money he took from their pay. A dime out of every dollar was his take. He stuck to it. And he charged a couple of dollars for each job he got them, and there were no more than three or four a season. While they were on the road, he got them to "help on the gas." When he deducted for social security, he always turned it in, as he was supposed to. If there was a big shopping center near the camp, he'd stop on the way back from the field so that the crew could do their shopping there instead of in the little stores near the camps, which always overcharged.

His wife thought he was stupid to pass up any chance to make money. So he sold moonshine. There was a good profit in that. "I   409 keep a little around because some of them—they won't work without it. If you don't have it for them, they'll go out and get it." He bought from a bootlegger for $1.00 a quart and sold it in the fields at $.50 a shot. A heavy drinker gets thirsty in the field. But Little Jim had to be careful not to give a bad drinker too much. He had one worker named Leroy Small, who was a mean drunk. He pulled out a home-made machete one afternoon and almost took a man's head off. After that Little Jim was more careful.

He was usually on the road with the crew four to five months a year. During that time, he was the crew's official representative. It is the crew leader, not the grower or the corporate farm, who is recognized as the employer. Whether or not a migrant ends the season money ahead or money behind often depends on his crew leader.

There are more than 8,000 crew leaders in the migrant streams. They come in all shades of reliability and honesty. Good or bad, the crew leaders perform a service that is invaluable to the grower. A grower in Maryland can make a simple agreement with a crew leader to supply a given number of migrants at a specified date and for a stipulated price. The farmer, theoretically, can rest assured that his labor problems will be taken care of. In practice, however, he can never rest easy until he sees the crew pull into camp. An unscrupulous crew leader can shift his crew to a higher-paying farm at the last minute. The first farmer can easily lose his crop for lack of a harvest crew. Because both the migrants and the farmers depend on the crew leader, he is in a good position to take advantage of both. Hamilton Daniels was like that.

You had to admire Hamp. He was a thorough professional, with imagination and style. He usually honored his obligations to deliver the promised number of workers at the agreed price and time. Sometimes he came a little late though, because he would stop for a few small unscheduled jobs on the way. Born in New Orleans, a diplomat and a shrewd judge of character, Hamp had a quick intelligence far beyond what five years in school had given him. He knew how to get along with the white growers. He just played Uncle Tom.

Sometimes when the grower was around, Hamp would ride herd on the crew just to let the man know he was in charge. But the growers knew that. They depended on Hamp to bring the migrants in on time and get them out when the work was done. Neither Hamp nor the grower would profit by argument. His dealings with the growers were usually cordial; a balance of power existed that neither cared to test.

Hamp could make a flat price for harvesting and then cut the crew's pay as low as they'd stand for. On a flat-fee basis, Hamp's profit was the difference between what the grower paid him and what he paid the crew. Hamp didn't care for this because if the weather was too hot or it rained too much, he might even lose money. 410

If there was a good crop and a high market, the grower might agree to an hourly rate so the crew would take their time and not damage the crop. But the usual agreement was a piece rate. This fixed the cost for Hamp and the grower. The rates were usually set up on a sliding scale. When the crop was good, the rates were lower, and as the fields thinned out, the rates went up. When the fields thinned out, the crew didn't want to work them because it was hard to make any money. So the grower would pay a bonus at the end of the harvest to all the workers who stayed on the job. But it really wasn't a bonus. He just withheld some of their money until the job was finished.

Whatever arrangement was made, the crew seldom knew the details. If the grower gave his camp rent free as part of the payment, Hamp might still charge the crew rent. He was careful never to cut into a man's pay directly, except to take out social security, which he never turned in to the government.

His dealings with the migrant crew were complex. For one thing, he lived closely with them. His impression on them was important. If a crew leader looked too prosperous, the crew might think he was crooked. If he looked too poor, they might doubt he was a good crew leader. Hamp managed to look just right. He has a pair of brown pants and a red shirt that were ragged to the point of fascination. He was the raggedest man they'd ever seen. Close examination of this costume would have revealed patches sewn over whole cloth, but the effect was one of arresting poverty. To contrast with this, Hamp drove a Cadillac. His garments attested to his humility and his car to his success.

In picking a crew, Hamp seemed to work with little thought or design. Actually, he was very careful about whom he took on. He wouldn't take boys who looked as if they were trying to save money for college in the fall. They held too tight to their money, and most of them would leave the crew to go back to school before the season was over.

Hamp looked for the quirk, the twist: the reason this man or that woman wanted to work the crops. He preferred workers, either male or female, in the first stages of alcoholism. Some crew leaders wouldn't hire the drinkers, but Hamp knew better. You had to wait until a man was hooked. Then he didn't seem to know or care what you took out of his pay as long as he had enough to eat and drink. He might get mad, but he didn't leave. Of course, a hardened wino was worthless. He couldn't stand the pace. It isn't easy to bend over in the broiling sun all day.

Hamp kept a good supply of white mule and had places along the way where he could get it. There was good money in it. He also kept little white packets of dope. There was the real money. But sometimes it was hard to get. You really had to push it all the time to make 411 it pay, and it was too bad if the government men caught you with junk.

He kept his hand in the ordinary rackets, too. He got a 15 percent cut from the grocery store near the camp. If the storekeeper refused to pay a kickback, Hamp would take the crew to another store. The crew seldom had cash, so Hamp worked out a credit system with the storekeeper. The crew members were never shown an itemized bill; they just paid what Hamp said they owed. Hamp also had beer and cigarettes in his trailer at double the store prices. For a $.50 bottle of wine, he charged $1.45. None of the crew stocked up on these things because they never had cash. With one thing and another, Hamp cleared about $20,000 in a fair year.

On the West Coast, the crew leader is called a labor contractor. (The term "crew leader" refers to the foreman.) Nick Peronni is a labor contractor in California. He has a fleet of buses and trucks that haul workers in and out of the San Joaquin Valley. He operates out of the "slave market," a big fenced-in lot that serves as a hiring hall, just up the street from the Farm Placement Service in the skid-row section. Before a man can work, he has to get a white card from the placement office. If he changes crews, he can't get another card. Even if the grower cheats him, he can't quit without losing his white card.

Most of the growers that Nick works for prefer to contract workers from elsewhere. Part of Nick's job is to keep too many of the local workers from getting on the crews. Nick does not travel with the crews. He loads the buses out of the slave market each day for short hauls into the valley. He also handles the paper work. No one is sure how much Nick makes, but estimates run high. As he himself puts it, "If this thing blows up tomorrow, I'll go fishing. It'll be a long time before I get cold and hungry."

These men are representative of crew leaders. For the most part their lives are hard to trace. Some use colorful pseudonyms like Sugar Daddy, Cool Breeze, or Meatball. A few years ago, the New York *Times* reported that only half of the crew leaders coming into New York State gave addresses that could be located. Tax investigators in Oregon found that relatively few crew leaders had ever filed personal income taxes, and almost none had filed social security returns for the crew, even though all presumably deducted from their migrants' paychecks.

In 1964, Congress passed a crew-leader registration law designed to put dishonest crew leaders out of business. The crews have just started to move now. It remains to be seen what effect the new law will have.

THE TAR-PAPER CURTAIN

Across America there are tens of thousands of migrant camps. They are in the valleys and in the fields, on the edges of cities and towns. Some are half deserted. Some are behind barbed wire and even pa- 412 trolled by armed guards. Migrant camps are within commuting distance of Times Square, under the vapor trails of Cape Kennedy, and surrounded by missile sites in the Southwest. They have names like Tin Top, Tin Town, Black Cat Row, Cardboard City, Mexico City, The Bottoms, Osceola (for whites), Okeechobee (for blacks), and Griffings Path.

Negroes from the Black Belt are dismayed by camps they find up North. Okies and Arkies who migrate today find camps much like those the Joads found in *The Grapes of Wrath*. You can drive from New York to California and never see a migrant camp. You have to know where to look. To borrow a popular analogy, a tar-paper curtain separates the migrants from the rest of America.

Let us look at a typical migrant camp which we will call Shacktown. Shacktown is owned by a corporate farm, one of whose foremen is in charge of the camp. "But mostly," he says, "we just turn it over to the people to run for themselves." In other words, no one collects garbage or maintains the camp in any way. The camp is built on the grower's sprawling farm. It cannot be reached without trespassing, and several signs along the road remind the visitor of this fact. Even finding it is difficult. Local residents are suspicious of outsiders who are interested in migrant camps. Requests for directions are met with icy stares.

Shacktown was built about fifteen years ago. No repairs to speak of have been made since then. Most of the screen doors are gone. The floors sag. The roofs leak. The Johnsons, a Shacktown family, have a six-month-old baby and five older children. "When it rains," says Mr. Johnson, "it leaks on our bed and all over the room. At night when it rains, we have to stand up with the baby so he don't get wet and catch pneumonia."

All the rooms in Shacktown are the same size, eight foot by sixteen. When the Johnsons moved in, they found they needed much more space. They sawed through the wall, a single thickness of one by six inch pine, and made a door to the next cabin, which was not occupied. The exterior walls are unpainted and uninsulated. They keep out neither wind nor rain, sight nor sound. Cracks between the boards are big enough to put your hand through. There is no privacy, and the Johnsons, like most Shacktown families, have learned to live without it. The windows are simple cutouts with a hatch propped open from the bottom. Some have a piece of clothlike screening tacked on.

The only touch of the twentieth century in the Johnsons' cabin is a drop cord that hangs down from the ceiling. It burns a single light bulb, plays a small worn radio, and when it works, an ancient television set that Mr. Johnson bought for ten dollars, through which they get their only glimpse of urban, affluent America.

Although there are trees nearby, the camp is built on a barren red-clay hill, baked by a blazing summer sun. There are four barrack-type 413 frame buildings, divided into single rooms. Behind the barracks are two privies, both four-seaters. The door to the women's privy is missing, but the rank growth of weeds serves as a screen. There are no lights, and no one uses the toilets after dark. The Johnsons use a slop jar at night. It is kept in the kitchen and used for garbage, too.

There is virtually no hope of keeping out the flies that swarm around the privies. But one county health inspector found an unusual way of getting the growers interested in the problem. The inspector would drop by the grower's house just before lunch and ask to see the migrant camp. When they came to the privy, the inspector would throw a handful of flour over the seats, which invariably swarmed with flies. On the way back to the house, the inspector would manage to get invited to stay for lunch. At the table he would remark, "Well, I'm sure glad you asked us all to lunch." And there crawling around on the fried chicken would be a floured, white-backed privy fly.

During most of the season in Shacktown there will be several full- or part-time whores. The going price is $3.00. Prostitution thrives behind open doors. Venereal diseases are sometimes epidemic. In a crew near Morehead City, North Carolina, one woman infected ten men in the course of three days. Six out of eight crews working in the area had at least one syphilitic.

There are two hasps on the Johnson's door in Shacktown. One is for the family to use. The other is for the grower. If the rent is not paid, the family will find when they return from the field that they have been locked out. Some growers provide cabins free. Some charge according to the number of able-bodied workers. Rents run from as low as $10 a month to as high as $50.

The Johnsons, like most Shacktown families, do their own cooking. But grocery shopping is not easy. There is a small cracker-barrel store near the camp, run by the grower, but the prices are a third higher than in town. "We got a ten-cent raise," says Mr. Johnson, "and everything in the store went up a quarter. He wants us to buy from him or move out. It don't seem right."

Cooking is done on a small, open-flame, unvented kerosene stove which serves as a heater in the cold weather. Fires and explosions are not uncommon. The cabins are not wired for electric heaters; natural gas is not available. Bottled gas requires a deposit and an installation fee. Asked if the tenants didn't suffer from the cold nights, the camp manager replied, "Oh, heat's no problem. You'd be surprised how hot it gets in one of them little cabins with so many people."

For most of the year the cabins are miserably hot. Refrigeration is nonexistent, and perishable foods seldom find their way to the migrant's table. The baby's milk sours quickly, and he is given warm Coke. Good water is always scarce in Shacktown. Between the long buildings there is a single cold-water tap. The faucet leaks, and there is no drainage. A small pond has developed, and the faucet is reached 414 by a footbridge made of boards propped on rocks. This is the only water in camp.

Just keeping clean is a struggle. Water must be carried in from the spigot, heated over the kerosene stove, and poured into the washtub. In the evening, the oldest children are sent out with buckets to stand in line for water. Sometimes when the line is too long, the Johnsons buy their water from a water dealer, who sells it by the bucket. "We get some of our water down the road about five miles," says Mrs. Johnson. "Sometimes I get so tired I'd just like to go in and die. We have to boil the water and then take it to the tub to wash the clothes. We have to boil water for washing dishes. The last camp we was in had a shower, but you had to stand in line for it half a day, especially in the summer."

The problem of getting water is widespread in migrant camps. A Mexican national in California said his camp was without water for a week. "The contractor said the pump broke. There was a small rusty pipe that brought enough water for washing the hands and the face, but we could not wash our clothes, and we could not take a bath for a week. The inspector ordered the pump be fixed right away. Now the water from the baths is pumped out of a big hole, and it flows through a ditch between the bunkhouse and the tents. When it makes warm weather it smells very bad. To me it looks like the contractor is not afraid of the inspector."

When several children in a Swansboro, North Carolina, camp became ill, a young minister named Jack Mansfield had the water in the camp tested. It was found to be contaminated. He reported this to the county health office, but they said nothing could be done since the camp had been condemned long ago.

Shacktown is a typical migrant camp, but not all migrants live like the Johnsons. Some find better camps. Many will find no room at all, and unfortunate workers will live, as they say in Arkansas, "under the stars." Three hundred migrants were stranded in Nevada when the harvest was late. "For days they had barely enough food to keep alive," the Associated Press reported. "They camped—men, women and children—in the open, along ditch banks, without protection from winter rains and freezing night temperatures. They took their drinking water from irrigation ditches used by cattle. Many children were sick. And they had no work."

Migrant workers are often housed with the livestock. A Mexican worker in California described his camp this way: "We are installed in a barn which was used for the cows when we moved in. You have to slide the big door and go in and out the same as the cows. The cracks between the wall planks are about eight or ten centimeters wide. This makes very good ventilation for the cattle, but it allows the wind to pass over our bunks at night. It is strong and fresh cow smell. It is necessary to use much Flit, and the smell of this chemical also   415 affronts us. The Americans are very inventive. Perhaps someday they will invent a Flit with perfume. . . . The only person who comes to see us is the Father, who hears confessions and says the Rosary. We are ashamed to have him come on account of the smell of the cows and the stink of the Flit."

As bad as conditions are in the camps where the migrants live, they are worse in the fields where they work. A Florida Health Department report noted that at times crews refused to harvest fields because of the human waste deposited there by an earlier crew.

Americans are probably the most dirt-conscious people in the world. We are a bathroom-oriented society. Chains of restaurants, motels, and hotels across the country appeal to customers almost solely on the contention that their establishments are spotlessly clean. In such a society, it is not pleasant to imagine that beneath the cellophane wrapper lies a head of lettuce that has been urinated on. A storm of controversy erupted when a labor union showed a movie of field workers urinating on a row of lettuce. Growers charged that the picture was posed by union men in old clothes. Perhaps it was, but it need not have been faked.

The fields of the modern factory farm are immense. And there are no bathrooms. A Catholic priest observed that "most consumers would gag on their salad if they saw these conditions, the lack of sanitary conditions, under which these products are grown and processed."

After a tour of leading farm states, Senator Harrison Williams of New Jersey said: "In the fields . . . sanitation facilities are a rarity. Unlike other sectors of our commerce, agriculture generally does not provide migrant farm workers with field-sanitation facilities such as toilets, hand-washing facilities, and potable drinking water.

"We as consumers have good reason to be uneasy about this situation. Much of our soft food and other products are picked, and often field packed, by migratory farm workers. If we object to filth anywhere, we certainly should object to it in any part of the process that brings the food from the fields to our tables."

One grower, a woman, docked the workers an hour's pay if they left the field to go to the bathroom. The woman stayed with the crew most of the day. The men had to relieve themselves in front of her. They found this humiliating but were unwilling to lose the wage.

Antonio Velez, a field worker in the San Joaquin Valley, said he was told by the grower to drive a pickup truck into the fields which carried two chemical toilets. The grower told him to drive fast so that the toilets would slosh around and be dirty, and no one would want to use them. He was afraid the workers "would lose too much time going to the bathroom." The idea of providing field workers with toilets and clean water strikes most growers as an unnecessary refinement. Consumers who realize that diseases such as amebic dysentery, polio, and infectious hepatitis (to name only a few) can be transmitted 416 through human excreta may not be so convinced of the frivolity of field sanitation.

Dysentery is often considered a joke. It is called by a host of humorous euphemisms. The facts about dysentery are not funny. It kills 6000 Americans a year, finding its heaviest toll among children less than two years old, many of whom are the children of migrant workers.

It will be argued that to supply field workers with rest rooms would be prohibitively expensive. In 1955, as a result of newspaper articles and state investigations about the lack of bathrooms and hand-washing facilities, a group of Western lettuce growers started a voluntary program. A novel type of mobile toilet and hand-washing facility was developed and tried out in the lettuce fields and found to be successful. Forty of the units were built and put into the fields in the spring of 1956. None of the other growers picked up the idea; so when the pressure abated, the project was abandoned.

THE CHILDREN OF HARVEST

The man put down his hamper. "It sure looks like rain," he said. The skies were a bright crystal blue, with only a trace of clouds to the east. The crew kept working, but a few looked up and saw the three men coming down the row. One was the grower, who seldom came around. The other was the crew leader. The third man was a stranger. He carried a brown leather case and a clipboard. The men just nodded as they passed.

They went up and down the rows, the first two walking easily. The third man, the stranger, stumbled now and then—a city man used to flat sidewalks. They crossed the red-clay road and went into the south field. A woman looked up as they came past the stacks of empty crates. Before they were close enough to hear, she turned to the busy crew. "Sure looks like rain." Two small pickers dropped their boxes and darted through the vines and ran into the woods. Someone on the next row passed the word. "Sure looks like rain." Two more children ducked into the vines and ran.

The children hid beyond the road in a small clearing in a clump of scrub oaks. From here they could see the man leave. It was their favorite game. Hiding from the inspector was about the only thing that broke up the long hours in the field. In the camp they played hide and seek this way. When you were "it" you were the inspector. But it was more fun when there was a real inspector.

Luis at twelve was the oldest of the children. He had been to school off and on since he was six, but he was only in the fourth grade. If he ever went back he would be in the fifth grade, because he was older and bigger now. But Luis didn't want to go back. He wanted to run away. He had been around the country a lot. Last year his family went 417 to California and Oregon. One year they went to Arkansas. Once long ago—he was too young to remember when—his father took them to Florida for the winter citrus harvest. Luis was an ageless child. He had a way of taking a deep weary drag on a cigarette, and after a long while letting the smoke curve slowly out of his nostrils. His face was wrinkled, marked with a tiny network of fragile lines at the corners of his eyes and deeper lines across his forehead.

Still a child, he liked to play games. He enjoyed the gaiety at the Christmas feast. But at the end of the working day, he would stand stooped over slightly with his hands stuck flat into his back pockets. From behind he looked like a dwarf, a tiny old man whose bones had dried up and warped with age.

Billy was the youngest of the children. He was not quite five but old enough to do a little work. He didn't earn much, but it was better, his father said, than having him sit around the day-care center costing them $.75 every single day. His mother kept the money he earned in a mason jar. When fall came, he'd get a pair of shoes if there was enough money. He could start school, if there was one nearby, in new shoes.

His brother lay beside him in the clearing. John was ten. In the years that separated Billy and John, a brother and sister had died, unnamed, a day after birth. John kept them alive in his imagination. There were few playmates in the camps and fields that he ever got to know.

"I got two brothers and a sister," he would say. "And they's all in heaven but Billy there."

He called his invisible brother Fred, which is what he wanted to be called instead of John. Faith was the name he gave his sister. He saw her as soft and gentle, wearing a dress with white frills, like a china doll. He played over in his mind a single drama with endless variations. Faith was hurt or being picked up by some bully. He would come to her side to help or defend her. Then he and Faith and Fred would sit beneath a tree, and they would praise him for his bravery, and he would say it was nothing. They would have something cold to drink and maybe some candy to eat. He retreated more and more into this pleasant world. His mother had noticed his blank gaze many times and had heard him say "Faith." She thought he was going to be called to the ministry to be a gospel preacher or a faith healer.

Robert was almost as old as Luis. He had been on the season for two years. His father came from the sawmill one day and said, "They don't need me any more. They hired a machine." His father had tried to make a joke of it, but late at night Robert could hear his mother crying. He knew it wasn't a joke about the machine being hired. They sold their house and packed everything into the car. Robert left school, and now they lived in one camp after another. Sometimes they slept in the car.

418

The man with the clipboard left. The children came out of the bushes, picked up their boxes. They bent over in silence and began to pluck at the vines. These are the children of harvest. "The kids that don't count" they are sometimes called. "The here-today-gone-tomorrow kids."

Inspectors from the Department of Labor find children working illegally on 60 percent of the farms they inspect. And no one knows how many hide in the woods when it "looks like rain." No one really knows how many migrant children there are. Estimates run from 10,000 to 600,000. The most frequently used figure is 150,000. One survey in the olive groves of California showed that nearly three fourths of the workers were children. An Oregon survey showed the importance of the child's labor to the family. There the average migrant worker earned $32 a week during the weeks he worked. But his wife and children together earned $48. In some crops women and children do more than half the harvest work.

The birth of the migrant child will most likely be in a migrant shack or, at best, in the emergency room of a county hospital. His nursery is the field and his toys the things that grow there. A few camps have day-care centers. There are twenty-four such registered centers in the United States, with a total capacity of less than a thousand children.

The migrant child may never develop any idea of home. His family is never in any place long enough, and home to him is wherever he happens to be. He seldom sees a doctor. It is almost certain that he will have pinworms and diarrhea. Other common ailments untreated are contagious skin infections, acute febrile tonsillitis, asthma, iron deficiency anemia, and disabling physical handicaps. A poor diet condemns the child from the start. A report on a camp in Mathis, Texas, showed that 96 percent of the children had not drunk milk in six months. Their diet consisted mainly of cornmeal and rice. A doctor commenting in the report said there was evidence of ordinary starvation. The migrant child is prone to scurvy, rickets, and kwashiorkor—a severe protein deficiency. Some reports have put the incidence of dental abnormalities at 95 percent, and others said that bad teeth were universal.

Epidemics, like the one in the San Joaquin Valley a few years ago, take a heavy toll. Shigellosis, a form of dysentery, had been rampant in the valley for years. The infant mortality rate was extremely high. Within a short time, twenty-eight babies died of dehydration and malnutrition. The migrant child is also prey to a host of diseases now rare in the nonmigrant world: smallpox, diphtheria, and whooping cough. A medical survey in California showed that two thirds of the children under three years of age were never immunized against diphtheria, whooping cough, lockjaw, or smallpox. Two thirds of the children under eighteen had not received polio shots.

419

There have been many brave attempts to provide migrant workers with medical service, usually on a shoestring budget and through the energy of a few determined people in a community. In the little farming towns around Morehead City, North Carolina, the Reverend Jack Mansfield got together the first mobile medical clinic, a white trailer called the Rocking Horse, equipped with the rudiments of a doctor's office. The Rocking Horse—so named because it tilted back and forth when you walked around in it—was staffed by a group of local doctors who took turns going out to the migrant camps. The welfare department was persuaded to provide a social worker. The National Council of Churches provided a migrant minister.

By the light of a flickering kerosene lantern, the lines of workers waited to see the doctor. Some had unnamed miseries of the head and the chest, aches and pains that move up the back and sieze the neck in a vise. Colds, bad teeth, rheumatism, and chronic headaches could only be treated by the same white pills.

It would take a full staff of psychologists to evaluate the psychic condition of the migrant children. But even in the absence of any thorough-going study, the symptoms of frustration, bitterness, and disorganization are easy to see. A day-care center was started in the basement of an Arkansas church for migrant children. One of the most successful parts of the center was a workshop run by a young man named Alec Johnson. The shop was set up in a corner room with small windows for ventilation at the top. It was cool and pleasant on the hottest days.

Alec had assembled the usual carpentry tools and some leatherworking tools. By the end of the season, when the migrants pulled out, he had learned several things about migrant children by watching them at play. Joey Smith was a blond blue-eyed boy from Kentucky. The family had been on the road for almost ten years, which was most of Joey's life. He was two when the coal mine was closed and his father lost his job. When Joey first came to the shop, he was quiet; by the end of the second week, he was racing around the room banging the chairs with a hammer. Alec had to take the hammer away from him, and Joey sulked and refused to do anything.

Alec got Joey interested in making a leather billfold. "I got all the material together," said Alec, "and Joey started with a flurry of energy. But within an hour, he had put it aside and was toying with some pieces of lumber. I started him back on the billfold. Joey hit it a few whacks with the mallet and then looked around for something else to do. Joey wanted the billfold and had been excited about making it. But he didn't seem to be able to stay with it and finish. There were many of the kids who were like this. It seemed to be a characteristic. They start out with great enthusiasm, but as soon as they hit a snag, they toss whatever it is aside and go to something else. They haven't had any experience in building anything or in solving problems. They 420 have no confidence in themselves." Teachers, doctors, and ministers have the most contact with the migrant children. They are, understandably, not optimistic about the future.

Children have worked on farms since the first farmer had a son, and it has always been considered part of the rural way of life. But there is a difference between the farmer's boy doing his chores and the migrant child topping onions and digging potatoes. The two are blurred together in the minds of people outside agriculture. The blurring gets help from such spokesmen as North Carolina's Congressman Cooley, who enunciated the Blue Sky Doctrine: "There are no sweat shops on the farms of America," he said. "On the farms of our nation, children labor with their parents out under the blue skies."

Under the blue skies of Idaho, a twelve-year-old girl got her ponytail caught in a potato-digging machine. It ripped off her scalp, ears, eyelids, and cheeks. She died shortly afterward in a hospital. On a farm in California, a ten-year-old girl came back from the fields exhausted from a day's work. She fell asleep on a pile of burlap bags as she waited for her parents. As other workers returned from the fields, they tossed the empty bags on the stack, and the little girl was soon covered up. A two-ton truck backed across the pile and drove off. They did not find her body until the next day.

If children were mangled in steel mills, there would be a storm of public protest. But death and injury on the mechanized farms seem to pass unnoticed. Under the blue sky of the farm factory is no place for little children. Agriculture is one of the three most hazardous industries. In California alone, more than five hundred agricultural workers under the age of eighteen are seriously injured every year.

The migrants who follow the harvest are the only people in America who are desperate enough for this work to take it. Their children will be another generation of wanderers, lost to themselves and to the nation.

FACTORIES IN THE FIELD

The family farm used to be the citadel of virtue in the American rural tradition. Life was made hard by the vagaries of the weather and complicated only by the bureaucrats in Washington, who always meddled with farming. In 1900, when the population of the United States was under seventy-six million, 40 percent of the people lived on the farm. Today, only 8 percent live on farms, and more leave every year.

Today, the important farms, as units of production, are more like factories. Great cultivators and harvesting machines lumber through endless fields. Gangs of workers bring in the harvest. One cannot ride past these giant farms after the harvest is over and the crew has left without an eerie feeling of being in a land without people. A verse 421 from Isaiah rides the wind: "Woe to those who join house to house, who add field to field, until there is no more room, and you are made to dwell alone in the midst of the land."

The importance of making the distinction between the big farm and the little farm—between the homestead and the factory in the field—is essential to the story of migrant labor. To begin with, the family farmer and the migrant worker are in the same sinking boat. The family farm, while providing an income and a place to live, no longer contributes significantly to America's food production.

If the earth suddenly swallowed up a million and a half small family farms in America—nearly half the total number—food production would drop by only 5 percent. Half of our food is produced by only 9 percent of the farms. These highly mechanized, capitalized, and integrated companies use most of the seasonal labor. Only a relatively few big growers (5 percent of the total number) use more than $2000 worth of labor a year. The real giants—the top 3 percent—hire more than a third of all farm labor.

It is through the fields of the farm factories that the migrant stream flows. And these are the growers that have brought foreign farm workers to America each year. The growth of corporation farming and its effect on the traditional family farm have been watched with concern for many years. In 1923 a North Carolina land commission issued a still-urgent report: "It is quite conceivable that under capitalistic or corporation farming, greater gains might be secured than under a system of small individual holdings.

"It is quite inconceivable, however, that the . . . farmer would be as good or as efficient a citizen, that he would get as much contentment and happiness for himself and his family out of his home, or that he could develop as satisfactory a community for himself and neighbors as he could and would if he owned the house in which he lives and the farm he cultivates. The problem, then, is that of life on the farm, the development of rural communities and the building of rural civilization with which, after all, we are most concerned. . . . The late Governor Bicket said: 'the small farm owned by the man who tills it is the best plant-bed in the world in which to grow a patriot. . . .' Every consideration of progress and safety urges us to employ all wise and just measures to get our lands into the hands of many and forestall that most destructive of all monopolies—the monopoly of the soil."

The policy of the federal government has always more or less agreed with this. Nearly every administration has declared itself in favor of preserving the family farm. It is ironic that each, in turn, has brought it closer to extinction.

In 1963 the government spent $4.7 billion on surplus commodities. Most of the money went to prosperous commercial farms, with only pennies trickling down to the hard-pressed family farms. The government-support price is often more than the production costs of the big commercial farms. This means they can produce without worrying about the market since "Uncle Sucker"—as some of the farmers say—will buy what they can't sell elsewhere.

In 1961 two corporate cotton farms received government subsidies of $2 million each; thirteen great farms each received $649,753 on the average; and 332 farms received $113,657 each. By contrast, 70 percent of the cotton farms were given an average of $60.

The government has subsidized the big operators in a more important way. Until this year the commercial farms have been allowed to draw on the pools of cheap labor from other countries, principally Mexico. The presence of hundreds of thousands of foreign workers has naturally disrupted the domestic labor market, resulting in low wages and poor working conditions. The family farmer, who hires little outside help, has to value his and his family's labor at no more than the commercial farmer pays for gang labor.

The exodus from the farm is proceeding at the rate of about 800,000 people a year, although cities and towns have as little immediate need for surplus rural populations as the nation does for surplus farm production. It has been seriously proposed many times that overproduction is caused by a surplus of farmers and that we should let the natural laws of competition weed out the less successful. This way, the problem of surplus production and surplus farmers would solve itself at no expense to the taxpayers. But, as we have already seen, most of the food is produced by a relatively few big farms. And, of course, when the small farmer finally gives up and goes to the city, his land is taken over eventually by another farmer and remains in production.

As a unit, the larger family farm is not without merit. According to a 1962 government report, "Family farms [in this case those using 1.5 man-years of hired labor] are more efficient than large corporate-type farms . . . . When the management of a farm is taken away from those who supply the labor, there is a loss of incentive, diligence, skill and prudent judgment which are necessary to maintain efficiency." The report said that the advantages of the corporate farm lay primarily in superior financing and control of the market.

No farmer, of course, whether big or small, can dominate the market. But the vertically integrated farm is its own market. The perishable harvest from the field goes to the farm's own processing and canning plants and is sold canned or frozen under less urgent conditions. (In 1962, however, the government bought up $1.3 million worth of California canned apricots.) The small farmer selling perishable produce is completely at the mercy of the market, or specifically, the buyer.

Today the position of the buyer is stronger than it has ever been. In 1958, supermarket buying agencies handled 60 percent of the food dollar. At the present time, it is said that chain buyers account for 90 percent of the food dollar.

There are about 3.7 million farms in the United States. What seems 423 to be happening is this: the 312,000 first-class farms are big and getting bigger; the 1,755,000 middle-class farms are struggling, and to survive they need a more equitable marketing structure, some government aid, and an orderly farm labor force; the third-class farms, of which there are 1,641,000, are marked for certain death if agriculture continues for much longer on its present path.

The farm of the classic rural tradition, the family farm, required little outside labor. A hired man or two were enough on the bigger farm for most of the year. And at planting or harvest, neighboring farm families joined together and did the work, going from farm to farm.

THE EXPLOITATION OF LABOR

The history of migrant labor is sketchy, but its dominant themes are quite clear. The rise of the corporate farm and the growth of the migrant labor force were twin developments. It is arguable which came first. Some say the industrialized farm developed because growers saw a chance to utilize a growing pool of unemployed labor. Others say that the development of the giant farm created a demand for gangs of itinerant labor, and the migrants came to fill the need. Whichever way it happened, the result has been that the corporate farm is, and always has been, dependent on cheap, migrant labor.

The migrant force of today still bears the marks of our history. Since early America was largely rural, farm interests dominated the government. While manufacturers adjusted to the industrial revolution early, agriculture was able to win exemption from most of the social legislation passed since the turn of the century. Agriculture has grown from a society, or way of life, into a complex food industry without coming to terms with its labor force. Had the automobile industry been able to import cheap labor from underdeveloped countries, it is unlikely that the automobile union would have made much headway.

The commercial farm has never adjusted to the realities of modern labor conditions or wages. Furthermore, the modern commercial farmer holds on to the idea that he somehow has a God-given right to unlimited cheap labor. Never has he had to enter the labor market and make serious efforts to attract farm labor. If anything characterizes the history of the seasonal farm worker, it is this—fate, through famine or depression, war or revolution, has time and again delivered to the commercial grower an ample supply of cheap and docile labor.

The migrant drama caught the nation's attention in the thirties. Great dust storms swept the plains and dimmed the sun as far away as the east coast. Long lines of tenant families, the gasoline gypsies, crossed the desert into California looking for work. The dust bowl refugees were only one set of characters in the migrant epic that began long before the Joads of *The Grapes of Wrath*.

424

By 1934 the Anglo population in the labor camps reached 50 percent. As the bitter years of dust storms and depression set in, Okies and Arkies continued to stream into California in caravans of jalopies. It was ironic that after so many years of coolies and peons, American workers took over in a time of widespread unemployment. Hence wages and working conditions, bad as they were, got worse. For every job that was open, there was a hungry carload of migrants. Men fought in the field over a row of beans. For the first time Western growers admitted there was a labor surplus. The Farm Security Administration reported that by 1938, 221,000 dust bowlers had entered California.

THE BRACEROS

With the coming of World War II, shipyards and aircraft industries drained off the surplus labor left by the Draft Board. Food demands climbed to wartime levels. Another source of cheap labor had to be found. The government was induced to sanction the wetbacks. And in 1944 the United States spent nearly $24 million to supply the growers with 62,170 braceros—Mexican farm laborers.

. As the war progressed, prisoners of war were turned over to growers, along with convicts. Japanese-Americans, impounded in concentration camps, were released to the custody of the big growers. Armed guards patrolled the fields. When the war ended, the P.O.W.'s went back to Italy and Germany, and the convicts went back to their cells.

The wetbacks remained, and their questionable legal position became more and more evident. Border patrols, 'on orders from Washington, looked the other way during the harvest season, and the wetbacks streamed in. The federal government not only condoned wetback traffic during the harvest season but actually encouraged it. The President's commission studying the problems of migratory labor discovered this incredible situation:

> . . . wetbacks (who were apprehended) were given identification slips in the United States by the Immigration and Naturalization Service which entitled them, within a few minutes, to step back across the border and become contract workers. There was no other way to obtain the indispensable slip of paper except to be found illegally in the United States. Thus violators of law were rewarded by receiving legal contracts while the same opportunities were denied law-abiding citizens of Mexico. The United States, having engaged in a program giving preference in contracting to those who had broken the law, had encouraged violation of the immigration laws. *Our government thus has become a contributor to the growth of an illegal traffic which it has the responsibility to prevent* [Italics mine].

In 1950 when the "police action" began in Korea, President Truman appointed a commission to study the problems of migrant labor. The 425 pressure was building up for more cheap labor to meet the anticipated new demands for food. The McCarran-Walter Act (Public Law 414) had just been passed over the President's veto. This was a new Immigration and Naturalization Act, which permitted the temporary importation of foreign labor under contract for periods up to three years.

Following completion of the report of the President's commission, the 82nd Congress, on July 12, 1951, passed Public Law 78. The commission had recommended a few months earlier that "no special measures be adopted to increase the number of alien contract workers beyond the number admitted in 1950." In that year 192,000 legal braceros (literally arm-men) came in under contract to work in the fields of the Southwest. Illegal wetback traffic began to decline, but by the end of the decade the number of braceros had risen far above the wartime emergency levels of either World War II or the Korean War. In 1959 there were 437,000 Mexican nationals scattered across the United States from Texas to Michigan.

Over the years growers have shown a decided preference for the foreign farm workers. The reasons are many. The foreigner many times does not speak English. He is uninformed about his rights and in a poor position to defend them if they are violated. He is willing to work for less and under poorer conditions. Imported farm workers are always single males. Housing and transportation are simpler. And when the farmer has done with them, they can be shipped back where they came from. And if any of them make trouble, they can be shipped home a little early.

Shortage of workers amid mass unemployment; foreign workers in record numbers while American workers can't find jobs—these are long-standing contradictions in farm labor. Growers say they can't find workers. Workers say they can't find jobs. Part of the answer lies in the definition of the terms. A shortage of labor exists for many growers when they don't have more than twice the number of workers they can get by with. Extra hands keep the wages down and the union out. The workers' idea of the proper labor supply is when he can choose between jobs and take the one that pays the most.

The theory of the laws that enable growers to import labor was that both worker and grower could be served. In practice these laws crushed the worker and gave the grower an almost limitless supply of cheap labor. Obviously, when a worker refuses a job at $.35 an hour (the prevailing wage for field workers in Arkansas, for example), he only makes it possible for the grower to get Mexicans. Until very recently, Arkansas was the third-largest user of braceros, employing about 40,000 annually.

An interesting example of the law in action was the shifting wages in the Imperial Valley. For many years domestic workers in the winter lettuce harvest were paid a piece rate of a penny a head for 426 harvesting lettuce. This amounted to an hourly wage of from $1.25 to $2.00, good money for harvesting.

As growers began to use more braceros, the piece rate was finally dropped and the wage level in the valley fell. For several years prior to 1961, it was frozen at about $.70 an hour. When President Kennedy signed the extension of Public Law 78 in 1961 (for two years), he instructed the Secretary of Labor to see to it that the program had no adverse effect on domestic labor. As a result, Imperial Valley growers who sought to use braceros were instructed to reinstate the old piece rate of a penny a head. (It can be noted in passing that if harvest wages were doubled, the labor cost would be only $.02 a head.)

In anticipation of this change, growers had increased the hourly wage from $.70 to $1.00. But as soon as the Labor Department called for the old piece rate, 200 growers flew to Washington to protest. The department backed down and agreed that the growers could pay either $1.00 an hour *or* the piece rate of $.24 a carton. *The choice was to be left to the worker.* That the growers were satisfied with the new arrangement indicated that they didn't intend the workers, most of whom were braceros, to have much say in the matter after all. And the nature of the choice—between $1.00 an hour or $2.00 an hour—indicated that the Department of Labor was either naïve or cynical.

The mystery was cleared up when an accountant employed by an El Centro lettuce company announced that she had falsified the payroll records. What she had done, on the orders of the company owners, was to pad the hours reported by the labor crews. This lowered, on paper, the hourly wage. Thus the Labor Department was unaware of what the piece rate earnings actually were. Apparently the wage surveyors had asked the growers what they were paying. But no one bothered to ask the workers what they were earning. If it had been discovered that the piece rate was equal to $2.00 an hour, then the bracero wage of $1.00 would have had to be doubled. It would have been clear that the use of the Mexicans had definitely had an adverse effect on other wages in the valley.

The low wages in agriculture may seem to be of little importance to the rest of society. But "agriculture as a whole," according to the California Democratic Council, "still remains our largest single industry. Depressed farm purchasing power contributes directly and significantly to fewer sales, fewer jobs, lower business profits, and a lower general level of national output and income than what the U.S. economy should be producing."

MEASURED IN PENNIES

The marketing of agriculture products needs a thorough investigation. In many cases neither the grower nor the worker is getting a fair 427 shake. Tomatoes grown in McAllen, Texas, and sold in Denver, for instance, produced a net income to the grower of $68.85 per acre. But the consumers paid $9,660 for this acre of tomatoes. Only a small fraction of retail food prices reflects farm crop prices. And a much smaller fraction represents harvesting wages.

There is room here for fair profits to growers and honest wages to workers. What the harvesters need is the dignity of work done under conditions meant for farm workers, not farm animals. The issues that are fought over are cabin space, hot water, and piece rates, but the real issues are basic human rights and fair play. The migrant doesn't want charity or handouts. He wants a chance, a start, to build his strength and manage his own life.

The wages paid harvest labor constitute a tiny fraction of the retail cost of food. In many cases, an increase in wages as much as 100 percent would barely affect the retail price. The price to consumers of eliminating migrant poverty is measured in pennies.

Legislation designed to help migrant labor is urgently needed. In 1964 a number of bills were enacted which will help states improve migrant education, expand the restrictions on child labor, provide some new day-care centers for children, and help farmers provide field sanitation. Congress could, if it would, establish a minimum wage for migratory workers, improve the methods of recruiting, training, transporting, and distributing farm workers, and extend the National Labor Relations Act to cover agriculture.

The ingrained poverty and underemployment that exist among the seasonal farm workers will be difficult to eliminate. Our agricultural system has made harvest work shameful. It has made the welfare check often more honorable than harvest work. It has made pride and satisfaction impossible. No man goes into a field to harvest crops if there is any other choice open to him. The new laws passed in 1964 do not constitute a complete solution. But they would make a start.

NOTHING BUT DESPAIR

The Brent family is typical of many thousands of migrant families. They were forced off their land in Georgia. They blundered into the migrant stream when the owner combined it with five other "mule and nigger" farms. One afternoon a placard appeared in the window of the filling station-grocery store near their home. It offered "employment opportunities" in the harvest in Homestead, Florida. The family was desperate for work. They loaded their household goods into their 1940 Dodge and started for Homestead.

After a long, hot, and dusty trip, they stopped in Belle Glade, north of Homestead, where the harvest was under way. Once there, they found plenty of work, and the whole family went to the fields. 428

In a month it was all over. They never got to Homestead. Work was finished there, too. They realized, too late, that they would have to go where the crops were. They sold their car and joined a crew headed for Pennsylvania. They had become migrants.

Crew leaders and roving bus drivers make recruiting drives into the South, and many workers enter the migrant stream this way. The promise of "a hundred dollars a week and live in a ho-tel" sounds good. A favorite target of the recruiters is the debt-ridden tenant family. Cash earnings and a place to live are heady inducements.

Some families enter the stream to search for a better place to live. One member will go on the season to look around up north or out west. Still, many of them wind up in the rural slums that lie at the fringes of the suburbs across the land. There are, for example, many Negroes from North Carolina living in Riverhead, Long Island. They came with migrant crews first and later brought their families.

Settling is a slow and difficult process. A Long Island woman explained it this way: "A man comes alone with a crew and picks a place to settle down. Next season, he may come back with another of the men in the family. If they decide it's OK, he'll come next year with his wife. At the end of the season, they stay in Riverhead. No one wants to hire a migrant because they're supposed to be wild and unstable; no one will rent him a house for fear he'll tear it up. So the first place the family lives is a real chicken house. If he finds a job, he can move his family out of the ex-migrant slum into a regular slum. After that, he's got it made. A lot of them don't, and they get stranded. Sometimes the husband has to leave so the wife can get welfare."

The valleys of California and Arizona and the suburbs of the Middle West are filled with the cabin slums of Mexican-Americans, Negroes, and poor whites trying to settle down. After a few years a migrant who cannot escape the stream is broken by it. The poverty, anxiety, homelessness, and isolation wear away his spirit. It is this apathy that is often called acceptance and makes people say, "They like things that way."

"We're always goin' someplace," said a sandy-haired Oklahoma migrant, "but we never git noplace." In a tired, flat voice, an old woman in a Michigan field put it only a little differently: "I been ever' place, and I got no place."

A migrant minister in a Belle Glade camp asked a woman in his camp church if she was going on the season again. "I don't know. Ever' year I go up broke, and I come back broke. I don't know why I go even."

A migrant in Arkansas sat on the steps of his one-room cabin. For an hour he had talked about where he had been, and the things he had done to keep his family alive. Suddenly it seemed as if the 429 memory of the years crushed him. "I get sick of the world sometimes and ever'body in it. I don't know what's goin' to happen. Used to make a livin' pickin' cotton. Then they started bringin' in them Mexicans by the truckload. Now they're gettin' them machines every day."

Few urban Americans have any awareness of this vast impoverished army that tramps through their country to bring the crops in from the fields. It cannot be seen except as a broken-down car or bus here, a truck there, a ragged crew working somewhere off in a field.

But the harvest cycle yields its own fruits: ignorance, poverty, death, and despair. Until we see the connection between migrancy —the corpses piled up on the roadway, the children left to the darkness of ignorance and illiteracy, the despairing, destitute families groping for a way to live—and the bountiful supply of fruits and vegetables on every corner fruit stand or in every supermarket, no changes will come. Without this understanding, no war on poverty can hope to win more than a few skirmishes.

Daniel P. Moynihan

The President & the Negro:
The Moment Lost

For anyone with even a moderate concern for the sources of stability in American government, the results of the 1966 elections will appear on balance a good thing. The Republican party reemerged as a strong and competent force in national life. Republicans now govern half the states of the union, are clearly seen as eligible to assume control of the national government, and increasingly are likely to do so before too many elections have passed.

The liberal Republicans whose successes were most prominent on November 8th do not normally take positions as "advanced" as have recent Democratic Presidents; but then over the years neither have Democratic Congresses, or the nation at large. We have just gone through one of those special periods in the American political cycle of high receptivity to new ideas and new social policies. This period, roughly from November 1963 to November 1966, was a consequence, as James L. Sundquist argues, of two tremendous accidents: the assassination of John F. Kennedy, and the nomination of Barry Goldwater. Much as we will remember the thousand days of Kennedy as a moment of brilliance in American life, it was nonetheless a time of modest legislative achievement. New ideas were conceived, new programs put forth, but the congressional response was cautious and toward the end hostile. At the time of the President's death, his legislative program was in trouble. It was only in the period that followed, in a spasm of remorse, guilt, fear, and something like exultation when

Reprinted from *Commentary*, February 1967, pp. 3–17, by permission of the author and publisher; copyright © 1967 by the American Jewish Committee. Daniel P. Moynihan, a former Assistant Secretary of Labor, is now director of The Joint Center for Urban Studies of The Massachusetts Institute of Technology and Harvard University.

what looked like disastrous fate was overcome and transformed indeed into triumph, that attention was turned to the unfinished business of the nation. Not long thereafter, the immense Democratic pluralities in Congress brought about by Goldwater's defeat provided a margin of votes for measures that had been stalemated for years. In three tremendous sessions, Congress cleaned up the agenda of the Roosevelt and Truman eras, while adding a number of important programs conceived in the present era, out of its special problems. The Republican resurgence in part almost certainly reflects a feeling that enough new things are underway for the time being; and there is truth in this. The demand for innovation and experiment has been more than met: a pause is hardly out of order, and with a major war being fought, such a pause was scarcely to be avoided regardless of party balance. In general, the newly elected Republicans are men who have no intention of reversing what progress has been made, nor even of standing still. It is just that the recent period of accelerated, intensive innovation is over.

Few groups in the nation have much to complain about in terms of how they fared during those thirty-six months; few can point to large and clearly formulated expectations that have been left unsatisfied. With one exception. For Negro Americans the election may turn out to have been a calamity. For the second time in their history, the great task of liberation has been left only half-accomplished. It appears that the nation may be in the process of reproducing the tragic events of the Reconstruction: giving to Negroes the forms of legal equality, but withholding the economic and political resources which are the bases of social equality.

The election was not a vote to undo any of the civil-rights advances of the past several years. Indeed, some of the most dramatic outcomes involved the choice of a Republican moderate over a segregationist or even racist Democrat. (Republicans nominated twice as many Negro candidates for the House as did Democrats, who put up only their six incumbents, and of course Republicans nominated and elected a Negro senator.) But the vote was a clear instruction to elected officials everywhere that the country has gone about as far as it wishes in providing social welfare and economic assistance to the Negro masses. The vote, moreover, was a bruising declaration that the electorate is fed up to the teeth with demonstrations and riots and perhaps more particularly with the assertion of the *right* to riot and open threats of violence that have increasingly accompanied even the most routine requests of Negro leaders. The voters think Negroes have received enough for the time being. This was manifest in countless election details, from the popularity of Ronald Reagan's disquisitions on welfare mothers and color television sets, to the startling turnout for the Conservative party in New York and the staggering, near two-to-one defeat of the civilian-dominated police review board by the citizens of New York City.

Even before the elections this mood had been telegraphed to the Congress, which refused to enact a civil-rights measure in its second session and which in many other ways indicated a withdrawal of sentiment from the Negro cause.

It was unavoidable that some such shift in attitude should have occurred eventually; the tragedy is that it came before the true destiny (if such terms are permitted) of this moment in history was fulfilled. Negroes did get a good deal out of this period. But not enough. They now have enforced legal rights as never in their history, but they remain terribly weak in economic and social terms—a situation that is, if anything, more conspicuous in the face of a booming, full-employment economy now entering its seventh year of unbroken expansion. The basic social legislation and, more importantly, adequate income levels for the Negro poor and the Negro working classes—legislation that would have meant for them what the New Deal measures meant for the population at large—were not enacted. They were, indeed, not even introduced. So long as war persists, economic conditions for Negroes are likely to be tolerable, but peace is more than likely to bring a return to the conditions of, say, the 1950's, conditions which they are no longer willing to accept, but no more than ever, as a group, able to avoid.

The misery is that it did not have to happen. The moment came when, as it were, the nation had the resources, and the leadership, and the will to make a *total* as against a partial commitment to the cause of Negro equality. It did not do so. But it was not Northern conservatives or Southern segregationists who stood in the way. For that one brief moment their opposition would not have prevailed. This time the opposition emanated from the supposed proponents of such a commitment: from Negro leaders unable to comprehend their opportunity; from civil-rights militants, Negro and white, caught up in a frenzy of arrogance and nihilism; and from white liberals unwilling to expend a jot of prestige to do a difficult but dangerous job that had to be done, and could have been done. But was not.

One may be confident that Lyndon Johnson will be blamed for this, and with perhaps especial vehemence inasmuch as more than any man in American public life, and any President in American history, he tried to see that the job did get done. Hence the events that led to his effort, and to its subsequent failure, are worth noting: very likely to no greater purpose than the satisfaction of curiosity, but possibly in some small way as a lesson.

In a pattern that has become familiar for major Presidential initiatives, the effort began with an address to a university audience, in 433 this instance the graduating class of Howard University on June 4, 1965. The timing here was perfect. The President had been overwhelmingly elected the preceding fall, and given the largest majorities in the House and Senate since those of the early Congresses that enacted the New Deal. Johnson had sent up a substantial, if not particularly radical, legislative program which was going along nicely. The one measure that promised to reapportion power in a part of American society, the Voting Rights Bill, was also well on its way to enactment. This latter was but one indication of the extraordinarily favored political position which Negro Americans enjoyed at that moment. The nation was proud, in a way, of having so resoundingly turned back the challenge of the Republican right wing, with its penumbra of reaction and racism. The Negro leaders had acted with great wisdom throughout that episode (and by successfully calling off demonstrations had seemed to evince genuine control of the Negro masses). The events in Selma had been almost a caricature of all that is stupid and intolerable in the South, and again the Negro performance was flawless. These events having in effect taken place on television, there was no longer any doubt that the country understood what things could be like in the South, and was determined to place the power of the federal government behind the protection of Negro civil rights in the region.

For just the reason that things were going so well, this was also the moment of maximum danger. To anyone who troubled to look closely at the situation it was clear that the disabilities of Negroes in the North were far wider and of a different order than those involving the deprivation of civil rights in the rural South. Assuring the franchise to Negroes in the South would help them; abolishing the public forms of segregation would also help them. But none of these measures would make any significant difference in the North, and not even that much in the South where Negroes were hopelessly outnumbered and, given the disparities of wealth and position, in important ways outclassed in the competitive struggle for position and wealth. In the meantime, a Negro proletariat was swelling to the bursting point in the cities of the North, its reach so far exceeding its grasp as to force any but the most indomitably complacent to see that trouble was in the offing.

The demand of Negroes in the South had been traditional, orderly, and unassailable in their justice: American citizens were asking that their constitutional rights be observed. Once the facts became clear, middle-class America agreed—instinctively, automatically. This was about the point—granting the looseness of any historical analogy— where things were left after the Civil War: the slaves were emancipated, and that was that. That they might remain penniless and dependent was not an issue touched upon either by John Locke or the American 434

Constitution, and therefore of no concern to government. Just as almost everyone was free in 1863, almost everyone was able to vote a century later. On the other hand, no one had a "right" to own a farm in 1865, and no one had the "right" to hold a job in 1965. Then, as now, going beyond legal entitlements to rights of this kind meant getting involved in large social change—something far more radical than merely eliminating the major inconsistency of the existing system by bringing Negroes into it. Many of the groups now so insistent that the poll tax be abolished and school segregation ended (in the South) would not normally be prepared to support such a change. Moreover, compassion for the suffering, Christlike, non-violent Negro demonstrators of the South was a different thing from loving and understanding the frequently debased and disorderly slum-dwellers of the North. This was a point that anyone who had watched the emergence of "crime-in-the-streets" as a major political issue in New York City would have grasped.

Thus the danger signs were there. Nevertheless, the plain and ascertainable fact was that the nation was going through a moment that had never occurred before—and could not persist indefinitely—in which a willingness to accept a considerable degree of social innovation was combined with genuine feeling for the problems of Negroes. The world was at peace. The President had enormous majorities in Congress. The success of the New Economics was by then manifest: the Bureau of the Budget was already forecasting a $45 billion increase in the level of federal revenues by 1970— an increase, further, which doctrine ordained had to be spent in order to accrue. It was, in addition, a moment of racial calm. No demonstrators were abroad, no confrontation between white power and black protest was building up anywhere. In this atmosphere of maximum reasonableness and calm, an atmosphere in which the President could without great risk do nothing, and which for that very reason provided an opportunity for history to be made, the President, seizing the opportunity, set in motion a major initiative.

He went before an audience of fourteen-thousand persons on hand for the graduating ceremonies at Howard University and made the most advanced commitment to the cause of Negro equality of any President in history. Citing Churchill, he declared that the soon-to-be-enacted Voting Rights Bill, generally deemed at the time the ultimate in civil-rights achievement, was "not the end . . . not even the beginning of the end . . . perhaps the end of the beginning." Once again Negroes were being given their freedom, but, said the President:

> . . . freedom is not enough. You do not wipe away the scars of centuries by saying: Now you are free to go where you want, do as you desire; choose the leaders you please.

435

You do not take a person who for years has been hobbled by chains and liberate him, bring him up to the starting line of a race and then say, "You are free to compete with all the others," and still justly believe that you have been completely fair.

Thus it is not enough just to open the gates of opportunity. All our citizens must have the ability to walk through those gates.

For many Negroes there had been great progress, the President continued (speaking in a setting that made that clear enough). "But for the great majority of Negro Americans—the poor, the unemployed, the uprooted and the dispossessed—there is a much grimmer story. They still are another nation. Despite the court order and the laws, despite the legislative victories and the speeches, for them the walls are rising and the gulf is widening." He went on to recount the facts of this widening gulf, and to insist that "Negro poverty is not white poverty"—the past had been too brutal, the present too distorted, racial prejudice too real for any useful analogy. The disadvantages of the Negro had become "a seamless web. They cause each other, they result from each other. They reinforce each other."

To argue this point, the President then turned to a subject never before mentioned by an American President, never before an acknowledged issue of public concern: the condition of the Negro family, the central fact and symbol of the "one huge wrong of the American nation," a condition that had vastly improved for some, but which remained anguished for many:

For this, most of all, white America must accept responsibility. It flows from centuries of oppression and persecution of the Negro man. It flows from long years of degradation and discrimination, which have attacked his dignity and assaulted his ability to provide for his family.

This, too, is not pleasant to look upon. But it must be faced by those whose serious intent is to improve the life of all Americans.

Only a minority—less than half—of all Negro children reach the age of eighteen having lived all their lives with both of their parents. At this moment a little less than two-thirds are living with both of their parents. Probably a majority of all Negro children receive federally aided public assistance sometime during their childhood.

The family is the cornerstone of our society. More than any other force it shapes the attitude, the hopes, the ambitions, and the values of the child. When the family collapses it is the children that are usually damaged. When it happens on a massive scale the community itself is crippled.

So, unless we work to strengthen the family, to create conditions under which most parents will stay together—all the rest: schools and playgrounds, public assistance and private concern, will never be enough to cut completely the circle of despair and deprivation.

436

The President proposed "no single easy answer." Some measures were obvious enough: jobs that enable a man to support his family, decent housing, welfare programs better designed to hold families together, health care, compassion. "But there are other answers still to be found." To seek them out, he announced, he would convene in the fall a White House Conference of scholars and experts, outstanding Negro leaders and government officials. Its theme would be "To Fulfill These Rights," a phrase echoing the great assertion of the Declaration of Independence. And he dedicated his administration to this epic undertaking:

> To move beyond opportunity to achievement. To shatter forever not only the barriers of law and public practice, but the walls which bound the condition of man to the color of his skin.
> This is the next and more profound stage of the battle for civil rights. We seek not just freedom but opportunity—not just legal equity but human ability—not just equality as a right and a theory, but equality as a fact and as a result.

His audience was not in the least prepared for such a speech, nor was the press. The first accounts were routine enough: the President had promised equality, the ovation was "stunning," he had received an honorary degree. A Gemini flight was the big news of the moment. But over the weekend the reporters thought again and began to assess what they had heard. Douglas Kiker described it in terms of the reaction of an audience "accustomed to hearing national political leaders speak in traditional ways about civil rights":

> At first they applauded the traditional lines. Then they sat in stunned silence. And finally they applauded out of shock and self-identification.
> Mr. Johnson . . . [spoke] as no President ever has spoken before, but as a result it is doubtful that any future, serious discussion of the problem can be attempted without consideration of what he said.

Tom Wicker described the speech in terms of the Supreme Court decision on school segregation:

> At Howard University . . . Mr. Johnson laid down much the same principle on a much broader scale.
> Providing for the Negro an equal "right" to vote, to get a job, to go to unsegregated schools, to due process of law, Mr. Johnson was really saying, is providing him with no more than "separate but equal" citizenship. And just as had been true in education, so it is true in the broader view that "separate" is inherently "unequal."
> Thus did President Johnson face squarely what must be ranked

as the most difficult problem in American life. That problem is not the enforcing of legal equity for the Negro. It is rather the acceptance of the Negro as an equal human being rather than a "separate but equal" human being—a man with a darker skin rather than a "black man."

It was a bold beginning. The speech seemed to attract more attention as time passed, and indeed is almost certain to find a place in the history of Presidential papers. Yet before half-a-year had passed the initiative was in ruins, and after a year-and-a-half it is settled that nothing whatever came of it.

Why? The reasons vary. Within weeks of the speech the President was caught up in the series of decisions that led to the large-scale introduction of ground forces into Vietnam later that summer. The address at Howard was in a sense his last peacetime speech. Thereafter, one would assume, his mind was increasingly preoccupied with war in Asia. This did not entail any backtracking on the commitment "To Fulfill These Rights," but it did mean that the White House was not going to think up a program to do so. The energies of that tiny group at the apex of government were now directed elsewhere. If a program was to be forthcoming, it would have to be the work of the civil-rights movement, with whatever assistance it could muster in government departments and universities. There was no reason to assume that the movement would fail in this, but in fact it did so: totally. The civil-rights movement had no program for going beyond the traditional and relatively easy issues of segregation and discrimination, and could not organize itself to produce one within the life of the 89th Congress. And in any event it did not do so because it allowed the question of developing a program to be superseded by a preposterous and fruitless controversy over a Department of Labor report which had been the original precipitant of the Howard speech.

The report was entitled. *The Negro Family: The Case for National Action.* It was written by me (I was then Assistant Secretary of Labor for Policy Planning and Research), with the assistance of Paul Barton and Ellen Broderick of the Policy Planning Staff. It was an internal document entirely: intended for the Secretary of Labor, the President, and the members of their staffs who would accept or reject its proposals and implications. A hundred copies were produced, but with no expectation of using even that few. The objectives of the report were twofold. First: to argue the need for seizing the opportunity of the moment to make the kind of commitment the President did in fact subsequently make. Second: to urge consideration of a new and different kind of policy, *in addition to* the more familiar ones—namely, a national family policy.

A word about these objectives: traditionally, the American legal 438 and constitutional system has been based on a deliberate blindness to any social reality other than the reality of individuals. Deriving partly from the metaphysics of classical liberalism, and partly from the relative ethnic homogeneity of American society before the Civil War, this emphasis has been a source of much vitality and initiative, but also an obstacle to the entry of a number of groups into a full sharing of the rewards of American life. It was simply not enough, as Anatole France observed, that the law in its majestic equality should forbid the rich equally with the poor to sleep under bridges and to beg bread in the streets. The reality of class had to be acknowledged, for example, in order for the labor movement to make the gains it did under the New Deal. But if this understanding of the Negro in group terms has been widespread enough among scholars, it has not been a consideration in the framing of programs. The report on the Negro family was intended to demonstrate its relevance and thereby to persuade the government that public policy must now concern itself with issues beyond the frame of individualistic political thinking.

The second objective was connected with and flowed from the first. Family is not a subject Americans tend to consider appropriate as an area of public policy. Family affairs are private. For that very reason, to raise the subject in terms of public policy is to arouse immediate interest: edged with apprehension, but interest nonetheless. That was the simple purpose of the report: to win the attention of those in power. The government no less—in fact, more—than the nation at large was caught up in the euphoria and sense of achievement of the moment. This was, after all, an administration of Texans who could hardly help exaggerating the importance of the dismantling of the segregationist social structure that had been the shame and the burden of the South for so long. It was necessary to depict, and in terms that would be felt as well as understood, the internal weakness of the Negro community and the need for immense federal efforts if that community was to go beyond opportunity "to equality as a fact and as a result." Another discourse on unemployment, on housing, on health would not have accomplished this. It would have added little to what persons thought they generally knew. In any event, unemployment was going down, housing was by any criteria improving, health standards were higher than ever. Yet social indicators such as these are relative, while family in a sense remains an absolute: a broken family is broken; a deserted wife is alone; an abandoned child needs help. Describing the plight of so many Negro families appeared the surest way to bring home the reality of their need. And, should the argument carry within the administration and be extended beyond, it seemed that programs aimed at the family might hope to enlist the support of the more conservative and tradition-oriented centers of power in American life whose enthusiasm for class legislation is limited indeed. To do anything for Negro families would entail assisting the 439 entire population. Certain groups might be hesitant at first, but if the European or Canadian experience was any guide, such programs could quickly become a matter of solid consensus.

However little explored as a subject of public policy, the question of the Negro family has been perhaps the central subject of Negro scholarship in America. The first and in ways the best book, now forgotten, was written by W. E. B. DuBois in 1908, under the title, *The Negro American Family*. A generation later, E. Franklin Frazier published his classic work, *The Negro Family in the United States*. A number of others have contributed important studies since. The destruction of the family under the form of capitalist slavery practiced in the American South was, after all, the unique experience of the Negro American. It was the supreme fact of bondage and, if one likes, the unredeemable sin of the slaveholders. The gradual formation of families by freedmen before emancipation and others thereafter was a central element in the great transformation of the Negro people, but while eminently successful for some, it was slow and painful for many, and from the beginning, Negro families have been exposed to every variety of internal travail and external pounding. Frazier ended his work, which appeared in 1939, on an ominous note. The uprooted, marginal, Southern peasants were then moving To the City of Destruction. "The travail of civilization," he wrote, "is not yet ended."

> First, it appears that the family which evolved within the isolated world of the Negro folk will become increasingly disorganized. Modern means of communication will break down the isolation of the world of black folk, and, as long as the bankrupt system of Southern agriculture exists, Negro families will continue to seek a living in the towns and cities of the country. They will crowd the slum areas of Southern cities or make their way to Northern cities where their family life will become disrupted and their poverty will force them to depend upon charity.

The plan of the Labor Department report was to pick up from Frazier and record what had happened. As the data were assembled—data which had not previously been brought together—a compelling hypothesis began to emerge: *Frazier had been right*. It could not be described as a conclusion, since the information was not that solid, but the impression arose that the Negro community might be dividing. A middle class was clearly consolidating and growing, and yet the overall indicators continued to worsen, not precipitously but steadily. These two things could not be true unless a third fact—that things were falling apart at the bottom—was also true. And that meant trouble in the Northern slums.

The last point is essential to understanding the initial impact of the report and later the reaction to it. The kind of female-headed, female- 440 based family now so common in Negro slums is nothing new. It has been and in places remains a commonplace feature of lower-class life in industrial societies. The Negro experience may be a particularly intensive one, but San Juan and Copenhagen, Glasgow and Dublin have or have had their counterparts. Further, it has its equivalents in primitive societies. In the view of a wide range of anthropologists and sociologists and, of course, of psychiatrists, these families and the communities they make up tend to transmit from one generation to the next, traits and circumstances which help perpetuate their condition. There is nothing absolute about this: as many individuals, no doubt, leave the culture as remain in it, and on one level the proposition amounts to little more than the assertion that the poor rarely inherit large estates. But anyone who has lived in or near the condition knows it to be real. The dissolution, the carelessness, the matriarchy, the violence, the "protest masculinity" are all there. The "massive deterioration of the fabric of society and its institutions," in Kenneth Clark's phrase, sets in and children get caught up in the "tangle of pathology" early. In any event, if, as Kennedy used to say, to govern is to choose, to advise those who govern is to choose positions and press them, and I pressed this one.

The report began: "The United States is approaching a new crisis in race relations." An opening section, "The End of the Beginning," proposed that the Negro demands for liberty in the South would now be met regardless of sporadic opposition, and that the nation must now turn to the issue of equality. On that issue no similar consensus existed. Yet mere equality of opportunity would not be sufficient, for in present terms Negroes were simply not competitive. "The principal challenge of the next phase of the Negro revolution is to make certain that equality of results will now follow. If we do not, there will be no social peace in the United States for generations."

With the warning: "Data are few and uncertain, and conclusions drawn from them, including the conclusions that follow, are subject to the grossest error," the report went on to declare that "At the heart of the deterioration of the fabric of Negro society is the deterioration of the Negro family." A combination of charts and text illustrated the way in which unemployment, in particular, had controlled family stability and welfare dependency, with the latter rising and falling in response to the non-white male unemployment rate, and the prevalence of broken families rising with the long-term rise in unemployment. But then in the 60's employment began to improve, but family conditions did not. *The possibility was real that the situation had begun feeding on itself.* The large number of children born to lower- and working-class Negro parents, combined with the low skills of Negro workers and the sluggishness of the wage structure, argued most powerfully that even full employment would not provide the economic 441 stability that was clearly the basis of family stability for this group. (There are other groups with different traditions—Appalachian miners, for instance—who can take a lot of punishment without much impact on family structure. But urban Negroes cannot, and that is really all there is to it.) The report concluded that a new and vast national effort was required to enhance "the stability and resources of the Negro American family."

A series of recommendations was at first included, then left out. It would have got in the way of the attention arousing argument that a crisis was coming and that family stability was the best measure of success or failure in dealing with it. The program response was anyhow obvious enough: guaranteed full employment, birth control, adoption services, etc. *But first of all a family allowance.* The United States is the only industrial democracy in the world without a system of automatic income supplements for people living with their children. It is the simplest and possibly the most effective of all social-welfare arrangements, not least because its administration involves no judgments as to whether or not the recipients are worthy and entitled to assistance. If the children are alive, the allowance is paid. The United States has, of course, a family allowance for *broken* families, the AFDC program. It was past time we came to our senses on the subject, and stopped penalizing families with a father in the home. In that far-off spring of 1965 it appeared we might. It was absurd to think that such a precious moment of legislative opportunity would pass without some measure of income redistribution. A family allowance was surely the most promising candidate. It would have cost $5 to $10 billion per year according to the scheme adopted *but we had the money.* To have enacted it would have been a first step in the necessary movement from the "civil-rights" phase—the phase involving legal equality for Negroes—into the phase of "equality as a fact and as a result."

The report was sent to the President by Secretary of Labor Wirtz on May 4th, along with a nine-point program. On May 30th, the White House asked for a draft of a speech at Howard to put forward its thesis. On the night of June 3rd, the draft was rewritten and after being read in the morning to Roy Wilkins, Whitney Young, and Martin Luther King, was delivered without further ado that afternoon.

Lee Rainwater and William L. Yancey have written a book about the controversy that ensued[1] and much that here follows draws on them. Predictably, albeit unbeknown to the White House, trouble began within the permanent government, as Arthur Schlesinger Jr. calls the

[1]*The Moynihan Report and the Politics of Controversy,* M.I.T. Press (forthcoming).

civil-service bureaucracies. The report and the speech were wholly the product of the Presidential government. The welfare bureaucracy knew nothing of either, but as closer inquiry put the two together it was instantly perceived that the adequacy of the welfare bureaucracy's efforts and even the integrity of its view of events had been roundly condemned. The civil service is in an untenable position in this area: they know well enough the inadequacy of the programs they administer, and the ways in which Negroes are discriminated against even within the context of inadequate programs. Rainwater and Yancey write:

> Over many years one of the most important ways of coping with this difficult situation has been to try to fuzz it over. Under the guise of civil libertarian reasoning, welfare organizations, both national and local, have tried to "wish away" race as a category, and this has had the latent function of concealing the extent to which discrimination continues. One of the early civil-rights activities of the Kennedy administration was to try to reverse this trend so that at least the government could be informed about the extent to which Negroes were disadvantaged. Having this "color blind" point of view built into their ideology, it was relatively easy for welfare personnel to find Moynihan's intransigent emphasis on color reactionary rather than radical.

Word began to flow forth from the recesses of the Department of Health, Education and Welfare that I was a "subtle racist," that the Negro people had been insulted, and further that the facts were wrong. The Children's Bureau awoke from its torpor to join this effort with singularly feline earnestness.

For the record let it be said that such new information as has come to light since the report was written has substantially confirmed the thesis that the prevalence of family disruption among lower-class Negroes has been on the increase. The weakest statistic in the report had to do with the actual proportion of female-headed non-white families, which had increased only from 18 per cent in 1950 to 21 per cent in 1960. It happens that in March 1965, the month the report was finished, another census was being taken which showed the proportion of female-headed Negro families to have increased to 25 per cent—a sharp acceleration. This is the prevalence at the moment; the incidence over time is, of course, much higher. Probably not much more than a quarter of lower-class Negro children live with both parents during their entire youths. There are more broken families and they are breaking up earlier. Analyzing the non-white data in a paper delivered last summer, Daniel O. Price reported that 1970 will see "significant increases in the percent married with spouse absent. These increases are doubtless related to many factors such   443 as increased urbanization, lack of economic opportunities for non-white males, welfare programs that reduce the financial strains on many female-headed households, differential cultural values, etc."

The white/non-white differential in marriage stability seems to hold at all economic and social levels, but the recent deterioration is clearly concentrated at the lowest ones. In Watts, for example, the proportion of children under 18 living with both parents dropped from 56 per cent in 1960, which was nothing to brag about, to 44 per cent in 1965. Most strikingly, family income levels have also been dropping in these areas. Between 1960 and 1965, family income in America rose 14 per cent. *Non-white* family income rose 24 per cent. But in South Los Angeles, it declined 8 per cent, from $5,122 to $4,736 in constant dollars. The Negro community in that area was going through a serious increase in disorganization; this was not, however, happening to the Mexican American community alongside them in East Los Angeles. In the Hough section of Cleveland, a similar process was underway. In 1959, family income there was $4,732; by 1964, this had dropped to $3,966, a decline almost entirely accounted for by the increase in female-headed households, which rose from 22.5 per cent in 1960 to 32.1 per cent in 1966.

It is plain enough that anyone seeking to discredit a political initiative based on as sensitive a subject as family structure, particularly that of Negroes, will have no difficulty devising arguments. For generations, Negroes have labored under the attribution of genetic inferiority; to raise the question of a "deviant subculture" is to invite the charge of raising the same old canard of innate differences in a more respectable guise. The subject of family introduces the subject of sex, in this instance Negro sex, an issue of intense and not always acknowledged sensitivity for all parties. The subject of broken families raises the specter of welfare cheating charges, an issue to which Newburgh, New York, gave its name, but which Governor Reagan has brought to a point of high political style. Further, Negro leaders and activists are apt themselves to come from the most solid, even rigid family backgrounds and probably have real difficulty perceiving or acknowledging the realities of lower-class life. And so on, down a long list of reasons, any one of which is sufficient to explain why, even when the subject is broached, as in the Howard speech, it barely makes its way into the press accounts, being an issue, as the *Economist* noted at the time, that liberals prefer to "skirt."

The attack, as is usual in such cases, came from the outside, in the form of a paper prepared early in the fall by a member of CORE, William Ryan (not the Manhattan congressman) and published in the *Nation*. Ryan, a psychologist, was a consultant to the Massachusetts Committee on Children and Youth, whose head is a former director of the Children's Bureau. He charged the report with providing grounds for a massive white "cop out" by means of "a new form of subtle racism that might be termed 'Savage Discovery,' and seduces the reader into believing that it is not racism and discrimination but the weaknesses and defects of the Negro himself that account for the present status of inequality. . . ." One recalls the character in a Disraeli novel said to have been "distinguished for ignorance, in that he had but one idea and that was wrong." Ryan's one idea was that I was obsessed with illegitimacy; I should never have raised the subject, he said, and moreover was inaccurate in my facts. He may have been right about the first allegation, but he was wrong about the statistics. For illegitimacy—which Myrdal judged the best measure of family stability—*is* a serious problem for Negroes (and increasingly for whites as well). A quarter of all non-white births and almost half of first births (and in one large city for which data are available, near to two-thirds of first births) are out of wedlock. The illegitimate first child (the non-white rate rose from 39.5 per cent in 1955 to 47.4 per cent in 1964) seems a particularly poignant problem, as it almost certainly decimates the bargaining power of a young Negro girl with the world around her. Illegitimacy is a painful subject, but one is surprised in this age of the Foul Speech Movement to find that it is also thought to be a dirty word.

Thomas Pettigrew, of Harvard University, author of *Profile of the Negro American,* wrote the editor of the *Nation* describing the Ryan article as "trash . . . replete with errors and written by a man with no past experience in race relations. . . ." But it was widely distributed within the civil-rights movement and seemingly accepted as truth. At the year's end it was reprinted in *Crisis,* the official organ of the NAACP, under the title, "The New Genteel Racism."

The article was a blow to the Howard initiative, but not yet a deadly one. Roy Wilkins wrote to say he had not known the NAACP was reprinting it. "My opinion of the Ryan piece and of similar reasoning is well known to my immediate associate here. . . . It is a silly and sinister distortion to classify as racist this inevitable discussion of a recognized phase of our so-called race problem." Wilkins's attitude was shared by other Negro leaders. During the summer, Whitney Young, Jr. several times noted, properly, that he had for years been writing about just such questions. In October in a speech in Westchester, Martin Luther King, Jr. summed up a general position:

> As public awareness [of the breakdown of the Negro family] increases there will be dangers and opportunities. The opportunity will be to deal fully rather than haphazardly with the problem as a whole—to see it as a social catastrophe and meet it as other disasters are met, with an adequacy of resources. The danger will be

445

that problems will be attributed to innate Negro weaknesses and used to justify neglect and rationalize oppression.

Just so. The Howard speech was playing for high stakes.

The fact was that the civil-rights movement was beginning to think in these terms. The President of a new Asian nation once remarked to an American Assistant Secretary of State that his predecessor, the first President, had had a glorious job. "He had only to go about the country shouting, 'Freedom!' For me it's different. For me it's all arithmetic." Just such a day was approaching for the Negro leaders. On April 3, 1965, in a staff memorandum entitled "Suggested Guidelines for Future Organizational Expansion," James Farmer, then the national head of CORE, had opened the subject: "In the past," he wrote, "any talk of upgrading and improving the Negro community would immediately have been labeled anti-integrationist, separationist, reactionary, and lending grist to the mill of those who cry, 'Not Ready Yet.' But even if such accusations come from thoughtless quarters, we must not delay motion in this direction."

In other circumstances, the Howard speech and even the report might have served to give direction to this developing attitude. Yet just the opposite occurred. The reasons are no doubt many, but an important one seems to have been the war in Vietnam. The political Left that had been associated with and indeed was part of the movement now began turning on the President and all his works. Thus, *Ramparts* published an editorial written by Marcus Raskin, evincing great concern that I seemed to think more Negroes should be in the armed forces (I do); and indicting me further as a lackey of the "social welfare monopoly—with its cop and spying attributes" that now proposed to force decent proletarian Negroes to live like the white bourgeoisie and to "torture" them with birth control. I had become a most suspect person indeed in the ranks of SNCC and CORE, and the Presidential initiative suffered accordingly.

The real blow was Watts. It threw the civil-rights movement entirely off balance. Until then, theirs had been the aggrieved, the just, the righteous cause. In the South an old game had been going on with a new rule, imperfectly understood by whites, that the first side to resort to violence—lost. Now in the North the Negroes had resorted to violence, in a wild destructive explosion that shattered, probably forever, the image of non-violent suffering. And within hours of the signing of the Voting Rights Act. The same new rule applied. The civil-rights movement could not explain Watts, and could not justify it. Then, of a sudden, the report on the Negro family was being used to do so. Watts made the report a public issue, and gave it a name. Or rather the columnists Rowland Evans and Robert Novak did in their column of August 18, which began:

446

Weeks before the Negro ghetto of Los Angeles erupted in violence, intense debate over how to handle such racial powder kegs was under way deep inside the Johnson administration.

The pivot of this debate: the Moynihan report, a much suppressed, much leaked Labor Department document that strips away usual equivocations and exposes the ugly truth about the big-city Negro's plight.

The report, said they, had raised, as indeed it had, the explosive question of preferential treatment, "a solution far afield from the American dream."

I had by this time left Washington for New York politics and was not at all involved with what was then going on in the capital, but it does appear that after Watts the report gained notoriety as an explanation of the internal problems revealed by the riots, and in that measure angered and repelled just those Negro leaders who had been on the point of turning to just such problems. Before long I was being denounced, for example, by James Farmer, in terms not at all consistent with his staff memorandum of April 3. "We are sick unto death," he wrote in a syndicated column, "of being analyzed, mesmerized, bought, sold, and slobbered over. . . . Moynihan has provided a massive academic copout for the white conscience and clearly implied that Negroes in this nation will never secure a substantial measure of freedom until we stop sleeping with our wife's sister and buying Cadillacs instead of bread. . . . Nowhere does Moynihan suggest that the proper answer to a shattered family is an open job market where the 'frustrated' Negro male can get an honest day's work." (The gist of the report was, if I may, that full employment, while indispensable, was no longer enough.)

Watts also threw off the White House, which found the moment for the conference "To Fulfill These Rights" almost upon it, but with no adequate preparations for a full-scale meeting. It was decided to hold first a small planning session. This met in November in an atmosphere of near frenzy over the report, which was all the militants seemed able to think of: indeed, at one of the plenary sessions the secretary to the conference felt called on to announce, "There is no such person as Daniel P. Moynihan." The conference was in truth a shambles; in the aftermath, one Chicago militant declared it had been entirely too much dominated by "whites and Jews," and from within the administration came the verdict: "A disaster." Rainwater and Yancey found one "close observer of Washington civil-rights events" who saw behind it all the "benign Machiavellianism" of Lyndon Johnson. They themselves suggest that "failure to treat the conference as the important event it had first seemed served several functions. First of all, it strongly disorganized the civil-rights forces who in the end managed to bring about a show of unity only in   447 opposition to the Moynihan report, *not in effective demands on the administration.*" But this kind of calculation is rarer in government than those outside tend to suppose. The essential fact is that neither the government nor the civil-rights movement had the resources to prepare a program in response to the Howard speech. This was the point of unparalleled opportunity for the liberal community and it was exactly the point where that community collapsed.

The collapse had been presaged just before the planning session met in November. A "Pre-White House Conference on Civil Rights" was convened in New York by the Office of Church and Race of the Protestant Council in cooperation with the Commission on Religion and Race of the National Council of Churches. A distinguished group of religious leaders, including Catholics and Jews and a scattering of liberal professors, was in attendance. The key figures were Dr. Robert Spike, Executive Director of the Commission on Religion and Race which had been established in 1963 in the midst of the Birmingham crisis, and Dr. Benjamin F. Payton, a young Negro sociologist and minister, then with the New York Protestant Council, and who a month later succeeded Spike in the national post. The larger purpose of the meeting was to propose that an "Economic Development Budget for Equal Rights in America," to cost $32 billion per year, be placed on the agenda of the White House Conference. But the real heat of the gathering was in the demand "that the question of 'family stability' be stricken entirely from that agenda. . . ."

This demand was supported by a paper written by Dr. Payton analyzing the report. It had already, he said, "had an impact upon the civil-rights movement and upon more general American politics that is quite deadening and utterly misleading." At the outset of a confused and confusing document, he seemed to suggest that the report had been written to explain Watts:

> Based largely upon Bureau of Census statistics, it summarizes very incomplete data in the form of some highly questionable conclusions, the most important of which are: (1) Since unemployment in general is decreasing in America, the riots breaking out in cities across the land cannot be positively associated with lack of jobs on the part of Negroes; (2) The major causal factor behind the riots, therefore, cannot be associated with *present and continuing* discrimination, or with an inadequate supply of job-training. . . .

Dr. Payton's main assertion was that the report had declared that the employment and income gap between Negroes and whites was closing (where, in fact, the report had said exactly the opposite). Also bewildering was the end of the paper where, describing the President in Neustadtian terms as "the Great Initiator" who may not wait for 448 information to make its way through the labyrinthine corridors of Washington offices, but rather must reach out for it "at the level of detail," Dr. Payton concluded:

> That President Johnson reached to significant social experts for the [Howard speech] . . . is evident from the quality of the speech. . . . The President sketched, in broad outline, an approach to the question of civil rights that promised to lift the whole issue to a new level of discussion, and provide a more meaningful framework within which action might be planned for its resolution. Pointing to the complex interrelationship among social and economic factors to the achievement of meaningful constitutional rights, Johnson became the first Chief Executive to maintain intact the issues pertaining purely to *racial* justice, and at the same time, to connect those issues with a category broader than the somewhat misleading genus of "race-relations"; hence giving them an adequate context.
> With an impressive array of technical data, shaped by imaginative ethical insight into an instrument of incisive social analysis, the speech provided a devastatingly clear rationale of why, at precisely the moment when unprecedented rights for the Negro are being secured by law, the nation needs to make a new departure if those rights are to become something more than mere ideal possibilities.

That the speech had had a direct relation to the report he seemed not to know, and the whole matter became even more curious two weeks later when I met Dr. Payton and he informed me that his paper was really an attack on President Johnson but that he had named me for "strategical purposes."

In truth, the Payton paper bordered on the psychopathological. (Although perhaps not: it was broadcast by the hundreds at the time, and achieved its objective brilliantly. But when Rainwater and Yancey recently asked to reproduce it in their book, Payton declined.) Charles M. Silberman, author of *Crisis in Black and White,* called it "the most blatant distortion that I can remember seeing in a long time." In a letter to a Presbyterian minister he wrote:

> Moynihan's whole emphasis is on the crucial role of unemployment in understanding all of the problems of Negro pathology; he presents one statistical correlation after another, showing that illegitimacy, desertion, and all the other symptoms show an unbelievably high correlation with changes in Negro unemployment; he marshals an enormous amount of evidence demonstrating—completely contrary to Payton's allegations throughout his essay—that Negro unemployment is very much more serious than the unemployment statistics indicate.

449

And so on. The Presidential assistant most directly responsible for civil-rights matters, a devout Protestant layman, described Payton's paper as "the apotheosis of the big lie." But somehow a nerve had been touched in Liberal Protestantism and there was no undoing the effects. Given the national prominence and the position of the persons who convened the Payton-Spike meeting, and given the absence of any protest or correction from within the church community, it had to be taken as the voice of American Protestantism. The issue of the Negro family was dead.

The plans for the November session were already fixed when the New York meeting took place, so that in fact one of the eight panels which met in Washington was on "The Family: Resources for Change." Chaired by Constance Baker Motley, it was a lively and useful session, on a subject that had not been talked to death. The panel report calling for the establishment of a national family policy might have been an important document, had it not been for the Payton-Spike intervention. But in February, the President appointed a thirty-member group to organize the White House Conference "To Fulfill These Rights." Reverend Spike was put on this Council and the subject of family—raised by an accused and thereby half-convicted "crypto-racist"—was taken off the agenda. The Department of Labor, the Department of Health, Education and Welfare, and the Office of Economic Opportunity set to work destroying all traces of the original policy, while producing tract on tract to demonstrate that what the President had said at Howard University was not so. The White House dissociated itself from the report and the subject. Order was restored, and soon the old orthodoxies were securely back in place: the problems of Negroes derived from the behavior of whites, and laws would change that behavior. A civil-rights message was sent to Congress proposing a ban on discrimination in housing in about the terms Governor Dewey used to address the New York State legislature in the 1940's.

The Conference, when it met, was a lifeless affair. The Council submitted a long report of unflinching orthodoxy, that missed entirely the import of the Howard speech. It reflected throughout what Rainwater has called "the services strategy," as against an income strategy in dealing with problems of poverty. Thus, the section on public welfare proposed, "There should be a sharp reduction of the number of clients served by each case worker." This is a common enough American approach to social problems, but there is perhaps a special significance in this particular area: a quite disproportionate number of middle-class Negroes, and of whites involved in civil-rights activities, are themselves members of the service professions. It is too much to expect that such persons will be oblivious to the advantages that might accrue to them from bidding up the demand for their services.

450

A more cynical person might describe the strategy as one of feeding the sparrows by feeding the horses. The Education section proposed that public expenditure per pupil be increased from $532 to $1,000. This would reflect an increase of tax outlay per Negro family of $1,404, or 37.5 per cent of average Negro family income. But almost every last penny of this increase would go to middle-class persons whose salaries are already well above the poverty level. The thought of giving the money directly to the Negro family in the form of a family allowance is not even suggested in the report, a document in any event destined for instant obscurity. The delegates were bored from the outset, and contented themselves with passing resolutions of no greater political realism than the report itself: "That J. Edgar Hoover be fired," "That the President ask for $2 billion to enforce Civil Rights laws." The President spoke briefly and warned his hearers not to expect miracles.

The question will be asked whether the subject of family was that essential. The answer will depend on a judgment as to the nature of the Negro problem. If one sees it as wholly a white problem, a matter of racial discrimination and oppression which can and should be stamped out, then it will be held that any internal troubles Negroes may have will thereafter take care of themselves. If, on the other hand, one sees it as a systemic problem which, *whatever its origins,* is now producing results that no significant portion of the population intends, then family becomes a relevant and politically *useful* issue. I believe it fair to say that family disruption is both a valid measure of the overall impact of external forces on a group such as urban Negroes, and it is also a measure whereby outside groups—white Americans—can be brought to see the realities of life in terms that command attention and demand response. In these terms, the subject of family does not, as has been charged, distract from issues like employment, but rather gives them a reality and urgency which normally they do not command among certain segments of the population. Writing in *Christianity and Crisis* in February 1965, Reverend Spike took particular exception to the fact that *Life* magazine seemed to approve the report. But that was just the point: family is an issue that comes home to responsible and influential, but conservative, persons such as the editors of *Life*. (Reverend Spike was murdered in tragic circumstances last summer, and cannot rebut anything I might say; so no more of him, although his influence in this matter was considerable and in ways decisive.)

But the essential fact about the subject of family in this connection was that upon it turned the issue of whether the conference and the administration would be kept to the President's proposition that a crisis was in the making within the Negro community. Rainwater and Yancey put it as follows:

451

For a government that wanted to move vigorously on social and economic reform to benefit Negroes, the Moynihan *report* provided a strong justification. For a government that wanted to "cool it," to avoid action that could no longer be afforded without having to take the blame for inaction, the Moynihan *controversy* provided an ideal distraction. The President and his aides could relax. A civil-rights strategy of "getting Moynihan" would obviously distract from "getting" the White House in the sense of either pressing for expanded federal commitments or protesting the lack of action.

I happen not to accept this interpretation. The administration was, and is, as much committed to the goals of the Howard speech as when it was delivered. But it lacked the resources of time and political capital to force the issue. (Remember that at this point, the civil-rights militants, Negro and white, were also bitterly attacking the war in Vietnam. The White House *had* to placate them, and in this instance all that was asked, ironically, was that it not move forward on the vast and expensive program of social reform to which in the wake of the report it had committed itself.) The most that could be hoped for was that the businessmen and liberal leaders on the President's new Council should stick by the Howard thesis and press the matter. They did nothing of the sort. In retrospect it is clear that civil rights had become for them a cause that could no longer stimulate or inspire them to take any grave risks. Their strategy now consisted of appearing to take an "advanced" social position, while remaining entrenched behind the most solid of orthodoxies. But faced with the prospect that this time there might be some real danger, that a genuinely—horrid word—controversial issue was being raised, the President's Council—persons solidly representative of the civil-rights establishment of that time—did not consider the matter even long enough for it to be said that it collapsed. It did not consider the matter at all. The subject was not dropped, it was never even raised.

The President's Council failed because in the end it had no views: all it sought was agreement. A quest for peace of this kind gives maximum leverage to the group with the most intransigent and assertive opinions, and the greatest ideological discipline. At the moment in question, in matters concerning civil rights, this was a position conspicuously enjoyed by the liberal Left. If that term is vague, anyone with experience in politics will nonetheless recognize the reality behind it. For the first half of the 1960's, the liberal Left, for the most part white, very nearly dominated the civil-rights movement, most conspicuously of course in SNCC and CORE, but also in the older-line organizations. The relation was not unlike that of the Marxist Left to the trade unions of the 1930's. The mass of the movement in each instance was made up of rank-and-file persons, with, on the whole, quite conventional views and expectations. But surrounding the leaders was an echelon of intense, purposeful, powerful, and dedicated persons 452 of a quite different character. And behind them was a community of sorts, in universities, in churches, in large cities, small businesses, and assorted journalistic enterprises that provided funds, ideas, support, followings: all those things that make for effective political action. There is no need to exaggerate its coherence in order to perceive that something like a community of opinion has existed here. More than most tendencies, this one is ridden with argument and controversy, but not uncommonly such strife ends up with substantial accord that can shift quite dramatically. Thus, one moment the war in Vietnam is a monstrously immoral adventure forced on the nation by a half demented President in the hands of a paranoid military, and the next instant the war is become a routine, on-going affair that provides no excuse whatever for not allocating the billions necessary to implement the Freedom Budget at home.

The nation needs the liberal Left. It has provided a secular conscience in a civilization where the immorality of large organizations has become, as Niebuhr warned us it would, almost the central danger of the age, and where the older voices of conscience have grown confused or silent or worse. Moreover, it has begun to affect and even to "infiltrate" religious institutions in many areas so that, of a sudden, churches stand for something in American public life other than that which is trivial, vulgar, or both. Had it not been for the liberal Left, it is unlikely that the civil-rights movement would have had the extraordinary impact and success of the past decade. But if one accepts the thesis that that was a first phase which now *must* be followed by a second, then the matter becomes more difficult. In the first phase, where issues of principle, of justice, of witness were involved, the liberal Left was an indispensable ally. In the second phase, however, where it becomes necessary to confront the realities of lower-class life, the liberal Left can be a disaster. Consider its reaction to the Watts riot. Anyone with a minimal sense of American social history would have instantly seen this as a calamity. Yet in no time, the liberal Left was depicting the participants not as a mob (and rather a merchandise-minded mob at that) but as an avenging, exultant proletariat. In the March 1966 COMMENTARY, Bayard Rustin explained that it had not been a riot at all, but rather a "Manifesto," a nicely articulated and discriminating statement of a political viewpoint. For a period after Watts it was not unusual to encounter middle-class civil-rights militants not only repeating the threats and predictions of further violence which had become commonplace on the part of Negroes, but actually enjoying the prospect. (How much of the backlash may be explained by Kipling's dictum: "If once you have paid . . . the Danegeld, you never get rid of the Dane"?)

The liberal Left wishes, on paper at least, to transform American society. It is largely made up of individuals who have passed through 453 most of the stages of routine affluence, and in certain ways, again on paper, now want out. Negroes want in. Read *Ebony*. Read Myrdal. Read the election returns from Lowndes County. The great, guilty, hateful secret is that Negroes are not swingers. They are Southern Protestants. They like jobs in the civil service. They support the war in Vietnam, approve the draft, back the President. And all this in greater proportion than any other group in the nation. Negroes are other things, too—but at this point in their history, only in quite limited numbers. (Note that when in October 1966 the old-line civil-rights leadership in effect dissociated itself from CORE and SNCC and Black Power, the statement was signed by the heads of the Negro Elks and the Negro Masons—two gentlemen who had not heretofore appeared as civil-rights leaders, but who represent a very considerable number of Negroes.)

The reaction of the liberal Left to the issue of the Negro family was decisive (the Protestant reaction was clearly triggered by it). They would have none of it. No one was going to talk about their poor people that way. Next ensued a discouragingly familiar form of whipsawing. On the one hand, the problems did not exist, the whole affair was a calculated slander; on the other hand, these were not problems at all, but healthful adaptations to intolerable social conditions imposed by an unfeeling racist society. College professors waxed absolutely lyric on the subject of the female-headed household. One of the persisting themes was first sounded by William Ryan who, in his *Nation* article, introduced a novel social indicator, the illegitimacy conception rate. This rate reveals that white bourgeois females fornicate as much as, or even more than (although not of course so well as), Negro girls, and conceive almost as often. But thereafter they resort to (Park Avenue) abortionists. Thus the point becomes to establish *guilt* instead of to deal with a problem.

This is terrifyingly reminiscent of Stanley Elkins's abolitionists who seem never to have seen slavery as a social problem for slaves, but only as an ethical problem for slaveholders. Once legal bondage was at an end, the subject was closed so far as the Northerners were concerned. The fact that the slaves lived on, and the child is born—and needs help—is a matter somehow to be passed over. This is the crux of it. Typically, the refusal of the liberal Left to accept the unpleasant facts of life for the poor—there is delinquency in the slums, but those kids in the suburbs are just as bad and don't get arrested, etc. etc.—leads to the same position as does the insistence of the extreme conservatives on just such facts: namely, to do nothing. The liberal Left will acknowledge the relevance of these facts only to the extent that they serve as an indictment of American society; after that it loses interest. The extreme conservatives harp on these facts in order to indict the poor; after that, *they* lose interest. It does 454 not occur to the liberal Left, for example, that the issue of illegitimacy has nothing to do with whether black women are more or less promiscuous than white women; it has to do with the number of children on the welfare rolls. This is a legitimate concern of public policy. At Howard, however, the President in a radical initiative made the damage to the life-chances of those children a further concern of public policy for the first time in American history. And the liberal Left responded by denying the facts of the damage ("the statistics are wrong") and/or denying that the damage was real ("it is a cultural pattern superior in its vitality to middle-class mores") and/or by arguing about the comparative sexual morals of white and black women.

The insistence, in short, of the liberal Left that the issue of disorganization in Negro lower-class life not be made a matter of public concern resulted directly in its not being made a matter of public action.

This is nowhere near as infrequent an outcome as might be thought. Thus, in recent months it has become clear that a combination of quite conservative and super-liberal forces is attempting to oppose efforts that might raise the number of Negroes in the armed forces to something like their proportion of the population. (They are overrepresented in infantry platoons, but seriously underrepresented in the good jobs elsewhere.) It doesn't matter that Negroes may like the army as a career. No one is *allowed* to like the army.

With all its virtues as a secular conscience, the liberal Left can be as rigid and destructive as any force in American life. One is reminded, in reading some of their remarks about the report on the Negro family, of Hannah Arendt's description of the totalitarian elites of Europe between the wars: "Their superiority consists in the ability to dissolve every statement of fact into a declaration of purpose." The report was neither a long nor a complicated document. It consisted for the greater part of social statistics combined with excerpts from social-science research papers. There was little interpretation, the object being to let the correlations speak for themselves, and the reputations of the authors cited carry the rest. The intention was to arouse a will to action, rather than to propose specific actions. Yet for a year I found myself the object of incredible accusations, some of them, from academia, going quite beyond the border of fair comment. Just before the White House Conference met in June, for example, a publication of the Ferkauf Graduate School of Education at Yeshiva University devoted itself to the subject: "The Moynihan Report and Its Critics: Which Side Are You On?" The publication was not on my side, heaven knows, but, more importantly, it depicted "my" side in terms near to absolute distortion: as against those who say lower-class youths lack employment opportunities. I was one of those who say they lack employability, etc. Now, even supposing that the report was not sufficiently clear on this point and others, it happens that in the two years or so preceding, I had contributed papers to three different books on the subject, and had preached on the problem of increasing job opportunities in at least a dozen articles in periodicals ranging from *Daedalus* ("Employment, Income, and the Ordeal of the Negro Family") and the *American Scholar* to *Commonweal, Look,* the Washington *Post,* even *Vocational Guidance Quarterly.* Yet in a three-page bibliography at the end of the Yeshiva bulletin, among 117 citations, there is not one item under my name, nor any reference to articles by Negro scholars such as C. Eric Lincoln's "The Absent Father Haunts the Negro Family," which appeared in the Sunday *Times* Magazine. This is the scholarship of Che Guevara. But it must be understood that the persons who put the bulletin out (it was signed by a Mr. R. G. Goldberg) unquestionably thought they were protecting the good name and furthering the best interests of a poor and victimized class. This was a time of great expectations, and, if one may be permitted, a certain arrogance on the Left. In the face of all reason, fact, and history, the more fashionable theoreticians were reviving the old dream of a vast coalition of Negroes, intellectuals, peace workers, migrant laborers, and the CIO that would take over and purify the nation. It was a time when, for example, Professor Richard A. Cloward of the Columbia School of Social Work propounded a "strategy of crisis" whereby civil-rights activists would enroll so many eligible Negroes on welfare rolls that city finances would collapse and the federal government would be forced to institute a guaranteed annual income. (Such a movement actually began. Had it made its way across the country quickly enough, Mr. Reagan might have won by two million votes.)

It would be entirely wrong to suggest that resentment over the report was confined to white intellectuals in New York. A great many Negro activists became quite incensed over it, and remained so. A clear concern on the part of many was that the issue would be picked up and used by racists. But there is almost no indication that this occurred, and on the other hand much evidence that Negroes in more ordinary walks of life both recognized what the report was about, and hoped something would come of it. In January, as an instance, the Jewish Labor Committee in Detroit sponsored a meeting at which a Wayne State University sociologist, Arthur Lipow, denounced the report as a "distorted . . . disgraceful . . . ideological rationalization to avoid the basic problem of Negro Americans." But the *Free Press* reporter who covered the occasion wrote that "most of those in the audience, which included top civil-rights leaders in Detroit, were openly hostile to Lipow's analysis. One Negro woman charged him with being blind to the harsh realities of the situation of many Negro

Americans." And this is the point: the situation *is* real. To deny that it exists, or that anything can be done about it, is not very far from denying that anything *should* be done about it. (Harold Shephard has pointed out that liberals who today insist that government policies can have no effect on family stability are curiously reminiscent of conservatives of the 1930's who held that government could do nothing about unemployment.)

The urgency of a serious national commitment in the area of income support and guaranteed employment (which would be the central goals of a national family policy) increases as other options close. At the moment, Negroes are placing enormous confidence in the idea that quality education can transform their situation. But it is not at all clear that education has this potential. Last summer, the U.S. Office of Education issued its report on "Equality of Educational Opportunity" based on the study—the second largest in the history of social science—ordered by the Civil Rights Acts of 1964 of the educational facilities available to Negroes and other minority groups as compared with the white majority. The report, of which James S. Coleman of Johns Hopkins was the principal author, radically confounded expectation. Negroes, it turned out, tested badly at the outset of their schooling, and worse at the end of it. But the quality of the schools they attend—shockingly segregated schools—was not in fact significantly different from that of schools attended by whites and others. More important, the regression analyses carried out for the study produced the astounding proposition that the quality of the schools has only a trifling relation to achievement:

> Differences in school facilities and curriculum, which are the major variables by which attempts are made to improve schools, are so little related to differences in achievement levels of students that, with few exceptions, their effects fail to appear even in a survey of this magnitude.

These findings may be modified by further analysis, and it should be noted that for the worst-off groups, better schools do show a distinct if small relation to achievement, and in the right direction. Nonetheless, the two great determinants of outcome turned out to be family background and social peer group. In a later article in *The Public Interest,* Coleman wrote:

> Two points, then, are clear: (1) These minority children have a serious educational deficiency at the start of school, which is obviously not a result of school; and (2) they have an even more serious deficiency at the end of school, which is obviously in part a result of school.
> Altogether, the sources of inequality of educational opportunity appear to lie first in the home itself and the cultural influences im-

457

mediately surrounding the home; then they lie in the school's ineffectiveness to free achievement from the impact of the home, and in the schools' cultural homogeneity, which perpetuates the social influences of the home and its environs.

Coleman's study is probably the best statistical case for integration ever made: pouring conscience money into slum schools is simply not likely to do the job. He provides strong support for the thesis of Otis Dudley Duncan (as expressed in a forthcoming article) that despite the many paper gains that Negroes have been making (and some of course more real than that), "There are two areas of bedrock resistance to 'the progress of the Negro race': residential segregation and the weakness of the Negro family structure." Coleman's data argue that both must be overcome, while the data relating to Duncan's thesis declare that this is not happening. It now appears it could be a generation before any extensive neighborhood integration is achieved. For the moment, the trend is in the opposite direction, owing to changes in the South. Unfortunately, housing integration presents itself as a deceptively simple matter: pass a law. It is likely therefore to preoccupy civil-rights forces, even though it is the area of the most adamant and resourceful opposition. In the meantime, measures to enhance the stability and resources of the family, which might in fact be easier to achieve, will probably continue to be neglected: those who want housing integration most are likely to support these measures least, and very possibly nothing will be achieved on either count.

Given this stalemate, it is altogether possible that the nation will spiral downward into a state of protracted violence and unrest. One infant in six in this country is Negro: the problem will not go away. Yet it may also be that recent events foretell a different outcome. The nation is turning conservative at a time when its serious internal problems may well be more amenable to conservative solutions than to liberal ones—or to solutions carried out by conservatives. It may be that conservatives have more stomach for dealing with the problems of poverty and disorganization in the necessary terms. Republican ranting about welfare contains much meanness and demagoguery, but it is also true that the number of families on welfare in this country *is* a scandal. They ought to be off the dole—not for the sake of the taxpayers, but for *their* sakes. The challenge is to find viable ways of doing this, but that will be impossible unless we first allow that the problem does exist.

The New York experience may be relevant here. Two of the more spectacular political victories of recent times were the election of the Republican John V. Lindsay as Mayor of New York City in 1965 and a year later, the re-election for a third term of Governor Nelson A. Rockefeller. It was not commented upon, but the issue of race was as

458

much present in their campaigns as it was in the more obvious "backlash" affairs elsewhere. In just about every subway car in the New York transit system in 1965 there was a large advertisement that said simply *"Breathe* easier, *Sleep* better, *Feel* safer, with the Lindsay Team." Anyone who does not know what that poster was about is really not eligible to vote. Similarly in 1966 Governor Rockefeller, as the New York *Times* reported, switched his campaign in the last weeks to concentrate almost entirely on crime in the streets.

Lindsay and Rockefeller are humane, progressive men with impeccable records of leadership in civil rights. But they perceive the reality of the internal problems of the slums, and are willing to get elected on that basis. It remains to be seen whether they and others like them will come forward with programs that will command conservative support for doing something about those problems: not necessarily out of compassion for the oppressed, but out of concern for the stability of society.

But to repeat, this is not a likely outcome. There are never enough Disraelis to go round. The more likely future is one dominated by hyper-conservatives unwilling to solve problems of the kind Negroes face, hyper-liberals reluctant to acknowledge the existence of such problems, and persons of the center increasingly aware that they are probably not competent and certainly not eligible to propose solutions of their own devising. The era of white initiatives on behalf of Negroes is over. The controversy over the report on the Negro family had at least this useful outcome: it raised for Negroes the question of what terms they are willing to accept as grounds for social action. The continuing controversy among Negroes themselves over the issue, which for a year now has been dead and forgotten in Washington, suggests that some at least are finding this a timely and useful development.

Two fairly clear points of view have emerged. On the one hand, there is that of Martin Luther King, Jr., who is willing to describe the present conditions of life in the lower classes as a "social catastrophe" and to say in effect to the white world, "Put up or shut up." The basic idea is that there can and ought to be change. This is a view widely held by scholars and activists alike. Thus, Parren Mitchell, head of the Baltimore poverty program, declared at the height of the controversy: "Slavery depended upon preventing the Negro family from forming, and over the centuries since, that tradition hung on. Now what we need is a better tradition. We need to hold our families together in a stronger kind of responsibility." But just as many—more —have taken quite a different view, namely that the family structure of the lower classes is a natural and essentially healthful adaptation to special conditions of life. In an interview in November 1966 the novelist Ralph Ellison, expressing his annoyance with the report, said: 459

> Moynihan looked at a fatherless family and interpreted it not in the context of Negro cultural patterns, but in a white cultural pattern. He wasn't looking at the accommodations Negroes have worked out in dealing with fatherless families. Grandmothers very often look after the kids. The mother works or goes on relief. The kids identify with stepfathers, uncles, even the mother's boyfriends. How children grow up is a cultural, not a statistical pattern.

I would argue that this is a perfectly tenable position. There is no reason Negroes need conform to anyone's standards but their own, and like no one else, Ellison has evoked the qualities of endurance and holding-on which are as much the fact of Negro character in white America as are the extremes of respectability or disorganization. On the other hand, in order for this to be a *viable* position as well as a tenable one, it must reject not only conformity but dependency. It is all very well to point out with whom it is that impoverished Negro youth identifies: the public issue is who supports them. So long as exceptional numbers of Negro children are dependent on Welfare (recently the U.S. Commissioner of Welfare reported that the majority of families receiving AFDC payments now are non-whites) and so long as vast numbers of Negro youths have to be helped along with Head Start, Upward Bound, Job Corps, and so on, Negroes will be at the mercy of whites demanding an end to "welfare chiseling" and "immorality," and also, no doubt, of the unwelcome ministrations of meliorists in the subcabinet. These things ought not to be so, but they are so. As the report said on its first page: "The racist virus in the American blood stream still afflicts us: Negroes will encounter serious personal prejudice for at least another generation." If at the moment educated, middle-class Negroes are much in demand and doing nicely, this is not so for the lower class and is likely never to be. This country is not fair to Negroes and will exploit any weaknesses they display. Hence they simply cannot afford the luxury of having a large lower class that is at once deviant *and* dependent. If they do not wish to bring it into line with the working class (*not* middle-class) world around them, they must devise ways to support it from within. It is entirely possible that this could happen, and it might be an eye-opener for all concerned. In all events, one of the most galling forms of dependency is surely behind us. The time when white men, whatever their motives, could tell Negroes what was or was not good for them, is now definitely and decidedly over. An era of bad manners is almost certainly begun. For a moment it had seemed this could be avoided, that the next two decades could be bypassed in a sweep of insight and daring. But the destiny reasserted itself. The Physiocrats never did have much luck.

460

Laura Carper

The Negro Family and the Moynihan Report

MRS. BOYLE: We'll go. Come, Mary, an' we'll never some back here agen. Let your father furrage for himself now; I've done all I could an' it was all no use—he'll be hopeless till the end of his days. I've got a little room in me sisther's where we'll stop till your throuble is over, an' then we'll work together for the sake of the baby.
MARY: My poor little child that'll have no father!
MRS. BOYLE: It'll have what's far betther—it'll have two mothers.

(*Juno and the Paycock*, Act III, Sean O'Casey)

The culmination of intensive efforts to codify the life of the hapless is a document published by the Department of Labor entitled *The Negro Family: The Case for National Action* and commonly referred to as "The Moynihan Report," after the reputed head of the investigation—the sociologist Daniel Moynihan. With the publication of this document a sociological theory which borders on an ideology has become a political weapon which we are all obliged to examine. In order to understand the theoretical framework within which this document was written, we must take a cursory look at sociological thought in the recent period.

In 1960, Dreger and Miller published in the *Psychological Bulletin* a critical evaluation of the "Comparative Psychological Studies of Negroes and Whites in the United States," which was an examination of the relevant contributions in the field between 1943 and 1958. They concluded that "in the areas of psychological functioning most closely related to the sociological, social class differences show up

Reprinted by permission of the author and publisher from *Dissent*, March-April 1966, pp. 133–140.

461

POVERTY AND INEQUALITY

more clearly as a basis for differentiation between the two groups. Leadership, family life, child rearing practices, fertility and mate selection all seem to conform to social structure rather than to racial lines per se."

Dreger and Miller's conclusion reflected the intensive efforts of liberal sociological and psychological thought of the period. It was the culmination of a thoroughgoing examination of the corrosive effects of our peculiar social organization and value system on the Negro as compared to the white. They were unable to find a uniquely Negro personality or Negro psychology in any class. Their conclusion became a landmark in the field with which every investigator has been forced to contend.

In April 1964, however, *The Journal of Social Issues* published a collection of studies with an introduction by Thomas Pettigrew and Daniel C. Thompson and a lead article by Thomas Pettigrew which sought to delineate what Dreger and Miller were unable to locate—a Negro personality and a Negro psychology. Frankly admitting that in this effort social psychology was whistling in the dark since the Negro was notorious for his refusal to reveal his inner self to the social investigator and since it was virtually impossible to establish control groups of whites, Pettigrew nevertheless argued that past findings have "underestimated the corrosive effects on young children of impecunious ghetto living." This may indeed be true, but the theoretical basis of the issue is that due to the vicissitudes of his history and the brutality of white society, the Negro has developed a recognizable psychology and a recognizable personality which emerged under slavery, and that this psychology is self-sustaining and transmitted from generation to generation. The studies, together with the introduction, almost seem to argue for the existence of a racial unconscious.

The thinking here represents a powerful tendency in modern sociological thought; and it is this thinking, shorn of its somewhat hesitant and carefully hedged tone, which characterizes the ideological commitment of *The Report on the Negro Family* and the direction its authors feel national action should take.

The thesis of the Report is that the Negro poor "confront the nation with a new kind of problem. Measures that have worked in the past, or would work for most groups in the present will not work here. A national effort is required that will give unity and purpose to the many activities of the Federal government in this area, directed to a new kind of national goal: the establishment of a stable Negro family structure." The presumption is that the Negro poor are no longer merely the victims of white institutional corruption but also, to an undetermined extent, of their corrosive family life; that despite the enactment of the voting rights bill, the creation of the "Manpower

462

Retraining Program, The Job Corps, and Community Action—et al,"
fifty per cent of the Negro population is incapable of profiting because
of a psychological distemper.

The argument is supported with an array of statistics but without
any effort to come to terms with the fact that variations in life style
and social adjustment *within* the ghetto and between the Northern
and Southern Negro poor are far more varied than between all of them
and society at large. Fifty per cent of the Negro population is identified
as reflecting the "social pathology" these statistics itemize, and the
Negro family is recognized as its "source."

On page thirteen of the report there is a graph charting the non-
white male unemployment rate and the number of AFDC (Aid to
Families with Dependent Children) cases opened each year. This
graph is the strongest argument the report offers to substantiate its
thesis that the Negro poor have been so crippled by their situation
and history that ordinary measures—which I suppose would be full
employment, a radical revision of the ghetto school system, integrated
education, decent housing, and a rigorously controlled police force—
will no longer suffice; that what is now needed is a national effort not
to alter our white social institutions but the way the Negro poor relate
to each other on the primary personal level—the family.

The graph shows a direct correlation between the non-white male
unemployment rate and AFDC cases opened each year between 1948
and 1961. As the unemployment rate drops, AFDC cases drop; as the
unemployment rate rises, AFDC cases rise. But in 1962 a negative
correlation begins to emerge; in 1963 the lines for each cross; in 1964
AFDC cases continue to rise as the unemployment rate continues to
drop. Presumably, the negative correlation after 1962 shows or suggests
that giving the Negro male a job will no longer insure or help insure
family stability. The conclusion is that something more is needed.

I am not prepared to argue an economic determinist thesis. It is
not my contention that the area of full employment is the only front
on which we should fight. But I would like to attempt to explain the
graph, particularly since the authors of the report direct the reader's
attention to the negative correlation and argue that no government
program should be instituted which aims at relieving the plight of the
Negro poor until the reasons for the reversal are understood.

The first consideration in evaluating statistics is to understand their
relevance. *New* AFDC cases must therefore be compared with the
unemployment rate of young Negroes. A little investigation shows
that the unemployment rate for non-white males as a whole is not
reflected in the unemployment rate of non-white youth. Non-white
youth, male and female, show a radically different set of statistics;
and it is of course the young and not the mature Negro woman who
would be a new AFDC case. The unemployment rate for eighteen and   463

nineteen year old non-white men rose from 23.9% in 1961 to 27.4% in 1963, and for eighteen and nineteen year old women who would be obliged to assist in the support of their families from 28.2% to 31.9%. Taken as a whole, the unemployment rate of non-white men between the ages of sixteen and twenty-four during the years in question fluctuates but shows little over-all change. In 1963, the year the lines for AFDC cases and the unemployment rate converge, the rates were especially high. Where the over-all non-white male unemployment rate went down in 1963, the unemployment rate for youth went up and then went down a little in 1964. The picture for young non-white women is comparable. Their rate showed a general tendency to increase.

These figures, although they radically temper the implications of the graph, do not account for the extent of the reversal. A complete explanation must include the famous 1962 change in the social security law. There is a remarkable correlation between AFDC figures and the date of the new law, which authorized greater social and case work service to the poor. In the state of Michigan at least (I choose Michigan arbitrarily, only because I live there and was in a position to discuss the graph with the welfare department), the department has interpreted this law as a directive to alter its standards. Prior to 1962, if an applicant was a poor housekeeper, mentally disturbed, or evidence of a male friend could be found, her application for AFDC was denied; after 1962 she was accepted if she showed need, regardless of her housekeeping practices, her mental health or her social life. Whereas between July 1960 and June 1961 33.4% of the applications were denied, only 28% were denied between July 1963 and June 1964. The strange graph in the Moynihan Report is the result of graphing the wrong things. The negative correlation is due to an inconsistency between youth unemployment rate and the unemployment rate of the non-white male population as a whole and to an important change in policy on the part of the welfare authorities. As a staff member of the department informed me, "it is our policy to give everyone a chance now." The thinking behind the new policy is that by accepting the "undeserving" poor as well as the "deserving" poor, case-work service is made available to those who need it most. It is inevitable that as news of this policy change spreads among the Negro poor and as each of the states slowly alters its policy to conform to this new view, AFDC cases will continue to rise.

The Negro family is not the source of the "tangle of pathology" which the report attributes to the Negro community. It is the pathological relationship between white social institutions and the Negro community which has bred the statistics the report cites—from low scholastic averages to drug addiction to arrest records to illegitimacy to unemployment rates. This is the reason the Black Muslims have 464 chosen to withdraw, and this is the reason the civil rights movement has chosen to confront us.

The statistics I have tried to examine are the supportive evidence the report offers in defense of a social psychological theory. In brief the argument is that American slavery stripped the Negro of his culture and his most minimal human rights; and that the Negro, under continued oppression, developed a matriarchal family organization within which the male played an inadequate role, if any. The argument continues that since American family life is patriarchal, the matriarchal family formation is pathological and is perpetuating a pathological Negro culture—as the statistics show. But I cannot help wonder with James Tobin, who published an interesting economic study in the Fall 1965 issue of *Daedalus,* why "personal attributes which doom(ed) a man to unemployment in 1932 or even 1954 or 1961 did not handicap him in 1944 or 1951 or 1956." Peter Townsend has pointed out that in 1930 many Englishmen estimated that as many as a million of their fellow-countrymen were unemployable because of their personal problems and only a decade later found that only 100,000 could be characterized in this way. There was a manpower shortage in 1940. What appears to be a social malformation in one period becomes the problem of isolated individuals in another.

The Negro poor are distinguished from the middle class primarily by the fact that they are poor. The father is haphazardly employed and at a very low wage. He is frequently absent from the family scene. He has either deserted or been thrown out by the mother. If he is present and works, he may squander his income. The children are raised by an extended family of adult women. This picture does not focus fifty per cent of the Negro families. But it does include a significant section of the Negro poor. Is it peculiar to them?

"Matriarchy" is a cultural formation common to many oppressed people throughout the history of western civilization—regardless of their own past history and regardless of the values they themselves held. A brilliant and moving characterization of how and why such a family constellation developed among the Irish poor can be found in Sean O'Casey's play *Juno and the Paycock,* from which I took the quotation which precedes this piece. The Irish matriarchal family formation is noteworthy because it existed in conflict with an Irish patriarchal ideal.

Both Patricia Sexton and Oscar Lewis have shown that the poor Puerto Rican family is beginning to move toward the same "pathology" as the Negro: illegitimacy and families with a woman at the helm.

The same can be said of Jewish family life in the *shtetl.* Although illegitimacy was not a problem (partly because divorce merely involved a witnessed statement placed in the hand of the wife) the 465 father was frequently absent, either as a peddler on the road, as an immigrant in America, or as a permanent resident of the house of study who came home only to eat. Newly married couples usually moved into the home of the bride's parents. Among the Hassidic Jews (Hassidism was a movement initiated by the poor), it was common for the father to leave his wife and children without a kopek or a groshen in the house and depart for the Rebbe's court where he would dance and drink and spend all his money. As among the American poor, relations between husband and wife were cold and the roles of each clearly defined. The wife worked and assumed the main burden of supporting the family, and children became adults before they had ever had an opportunity to be children. The man either struggled desperately to make a living with little success or withdrew entirely into a private male society based on discourse or ecstacy and left the family to shift for itself. What the Jewish man succeeded in doing that the Negro man has failed to do is place a positive value on family desertion and personal withdrawal.

Since the Negro man does not rationalize his role as being a desirable religious achievement, it seems to me he would be easier to integrate into the surrounding culture than the Jew. After all, once integration became a viable possibility, even the *shtetl* Jew cast off what no longer served him. And the depth and extent to which oppression and poverty reduced the Jew can be measured by the disintegrative effects of the widespread Messianic movements, two of which emphasized orgiastic sexual practices as a means of insuring the coming of the Messiah.

I have chosen to detail the matriarchal organization of the Jewish family life not because it corresponds to the Negro family but because sociologists look upon Jewish family life as remarkably cohesive. Is the caricature I have drawn of the *shtetl* family accurate? Of course not. I have applied Mr. Moynihan's method of describing the Negro to a description of the Jew. I lumped a few hundred years of history together and failed to distinguish between people. Pathology is in the eye of the beholder. If one eliminates the positive social function of a cultural constellation, if one ignores the meaning personal relations have to the people involved, if one, in short, uses science to depersonalize, what emerges is always pathology. For health involves spontaneous human feelings of affection and tenderness which the Moynihan Report, like my deliberate caricature of Jewish family life, cannot encompass.

Let me also add that I am not trying to draw any direct analogies between the Irish poor, the Jewish poor, or even the Puerto Rican poor, and the Negro poor. I am seeking to show that "matriarchy" within the larger social context of what the report calls "patriarchy" is common to the way of life of poor people. And further, that people 466 living under oppression always develop social formations which appear to the surrounding oppressive culture to be excessive or pathological. The form these so-called excesses take varies from culture to culture and person to person within the culture—but no matter how extreme the nature of the adjustment, once the social pressure which created it is removed, a new adjustment develops. A people is not destroyed by its history. What destroys a people is physical annihilation or assimilation, not its family life.

The question the report raises is the direction a government program would take to insure family stability. What is the quality of the solutions Mr. Moynihan has in mind? The report includes a detailed description of the therapeutic effects of military service. Mr. Moynihan argues that the armed forces are educational and that they "provide the largest single source of employment in the nation." He admits that "for those comparatively few who are killed or wounded in combat, or otherwise, the personal sacrifice is inestimable. But on balance, service in the Armed Forces over the past quarter-century has worked greatly to the advantage of those involved. . . . Service in the United States Armed Forces is the *only* [author's italics] experience open to the Negro-American in which he is truly treated as an equal: not as a Negro equal to any white, but as one man equal to any man in a world where the category 'Negro' and 'white' do not exist." Mr. Moynihan further states that for the Negro "the armed forces are a dramatic and desperately needed change: a world away from women, a world run by strong men of unquestioned authority, where discipline, if harsh, is nonetheless orderly and predictable and where rewards, if limited, are granted on the basis of performance." This view of the desirability of army life is patently absurd. Underlying the Report's understanding of the problems of the Negro family is its author's concept of masculinity. According to the Report "the essence of the male animal, from the bantam rooster to the four-star general, is to strut."

I cannot here counterpose my taste in men or my concept of the good life against Mr. Moynihan's—but it seems clear to me that it is for the Negro male himself to determine his sexual and social style —whether strutting or not.

The challenge to the Negro community is political. It remains to be seen whether we can make room for the poor to acquire social and economic power. This is our social problem—and not the existence of a matriarchal family organization. What is more, Frank Riessman has found that involving emotionally disturbed people among the Negro poor in the civil rights movement can resolve their personal problems. What is destructive to the Negro man and woman is social impotence here and now, and what rehabilitates them is social power and the struggle for it. It is not new for a ruling elite to characterize 467 its poor as incontinent and shiftless. It is the characteristic way in which those on top describe those on the bottom, even when sincerely trying to uplift them. My Negro landlady encountered a helpful woman who tried to tell her that Negro culture was rooted in the life style of slavery and fixed by history. In telling me about the conversation my landlady said, "That woman thinks that if she handed me a bail of cotton, I'd know how to make a dress out of it!" The Negro is not grappling with the social system under which he lived over a hundred years ago, or even with the social system under which he lived ten years ago. He is grappling with the social system under which he lives today.

Bayard Rustin

The Watts "Manifesto" & the McCone Report

The riots in the Watts section of Los Angeles last August continued for six days, during which 34 persons were killed, 1,032 were injured, and some 3,952 were arrested. Viewed by many of the rioters themselves as their "manifesto," the uprising of the Watts Negroes brought out in the open, as no other aspect of the Negro protest has done, the despair and hatred that continue to brew in the Northern ghettoes despite the civil-rights legislation of recent years and the advent of "the war on poverty." With national attention focused on Los Angeles, Governor Edward P. Brown created a commission of prominent local citizens, headed by John A. McCone, to investigate the causes of the riots and to prescribe remedies against any such outbreaks in the future. Just as the violent confrontation on the burning streets of Watts told us much about the underlying realities of race and class relations in America—summed up best, perhaps, by the words of Los Angeles Police Chief William Parker, "We're on top and they're on the bottom"—so does the McCone Report, published under the title *Violence in the City—An End or a Beginning?*, tell us much about the response of our political and economic institutions to the Watts "manifesto."

Like the much-discussed Moynihan Report, the McCone Report is a bold departure from the standard government paper on social problems. It goes beyond the mere recital of statistics to discuss, somewhat sympathetically, the real problems of the Watts community —problems like unemployment, inadequate schools, dilapidated housing—and it seems at first glance to be leading toward constructive programs. It never reaches them, however, for, again like the Moyni-

Reprinted from *Commentary*, March 1966, pp. 29–35, by permission of the author and publisher; copyright © 1966 by the American Jewish Committee. Bayard Rustin, the noted civil-rights leader, is executive director of The A. Philip Randolph Institute in New York.

han Report, it is ambivalent about the basic reforms that are needed to solve these problems and therefore shies away from spelling them out too explicitly. Thus, while it calls for the creation of 50,000 new jobs to compensate for the "spiral of failure" that it finds among the Watts Negroes, the McCone Report does not tell us how these jobs are to be created or obtained and instead recommends existing programs which have already shown themselves to be inadequate. The Moynihan Report, similarly, by emphasizing the breakdown of the Negro family, also steers clear of confronting the thorny issues of Negro unemployment as such.

By appearing to provide new viewpoints and fresh initiatives while at the same time repeating, if in more sophisticated and compassionate terms, the standard white stereotypes and shibboleths about Negroes, the two reports have become controversial on both sides of the Negro question. On the one hand, civil-rights leaders can point to the recognition in these reports of the need for jobs and training, and for other economic and social programs to aid the Negro family, while conservatives can find confirmed in their pages the Negro penchant for violence, the excessive agitation against law and order by the civil-rights movement, or the high rates of crime and illegitimacy in the Negro community; on the other hand, both sides have criticized the reports for feeding ammunition to the opposition. Unfortunately, but inevitably, the emphasis on *Negro* behavior in both reports has stirred up an abstract debate over the interpretation of data rather than suggesting programs for dealing with the existing and very concrete situation in which American Negroes find themselves. For example, neither report is concerned about segregation and both tacitly assume that the Civil Rights Acts of 1964 and 1965 are already destroying this system. In the case of the McCone Report, this leaves the writers free to discuss the problems of Negro housing, education, and unemployment in great detail without attacking the conditions of de facto segregation that underly them.

The errors and misconceptions of the McCone Report are particularly revealing because it purports to deal with the realities of the Watts riots rather than with the abstractions of the Negro family. The first distortion of these realities occurs in the opening chapter—"The Crisis: An Overview"—where, after briefly discussing the looting and beatings, the writers conclude that "The rioters seem to have been caught up in an insensate rage of destruction." Such an image may reflect the fear of the white community that Watts had run amok during six days in August, but it does not accurately describe the major motive and mood of the riots, as subsequent data in the report itself indicate. While it is true that Negroes in the past have often turned the violence inflicted on them by society in upon themselves —"insensate rage" would perhaps have been an appropriate phrase 470 for the third day of the 1964 Harlem riots—the whole point of the outbreak in Watts was that it marked the first major rebellion of Negroes against their own masochism and was carried on with the express purpose of asserting that they would no longer quietly submit to the deprivation of slum life.

This message came home to me over and over again when I talked with the young people in Watts during and after the riots, as it will have come home to those who watched the various television documentaries in which the Negroes of the community were permitted to speak for themselves. At a street-corner meeting in Watts when the riots were over, an unemployed youth of about twenty said to me, "We won." I asked him: "How have you won? Homes have been destroyed, Negroes are lying dead in the streets, the stores from which you buy food and clothes are destroyed, and people are bringing you relief." His reply was significant: "We won because we made the whole world pay attention to us. The police chief never came here before; the mayor always stayed uptown. We made them come." Clearly it was no accident that the riots proceeded along an almost direct path to City Hall.

Nor was the violence along the way random and "insensate." Wherever a store-owner identified himself as a "poor working Negro trying to make a business" or as a "Blood Brother," the mob passed the store by. It even spared a few white businesses that allowed credit or time purchases, and it made a point of looting and destroying stores that were notorious for their high prices and hostile manners. The McCone Report itself observes that "the rioters concentrated on food markets, liquor stores, clothing stores, department stores, and pawn shops." The authors "note with interest that no residences were deliberately burned, that damage to schools, libraries, public buildings was minimal and that certain types of business establishments, notably service stations and automobile dealers, were for the most part unharmed." It is also worth noting that the rioters were much more inclined to destroy the stock of the liquor stores they broke into than to steal it, and that according to the McCone Report, "there is no evidence that the rioters made any attempt to steal narcotics from pharmacies . . . which were looted and burned."

This is hardly a description of a Negro community that has run amok. The largest number of arrests were for looting—not for arson or shooting. Most of the people involved were not habitual thieves; they were members of a deprived group who seized a chance to possess things that all the dinning affluence of Los Angeles had never given them. There were innumerable touching examples of this behavior. One married couple in their sixties was seen carrying a couch to their home, and when its weight became too much for them, they sat down and rested on it until they could pick it up again. Langston Hughes tells of another woman who was dragging a sofa through the   471 streets and who stopped at each intersection and waited for the traffic light to turn green. A third woman went out with her children to get a kitchen set, and after bringing it home, she discovered they needed one more chair in order to feed the whole family together; they went back to get the chair and all of them were arrested.

If the McCone Report misses the point of the Watts riots, it shows even less understanding of their causes. To place these in perspective, the authors begin by reviewing the various outbursts in the Negro ghettoes since the summer of 1964 and quickly come up with the following explanations: "Not enough jobs to go around, and within this scarcity not enough by a wide margin of a character which the untrained Negro could fill. . . . Not enough schooling to meet the special needs of the disadvantaged Negro child whose environment from infancy onward places him under a serious handicap." Finally, "a resentment, even hatred, of the police as a symbol of authority."

For the members of the special commission these are the fundamental causes of the current Negro plight and protest, which are glibly summed up in the ensuing paragraph by the statement that "Many Negroes moved to the city in the last generation and are totally unprepared to meet the conditions of city life." I shall be discussing these "causes" in detail as we go along, but it should be noted here that the burden of responsibility has already been placed on these hapless migrants to the cities. There is not one word about the conditions, economic as well as social, that have pushed Negroes out of the rural areas; nor is there one word about whether the cities have been willing and able to meet the demand for jobs, adequate housing, proper schools. After all, one could as well say that it is the *cities* which have been "totally unprepared" to meet the "conditions of *Negro* life," but the moralistic bias of the McCone Report, involving as it does an emphasis on the decisions of men rather than the pressure of social forces, continually operates in the other direction.

The same failure of awareness is evident in the report's description of the Los Angeles situation (the Negro areas of Los Angeles "are not urban gems, neither are they slums," the Negro population "has exploded," etc.). The authors do concede that the Los Angeles transportation system is the "least adequate of any major city," but even here they fail to draw the full consequences of their findings. Good, cheap transportation is essential to a segregated working-class population in a big city. In Los Angeles a domestic worker, for example, must spend about $1.50 and 1½ to 2 hours to get to a job that pays $6 or $7 a day. This both discourages efforts to find work and exacerbates the feeling of isolation.

A neighborhood such as Watts may seem beautiful when compared to much of Harlem (which, in turn, is an improvement over the Negro section of Mobile, Alabama)—but it is still a ghetto. The housing is

472

run-down, public services are inferior, the listless penned-in atmosphere of segregation is oppressive. Absentee landlords are the rule, and most of the businesses are owned by whites: neglect and exploitation reign by day, and at night, as one Watts Negro tersely put it, "There's just the cops and us."

The McCone Report, significantly, also ignores the political atmosphere of Los Angeles. It refers, for example, to the repeal in 1964 of the Rumford Act—the California fair-housing law—in these words: "In addition, many Negroes here felt and were encouraged to feel that they had been affronted by the passage of Proposition 14." Affronted, indeed! The largest state in the Union, by a three-to-one majority, abolishes one of its own laws against discrimination and Negroes are described as regarding this as they might the failure of a friend to keep an engagement. What they did feel—and without any need of encouragement—was that while the rest of the North was passing civil-rights laws and improving opportunities for Negroes, their own state and city were rushing to reinforce the barriers against them.

The McCone Report goes on to mention two other "aggravating events in the twelve months prior to the riot." One was the failure of the poverty program to "live up to [its] press notices," combined with reports of "controversy and bickering" in Los Angeles over administering the program. The second "aggravating event" is summed up by the report in these words:

Throughout the nation unpunished violence and disobedience to law were widely reported, and almost daily there were exhortations here and elsewhere, to take the most extreme and illegal remedies to right a wide variety of wrongs, real and supposed.

It would be hard to frame a more insidiously equivocal statement of the Negro grievance concerning law enforcement during a period that included the release of the suspects in the murder of the three civil-rights workers in Mississippi, the failure to obtain convictions against the suspected murderers of Medgar Evers and Mrs. Violet Liuzzo, the Gilligan incident in New York, the murder of Reverend James Reeb, and the police violence in Selma, Alabama—to mention only a few of the more notorious cases. And surely it would have been more to the point to mention that throughout the nation Negro demonstrations have almost invariably been non-violent, and that the major influence on the Negro community of the civil-rights movement has been the strategy of discipline and dignity. Obsessed by the few prophets of violent resistance, the McCone Commission ignores the fact that never before has an American group sent so many people to jail or been so severely punished for trying to uphold the law of the land. 473

It is not stretching things too far to find a connection between these matters and the treatment of the controversy concerning the role of the Los Angeles police. The report goes into this question at great length, finally giving no credence to the charge that the police may have contributed to the spread of the riots through the use of excessive force. Yet this conclusion is arrived at not from the point of view of the Watts Negroes, but from that of the city officials and the police. Thus, the report informs us, in judicial hearings that were held on 32 of the 35 deaths which occurred, 26 were ruled justifiable homicides, but the report—which includes such details as the precise time Mayor Yorty called Police Chief Parker and when exactly the National Guard was summoned—never tells us what a "justifiable homicide" is considered to be. It tells us that "of the 35 killed, one was a fireman, one was a deputy sheriff, and one was a Long Beach policeman," but it does not tell us how many Negroes were killed or injured by police or National Guardsmen. (Harry Fleischman of the American Jewish Committee reports that the fireman was killed by a falling wall; the deputy sheriff, by another sheriff's bullet; and the policeman, by another policeman's bullet.) We learn that of the 1,032 people reported injured, 90 were police officers, 36 were firemen, 10 were National Guardsmen, 23 were from government agencies. To find out that about 85 per cent of the injured were Negroes, we have to do our own arithmetic. The report contains no information as to how many of these were victims of police force, but one can surmise from the general pattern of the riots that few could have been victims of Negro violence.

The report gives credence to Chief Parker's assertion that the rioters were the "criminal element in Watts" yet informs us that of the 3,438 adults arrested, 1,164 had only minor criminal records and 1,232 had never been arrested before. Moreover, such statistics are always misleading. Most Negroes, at one time or another, have been picked up and placed in jail. I myself have been arrested twice in Harlem on charges that had no basis in fact: once for trying to stop a police officer from arresting the wrong man; the second time for asking an officer who was throwing several young men into a paddy wagon what they had done. Both times I was charged with interfering with an arrest and kept overnight in jail until the judge recognized me and dismissed the charges. Most Negroes are not fortunate enough to be recognized by judges.

Having accepted Chief Parker's view of the riots, the report goes on to absolve him of the charge of discrimination: "Chief Parker's statements to us and collateral evidence, such as his fairness to Negro officers, are inconsistent with his having such an attitude ['deep hatred of Negroes']. Despite the depth of feeling against Chief Parker expressed to us by so many witnesses, he is recognized even by many

474

of his vocal critics as a capable Chief who directs an efficient police force and serves well this entire community."

I am not going to stress the usual argument that the police habitually mistreat Negroes. Every Negro knows this. There is scarcely any black man, woman, or child in the land who at some point or other has not been mistreated by a policeman. (A young man in Watts said, "The riots will continue because I, as a Negro, am immediately considered to be a criminal by the police and, if I have a pretty woman with me, she is a tramp even if she is my wife or mother.") Police Chief Parker, however, goes beyond the usual bounds. He does not recognize that he is prejudiced, and being both naïve and zealous about law and order, he is given to a dangerous fanaticism. His reference to the Negro rioters as "monkeys," and his "top . . . and bottom" description of the riots, speak for themselves, and they could only have further enraged and encouraged the rioters. His insistence on dealing with the outbreak in Watts as though it were the random work of a "criminal element" threatened to lead the community, as Martin Luther King remarked after the meeting he and I had with Chief Parker, "into potential holocaust." Though Dr. King and I have had considerable experience in talking with public officials who do not understand the Negro community, our discussions with Chief Parker and Mayor Samuel Yorty left us completely nonplussed. They both denied, for example, that there was any prejudice in Los Angeles. When we pointed to the very heavy vote in the city for Proposition 14, they replied, "That's no indication of prejudice. That's personal choice." When I asked Chief Parker about his choice of language, he implied that this was the only language Negroes understood.

The impression of "blind intransigence and ignorance of the social forces involved" which Dr. King carried away from our meeting with Chief Parker is borne out by other indications. The cast of his political beliefs, for example, was evidenced during his appearance last May on the Manion Forum, one of the leading platforms of the radical right, in which (according to newspaper reports) he offered his "considered opinion that America today is in reality more than half pagan" and that "we have moved our form of government to a socialist form of government." Such opinions have a good deal of currency today within the Los Angeles police department. About a month before the riots, a leaflet describing Dr. King as a liar and a Communist was posted on the bulletin board of a Los Angeles police station, and only after the concerted efforts of various Negro organizations was this scurrilous pamphlet removed.

Certainly these were "aggravating factors" that the McCone Report should properly have mentioned. But what is more important to 475 understand is that even if every policeman in every black ghetto behaved like an angel and were trained in the most progressive of police academies, the conflict would still exist. This is so because the ghetto is a place where Negroes do not want to be and are fighting to get out of. When someone with a billy club and a gun tells you to behave yourself amid these terrible circumstances, he becomes a zoo keeper, demanding of you, as one of "these monkeys" (to use Chief Parker's phrase), that you accept abhorrent conditions. He is brutalizing you by insisting that you tolerate what you cannot, and ought not, tolerate.

In its blithe ignorance of such feelings, the McCone Report offers as one of its principal suggestions that speakers be sent to Negro schools to teach the students that the police are their friends and that their interests are best served by respect for law and order. Such public-relations gimmicks, of course, are futile—it is hardly a lack of contact with the police that creates the problem. Nor, as I have suggested, is it only a matter of prejudice. The fact is that when Negroes are deprived of work, they resort to selling numbers, women, or dope to earn a living; they must gamble and work in poolrooms. And when the policeman upholds the law, he is depriving them of their livelihood. A clever criminal in the Negro ghettoes is not unlike a clever "operator" in the white business world, and so long as Negroes are denied legitimate opportunities, no exhortations to obey the rules of the society and to regard the police as friends will have any effect.

This is not to say that relations between the police and the Negroes of Watts could not be improved. Mayor Yorty and Police Chief Parker might have headed off a full-scale riot had they refrained from denouncing the Negro leaders and agreed to meet with them early on. Over and over again—to repeat the point with which we began—the rioters claimed that violence was the only way they could get these officials to listen to them. The McCone Commission, however, rejects the proposal for an independent police review board and instead recommends that the post of Inspector General be established —under the authority of the Chief of Police—to handle grievances.

The conditions of Negro life in Watts are not, of course, ignored by the McCone Report. Their basic structure is outlined in a section entitled "Dull, Devastating Spiral of Failure." Here we find that the Negro's "homelife destroys incentive"; that he lacks "experience with words and ideas"; that he is "unready and unprepared" in school; and that, "unprepared and unready," he "*slips* into the ranks of the unemployed" (my italics).

I would say, *is shoved.* It is time that we began to understand this "dull, devastating spiral of failure" and that we stopped attributing it to this or that characteristic of Negro life. In 1940, Edward Wight   476

Bakke described the effects of unemployment on family structure in terms of the following model: The jobless man no longer provides, credit runs out, the woman is forced to take a job; if relief then becomes necessary, the woman is regarded even more as the center of the family; the man is dependent on her, the children are bewildered, and the stability of the family is threatened and often shattered. Bakke's research dealt strictly with white families. The fact that Negro social scientists like E. Franklin Frazier and Kenneth Clark have shown that this pattern is typical among the Negro poor does not mean, then, that it stems from some inherent Negro trait or is the ineluctable product of Negro social history. If Negroes suffer more than others from the problems of family instability today, it is not because they are Negro but because they are so disproportionately unemployed, underemployed, and ill-paid.

Anyone looking for historical patterns would do well to consider the labor market for Negroes since the Emancipation. He will find that Negro men have consistently been denied the opportunity to enter the labor force in anything like proportionate numbers, have been concentrated in the unskilled and marginal labor and service occupations, and have generally required wartime emergencies to make any advances in employment, job quality, and security. Such advances are then largely wiped out when the economy slumps again.

In 1948, for example, the rates of Negro and white unemployment were roughly equal. During the next decade, however, Negro unemployment was consistently double that of whites, and among Negro teenagers it remained at the disastrously high figure which prevailed for the entire population during the Depression. It is true that the nation's improved economic performance in recent years has reduced the percentage of jobless Negroes from 12.6 per cent, which it reached in 1958 (12.5 per cent in 1961) to roughly 8.1 per cent today. Despite this progress, the rate of Negro unemployment continues to be twice as high as white (8.13 per cent as against 4.2 per cent). In other words, job discrimination remains constant. These statistics, moreover, conceal the persistence of Negro youth unemployment: in 1961, 24.7 per cent of those Negro teenagers not in school were out of work and it is estimated that in 1966 this incredible rate will only decline to 23.2 per cent. What this figure tells us is that the rise in Negro employment has largely resulted from the calling of men with previous experience back to work. This is an ominous trend, for it is estimated that in the coming year, 20 per cent of the new entrants into the labor force will be Negro (almost twice as high as the Negro percentage of the population). Approximately half of these young Negroes will not have the equivalent of a high-school education and they will be competing in an economy in which the demand for skill and training is increasing sharply.

Thus there is bound to be a further deterioration of the Negro's   477 economic—and hence social—position, despite the important political victories being achieved by the civil-rights movement. For many young Negroes, who are learning that economic servitude can be as effective an instrument of discrimination as racist laws, the new "freedom" has already become a bitter thing indeed. No wonder that the men of Watts were incensed by reports that the poverty program was being obstructed in Los Angeles by administrative wrangling. (As I write this, the New York *Times* reports that political rivalries and ambitions have now virtually paralyzed the program in that area.)

How does the McCone Report propose to halt this "dull, devastating spiral of failure"? First, through education—"our fundamental resource." The commission's analysis begins with a comparison of class size in white and Negro areas (the latter are referred to throughout as "disadvantaged areas" and Negro schools, as "disadvantaged schools"). It immediately notes that classes in the disadvantaged schools are slightly smaller; on the other hand, the more experienced teachers are likely to be found in the *non*-disadvantaged areas, and there is tremendous overcrowding in the disadvantaged schools because of double sessions. The buildings in the "disadvantaged areas are in better repair"; on the other hand, there are "cafeterias in the advantaged schools" but not in the disadvantaged schools, which also have no libraries. This random balance sheet of "resources" shows no sense of priorities; moreover, despite the alarming deficiencies it uncovers in the "disadvantaged schools," the McCone Report, in consistent fashion, places its emphasis on the Negro child's "deficiency in environmental experiences" and on "his homelife [which] all too often fails to give him incentive. . . ."

The two major recommendations of the commission in this area will hardly serve to correct the imbalances revealed. The first is that elementary and junior high schools in the "disadvantaged areas" which have achievement levels substantially below the city average should be designated "Emergency Schools." In each of these schools an emergency literacy program is to be established with a maximum of 22 students in each class and an enlarged and supportive corps of teachers. The second recommendation is to establish a permanent pre-school program to help prepare three- and four-year-old children to read and write.

W. T. Bassett, executive secretary of the Los Angeles AFL-CIO, has criticized the report for its failure to deal with education and training for adolescents and adults who are no longer in school. Another glaring omission is of a specific plan to decrease school segregation. While most of us now agree that the major goal of American education must be that of quality integrated schools, we cannot, as even the report suggests, achieve the quality without at the same time moving toward integration. The stated goal of the 478

McCone Commission, however, is to "reverse the trend of de facto segregation" by improving the quality of the Negro schools: in short, separate but equal schools that do not disturb the existing social patterns which isolate the Negro child in his "disadvantaged areas."

That the commission's explicit concern for Negro problems falls short of its implicit concern for the status quo is also evident in its proposals for housing. It calls for the liberalization of credit and FHA-insured loans in "disadvantaged areas," the implementation of rehabilitation measures and other urban-renewal programs and, as its particular innovation, the creation of a "wide area data bank." Meanwhile it refuses to discuss, much less to criticize, the effect of Proposition 14 or to recommend a new fair-housing code. To protect the Negro against discrimination, the McCone Report supports the creation of a Commission on Human Relations, but does not present any proposals that would enable it to do more than collect information and conduct public-relations campaigns.

The most crucial section of the report is the one on employment and, not unexpectedly, it is also the most ignorant, unimaginative, and conservative—despite its dramatic recommendation that 50,000 new jobs be created. On the matter of youth unemployment, the report suggests that the existing federal projects initiate a series of "attitudinal training" programs to help young Negroes develop the necessary motivation to hold on to these new jobs which are to come from somewhere that the commission keeps secret. This is just another example of the commission's continued reliance on public relations, and of its preoccupation with the "dull, devastating spiral" of Negro failure. The truth of the matter is that Negro youths cannot change their attitudes until they see that they can get jobs. When what they see is unemployment and their Economic Opportunity programs being manipulated in behalf of politicians, their attitudes will remain realistically cynical.

Once again, let me try to cut through the obscurantism which has increasingly come to cloud this issue of Negro attitudes. I am on a committee which administers the Apprenticeship Training Program of the Workers Defense League. For many years the League had heard that there were not enough Negro applicants to fill the various openings for apprenticeship training and had also repeatedly been told by vocational-school counselors that Negro students could not pay attention to key subjects such as English and mathematics. The League began its own recruitment and placement program two years ago and now has more than 500 apprentice applicants on file. When, last fall, Local 28 of the Sheetmetal Workers Union—to take one example —announced that a new admission test for apprentices was to be given soon, the League contacted those applicants who had indicated an interest in sheetmetal work. The young men came to the office, 479 filled out a 10-page application form, filed a ten-dollar fee, and returned it to the Local 28 office. Then, five nights a week for three weeks, they came to Harlem, in many cases from Brooklyn and Queens, to be tutored. Most of the young men showed up for all fifteen sessions, and scored well on the test. At their interviews they were poised and confident. Eleven of these men finally were admitted to a class of 33. The WDL doesn't attribute this success to a miraculous program; it merely knows that when young people are told that at the end of a given period of study those who perform well will obtain decent work, then their attitudes will be markedly different from those who are sent off to a work camp with vague promises.

To cut the cost of job training programs, the McCone Commission avers that compensation "should not be necessary for those trainees who are receiving welfare support." Earlier in the report the authors point out that welfare services tend to destroy family life by giving more money to a woman who lives alone; yet they have the audacity to ask that the practice of not allowing men who are on family relief to earn an additional income be maintained for young men who are working and being trained. How is a young man to be adequately motivated if he cannot feel that his work is meaningful and necessary? The McCone Report would have us say to him, "There, there, young man, we're going to keep you off the streets—just putter around doing this make-work." But the young man knows that he can collect welfare checks and also hustle on street corners to increase his earnings. A man's share of a welfare allotment is pitifully small, but more than that, he should be paid for his work; and if one is interested in his morale, he should not be treated as a charity case.

Continuing with the problem of employment, the report recommends that "there should immediately be developed in the affected area a job training and placement center through the combined efforts of Negroes, employers, labor unions and government." In the absence of actual jobs, this would mean merely setting up a new division, albeit voluntary, of the unemployment insurance program. "Federal and state governments should seek to insure through development of new facilities and additional means of communication that advantage is taken of government and private training programs and employment opportunities in our disadvantaged communities." Perhaps the only thing the Job Corps program doesn't lack is publicity: last summer it received ten times as many applications as it could handle. Nor can new types of information centers and questionnaires provide 50,000 new jobs. They may provide positions for social workers and vocational counselors, but very few of them will be unemployed Negroes.

The report goes on: "Legislation should be enacted requiring employers with more than 250 employees and all labor unions to report annually to the state Fair Employment Practices Commission, 480 the racial composition of the work force and membership." But an FEP Commission that merely collects information and propaganda is powerless. And even with the fullest cooperation of labor and management to promote equality of opportunity, the fact remains that there are not enough jobs in the Los Angeles area to go around, even for those who are fortunate enough to be included in the retraining programs. As long as unions cannot find work for many of their own members, there is not much they can do to help unemployed Negroes. And the McCone Report places much of its hope in private enterprise, whose response so far has been meager. The highest estimate of the number of jobs given to Los Angeles Negroes since the Watts crisis is less than 1,000.

The Negro slums today are ghettoes of despair. In Watts, as elsewhere, there are the unemployable poor: the children, the aging, the permanently handicapped. No measure of employment or of economic growth will put an end to their misery, and only government programs can provide them with a decent way of life. The care of these people could be made a major area of job growth. Los Angeles officials could immediately train and put to work women and unemployed youths as school attendants, recreation counselors, practical nurses, and community workers. The federal government and the state of California could aid the people of Watts by beginning a massive public-works program to build needed housing, schools, hospitals, neighborhood centers, and transportation facilities: this, too, would create new jobs. In short, they could begin to develop the $100-billion freedom budget advocated by A. Philip Randolph.

Such proposals may seem impractical and even incredible. But what is truly impractical and incredible is that America, with its enormous wealth, has allowed Watts to become what it is and that a commission empowered to study this explosive situation should come up with answers that boil down to voluntary actions by business and labor, new public-relations campaigns for municipal agencies, and information-gathering for housing, fair-employment, and welfare departments. The Watts manifesto is a response to realities that the McCone Report is barely beginning to grasp. Like the liberal consensus which it embodies and reflects, the commission's imagination and political intelligence appear paralyzed by the hard facts of Negro deprivation it has unearthed, and it lacks the political will to demand that the vast resources of contemporary America be used to build a genuinely great society that will finally put an end to these deprivations. And what is most impractical and incredible of all is that we may very well continue to teach impoverished, segregated, and ignored Negroes that the only way they can get the ear of America is to rise up in violence.

NINE

PROGRAMS, POWER, AND THE POOR

The previous section dealt with the current form of domestic poverty and the relation of this poverty to racial inequality and injustice. In this section the emphasis will be upon the programs which have emerged to combat poverty and upon those aspects of the new poverty which have not been met by existing programs. The new poverty is clearly related to the cybernetic revolution which is in turn related to the development of technological militarism. The latter encourages the technician, displaces the untrained, and invests federal funds into the area of defense which does not benefit the poor. Also new is the fact that poverty is occurring at a time of general prosperity which is clearly visible to the poor.

By and large, the modern poor are trapped in islands of rural and inner-city poverty. They own neither the land, nor the shops nor industries which they sometimes occupy. The employers, shop-keepers, store managers, landlords, lending agencies, as well as the police, social workers, hospital workers, and teachers who work in these pockets of poverty, represent a culture different from and sometimes alien to the ways of life of the poor residents. These outsider helpers and entrepreneurs who live in ways strangely dependent upon the culture of continuous poverty, are carriers of a different set of norms and values. The values of their culture (the dominant middle-class culture) are that individual success in the competitive marketplace is the mark of individual worth. That the dominance of large organizations dependent on long-range planning has made such a criterion for success illusory does not prevent these culture carriers from retaining the view, or from assuming that it has universal applicability to the large number of disadvantaged. The culture carriers themselves have reached a moderate success in the culture. Why can the impoverished not do the same?

The answer given to this question varies with one's ideology. A con-

482

servative will say that the poor are deficient in the motivation or directed intelligence requisite for reaching the good life and therefore are themselves to blame. The liberal will transplant the blame for the deficiencies to inadequate opportunities to develop the appropriate motivation and patterns of thought by which an individual is sometimes capable of raising himself from humble origins. Whatever the cause or the source of blame for the deficiencies may be, this process of transformation from impoverished existence is by no means an easy one. The Negro child who, by four years of age, shows his self image by selecting the white doll as nicer and more attractive, the child whose father has deserted because the experience of not being a good provider became too great a threat to his manhood—these children are impaired before the agencies of society can reach them. Many other situations make mobility difficult for the poor: jobs are dependent upon good education, education is dependent upon access to good schools, good schools are dependent upon access to good neighborhoods which is curtailed by discrimination and by poverty itself. This is what is meant by the cycle of poverty.

Where the conservative and liberal statements merge is in the shared view that the poor are individuals who for some reason suffer deficiencies in achievement-motivation, stimulation, education, scholastic ability, training, capacity for saving or for delayed gratification, or employment opportunity. Given such a philosophy the poor are seen as a problem because they lack the virtues and assets of the middle class. Programs for the general welfare have generally been geared for those sufficiently imbued with middle-class characteristics to have the desire and know-how to gain from them. There has developed a communication gap between those who are poor and the agencies which are supposed to help them. Such a gap was clearly in evidence when a convention of representatives of the poor hooted down Sargent Shriver, the Director of the Office of Economic Opportunity, an official and spokesman for the nation's anti-poverty program.

The problem stems from the fact that the poor do not see themselves as problem cases in need of restitution. Rather they are inclined to see their better-off peers not as superior in virtue or competence but rather as better placed, more powerful, and wealthier to begin with. Lacking such position, power or wealth in the dominant culture the poor have been prone to establish subcultural adjustments. This is not to say that life in the ghetto or in the tenant farm is a tolerable experience or that the junkie culture, the gang culture, the revivalist sects or even the strong familial ties that sometimes develop can compensate for the degradation of poverty. We are trying to say rather that many of the poor see themselves as people rather than as problem cases; they see the adjustment patterns relevant to living in the slum or amidst a band of sharecroppers as meaningful to their real problems. They see the ways of the middle-class world as lacking in any special

483

virtue, hypocritical in its professions of equality, and certainly irrelevant to the immediate problems of life among the deprived.

This country is now engaged in numerous programs to combat poverty and inequality. Whether these programs were motivated by the United States' embarrassment at having a domestic poor while involved in a cold war struggle for influence over the poorer countries, or by fears of domestic disorder and violence, or by a long overdue concern for human decency, the programs have not been markedly successful either in the objective raising of living standards or in the subjective change of the opinions of the poor.

What is at issue in the various instances of disapproval and unrest is who sets the terms (the conditions, the priorities for the administration of anti-poverty programs), and who is to be protected or sacrificed in the rush of the deprived for greater control over the police, housing, welfare, political, or commercial institutions which establish the constraints under which the poor live.

Awareness that the poor have developed their own subcultural adjustments which are highly resistant to change, and the issue of power or control over approaches to combat poverty are matters discussed in this chapter. Miller's article in this section is based on some of the most important studies which have helped to define the poverty of the 1960's. The implication of his article is that the traditional methods of assisting the needy and the existing professional services charged with such assistance are unequal to the task. What may be needed are methods that approach the very young through schools or day-care centers before the grip of poverty has taken hold. Miller places great emphasis on the educational system to fulfill this need. In the article that follows, however, Friedenberg points a critical finger at the goals and techniques of the educational system. He feels that the shortcomings of the educational system cut even more deeply than the pressing need for more teachers and classrooms or better pay for teachers. These shortages which result in routinized mechanical procedures are less the target of Friedenberg's critique than the school system geared not to education but to advancement for the child least in need of help. For the child in poverty the system has almost nothing relevant to offer.

One problem in working at poverty through the children is that poor children have already suffered deprivation and enter school with a handicap which tends to increase with time. Another problem is that effective school programs require participation and support from the home and other parts of the community. These requirements mean that programs must come closer to the particular perceptions and strivings of the deprived communities. This is difficult to do; the Negro poor have learned to distrust "whitey."

A number of new and experimental programs have begun to help bridge the gap in communication. Some, like the use of the poor

484

themselves as subprofessional workers in their own areas, have been promising. Frequently, however, the projects lack the resources to do complete jobs. Occasionally they are demonstration projects designed without plans for adequate evaluation or for continuation or implementation elsewhere should they prove successful. Such projects are more convincing to the politician or to the professional who can say that something is being done, than they are to the large number of underprivileged people. The manner in which demonstration projects hinder effective social action by providing token measures to meet popular pressures is described in an article by Rein and Miller (1966).

Insufficient funds and a lack of follow-through have been much more a part of the welfare programs designed to be part of a war on poverty than they have been to defense-related programs like the space and anti-ballistic-missile programs. These priorities reflect the process of political decision-making at the highest levels. The process has its counterpart at state and local levels. The Mississippi legislature recently met in special session to consider a special dispensation for a large industrial firm. This is not particularly striking except that one week before, a group of physicians had released the findings of their study of health needs in Mississippi. The report stated that a sizable number of rural Mississippians were living under conditons where extreme malnutrition was a cause of death and disease, particularly among the young. No special session was called to remedy this circumstance.

Most federal projects which are intended to provide jobs, or special education, or voting rights to the disadvantaged have been administered by local authorities and local leaders of the community. These authorities and these leaders reflect the positions of the prevailing loci of power in their communities. Programs have not been used to make dramatic changes in power or wealth of the poorer community. They have been inclined rather to reinforce existing lines of power by providing a system of rewards, jobs, ballots, surplus food or welfare checks which can be used as a means of pacification or for the purchase of patronage. Such use is not conducive to acceptance of the agent of welfare into the poor community and makes little inroad into the cycle of poverty previously described. Again, it is clearly evident that certain dedicated professionals and certain leaders among the poor have not accepted a definition of the program which leaves its direction in the hands of existing authorities. It is to the credit of one Head Start program in particular, the Child Development Group of Mississippi (described in the article by Levin), that it sought direction and leadership from the poor community and consequently won the support and community involvement needed for educational improvement. However, the strong sense of community involvement proved too great a threat to the existing power alignment of the state. Levin, the program director, was obliged by O.E.O. to resign and finally the en- 485 tire program was attacked and forced to curtail its activities. The problem is one of power conflict between an existing social order favoring a status quo and an ascending order demanding change. It is not particularly a southern problem as the example may suggest, for Mobilization for Youth in New York City ran into similar conflicts with the existing educational and political hierarchies.

In some instances O.E.O. has successfully created a federally sponsored organization of the poor which has been effective in wresting control from local interests. In Western Kentucky it was to the interest not only of the impoverished Appalachian miner but also of the liberal governor and of the larger corporations seeking to enter the area to drive out the extremely conservative, independent mine operators whose strip mining techniques have not only defaced the land but also have displaced the people. Such coalition of interests is not the ordinary case nor does it seem destined to last once the strip miners and small landowners are successfully fought in the courts and driven from the area.

The final article by Kopkind is included in this section to illustrate the difference in philosophies between service and action programs. A service program either directly or implicitly accepts the criterion of material well being as the measure of success and assumes the poor to be deficient. An action program assumes that the poor community has resources adequate to its own well being, providing that obstacles to organization and advancement can be removed. The service approach asks, "What can we do to keep your family together, to keep you from dropping out of school, or to turn your gang into a constructive club?" The activists ask, "What are the strong points of your way of life, what is wrong with the school system or the job system which prevents it from meeting your needs?" From the activists' position a potential leader of the deprived community who makes it into a high position in the military or in industry, or an actual leader, whose demands grow more cautious as he is employed on some federal program are examples of failure. For the activist the illness is not poverty but rather the larger social system which permitted it to develop even amidst plenty. For the student organizers who have forsaken their own careers to work among tenant farmers or ghetto residents, the program which takes steam out of the protest serves only to amalgamate a few more cases into a social system with extremely low priorities for human needs. The tenor of the activists will be seen in our last section on the revolution in expression. What is relevant in this section is the effort to develop programs in which "maximum feasible participation" is not a substitute for complete control by the poor of their own programs. Such programs are radical in their objectives and sometimes in their methods. They are highly relevant to the theme of this book because they make explicit the basic difficulty that an automated and impersonal society, geared to wasteful productivity

486

and to globalism in foreign policy, may not have the human resources to deal with a struggle which demands not only goods but a share in the nation's power and a sense of self direction and respect.

REFERENCES AND ADDITIONAL READING

Saul D. Alinsky, "The War on Poverty—Political Pornography," *Journal of Social Issues*, 21, 1965, 41–47.

David Caplovitz, *The Poor Pay More*, New York: Free Press, 1963.

Jack Minnis, "The Care and Feeding of Power Structures," *New University Thought*, 4, 1964, 73–79.

Raymond J. Murphy and Howard Elinson, eds., *Problems and Prospects of the Negro Movement*, Belmont, California: Wadsworth Publishing Co., 1966.

Martin Rein and S. M. Miller, "Social Action on the Installment Plan," *Trans-action*, January-February, 1966, 31–38.

Alvin L. Schorr, *Slums and Social Insecurity*, Washington, D. C.: U. S. Department of Health, Education, and Welfare, 1963.

487

S. M. Miller

Poverty and Inequality in America: Implications for the Social Services

AN ESSAY REVIEW OF "THE OTHER AMERICA"

In recent months a rediscovery of poverty in the United States has upset some comforting myths. Two factors—the expansion of gross national product, and the misreading of Galbraith[1] to believe that he was describing America as the affluent society rather than predicting possibilities—have led to an easy complacency that the poor were few in number and declining through the "natural" operation of the economy. It was believed that we were living in an "income revolution" that not only was rapidly eliminating poverty but reducing inequalities of income and wealth as well. This Panglossian picture has been battered by a number of recent books that have underlined the extent of poverty in the United States, the recent slowness of movement toward its elimination, the growing inequality in income and wealth, and the corrosive character of poverty in a generally high-income society.[2]

Reprinted by special permission of the author and Child Welfare League of America from *Child Welfare*, Vol. XLII, No. 9, pp. 442–445, November 1963. S. M. Miller is professor of sociology at New York University.

[1]John Kenneth Galbraith, *The Affluent Society* (Boston: Houghton Mifflin Co., 1960).

[2]Conference on Economic Progress, *Poverty and Deprivation in the United States* (Washington, D.C.: Conference on Economic Progress, 1962).
488

Discussions of poverty sometimes seem unclear when we do not recognize that poverty can be measured from two viewpoints: (1) the standard approach—an income level is specified as a poverty line and those below this level are considered poor—and (2) the relative approach—a specified percentage of the population (say 20 percent) is thought of as poor and the concern is with changes in their condition relative to that of other groups in society, since these changes reflect trends in equality. Most studies of poverty utilize the first principle. Obviously, one can argue about where the poverty line should be placed for consuming units of different sizes and types. The surprising thing about the recent studies of poverty is that they come to a fair degree of agreement in placing the number of the poor at 20 percent to 25 percent of the total United States population. If the poverty line were raised—and Harrington and Keyserling believe it to be too low by current American standards—then more people would be considered poor.

Harrington's book prevents us from looking at poverty as a "genteel" condition in which people are just somewhat worse off than we are in the main society of relatively high income and affluence. He feelingly describes what it means to be poor—the toll, the frustration. After reading his book, one cannot feel that even a smaller poor can be ignored. His message is that it is a disgrace for a rich society to have a poor.

Morgan's conclusion is that this disgrace can be overcome with comparative ease in an economy that annually produces over $500 billion of goods and services. Since $10 billion a year would lift all families above the poverty line, poverty has never before been so financially easy to eliminate.

INEQUALITY

Inequality, however, is another matter. Kolko's and Lampman's works indicate that inequality is not now declining in the United States. Since 1949, Lampman's data show, the concentration of wealth in the hands of the upper 1 percent has grown. The proportion of income going to the bottom 20 percent of society is less today, Kolko charges, than it was in 1910. The upper 10 percent, relative to other economic group-

---

[the main author of this analysis is Leon Keyserling, and it is known as the "Keyserling Report"]; Michael Harrington, *The Other America: Poverty in the United States* (New York: Macmillan and Company, 1962); Gabriel Kolko, *Wealth and Power in America* (New York: Frederick Praeger, 1962); Robert J. Lampman, *The Share of Top Wealth-Holders in National Wealth* (Princeton, N.J.: Princeton University Press, 1962); and James N. Morgan, *et al., Income and Welfare in the United States* (New York: McGraw-Hill Book Co., 1962).

ings, are not doing as well as in 1910 because the middle-income groups have advanced the most from the expansion of the economy. As Herman Miller pointed out in a memorable article,[3] the income of Negroes is no longer improving relative to that of whites. Although the general level of Negroes' incomes has been advancing, the income of whites has moved up at least as rapidly. The data assembled by Keyserling and Herman Miller suggest that there was a real improvement in the income position of low-income groups during World War II, but since then the economy has not drastically improved the conditions of the low-income population.

While Galbraith pointed out that our poor was a minority of the population, unlike the majority poor of India, and that we had the best-dressed poor in the history of the world, he underplayed the possibility that the relative effects of poverty—relative deprivation—grows when a poor are a special part of the population. The Cloward-Ohlin theory of juvenile delinquency[4] is based in part on recognizing this relative frustration. Material on revolutions indicates that a population is most likely to act not when its position is the worst in absolute terms but when conditions are improving but not as rapidly as they are expected to. As the poor expect more—even though they may have more than the poor of other lands or than they themselves had at an earlier point—they feel their deprivation most keenly. Obviously, this analysis is pertinent to the current Negro revolution.

The American poor are an extremely varied group. The Morgan and Keyserling data indicate that about 60 percent live outside central cities and their suburbs. Over a quarter, on the other hand, are in the central cities. Two-thirds of the heads of poor families are in the labor force, one-third are not. And while 60 percent of all Negroes are poor, most of the poor (80 percent) are white. Only 10 percent of the poor are people who are customarily employed but now unemployed. About 25 percent of the poor are in families headed by individuals over 65. Poverty is concentrated, however—almost 50 percent of the poor live in the South.

A surprising finding of the Morgan study is that only one-fifth of the poor receive welfare aid. But one-tenth of all Americans have been "on welfare" at some time in their lives. The inadequacy of social security (note that 27 percent of the poor are in families headed by aged individuals) and welfare payments indicates the significance of public policy in permitting the existence of poverty.

[3]H. P. Miller, "Is the Income Gap Closing? No," *The New York Times Magazine,* November 11, 1962, p. 50 ff.

[4]Richard A. Cloward and Lloyd E. Ohlin, *Delinquency and Opportunity: A Theory of Delinquent Gangs* (Glencoe, Ill.: The Free Press of Glencoe, 1960).

490

Other causes of poverty lie in the great changes taking place in the American economy. Rural areas are producing the majority of the new poor, many of whom migrate to large cities. These cities already contain large numbers of poor (about one-third of the cities' populations), but they have no economic function to provide for the newly arriving poor. Also, the changes in technology and in American industry are transforming American communities. Some industries are declining, which means the end of many one-industry towns, and old plants are being closed down, thereby further aggravating the problems of many communities.

The skill and education that industries require of their employees are increasing. Whether industry really needs the level of skill it demands is not the issue; the important fact is that industry thinks it does and believes that it can get such labor. The effect is to make old skills obsolete, thereby taking away the jobs of many workers as the demand for industrial labor declines. New labor is employable only if it is highly skilled or educated. Consequently, those with little education, especially the young, are more disadvantaged in relation to the economic system today than their counterparts were a generation or two ago. The second industrial revolution that is happening now is destroying the economic potential of vast segments of the American population. Increasingly, formal schooling—not necessarily the ability to perform certain tasks—is the credential required for entry into the main economic system.

IMPLICATIONS FOR PROFESSIONALS

What are the implications of these findings for professionals dealing with the poor and their families? First of all the poor in America have not received sufficient attention. Richard Cloward writes of social work's increasing disengagement from the poor.[5] Other professions have never engaged themselves or have insufficiently engaged themselves with the plight of the poor. Each profession and social service has to confront the issue of how much existing practice is aimed at dealing with the problems of the poor as they presently exist in the United States.

The "welfare state" is a slogan rather than a reality. As Harrington has pointed out for the United States and Richard Titmuss for Great

[5]Richard A. Cloward and Irwin Epstein, "Private Family Agencies and the Poor," paper presented at the Conference on Low-Income Culture, June 1963.

Britain,[6] the extension of welfare services in the "semi-affluent society" has not primarily benefited those at the bottom of the economic ladder. Mainly the upper working class and especially the middle classes have gained from the extension of social services.

The varied character of the poor suggests that differential policies must be carried out to deal effectively with particular segments of the poor—no one measure will be effective with all. For example, "heating up the economy" so that more jobs will be generated will not benefit those of the poor who are unable to work, whether for physical or familial reasons (for example, female heads of households). On the other hand, improvement in social services will not basically solve the problems of unemployment in distressed areas, even though it might alleviate them.

Consequently, it becomes especially important today to clarify the goals of professionals and of the social services. If many of the poor are likely to be a permanent poor, there must be a search for the kind of programs that will be most effective in ameliorating their conditions. On the other hand, those of the poor who can be helped to improve their conditions—who have some economic potential—need a kind of help that is aimed at this potential.

We do not have a coordinated and well-aimed set of policies to deal with the extent and character of poverty today. We are not dealing with the poverty of the 1930's nor with the poverty of the turn of the century when all immigrant groups were to be helped to "Americanize," with the facile idea that they would then rapidly work their way up the occupational ladder.

The goals of various social services have to be redirected to meet the changed conditions of the sixties. Many of the poor will be permanently poor, and so will their children; others may escape into the main economy. Are the strategies and tactics of the social services differentiated enough and suitable to deal with the varied kinds of poor with their different prospects and conditions?

Services aimed at individual treatment are not enough. Professionals and their organizations must support and encourage action that will deal with the larger American scene in which poverty is being produced and maintained. The professional role cannot end with the limited services that the profession provides; it must extend itself to pressure for social changes that will make individualized professional services more meaningful and effective. Concentrating on individualized services, without concern for the forces outside the profession that are molding and limiting possibilities, is tantamount to adopting professional blinders. These blinders may promote confidence in one's expertise and effectiveness, but they force the professional to ignore

[6]Richard M. Titmuss, *Essays on "The Welfare State"* (London: George Allen and Unwin, 1958).

the barriers to deep and continuing change among the clientele.

Casework services have to be flexible, adaptive, and able to range over a variety of activities. Are services predicated on the likelihood that, in the near future, the number of female-based families will not decrease and that most of them are permanently without a male figure? Have we developed unmechanical "functional equivalents" to provide the kinds of experiences and feelings that a father might give to his children? And are we even certain what these "experiences and feelings" are? In the effort to deal with such questions, casework services must be remolded to handle more effectively the pressing and continuing problems of today.

NEW SOLUTIONS REQUIRED

There is inadequate understanding of the styles of life of low-income groups. Programs of professional action are frequently not based on and oriented to these styles of life—sometimes the professional strategies and tactics are extensions of what is believed to be important for middle-class individuals.

Education is the escape route from poverty. Therefore, many services to families should be more directly oriented to improving the educational chances and performances of the youth and, perhaps, also the adults in low-income families. In this connection, it is important to recognize that many low-income families, especially Negro families, have a very high regard for education. Nonetheless, many children of these families are early school-leavers. Among other reasons, this is because of the parents' inability to translate their general strong interest in education into effective support of the children in school, and the inability (and frequent indifference) of schools to capitalize on the particular emphasis on education in many low-income families.

Public and private agencies dealing with low-income groups might seek to orient and concentrate their services on enhancing the educational prospects of low-income youth rather than having a less specific and less efficient emphasis on a "general improvement" in family and individual functioning.

The example of education underlines the importance of stressing the positive elements in low-income life.[7] In contrast to Harrington's pessimistic portrait of a "culture of poverty," of apathy, indifference, and of withdrawal, the professional must seek out the signs of strength and accentuate them. Recent political events in Negro and Spanish-speaking communities point up the lack of attention to and understanding of these strengths.

[7]For one of the few attempts to pursue this emphasis, see Frank Riessman, *The Culturally Deprived Child* (New York: Harper & Row, 1962).

Edgar Z. Friedenberg

An Ideology of School Withdrawal

Compulsory school attendance in the United States has been justified from the beginning as essential to democratic polity. Everyone knows Madison's statement to the effect that popular government without popular education is the prelude to a tragedy, or a farce, or both. We have had both, continuously ever since. I have just finished Theodore White's *The Making of the President, 1960;* and I think this book is the strongest indictment of American public education I have ever seen, though Mr. White does not discuss the issue directly. Still, the laws are on the books. Within a century, with the Kalamazoo decision (1874), the legal basis had been laid for what Madison thought so necessary.

And, be it noted, for the reasons he gave. So far as I know, public support of education in this country has never been justified on the grounds that education was beneficial to the individual student, except to the extent that this pertained to equality of opportunity. It is logical to argue that the individuals who share the responsibilities of citizenship must learn what they have to do in order to discharge them. I wouldn't say the logic was watertight. In Louisiana, where I was raised, we have never regarded either ignorance or lunacy as a bar to high public office; and this liberalism has permitted us to enjoy unusually creative leadership. But, on the whole, the point is well taken. If public education can be justified on the grounds that it is essential to citizenship, it can also claim, for that reason, to be good for the future citizens themselves.

School attendance laws, however, are a very distorted reflection of the purpose implicit in Madison's phrase. They are not *licensing* laws. They do not require attendance until a specified minimum level of

Reprinted from *Commentary*, June 1963, by permission of the author and publisher; copyright © 1963 by the American Jewish Committee. Edgar Z. Friedenberg is associate professor of sociology at The State University of New York at Buffalo.

competence deemed essential to the conduct of adult life has been attained; this would mean a life sentence for some. Nor are they *contractual*: they do not assure the student any outcome or even any minimum standard of educational service or decent treatment in exchange for his obligation to attend. Other laws, to be sure, do set up such standards, but the student has no remedy against their breach. Even if he can establish that the school is sub-standard and that he personally is mistreated there, he cannot legally withdraw; he can only try to force the school authorities to make improvements which, usually, they would already have made long ago if they possibly could.

From this point of view, compulsory school attendance appears as a gross violation of civil liberty: a bill of attainder against a specific age group that guarantees no compensation in return. The school may, indeed, benefit the child; but it doesn't have to in order to earn the right to retain him. In talking about the youngsters who drop out, therefore, I am not going to start with the assumption that they ought to be retained. My hunch is that a large proportion of the dropouts may be doing what is best for themselves under the atrocious circumstances that exist. But I do want to analyze those circumstances, and see why the schools have so little to offer these youngsters.

In the small Southern Methodist college I attended, we had chapel services twice a week; and after the opening hymn there was a responsive reading. The Dean—it was a poor school and could only afford one—would read a portion of Scripture aloud; and the students, assembled as a congregation, would read the following portion: his in light-faced type, ours in bold. There was one of these that I liked especially well, and I remember fragments of it distinctly—not accurately, but distinctly. It began:

> DEAN: *Whereof from a young man's fancy shall he wend his way?*
> STUDENTS: *By taking heed unto the Lord, and the firmament thereof.*

This responsive reading, in the version in which I recall it, is admirably suited to its purpose. The first line reveals real evidence of poetic influence. It ties in with the culture, showing that we share in its heritage, and it alludes to the necessity for progress and achievement; while the second line asserts the necessity of basing these on a sound moral imperative. By saying it over together we experienced a feeling of mutuality and belonging, of being the same kind. Yet we ran no risk of binding ourselves to too literal an interpretation of its mandate, because it doesn't actually make any sense at all.

For the types of students it is designed for, the public high school and junior high school curriculum serves, I believe, exactly the same purpose as this responsive reading. Its function is liturgical. This is not as true of elementary school, because the basic skills really work. If 495 you read as you are taught there, you will understand at least the words; if you write, your words will be understood; if you follow the rules of arithmetic, your calculations will check out and your books will balance, though you may never have the remotest conception of mathematics.

High school, however, is another matter. What would happen to the businessman, or just citizen, who attempted to apply what he was taught in high-school civics to the actual power structure of his community or his country? Who learns to love reading, or to find the kind of reading he can love among the classics and the bitty anthologies of the high-school English course? High-school history, by and large, is not even propaganda, because nobody is expected to believe it or to be moved by it; it is received as official myth. We tell youngsters that the Pilgrims came to New England searching for religious freedom not in order to give them an understanding of the actual root values of Colonial New England, but in order to provide them with the relevant cliché about the relation of church and state in America, and to let them know that a good middle-class American thinks of "my religious affiliation" or "the faith of my choice." This keeps the youngsters from getting hung up on religion, like an Italian peasant or rural Southerner. As for high-school science, it has, since Sputnik, increased its work load enormously and often tries to duplicate the content of college science courses. But essentially, it serves not as an introduction to science but to legitimate the American middle-class epistemology; science proves that Truth is an aggregate of general principles induced from empirical data that observers can agree on. The function of science is to protect people from odd-balls by setting up the rules so that subjective feeling is discounted. The scientific method, then, becomes a way of separating ends and means. When we want to win an election, or spy on the Soviet Union, or redevelop a slum, we go about it scientifically—i.e., by defining what we are trying to do as a technical problem. Naturally, we care about the feelings of the people affected; people's emotions are a very important factor. That's why we have psychologists on our team.

It is even truer than the progressives have always maintained that there is no valid distinction between the curriculum and the extra-curriculum. What counts is the total experience of the student, and what he learns in both the classroom and the playing field is a posture, a pattern of anxieties and a pattern of responses for dealing with it. There is seldom any pleasure in scholarship or ideas as such; the classroom and the playing field alike are places where you try to make it, and learn the techniques for making it that alienate you least from your peers. The over-all rules are the same in both: learn the ropes; don't get hung up; always be friendly, sincere, and creative. And win!

The important thing about this familiar picture is that it is a picture of a totally instrumental institution. Nothing about the institution is meant to be valuable, here and now, for its own sake. I don't mean that high school students don't have any fun. Of course they do; in the suburbs, at least, the high school is a "fun place." But this sort of fun is a part of the social pattern to be learned; being "fun" helps you to make it as well or better than anything, and it takes a great deal of social skill which American adolescents, notably, do learn.

We have never had much interest in what education means and feels like to the youngsters who are subjected to it; only in what it might help them to make of themselves. Even the Supreme Court, in its decision against segregation, could not rest on the moral obloquy and insult that segregation imposes on Negro children; that was not enough. It had to support its position further by pointing out that a major reason why separate schools could not be equal even if they were identical was that the Negro students couldn't make the same contacts there that white students could in their school, and that this was what people really go to school for.

So it is: the Court has done our motives no discredit, but merely reaffirmed our tradition. The public school gives poor boys a chance to develop their potentialities, both by formal education and by providing an opportunity to mingle with and learn from their social superordinates. The commonwealth is then the richer for the skills they later contribute, which would otherwise have been forever lost. This is exactly the opportunity our dropouts need, and which they ought presumably to welcome. So what has gone wrong?

What has gone wrong is pretty complicated; but basically I think one might locate it in the schools' perennial assumptions about the nature of what they have had to offer the children of the poor. These assumptions were probably never valid; but both the school and the poor once believed them. Now, only the school continues to assert them, though no longer with much conviction.

The schools assumed that in order to get ahead in America the student had to learn not only a body of skills, but also a set of social conventions, increasingly subtle and refined as he climbed up the ladder. In school he was taught techniques for handling things and manners for getting along with people. The teachers were the transmitters of an alien culture—alien to them, too. Social mobility was a process like preparing to get a job as a rice farmer in China or a coffee-grower in Brazil. There was a strange language to be learned—from instructors who didn't speak it too well themselves; a strange body of techniques to be mastered—from teachers who had never practiced them at first hand. It would all have to be learned over again when he got there; but at the time it seemed relevant, and made the student feel that he was well on his way.

Now, there are three important ways in which this situation differs from the condition in the high school today. In the first place, the 497 problem of dropouts did not then exist. Most of the students who drop out today would never have been in high school fifty years ago; the school-leaving age has risen irregularly over the past decades, and a more rigid and self-confident school policy would not have hesitated to keep students in grade school until they reached it, whatever it was, if they did not pass. A good many of these dropped out, and took unskilled jobs, which existed; and that was the last anyone thought of them till election day six or seven years later. They weren't a dropout problem; they were the working class.

But those who didn't drop out, even though they came from a working-class background, did not feel at the time that they were losing their identity. This happened later, after they had made it, in the classical discovery of the loneliness of the long-distance runner. In school you were still you: *striving* didn't separate you from other poor, immigrant boys; it was exactly what poor, immigrant boys were supposed to do. There was no intimation at the time that you were leaving yourself behind. It wasn't that you were becoming a different person; the old *you* was learning new tricks. Education was instrumental, all right—it has always been that in America—but the instruments were thought to be in the curriculum. The student didn't have to learn to think of *himself* as one.

And finally, nobody doubted what the norms were. It seemed very clear that the people in the next stratum up were the ones who knew what the student had to learn; he had to be able to do what they did. This wouldn't make them accept him willingly; but it would allow him to work his way in even if they didn't.

I don't mean to imply that the school actually delivered the social mobility it promised; sometimes it did, more often it didn't. But this was the way it was supposed to work, and why there was so little controversy over whether compulsory school attendance was good for the individual as well as for the commonwealth. As long as the students who stayed in school believed in education naïvely, it served—much better than religion could have in this heterogeneous country—as the opiate of the people. And opium vendors don't have dropout problems.

Apparently, however—to judge by the present situation—they can: the American poor are getting over their addiction.[1] It takes more and

---

[1]Thus, in her recent study of the schools in Big City, Patricia Sexton reports dropout rates even in *elementary school* of 15.5 per 10,000 children from families earning from $3,000-5,000 annually, falling to 3 children per 10,000 for families earning $5,000-7,000. For families making more than $9,000, the rate was less than 1 child per 10,000. In high schools, of course, the rate is enormously greater, but follows the same pattern. There is no high school in Big City whose median family income is less than $5,000. For schools with median family incomes ranging from $5,000-

more education every year to invoke the same dream; and reality breaks through too often, leaving them sick, mean, and edgy. The educational establishment, fearful of losing popular support, is naturally much concerned with the possibilities of a *rapprochement,* of which two have already been tried. The simplest of these is an effort to beef up the traditional, but paradoxically faltering, economic appeal of education. Students are reminded over and over that today, more than ever, you need a high school diploma to get any sort of job and a college degree to get a good one. They are given the statistics on the fabulous return education, as an investment, brings in over a lifetime in increments of annual income. The unemployment data on adolescents and unskilled labor are stressed so that the youngsters will understand how hopeless things will be for them if they drop out of school. If they and their teacher are sophisticated enough, the demographic shift in job-type may be explained: how unskilled and blue-collar work has fallen off, while service and white-collar jobs, demanding a higher level of school achievement, have enormously increased in proportion.

All this is true enough; but the implication is false. It does not follow that most of the students now dropping out would have a better chance, even economically, if they stayed in school. As S. M. Miller and Frank Riessman have pointed out in a recent WBAI broadcast, the illusory success of some of these school-retention efforts in leading students to better jobs is based on the fact that they made hardly a dent in the number of school dropouts; if the programs had been successful in reaching the students they would inevitably have failed in delivering the jobs. In our economy, the demonstrable economic value of an education is partly a consequence of its scarcity. The blue-collar–white-collar figures are relative, and one loses sight of how much smaller the white-collar one was to begin with. The absolute increase in white-collar opportunity does not compensate for the absolute loss in blue-collar jobs—a discrepancy which is rapidly increasing in magnitude as automation proceeds. Today's dropouts are, perhaps fortunately, pretty skeptical kids; if they all believed that the school could deliver them to a brighter economic future we would soon have unemployed IBM operators and technicians hanging around the way India and Africa have lawyers.

The other, and more sophisticated, *rapprochement* is represented by the Higher Horizons Program, about which I wish I could bring myself to be less doubtful, for it is a program that seems to me char-

---

5,999, Sexton found a dropout rate of 19.2 per cent of the total registration, falling to 7.9 per cent for schools whose students had a median family income of $7,000-7,999, and to 3.6 per cent for the school whose students came from families having median incomes above $9,000. (*Education and Income,* Viking, 1961, pp. 97 and 202.)

acterized by much intelligence, ingenuity, enthusiasm, and sheer good will. Its appeal, moreover, is not purely economic. I understand it to be an attempt to convey to students that middle-class culture, *in toto,* is not beyond their grasp. It can be theirs, if only they do their work. As the title implies, the Higher Horizons approach seeks to make education appear more worthwhile to the student, and encourages him to remain in school to develop his potentialities, by raising his level of aspiration not just economically but culturally. As the boy lifts himself to gaze beyond the slum there comes into view the Museum of Modern Art.

It is heartening to find the middle class so generously willing to share its resources, and, for once, apparently confident of their value. It is also obvious that if the middle class cannot somehow make public educational acceptable to the poor on its terms rather than theirs, middle-class dominance of public education—a long established fact of American life—is doomed. But if the effort is successful, it will remind me of a story that a very intelligent, very British, very working-class hospital orderly used to tell, in a sensitive effort to ease his middle-class patients' embarrassment at the services he was obliged to perform for them. This story concerned a small pharmaceutical firm that was facing bankruptcy. It had an established reputation as Britain's most reputable manufacturer of suppositories. But respect for craftsmanship, as is well known, was declining; their customers, apparently, were turning to other sources for satisfaction. Things looked black. Then the firm consulted one of Madison Avenue's most resourceful advertising agencies. And the agency, after much brain-storming, came up with a slogan that at once opened vast markets to the company by motivating the very segment of the population which had hitherto most successfully resisted its appeal. The slogan was, very simply, "If you don't like our suppositories, you know what you can do with them!"

The dropouts, by and large, don't like middle-class culture; and they know quite well what we can do with it. Dropping out is one way of telling us, and it is about time we turned our attention to the things about the school that are bugging them. The school is the arena in which these youngsters encounter middle-class life; this is where the dropouts fight the ten-year's ideological war that ends in their defeat and rout. In this warfare the core values of their culture and the values the school represents are at issue, and any one that we start by considering will lead to the others. I think the most fruitful might be the familiar question of deferred gratification, or impulse control, which is the source of so much conflict with the school authorities.

We all know the school's side of the question; and know that lower-class youngsters act out their conflicts. Retention programs try to face up to this by helping the youngsters learn more self-control and giving them some valid experience of being rewarded for it, so that they will 500 discover for themselves that certain very desirable goals exist that can only be achieved by people who plan, save, and give a soft answer to wrath-provoking circumstances. In this way the kids learn that there may be more desirable rewards than the immediate pleasure of blowing up and shooting your bolt. "Now, Dionysus, let's think about what we're really trying to get done here," friendly Apollo is always urging; and of course he is right. The difficulty lies in getting Dionysus to listen.

Or does it? Let me return for a moment to Mr. White's account of the 1960 election, and the Apollonian behavior it elicited from the Republican candidate.

> And this, finally, was the only summary one could make of the campaign that Richard M. Nixon had so valiantly waged, under such personal suffering: that there was neither philosophy nor structure to it, no whole picture either of the man or of the future he offered. One could perceive neither in this last climactic proposal nor in his prepared speeches nor in his personal discourses any shape of history, any sense of the stream of time or flow of forces by which America had come to this point in history and might move on. Nixon's skill in politics was enormous, his courage unquestioned, his endurance substantial. But they were the skills, courage, and endurance of the sailor who knows the winds and can brave the storm and recognize the tide. There was missing in him always the direction of the navigator. . . . Thus, it is impossible to distinguish, from his campaign performance, what Nixon's personal political attitude was to the arrest of Martin Luther King when that hero figure of American Negroes was arrested in the last days of the campaign. . . . On the afternoon of the sentencing of Martin Luther King to four months of hard labor in Georgia, the Department of Justice—at the suggestion of a wise yet shrewd Republican Deputy Attorney-General— composed a draft statement to support the application for release of the imprisoned Negro minister. Two copies of the draft were sent out immediately for approval—one to the White House, one to Mr. Nixon's traveling headquarters. No one has yet revealed who killed this draft statement that was so critically important in the tense politics of civil rights. Either President Eisenhower or Vice-President Nixon could have acted—yet neither did. However obscure Eisenhower's motivations were, Nixon's are more perplexing, for he was the candidate. He had made the political decision at Chicago to court the Negro vote in the North; only now, apparently, he felt it quite possible that Texas, South Carolina, and Louisiana might all be won to him by the white vote and he did not wish to offend that vote. So he did not act—there was no whole philosophy of politics to instruct him.

> There could never be any doubt of the Vice-President's pugnacity or innate courage; yet it was a pugnacity and courage committed without a framing strategy to make them effective.

501

The terms of Mr. White's criticism are interesting as the incident itself. No philosophy of politics? No framing strategy? On the contrary, he was all strategy. What he lacked was heart and a sense of outrage: the capacity to make moral judgments. Yet, Mr. White cannot say this because his whole book, though very sensitive to moral factors in the contest, shares the assumption that a candidate's first duty is to get elected. Nixon lost, and the figures do indeed show that his expediency on this issue may have cost him the election. But to infer from this fact that the worst thing about Mr. Nixon's behavior was that it didn't work is to share his posture.

Earlier on, Mr. White describes the situations in the campaign that found Mr. Nixon at his best.

> One had to see Nixon entering a small Iowa village—the streets lined with school children, all waving American flags until it seemed as if the cavalcade were entering a defile lined by fluttering, peppermint-striped little banners—then see him stop at a Harvest Festival (in Red Oaks)—where on the festival tables lay the ripened ears of field corn . . . to see him at his best. For in such small towns he found an echo. These people were his natural constituency, his idiom their idiom. . . . He woke in Marietta, Ohio, on Monday, October 25th, to begin his last "peak" effort, and it was clear from his first speech of the day that he was at one with his audience as he had not been since he had passed through the corn fields of Iowa in the first week of the campaign. A sign outside the courthouse of Marietta, Ohio, read: HIGH SCHOOL DEBATERS GREET WORLD DEBATER—the sign was apropos and of the essence of this last trip as he revived. For he *was* a high-school debater, the boy who had some thirty years before won a Los Angeles *Times* prize for his high-school oration on the Constitution. He was seeking not so much to score home a message as to win the hearts of his little audiences; his style was homestyle and during the next two weeks told much about him.

In Red Oaks and Marietta they don't have much of a dropout problem. Good, solid communities, with woodsheds ample to the needs of youth, they turn out clean-cut boys and girls among whom Mr. Nixon is right at home. It was the urban proletariat, and overwhelmingly the Negroes, who refused to take part in his Harvest Festival, though the corn be ripe and the harvest long overdue.

To carry this illustration further would not make my point clearer; in any case, it is simple enough. I think the youngsters who drop out are probably, in many ways, a more promising moral resource than those who stay in, and I think they are driven out in part by moral revulsion from the middle-class life of the school. They could never, themselves, identify their feelings as moral repugnance because they view morality as being on the side of the enemy and therefore square; 502

they imagine they dislike morality and have never been allowed to realize that they have morals of their own. They don't have a complete moral *system,* because they are not systematic; they are unprincipled in their behavior, because principles are too abstract for them to handle. But in a concrete situation they can be trusted more safely than their middle-class peers who are trying to make it.

Mr. Nixon and his silent superior are symbols, too; and I am not naïve enough to attribute the lower-class response to them solely to the revulsion they arouse in the breast of the noble savage. The opposition was well-organized and well-manipulated. But there are natural affinities and polarities in politics that set limits to what manipulation can achieve, and these, among other things, are reflected in the class structure of American society. Officially, American society is, however, middle-class and opportunistic—in the Land of Opportunity these are the values that receive official support and that in fact prevail. It is surely fair enough to take Mr. Eisenhower, and Mr. Nixon at the zenith of his presidential aspirations, as representative of what is most American. But one need not be wholly partisan. President Kennedy has also stated emphatically that we need technical rather than ideological or philosophical approaches to the problems that confront us.[2]

This moral attitude dominates our life. We are caught in it in crisis after crisis: in the U-2 incident, the Cuban invasion, the presence of our observers in Vietnam organizing the forced evacuation of peasants so that their farms can be burned, and helping the government see to it that the Viet Cong guerrillas don't get any antibiotics. Time after time the world finds a nice, friendly American standing in the middle of somebody else's ruins, with no more to say for himself than a rueful "It shoulda worked, but somebody must have goofed!"

I have a name for this boy. I call him Edsel, and I think it is time we withdrew him from production and got out a more responsive and less hazardous model. Even the practical-minded may not have much use for him any more; the locals seem to be getting pretty tired of Edsel and are about ready to get him out of there, with a hammer and sickle if necessary. But if we are to grow anything better, the dropouts are the kids to start with, for they have come part way on their own, against heavy opposition, already. They are ill-disciplined. They have no basic skills. They are so sore that any place you touch them hurts, and when they are hurt they hurt back. They are extremely parochial, limited in their experience of the world to a few city blocks of desolate slum, and therefore both gullible and suspicious about anything beyond it. They are sometimes homeless, and never have any quiet place to study and think. They are inconveniently aware of their

[2]In the 1962 Commencement Address at Yale. See William Lee Miller, "Some Academic Questions About a New Yale Man," *Reporter,* July 5, 1962.

own sexuality and inconveniently skilled at bringing it to the attention of others. They live, their teachers sometimes say, like animals; and as they say it, a ghost sobs, harshly. But if these youngsters are trapped, it is not in their apprehensions of pseudo-events. They are not alienated from themsleves. They still have access to their sense-data, and, on their own terms, they are accustomed to fidelity.

These are the qualities that, I believe, we hoped to preserve and continually renew by building an open society in which a sensitive, compulsively masculine boy could become an Ernest Hemingway and a poor but beautiful waif a Marilyn Monroe. But at this juncture, less fatal alternatives to mediocrity are needed. Can a school geared to success and social mobility help formulate them? Its traditions are against it, its staff is against it, its relationship to the community power structure is against it.

To reach the dropouts and give them a reason for staying, the school would have to start by accepting their *raison d'être*. It would have to take lower-class life seriously as a condition and a pattern of experience—not just as a contemptible and humiliating set of circumstances that every decent boy or girl is anxious to escape from. It would have to accept their language, and their dress, and their values as a point of departure for disciplined exploration, to be understood, not as a trick for luring them into the middle class, but as a way of helping them to explore the meaning of their own lives. This is the way to encourage and nurture potentialities from *whatever* social class. Talent, and genius, when real, are expressions of individual experience and the inner life. But success and higher status are not the first goal to which talent or genius is devoted—though they are sometimes the last.

I do not mean to imply that I accept Sitwell's Fallacy: that the poor are happier in their station in life and should be left to enjoy it. Most lower-class people of whatever age hate lower-class life, I am sure: the noise, and the filth, and the crowding, and the vulnerability to the police and illness; never feeling quite well or quite rested. Worst of all, perhaps, is the constant din of the mass media—including the school—telling them that if they were any good at all they would be middle-class like everybody else, and live in loveliness in Larchmont. But the fact that they have reason to hate their life of fear and deprivation does not give us the right to force ours on them as the only acceptable alternative to it. This is something they must work out for themselves, and the school's job is to help them understand most fully the meaning and nature of what they have to work with. Basically, the problem of reaching the dropout is analogous to that faced by the Peace Corps in reaching the peoples of under-developed countries. Can we—do we even really wish to—help them deal with their situation on their terms with our resources, while leaving our way of life aside till somebody asks for it?

504

Frankly, I doubt it. This is not how the teachers I know approach lower-status youngsters. They are afraid of them, for one thing. The principal is afraid of disorder which looks bad in his record and in the records of his teachers, and they each have their careers to think of, too. So they learn early to keep the kids in line; this comes first. Order *is* helpful to learning, but it doesn't come first, it grows out of the common task; and teachers who put it first are not enthusiastic allies in keeping disorderly youngsters in school till a basis for order can be created. Order is not, to be sure, the central issue, but it will serve to symbolize the sharpness of the issue between those whose security depends on the suppression of impulse, and those who depend on its expression.

In the urban public school today, the former predominate, and I don't think they can be easily changed, within the limits of personality and bureaucracy that characterize the school. If they can be, there is no fundamental reason why the kinds of youngsters who now drop out may not be well served. But this is a big *if*, for the public school, as it is, is profoundly expressive of our culture. And the fate of the "dropouts" is just one more expression of their actual status in our democracy.

The answer, then, may be "No; this plant makes only Edsels." But if it is, I see no dropout problem. Let them go, let them go, God bless them. They may pop up again. St. James (or Santiago, as this chiliastic figure is known in Spanish) is not merely more merciful than the school system; he is far more flexible and versatile. He can accommodate a wider range of talent; he has a great Court, as well as an Infirmary, and though no familiar avenue bears his name, he has, like James Madison, been thus honored by the inhabitants of certain cities. The nearest, unfortunately, in Cuba.

Tom Levin

The Child Development Group of Mississippi: A Report from a Hot Sector of the Quiet Front in the War on Poverty

The war on poverty is being fought using the poor. It is not being fought by the poor. The poor largely remain pacifists. Some, though conscientious objectors, have been drafted by the iron-grip of hunger. They move like so many pawns on a chess-board, pushed and shoved from above without volition or creativity. Others, excluded from a poor-peoples army, stand by, neither assisting, nor in sympathy with their drafted neighbors. The magnificent concepts of a drive toward a great society leave them untouched and disinterested. The older poor compare the war on poverty with the WPA; the younger people talk about welfare and charity. The war on poverty has not sparked their imaginations because it is not their war.

One O.E.O. program gained immediate enthusiastic response from the poor—Project Head Start. Indeed, Project Head Start far exceeded the expectations of its planners. These expectations were, however, in terms of established community acceptance, public support and numerical enrollment.

Significantly, Head Start was a semi-autonomous program operating outside of the usual CAP community coalition concept. While Head Start descriptive literature encouraged community participation, the emphasis was on parental involvement. The Head Start bulletin entitled "Staff," strongly emphasized the professionalism of the pro-

From the *American Journal of Orthopsychiatry*, Vol. XXXVII, No. 1, January 1967, pp. 139–145. Copyright, the American Orthopsychiatric Association, Inc. Reproduced by permission of the author and publisher. Tom Levin, formerly Director of the Child Development Group of Mississippi, is one of the faculty of the National Psychological Association for Psychoanalysis Training Institute.

gram and, with some notable exceptions, the non-professional in most projects was confined to ancillary and non-creative functions. With few exceptions, Head Start programs were organized through existing school systems or agencies with previous professional involvement in child care.

It is apparent that the original planners did not frame Project Head Start as a community action endeavor. Project Head Start's emphasis on jobs for the poor and services to children of the poor with a strong professionalism dominating the program, while a significant contribution to the welfare of the poor, perpetuated the donor-donee relationship of established social service concepts. It may very well be that this concept of Project Head Start facilitated its wide acceptance by the public, the established educational and social agencies, and state and city governments. However, the price paid to establish this "quiet front" in the war on poverty was the surrender of an aggressive community action-oriented approach in a program which could have achieved a victory for community action as a viable concept.

The Child Development Group of Mississippi, using action-oriented concepts, succeeded in organizing 84 centers in over 50 urban and rural impoverished Negro communities in Mississippi. Each one of these centers was run by a local committee of poor people which was responsible for the planning, program, hiring, administration, and ultimately the success or failure of the center.

In the original announcement of the CDGM project the following statement appeared:

> We will measure the success of the project by two criteria:
> 1. Have we helped the children to a sense of freedom, responsibility and self-worth? Have they experienced an expansion of their horizons and skills?
> 2. Has the community experienced their own efforts and resources as the central force in the activities of the child development centers? *Has this been demonstrated by intention to continue the center?* (italics, T.L.)

It is not the province of this paper to validate the success of Point #1. However, it might be noted that at hearings before the Appropriations Committee of the U.S. Senate, Sargent Shriver and a number of expert witnesses attested to the high level of educational success of the Child Development Group program for 6,500 disadvantaged children.

Point #2 can be validated. Without any prior existing organizational structure, resources, or cooperation from the power structure of Mississippi—on the contrary, in the face of a non-cooperative and frequently hostile white community—CDGM procured and repaired shacks to establish centers, converted old farm trucks to buses, re- 507 cruited a staff of 1,200 poor Mississippians and maintained every one of the original 84 centers throughout the summer. Over 40 centers conducted full time programs for 6 months without any outside funds after the expiration of the grant on August 28, 1965, and by January 1966 a total of 143 centers had been established throughout Mississippi, all under local committees of the poor. The Child Development Group of Mississippi is the only O.E.O. program in Mississippi which succeeded in achieving such active participation of the communities of Negro poor.

The Mississippi poor have too many needs to be met through the constricted funnel of present poverty program positions. Five confrontation positions are presented here as a basis for re-evaluation of our obligations and our commitments to the poor.

Position 1

POVERTY PROGRAM RUN FROM ABOVE WITHOUT THE DISABILITIES AND VITALITY OF THE POOR

versus

CHAOTIC MOVEMENT WITH DIRECTION DEVELOPING THROUGH LEARNING

The poor are not motivated by self-help. The poor are not motivated by tomorrow. The poor are not motivated by abstractions. They are motivated by that beautiful fundamental drive of the "have nots" to "have." The poor of Mississippi initially joined the program of CDGM because they wanted to have the money, the jobs and the services for their children. In order to obtain these, certain minimal requirements were established by CDGM. Each center must be run by an elected committee of that community who would be required to plan and execute the program. At first the committees saw themselves as simply window-dressing. It was only when central administration refused to give directives, solve problems, or resolve conflicts that the committees developed vitality. The motivation was simple and direct. To have a center and consequent jobs, supplies and a program for their children, the committees would have to do the work.

On the first day of the program, the Director of CDGM visited a newly opened center in the Delta. During the organizational stages the center had been run by a powerful matriarch who assigned all jobs and made all decisions without planning or decision-making being shared in the community. During the intervening orientation we had stressed that centers must be run with full community participation. The Director arrived at 10:45 a.m. to find the children being sent home. The community people had refused to participate in the transportation and food preparation since they had never been consulted 508 in its planning. The center had not succeeded in achieving its proposed enrollment the first day because of the inefficiency of a boss system with these Delta poor. The Aides, trainees, and teachers knew they could not keep their jobs nor service their children unless they could function. Yet they would not sacrifice their aspiration for real participation in order to hold on to their jobs. In the ensuing discussion the Director refused to resolve the conflict between the chairman, staff, and committee. The Director simply stated that everyone was allowed mistakes and if this center was a mistake we would open another center. The following morning committees had been elected, the food and transportation problem resolved and the center was in full operation.

The poor want money, as well as opportunities for themselves and their children, and will be creatively activated if they have a real part in functioning, decision-making and resulting consequences.

Position 2

THE "COMMUNITY" DEFINED AS A POLITICAL SUB-DIVISION RESULTING IN A SOCIOLOGICAL MONSTROSITY

versus

ORGANIC INTEGRITY OF THE NATURAL COMMUNITY

The concept of a Community-Action Program is as sound as the concept of "community" it is based upon. To define community as being a city or a county is to require that the existing power structure be incorporated into, and inevitably become the dominating influence of, a CAP. This effectively disenfranchises the black poor of Mississippi.

The people of the communities of Hudsonville or Mount Peel cannot work with the Mayor of Holly Springs. The reasons are multitudinous. The Mayor is not part of their community. Many are intimidated by him. All distrust his ability to understand or participate in their real community affairs. The accident or manipulation which results in the map lines of electoral districts defining community effectively disenfranchises total communities.

A community is a group of people who are held together by common reality interests, not the abstractions of political subdivisions. In Bolivar county the Negro community has organized itself into a prototype CAP. While the poor of Winstonville, Mound Bayou, Rosedale and Cleveland find they may be able to develop an alliance of natural communities, injecting the white power structure into this new political womb would bring immediate abortion. In Mississippi there exist many such vital Negro communities. They must be the base for a new CAP concept.

509

THE CONCEPT OF "QUALIFIED" AS A WAY OF RELE-
GATING THE POOR TO MENIAL AND SUBSERVIENT
FUNCTIONS

versus

AN APPRECIATION OF THE POTENTIAL FOR "QUALITY"
TEACHING AVAILABLE THROUGH FULL UTILIZATION OF
THE SKILLS OF THE INDIGENOUS POOR

Integration will not afford the Negro child an opportunity for an altered home and community environment. The child's parents and neighbors will continue to be subjected to the disenfranchisement of the "unqualified." CDGM, as part of our concept of "maximum feasible participation of the poor," discarded the shibboleth that "qualified," in terms of academic and state credentials necessarily coincided with "quality." While each teaching unit was assigned a professional "resource teacher," the professional was directed to the challenge of guiding the trainee and aide who were charged with actually conducting the class. Our centers did not have an appointed professional director, but rather a central program development staff which took up the challenge of assisting the communities in developing a preschool program, jointly determined by committee, community and staff. In addition, CDGM obtained permission from O.E.O. to conduct its own training and orientation program where we emphasized program development and teaching methods based upon the strengths of the community. We felt that this "quality" was much more significant than abstract qualifications.

In retrospect our attempt at training left many gaps. However, it did instill the concept of the dignity and validity of the contributions of the poor. A teacher development program, undertaken by CDGM in the fall under a Field Foundation grant, building upon the experiences and spirit of the summer, developed a core of teachers who later attended O.E.O. sponsored university preschool training programs. The CDGM teachers at these programs participated with a vigor, dignity, professional proficiency and receptivity, which earned astonished admiration from the university staff.

For a proverty program to reach the poor, we must redefine our concept of "qualified" so that we do not disenfranchise the poor themselves.

Position 4

INTEGRATION AS A PROCESS REMINISCENT OF THE
INGESTION OF THE LAMB BY THE WOLF

INTEGRATION POSTULATED ON EQUIVALENT ECONOMIC
AND SOCIAL POWER

The black poor of Mississippi do not yearn to be "integrated" by submission to the white power structure. They have their own natural communities, their own pressing needs and their own trusted leaders. To many such communities, indiscriminate and mass "integration" is a liberal misconception which will destroy the rising role of their own community organizations and leadership. They do not wish forced integration. They do wish *not* to be excluded.

Floyd Bixler McKissick, the Director of CORE, indicated in an interview following his appointment, the Negro community wishes ". . . total equality—the freedom to be integrated if you want to, and the freedom to develop your own culture patterns if you want to." For many communities, solidification of their emerging political, social and economic strength depends upon a period of congregation in which their community can develop power. An integration program which denies the communities their legitimate aspirations for power is viewed as, at the best, misguided; and, at the worst, and more commonly, betrayal.

From afar, the right to eat at the local Holiday Inn, or to transfer patronage to downtown stores, might appear as a primary drive of the Negro community. But what will happen to the small independent Negro entrepreneur if this "integration" is accomplished? What the dynamiters could not achieve by force, the destruction of an independent economic Negro competition could achieve under the guise of "integration." The middle class allies of the poor will be destroyed. They do not have the power economically, socially or politically to survive. The communities will not betray these allies of the movement.

Before the 1954 Supreme Court school desegregation decision, Negro communities throughout Mississippi contained schools which were governed by school boards of local Negro leadership. While it would be romantic to describe these boards as always serving the best interests of the Negro communities, and it must be recognized that they were largely dominated by local "Toms," this condition obtained because of the effective veto of a white supremist county school structure. As school desegregation proceeds hundreds of Negro teachers, rejected by the white schools find themselves without jobs, their places taken by the higher "qualified" white teachers.

School integration of children is a fragment of a true concept of educational integration. It does not provide for integration of Negro leadership into the governing bodies of the schools; it does not provide for the adequate integration of Negro teacher and administrator into   511 the professional structure, and does not provide any incentive or avenue for the participation of the Negro parent in educational affairs.

Pupil integration will, in most Negro communities in Mississippi, result in the Negro community being asked to turn their young over to an all "white" school system—a system from which they can expect only hostility and exclusion.

There will be exceptions, however. Throughout Mississippi as the result of activities of NAACP, SNCC, CORE, Mississippi Freedom Democratic Party, and the work of CDGM this summer, parents have met and organized themselves around education as a community action. These parents are determined that their children will not be deserted to be educated by the white power structure.

One of the most marked successes of the CDGM was to create a group of the Negro poor who, through CDGM, learned to trust their abilities to engage with professional educators and teachers. They will not be intimidated into submission to the power structure school system for they have learned that they too can run their own schools.

Position 5

"FEAR AND TREMBLING" OF THE LAW-ABIDING IN THE
PRESENCE OF THE "LAW-ABIDERS"

versus

AN ACCEPTANCE OF "THE MOVEMENT" (WITHIN ITS
REALITY DEFINITION) AS THE ONLY CHANNEL OF
COMMUNICATION WITH THE NEGRO POOR AND THE ONLY
SOURCE OF ACCEPTABLE LEADERSHIP

A strangely nefarious situation develops when O.E.O., an agency of the federal government pledged, committed and bound by the principles of the Civil Rights Compliance Act, is able to bargain, compromise, and justify its dealings with a Mississippi power structure equally committed and dedicated to evade, destroy and subvert these very principles; while at the same time they tremble apologetically at the constructive efforts of the law-abiders, otherwise known as "the movement."

"The movement" is defined by the Mississippi structure as a group of bearded beatnik "outsiders" dedicated to overthrow of the government. This is not "the movement." In CDGM's application form, civil rights activity has been described by Mississippi applicants as "I work with the movement," "I went to register last month," "I have gone to voter classes," "I give money to NAACP." These answers define the heart of the movement.

The movement is composed of people who identify themselves with 512 the growing awareness that a basic change must take place in the social, economic and political structure of the South. The activists of the movement are those who bring to the people the message that President Johnson's Voter Registration Act says they can vote. The activists are those who spread the message of Title 6. The activists take up the battle for "maximum feasible participation of the poor." While the State of Mississippi forfeited 60% of the O.E.O. funds available to it rather than abide by Federal law, the movement people struggled to bring the third largest Head Start program in the United States to the impoverished and isolated Negro communities. It was the movement that stimulated the leadership that organized the local committees.

It is only through these movement people that Head Start, and the poverty program generally will be able to reach into the urban and rural communities of Negro poor of Mississippi and enlist their support for a great society.

In a farewell message to the project published in the CDGM newsletter, the Director summarized the relationship between CDGM and the movement as follows:

> This summer in Mississippi we have built upon the struggles of past years. We built CDGM upon the ashes of churches where poor people spoke out for equality. We built CDGM upon the bodies of Negro and white workers for the poor who were killed because they would not stay quietly at home to live in peace with injustice. We built CDGM upon the hunger and humiliation of men and women who were not allowed to work at a decent job because they would not give up being free. We built upon hundreds of years of the suffering and courage of mothers and fathers throughout the state of Mississippi who wanted something human and decent for their children and themselves. If we are proud of what we have done we must remember that we could not have schools run by the poor people, schools with black and white working together, if a place in history had not been won for us by brave men and women before this summer—men and women who said loudly and clearly "All Men Must Be Free." We have a large debt to these brave people of the "Movement." We can only pay it by never being satisfied until all men in Mississippi have political, social, and economic freedom.

In summary, the experience of the CDGM summer project suggests we must re-examine our total position vis-a-vis Poverty Program concepts. The children of the poor cannot be redeemed without redeeming the communities they live in. We must re-assess the poor, their talents, their allies, and their motivations. Head Start must be rescued from the "Quiet Front" and education must be recognized as a legitimate and vital area for total community involvement and community action. 513

We must assault the political and professional shibboleths which, while serving narrowed self interest, perpetuate an intimidated and powerless poor. The war against poverty cannot be fought as though it were directed at some distant and external enemy. An effective war on poverty must be an internal social revolution which will jar all structures of our society, professional as well as governmental.

Andrew Kopkind

Of, By and For the Poor
THE NEW GENERATION OF STUDENT ORGANIZERS

More than anything, the new generation of students cares about democracy. They have talked about it, written about it, demonstrated about it. Now they have begun to organize people to change their communities into more democratic forms. Their theories of change are being put into practice in Mississippi and parts of a few other Southern states by SNCC (the Student Nonviolent Coordinating Committee) and its followers, and in 11 Northern cities by SDS (Students for a Democratic Society). Its practitioners are almost all in their twenties (or younger), and their education and experience is not exceptional. But they have—perhaps uniquely in this generation—grasped the enormity of the contradictions in the American experience, and they have committed themselves to work for basic social change. They may not succeed; the odds against a significant shift in a huge technological society of 200 million people are incalculably high. But already the new organizers have had an impact greater than the modesty of their numbers would suggest.

Their movement, like all "ferment" on college campuses in the past half-decade, has to be understood in the context of the civil rights movement. The struggle for minimal participation by American Negroes in American democracy "peeled away the façade" (in the current jargon) from the architecture of society, and those who were in the fight saw that there was more to discrimination than weak laws or racial prejudice. For the students of the 'sixties, Birmingham and Albany and the Mississippi Summer was the new American Revolution. At the core of the Berkeley Free Speech Movement last fall was the

Reprinted by permission of the author and *The New Republic* from *The New Republic*, June 19, 1965, pp. 15–19. © 1965, Harrison-Blaine of New Jersey, Inc. Andrew Kopkind is a contributing editor of *The New Republic*. 515

same battle cry that had been heard in the counties of Mississippi: "Let the people decide."

It is the same slogan that the SDS organizers wear on buttons as they work with the Negroes of Clinton Hill, a slum in the South Ward of Newark, New Jersey. It is the same phrase that SDS organizers in Cleveland's Near West Side, a poor white slum, use in protesting the politician-run poverty program.

SDS has a prehistory as the unfortunately-named SLID—the Student League for Industrial Democracy. Without the students, the parent league is a kind of camp for itinerant old leftist intellectuals—or those who think old. In the summer of 1962, the new SDS students met near Port Huron, Mich., and approved a statement of ideas and principles. The "Port Huron Statement" is the seminal document of the new left—or "the movement." Its analysis of society was blunt: "America rests in national stalemate . . . its democratic system apathetic and manipulated rather than 'of, by and for the people'." The framers had no detailed prescription for a change, but a determination to "search for truly democratic alternatives to the present, and a commitment to social experimentation with them. We seek the establishment of a democracy of individual participation governed by two central aims: that the individual share in those social decisions determining the quality and the direction of his life; that society be organized to encourage independence in men and provide the media for their common participation."

SDS chapters opened on several campuses—there were 23 with 900 members at the beginning of the academic year; there are now about 75, with 2,000 members—but except for crisis breaks for civil rights activities in the South, the students had no program for putting the Port Huron concepts into practice. In fact, the distrust of authority and dislike of manipulation were so strong and so pervasive that the idea of any program at all was suspect. Programs imply leaders, strategy, preconceived notions of what is good for people. But somehow the students got that particular philosophical fly out of the bottle, and in early 1964 began setting up SDS projects in a number of Northern cities. A special department called ERAP (Economic Research and Action Project) administered the community organizing work, initially with a $3,000 grant from the United Auto Workers.

CHANGING LIVES

They moved into the communities in groups of six or a dozen. In Cleveland, they rented an apartment in a tacky old frame house in one of the poorest white neighborhoods. They had an idea that they would help the local "community people" to change the condition and quality of their lives, but they were not at all sure how they would do it. ERAP was committed to building an "interracial movement of the   516 poor"; it was thought reasonable to begin reshaping the community among the classes who had the least stake in its preservation, and the most immediate need for improvement. The Near West Side of Cleveland looked at first like a fertile ground. Poor whites from Southern Appalachia lived in squalid "hillbilly heavens," in small, roach-infested apartments that rented for $25 a week. There was a WPA-vintage housing project nearby, with an unobstructed view of a clangorous barge-loading canal, and easy access to the city's most notorious rat-breeding grounds.

For three weeks, the SDS kids (they are called that, or "students," by their friends in the community, and while the terms are, strictly speaking, inaccurate, they do not object) canvassed the neighborhood on a voter-registration drive. They were able to get into hundreds of living rooms, and they talked easily about the concerns people had. In late July, they put together their findings. There were three major problems the people of the Near West Side had more or less in common: the inadequacy and mindless application of public welfare (particularly Aid to Dependent Children), unemployment among men, and conditions in the public housing project.

Organization of the community was to begin around these issues. First off, the staff helped women on welfare to revitalize an organization called CUFAW (Citizens United for Adequate Welfare), which had been active two years previously when Ohio's Governor Rhodes cut welfare payments drastically as an "economy move." The cut had never been restored, but CUFAW was dormant.

"We just talked with the women. They decided they wanted to do something. We said we'd help them do whatever they wanted," said one of the SDS staff. CUFAW's first target—less ambitious than the restoration of full welfare payments—was the institution of a free school lunch program in Cleveland public schools. With the SDS kids always in the background (but with the assurance of their support), the CUFAW women held rallies and meetings, protested to official boards, and complained so loud in public—and with such force—that the city caved in.

The students advised against setting up a hierarchic leadership in CUFAW. As in their own staff meetings, chairmanship rotated among the members, and there was no permanent bureaucratic structure. "Things are done as they need to be," one student explained. The anarchy, which is so characteristic of the SNCC-SDS movement, was a bit much for the older women of CUFAW. Later in the year they moved to formalize their group. Chairmen were elected to terms of a few months instead of a few weeks, but the basic premise of full participation by all the members remained.

The housing project was organized around the lack of recreation facilities. The SDS kids talked with residents, and a tenants' meeting was held. The housing project officials were terrified, but the rec- 517 reation director—whose enthusiasms had not previously included an interest in recreation—was convinced to make immediate reforms. The tenants' meeting became the Tenants' Council, but the whole movement in the project touched a sensitive nerve in Cleveland officialdom. SDS activities were investigated by the city's "Red Squad," a kind of miniature FBI. Some older women residents of the housing project were convinced that the students were Communists, and the first of a continuing series of red-baitings began. The pressure finally became so strong that SDS withdrew its support from the Tenants' Council, the president of the Council resigned, and organizing was abandoned.

The unemployment issue proved difficult to "organize around." As it turned out, unemployed men in the neighborhood had little in common. In the process, though, some of the SDS students spent days in "spot labor" employment offices, and began to learn what it was like to be in the lowest ranks of American life. They also saw how uninterested organized labor was in reforming the employment patterns of the area. "Spot labor"—short-term or part-time jobs for minimum wages and less—was non-unionized, but the spot laborers could work in union shops, often for long periods of time under gentlemen's agreements between the employers and the unions.

Organizing in a poor white community was much tougher than the SDS kids had feared, but they had already made their existence felt in Cleveland. They fought the official anti-poverty program (like most in the country, it was controlled by politicians for whatever political benefits it might bring), and helped residents draw up alternatives. They also made friends in the Negro near-slum area of Glenville, across town from their original headquarters, and made plans to start an organizing project there this summer.

As the year progressed, the SDS staff—which now included one local young mother on welfare—were attracted more and more to the idea of a "community union" rather than specific issue-groups as a basis for organizing. Their model was the SDS project in Newark, which had gathered scores of local Negroes into the Newark Community Union Project (NCUP), called by everyone "en-cup."

NCUP began at the same time as the Cleveland project, but the SDS kids found more immediate response in the Negro ghetto than their friends had among the Cleveland poor whites. The Negroes of Clinton Hill had a wide range of grievances: housing, education, police harassment, welfare—and simply the feeling of being "left out." The organizers easily found local residents to work with them, and there are now about as many Negroes as "students" on the staff.

The students roamed the streets of the "lower hill" neighborhood in Newark; they took "housing surveys" and met the residents. Those who were most eager to "do something" were encouraged to have informal meetings of their neighbors, and soon a system of organized

518

streets—called "blocks"—developed. Hunterdon Street held weekly meetings, so did Hillside, and Peshine; and every Tuesday there would be a general NCUP meeting for all the blocks.

Housing was the obvious first concern, and when the tenants in a slum building met they realized that together they might have the leverage to compel improvements. There were rent strikes, and there were repairs. There was also increased harassment from city officials and the police, and a round of court cases began—against NCUP organizers—which have yet to be resolved. As they did by probing the Cleveland housing project, the students touched raw spots by attacking politically-connected slumlords in Newark.

There had been some hope that NCUP would attract whites as well as Negroes, but it has not so far. There are still whites in Clinton Hill—it was once a middle class Jewish neighborhood, and some older white residents still live on the "upper hill." They are not in NCUP. There had been a neighborhood council before NCUP, but its main effect was to preserve as long as possible the "nice" parts of the Hill and avoid contact with the new poor Negroes.

It is difficult to measure the extent of NCUP's effect on Clinton Hill. In the way of immediate improvements, there have been a number of building repairs made by landlords, and at least detectable housing inspection and code enforcement by the city. Sanitation and garbage pick-up (NCUP demands) have been improved, and an urban renewal scheme which would have turned much of the area into an industrial zone—with drastic results for the poorest residents—has been quietly shelved. These are small victories, but they have done something more for the Negroes of Clinton Hill: they expect something will happen.

FROM THE BOTTOM UP

Organizing the poor is not so much a political act as a psychological process. There is no street haranguing, no cadre discipline. Spontaneity is all-important. "The most significant thing," says Tom Hayden, who drafted the Port Huron Statement and is now an NCUP organizer in Newark, "is the development of a group of people with no previous political connections who are able to speak and act without being embarrassed or dependent on the higher-ups."

It is a long jump from a statement of theories to a block meeting, but they are jumping in Newark. Last week, after she and her son were arrested by Fifth Precinct policemen in Clinton Hill, Mrs. Georgia Lewis sat in the office of an aide to Mayor Hugh J. Addonizio, and told him she didn't want to take any more harassment, that she was tired of arbitrary arrests and threats and brutal treatment (Mrs. Lewis's daughter was arrested in front of the NCUP staff's apartment a few months ago, also for no apparent reason). With her in the 519 office were a dozen NCUP members—both students and community people. Mrs. Lewis, a shy, frail Negro, was suddenly not afraid to speak back to the "higher-ups." The mayor's aide was annoyed, but he could not help being impressed.

To visit with the SDS projects for a week is a wrenching experience. Someone said the official war on poverty might be far more effective if Sargent Shriver spent a few days—perhaps incognito, like Peter the Great among shipwrights in Amsterdam—with the poor whites on the Near West Side, or the Negroes in Newark. Long before Adam Clayton Powell thought of it, the SDS kids knew that social change cannot come from the top-down and decided they had to become as nearly as possible part of the community they are helping.

Hardly anyone on the "outside" can imagine the completeness of their transformation, or the depth of their commitment. They are not down there for a visit in the slums. They are part of the slums, a kind of lay-brotherhood, or worker-priests, except that they have no dogma to sell. They get no salary; they live on a subsistence allowance that the project as a whole uses for rent and food. Most of the time they are broke. In the dining room of the Cleveland "project house" last week was a sign: "Panic point. Bank balance $4.09." Newark project workers have to call "friends in the suburbs" every so often for $5 or $10, so the necessities of life can continue. The kids are the very antithesis of paid organizers the unions or political parties have to hire. Most of them have committed their lives to "the movement"; no matter if in a few years they change their minds. It is important that they now have the expectation of remaining.

Most of them went to college. Their experience runs from drop-out to PhD. The two major collegiate springs were Swarthmore (where students started an organizing project in nearby Chester, Pa., which became one model and later an affiliate of ERAP) and the University of Michigan. Most of them come from middle-class and professional-class families; many of their parents do not approve. They are subject to the same psychological motivations as everyone else of their age in America. They believe it is their conscience, not their psychology, which counts in their society. They hear about SDS at college and the projects cannot absorb all the organizers who apply to work. The urge to *act* is the strongest force of the new left. Students can read in a brochure distributed by the National Student Association of 30 or more action projects they can join, for the summer or longer.

In some instances, they are more proletarian than the proletariat: they eat a spartan diet of one-and-a-half meals a day, consisting mainly of powdered milk and large quantities of peanut butter and jelly, which seems to be the SDS staple. Occasionally, they cadge much more appetizing (and, presumably, more nourishing) meals from their poor local friends.

They will never, of course, assimilate themselves entirely into the 520 poor community. There is a psychological distance between the new-comers and the older residents, and even though it is shorter than one would imagine, it bothers some of the kids. A few of the NCUP students have gone to another New Jersey city, have taken low-paying jobs, much as the indigenous poor would have, and they lead an "ordinary" life without any kind of plan for organizing. It is more than the Fabian idea of "getting to know the poor," and much less than the old Communist idea of infiltrating the proletariat. One girl has gone to work in a garment shop; when her friends and co-workers learn she is a college graduate and ask why she is working for $1.25 an hour as an unskilled laborer, she replies truthfully, "because I was tired of the rat-race."

But most of the SDS kids do not go so far. They balance their desire to build a working movement with their anti-strategy and anti-leadership beliefs. They hate the system of manipulation and authoritarianism more than they dislike the injustices it produces.

REPUDIATING THE PAST

It is hard for liberals traumatized by both Stalinism and McCarthyism to understand the new left's attitudes about Communism. First, SDS called itself a "non-Communist organization." The students dropped the designation a few months ago, because no one could see its relevance. (The Daughters of the American Revolution does not call itself a non-Communist group.) They do not seek allies in the middle-class liberal world, because their analysis of society tells them that the liberals have as much stake in the *status quo* as the conservatives, and are equally as biased against change. The red-baiting in Newark has come from "liberal Democratic" politicians—and from some of the older civil rights organizations.

Relations with the League for Industrial Democracy are far from friendly. League leaders—especially Bayard Rustin—want a coalition of liberal movements (unions, civil rights groups, the churches) to improve the condition of the poor. The students see the coalition idea as merely an extension of New Deal welfare politics. They want to do more than lift a few poor people into the middle class. "The New Deal brought socialism to the middle class and free enterprise to the poor," a Protestant minister who works with SDS in Cleveland said.

The organizers are anything but apolitical. But they believe they must shake up the politicians before any changes can be made, that they must start the poor moving—as the civil rights movement got the Negroes in the South moving—before the "power structure" will acknowledge their existence. SNCC workers in Mississippi march with Negroes to courthouses every day in a futile attempt to register to vote, not because they think that the rolls will suddenly open, but because the Negroes learn that they are systematically excluded from 521 democratic participation. SDS organizers march with the poor in Newark for the same reason. If Mayor Addonizio thinks that is a subversive development, he is right.

The temptation to direct the course of the movement is strong, and the SDS workers have all they can do to stay in the background. In Cleveland, there is a strong feeling for the project "group." Some have called it a kind of kibbutz, or a commune. The staff lives and eats together. They have no project office; if their organizing produces a community organization, they want the local people, not the SDS kids to run it. Long staff meetings that characterize the whole movement, North and South, sometimes sound like group therapy sessions.

Newark's project is much more free-wheeling than Cleveland's, perhaps because it includes so many community people already. The original SDS students are now merged with the local Negro staff in NCUP, and together they spend much of the day talking with people in their neighborhood. Sometimes in pairs (often interracial) they walk up and down the blocks, ringing doorbells of apartments they have not yet visited, or dropping in on NCUP stalwarts. There is a staff apartment, but some members are leaving to find separate quarters in the neighborhood, and eventually that may become the pattern.

This summer, all the SDS projects—in Cleveland, Newark, Hudson County, N.J., Chicago, Baltimore, Cairo, Ill., Boston and Oakland, Calif., and affiliates in Chester, Pa., San Francisco, and New Haven— will get an influx of new students, some working *à la* Mississippi between school years, and others who will stay on through the year. In Cleveland, the project is starting a community theater, which will get community people to act in loose-scripted plays around the neighborhood—on food stamp lines, in front of unemployment offices, and wherever else a crowd is likely to gather. In Newark, dozens of SDS kids will work with NCUP on extending the block organization and trying to steer the official Newark anti-poverty program around to involvement of the poor.

THE USES OF POWER

At the April 17 "March on Washington to End the War in Vietnam," which SDS sponsored, the organization's president, Paul Potter, asked the demonstrators as they massed at the base of the Washington Monument, "What kind of system is it that disenfranchises people in the South, leaves millions . . . impoverished and excluded from the mainstream and promise of American society, that creates faceless and terrible bureaucracies . . . that consistently puts material values before human values—and still persists in calling itself free and in finding itself fit to police the world? What place is there for ordinary men in that system and how are they to control it, makes it bend itself to their wills rather than bending them to its? We must name that 522 system. We must name it, describe it, analyze it, understand it, and change it."

Someone in the crowd yelled "capitalism," and he was shouted down by others. The system Potter means to name—and change—is much more complicated than that. It is an intricate set of interlocking relationships that is called "power." It doesn't really matter who is holding it—a Negro leader or a white, a liberal or a conservative.

The old left says that community organization was tried in the 'thirties, among the unemployed, and it did not grow into a movement then, and will not in this generation. They suspect that the students would not know what to do with power if they should suddenly achieve it—and they think that indeed the students would rather remain in opposition than start planning. More than that, they do not know how in the world a community union or a group of protesting welfare mothers can win over the entrenched power of city or state administrations, and the vast economic allies they have.

What is to be done with power is the crucial question in SDS, as it is with SNCC. Last week in Newark, a slate of NCUP community members (including some SDS staff organizers) was elected to run one of the area boards of the city's official war on poverty. Newark's machine politicians were aghast, but NCUP's joy at political victory (the slate won a vote of area residents by two-thirds majority) was not unalloyed. Running even part of an anti-poverty program (the area board will determine the needs of its neighborhood, and then help administer the funds granted) might lead to the creation of the kind of bureaucratic, leader-heavy organization which the students abhor. In Cleveland, the SDS staff shies away from attaching itself too closely even to the opposition anti-poverty plan, which calls for the participation of the poor. The tension within the "freedom movement," between those who want more freedom, and those who want more movement, will surely increase as the doors to power open. "The kids will have to decide whether they want to save their own souls, or change other people's lives," said an older-left critic.

Perhaps the students have not come to grips with that central problem. Still, there is no other movement, no other source of action in the US that is so doggedly exploring methods of social change, and putting them into practice.

TEN

DISPENSING JUSTICE
AND DIGNITY

In January, 1965, a project entitled Neighborhood Legal Services (NLS) was started in Washington, D. C. funded by the Office of Economic Opportunity. The NLS provides lawyers to defend poor clients who are facing legal action, and to represent clients in legal actions to protect their own interests. The impact of the NLS was described in the October 3, 1966, issue of the Washington Post.

> Imagine a Washington where slum tenants can legally refuse to pay rent until landlords bring their housing up to city standards;
> Where public housing tenants can go to court and force the National Capital Housing Authority to eliminate rats from their homes;
> Where Welfare Department investigators are banned from homes of public aid recipients unless they are invited inside or have a search warrant;
> Where finance companies dealing largely with the poor suddenly find they can no longer collect on questionable high-interest contracts.
> Imagine a Washington where the quarter of a million poor people now hailed without lawyers into Landlord and Tenant, Small Claims, Traffic, Drunk and Juvenile courts each year started showing up with attorneys, demanding full court hearings and winning 10, 20, even 50 times as many cases as they do now.

In response to the activities of the NLS, lawyers for landlords have complained that the NLS lawyers have frequently requested jury trials to earn more time for their clients in avoiding evictions; lawyers in private practice have filed suit against the NLS charging unfair competition; lawyers representing landlords and finance companies who have been used to winning scores of judgments without trials now find themselves confronted with long court trials; and city judges looking at their clogged court docket complain about the NLS lawyers who

524

"are trying to take every 15-cent case all the way up to the Supreme Court."

The effects of the Neighborhood Legal Services project are most striking when one considers that all this represents is a situation where the poor have an opportunity to enjoy all the legal rights generally available to more prosperous and more knowledgeable citizens. It also dramatically describes how easily social institutions—in this case the legal institutions—become adapted to a condition of established legal inequality for some citizens and at the same time resistant to attempts to restore those rights.

The legal system is one activity of the national state that has the manifest purpose of protecting the rights of its citizens. Another activity that is manifestly designed to serve the needs of citizens of the state is the system of public welfare. Both activities have in common a grounding in philosophical principles that see men as beings of special worth and value, with certain fundamental rights that must be preserved. However, both activities also share the dubious honors of falling very far short of their noble purposes and destroying the ends they seek to achieve.

Constitutional guarantees of equal protection under the law, legal counsel, grand jury indictment, and trial by jury have been found frequently to be guarantees more for some citizens than for others. The complex machinery of the law concerning bail, parole, appeals, grand jury hearings, preliminary hearings, and rights to counsel can be overwhelming to the person who has little knowledge of the law or little money to employ the services of legal representatives. The poor do not fare well in obtaining the benefit of many of their legal guarantees. They are more likely not to get preliminary hearings, not to get bail, to be in jail longer awaiting trial, not to get a grand jury hearing, to have fewer jury trials, and to be found guilty more frequently (Nagel, 1966).

The Blumberg article in this chapter provides a close-up look at the legal process in terms of the relationships among the lawyer, client, and court. The author provides a description of the pre-trial process that is far-removed from popular conceptions of the adversary system of a lawyer representing his client. Here we have a version of the lawyer-client relationship played as a confidence game, with the lawyer choosing legal strategies that will lead to a speedy conclusion and an assured fee. The client is caught between two bureaucratic structures —the legal profession and the courts—each of which has an interest in preserving the other and in developing an efficient system for processing defendants. Blumberg's argument raises some doubt as to the effectiveness of Supreme Court decisions which have extended guarantees to counsel to all citizens; he questions whether the poor defendant is any better off with a lawyer than he is without one.

Efforts to extend Constitutional guarantees to the poor have not been   525 limited to the trial phase of the legal process. There have also been important Supreme Court decisions designed to protect defendants in the earliest phase of the legal process—while they are in the hands of the police. In 1957, the Supreme Court in the Mallory decision ruled that police in the District of Columbia could only hold a suspect for the shortest time possible before bringing him before a judge. In 1963, the Gideon decision provided a blanket rule on the individual defendant's right to a lawyer. The most far-reaching decision in 1964 —the Escobedo case—ruled that an accused person in the custody of the police could not be subjected to a station-house interrogation until his request to see his lawyer was granted.

These decisions have thrust the Court into a position of making policy for running police departments. This has occurred as the Courts decisions on specific cases have tended to become extended as a general standard governing all cases. As Packer (1965) has noted in speaking of the new decisions by the Court:

> It is one thing to say: This defendant's confession was illegally co-erced because he was illiterate, unadvised of his rights, held incom-municado, subjected to threats, beaten, or whatever. It is quite another to say: No person who is arrested may be questioned by the police until he has been advised of his right to remain silent and to have the assistance of a lawyer and until he has had the chance to see a lawyer if he wants to.

According to Packer, the increasing tendency of the Supreme Court to make the second type of ruling results from the failure of police departments and appropriate state and federal legislative bodies to develop a system of internal controls to protect the rights of accused citizens.

The response of law enforcement agencies to the court decisions has been to point out how police effectiveness in crime control has been hampered. It is probably true that police interrogation has helped to detect many crimes and criminals. It is probably equally true that interrogation leads to abuse of individual rights and tragic errors in dispensing justice. The tendency to bend in the direction of the accused rather than the police stems from the absence of any effective civilian control over police activities. The complaints of minority groups concerning police brutality reflect a situation where the police are generally unaccountable for their actions, and certainly unaccountable to powerless minority group members.

Another reason to be concerned over the abuses of individual rights in a situation of unrestrained interrogation is the growing use by police of sophisticated behavior control techniques in their investigative procedures. The article by Zimbardo describes police techniques in interrogations and enhances our understanding of a legal situation which 526 seems highly implausible: that an innocent man can confess to a crime he did not commit.

Turning to the system of public welfare in the United States we often find that what is intended as a device to help the less fortunate becomes a way of punishing those whose misfortunes are seen as signs of immorality and fundamental deficiencies in character. There are today in the United States nearly 8,000,000 persons on public welfare rolls; over one-half of these are children, while another third are the aged and the incapacitated. These figures do not include millions of others who live on substandard incomes but are not eligible for public assistance. The two million migrant workers do not meet residency requirements in most states and are ineligible for benefits.

Welfare issues seem to have gained public attention in recent years, and the attention has paralled the migration of poor whites and Negroes to urban centers, the increased agitation of civil rights groups for protection against rising unemployment rates, and the increasing public welfare budgets.

Many of the issues surrounding public welfare were given national prominence in 1960–1961 in Newburgh, New York, in a series of events that was characterized as *The Battle of Newburgh* (the title of a CBS television report on the subject). Not only did Newburgh spark a national debate over public welfare but it also gave public attention to the manner in which a welfare system can be used to punish and degrade those persons it is designed to assist. In an effort to discourage the alleged inflow of more welfare cases and get rid of its reputation as a welfare resort (according to the city manager who proposed the plan) the city required welfare recipients to pick up their checks at the police department rather than in the mail and proposed a list of thirteen operating procedures governing the welfare programs:

1. All cash payments which can be converted to food, clothing and rent vouchers and the like without basic harm to the intent of the aid shall be issued in voucher form henceforth.

2. All able-bodied adult males on relief of any kind who are capable of working are to be assigned to the chief of building maintenance for work assignment on a 40-hour week.

3. All recipients physically capable of and available for private employment who are offered a job but refuse it, regardless of the type of employment involved, are to be denied relief.

4. All mothers of illegitimate children are to be advised that should they have any more children out of wedlock, they shall be denied relief.

5. All applicants for relief who have left a job voluntarily, i.e., who have not been fired or laid-off, shall be denied relief.

527

6. The allotment for any one family unit shall not exceed the take-home pay of the lowest paid city employee with a family of comparable size. Also, no relief shall be granted to any family whose income is in excess of the latter figure.

7. All files of all Aid to Dependent Children cases are to be brought to the office of the corporation counsel for review monthly. All new cases of any kind will be referred to the corporation counsel prior to certification of payment.

8. All applicants for relief who are new to the city must show evidence that their plans in coming to the city involved a concrete offer of employment, similar to that required for foreign immigrants. All such persons shall be limited to two weeks of relief. Those who cannot show evidence shall be limited to one week of relief.

9. Aid to persons except the aged, blind and disabled shall be limited to three months in any one year—this is a feature similar to the present policies on unemployment benefits.

10. All recipients who are not disabled, blind, or otherwise incapacitated, shall report to the Department of Public Welfare monthly for a conference regarding the status of their case.

11. Once the budget for the fiscal year is approved by the Council, it shall not be exceeded by the Welfare Department unless approved by Council by supplemental appropriation.

12. There shall be a monthly expenditure limit on all categories of Welfare Aid. This monthly expenditure limit shall be established by the Department of Public Welfare at the time of presenting its budget, and shall take into account seasonal variations.

13. Prior to certifying or continuing any more Aid to Dependent children cases, a determination shall be made as to the home environment. If the home environment is not satisfactory, the children in that home shall be placed in foster care in lieu of Welfare aid to the family adults. (May, 1964, 25–26)

Other proposals that were considered and rejected by the city council included a requirement that applicants for relief be photographed and thumbprinted before eligibility is established and a plan to publish the names, addresses and amount of assistance received by all welfare recipients in the city newspaper.

While the motives for such measures as were employed in the Newburgh case are, at least in part, to guard against misuse, the effects of such a program are not only degrading to the recipients but they make him a pawn in the hands of agencies on which he depends. Moreover, such policies effectively block the payments to many individuals whose particular pattern of needs just do not fit the requirements laid out.

The articles by Barr and Lebeaux in this chapter provide documentation of the position that the present social welfare system is not only an

528

inadequate solution to poverty, but that the manner in which welfare is administered is also degrading. Greater dependence on welfare by the poor is fostered by the current welfare programs since the budgets allotted are not sufficient to provide opportunities for realistic planning, nor are they enough to provide the children of the poor with much hope for themselves. Some of the shortcomings of the welfare programs give support to those who propose the guaranteed income as the main solution to poverty. The guaranteed income could help to reverse the growing tendency toward the development of a centralized state, exercising control over the detailed choices of daily existence among a significant portion of its population.

REFERENCES AND ADDITIONAL READING

Richard A. Cloward and Frances Fox Piven, "We've Got Rights! The No-Longer Silent Welfare Poor," *The New Republic,* August 5, 1967, 23–27.

Edgar May, *The Wasted Americans,* New York: New American Library, 1964.

Stuart S. Nagel, "The Tipped Scales of Justice," *Trans-action,* May-June, 1966, 3–9.

Herbert L. Packer, "Policing the Police: Nine Men are not Enough," *The New Republic,* September 4, 1965, 17–21.

Jerome A. Skolnick, *Justice Without Trial,* New York: John Wiley, 1966.

Abraham S. Blumberg

Covert Contingencies in the Right to the Assistance of Counsel

A recurring theme in the growing dialogue between sociology and law has been the great need for a joint effort of the two disciplines in illuminating urgent social and legal issues. Having uttered fervent public pronouncements in this vein, the respective practitioners go their separate ways. Academic spokesmen for the legal profession are somewhat critical of sociologists of law because of what they perceive as the sociologist's preoccupation with the application of his methodology to the solution of legal problems. Further, it is felt that ". . . contemporary writing in the sociology of law . . . betrays the existence of painfully unsophisticated notions about the day-to-day operations of courts, legislatures and law offices."[1] Regardless of the merit of this seemingly harsh criticism, it is evident that scant attention—apart from explorations of the legal profession itself, has been given to the sociological examination and understanding of legal institutions,

A slightly abridged version of the paper presented at The American Sociological Association Meetings (Miami, Florida, August 30, 1966) and subsequently published in *Law and Society Review*, Vol. 2, pp. 15–39, 1967, is used here by permission of the author and *Law and Society Review*. Abraham S. Blumberg is associate professor of law and sociology at the John Jay College of The City University of New York.

[1]Harry W. Jones, "A View From the Bridge," *Social Problems* Law and Society Supplement, Vol. 13 (Summer, 1965) p. 42: See Gilbert Geis, "Sociology, Criminology, and Criminal Law," *Social Problems* Vol. 7, No. 1 (Summer, 1959) pp. 40-47, and N. S. Timasheff, "Growth and Scope of Sociology of Law" in Howard Becker and Alvin Boskoff, eds., *Modern Sociological Theory in Continuity and Change* (New York: Dryden Press, 1957) pp. 424-449, for further evaluation of the strained relations between sociology and law.

or their supporting ideological assumptions. Thus, for example, very little sociological effort is expended to ascertain the validity and viability of important court decisions, which may rest on wholly erroneous assumptions in the light of the contextual realities of social structure. A particular decision may rest upon a legally impeccable rationale: at the same time it may be rendered nugatory by contingencies imposed by aspects of social reality of which the lawmakers are themselves unaware.

It is in this context that I wish to examine two recent landmark decisions of the United States Supreme Court, which have been hailed as destined to effect profound changes in the future of criminal law administration and enforcement in America. The first of these, *Gideon* v. *Wainwright,* 372 U.S. 335 (1963), was a historic milestone in that it requires states and localities henceforth to furnish counsel in the case of indigent persons charged with a felony.[2] The Gideon ruling raised an interesting question: What is the precise point in time at which a suspect is entitled to counsel?[3] The answer came relatively

[2]This decision represented the climax of a line of cases which had begun to chip away at the notion that the VIth Amendment of the Constitution (right to assistance of counsel) applied only to the federal government, and could not be held to run against the states through the XIVth Amendment. An exhaustive historical analysis of the XIVth Amendment and the Bill of Rights will be found in Charles Fairman, "Does the Fourteenth Amendment Incorporate the Bill of Rights? The Original Understanding." *Stanford Law Review* Vol. 2 (December, 1949), pp. 5-139. Since the Gideon decision, there is already evidence that its effect will ultimately extend to indigent persons charged with misdemeanors—and perhaps ultimately even traffic cases and other minor offenses. For a popular account of this important development in connection with the right to assistance of counsel see, Anthony Lewis, *Gideon's Trumpet,* (New York: Random House, 1964). For a scholarly historical analysis of the right to counsel see, William M. Beaney, *The Right To Counsel in American Courts,* (Ann Arbor: University of Michigan Press, 1955). For a more recent comprehensive review and discussion of the right to counsel and its development see, Note, "Counsel at Interrogation," *Yale Law Journal,* Vol. 73, (May, 1964) pp. 1000-1057.

With the passage of the Criminal Justice Act of 1964, indigent accused persons in the federal courts will be defended by federally paid legal counsel. For a general discussion of the nature and extent of public and private legal aid in the United States prior to the Gideon case, see Emery A. Brownell, *Legal Aid in the United States,* (Rochester: The Lawyers Cooperative Publishing Co., 1961); also Robert B. vonMehren, *et al., Equal Justice for the Accused,* (Garden City: Doubleday and Co., Inc., 1959).

[3]In the case of federal defendants the issue is clear. In *Mallory* v. *United States,* 354 U.S. 449 (1957) the Supreme Court unequivocally indicated that a person under federal arrest must be taken "without any unnecessary delay" before a U.S. commissioner where he will receive information as to his rights to remain silent and to assistance of counsel which will be furnished, in the event he is indigent, under the Criminal

531

quickly in *Escobedo* v. *Illinois,* 378 U.S. 478 (1964), which has aroused a storm of controversy. Danny Escobedo confessed to the murder of his brother-in-law after the police had refused to permit retained counsel to see him, although his lawyer was present in the station house and requested to confer with his client. In a 5–4 decision, the court asserted where the process of police investigative effort shifts from merely investigatory to that of accustory— "when its focus is on the accused and its purpose is to elicit a confession—our adversary system begins to operate, and, under the circumstances here, the accused must be permitted to consult with his lawyer."

As a consequence Escobedo's confession was rendered inadmissible, triggering a national debate among police, district attorneys, judges, lawyers and other law enforcement officials, which continues unabated, as to the value and propriety of confessions in criminal cases.[4] Regardless of the relative merit of the various shades of opinion as to the role of counsel in criminal cases, the issues generated thereby will be in part resolved as additional cases move toward decision in the Supreme Court in the near future.[5] They are of peripheral interest

---

Justice Act of 1964. For a most interesting and richly documented work in connection with the general area of the Bill of Rights, see Claude R. Sowle, *Police Power and Individual Freedom,* (Chicago: Aldine Publishing Co., 1962).

[4]See *New York Times,* November 20, 1965, page 1, for Justice Nathan R. Sobel's statement to the effect that based on his study of 1,000 indictments in Brooklyn, N.Y. from February-April, 1965, fewer than 10% involved confessions. Sobel's detailed analysis will be found in six articles which appeared in the *New York Law Journal,* beginning November 15, 1965, through November 21, 1965, titled "The Exclusionary Rules in the Law of Confessions: A Legal Perspective—A Practical Perspective." Most law enforcement officials believe that the majority of convictions in criminal cases are based upon confessions obtained by police. For example, the District Attorney of New York County, (a jurisdiction which has the largest volume of cases in the U.S.A.), Frank S. Hogan, reports that confessions are crucial and indicates "if a suspect is entitled to have a lawyer during preliminary questioning . . . any lawyer worth his fee will tell him to keep his mouth shut," *New York Times,* December 2, 1965, page 1. Concise discussions of the issue are to be found in, David Robinson, Jr., "Massiah, Escobedo and Rationales For the Exclusion of Confessions," *Journal of Criminal Law, Criminology and Police Science,* Vol. 56, No. 4, (December, 1965) pp. 412–431; Donald C. Dowling, "Escobedo and Beyond: The Need for a Fourteenth Amendment Code of Criminal Procedure," *Journal of Criminal Law, Criminology and Police Science,* Vol. 56, No. 2 (June, 1965) pp. 143-157.

[5]On June 13, 1966, the Supreme Court in a 5-4 decision underscored the principle enunciated in Escobedo in the case of *Miranda* v. *Arizona*-U.S.-Police interrogation of any suspect in custody, without his consent, unless a defense attorney is present, is prohibited by the self-incrimination provision of the FIFTH AMENDMENT.

and not of immediate concern in this paper. However, the *Gideon* and *Escobedo* cases pose interesting general questions. In both instances, the Supreme Court reiterates the traditional legal conception of a defense lawyer which is reflective of the ideological perception of a criminal case as being an *adversary, combative* proceeding, in which counsel for the defense assiduously musters all the admittedly limited resources at his command to *defend* the accused.[6] The fundamental question to be asked is does the Supreme Court's conception of the role of counsel in a criminal case square with social reality? That is the focus of my concern, and it shall be the task of this paper to furnish some preliminary evidence toward the illumination of that question. For it would seem, that there exist only some ideologically oriented generalizations and commitments, but limited empirical apprehension of the function of defense counsel.

There is by now ample evidence that the overwhelming majority of convictions in criminal cases (usually over 90%) are not the product of a combative, trial-by-jury process at all, but instead merely involve the sentencing of the individual after a negotiated, bargained-for plea of guilty has been entered.[7] Although more recently the overzealous role of police and prosecutors in producing pretrial confessions and admissions has achieved a good deal of notoriety, scant attention has been paid to the organizational structure and personnel of the criminal court itself. Indeed, the extremely high conviction rate produced

[6]Even under optimal circumstances a criminal case is a very much one-sided affair, the parties to the "contest" being decidedly unequal in strength and resources. See Abraham S. Goldstein, "The State and the Accused: Balance of Advantage in Criminal Procedure," *Yale Law Journal,* Vol. 69 (June, 1960) pp. 1149-1199.

[7]F. James Davis *et al., Society and the Law: New Meanings for an Old Profession,* (New York: Free Press of Glencoe, 1962) p. 301; Lester Orfield, *Criminal Procedure from Arrest to Appeal,* (New York: New York University Press, 1947) p. 297.

Donald J. Newman, "Pleading Guilty for Considerations: A Study of Bargain Justice," *The Journal of Criminal Law, Criminology and Police Science,* Vol. 46, No. 6, (March-April, 1954), pp. 780-790. Newman's data covered only one year, 1954, in a midwestern community; however, it is in general confirmed by my own data drawn from a far more populous area, and from what is one of the major criminal courts in the country, for a period of fifteen years from 1950 to 1964 inclusive. The English experience tends also to confirm American data, see Nigel Walker, *Crime and Punishment in Britain: An Analysis of the Penal System.* (Edinburgh: Edinburgh University Press, 1965). See also Donald J. Newman, *Conviction: The Determination of Guilt or Innocence Without Trial.* (Boston: Little, Brown and Co., 1966) for a comprehensive legalistic study of the guilty plea sponsored by the American Bar Foundation. The criminal court as a social system, an analysis of "bargaining" and its functions in the criminal court's organizational structure, are examined in my forthcoming Book. *The Criminal Court: A Sociological Perspective,* to be published by Quadrangle Books, Chicago, Ill.

533

without the features of an adversary trial in our courts would tend to suggest that the "trial" becomes a perfunctory reiteration and validation of the pretrial interrogation and investigation.[8]

For it is in that institutional setting that the actual role of defense counsel in a criminal case is radically different from the one traditionally depicted.[9] Sociologists and others, have focused their attention on the deprivations and social disabilities of such variables as race, ethnicity, and social class as being the source of an accused person's defeat in a criminal court. Largely overlooked is the variable of the court organization itself, which possesses a thrust, purpose and direction of its own. It is grounded in values, bureaucratic priorities and administrative instruments, which exalt maximum production and the particularistic designs for career enhancement of organizational incumbents, whose occupational and career commitments tend to generate a set of priorities, exerting a higher claim than the stated ideological goals of "due process of law," and is often inconsistent with them. . . .

At the outset, one must distinguish between the "lawyer regulars," i.e., those defense lawyers, who by virtue of their continuous appearances in behalf of defendants, tend to represent the bulk of a criminal court's non-indigent case workload, and those lawyers who are not "regulars," who appear almost casually in behalf of an occasional client. Some of the "lawyer regulars" are highly visible as one moves about the major urban centers of the nation, their offices line the back streets of the courthouses, at times sharing space with bondsmen. Their political "visibility" in terms of local club house ties, reaching into the judge's chambers and prosecutor's office, are also deemed essential to successful practitioners. . . .

However, lawyers whether privately retained or of the legal-aid, public defender variety, have close and continuing relations with the prosecuting office and the court itself through discreet relations with the judges via their law secretaries or "confidential" assistants. . . .

The client, then, is a secondary figure in the court system as in

[8]George Feifer, *Justice in Moscow*, (New York: Dell Publishing Co., 1965). The Soviet trial has been termed "an appeal from the pretrial investigation," and Feifer notes that the Soviet "trial" is simply a recapitulation of the data collected by the pretrial investigator. The notions of a trial being a "tabula rasa" and presumptions of innocence are wholly alien to Soviet notions of justice. . . . "The closer the investigation resembles the finished script, the better . . ." p. 86.

[9]For a concise statement of the constitutional and economic aspects of the right to legal assistance, see Monrad G. Paulsen, *Equal Justice for the Poor Man*, (New York: Public Affairs Pamphlets, No. 367, 1964); for a brief traditional description of the legal profession see Paul A. Freund, "The Legal Profession," *Daedalus* (Fall, 1963) pp. 689-700.

certain other bureaucratic settings.[12] He becomes a means to other, larger ends of the organization's incumbents. Doubts, contingencies and pressures he may present which challenge existing informal arrangements or are disruptive of them, tend to be resolved in favor of the continuance of the organization and its relations as before. There is a greater community of interest among all the principal organizational structures and their incumbents than exists elsewhere in other settings. The accused's lawyer has far greater professional, economic, intellectual and other ties to the various elements of the court system than he does to his own client. The court is a closed community. This is more than just the case of the usual "secrets" of bureaucracy which are fanatically defended from outside view. Even all elements of the press are zealously determined to report only that which will not offend the board of judges, the prosecutor, probation, legal-aid, or other officials, in return for privileges and courtesies granted in the past and to be granted in the future. Rather than any view of the matter in terms of some variation of a "conspiracy" hypothesis, the simple explanation is one of an ongoing system dealing with delicate, tension and trauma producing law enforcement and administration, which requires the almost pathological distrust of "outsiders" bordering on group paranoia.

The virtually hostile attitude toward "outsiders" is in large measure engendered by a defensiveness produced by the inherent deficiencies of assembly line justice, so characteristic of our major criminal courts. Intolerably large case loads of defendants which must be disposed of in an organizational context of limited resources and personnel, potentially subject the participants in the court community to harsh scrutiny from appellate courts, and other public and private sources of condemnation. As a consequence, an almost irreconcilable conflict is posed in terms of intense pressures to process large numbers of cases on the one hand, and the stringent ideological and legal requirements of "due process of law," on the other hand. A rather tenuous resolution of the dilemma has emerged in the shape of a large variety of bureaucratically ordained and controlled "work crimes," short cuts, deviations, and outright rule violations on the part of court occupational incumbents ranging from judges to stenographers in order to meet production norms. Fearfully anticipating criticism on ethical as well as legal grounds, all the significant participants in

[12]There is a real question to be raised as to whether in certain organizational settings, a complete reversal of the bureaucratic-ideal has not occurred. That is, it would seem, in some instances the organization appears to exist to serve the needs of its various occupational incumbents, rather than its clients. Amitai Etzioni, *Modern Organizations,* (Englewood Cliffs, N.J.: Prentice-Hall, Inc., 1964) pp. 94-104.

535

the court's social structure are bound into an organized system of complicity. This consists of a work arrangement in which the patterned, covert, informal breaches, and evasions of "due process" are institutionalized, but are, nevertheless, denied to exist.

These institutionalized evasions will be found to occur to some degree, in all criminal courts. Their nature, scope and complexity will be largely determined by the size of the court, and the character of the community in which it is located, e.g., whether it is a large, urban institution, or a relatively small rural county court. In addition, idiosyncratic, local conditions may contribute to a unique flavor in the character and quality of the criminal law's administraton in a particular community. However, in most instances a variety of stratagems are employed—some subtle, some crude, in effectively disposing of what are often too large caseloads. A wide variety of coercive devices are employed against an accused-client, couched in a depersonalized, instrumental, bureaucratic version of due process of law, and which are in reality a perfunctory obeisance to the ideology of due process. These include some very explicit pressures which are exerted in some measure by all court personnel, including judges, to plead guilty and avoid trial. In many instances the sanction of a potentially harsh sentence is utilized as the visible alternative to pleading guilty, in the case of recalcitrants. Probation and psychiatric reports are "tailored" to organizational needs, or are at least responsive to the court organization's requirements for the refurbishment of a defendant's social biography, consonant with his new status. A resourceful judge can, through his subtle domination of the proceedings, impose his will on the final outcome of a trial. Stenographers and clerks, in their function as record keepers, are on occasion pressed into service in support of a judicial need to "rewrite" the record of a courtroom event. Bail practices are usually employed for purposes other than simply assuring a defendant's presence on the date of a hearing in connection with his case. Too often, the discretionary power as to bail is part of the arsenal of weapons available to collapse the resistance of an accused person. The foregoing is a most cursory examination of some of the more prominent "short cuts" available to any court organization. There are numerous other procedural strategies constituting due process deviations, which tend to become the work style artifacts of a court's personnel. Thus, only court "regulars" who are "bound in" are really accepted, others are treated routinely and in almost a coldly correct manner.

The defense attorneys, therefore, whether of the "legal-aid," public defender variety, or privately retained, although operating in terms of pressures specific to their respective role and organizational obligations, ultimately are concerned with strategies which tend to lead to a plea. It is the rational, impersonal elements involving economies of

536

time, labor, expense and a superior commitment of the defense counsel to these rationalistic values of maximum production[13] of court organization that prevail, rather than any particularistic, affective ties an accused may have reasonably expected to be the character of his relationship with his lawyer. The lawyer "regulars" are frequently former staff members of the prosecutor's office and utilize the charisma, "know-how" and contacts of their former affiliation as part of their stock in trade. But an accused and his kin, as with others outside the court community, are unable to apprehend the nature and dimensions of the close and continuing relations between the lawyer "regular" and his former colleagues in the prosecutor's office. Their continuing colleagueship is based on real professional and organizational needs of a *quid pro quo,* which goes beyond the limits of an accommodation or *modus vivendi* one might ordinarily expect under the circumstances of an otherwise seemingly adversary relationship. Indeed, the adversary features which are manifest are for the most part muted and exist even in their attenuated form largely for external consumption. The principals, lawyer and assistant district attorney, rely upon one another's cooperation for their continued professional existence, and so the bargaining between them tends usually to be "reasonable" rather than fierce.

The real key to the apprehension of the role of defense counsel in a criminal case is to be found in the area of the fixing of the fee to be charged and its collection. The problem of fixing and collecting the fee tends to influence to a significant degree the criminal court process itself, and not just the relationship of the lawyer and his client. In essence, a lawyer-client "confidence game" is played. Almost everyone is familiar with the oft-told tale of "The Emperor's New Clothes." A true confidence game is unlike the case of the emperor's new clothes wherein that monarch's nakedness was a result of inordinate gullibility and credulity. In a genuine confidence game,

[13]Three relatively recent items reported in the New York Times tend to underscore this point as it has manifested itself in one of the major criminal courts. In one instance the Bronx County Bar Association condemned "mass assemblyline justice," which "was rushing defendants into pleas of guilty and into convictions, in violation of their legal rights." *New York Times,* March 10, 1965, p. 51. Another item, appearing somewhat later that year reports a judge criticizing his own court system (the New York Criminal Court), that "pressure to set statistical records in disposing of cases had hurt the administration of justice." *New York Times,* November 4, 1965, p. 49. A third, and most unusual recent public discussion in the press was a statement by a leading New York appellate judge decrying "instant justice" which is employed to reduce court calendar congestion. . . . "converting our courthouses into counting houses. . . . , as in most big cities where the volume of business tends to overpower court facilities." *New York Times,* February 5, 1966, p. 58.

the perpetrator manipulates the basic dishonesty of his partner, the victim or mark, toward his own (the confidence operator's) ends. The two phenomena must be distinguished—the case of the emperor's clothes and the true confidence game. In the case of the emperor, who was possessed of great personal vanity, cupidity and naiveté, a fraud was perpetrated by some crafty operators who duped him and his subjects. For truly, up to a point, everyone believed that the reality of the emperor's nakedness was but the most clever, artful, and miraculously wrought gossamer. However, in the confidence game, the victim is not an innocent dupe, for he seeks some undue advantage or some shady, illegitimate goal of his own. Thus, "the victim of a con scheme must have some larceny in his heart."[14]

In many of the so-called "server-served" relationships for a fee, which include not only the practice of law, medicine, or dentistry, but also plumbing, there is not always a visible end product or tangible service involved. Usually, a plumber will be able to demonstrate empirically that he has performed a service by clearing up the stuffed drain, repairing the leaky faucet or pipe—and therefore merits his fee. He has rendered, when summoned, a visible, tangible boon for his client in return for the requested fee. A physician, who has not performed some visible surgery or otherwise engaged in some readily discernible procedure in connection with a patient, may be deemed by the patient to have "done nothing" for him. As a consequence, medical practitioners may simply prescribe or administer by injection a placebo to overcome a patient's potential reluctance or dissatisfaction in paying a requested fee, "for nothing."

In the practice of law there is a special problem in this regard, no matter what the level of the practitioner or his place in the hierarchy of prestige. Much legal work is intangible in its dimensions either because it is simply a few words of advice, some preventive action, a telephone call, negotiation of some kind, a form filled out and filed, a hurried conference with another attorney or an official of a government agency, a letter or opinion written, or a countless variety of seemingly innocuous, and even prosaic procedures and actions. These are the basic activities, apart from any possible court appearance, of almost all lawyers, at all levels of practice. Much of the activity is not in the nature of the exercise of the traditional, precise professional skills of the attorney such as library research and oral argument in connection with appellate briefs, court motions, trial work, drafting of opinions, memoranda, contracts, and other complex documents and agreements. Instead, much legal activity, whether it is at the lowest or highest "white shoe" law firm levels, is of the brokerage, agent, sales representative, lobbyist type of activity, in which the lawyer

[14]Robert L. Gasser, "The Confidence Game," *Federal Probation,* Vol. 27, No. 4 (December, 1963) p. 47.

acts for someone else in pursuing the latter's interests and designs, furnishing an intangible service.[15]

The large-scale law firm may not speak as openly of their "contacts," their "fixing" abilities, as does the lower level lawyer. They trade instead upon a facade of thick carpeting, walnut paneling, genteel low pressure, and superficialities of traditional legal professionalism. There are occasions when even the large firm is on the defensive in connection with the fees they charge because the services rendered or results obtained do not appear to merit the fee asked.[16] Therefore, there is a recurrent problem in the legal profession in fixing the amount of fee, and in justifying the basis for the requested fee.

Although the fee at times amounts to what the traffic and the conscience of the lawyer will bear, one further observation must be made with regard to the size of the fee and its collection. The defendant in a criminal case and the material gain he may have acquired during the course of his illicit activities are soon parted. Not infrequently the ill gotten fruits of the various modes of larceny are sequestered by a defense lawyer in payment of his fee. Inexorably, the amount of the fee is a function of the dollar value of the crime committed, and is frequently set with meticulous precision at a sum which bears an uncanny relationship to that of the net proceeds of the particular offense involved. On occasion, defendants have been known to commit additional offenses while at liberty on bail, in order to secure the requisite funds with which to meet their obligations for payment of legal fees. Defense lawyers condition even the most obtuse clients to recognize that there is a firm interconnection between fee payment and the zealous exercise of professional expertise, secret knowledge, and organizational "connections" in their behalf. Lawyers, therefore, seek to keep their clients in a proper state of tension, and to arouse in them the precise edge of anxiety which is calculated to encourage prompt fee payment. Consequently, the client attitude in the relationship between defense counsel and an accused is in many instances a precarious admixture of hostility, mistrust, dependence and sychophancy. By keeping his client's anxieties aroused to the proper pitch, and establishing a seemingly causal relationship between a requested fee and the accused's ultimate extrication from his onerous difficulties, the lawyer will have established the necessary preliminary groundwork to assure a minimum of haggling over the fee and its eventual payment.

In varying degrees, as a consequence, all law practice involves a manipulation of the client and a stage management of the lawyer-

[15]C. Wright Mills, *White Collar*, (New York: Oxford University Press, 1951) pp. 121-129; Jerome E. Carlin, op. cit. passim.

[16]Erwin O. Smigel, *The Wall Street Lawyer*, (New York: The Free Press of Glencoe, 1964) p. 309.

539

client relationship so that at least an *appearance* of help and service will be forthcoming. This is accomplished in a variety of ways, often exercised in combination with each other. At the outset, the lawyer-professional employs with suitable variation a measure of sales-puff which may range from an air of unbounding self-confidence, adequacy, and dominion over events, to that of complete arrogance. This will be supplemented by the affectation of a studied, faultless mode of personal attire. In the larger firms, the furnishings and office trappings will serve as the back-drop to help in impression management and client intimidation. In all firms, solo or large scale, an access to secret knowledge, and to the seats of power and influence is inferred, or presumed to a varying degree as the basic vendible commodity of the practitioners.

The lack of visible end product offers a special complication in the course of the professional life of the criminal court lawyer with respect to his fee and in his relations with his client. The plain fact is that an accused in a criminal case always "loses" even when he has been exonerated by an acquittal, discharge, or dismissal of his case. The hostility of an accused which follows as a consequence of his arrest, incarceration, possible loss of job, expense and other traumas connected with his case is directed, by means of displacement, toward his lawyer. It is in this sense that it may be said that a criminal lawyer never really "wins" a case. The really satisfied client is rare, since in the very nature of the situation even an accused's vindication leaves him with some degree of dissatisfaction and hostility. It is this state of affairs that makes for a lawyer-client relationship in the criminal court which tends to be a somewhat exaggerated version of the usual lawyer-client confidence game.

At the outset, because there are great risks of non-payment of the fee, due to the impecuniousness of his clients, and the fact that a man who is sentenced to jail may be a singularly unappreciative client, the criminal lawyer collects his fee *in advance*. Often, because the lawyer and the accused both have questionable designs of their own upon each other, the confidence game can be played. The criminal lawyer must serve three major functions, or stated another way, he must solve three problems. First, he must arrange for his fee; second, he must prepare and then, if necessary, "cool out" his client in case of defeat,[17] (a highly likely contingency); third, he

[17]Talcott Parsons indicates that the social role and function of the lawyer can be therapeutic, helping his client psychologically in giving him necessary emotional support at critical times. The lawyer is also said to be acting as an agent of social control in the counselling of his client and in the influencing of his course of conduct. See Talcott Parsons, *Essays in Sociological Theory,* (New York: The Free Press of Glencoe, 1954) pp. 382 et seq.; Erving Goffman, "On Cooling the Mark Out: Some Aspects

must satisfy the court organization that he has performed adequately in the process of negotiating the plea, so as to preclude the possibility of the occurrence of any sort of embarrassing incident which may serve to invite "outside" scrutiny.

In assuring the attainment of one of his primary objectives, his fee, the criminal lawyer will very often enter into negotiations with various members of the accused's kin group, including collateral relatives. In many instances, the accused himself is unable to pay any sort of fee or anything more than a token fee. It then becomes important to involve as many of the accused's kin group as possible in the situation. This is especially so if the attorney hopes to collect a significant part of a proposed substantial fee. It is not uncommon for several relatives to contribute toward the fee. The larger the group, the greater the possibility that the lawyer will collect a sizeable fee by exacting contributions from a diverse number of individuals.

A fee for a felony case which ultimately results in a plea, rather than a trial, may ordinarily range anywhere from $500 to $1,500. Should the case go to trial, the fee will be proportionately larger, depending upon the length of the trial. But the larger the fee the lawyer wishes to exact, the more impressive his performance must be, in terms of his stage managed image as being a personage of great influence and power in the court organization. Court personnel are keenly aware of the extent to which a lawyer's stock in trade involves the precarious stage management of an image which goes beyond the usual professional flamboyance, and for this reason alone the lawyer is "bound in" to the authority system of the court's organizational discipline. Therefore, to some extent, court personnel will aid the lawyer in the creation and maintenance of that impression. There is a tacit commitment to the lawyer by the court organization, apart from formal etiquette, to aid him in this. Such augmentation of the lawyer's stage managed image as this affords, is the partial basis for the *quid pro quo* which exists between the lawyer and the court organization. It tends to serve as the continuing basis for the higher loyalty of the lawyer to the organization; his relationship with his client, in contrast, is transient, ephemeral and often superficial.

The lawyer has often been accused of stirring up unnecessary litigation, especially in the field of negligence. He is said to acquire a vested interest in a cause of action or claim which was initially his client's. The strong incentive of possible fee motivates the lawyer to promote litigation which would otherwise never have developed. The

---

of Adaptation to Failure," in *Human Behavior and Social Processes,* edited by Arnold M. Rose, (Boston: Houghton Mifflin Co., 1962) pp. 482-505. Goffman's "cooling out" analysis is especially relevant in the lawyer-accused client relationship.

541

criminal lawyer develops a vested interest of an entirely different nature in his client's case: not to promote the litigation, but to limit its scope and duration. Only in this way can a case be "profitable." Thus, he enlists the aid of relatives not only to assure payment of his fee, but he will also rely on these persons to help him in his agent-mediator role of convincing the accused to plead guilty, and ultimately to help him in "cooling out" the accused if necessary.

It is at this point that an accused-defendant may experience his first sense of "betrayal." While he had perhaps perceived the police and prosecutor to be adversaries, or possibly even a judge could be cast in a somewhat similar role, the accused is wholly unprepared for his counsel's role performance as an agent-mediator. In the same vein, it is even less likely to occur to an accused that members of his own family or kin group may become agents, albeit at the behest and urging of other agents or mediators, acting on the principle that they are in reality helping an accused negotiate the best possible plea arrangement under the circumstances. Usually, it will be the lawyer who will activate next of kin in this role, his ostensible motive being to arrange for his fee. But soon latent and unstated motives will assert themselves, with entreaties by counsel to the accused's next of kin, to appeal to the accused to "help himself" by pleading. *Gemeinschaft* sentiments are to this extent exploited by a defense lawyer (or even at times by a district attorney) to achieve specific secular ends, that is, of concluding a particular matter with all possible dispatch.

The fee is often collected in stages, each installment usually payable prior to a necessary court appearance required during the course of an accused's career journey. At each stage, in his interviews and communications with the accused, or in addition, with members of his kin group, if they are helping with the fee payment, the lawyer employs an air of professional confidence and "inside-dopesterism" in order to assuage anxieties on all sides. He makes the necessary bland assurances, and in effect manipulates his client, who is usually willing to do and say the things, true or not, which will help his attorney extricate him. Since the dimensions of what he is essentially selling, organizational influence and expertise, is not technically and precisely measurable, the lawyer can make extravagant claims of influence and secret knowledge with impunity. Thus, lawyers frequently claim to have inside knowledge in connection with information in the hands of the DA, police, probation officials or to have access to these functionaries. Factually, they often do, and need only to exaggerate the nature of their relationships with them to obtain the desired effective impression upon the client. But as in the genuine confidence game, the victim who has participated is loath to do

542

anything which will upset the lesser plea which his lawyer has "conned" him into accepting.[18]

In effect, in his role as double agent, the criminal lawyer performs an extremely vital and delicate mission for the court organization and the accused. Both principals are anxious to terminate the litigation with a minimum of expense and damage to each other. There is no other personage or role incumbent in the total court structure more strategically located, who by training and in terms of his own requirements, is more ideally suited to do so than the lawyer. In recognition of this, judges will cooperate with attorneys in many important ways. For example, they will adjourn the case of an accused in jail awaiting plea or sentence if the attorney requests such action. While explicitly this may be done for some innocuous and seemingly valid reason, the tacit purpose is that pressure is being applied by the attorney for the collection of his fee, which he knows will probably not be forthcoming if the case is concluded. Judges are aware of this tactic on the part of lawyers, who, by requesting an adjournment, keep an accused incarcerated awhile longer as a not too subtle method of dunning a client for payment. However, the judges will go along with this, on the ground that important ends are being served. Often, the only end being served is to protect a lawyer's fee.

In still another way will the judge help an accused's lawyer. He will lend the official aura of his office and courtroom so that a lawyer can stage manage an impression of an "all out" performance for the accused in justification of his fee. The judge and other court personnel will serve as a backdrop for a scene charged with dramatic fire, in which the accused's lawyer makes a stirring appeal in his behalf. With a show of restrained passion, the lawyer will intone the virtues of the accused and recite the social deprivations which have reduced him to his present state. There is a speech which varies somewhat, depending on whether the accused has been convicted after trial or

[18]The question has never been raised as to whether "bargain justice," "copping a plea," or justice by negotiation is a constitutional process. Although it has become the most central aspect of the process of criminal law administration, it has received virtually no close scrutiny by the appellate courts. As a consequence, it is relatively free of legal control and supervision. But, apart from any questions of the legality of bargaining, in terms of the pressures and devices that are employed which tend to violate due process of law, there remain ethical and practical questions. The system of bargain-counter justice is like the proverbial iceberg, much of its danger is concealed in secret negotiations and its least alarming feature, the final plea, being the one presented to public view. See Arnold S. Trebach, *The Rationing of Justice,* (New Brunswick: Rutgers University Press, 1964) pp. 74-94, Dominick R. Vetri, Note, "Guilty Plea Bargaining; Compromises by Prosecutors to Secure Guilty Pleas," *University of Pennsylvania Law Review*, Vol. 112 (April, 1964), pp. 865-895.

has pleaded guilty. In the main, however, the incongruity, superficiality and ritualistic character of the total performance is understood by a visibly impassive, almost bored reaction on the part of the judge and other members of the court retinue. Afterward, there is a hearty exchange of pleasantries between the lawyer and district attorney, wholly out of context in terms of the supposed adversary nature of the preceding events.

The fiery passion in defense of his client is gone, and the lawyers for both sides resume their offstage relations, chatting amiably and perhaps including the judge in their restrained banter. No other aspect of their visible conduct so effectively serves to put even a casual observer on notice, that these individuals have claims upon each other. These seemingly innocuous actions are indicative of continuing organizational and informal relations, which, in their intricacy and depth, range far beyond any priorities or claims a particular defendant may have.[19]

Criminal law practice is a unique form of private law practice since it really only appears to be private practice.[20] Actually it is bureaucratic practice, because of the legal practitioner's enmeshment in the authority, discipline and perspectives of the court organization. Private practice, supposedly, in a professional sense, involves the maintenance of an organized, disciplined body of knowledge and learning; the individual practitioners are imbued with a spirit of

[19]For a conventional summary statement of some of the inevitable conflicting loyalties encountered in the practice of law see, Elliot E. Cheatham, *Cases and Materials on the Legal Profession,* 2nd ed. (Brooklyn: Foundation Press, Inc., 1955) pp. 70-79.

[20]Some lawyers at either end of the continuum of law practice appear to have grave doubts as to whether it is indeed a profession at all. Jerome E. Carlin, *op. cit.,* p. 192: Erwin O. Smigel, *op. cit.,* pp. 304-305. Increasingly, it is perceived as a business with widespread evasion of the Canons of Ethics, duplicity and chicanery being practiced in an effort to get and keep business. The poet Carl Sandberg epitomized this notion in the following vignette: "Have you a criminal lawyer in this burg?" "We think so but we haven't been able to prove it on him." *The People, Yes,* (New York: Harcourt, Brace and Co., 1936) p. 154.

Thus, while there is a considerable amount of dishonesty present in law practice involving fee splitting, thefts from clients, influence peddling, fixing, questionable use of favors and gifts to obtain business or influence others: this sort of activity is most often attributed to the "solo," private practice lawyer. See Arthur Lewis Wood, "Professional Ethics Among Criminal Lawyers," *Social Problems,* Vol. 7, No. 1 (Summer, 1959) pp. 70-83. However, to some degree, large scale "downtown" elite firms also engage in these dubious activities. The difference is that the latter firms enjoy a good deal of immunity from these harsh charges because of their institutional and organizational advantages, in terms of near monopoly over more desirable types of practice, as well as exerting great influence in the political, economic and professional realms of power.

544

autonomy and service, the earning of a livelihood being incidental. In the sense that the lawyer in the criminal court serves as a double agent, serving higher organizational rather than professional ends, he may be deemed to be engaged in bureaucratic rather than private practice. To some extent the lawyer-client "confidence game," in addition to its other functions, serves to conceal this fact.

The "cop-out" ceremony, in which the court process culminates, is not only invaluable for redefining the accused's perspectives of himself, but also in reiterating publicly in a formally structured ritual the accused person's guilt for the benefit of significant "others" who are observing. The accused not only is made to assert publicly his guilt of a specific crime, but also a complete recital of its details. He is further made to indicate that he is entering his plea of guilty freely, willingly and voluntarily, and that he is not doing so because of any promises or in consideration of any commitments that may have been made to him by anyone. This last is intended as a blanket statement to shield the participants from any possible charges of "coercion" or undue influence that may have been exerted in violation of due process requirements. Its function is to preclude any later review by an appellate court on these grounds, and also to obviate any second thoughts an accused may develop in connection with his plea.

However, for the accused, the conception of self as a guilty person is in large measure a temporary role adaptation. His career socialization as an accused, if it is successful, eventuates in his acceptance and redefinition of himself as a guilty person.[21] However, the transformation is ephemeral, in that he will, in private, quickly reassert his innocence. Of importance is that he accept his defeat, publicly proclaim it, and find some measure of pacification in it.[22] Almost

---

[21]This does not mean that most of those who plead guilty are innocent of any crime. Indeed, in many instances those who have been able to negotiate a lesser plea, have done so willingly and even eagerly. The system of justice-by-negotiation, without trial, probably tends to better serve the interests and requirements of guilty persons, who are thereby presented with formal alternatives of "half a loaf," in terms of at worst possibilities of a lesser plea and a concomitant shorter sentence as compensation for their acquiescence and participation. Having observed the prescriptive etiquette in compliance with the defendant role expectancies in this setting, he is rewarded. An innocent person, on the other hand, is confronted with the same set of role prescriptions, structures and legal alternatives, and in any event, for him this mode of justice is often an ineluctable bind.

[22]"Any communicative network between persons whereby the public identity of an actor is transformed into something looked on as lower in the local scheme of social types will be called a 'status degradation ceremony'." Harold Garfinkel, "Conditions of Successful Degradation Ceremonies," *American Journal of Sociology*, Vol. 61, No. 5 (March, 1956) pp. 420-424. But contrary to the conception of the "cop out" as a "status degradation ceremony," is the fact that it is in reality a charade, during the course of which an accused must project an appropriate and acceptable

545

immediately after his plea, a defendant will generally be interviewed by a representative of the Probation division in connection with a presentence report which is to be prepared. The very first question to be asked of him by the probation officer is: "Are you guilty of the crime to which you pleaded?" This is by way of double affirmation of the defendant's guilt. Should the defendant now begin to make bold assertions of his innocence, despite his plea of guilty, he will be asked to withdraw his plea and stand trial on the original charges. Such a threatened possibility is in most instances sufficient to cause an accused to let the plea stand and to request the probation officer to overlook his exclamations of innocence. The table that follows is a breakdown of the categorized responses of a random sample of male defendants in Metropolitan Court[23] during 1962, 1963 and 1964 in connection with their statements during presentence probation interviews following their plea of guilty:

TABLE NO. 1

*Defendant Responses as to Guilt or Innocence
after Pleading*

N=724   YEARS—1962, 1963, 1964

NATURE OF RESPONSE		NUMBER OF DEFENDANTS
INNOCENT (Manipulated)	"The lawyer or judge, police or DA 'conned me' "	86
INNOCENT (Pragmatic)	"Wanted to get it over with" "You can't beat the system" "They have you over a barrel when you have a record"	147
INNOCENT (Advice of counsel)	"Followed my lawyer's advice"	92

amount of guilt, penitence and remorse. Having adequately feigned the role of the "guilty person," his hearers will engage in the fantasy that he is contrite, and thereby merits a lesser plea. It is one of the essential functions of the criminal lawyer that he coach and direct his accused-client in that role performance. Thus, what is actually involved is not a "degradation" process at all, but is instead, a highly structured system of exchange cloaked in the rituals of legalism and public professions of guilt and repentance.

[23]The name is of course fictitious. However, the actual court which served as the universe from which the data were drawn, is one of the largest criminal courts in the United States, dealing with felonies only. Female defendants in the years 1950 through 1964 constituted from 7-10% of the totals for each year.

INNOCENT (Defiant)	"Framed"— Betrayed by "Complainant," "Police," "Squealers," "Lawyer," "Friends," "Wife," "Girlfriend"	33
INNOCENT (Adverse social data)	Blames probation officer or psychiatrist for "Bad Report," in cases where there was prepleading investigation	15
GUILTY	"But I should have gotten a better deal" Blames lawyer, DA, Police, Judge	74
GUILTY	Won't say anything further	21
FATALISTIC (Doesn't press his "Innocence," won't admit "Guilt")	"I did it for convenience" "My lawyer told me it was only thing I could do" "I did it because it was the best way out"	248
NO RESPONSE		8
TOTAL		724

It would be well to observe at the outset, that of the 724 defendants who pleaded guilty before trial, only 43 (5.94%) of the total group had confessed prior to their indictment. Thus, the ultimate judicial process was predicated upon evidence independent of any confession of the accused.[24]

As the data indicate, only a relatively small number (95) out of the total number of defendants actually will even admit their guilt, following the "cop-out" ceremony. However, even though they have affirmed their guilt, many of these defendants felt that they should have been able to negotiate a more favorable plea. The largest aggregate of defendants (373) were those who reasserted their "innocence"

[24]My own data in this connection would appear to support Sobel's conclusion (see footnote #3), and appear to be at variance with the prevalent view, which stresses the importance of confessions in law enforcement and prosecution. All the persons in my sample were originally charged with felonies ranging from Homicide to Forgery, in most instances the original felony charges were reduced to misdemeanors by way of a negotiated lesser plea. The vast range of crime categories which are available, facilitates the patterned court process of plea reduction to a lesser offense, which is also usually a socially less opprobious crime. For an illustration of this feature of the bargaining process in a court utilizing a public defender office see, David Sudnow, "Normal Crimes: Sociological Features of the Penal Code in a Public Defender Office," *Social Problems,* Vol. 12 (Winter, 1964) pp. 255-276.

following their public profession of guilt during the "cop-out" ceremony. These defendants employed differential degrees of fervor, solemnity and credibility, ranging from really mild, wavering assertions of innocence which were embroidered with a variety of stock explanations and rationalizations, to those of an adamant, "framed" nature. Thus, the "Innocent" group for the most part, it must be stressed, were largely concerned with underscoring for their probation interviewer their essential "goodness" and "worthiness," despite their formal plea of guilty. Assertion of his innocence at the post plea stage, resurrects a more respectable and acceptable self concept for the accused defendant who has pleaded guilty. A recital of the structural exigencies which precipitated his plea of guilt, serves to embellish a newly proffered claim of innocence, which many defendants mistakenly feel will stand them in good stead at the time of sentence, or ultimately with probation or parole authorities.

Relatively few (33) maintained their innocence in terms of having been "framed" by some person or agent-mediator, although a larger number (86) indicated that they had been manipulated or "conned" by an agent-mediator to plead guilty, but as indicated, their assertions of innocence were relatively mild.

A rather substantial group (147) preferred to stress the pragmatic aspects of their plea of guilty. They would only perfunctorily assert their innocence and would in general refer to some adverse aspect of their situation which they believed tended to negatively affect their bargaining leverage, including in some instances a prior criminal record.

One group of defendants (92), while maintaining their innocence, simply employed some variation of a theme of following "the advice of counsel" as a covering response, to explain their guilty plea in the light of their new affirmation of innocence.

It was a shorthand method of invoking a catch phrase to preclude any further discussion of an otherwise seemingly inconsistent position.

The largest single group of defendants (248) were basically fatalistic. They would only verbalize weak suggestions of their innocence in rather halting terms, wholly without conviction. By the same token, they would not admit guilt readily and were generally evasive as to guilt or innocence, preferring to stress aspects of their stoic submission in their decision to plead. This sizable group of defendants appeared to perceive the total court process as being caught up in a monstrous organizational apparatus, in which the defendant role expectancies were not clearly defined. Reluctant to offend anyone in authority, fearful that clear cut statements on their part as to their guilt or innocence will be negatively construed, they adopt a stance of passivity, resignation and acceptance. Interestingly, they would in most instances invoke their lawyer as being the one who crystallized the 548 available alternatives for them, and who was therefore the critical element in their decision making process. . . .

Based on data which are admittedly tentative and fragmentary, the furor over confessions, whether of the coerced or voluntary variety, would appear to be not too meaningful. It is suggested that the process of criminal law enforcement has always depended, and will continue to do so in the foreseeable future, on judicial confessions in open court (i.e., pleas of guilty), rather than on confessions wrung from an accused in the back room of a police station. The decision of *Gideon* v. *Wainwright,* requiring states and localities to furnish counsel in the case of indigent persons charged with a felony, has been regarded in legal circles as a most important development in American jurisprudence. No doubt, in time, the various states will make administrative provisions to implement this decision. Although there has been great enthusiasm expressed in connection with the decision, my limited data would appear to suggest that results at the felony level in the future will not be significantly different from those which presently obtain in the respective communities affected by the *Gideon* decision.

The organizational and structural variables of the criminal court will continue to be present, and perhaps be even further augmented, in addition to any race, class, ethnic or other socio-demographic variables which are to be found in the respective jurisdictions. Together, these are formidable. The organizational features which in the pursuit of rationality tend to promote the present system of justice, will not be easily overcome by additional counsel and similar resources,[28] for they may in turn be co-opted and become part of the organizational structure, if they are not already.

[28]Some of the resources which have become an integral part of our courts, e.g., psychiatry, social work and probation, were originally intended as part of an ameliorative, therapeutic effort to individualize offenders. However, there is some evidence that a quite different result obtains, than the one originally intended. The ameliorative instruments have been co-opted by the court in order to more "efficiently" deal with a court's caseload, often to the legal disadvantage of an accused person. See Francis A. Allen, *The Borderland of Criminal Justice,* (Chicago: University of Chicago Press), passim; Thomas S. Szasz, *Law, Liberty and Psychiatry,* (New York: Macmillan Co., 1963) and also Szasz's most recent, *Psychiatric Justice,* (New York: Macmillan Co., 1965): Lewis Diana, "The Rights of Juvenile Delinquents: An Appraisal of Juvenile Court Procedures," *Journal of Criminal Law, Criminology and Police Science,* Vol. 47, No. 5 (January-February, 1957) pp. 561-569.

Philip G. Zimbardo

Coercion and Compliance:
The Psychology of Police Confessions

The fascination that the police have for the thief is manifested by the thief's temptation to confess when he is arrested. In the presence of the examining magistrate who questions him, he is seized with giddiness: the magistrate speaks gently to him, perhaps with kindness, explaining what is expected of him; practically nothing: an assent. If only once, just once, he did what was asked of him, if he uttered the "yes" that is requested, harmony of minds would be achieved. He would be told, "That's fine," perhaps he would be congratulated. It would be the end of hatred. The desire to confess is the mad dream of universal love; it is, as Genet himself says, the temptation of the human.

From *St. Genet*, by Sartre
New York: George Braziller, 1963

PART 1. INTRODUCTION TO THE PROBLEM

The basic issue with which I will concern myself in this paper raises the question of whether the protection of our "great society" by means of quick and efficient law enforcement is more important than the loss of individual freedoms and rights which may result from such "protection." More specifically, how far is it permissible for the police to go in interrogating a suspect or a witness in order to guarantee public safety and the swift execution of justice?

Usually we don't consider that "most defendants have, in effect, two trials. They are first tried by the police. If found guilty by the

A slightly abridged version of the paper presented at The American Psychological Association Meetings, New York, September 3, 1966, published here with the author's permission. Philip Zimbardo is associate professor of psychology at New York University.

police, they are held for trial by the courts. If found innocent by the police, they are acquitted then and there. This procedure has no basis in law . . . but we know from practical experience that far more cases are disposed of in this manner than ever reach our courts" (Kidd, #3, pp. 15–16). Consequently, the question of police procedures becomes one of the most complex legal issues ever to face the courts.

Critics of the police claim that due process of law and constitutional rights are being abrogated by police techniques and are calling for reforms. On the other hand, law enforcement agencies point to the rising tide of crime and violence in our society and the need to control it before it engulfs us. They want to pursue what they see as "their job" unhampered by restrictions imposed by the Supreme Court.

In the last national election the Republican vice-presidential candidate ascribed the increase in crime and Northern race riots to the moral atmosphere engendered by "so-called liberals of this Administration, and some of the bleeding hearts who often center more sentiment and concern on the criminal than the victim" (*New York Times*, #30, October 10, 1964).

What makes the problem an especially difficult one legally is that the basic questions to be resolved are not inherently legal but psychological in nature, and psychologists have ignored the problem and been ignored by those who would solve it. How can the court formulate criteria to assess "psychological coercion," "voluntariness of a confession," "ability to resist pressure" and similar concepts without reference to psychology? Central in the definition and analysis of these concepts is a knowledge of personality, behavior deviations, performance under stress and deprivation, the effects of social demand characteristics, research on persuasability and attitude change, and many other areas of psychology in which many of the readers of this paper are expert.

One of the few limitations imposed upon the interrogators is self-imposed; interrogation techniques are legally acceptable, they assert, so long as the interrogator believes they would not make an innocent man confess (Inbau & Reid, #6). However, the *only* evidence that this indeed is a limitation, that an innocent man would *not* confess, is the "feeling" of the authors of the police interrogation manual, unreliable by any standard of judgment.

We know from our close study of American prisoners of the Korean War in Communist interrogation camps (cf., Hinkle & Wolff, #13; Schein, #22; Schein, *et al.*, #23) that many good soldiers gave false confessions, incriminated themselves, and betrayed their fellow soldiers. "Prior to the confessions in the Korean War we usually refused to recognize how easy it was to break the will of individual human beings" (Rogge, #20, p. 201). "It has appeared that they [the communists] can force men to confess to crimes which have not been committed, and then, apparently, to believe in the truth of their 551 confessions and express sympathy and gratitude toward those who have imprisoned them" (Hinkle & Wolff, p. 116).

What I will contend in this essay is that the techniques employed by our American police are more highly developed, more psychologically sophisticated and more effective than the Chinese Communist "brainwashing" techniques which we have denounced.

It is the primary intention of this paper to convince the psychologists among my readers of the theoretical and practical importance of the phenomena of police-elicited confessions. As psychologists concerned with discovering truths about human behavior and establishing valid generalizations based upon sound evidence, I hope they will become sufficiently concerned to contribute their talents to illuminating with relevant research an area of confusion and error. But more important, I expect that any citizen of this country will react with surprise and disgust at the canker we have allowed to grow within our system of justice by our indifference.

The recent Supreme Court decisions which make it mandatory to warn a suspect of his right to remain silent and of his right to counsel might seem to many of you to vitiate not only my remarks but any serious questioning of the legal issues involved. I will present evidence to show that this ruling has had only the slightest effect on the exceedingly high confession rate police obtain. Secondly, Senator Sam J. Ervine of North Carolina has proposed to overturn the Supreme Court ruling by means of a constitutional amendment. He is against "unfair, illegal or reprehensible pressure" but not for the "removal of all pressure." I will leave it to your judgment to determine whether the techniques the police secretly use qualify for what the senator is against. Finally, and most important for us as Americans, is the fundamental issue of democratic guarantees for the individual regardless of the public's demands to get a loose killer, the insistence by the House Un-American Activities Committee on finding Communists in all protest movements, or the President's demand that we unquestioningly support his foreign policies during this time of national emergency (Vietnam).

My paper will first consider a case familiar to many of you in which a "voluntary" confession of murder was subsequently proven false. Then I will examine at length a selection of specific techniques, tactics and approaches which the police employ in order to secure confessions. Each of these should be viewed in light of the degree to which it violates what you consider to be a fundamental human right. Following this there will be a brief assessment of the allegation that police enforcement demands "efficiency," which in turn justifies the use of such interrogation tactics. Finally, I would like to suggest some lines of research which psychologists ought to be doing in their labs, in the field, or better yet, with the help of their local police academies.

552

PART 2. A CASE OF A FALSE CONFESSION—
THE WHITMORE CASE

Can a man be induced to give a confession which virtually sentences him to the electric chair when in fact he is "innocent?" If this extreme statement of the proposition can be shown to be true, then it is likely that under appropriate circumstances men will admit to lesser crimes bearing less severe penalties when they are not guilty. The interrogative tactics and techniques (to be described in the next section of this paper) do, according to the authors of police manuals, "certainly measure up to the fundamental test that not one of them is apt to induce an innocent man to confess" (Inbau & Reid, #6, Preface). Since the authors present no evidence except their own personal opinion to support this sweeping generalization, I will leave it to you to judge the validity of the assertion by exposing for you a sampling of the recommended interrogation tactics. However, before doing so, let us consider our initial question of whether a man would falsely confess to murder by examining a recent concrete instance of such confession.

Two years ago a policeman, Patrolman Frank Isola, came to the aid of a woman who was being molested in the Brownsville section of Brooklyn, New York City, but was unable to apprehend the attacker. The woman, Mrs. Elba Borrero, reportedly described her assailant as a Negro, 5 feet 9 inches, 165 pounds, pock-marked face, wearing a raincoat from which she had torn a button.

The next day the patrolman and a detective, Richard Aidala, picked up George Whitmore, Jr. in the vicinity of the crime, since he vaguely fit the description (although 4 inches shorter and 25 pounds lighter, he was a Negro with a button missing from his raincoat). He was asked to go to the police station for questioning, which he agreed to do. The probable cause for taking him into custody was stated in the vaguest possible terms in the affidavit as "a reasonable ground for suspicion supported by circumstances sufficiently strong in themselves."

After viewing him through a peephole, the woman identified him as her attacker, and then the interrogation began in earnest. Within a few hours he had confessed to the attempted rape.

Armed with this confession, Whitmore's coat with the missing button, Brooklyn District Attorney S. A. Lichtman was able to say in his summation to the jury, "We have nailed George Whitmore on the button, so to speak." However, the prosecution had conveniently suppressed a report from the F.B.I. laboratory, stating that the remaining buttons on Whitmore's coat were "different in size, design and construction" from the one torn off the coat of the molester.

But this is the least interesting aspect of this case. Let us return to the East Brooklyn precinct house where Whitmore was being questioned. He was picked up at 8 A.M., had confessed by 10:30, then   553 around noon made a second confession of a knife slaying of a Mrs. Edwards. At this time a detective from the Brooklyn North Homicide Squad, E. J. F. Bulger, had witnessed the confession and in looking over the suspect's belongings, noticed a picture of a white girl. He, along with many other detectives had been working without success for the previous eight months on the sensational dual killing of Janice Wylie and Emily Hoffert (slain August 28, 1963, on East 88th Street in New York City). The detective identified the girl in the photo as Miss Wylie, and then the interrogation began with renewed intensity.

By 4 A.M. the next morning, after 26 hours of questioning, Whitmore "broke" and confessed for a third time, to the slaying of the two girls. The press, and undoubtedly the public, were delighted by the announcement of Chief of Detectives (now Chief Inspector) L. J. McKearney, "We've got the right guy, no question about it."

Just to be sure there was no question about it, Manhattan Assistant District Attorney Peter Koste, who took the confession, noted that Whitmore was "composed" and "alert" at the end of the interrogation. In addition, the principal interrogator, Detective Bulger, swore to District Attorney Hogan's aides that he obtained the confession without "feeding" any information to Whitmore.

These statements are remarkable when one considers the nature of the confession, what we have learned of the interrogation procedures used, and subsequent events which proved Whitmore was innocent.

The confession "was quite persuasive and convincing" and went into such great detail that it required *61 typed pages!* It included drawings of the apartment and innumerable minor details that only someone at the scene of the crime could know.

Although Whitmore claimed that the police beat him, they denied the charge, and who would take the word of a rapist-killer to that of our police? In an excellent article (cf., #36), *New York Times* reporter Sidney E. Zion (formerly an Assistant United States Attorney for the State of New Jersey) noted that the police used to advantage a technique to be described in the next section of this paper as "the Mutt and Jeff" approach. Arresting Detective Aidala was the "heavy" —mean stern demanding while Detective Joseph Di Prima (present at all three confessions) was the sweet guy with whom Whitmore was able to develop "rapport." Whitmore is reported to have said that Di Prima was nicer to him than his own father had been!

Two weeks later the police concluded that the photo which had started all the gears going was *not* of Miss Wylie. They then spent the rest of the summer trying to prove that nevertheless it did come from her apartment, where Whitmore must have found it and thus he still had to be guilty.

In October the police were informed by one Nathan Delaney that his friend, Richard Robles, admitted to the murder of the two girls. Now mildly suspicious of the validity of the confession, the police engaged in some brilliant investigatory work and pinpointed the locale of the photo as the picnic area in the Belleplain State Forest, northwest of Wildwood, New Jersey, and the girl in the photo as Arlene Franco. Whitmore lived in Wildwood and had claimed he found the photo, which the girl admitted she threw away.

Only after two witnesses reported that Whitmore was seen in Wildwood on the eve of the murder, and Robles had confessed to the Wylie-Hoffert murders was George Whitmore released in January, 1965—after eight months in jail.

How could it be that a man confesses—61 pages worth—to murders which he did not commit? Whitmore was quite lucky, for as one assistant district attorney said (cf., #31): "If this was what we so-called professionals call a run-of-the-mill murder, Whitmore might well have been slipped into the electric chair and been killed for something he didn't do. Let's face it. We've had executions in the past based on nothing more than a dead body and a confession."

An officer in the Police Department was concerned about the unfavorable publicity and the consequences this case might have on the public's image of the police (to be discussed later). He said, "It's an awful thing, but sooner or later things like this happen. I hate to say this but I'm sure that sometime in history we've sent innocent men to their death by an unjust verdict."

But *why* did Whitmore confess? "Call it what you want, brainwashing, hypnosis, fright. They made him give an untrue confession" is what one assistant district attorney close to the case reported (cf., #31). A second assistant district attorney confessed, "I am positive the police prepared the confession for Whitmore. . . . I am also sure that the police were the ones who gave Whitmore all the details of the killings that he recited to our office" (cf., #31).

Finally, it is also instructive to note the remarks at Robles' trial of Lieut. T. J. Cavanaugh, commander of the Manhattan detective squad investigating the Wylie-Hoffert murders. He stated that he always believed that the interrogation was "improper" because the confession was inconsistent with the known facts (cf., #34).

But perhaps it is not fair to argue a general point with the evidence from one isolated case which happens to provide an affirmative answer to the question I posed: Do innocent men falsely confess to murder?

Time does not permit me to present much more of the available evidence, but it may be adequate to note that last year in New York State alone there were over 500 appeals made by prisoners to reopen cases which were based on confessions (cf., #33). A specific instance of these appeals is the case of a Bronx, New York factory worker who confessed to the murder of a woman, and after spending a year in jail was found innocent by polygraph data which contradicted his confession. The accused, Santo Sanchez, a 40-year-old Puerto Rican   555 father of six children who speaks little English, went into the 41st Street Precinct in good physical condition, and after his indictment on December 21, 1964, was hospitalized for bruises, etc. on Riker's Island for more than six weeks. Incidentally, the major link to the crime was a photo of the accused which was found in the dead woman's apartment. But since they were relatives this does not seem like such a strange phenomenon (cf., #38).

There are many other cases of false arrest and conviction which have been uncovered, but how many have not and will never be? This is an idle conjecture for which we have no answer.

Suppose for a moment that you wanted more information about the nature of the interrogation to which Whitmore was subjected. You'd like to know what were the conditions which could exercise such extreme control over a human being's behavior that he would change his overt behavior, admit to murder, and "voluntarily" sign a written confession of it. There are only two direct sources of information available to you: the accused, Whitmore, and his accuser, the interrogating detective.

Whitmore says he was beaten, the interrogator says he was not. The police claim the confession was a voluntary, uncoerced document freely given by the suspect; he claims it was forced out of him. "Since no outsider is permitted in the interrogation room, it is not possible to know for a certainty what methods the police use in obtaining confessions" (cf., #37). What develops is a swearing contest in which almost everyone prefers to believe the law enforcer.

In this vein it was surprising to read that Chief Justice Joseph Weintraub of the New Jersey Supreme Court, called for a study of what goes on in "squad rooms" (cf., #40, December 11, 1965). "So far all we have are opinions and what we read in the press. . . . What we need are the facts. Do judges really know what goes on in squad rooms?"

PART 3. POLICE INTERROGATION TECHNIQUES

If judges do not know what happens during police interrogations, then how can we as merely interested citizens ever find out? One secondary source of evidence which was pointed out to me a number of years ago by Abraham Goldstein, Professor of Law at Yale, are the manuals* used by the police to train detectives and interrogators. These manuals, written largely by police officers, detectives, or former staff members of police scientific crime detection laboratories, all include at least a chapter or a whole section on techniques of interrogation. The most recent book, a 1962 revision of an earlier 1953

*All references are to police manuals listed in the references, especially items numbered 2 through 9.

book written by Fred Inbau and John Reid, is entirely "devoted to a discussion of the psychological tactics and techniques of effective interrogation." I verified that these manuals are used in training interrogators by calling several police academies and requesting source material that I could use in a college course on interviewing.

Although it is not the purpose of this paper to enumerate all of the many different approaches suggested and used by the police in questioning informants, witnesses and suspects, it will be necessary to present a sampling of them in order to permit you to evaluate whether or not they are "psychologically coercive," and thereby deprive an individual of his fundamental rights and maybe even of his human dignity.

While there are many ways of organizing this material, I have arbitrarily chosen to classify my sample into the following categories:

1. *Demand characteristics of the interrogation environment*—which includes all attempts to manipulate the *current stimulus* environment in order to create a given set or expectation in the person being questioned.

2. *Perceptual and judgmental distortion*—which includes all attempts to manipulate the suspect's perception of the *past crime* and events associated with it.

3. *Distortion of the social psychological situation*—which includes all attempts to: (a) manipulate the interpersonal relationship between interrogator and suspect to achieve a desired goal, and also (b) attempts to capitalize on social variables or social characteristics of the suspect.

4. *Utilization of personality and clinical psychology phenomena*— which includes all attempts to control the subject's personal motives and needs, to establish a therapeutic relationship, and to tailor tactics to personality traits.

5. *Semantic and verbal distortion*—which includes all attempts to create a given impression by use of specific verbal formulae or words charged with emotion and affect.

It will be obvious that these are not exclusive nor exhaustive categories, but will suffice for our present limited interest which is focused on questions of the "voluntariness" of confessions obtained using these approaches, the degree of coercion and psychological force implied, and also the extent to which they violate what we believe are our basic constitutional and human rights.

Do *you* think they could make a guilty man incriminate himself against his will? Do *you* think they could make a reluctant witness reveal the known identity of a criminal? Do *you* think they could make an innocent man confess falsely?

1. Demand characteristics of the situation

Our image of the "squad room" from old movies as a dingy office with a light shining in the eyes of the suspect while a team of police 557 shout questions and accusations has gone the way of Humphrey Bogart. Modern psychology has entered and alerted the police to the potential significance of every detail in the stimulus situation which they can manipulate and control.

(a) *The environment*. The interrogation should never take place in an environment familiar to the suspect or with anyone he knows present. "By going to the police station the suspect has made the first act of yielding" (Kidd, #3). The suspect is the "guest" of the police and never should the reverse be true; all psychological support from a familiar environment is thereby destroyed. The room must be quiet, free of all external and internal distractors. It must guarantee privacy for the interrogator and not permit of unplanned interruptions.

It is suggested that since most of the appeals (to be mentioned later) depend upon dissociating the interrogating officer from his law-enforcing police officer function, the room itself should not resemble a jail or police office. While it is preferable that it should not have windows, if they do exist, then bars on them should be of an ornamental nature. In fact, one author (Mulbar, #7) suggests Italian garden gate as a particularly suitable style. The bareness of the room (no pictures, only two chairs and maybe a desk) should all serve to focus attention on the purpose it is serving. No "tension-relieving" activities or objects (paper clips, etc.) should be allowed the suspect or available (Inbau & Reid, #6). There should not even be ash trays present, since they "represent a tacit invitation to smoke"—a distracting tension-reliever (Inbau & Reid, #6). No phone should be present because it permits interference with a line of questioning, and represents a symbolic "object of contact with the outside world" (Mulbar, #7). Another investigator (O'Hara, #8), on the other hand, feels that a fake telephone should be present so that the interrogator can surreptitiously ring it when he feels he needs a break and wants an excuse to leave the room. He also feels that "since the subject should be deprived of every psychological advantage," the atmosphere should suggest the invincibility of the law.

It is also good practice to sit the suspect in an armless, straight-back chair so that he cannot become too comfortable, and so all of his bodily movements are observable.

(b) *The interrogator*. Since relay questioning is less effective than intensive questioning by a single interrogator, the interrogator should be alone with the suspect and "the full weight of his personality must be brought to bear on the emotional situation" (O'Hara, #8). He should sit or stand as close to the suspect as possible, with no furniture intervening. "When a person is close to another one physically, he is closer psychologically" (Inbau & Reid, #6).

He should not be dressed in uniform and no guns or police symbols should be present. The interrogator should wear a conservative suit, avoid loud ties or conspicuous clothing. "A short-sleeved interrogator does not command the respect his position requires" (Inbau & Reid, #6). Moreover, he should not offend or distract the suspect by unpleasant breath odors, which should be checked first by a fellow officer, and remedied with mouth wash or "a chlorophyll mint" (Inbau & Reid, #6).

The interrogator must at all times be in full control of the interview and possess no distracting mannerisms or lose his composure. With a difficult subject he can immediately establish his authority by small gestures like prohibiting smoking or directing the suspect where to sit, etc. (O'Hara, #8). Whenever a witness or other prospective informant refuses to cooperate, the bond of loyalty between him and the offender should be weakened by accusing *him* of the offense, and proceeding to interrogate him as if he were the criminal until he agrees to cooperate. . . .

Thus psychology has generally replaced the physical abuses of the third degree, not only because the courts have made invalid physically coerced confessions, but largely because the third degree is not as effective. "When you break a man by torture, he will always hate you. If you break him by your intelligence, he will always fear and respect you" (Kidd, #3, p. 49). To this end an environment is created which minimizes sensory stimulation for the suspect, maximally exposes the suspect's vulnerability, and provides for complete control and domination by the interrogating officer. . . .

2. Perceptual and judgmental distortion techniques

Confessions are often obtained by either minimizing the seriousness of the offense and allowing the suspect a "face-saving" out, or by the opposite through misrepresenting and exaggerating the seriousness of the crime.

The first approach can be accomplished through "extenuation"— in which the investigator reports that he doesn't take too seriously a view of the subject's indiscretion, since he's seen thousands of others in the same situation. Or he may "shift the blame" to circumstances, the environment, a subject's weaknesses, any of which might lead anyone to do what the suspect did. A more morally acceptable motive may be suggested for the crime, such as self-defense, an accident, a mistake, heat of passion, etc. In order to "open up" a suspect, it is recommended that good "bait" is blaming anyone who might be associated with the crime other than the suspect, e.g., an accomplice, a fence, a company, loan sharks, or even the victim.

Some provocative examples of the way in which experts use this approach in order to misrepresent the nature of the crime to the suspect in order to get him to talk about it are provided by Inbau and Reid (cf., #6).

(a) A 50-year-old man accused of having taken "indecent liberties" with a 10-year-old girl was told: "This girl is well developed for her age. She probably learned a lot about sex from the boys in the neigh- 559 borhood and from the movies and TV; and knowing what she did about it, she may have deliberately tried to excite you to see what you would do" (p. 45).

(b) Or, they note that in forcible rape cases, "where circumstances permit, the suggestion might be offered that the rape victim acted like she might be a prostitute . . . that the police knew she had been engaged in acts of prostitution on other occasions" (p. 46).

(c) "During the interrogation of a married rape suspect, blame may be cast upon the subject's wife for not providing him with the necessary sexual gratification. 'When a fellow like you doesn't get it at home, he seeks it elsewhere' " (p. 51).

Once the suspect is in a state of emotional confusion, then "he is unable to think logically and clearly, since his sense of values has been disturbed and his imagination is distorting his perspective. It is possible for the investigator to obtain admissions or even a confession from the suspect by further misrepresenting the picture" (O'Hara, #8, p. 105). . . .

3. Distortion of social psychological phenomena

Even before the questioning begins, the interrogator is urged to role-play the position of the subject in order to be able to respond to him—"man to man, not as policeman to prisoner" (Inbau & Reid, #6, p. 19). The interrogator is cautioned that "it is a mistake . . . to look upon the subject as an animal" (ibid.).

Under this category would fall all the appeals which depend upon the interrogator being friendly, kind, sympathetic, understanding, "a Dutch uncle," or an older brother. He is the one who provides social approval and recognition, who accords the suspect status, and is aware of and able to manipulate the suspect because of his social values, feelings of pride and class or group membership.

We are told, "It is a basic human trait to seek and enjoy the approval of other persons" (Inbau & Reid, #6, p. 69). Therefore, it is wise to flatter some subjects, for example, by complimenting an accused driver of a get-away car for his maneuvering and "cornering," or compare a juvenile with his movie idol, or a member of a racial group with a respectable, outstanding member of that group. This approach apparently works best with "the uneducated and under-privileged," since they "are more vulnerable to flattery than the educated person or the person in favorable financial circumstances" (Inbau & Reid, #6, p. 72). . . .

To create rapport, the interrogator could pat the suspect on the shoulder, grip his hand or offer to do a favor for him—get water, talk to his wife, employer, etc. "Gestures of this type produce a very desirable effect. They impart an attitude of understanding and sympathy better than words."

In order to know what "to pit against what," one interrogator suggests that a suspect be asked to name all the people and ideals 560 that are important to the suspect, as well as all those to which he is violently opposed.

For suspects who have pride in their family, an attempt is made to get parents to cooperate. If they refuse, their attention is called to a (faked) circular being prepared for broadcast and distribution throughout the country. It not only describes the fugitive, but lists all of his known relatives' names and addresses as possible leads for apprehending him. Cooperation is quite often obtained in this way, Kidd (#3) notes.

It will be remembered that in the case of George Whitmore one of the techniques reportedly used involved the arresting detective instilling fear in him, while the interrogating detective was protective, supportive and sympathetic. Whitmore responded to this technique which the police call the *Mutt and Jeff* approach by actually believing that Jeff was sincerely concerned about his welfare. While Mutt is typically a big, cruel, relentless investigator, Jeff is a kind-hearted family man, perhaps with a brother in a similar scrape once. Jeff asks Mutt to leave the prisoner alone and get out of the room. He then confides that he, too, detests Mutt's tactics (which unfortunately will get worse), and the suspect's only hope is to cooperate quickly with his friend Jeff by telling the truth and confessing. . . .

These tactics and deceptions appear to support Hugo Munsterberg's classic analysis of untrue confessions (cf., #18). He said that there are a number of social motives which make it conceivable from the start that an accused makes of his own accord a confession against himself which is not true. In the face of seemingly overwhelming damaging circumstantial evidence, an individual may prefer to make a false confession in the hope of a recommendation of mercy. The brothers Boorn of Vermont confessed to a killing in order to have the charge changed from homicide to manslaughter, only to have the "corpse" turn up alive. He concludes, "The untrue confessions from hope or fear, through promises and threats, from cunning calculations and passive yielding, thus shade off into others which are given with real conviction under the pressure of emotional excitement or under the spell of overpowering influences" (p. 147).

Let us now consider how the personality and character of the suspect become prime instruments of coercion in the police's arsenal of psychological weapons.

4. Utilization of personality and clinical psychology phenomena

Theodore Reik's brilliant analysis of "the compulsion to confess" (cf., #19) focuses attention not only on the obviously mentally ill who flock to police stations to confess after every major crime is publicized, but on all of us who harbor some deep-seated guilt for some real or imagined childhood transgression. Since guilt can only be completely relieved by confession, punishment and absolution, he would hold that we all have a need to confess which, although varying

561

in intensity, is nevertheless there in every one of us. He compares the criminal suspect with the patient in therapy who he says confesses something and does not know what he has said in so doing. He notes further that the confession is often not an end in itself, but has the additional meaning of an appeal to one's parents or their substitutes —the police. Because the emotional processes which underlie our motives for a lifetime of petty crimes are largely unconscious, they are reflected in a compulsion to confess—in slips of the tongue, symptoms, self-incriminations, and even in criminal false confessions.

Part of the initial "sizing-up" of the suspect involves an assessment of his personality, his strengths and weaknesses (without the aid of standard psychological measuring instruments). Suspects who appear nervous are left alone to "sweat it" for a long time. For some "apparently guilty" subjects, it may be necessary to reduce their guilt feelings by providing justifications for their behavior in order for them to be able even to talk about their feelings and their crimes.

For subjects who don't appear nervous, it is well to point out supposed psychological and pysiological symptoms of guilt which they are manifesting. As any hypnotist will tell you, merely calling attention to and making salient some part of the body or bodily process causes the person to react in accordance with the suggestion. Thus, Inbau and Reid (#5, 6) say attention should be directed to the: (a) pulsation of the carotid artery (in the neck), (b) movement of the Adam's apple, (c) dryness of the mouth, (d) any movement of the limbs, and (e) a "peculiar feeling inside" which is due to a troubled conscience.

While practicing one or more of these tactics on the suspect, the interrogator must be constantly alert and able to recognize "moments of indecision, during which his [the suspect's] struggle to avoid the consequences of his criminal act will be partially overcome by, or temporarily deadlocked with, his impulse to confess" (Inbau & Reid, # 6).

This is the time to "move in" on him. If he is a youngster, the interrogator could play on shame by asking him if or how often he masturbates. This is so embarrassing for most youngsters that they will be eager to change the topic of conversation, and can easily be led into talking about the crime.

On the other hand, with sex offenders of the so-called "intellectual type," it may be helpful to note that the Kinsey reports reveal human beings are not so different from animals in matters of sex. Because female sex victims are usually reluctant to talk about the activities which transpired (and some may even be feeling some guilt at not being more disturbed than they are after having been raped), the interrogator may have them write out details rather than speak them or he may ease the situation for them by asking them to view him as their gynecologist whom they are consulting about "a sex organ problem" (Inbau & Reid, #6, p. 36).

It is also well (say Inbau and Reid) for an interrogator to ask the suspect if he ever dreamed about committing the offense in question, since there is an "obvious relationship between dreaming and acting out."

"Fears of novel contrivances" allow the police to capitalize on the public's belief in the validity of lie detector tests, truth serums, etc. The suspect is told he will have to undergo such tests and they will prove conclusively his guilt. If he refuses, then that too is taken as a sign of his guilt. It is also permissible to falsify the tests to make the subject think the machine singles him out as guilty. While this evidence obviously cannot be used in court, his confession based on it is admissible.

Before turning to the final category in this catalogue of interviewing techniques, it would be remiss not to mention the deception which Kidd (#3, p. 141) refers to as "fear of the insane asylum." He says that "we find that some mentally affected persons fear the asylum more than they do jail. Threat of confinement in an asylum may secure a ready admission in the hope that they will go to jail." . . .

PART 4. CONCLUSIONS, EXAMINATION OF ALLEGATIONS AND RECOMMENDATIONS

It is my professional opinion as a psychologist who has been concerned with the experimental modification of attitudes and behavior, that these techniques represent a highly sophisticated application of psychological principles which for many people are more compelling and coercive than physical torture. These techniques involve confusing the suspect, lying, misrepresenting the situation, perjury, arousing and manipulating his social values and personal needs, as well as capitalizing on repressed motives.

I feel that not only are they likely to make a guilty man incriminate himself *against his will*, but they also can lead to false confessions by the innocent and involuntary testimony by witnesses. It is for the courts to act on this problem as a legal issue, and for the reader to judge for himself whether he wants his police force to be empowered to use such techniques on citizens of this country, which is to say, ultimately, whether he wants his police force to be able to use such techniques on himself or some member of his family. As far as I am concerned, this catalogue of interrogation techniques represents a debasement of human nature and stands as a disgraceful slur on the American system of justice.

Obviously, I am on the side of the individual and feel that society's major function is safeguarding *his* rights, *your* rights. Apparently such 563 a position conflicts with the concepts of "efficiency" and "necessity." Fred Inbau and John Reid, the authors of the most recent textbook on criminal interrogation from which I have quoted so freely, declare that they "approve of such psychological tactics and techniques as trickery and deceit that are not only helpful but frequently necessary in order to secure incriminating information . . ." (#6, pp. 203–204).

In fairness to the positions of these men, it must be noted that crime is increasing at a phenomenal rate in America and in most countries of the world. Since 1958 serious crimes in the United States have increased by 60 per cent, six times the population increase! Statistics like these, as well as the mass murders, the "unmotivated" killing of innocent victims, the rapes and kidnappings (which are exploited for dramatic effect by our communication media) cause the public to be justifiably afraid and to demand quick vengeance. The police respond to public pressures and their concern centers on the immediate goal of convicting a particular suspect. In the course of responding to public fear they are in danger of losing their true function. They forget that they are the *enforcers* of our laws, *not* the makers of them, nor yet the judges of those who may have broken them. . . .

It is claimed by the police that over 80 per cent of all criminal cases are solved by confessions, so that these trials are mere formalities. This efficient system of justice in the face of our crime wave may be the major reason for the implicit conspiracy of silence and ignorance about police interrogation tactics by our judges and lawyers. *Why do we demand confessions?* It is also interesting to speculate why such a high premium is placed on confessions in our country. Even in the face of sufficient material evidence, the police insist on a confession. This overzealousness in securing a confession sometimes results in a guilty defendant going free (on a legal technicality) when the material evidence alone would have convicted him. It is my hypothesis that the police need to have the criminal *participate in his own destruction* and that a confession of guilt not only absolves the police of the man's subsequent punishment and maybe death, but also absolves the judge, the prosecuting attorney, the jury, the victim (and his relations). Reik (cf., #19) notes that the criminal reveals in his confession his intention to re-enter society by declaring himself deserving of punishment. Once done, then the court and police authorities function unconsciously as the "typical representative of the father who condemns and forgives, who judges and comforts." There is a strange similarity between our insistence on confessions from criminal suspects, and our forefathers' insistence upon a declaration of guilt and a renunciation of the devil before a woman suspected of being a witch was burned. "It is rare that a man is acquitted once his confession is admitted in evidence" (cf., #37).

The act of confession not only absolves the agents of society of the consequences of their sentence and punishment of the criminal, it does much more. It helps to reestablish (at least in their perception) the bond of human communication between society and one of its transgressors, between the many and the social outcast. Confession "personalizes" the criminal act and makes it an object lesson for all of us who could under other circumstances be judged rather than judging. For the criminal, the act of confession may alleviate not only the guilt of the particular crime, but also that stemming from other crimes which shade off into real or imagined childhood aggressions and sins against society. It is likely that for the nonhabitual criminal, confession leads to "an exhilarating sense of relief that may have the characteristics of a religious conversion" (Hinkle & Wolff, #13, p. 612, in describing the reactions of POW's of the Chinese Communists).

Will all hell break loose if police have to change their tactics? Recently critics have questioned the need for the police to rely on confessions, as well as the allegation that legal restrictions upon law enforcement only result in a weakened police force and a higher crime rate. Justice Nathan Sobel of the New York Supreme Court, after reviewing 1,000 Brooklyn indictments from February to April, 1965, concluded that fewer than 10 per cent involved confessions! (cf., #27). A *New York Times* reporter commented after the recent Supreme Court ruling (cf., #41) that "while a number of police departments have been issuing warnings, the method probably has been cursory with the words mumbled. Or, it has likely been done as a tactic to establish a rapport with the suspect." It is estimated that 60 per cent of United States criminal defendants cannot afford a lawyer, and an even larger percentage do not even know a lawyer or place any trust in lawyers. For most people of the so-called lower socio-economic classes, lawyers are not friends when in need, but rather fast-talking shysters who are in it only for the money. Moreover, some interrogation tactics explicitly suggest that a suspect's request for a lawyer is a sign of guilt, and a lawyer is only a "stranger" who will come between the "man-to-man conversation" of the suspect and his "friend in the police station." In addition, maintaining one's right to silence is countered by the police with statements that if the suspect didn't have anything to hide he could talk freely, and his silence is therefore incriminating.

A system of justice based upon secret trial by the police and confession-elicitation has, according to the late Justice Felix Frankfurter, "manifest evils." One evil is "the threat that a police system which has grown to rely too heavily on interrogation will not pursue or learn other crime detection methods, and the consequent danger that police will feel themselves under pressure to secure confessions" (cf., #28). It is not only more efficient to rely on confession-getting   565 than tracking down clues and material evidence, but it is simply easier for the police. The framers of the India Evidence Act back in 1872 recognized this when they eloquently stated that:

> It is far pleasanter to sit comfortably in the shade rubbing pepper into a poor devil's eyes than go about in the sun hunting up evidence.

Detroit's Chief Detective Vincent Piersante substantiated Justice Frankfurter's assertion with statistics showing that in the year prior to the ruling advising a suspect of his rights, confessions were deemed "essential" in 21 per cent of Detroit's murder cases. In 1965, with warnings to suspects of their rights, the absolute number of confessions *increased,* but they were "essential" in only 9 per cent of the murder cases—due to sharper sleuthing which uncovered additional, more solid evidence.

The contention made by many police officials that the Supreme Court rulings would "force them to close down" and abandon the city to the criminals receives little support from two other police sources. In Philadelphia the police began giving carefully worded verbal warnings to suspects last year, and since then 76 per cent of all felony suspects voluntarily confessed, 60 per cent of all robbery suspects, and 83 per cent of all murder suspects did likewise. A week after the most recent Supreme Court ruling, Lieut. A. E. Schultheiss of the 14th Detective Squad based at the West 30th Street station of New York City (which makes 1,500 arrests a year) said, "By and large they readily admit what they've been doing even after they've been told of their rights." It is only "the hardened criminal who won't talk" and who often has legal counsel available anyway (cf., #42).

Therefore, it appears that giving citizens their constitutional rights against self-incrimination and for legal counsel has not crippled or "shackled" police work, and they have not had, nor fear of having to "close down the shop" (cf., #43).

It is instructive, in fact, to note evidence to the contrary. In Washington, D.C., Police Chief Robert Murray complained that the Mallory decision "will result in a complete breakdown in law enforcement in the District of Columbia." In comparing crime rates in Washington, D.C., which has supposedly been "handcuffed" by having to follow federal rulings while its neighbors, Virginia and Maryland, operated under more lenient state court statutes, it was found that the overall felony rate increased by only 1 per cent in Washington from 1950 to 1960, while it went up 69 per cent in comparable Maryland and Virginia suburbs (cf., #16).

The techniques the police use alienate them from society. It should be mentioned in passing that one of the most serious consequences of the use of interrogation tactics and approaches like those mentioned in this paper is the debasement of the *police themselves* who have to employ them. When one human being aggresses against another either verbally or physically, deceives and tricks him, and finally "breaks his man" and does so under conditions where the "victim" is helpless to retaliate, then we have the conditions under which cognitive dissonance should be aroused in the aggressor. This state of psychological tension results from behavior which is discrepant with the police officer's ideals of fair play, of the rights of every citizen, of human dignity, and is contrary to any feelings of empathy and social/emotional comparison he may have toward the human being he is interrogating. According to Festinger's theory of cognitive dissonance (1957, #12a), the existence of the psychological state of dissonance will motivate the individual to behave in ways which will reduce its magnitude or intensity. Our interrogating officer can readily reduce his dissonance by modifying several of his cognitions; by derogating the suspect, seeing as necessity all coercive techniques designed to expose criminals, and feeling a moral obligation to persecute and convict those suspected of crimes.

Similar consequences have been observed in recent laboratory studies (summarized by Brock and Pallak, 1967, #11a) in which a person choosing to be aggressive toward a "victim" (who ostensibly benefits in some way from such aggression, e.g., his errors are punished), minimizes the seriousness of the pain inflicted, evaluates the victim negatively, and feels obligated to have acted in this way.

The long-range effects of such psychological coping mechanisms leave the typical police officer regarding "the public as his enemy," and feeling "his occupation to be in conflict with the community" (according to W. A. Westley, #25, p. 35). He comes to hate the petty criminal, to be suspicious of everyone, and to find a strange kinship with the smart, hardened criminal. Where the law "blocks the path from suspicion to disposition, the law becomes an enemy of its ostensible servants" (H. Toch, #24, p. 6). Eventually many police officers come to redefine for themselves the concepts of justice, criminals, and even graft. They cease using the "average person" as a source of social comparison, may lose the ability to empathize with him, feel compelled to operate "extra legally" when necessary, in order to harass prostitutes, homosexuals, "beatniks," Negroes, and other minority group members (as documented recently in the Danny Escobedo affair in Chicago, cf., #28). In so doing, they lose contact with the society they serve, and by feeling above most of its average citizens, alienate themselves from it. Part of this attitude of the police is succinctly summarized by Inbau and Reid: "Of necessity, criminal interrogation must deal with offenders on a somewhat lower moral plane than that upon which ethical, law-abiding citizens are expected to conduct their everyday affairs" (#6, p. 208).

567

Chief Circuit Judge David L. Bazelon, of the United States Court of Appeals, has said, "We must deter not only crime, but also the debasement of the individual" (#10a). This imperative should include *both* the suspected criminal and the police officer. . . .

It is clear, then, that because the phenomenon we have been discussing has such broad psychological implications, psychologists who insist on working within the secure confines of their self-defined fields of expertness can nevertheless make a significant contribution with their relevant research to the psychology of police-elicited confessions.

America is at a critical stage in her development (cf., Irving Sarnoff's analysis, #21), with the rights of the individual to protest being challenged all the way from Washington, D.C. to Texas and Sacramento. Responsible citizens and concerned professional psychologists must view the issues raised here in the broadest possible terms.

I prefer to see them in the light of Chief Justice Warren's wisdom:

> The methods we employ in the enforcement of our criminal law have aptly been called the measures by which the quality of our civilization may be judged (Cited in #16, p. 18).

REFERENCES

Police Manuals
1. Criminal investigation. *Dept. of the Army Field Manual,* FM 19-20, July, 1951.
2. Dienstein, W. *Technics for the crime investigator.* Springfield, Ill.: Thomas Publishing Co., 1952.
3. Kidd, W. R. Police interrogation. *The Police Journal,* New York, 1940.
4. Gross, H. *Criminal investigation.* Adapted by J. C. Adam, edited by N. Kendal (3rd ed.). London: Sweet and Maxwell, Ltd., 1934.
5. Inbau, F. E., & Reid, J. E. *Lie detection and criminal interrogation.* Baltimore: Williams & Wilkins, 1953.
6. Inbau, F. E., & Reid, J. E. *Criminal interrogation and confessions.* Baltimore: Williams & Wilkins, 1962.
7. Mulbar, H. *Interrogation.* Springfield, Ill.: Thomas Publishing Co., 1951.
8. O'Hara, C. E. *Fundamentals of criminal investigation.* Springfield, Ill.: Thomas Publishing Co., 1956.
9. Söderman, H., & O'Connell, J. J. *Modern criminal investigation.* New York: Funk & Wagnall, 1945.

Relevant "Professional" Sources
10. Arens, R., & Meadow, A. Psycholinguistics and the confession dilemma. *Columbia Law Rev.,* 1956, 56, 19-46.

568

10a. Bazelon, David L. "Law, Morality, and Individual Rights." Unpublished address to Juvenile Court Judges Institute and Juvenile Officers Institute, Minneapolis, Minn., Aug. 20, 1963, p. 10.

11. Bem, D. Inducing beliefs in false confessions. *J. Pers. soc. Psychol.*, 1966, 3, 707-710.

11a. Brock, T. C., & Pallak, M. S. The consequences of choosing to be aggressive. In P. G. Zimbardo (Ed.) *The cognitive control of motivation.* Chicago: Scott, Foresman, in press.

12. Carlton, C. O., Dillehay, R. C., & Holey, J. The criminal, the penalty and the crime: a study of social perception and judgment. Paper presented at the American Psychological Association, New York, September, 1966.

12a. Festinger, L. *A theory of cognitive dissonance.* Stanford, Calif.: Stanford Univer. Press, 1957.

13. Hinkle, L. E., & Wolff, H. C. Communist interrogation and indoctrination of "enemies of the state." *Arch. Neurol. Psychiat.*, 1956, 76, 115-174.

14. Horowitz, M. W. The psychology of confession. *J. clin. exp. Psychopath.*, 1957, 18, 381-382.

15. Johnson, N. Sources of distortion and deception in prison interviewing. *Fed. Probation,* 1956, 20, 43-48.

16. Kamisar, Y. The police chief, the college coach and the problem of "absentee management" . . . and other reflections on the tactics of "police persecution-minded critics of the courts." Paper presented at American Psychological Association, September, 1963.

18. Munsterberg, H. *On the witness stand.* New York: Clark Boardman, 1949.

19. Reik, T. *The compulsion to confess.* New York: Farrar Strauss, 1959.

20. Rogge, O. J. *Why men confess.* New York: Nelson & Sons, 1959.

21. Sarnoff, I. *Society with tears.* New York: Citadel Press, 1966.

22. Schein, E. H. Reaction patterns to severe, chronic stress in American army prisoners of war of the Chinese. *J. soc. Issues,* 1957, XIII, 21-30.

23. Schein, E. H., Hill, W. E., Williams, H. L., & Lubin, A. Distinguishing characteristics of collaborators and resisters among American prisoners of war. *J. abnorm. soc. Psychol.,* 1957, 55, 197-201.

23a. Skolnick, J. H. *Justice without trial.* New York: Wiley, 1966.

24. Toch, H. H. Psychological consequences of the police role. Paper presented at American Psychological Association, September, 1963.

25. Westley, W. A. Violence and the police. *Amer. J. Sociology,* 1953, 59, 34-41.

Relevant "Popular" Sources (Mass Media)

26. *Civil Liberties in New York.* March, 1963 issue.

27. The law section. *Time Magazine,* Dec. 3, 1965.

28. The law section. *Time Magazine,* April 29, 1966.

New York Times (arranged in chronological order)
29. "New York Curbs Third Degree." J. Roth, Nov. 7, 1963.
30. "Miller says 'Distorted' Idea of Goldwater Fades," Oct. 10, 1964.
31. "Hogan Clears Whitmore in Two East Side Murders," Jan. 28, 1965.
32. "Bar Leader Finds High Court Too Lenient in Criminal Cases." Edith E. Asbury, Jan. 30, 1965.
33. "Confession Cases May Rise Sharply." P. Benjamin, Feb. 15, 1965.
34. "Police Doubted Whitmore Story." T. Jones, April, 1965.
35. "High Court Scored in Crime Rulings." S. E. Zion, May 14, 1965.
36. "The Suspect Confesses—But Who Believes Him?" S. E. Zion, May 16, 1965.
37. "What About Confessions?" S. E. Zion, July 5, 1965.
38. "Confessed 'Slayer' Cleared After Year." B. Weinraub, Nov. 9, 1965.
39. "Confessions Held Crucial by Hogan." S. V. Roberts, Dec. 1, 1965.
40. "Study of Confessions Asked by Weintraub." R. Sullivan, Dec. 11, 1965.
41. "The Court on Confessions," June 19, 1966.
42. "Police Find Suspects Willing to Talk." B. Weinraub, June 25, 1966.
43. "No Shackles on the Law." Editorial, Aug. 15, 1966.
44. "Detroit Police Plan to Put Confessions on Television Tape," Jan. 20, 1967.

Sherman Barr

Budgeting and the Poor:
A View from the Bottom

The materials on which this paper is based are excerpts taken from over 200 taped interviews with poor persons residing in the Lower East Side of Manhattan. Almost all are receiving funds from the New York City Department of Welfare. These interviews were the major efforts of the Project on Poverty, a project of the Research Center of the Columbia University School of Social Work for Mobilization for Youth.[1]

LIFE STYLE OF THE POOR

The study, wholly impressionistic, engaged in three major lines of inquiry. The first sought information in regard to the life style of the poor. In this connection we were concerned with the management of such day to day activities as washing, shopping, housekeeping, child care, budgeting, and the like. A second line of inquiry was related to how the poor perceive and use the public and private services on which they are almost completely dependent. The third dimension of the study obtained information about poor persons' perceptions and

Reprinted from the October 1965 issue of *Public Welfare*, pp. 246–250, with the permission of the author and the American Public Welfare Association. Sherman Barr is Assistant Chief of Services to Individuals and Families at Mobilization for Youth, Inc., and a part-time faculty member at the Columbia University School of Social Work.

[1]Mobilization for Youth is an experimental action-research project in the field of juvenile delinquency and poverty prevention on the Lower East Side of Manhattan. It offers broad scale services in the field of employment, education, casework, group work and community organization. The opinions and judgments noted in this paper are the author's and do not reflect the policies or practices of Mobilization for Youth, Inc.   571

insights into the various individuals and groups which comprise the social, economic and political structures.

First, I will quote literally from several taped interviews and summarize other quotes that are particularly relevant to how the poor view what is called "budgeting." Time permits me to note only a portion of some of the most revealing interviews.

I will present some implications for services and programs which arise from the material.

Mr. P. is 67 years old and blind. In one interview he related how he uses surplus food. "Well, here's what I do with the surplus food. I don't use the lard and they give you so much cheese that it's impossible to use. So I sell some things to my neighbors and with this money I buy myself an extra chicken. When I cook up the chicken I take off the fat first. I make good chicken fat and sell it back to the butcher. I make a few cents, my neighbors a few cents and so does the butcher."

An eight year old boy in a nearby park responded as follows in regard to questions about savings. "Maybe one of these days I'll be able to save. But, if I had money, I would first buy two knives, two guns, and a holster, and then I'd kill the people who rob my apartment. And then I'd buy a hat and new pants for my father so he could look for a job. And then I'd buy cake, cookies, candy, toys, and furniture so we would have something to sit on in the living room."

A young pregnant mother said, "I'd wear a girdle to the unemployment office and as soon as I'd sign for the check, I'd run to the ladies room and take it off and thank God I had another check stacked away. What did I lie for? I'll tell you—to be able to buy my child's crib."

Another elderly gentleman had this to say: "What can you do if we are not lucky enough in the richest city in the world? We've got to go on Welfare and have the Welfare worker come up to see us and tell us how to live and then she looks in the ice box at what we have. They want to know what kind of clothes you have and when they see a telephone they want to know who is paying for it and why that money isn't being used for food. They try every way to get you. They make it hard for you and they don't want to know from nothing. But *they* get a big salary every week. Before you get the first check, you wait three or four weeks and when you get it you don't know what to do first. They should have on their bones how much they give you. But you've got to make the best of it. One of these days I'll go up to the top of the Brooklyn Bridge, yell 'Here I go' and then jump off. And you know what? Nobody will know! Nobody will care! Nobody will miss me. Maybe the Welfare would be happy because they wouldn't have to give me money any more. Who are you going to fight? City Hall? You've got to have pull and, if you don't have it, it's no good. If only people who get together would organize and put up a fight, maybe there would be something for them so they wouldn't have to suffer so much, so they won't be cranky."

Mrs. C. raises three energetic boys on AFDC funds. Three brief incidents tell us something about how she budgets. During one interview when we discussed what she read, she pointed out that the afternoon paper was delivered daily. When I questioned the expense of this method, she said that the delivery was the way she manipulated not having five cents to make a daily purchase. By having it delivered, she was assured of semi-monthly billing and thus was able to pay for it when the semi-monthly public assistance checks came. Mrs. C. was creative in other ways. When she received a used television set from her son's godmother, she no longer had the need to spend money for a clock. To know the time, she turns on the television. Finally, Mrs. C. told me of her failure to obtain funds for a communion suit from the Welfare Department after several weeks of frustrating negotiation. She finally got together seven dollars by asking many friends for small loans of ten to twenty-five cents each. Being without proper clothes for herself, she did not attend the communion. When her son returned home, he was proud of how he looked and asked permission to visit old friends in the neighborhood. She understood and agreed. He came back many hours later with over one dollar in change. When she pressed him for an explanation, he volunteered that when he arrived at his old haunts, he met the grocery man who offered him a commission for selling frozen fruit ices. Of course he agreed. And Mrs. C's last words for that interview were these: "And can you picture my little sweet Alex standing there in his communion suit selling ices to make some money. What a picture." She began to laugh. And she laughed and laughed and laughed, and as she looked at me, her cheek bones twitched, her lips trembled, and her tears of laughter dissolved into tears of weeping.

The F. family perceived the following ten choices they were faced with over a short period of time. Seven of the ten were related to budgeting.

(1) Complain to the landlord and face the possibility of being evicted or accept poor service.

(2) Complain to Welfare and possibly be cut off or insist on a revised budget.

(3) Leave lights burning all night to keep away rats and then have large utility bills or take a chance with the rats.

(4) Take a feverish child to clinic with inadequate clothes or stay home and hope for the best.

(5) Take the five children to a clinic and spend the carfare or stay home and hope for good health.

(6) Go to clinic for personal reasons and lose one-half day's pay or not go at all.

573

(7) Report a salary increase to the Housing Authority or pay off some debts and then notify them.

(8) Send the children to school with inadequate clothing or keep them home and face the embarrassment of answering notes from the attendance officers.

(9) Ask DW for camp clothing again so that the children can go to camp or, in the mother's words, "keep them home during the summer and have them drive me crazy."

(10) Tell the investigator that her parents in Puerto Rico are dead or tell the truth and let her parents find out that she never "made it" in the United States.

Mr. J. works and is out of the home from 8:00 a.m. to 6:00 p.m. Mrs. J. works and is out of the home from 5:00 p.m. to 11:00 p.m. From 5:00 p.m. to 6:00 p.m. the eight children are scheduled in Mrs. J.'s words, "like the Marine Corps." The rest of her life, particularly budgeting, is just as disciplined. She knows exactly which door to use in which department store on which day for which purpose. She travels from Manhattan to the Bronx to save a few pennies on meat. She knows personally the owner of every good second hand clothing store on the Lower East Side. Her sons get their haircuts at the Bowery barber schools where she saves one dollar over the regular price. She would never move from her over-crowded apartment in a low-income project to a different project because she is now living adjacent to a middle-income development populated largely by Jews because where Jews are, you can find better schools, better police protection, better shopping, better recreation and better support for various civic improvements. She knows which police station to go to for Christmas toys, which social agency for money, and which church to belong to because it offers more clothing than other churches. In short, she is everything some people in our society want poor people to be—thrifty, disciplined, and organized. However, after the seventh interview, she blurted out that all wasn't what it appeared to be. Occasionally, she and her husband engage in violent physical battles which sometimes result in the police being called in. "Something has to give," she said. "Something just has to give."

Mrs. G. is a mother of seven and after much negotiation was able to secure a washing machine in place of the regular laundry allowance. The machine is required to be a hand wringer type and after three weeks of use, she said: "I guess it makes no difference how you get a heart attack—bringing the clothes up and down the stairs or wringing until your guts come out. Maybe, if I had a heart attack, they'd get me an automatic."

Mrs. M. is a spry, energetic young mother of two. In telling us how she shopped wisely for a new bed for which she was granted $24.00, she pointed out the following.

574

(1) she visited four different second hand stores covering a distance of ten miles;

(2) she spent $1.20 for fares;

(3) she antagonized both her children whom she had to take with her on this expedition;

(4) the shopping trip took two days to complete;

(5) and finally, she said, and I quote, "And you can bet your life I got that receipt to show the investigator. She'd never believe I got such a good buy. Without that receipt she'd start asking all kinds of questions and then 'pop,' I get mad at her and I'm in trouble again."

WHAT POOR PERSONS TOLD US

More of the significant material is summarized. May I remind you that these statements are not presented as facts, but simply as a report on what poor persons have told us.

1. Poor persons see themselves as victimized by society and do not see themselves to blame for the variety of financial difficulties in which they find themselves. They believe that the affluent society can never know or understand the world of the poor, particularly the suffering and relentless recurrence of financial crisis.

2. Service agencies are seen as systems which must be manipulated if decent service is to be obtained. Similarly, personnel employed by these agencies are seen as "welfare adjusters," that is, persons who help you to adjust to the *status quo*. It is this feeling that dealing with the Welfare Department in particular requires power and a level of knowledge and sophistication which is impossible for them to obtain, learn and employ. Adhering to present budgeting procedures and standards requires a level of planning, coordination, and education which they feel is not within their ability, experience or life style.[2] Many welfare recipients employ some small "illegitimate" means to obtain additional funds, services or goods. In the welfare system is the embodiment of all of society's injustice, callousness, insensitivity, cruelty, and illogicalness. This perception is quickly incorporated by even the youngest member of the family. Thus, as we know, the welfare system bears the blame for all of society's ills.

[2]Orshansky, Mollie, "Counting the Poor: Another Look at the Poverty People," *Social Security Bulletin,* Social Security Administration, Department of Health, Education, and Welfare, Washington, D. C. 20201, January, 1965, pp. 3-29.

Mollie Orshansky arrives at a similar conclusion through another route. She notes that ". . . all the (food) plans, if strictly followed, can provide an acceptable diet, but—generally speaking—the lower level of cost, the more restricted the kinds and qualities of food must be and *the more the skill in marketing and food preparation that is required.*"

575

3. Some semblance of a broad prevailing pattern of budgeting seems to exist in that food is given top priority and rent lowest. There is a generalized belief that the city will "get you off the hook" so to speak and issue a duplicate check for rent, but not for food. Social pressures for jewelry, television set, clothing for special occasions and the like are so great that many families, who would be regarded as not budgeting adequately by present criteria, do amazingly well in regard to purchasing these items from their recurring allotments. Of course, these purchases are made at the expense of other important needs. All interviewees reported that they never receive any instructions in regard to budgeting requirements, allowances and procedures. Many of them did not have budgets.

4. A constantly recurring theme which our interviewees provided was that society in a sense evaluates them negatively by giving them inadequate grants to purchase monotonous, shabby clothing and worn furniture. Soon, the poor, too, begin to think this way negatively about themselves.

5. While money is considered as the most vital element in their lives, the interviewees do not necessarily equate the possession of money with personal qualities of intelligence or industry. As a matter of fact, there is a tendency to regard wealthy persons as people who have gotten their wealth through illegitimate means or at the expense of others, namely, the poor.

FIND INNOVATING WAYS

If these observations made by the poor have any merit, and I think they do, they have implications for how we deal with the specific problems of budgeting and the related larger problems of welfare services. How might our programs and practices be made more effective and responsive to the needs of the poor?

At the same time that we are constantly engaged in improving our welfare services, we also need to help clients find specific innovating ways of coping with a bureaucratic philosophy and bureaucratic system which allows 90 razor blades a year for employed males and 50 blades for unemployed males; a system which allows 12 haircuts a year for an employed male and nine haircuts for an unemployed male; a system which provides 20 cents a month for a 12 year old child's school expenses; a system which allows 48 bobby pins a year for a woman; a system which draws the line so finely that it allows two lipsticks annually for an employed woman and one for an unemployed woman.

Present methods of budgeting lock poor persons into a moral and social bind. On one hand, initiative and ambition are admired and desired traits in our society. We preach and teach them. However, if a struggling AFDC mother should earn a few unreported dollars 576 to maintain standards or even to provide herself with a little extra, if you will, she is then regarded by the public and by herself as well as being a welfare "chiseler." Similarly, the poor are taunted and reminded constantly by television, radio, and advertising of all the goodies which exist in the affluent society's treasure box. What were regarded as goodies only a short time ago are now necessities. Poor people, too, need to meet the increased economic and social demands of the school, the church, the special social functions and the like without having to deal with their aroused feelings of anxiety, fear, guilt, and frustration. Since various welfare departments across the country have recognized the value of incentive payments, certain activities now considered "illegitimate" could easly be legitimized by them relating to an incentive payment plan or perhaps a family allotment plan. Such a plan would not only provide needed additional funds to families but would, in addition, stimulate motivation and address itself in part to alleviating some of the social and psychological causes of stress within families.

BUDGETING STANDARDS AND TECHNIQUES

The material also indicates that perhaps we need a closer look at budgeting standards and techniques. The extremely difficult pressures under which we provide service can often make us forget that budgeting, when used well, is a differentially applied tool designed to assist a family to function more adequately. If this is so, then perhaps the supermarket may not be the best place to shop for a mother with many children or an aged person who lives on the sixth floor of a walk-up. Perhaps such people should shop at a store that delivers and the budget might reflect this extra cost. I have not always felt too comfortable as a social worker in helping a client obtain the poorest quality new merchandise or good second hand furniture. I have often felt that having something new, something good, something not specified in the manual of procedures is a much better morale booster for my client than the knowledge that she bought what she needed within the prescribed allowance. The latter may be better for my morale than for hers. And I have often felt that I have permitted myself to be "used" professionally to reinforce and promulgate budgetary standards which are in many cases far below what we know people need to have if they are to live not in minimal, but in good standards of comfort and safety.

Charles Lebeaux

Life on ADC: Budgets of Despair

In September 1962 a grave crisis occurred in 6,000 needy families with children in Detroit. These families were recipients of Aid to Families with Dependent Children (AFDC), the aid program commonly known as ADC (Aid to Dependent Children) until its title was changed in 1962. In the early 1940's the Detroit welfare departments began supplementing AFDC grants out of general relief funds, because the Michigan state grant in AFDC was in many cases too small for the family to live on, and because it was often *less* than the same family would receive from general relief.[1] But due to Detroit's financial straits, about four years ago the city began cutting the amount of the supplement. In September 1962 the supplement was out entirely. This last cut affected 6,000 of the city's 13,000 AFDC families—many more had been affected by earlier cuts. These many thousands of families are thus living below the minimum standards of health and decency, even as defined by this welfare program itself.

Few people in Michigan know about the plight of these families

Reprinted by permission of the author and publishers from *New University Thought*, Vol. 3, No. 4, 1963, pp. 26–35. Charles Lebeaux is on the faculty of the School of Social Work of Wayne State University.

[1]AFDC is one of five categorical public assistance programs set up in the Social Security Act, in which the federal government shares costs with the states. These programs (AFDC, Old Age Assistance, Aid to the Blind, Aid to the Disabled, and Medical Aid to the Aged) are separate financially, and for the most part administratively, from general relief, which is run by the states and localities with no federal involvement. Detroit is in Wayne County where there are three relief offices: the Wayne County Bureau of Social Aid, which administers the categorical aid programs (including AFDC) for the entire county; the Detroit Department of Public Welfare, which handles general relief in Detroit; and the Wayne County Department of Social Welfare, which handles general relief in the rest of the county.

and even fewer seem to care. The AFDC mothers themselves, many without the clothes or carfare to go out of their homes, have almost no power to influence public policy or opinions. Although in the fall of 1962 members of the Detroit Chapter of the National Association of Social Workers (NASW) organized and supported efforts of some Negro organizations (primarily the Trade Union Leadership Council and the Federation of AFDC Mothers, a group of the mothers themselves), none of their appeals to rescind the cut, either to the mayor or the welfare department, were successful. When these efforts failed, the following survey of the families affected by the cut was made, in order to arouse the moribund consciences of the city and state.[2]

THE PEOPLE ON AFDC

There are now about 7½ million people in the United States getting public assistance under all programs, special and general. Around four million of these are in AFDC families. There are about 33,000 AFDC families in Michigan; about 13,000 of these families, with some 40,000 children, live in Detroit. AFDC is the most controversial of the public assistance programs, not only because of its size and persistent growth, but because of the social characteristics of the recipients. When the program started in the late 1930's, death of the father was the most common cause for being in need of aid. Today, more than 60 per cent of AFDC cases are due to estrangement of parents—divorce, separation, desertion, or unmarried motherhood. The American public regards these as bad or unworthy reasons to be in need, and is less inclined to give help.

Over 40 per cent of AFDC families are Negro (compared to about 10 per cent of the general population). In northern industrial cities

[2]After we were unable to obtain a list of the 6,000 from city, county or state agencies, which made a full random sample impossible, the NASW decided that it had to proceed on its own, and quickly. A list of some hundred odd names was supplied by the Federation of AFDC Mothers, and a questionnaire was devised by faculty and students of the Wayne State University School of Social Work. Twenty-five members of NASW and twenty-five social work students volunteered to do the home interviewing, which was accomplished in April 1963. Ninety-three usable interviews were held, and are the basis of this report.

Because we could not obtain the list of 6,000 supplement cut cases, we could not pick a statistically correct sample; but when a population is quite homogeneous with respect to the characteristic under investigation, just a few cases may represent all. So with the poverty aspect of our AFDC families. In fact, my guess is that our group is better off than the typical AFDC family, because women who participate in the Federation of AFDC Mothers also probably will be better managers than the average woman receiving AFDC.

579

the caseload is largely Negro (about 81 per cent in Detroit), and in cities like Detroit, the proportion of illegitimate children is unusually high (although less than one-quarter of all illegitimate children in the country receive AFDC assistance).

The federal law says that to qualify under AFDC a child must be in "need," but the states define that status and determine the actual amount of money that each child and his family receive. The Michigan AFDC law says that they shall receive enough to permit them to live with "health and decency," at a level below which something suffers— health, church and school attendance, or self-respect. However, most states, including Michigan, interpret a health and decency standard to mean "minimum subsistence."

Dollar costs of a minimum subsistence budget are determined by home economists and other experts in the Federal Department of Agriculture, the State Department of Social Welfare, and home economics departments in universities by adding together minimum amounts for food, shelter, utilities, clothing, household supplies, and personal incidentals. For example, on the scale prepared by the Family Budget Council of the Detroit Visiting Nurses Association, $266.21 per month was the minimum income required in January 1960, by a family consisting of a mother age thirty-five, a boy age fourteen, and two girls, nine and four, with rent assumed to be $55 per month. For the identical family, paying identical rent, the Michigan State Department of Social Welfare in January 1961, has $223.05 as the monthly amount required to meet basic needs.

In practice, the welfare worker on the case adds up the amount needed to meet basic needs of the family according to state standards, subtracts any income there may be, and the unmet need should be the amount of the AFDC check. But in most cases in Detroit that is *not what the family gets.* The state sets ceilings on what each family can get, no matter what the budget figures show they need, according to the 1963 formula shown in Table 1.

Table 1: *Theoretical and actual grants*

FAMILY SIZE	BUDGET REQUIREMENTS[1]	MAXIMUM GRANT
Mother and 1 child	$151	$120
Mother and 2 children	191	140
Mother and 3 children	228	160
Mother and 4 children	263	180
Mother and 5 children	300	200
Mother and 6 children	334	220
Mother and 7 children	368	240 (absolute maximum)

[1]Includes food and incidentals allowance of $34 per person, $67 rent, and heat and utilities according to a standardized allowance based on family size.

Without important error, we can think of these families as living on the schedule of state ceiling grants. No income other than the relief grant was reported for seventy-nine families. This means that for 85 per cent of the group, income is fixed by the state ceilings—$120 for a mother and one child, $140 for a mother and two children, and so on. Whenever income plus the ceiling grant exceeds the state subsistence standard for the family, the grant is reduced accordingly.

Court-ordered or voluntary support payments by the absent fathers of families on relief is the weakest of financial reeds. In many cases they are not actually forthcoming, and families dependent on them are chronically on the verge of utter destitution. Children over seventeen are excluded from the state-federal AFDC program, and since September 1962 are also eliminated from city welfare support. There are at least six families among our ninety-three with an unemployed child over seventeen living in the home with no provision for his support.

Out of the ceiling grant rent and utilities must get paid, usually first. Table 2 shows the combined cost of rent and utilities to these families in the month of March 1963.

Table 2: Combined cost of rent and utilities—March 1963

DOLLARS	PUBLIC HOUSING	PRIVATE HOUSING	TYPE OF HOUSING NOT ASCERTAINED
40-59	44	3	1
60-79	6	10	1
80-99	2	18	2
100-above	0	5	0
Total	52	36	4

Fifty-two of the families live in city public housing projects, thirty-seven in private housing. Living in public housing projects is cheaper —the median rent and utility cost is $56, compared with $86 in private housing, but few public housing units are large enough for the biggest families, who naturally pay more for bigger private quarters.

What do these reasonable rent and utility costs mean to an AFDC family? Consider a mother with two children. Say that rent and utilities are $70 per month. Out of their $140 grant that leaves $70. But the state welfare department says that three people need $102 a month for food and incidentals. It is clear that for these families "something suffers."

One mother, three days after receipt of her check (and twelve days 581 before the next one would come), had 56¢ left. She had bought food and coal and paid the rent, but held off on the gas and electricity bills because there was no money to pay them. The gas and electricity may be cut off, she says, as they have been twice in the last two years. And what of school supplies, clothing, or carfare?

Sixteen mothers reported they were behind in rent. Half of these owed $50 or less, but one woman was $140 behind because her grant had stopped while the agency checked out a report that "a man was living with her." The lost income was never made up. Twenty-five families were behind in utilities; you need a roof overhead, at least in the winter, but you can exist without heat and light.

A surprising proportion of the mothers considered themselves not badly housed. In the words of the women:

(Private housing): *"It's good because the rent is fair and it's near school, relatives and shopping. But the house is too small and the neighborhood is unfriendly."* (High-rise public housing project): *"It's cold in winter, causing excess use of electricity. It's too far from the children outside, too small, and the elevators are a problem. But it is burglar and fire proof, and there's a good incinerator."* (Also high-rise): *"It's too crowded, noisy, and too high,"* (woman has hypertension), *"But it's warm, fire-proof, and the Neighborhood Service Organization has good programs for the kids."*

HOW DO AFDC FAMILIES EAT?

To get some detail on the quality of economic life on AFDC, we asked the mothers how much food they had on hand (meat, dairy products, and fresh or canned fruit). The information obtained was voluminous and interesting, but difficult to summarize and liable to misinterpretation. Just before check day, food stocks will naturally be low, and just after, there may be two weeks supply of food newly purchased. Averages here would make no sense.

However, the trend of the information gathered indicated that hardly any mother had as much as a half-gallon of milk on hand, and very little meat. Often the meat listed was an inexpensive cut like neck bones, or a canned variety. There was a nearly universal report, "No fruit," "No fruit." And something we didn't inquire into was frequently volunteered: "No vegetables either." And in home economics courses in the schools they teach children about balanced diets!

Asked "Is your family adequately fed?" forty of the mothers answered "yes," six answered "sometimes," and forty-seven answered "no." "Never enough near the time the check is due. Hungry at other times too." "Before transfer to AFDC (from Detroit welfare) we ate well, but now food is inadequate." So the mothers respond who feel 582 their families are inadequately fed. One mother had a doctor-prescribed high-protein diet (and TB too) that she has been unable to follow for two months.

Those that consider their families adequately fed have often given up something else. They say that they are getting behind in the rent, are without adequate clothing, and in one case without a phone, which was necessary because of a brain damaged child with frequent convulsions. Those who feel they are adequately fed usually go without fruit, and eat little meat and vegetables.

FOOD STAMPS IN THE AFDC PROGRAM

For many years now the federal government has been disposing of some of the surplus foods accumulated under the farm subsidy program, by giving it to local relief agencies across the country who distribute it to poor people. In 1962 the food stamp program, which had been used before World War II, was started in a number of localities including Detroit to test whether it was a better way of distributing surplus foods. As a result, in Detroit surplus commodities are not now given directly to families, but food stamps are distributed by the City Department of Public Welfare to all low income people who wish to participate. The participant takes his cash to a stamp office and buys stamps which are worth more than the cash paid—for example, you may get $14 worth of stamps for $10. The amount one may purchase depends mostly on the size of the family, but most AFDC families qualify for less than a 50 per cent bonus, e.g., for $30 cash, $43 in food stamps.

All AFDC families in Detroit are eligible to buy food stamps. Forty-seven out of our ninety-three families reported buying food stamps; forty-six did not. Most mothers who get the stamps say they are a great help. Those who do not get the stamps gave the following reasons (in order of frequency): not enough cash, restricts purchase selection, timing is off, and can't get to the stamp office.

Twenty-four families found the stamps restricted purchase selection. For example, the stamps don't buy soap, cleaning supplies, or toilet paper. They don't buy coffee or cocoa. These restrictions occur because the program, financed by the U.S. Department of Agriculture with farm subsidy funds, is designed to get rid of surplus food stores, not to help feed poor people. The resulting rules and procedures guard the interests of the farmers, who don't grow coffee or toilet paper, instead of the interests of the stamp users. Even a very careful home manager is penalized by the program's procedures; however, she still gains in dollars by using the stamps.

Not enough cash. This is the most important reason; and it causes 583 all kinds of difficulties even for the families that buy food stamps. What happens is this: A family of mother and three children when receiving its semi-monthly AFDC check of $80 is certified to buy $30 worth of food stamps. But the rent of $55 is due and must be paid first; there is not enough left to get the food stamps. Suppose they pay only half the rent now (which many do); but some utility bills are due and a child must have a pair of shoes—again, not enough cash to buy the food stamps. They are not permitted to buy less than the amount they are certified for by the welfare department (this would be against the Department of Agriculture regulations). And they must buy regularly. Every time a family fails to buy the stamps at the appointed time, it is automatically decertified and must go through the application procedure again. If the family is very irregular in buying stamps, it becomes ineligible for the program for a while—a Department of Agriculture penalty to force regular participation. Thus those who most need the added food-buying power of the stamps are least able to get them.

Some find the "timing is off"—that the fixed time for buying stamps comes several days after (or before) the check comes. Meanwhile you have to eat, and there is then insufficient cash to buy stamps when the time comes. This problem is much less severe now than it was when the program was started because local relief officials, after fighting a long battle with Washington, have been able to get the check and stamp buying dates into approximate coincidence.

WHAT DO THE CHILDREN WEAR?

As a further measure of the level of living on AFDC, information was obtained on the total wardrobe of the oldest school child in each family. As with the food data, the information obtained was voluminous and enlightening, but difficult to summarize and liable to misinterpretation. However, some startling facts emerged regarding what is one of the most critical problems in AFDC life, clothing for school children.

Only about half of the clothing is purchased, a good deal of it was bought before the supplement cut of September 1962, and a good deal of this purchased clothing is used. For the other half of their clothing the children depend on gifts, from relatives and neighbors, and from school teachers. About eight out of ten boys have but one pair of shoes; about half the girls have only one pair of shoes, and half have two pairs. About half the children have no rubbers or boots of any kind, and about three-fourths have no raincoats of any description. There is obviously no room in a state ceiling grant for clothing.

584

Although the grants hardly allow for it, the mothers are forced from time to time to spend money on things other than rent, utilities, and food. For the month prior to the interview they reported the following other expenditures—which, of course, are estimates from memory.

Sixty-nine had some expense for transportation, ranging in amount from under a dollar to $45 for a trip South to resettle a burned-out mother. Thirty spent one or two dollars, nineteen more spent three or four dollars. One woman said it cost $20 in carfare to make trips to the clinic for an asthmatic son. Twenty-four families apparently rode not at all.

A good deal of medical expense is reflected in the transportation figure, since the free clinic is their only medical provision. Many find Receiving Hospital care unsatisfactory because of long waits and responsibility for young children; thus we find thirty-one who had expenses for doctors, dentists, or medicines during the month. In twenty-four of these cases the amounts expended were less than $7, but one woman reported $48.68 for doctor and $4.25 for medicine, while another "pays what she can" on a $300 bill for braces for her son's teeth.

Eight families reported insurance premium payments of from $3 to $15 in the preceding month, and undoubtedly many more neglected to report such expenditures. Only ten families reported any expenditure for recreation, although all were specifically asked about this. Nine reported church expenses, from $1 to $6; nine had school expenses, from $1 to $10; eleven paid telephone bills; one paid $7.50 for house screens; one $2 for a horn mouthpiece for a child; one $3.09 for brooms and a mop; several had bought newspapers; one girl lost $10 from the sale of Girl Scout cookies and the mother had to make it good.

LIFE IN OUR "AFFLUENT SOCIETY"

The significance of these other expenditures is twofold. First, that they should exist at all, since there is usually no allowance at all for them in the grim budgets of these families; and second, even more important, that they should be so few and so small considering that we live in a money economy. What does it mean that families should spend nothing at all for transportation for a whole month in a city like Detroit? That most should spend nothing at all for recreation in families averaging over three children apiece? That with hundreds of school kids represented, only nine families reported expenses for school supplies?

585

As a refined measure of the economic situation of these families, they were asked the combined value of cash and food stamps on hand, and how many days until the next check came. AFDC checks are now issued twice monthly, rather than once as formerly, to help families spread their income over the entire month, although this interferes with rent payment and purchase of food stamps. The essence of the financial situation of these people is contained in the fact that thirty-one families had between nothing and $4 on hand to last from three to fourteen days. Asked if they ever ran out of money, they all answered yes.

When asked what they did about running out of money, two-thirds said they borrowed, either from relatives and friends or storekeepers, and one-third said they just "stayed run out." "Stay run out" is the theme of their lives—and for those who borrow too, because the loan must be paid back, and each month they sink a little deeper. Besides borrowing and staying run out, some found other ways to cope with the continuing crisis: One "lets the bills go." (Where does this end?) One cashes in bottles and borrows food. One cried in shame: "The lady downstairs gives us food." One said, "If the children get sick, I call the police to take them to Receiving Hospital."

One has been "borrowing" secretly from the funds of a Ladies' Club of which she is treasurer. The club is her one meaningful adult social contact. There is soon to be an election for new club officers and she will be exposed. Her children ask: "Mama, why are you always so sad?" Half crazy with worry, she feels sick; at Receiving Hospital they have referred her to the psychiatrist.

One was in despair because a retarded son who delights in his monthly visit home from the County Training School was coming tomorrow, and there was little food and no money or food stamps in the house. One said bitterly: "A woman could always get $10 if she had to. I prefer not to resort to this."

Consider our affluent society: in an economy generating wealth sufficient to supply every family of four with nearly $10,000 per year income, we reduce a family to cashing in pop bottles to get food, we push a woman to thoughts of prostitution to feed her children, we force an honest woman into theft and then provide her with $25 an hour psychiatric treatment.

IMPACT OF THE SUPPLEMENTATION CUT

As noted above, only about two-thirds of the ninety-three families received a supplement cut in September 1962. The families that had been cut were asked: Where did it hurt? What did you stop buying?

"No more clothes, fruit, milk. Clothes hurt most because mostly

for school boy. Borrowed clothes to go to church." "Got behind in utilities—over $100." "Had to cut out food stamps. Hurt because came at time when children needed school supplies and clothing." "Shoes. Children have hard to fit feet so can't buy cheap shoes. Special treats cut out. We used to go as a family for small treats on holidays, but no more." "School clothing. They are ashamed of their ragged clothing. No spending money in school. This makes my children want to quit." "Boy dropped out of Boy Scouts. No shows, no getting away from the house."

No clothing, no school supplies, no gym shoes, no church, no Boy Scouts, no movies, no little treats, no ice cream cones—nothing like this if you want to keep the roof overhead. But after a while you lose interest even in that, and you quit school, quit church, quit Boy Scouts, begin to steal, or perhaps take money from a boy friend. Every single family which has its supplement cut was seriously hurt by the income reduction—all gave stories like those above.

When the 6,000 AFDC cases were cut off supplemental relief in September 1962, it was expected at the welfare department that many would come to the department asking for reinstatement of supplementation. But few showed up. It was then suggested by some public assistance officials, "Maybe they are not so bad off as we thought. Maybe they don't really need it." As we have seen they are wrong.

But how many went, what happened, and why didn't the rest go? Actually thirty-one of the sixty-five mothers who had received a budget cut *did* go to the city welfare to ask for help. None got it. Why didn't the other thirty-four mothers go? Perhaps they were wiser in anticipating refusal; they decided to save the time, the carfare, and the effort. Of course, in refusing aid the intake workers are simply carrying out departmental policy. So often in the position of having to deny aid to people who in their heart they know need help, the workers tend to develop what one former worker calls "the culture of intake"—methods of denying aid without fully examining the circumstances of the family.

SOCIAL POVERTY

These people are not starving or out on the street. But in our world lack of buying power, even when it is not so absolute as to lead to starvation or death, leads to a very real social starvation and social death.

Well-off people easily forget that almost all social relationships depend on the ability to spend some money. To go to school costs money—for books, notebooks, pencils, gym shoes, and ice cream with the other kids. Without these the child begins to be an outcast. 587

To go to church costs money—for Sunday clothes, carfare to get there, and a little offering. Without these, one cannot go. To belong to the Boy Scouts costs money—for uniforms, occasional dues, shared costs of a picnic. Without these, no Scouts.

Poverty settles like an impenetrable prison cell over the lives of the very poor, shutting them off from every social contact, killing the spirit, and isolating them from the community of human life.

ELEVEN

DISSENT AND SOCIAL CONTROL

In an earlier section we dealt with the application of the new technology to the control of human behavior. Electronic wiretapping, computerized data banks, centralized wire service, concentrated ownership of the media, and the sophisticated application of the social and biological sciences provide a giant step toward the regulation of individual behavior. But these new technologies have not created the problem of social control. The coercive control of one group of people by another is a major theme of the human historical record.

The most abusive methods of control in modern history are identified with slavery and with the practices of the Nazis in Germany. The Nazi case is particularly illuminating because it took place in a "civilized" society like our own in many important respects. The very sadism of the atrocities inflicted by the Nazis helps us to isolate the case as something apart, something which could not conceivably happen here. The article by Hughes, written in 1948, provides a compelling analysis of the mutual interdependence of the relatively small number of human butchers who did the dirty work and the millions of disinterested bystanders who either condoned it as being the legal prerogative of the state or, even more frequently, refused either to be involved or to let themselves become aware of the distress of other people. The practice in the American media of presenting the daily "body count" or "kill ratio" in the Vietnam war suggests an immunity, in the general public, to the suffering of other people.

The case of Kitty Genovese who was assaulted three separate times while 38 persons turned on their lights to see but neither gave nor sought help, is frequently cited to demonstrate the unwillingness of Americans to get involved. And there are also some, including a small American Nazi party and the Minutemen armed against a communist plot (exactly as the Nazis in Germany first described their purpose), who can be counted upon, when the time is right, to do the dirty work.

589

The atmosphere conducive to a circumstance in which one group of people (in the American case those designated as communist or subversive) can become the scapegoats and victims of another has been greatly favored by the rapid growth of the radical right. Many a local community has found members of its school board, or particular teachers, or even particular books in its libraries fall victim to well-disciplined attempts of extremist organizations. Such groups seek to purge their country from what they sincerely believe to be the efforts of a conspiratorial movement. The extremist movement finds many adherents from stable middle-class families who feel alienated from meaningful participation in a mass society. A citizen of certain historically powerful empires might have substituted a nationalistic identification for his own failing sense of importance. Now one finds the substitution of national glory for personal pride made impossible by the revolutionary state of the world, the stalemate in nuclear weapons, and the gradual gain in authority or reputation of international agencies. Since 1955 the organizations of the extreme right have grown by an annual average of 22 percent. The budgets of the thirty largest of these organizations rose from close to 5 million dollars in 1958 to more than 14 million dollars in 1963. The vindictive message reaches its audiences through publications with a combined circulation of over one million and more than 7,000 radio broadcasts every week. Social scientists are not completely agreed upon the causes for this rapid expansion, but its growth is a fact.

The effects of a hostile super-patriot group upon the larger community are not always apparent. Certain individuals targeted for suspicion are ruined through techniques which were long associated with the name of Senator Joseph McCarthy. During the fifties, described by many as the McCarthy era, the issue of coercive control was particularly salient. This was the period of ascendance of the cold war.

Sociologists and other observers of the social setting were impressed by the general silence, apathy, and acquiscence of the American public at this time. It was the period of investigation and intimidation when Senator McCarthy and his counterparts discredited their opposition by using innuendo in charges made before the press and by hiring paid informants who produced what was wanted for money or out of fear of being subjected to abusive investigation themselves.

Certain procedures of the McCarthy era are strongly reminiscent of excesses during the Stalin era in the Soviet Union—many of which were substantially more extreme, more brutal and more direct. There is an important parallel to be drawn here between the conditions for military predominance and the condition for restriction in the rights of expression for individuals. Both military preparedness and witch-hunting are partly products of externally perceived threat. Ideologically sanctioned total warfare, whether hot or cold, helps to push both antagonists to measures which transgress the very values which the

590

society is said to be protecting. It is also clear from the Stalin example that totalitarian excesses may be reflections of left wing as well as right wing governments. In fact, as control techniques are improved it seems quite conceivable that a totalitarianism of the center, à la Huxley's *Brave New World,* could overcome the technologically advanced societies.

In America, in the fifties particularly, the effects upon those subjected to these procedures was enormous. One victim, a prominent millionaire named Edward Lamb, was subjected to intensive investigation in which he was faced by witnesses paid to perjure by attorneys for the Federal Communications Commission. It took Lamb, who was an attorney and businessman, three and one-half years of court fighting and $900,000 to clear his name and have the license for his radio and television stations renewed (Lamb, 1963). Hundreds of government workers, college professors and entertainers were ruined because they lacked such resources. But the major effects were caused by the larger number of silent people who just did not find the time or were a little frightened or didn't think anything good would come of being involved. It is this period of silence which prevented active critical discussion of the revolutionary forces of technological militarism, cybernation, race, and poverty which have shaped the present period.

During the late fifties, an important Supreme Court decision was made by a 5–4 vote against a defendent who had refused to answer before the House Committee on Unamerican Activities. Justice Black's dissent to the majority ruling provides an interesting documentation of the conditions under which the limits of free criticism are reduced.

The House Committee on Unamerican Activities as an agency of the federal government is granted great discretionary power and substantial fiscal support in the conduct of its investigations. So, too, is the authority of state and local government a strong adversary against even the most enterprising of dissenters. The state of Arkansas managed to "lynch" its most independent and critical newspaper through an intricate series of legal and financial maneuvers. The local sheriff and police and some of the more politically motivated court officials have great power to determine what persons and what action shall be impeded, which shall be punished severely, and which shall go unnoticed.

Martin Luther King once took the opportunity of his detention by local authorities in a Birmingham jail to answer some of his clerical colleagues who were critical of the methods he employed of sit-ins, marches, and boycotts. King's eloquent reply expressed the reasons why strong dissent is the lifeblood of social change. His view is that the stimulation of tension was a demonstrated necessity before the segregationist South would even open a dialogue. He points also to the crucial aspect of non-violent techniques in those instances where the practices do constitute violation of a law. The practitioner of this form of civil disobedience openly violates the unconscionable law and will- 591 ingly accepts the penalty. Such practice avoids the trap of the German citizens who carried out the Nazis' orders because they were legal.

King's response to the question of whether he has allowed due time for progress is particularly relevant to the functions of dissent. Time itself is neutral, King notes, and progress is not inevitable. Progress comes about through the tireless efforts of men. In the face of gross injustice the silence of good people proves as appalling as the hateful actions of the evil-doers.

Wherever the demand for change occurs there tends to be a reciprocal set of forces put in motion to retain or revert to some earlier state of equilibrium; hence, a major tool in any movement, including the contemporary revolution in human rights, is the right to dissent. A major weapon in the hands of forces resisting this revolution is the power of control.

One of the mainstays of power is the ability of the holders to monopolize the symbols of legitimacy (e.g., royal birth, electoral process, executive or officer's status, etc.). Under such circumstances dissent from a loyal subject, a disenfranchised voter, a lower-echelon clerk or an enlisted man is severely diminished. Furthermore, power tends to become imbedded in certain patterns of communication and certain fiscal transactions which go on behind the closed doors of the Joint Chiefs of Staff or at the local Business Development Councils. Thus, many significant decisions are made outside of the clear view of those who would be most disturbed by the dealings transacted. For this reason, verbal dissent is frequently without a platform for confrontation of the particular part of the social system which it would like to change. Before workers could effectively confront their employers it was necessary for them to go through a harrowing period of organization which resulted in acquisition of their own bureaucratic power structure. From positions of equal power, big labor and big business now do engage in direct negotiations and dialogues.

There are numerous examples of attempts by the existing power to prevent organized action that challenges established power. The British attempt to curtail town meetings that protested taxation without representation, the hiring of the Black Legion by major American corporations to use sniping, poison gas, and the fanning of ethnic hatreds to prevent unionization, and even the objectives of the American Project Camelot (see section Ic) to identify and deter insurgent elements in Latin America are important examples. The modernday examples of "The Crucible," Arthur Miller's drama of the Salem witch hunt in which those labeled as heretics are effectively smothered, are both numerous and tragic. Most relevant to the modern American struggle for human rights, however, are the methods of direct action employed by the "heretics" comprising the amorphous civil rights groups to induce change. One case, the Montgomery bus boycott, is of particular importance historically because it marked a turning point in the 592 participation of southern Negroes in what had, till then, been a very cautious, "respectable" organization of middle-class Negroes and whites. The details of the case described in the article by Reddick are particularly helpful in illuminating the interplay between the persistence of dissent and the measures devised by the powers of the community to resist the challenge. The case is remarkable, in retrospect, when one considers the extremely modest demands of the group to hire Negro drivers in all-Negro routes, and to change the seating customs to do away with segregation only in the middle sections of the buses, but to leave the front and rear reserved for whites and Negroes respectively. That such modest demands could create so great a reaction reveals the depth of conviction of those who would resist change. Sometimes, as in the jailing of King in Montgomery, in the slaying of three Mississippi summer project workers, or in the use of bull whips and cattle prodding devices, the intense conviction resulted in such provocative recriminations that the protestors become more unified and more militant.

Humor and music have both been factors in maintaining the morale of the civil rights movement. Negro comedian Dick Gregory suggested that Negro bus drivers need not interfere with segregated seating patterns on the buses if they could only be provided with a 30-foot long steering column.

The protestors, of course, are equally prone to errors of judgment which set back their own course. Even the most sophisticated forms of resistance to the protestors, such as the hiring of Negro policemen, the establishment of Job Corps training centers and integrated housing projects, attempts by the mass media to associate parts of the movement with communist leanings—even these attempts have been serving to fan the militancy of the civil rights movement. As a group, however, they have become increasingly strong as the techniques to control them evolved from the bull whip to the most benevolent tokens of equality. The reasons for this relate back to the very isolation and concealment of American poverty. Segregation itself helped keep the poor congregated in separate communities. This helped to fortify the people against a complete internalization of such dominant American values as the mystique of the do-it-yourself Horatio Alger legend, or the respect for order even above justice. When the protestors see measures organized from without ostensibly for the benefit of the deprived, they appear suspicious and strangely ungrateful.

When well-intentioned programs are not well received, the following questions emerge. Why can't they overcome their distrust of the political system which has long been unrepresentative of their interests? Why don't they respond to the ads to stay in school, seek out the job training programs, appear more respectable to earn the tolerance of white neighbors? Increasingly, among the dissenters the mood is militant and alienated. In the slums and on the university campuses there 593 is evidence, among the protestors, of an unwillingness to accept a groove, even an apparently desirable groove in a society which is geared, at best half-heartedly, to the provisions of human needs. For most the alternatives are either to enter the social ladder at the bottommost rung and remain dependent upon others for providing such limited opportunities as may exist or to assume responsibility themselves for the future of their own communities. The psychological rewards of the more militant and separatist attempts appear to be greater. Picketing realtors who charge exorbitant rents for inferior housing, destroying stores which charge high interest rates, engaging in a political struggle, demanding effective control of the Head Start program may seem more relevant to the poor person than job training, whether in or out of the military, to become a card punch operator for an electronics firm whose extensive defense contracts use the same funds which might otherwise go to the support of needed community programs. The issue of protest is more than a matter of material gains. It has become a matter of the search for meaningful activity related to the nature of one's problems. The participation in decisions is less easily achieved in a mass bureaucratic society than the initiation of particular welfare programs. If the objective of participation sought by the greater revolution for human rights is achieved it will probably be through new and imaginative ways of permitting people to have a say in the operation of their communities. Such at least is the hope of certain social critics who would see in the protest movement a means for aiding not only the protestors or the poor but the society as a whole.

It is difficult to make predictions about the future of protest and control in the revolution in human rights in this country. Eventually the rights movement is likely to develop its own sources of bureaucratized power and to be assimilated as a pluralist power group in American society. Until such time its message seems likely to be more revolutionary than reformist, its demands more embarrassing to the centers of American power, and its potential for violence exacerbated by increases in unemployment and the return of young Negro soldiers to their homes in urban ghettos or rural shanty towns. There is always danger that, with the disenchantment from slow progress, a proneness for demagoguery will develop leaving the entire race issue even more volatile than the summer rioting of 1965 through 1967 would lead us to anticipate.

While the protest increases its pitch it seems also likely that greater efforts at suppression will be attempted and, not inconceivably, that the entire apparatus of police control designed for assisting counter-revolutionary governments abroad will be tried in this country. Tighter police control, stiffer jail sentences and more harassment of "black power" sympathizers would not be an unreasonable prediction. Barring the unwanted, but possible, onset of nuclear war, the military revolution and the cybernetic revolution could probably go on indefinitely, gradually accommodating human beings to the non-human technologies. Where the clash and the essential crack in American society seems most likely is in the area in which the military and cybernetic revolutions run counter to the demands being expressed in the human rights revolution.

Conflict is probably a healthy sign in societies, provided that its toll from violence is low and its capacity to find meaningful and satisfactory compromises for conflicting demands remains high. But the prospects for the accommodation of a highly automated warfare-oriented state to meet the challenges behind the extraordinary forms of dissent in this country do not seem good. If we are in fact entering a period of increased suppression then it will do to bear in mind Hughes' warning about good people whose moderate dehumanization and detachment make possible the dirty work of others.

REFERENCES AND ADDITIONAL READING

Betty Chmaj, "Paranoid Patriotism: The Radical Right and the South," *The Atlantic,* November, 1962, 91–98.

Ralph J. Gleason and Paul Krassner, "Obituaries on Lenny Bruce," *Ramparts,* October, 1966, 34–38.

Edward Lamb, *Trial by Battle: Case History of a Washington Witch Hunt,* Santa Barbara, California: Center for the Study of Democratic Institutions, 1963.

Gene Marine, "Nobody Knows My Name," *Ramparts,* June, 1967, 11–16.

Thelma McCormack, "Intellectuals and the Mass Media," *American Behavioral Scientist,* December, 1965–January, 1966.

Robert Reed, "How to Lynch a Newspaper," *The Atlantic,* November, 1964, 59–63.

Everett C. Hughes

Good People and Dirty Work

"... une secte est le *noyau* et le *levain* de toute foule. . . . Etudier
la foule c'est juger un drame d'après ce qu'on voit sur la scène;
étudier la secte c'est le juger d'après ce qu'on voit dans les coulisses."
Sighele, S. *Psyhcologie des sectes.* Paris, 1898. Pp. 62, 63, 65.[1]

The National Socialist Government of Germany, with the arm of its
fanatical inner sect, the S.S., commonly known as the Black Shirts or
Elite Guard, perpetrated and boasted of the most colossal and dramatic piece of social dirty work the world has even known. Perhaps
there are other claimants to the title, but they could not match this
one's combination of mass, speed and perverse pride in the deed.
Nearly all peoples have plenty of cruelty and death to account for.
How many Negro Americans have died by the hands of lynching
mobs? How many more from unnecessary disease and lack of food
or of knowledge of nutrition? How many Russians died to bring about
collectivization of land? And who is to blame if there be starving

Reprinted by permission of the author and publisher from *Social Problems,* Vol. 10, No. 1, Summer 1964, pp. 3–11. Everett C. Hughes is professor of sociology at Brandeis University.

[1]". . . a sect is the nucleus and the yeast of every crowd. . . . To study
a crowd is to judge by what one sees on the stage; to study the sect is to
judge by what one sees backstage." These are among the many passages
underlined by Robert E. Park in his copy, now in my possession, of
Sighele's classic work on political sects. There are a number of references
to this work in the Park and Burgess *Introduction to the Science of Sociology,* Chicago, 1921. In fact, there is more attention paid to fanatical
political and religious behavior in Park and Burgess than in any later
sociological work in this country. Sighele's discussion relates chiefly to the
anarchist movement of his time. There have been fanatical movements
since. The Secret Army Organization in Algeria is but the latest.

596

millions in some parts of the world while wheat molds in the fields of other parts?

I do not revive the case of the Nazi *Endloesung* (final solution) of the Jewish problem in order to condemn the Germans, or make them look worse than other peoples, but to recall to our attention dangers which lurk in our midst always. Most of what follows was written after my first postwar visit to Germany in 1948. The impressions were vivid. The facts have not diminished and disappeared with time, as did the stories of alleged German atrocities in Belgium in the first World War. The fuller the record, the worse it gets.[2]

Several millions of people were delivered to the concentration camps, operated under the leadership of Heinrich Himmler with the help of Adolf Eichmann. A few hundred thousand survived in some fashion. Still fewer came out sound of mind and body. A pair of examples, well attested, will show the extreme of perverse cruelty reached by the S.S. guards in charge of the camps. Prisoners were ordered to climb trees; guards whipped them to make them climb faster. Once they were out of reach, other prisoners, also urged by the whip, were put to shaking the trees. When the victims fell they were kicked to see whether they could rise to their feet. Those too badly injured to get up were shot to death, as useless for work. A not inconsiderable number of prisoners were drowned in pits full of human excrement. These examples are so horrible that your minds will run away from them. You will not, as when you read a slightly salacious novel, imagine the rest. I therefore thrust these examples upon you and insist that the people who thought them up could, and did, improvise others like them, and even worse, from day to day over several years. Many of the victims of the Camps gave up the ghost (this Biblical phrase is the most apt) from a combination of humiliation, starvation, fatigue and physical abuse. In due time, a policy of mass liquidation in the gas chamber was added to individual virtuosity in cruelty.

This program—for it was a program—of cruelty and murder was carried out in the name of racial superiority and racial purity. It was

[2]The best source easily available at that time was Eugen Kogon's *Der SS-Staat. Das System der Deutschen Konzentrationslager,* Berlin, 1946. Many of my data are from his book. Some years later H. G. Adler, after several years of research, wrote *Theresianstadt, 1941–1945. Das Antlitz einer Zwangsgemeinschaft* (Tuebingen, 1955), and still later published *Die Verheimlichte Wahrheit, Theresienstaedter Dokumente* (Tuebingen, 1958), a book of documents concerning that camp in which Czech and other Jews were concentrated, demoralized and destroyed. Kogon, a Catholic intellectual, and Adler, a Bohemian Jew, both wrote out of personal experience in the Concentration Camps. Both considered it their duty to present the phenomenon objectively to the public. None of their statements has ever been challenged.

directed mainly, although by no means exclusively, against Jews, Slavs and Gypsies. It was thorough. There are few Jews in the territories which were under the control of the Third German Reich—the two Germanies, Holland, Czechoslavakia, Poland, Austria, Hungary. Many Jewish Frenchmen were destroyed. There were concentration camps even in Tunisia and Algiers under the German occupation.

When, during my 1948 visit to Germany, I became more aware of the reactions of ordinary Germans to the horrors of the concentration camps, I found myself asking not the usual question, "How did racial hatred rise to such a high level?", but this one, "How could such dirty work be done among and, in a sense, *by* the millions of ordinary, civilized German people?" Along with this came related questions. How could these millions of ordinary people live in the midst of such cruelty and murder without a general uprising against it and against the people who did it? How, once freed from the regime that did it, could they be apparently so little concerned about it, so toughly silent about it, not only in talking with outsiders—which is easy to understand—but among themselves? How and where could there be found in a modern civilized country the several hundred thousand men and women capable of such work? How were these people so far released from the inhibitions of civilized life as to be able to imagine, let alone perform, the ferocious, obscene and perverse actions which they did imagine and perform? How could they be kept at such a height of fury through years of having to see daily at close range the human wrecks they made and being often literally spattered with the filth produced and accumulated by their own actions?

You will see that there are here two orders of questions. One set concerns the good people who did not themselves do this work. The other concerns those who did do it. But the two sets are not really separate; for the crucial question concerning the good people is their relation to the people who did the dirty work, with a related one which asks under what circumstances good people let the others get away with such actions.

An easy answer concerning the Germans is that they were not so good after all. We can attribute to them some special inborn or in-grained race consciousness, combined with a penchant for sadistic cruelty and unquestioning acceptance of whatever is done by those who happen to be in authority. Pushed to its extreme, this answer simply makes us, rather than the Germans, the superior race. It is the Nazi tune, put to words of our own.

Now there are deep and stubborn differences between peoples. Their history and culture may make the Germans especially susceptible to the doctrine of their own racial superiority and especially acquiescent to the actions of whoever is in power over them. These are matters deserving of the best study that can be given them. But 598 to say that these things could happen in Germany simply because Germans are different—from us—buttresses their own excuses and lets us off too easily from blame for what happened there and from the question whether it could happen here.

Certainly in their daily practice and expression before the Hitler regime, the Germans showed no more, if as much, hatred of other racial or cultural groups than we did and do. Residential segregation was not marked. Intermarriage was common, and the families of such marriages had an easier social existence than they generally have in America. The racially exclusive club, school and hotel were much less in evidence than here. And I well remember an evening in 1933 when a Montreal business man—a very nice man, too—said in our living room, "Why don't we admit that Hitler is doing to the Jews just what we ought to be doing?" That was not an uncommon sentiment, although it may be said in defense of the people who expressed it, that they probably did not know and would not have believed the full truth about the Nazi program of destroying Jews. The essential underlying sentiments on racial matters in Germany were not different in kind from those prevailing throughout the western, and especially the Anglo-Saxon, countries. But I do not wish to over-emphasize this point. I only want to close one easy way out of serious consideration of the problem of good people and dirty work, by demonstrating that the Germans were and are about as good and about as bad as the rest of us on this matter of racial sentiments and, let us add, their notions of decent human behaviour.

But what was the reaction of ordinary Germans to the persecution of the Jews and to the concentration camp mass torture and murder? A conversation between a German school-teacher, a German architect and myself gives the essentials in a vivid form. It was in the studio of the architect, and the occasion was a rather casual visit, in Frankfurt am Main in 1948.

> The architect: "I am ashamed for my people whenever I think of it. But we didn't know about it. We only learned about all that later. You must remember the pressure we were under; we had to join the party. We had to keep our mouths shut and do as we were told. It was a terrible pressure. Still, I am ashamed. But you see, we had lost our colonies, and our national honour was hurt. And these Nazis exploited that feeling. And the Jews, they *were* a problem. They came from the east. You should see them in Poland; the lowest class of people, full of lice, dirty and poor, running about in their Ghettos in filthy caftans. They came here, and got rich by unbelievable methods after the first war. They occupied all the good places. Why, they were in the proportion of ten to one in medicine and law and government posts!"

At this point the architect hesitated and looked confused. He   599 continued: "Where was I? It is the poor food. You see what misery we are in here, Herr Professor. It often happens that I forget what I was talking about. Where was I now? I have completely forgotten."

(His confusion was, I believe, not at all feigned. Many Germans said they suffered losses of memory such as this, and laid it to their lack of food.)

I said firmly: "You were talking about loss of national honour and how the Jews had got hold of everything."

The architect: "Oh, yes! That was it! Well, of course that was no way to settle the Jewish problem. But there *was* a problem and it had to be settled some way."

The school-teacher: "Of course, they have Palestine now."

I protested that Palestine would hardly hold them.

The architect: "The professor is right. Palestine can't hold all the Jews. And it was a terrible thing to murder people. But we didn't know it at the time. But I am glad I am alive now. It is an interesting time in men's history. You know, when the Americans came it was like a great release. I really want to see a new ideal in Germany. I like the freedom that lets me talk to you like this. But, unfortunately that is not the general opinion. Most of my friends really hang on to the old ideas. They can't see any hope, so they hang on to the old ideas."

This scrap of talk gives, I believe, the essential elements as well as the flavor of the German reaction. It checks well with formal studies which have been made, and it varies only in detail from other conversations which I myself recorded in 1948.

One of the most obvious points in it is unwillingness to think about the dirty work done. In this case—perhaps by chance, perhaps not— the good man suffered an actual lapse of memory in the middle of this statement. This seems a simple point. But the psychiatrists have shown that it is less simple than it looks. They have done a good deal of work on the complicated mechanisms by which the individual mind keeps unpleasant or intolerable knowledge from consciousness, and have shown how great may, in some cases, be the consequent loss of effectiveness of the personality. But we have taken collective unwillingness to know unpleasant facts more or less for granted. That people can and do keep a silence about things whose open discussion would threaten the group's conception of itself, and hence its solidarity, is common knowledge. It is a mechanism that operates in every family and in every group which has a sense of group reputation. To break such a silence is considered an attack against the group; a sort of treason, if it be a member of the group who breaks the silence. This common silence allows group fictions to grow up; such as, that grandpa was less a scoundrel and more romantic than he really was. And I think it demonstrable that it operates especially against any expression, except in ritual, of collective guilt. The remarkable thing 600 in present-day Germany is not that there is so little reference to something about which people do feel deeply guilty, but that it is talked about at all.

In order to understand this phenomenon we would have to find out who talks about the concentration camp atrocities, in what situations, in what mood, and with what stimulus. On these points I know only my own limited experiences. One of the most moving of these was my first post-war meeting with an elderly professor whom I had known before the Nazi time; he is an heroic soul who did not bow his head during the Nazi time and who keeps it erect now. His first words, spoken with tears in his eyes, were:

"How hard it is to believe that men will be as bad as they say they will. Hitler and his people said: 'Heads will roll,' but how many of us —even of his bitterest opponents—could really believe that they would do it."

This man could and did speak, in 1948, not only to the likes of me, but to his students, his colleagues and to the public which read his articles, in the most natural way about the Nazi atrocities whenever there was occasion to do it in the course of his tireless effort to reorganize and to bring new life into the German universities. He had neither the compulsion to speak, so that he might excuse and defend himelf, nor a conscious or unconscious need to keep silent. Such people were rare; how many there were in Germany I do not know.

Occasions of another kind in which the silence was broken were those where, in class, public lecture or in informal meetings with students, I myself had talked frankly of race relations in other parts of the world, including the lynchings which sometimes occur in my own country and the terrible cruelty visited upon natives in South Africa. This took off the lid of defensiveness, so that a few people would talk quite easily of what happened under the Nazi regime. More common were situations like that with the architect, where I threw in some remark about the atrocities in response to Germans' complaint that the world is abusing them. In such cases, there was usually an expression of shame, accompanied by a variety of excuses (including that of having been kept in ignorance), and followed by a quick turning away from the subject.

Somewhere in consideration of this problem of discussion versus silence we must ask what the good (that is, ordinary) people in Germany did know about these things. It is clear that the S.S. kept the more gory details of the concentration camps a close secret. Even high officials of the government, the army and the Nazi party itself were in some measure held in ignorance, although of course they kept the camps supplied with victims. The common people of Germany knew that the camps existed; most knew people who had disappeared into

601

them; some saw the victims, walking skeletons in rags, being transported in trucks or trains, or being herded on the road from station to camp or to work in fields or factories near the camps. Many knew people who had been released from concentration camps; such released persons kept their counsel on pain of death. But secrecy was cultivated and supported by fear and terror. In the absence of a determined and heroic will to know and publish the truth, and in the absence of all the instruments of opposition, the degree of knowledge was undoubtedly low, in spite of the fact that all knew that something both stupendous and horrible was going on; and in spite of the fact that Hitler's *Mein Kampf* and the utterances of his aides said that no fate was too horrible for the Jews and other wrong-headed or inferior people. This must make us ask under what conditions the will to know and to discuss is strong, determined and effective; this, like most of the important questions I have raised, I leave unanswered except as answers may be contained in the statement of the case.

But to return to our moderately good man, the architect. He insisted over and over again that he did not know, and we may suppose that he knew as much and as little as most Germans. But he also made it quite clear that he wanted something done to the Jews. I have similar statements from people of whom I knew that they had had close Jewish friends before the Nazi time. This raises the whole problem of the extent to which those pariahs who do the dirty work of society are really acting as agents for the rest of us. To talk of this question one must note that, in building up his case, the architect pushed the Jews firmly into an out-group: they were dirty, lousy and unscrupulous (an odd statement from a resident of Frankfurt, the home of old Jewish merchants and intellectual families long identified with those aspects of culture of which Germans are most proud). Having dissociated himself clearly from these people, and having declared them a problem, he apparently was willing to let someone else do to them the dirty work which he himself would not do, and for which he expressed shame. The case is perhaps analogous to our attitude toward those convicted of crime. From time to time, we get wind of cruelty practiced upon the prisoners in penitentiaries or jails; or, it may be, merely a report that they are ill-fed or that hygienic conditions are not good. Perhaps we do not wish that the prisoners should be cruelly treated or badly fed, but our reaction is probably tempered by a notion that they deserve something, because of some dissociation of them from the in-group of good people. If what they get is worse than what we like to think about, it is a little bit too bad. It is a point on which we are ambivalent. Campaigns for reform of prisons are often followed by counter-campaigns against a too high standard of living for prisoners and against having prisons run by softies. Now the people who run prisons are our agents. Just how far they do or could carry out our wishes is hard to say. The minor prison guard, in boastful justification of some of his more questionable practices, says, in effect: "If those reformers and those big shots upstairs had to live with these birds as I do, they would soon change their fool notions about running a prison." He is suggesting that the good people are either naive or hypocritical. Furthermore, he knows quite well that the wishes of his employers, the public, are by no means unmixed. They are quite as likely to put upon him for being too nice as for being too harsh. And if, as sometimes happens, he is a man disposed to cruelty, there may be some justice in his feeling that he is only doing what others would like to do, if they but dared; and what they would do, if they were in his place.

There are plenty of examples in our own world which I might have picked for comparison with the German attitude toward the concentration camps. For instance, a newspaper in Denver made a great scandal out of the allegation that our Japanese compatriots were too well fed in the camps where they were concentrated during the war. I might have mentioned some feature of the sorry history of the people of Japanese background in Canada. Or it might have been lynching, or some aspect of racial discrimination. But I purposely chose prisoners convicted of crime. For convicts are formally set aside for special handling. They constitute an out-group in all countries. This brings the issue clearly before us, since few people cherish the illusion that the problem of treating criminals can be settled by propaganda designed to prove that there aren't any criminals. Almost everyone agrees that something has to be done about them. The question concerns what is done, who does it, and the nature of the mandate given by the rest of us to those who do it. Perhaps we give them an unconscious mandate to go beyond anything we ourselves would care to do or even to acknowledge. I venture to suggest that the higher and more expert functionaries who act in our behalf represent something of a distillation of what we may consider our public wishes, while some of the others show a sort of concentrate of those impulses of which we are or wish to be less aware.

Now the choice of convicted prisoners brings up another crucial point in inter-group relations. All societies of any great size have in-groups and out-groups; in fact, one of the best ways of describing a society is to consider it a network of smaller and larger in-groups and out-groups. And an in-group is one only because there are out-groups. When I refer to *my* children I obviously imply that they are closer to me than other people's children and that I will make greater efforts to buy oranges and cod-liver oil for them than for others' children. In fact, it may mean that I will give them cod-liver oil if I have to choke them to get it down. We do our own dirty work on those closest to us. The very injunction that I love my neighbor as   603 myself starts with me; if I don't love myself and my nearest, the phrase has a very sour meaning.

Each of us is a center of a network of in and out-groups. Now the distinctions between *in* and *out* may be drawn in various ways, and nothing is more important for both the student of society and the educator than to discover how these lines are made and how they may be redrawn in more just and sensible ways. But to believe that we can do away with the distinction between *in* and *out*, *us* and *them* in social life is complete nonsense. On the positive side, we generally feel a greater obligation to in-groups; hence less obligation to out-groups; and in the case of such groups as convicted criminals, the out-group is definitely given over to the hands of our agents for punishment. That is the extreme case. But there are other out-groups toward which we may have aggressive feelings and dislike, although we give no formal mandate to anyone to deal with them on our behalf, and although we profess to believe that they should not suffer restrictions or disadvantages. The greater their social distance from us, the more we leave in the hands of others a sort of mandate by default to deal with them on our behalf. Whatever effort we put on reconstructing the lines which divide in and out-groups, there remains the eternal problem of our treatment, direct or delegated, of whatever groups are considered somewhat outside. And here it is that the whole matter of our professed and possible deeper unprofessed wishes comes up for consideration; and the related problem of what we know, can know and want to know about it. In Germany, the agents got out of hand and created such terror that it was best not to know. It is also clear that it was and is easier to the conscience of many Germans not to know. It is, finally, not unjust to say that the agents were at least working in the direction of the wishes of many people, although they may have gone beyond the wishes of most. The same questions can be asked about our own society, and with reference not only to prisoners but also to many other groups upon whom there is no legal or moral stigma. Again I have not the answers. I leave you to search for them.

In considering the question of dirty work we have eventually to think about the people who do it. In Germany, these were the members of the S.S. and of that inner group of the S.S. who operated the concentration camps. Many reports have been made on the social backgrounds and the personalities of these cruel fanatics. Those who have studied them say that a large proportion were "gescheiterte Existenzen," men or women with a history of failure, of poor adaptation to the demands of work and of the classes of society in which they had been bred. Germany between wars had large numbers of such people. Their adherence to a movement which proclaimed a doctrine of hatred was natural enough. The movement offered something 604 more. It created an inner group which was to be superior to all others, even Germans, in their emancipation from the usual bourgeois morality; people above and beyond the ordinary morality. I dwell on this, not as a doctrine, but as an organizational device. For, as Eugen Kogon, author of the most penetrating analysis of the S.S. and their camps, has said, the Nazis came to power by creating a state within a state; a body with its own counter-morality, and its own counter-law, its courts and its own execution of sentence upon those who did not live up to its orders and standards. Even as a movement, it had inner circles within inner circles; each sworn to secrecy as against the next outer one. The struggle between these inner circles continued after Hitler came to power; Himmler eventually won the day. His S.S. bcame a state within the Nazi state, just as the Nazi movement had become a state within the Weimar state. One is reminded of the oft quoted but neglected statement of Sighele: "At the center of a crowd look for the sect." He referred, of course, to the political sect; the fanatical inner group of a movement seeking power by revolutionary methods. Once the Nazis were in power, this inner sect, while becoming now the recognized agent of the state and, hence, of the masses of the people, could at the same time dissociate itself more completely from them in action, because of the very fact of having a mandate. It was now beyond all danger of interference and investigation. For it had the instruments of interference and investigation in its own hands. These are also the instruments of secrecy. So the S.S. could and did build up a powerful system in which they had the resources of the state and of the economy of Germany and the conquered countries from which to steal all that was needed to carry out their orgy of cruelty luxuriously as well as with impunity.

Now let us ask, concerning the dirty workers, questions similar to those concerning the good people. Is there a supply of candidates for such work in other societies? It would be easy to say that only Germany could produce such a crop. The question is answered by being put. The problem of people who have run aground (gescheiterte Existenzen) is one of the most serious in our modern societies. Any psychiatrist will, I believe, testify that we have a sufficient pool or fund of personalities warped toward perverse punishment and cruelty to do any amount of dirty work that the good people may be inclined to countenance. It would not take a very great turn of events to increase the number of such people, and to bring their discontents to the surface. This is not to suggest that every movement based on discontent with the present state of things will be led by such people. That is obviously untrue; and I emphasize the point lest my remarks give comfort to those who would damn all who express militant discontent. But I think study of militant social movements does show that these warped people seek a place in them. Specifically, they are 605 likely to become the plotting, secret police of the group. It is one of the problems of militant social movements to keep such people out. It is of course easier to do this if the spirit of the movement is positive, its conception of humanity high and inclusive, and its aims sound. This was not the case of the Nazi movement. As Kogon puts it: "The SS were but the arch-type of the Nazis in general."[3] But such people are sometimes attracted for want of something better, to movements whose aims are contrary to the spirit of cruelty and punishment. I would suggest that all of us look well at the leadership and entourage of movements to which we attach ourselves for signs of a negativistic, punishing attitude. For once such a spirit develops in a movement, punishment of the nearest and easiest victim is likely to become more attractive than striving for the essential goals. And, if the Nazi movement teaches us anything at all, it is that if any shadow of a mandate be given to such people, they will—having compromised us—make it larger and larger. The processes by which they do so are the development of the power and inward discipline of their own group, a progressive dissociation of themselves from the rules of human decency prevalent in their culture, and an ever-growing contempt for the welfare of the masses of people.

The power and inward discipline of the S.S. became such that those who once became members could get out only by death; by suicide, murder or mental breakdown. Orders from the central offices of the S.S. were couched in equivocal terms as a hedge against a possible day of judgment. When it became clear that such a day of judgment would come, the hedging and intrigue became greater; the urge to murder also became greater, because every prisoner became a potential witness.

Again we are dealing with a phenomenon common in all societies. Almost every group which has a specialized social function to perform is in some measure a secret society, with a body of rules developed and enforced by the members and with some power to save its members from outside punishment. And here is one of the paradoxes of social order. A society without smaller, rule-making and disciplining powers would be no society at all. There would be nothing but law and police; and this is what the Nazis strove for, at the expense of family, church, professional groups, parties and other such nuclei of spontaneous control. But apparently the only way to do this, for good as well as for evil ends, is to give power into the hands of some fanatical small group which will have a far greater power of self-discipline and a far greater immunity from outside control than the traditional groups. The problem is, then, not of trying to get rid of all the self-disciplining, protecting groups within society, but one of

[3]*Op. cit.* p. 316.

keeping them integrated with one another and as sensitive as can be to a public opinion which transcends them all. It is a matter of checks and balances, of what we might call the social and moral constitution of society.

Those who are especially devoted to efforts to eradicate from good people, as individuals, all those sentiments which seem to bring about the great and small dirty work of the world, may think that my remarks are something of an attack on their methods. They are right to this extent; that I am insisting that we give a share of our effort to the social mechanisms involved as well as to the individual and those of his sentiments which concern people of other kinds.

Hugo L. Black

FROM JUSTICE BLACK'S DISSENT
(WITH WARREN AND DOUGLAS)
IN THE BRADEN CASE

"In July 1958 the House Un-American Activities Committee announced its intention to conduct a series of hearings in Atlanta, Georgia. . . . Petitioner, a long-time opponent of the Committee, decided to go to Atlanta for the purpose of lending his support to those who were fighting against the hearings. . . . Within an hour of his registration (in an Atlanta hotel as representative of the Emergency Civil Liberties Committee), petitioner was served with a subpoena. . . . When he appeared in response to this subpoena, petitioner was told that he had been subpoenaed because the Committee was informed that 'you were sent to this area by the Communist Party for the purpose of developing a hostile sentiment to this Committee'. . . .

"In my view, the majority by its decision today (upholding this contempt conviction) places the stamp of constitutional approval upon a practice as clearly inconsistent with the Constitution . . . as any that has ever come before this Court. . . . This case involves nothing more nor less than an attempt by the Un-American Activities Committee to use the contempt power of the House of Representatives as a weapon against those who dare to criticize it. . . .

The Easiest of Accusations

"So far as appears from this record the only information the Committee had with regard to petitioner was the testimony of a paid in-

Reprinted by permission of the author from *United States Reports, Cases Adjudged by the Supreme Court*, V. 365, pp. 415–423. Hugo L. Black is a member of The Supreme Court of the United States.

formant at a previous Committee hearing. The only evidence to the effect that petitioner was in fact a member of the Communist Party that emerges from that testimony is a flat conclusory statement by the informant that it was so. . . . When this fact is considered in conjunction with the fact that petitioner was not accorded the opportunity to cross-examine the informant or the protection of the statute permitting inspection of statements given to the FBI by paid informants, it seems obvious to me that such testimony is almost totally worthless for the purpose of establishing probable cause. For all we know, the informant may have had no basis at all for her conclusion and, indeed, the possibility of prejury cannot, in view of its frequent occurrence in these sorts of cases, be entirely discounted. . . . In the atmosphere existing in this country today, the charge that someone is a Communist is so common that hardly anyone active in public life escapes it. Every member of this Court has, on one occasion or another, been so designated. . . . If the mere fact that someone has been called a Communist is to be permitted to satisfy a requirement of probable cause, I think it plain that such a requirement is without value.

"The other such 'protection' afforded to critics of the Un-American Activities Committee under these decisions is included in the majority's so-called balancing test. The truth of the matter is that the balancing test . . . means that the Committee may engage in *any* inquiry a majority of this Court happens to think could possibly be for a legitimate purpose. . . . And under the tests of legitimacy that are used in this area, any first year law school student worth his salt could construct a rationalization to justify almost any question put to any witness at any time.

"Thus, in my view, the conclusion is inescapable that the only real limitation upon the Committee's power to harass its opponents is the Committee's own self-restraint, a characteristic which probably has not been predominant in the Committee's work over the past few years. The result of all this is that from now on anyone who takes a public position contrary to that being urged by the Un-American Activities Committee should realize that he runs the risk of being subpoenaed to appear at a hearing in some far off place, of being questioned with regard to every minute detail of his past life, of being asked to repeat all the gossip he may have heard about any of his friends and acquaintances, of being accused by the Committee of membership in the Communist Party, of being held up to the public as a subversive and a traitor, of being jailed for contempt if he refuses to cooperate with the Committee in its probe of his mind and associations, and of being branded by his neighbors, employer and erstwhile friends as a menace to society *regardless of the outcome of that hearing.* With such a powerful weapon in its hands, it seems quite likely that the Committee will weather all criticism, even though justifiable, that may

609

be directed toward it. For there are not many people in our society who will have the courage to speak out against such a formidable opponent. If the present trend continues, this already small number will necessarily dwindle as their ranks are thinned by the jails. Government by consent will appear to be replaced by government by intimidation. . . .

"I believe that true Americanism is to be protected, not by committees that persecute unorthodox minorities but by strict adherence to basic principles of freedom that are responsible for this Nation's greatness. . . . The principles of the First Amendment are stated in precise and mandatory terms and unless they are applied in those terms, the freedoms of religion, speech, press, assembly and petition will have no effective protection. Where these freedoms are left to depend upon a balance to be struck by this Court in each particular case, liberty cannot survive. For under such a rule, there are no constitutional rights that cannot be 'balanced' away."

"The petitioner . . . has for some time been at odds with strong sentiment favoring racial segregation in his home State of Kentucky. A white man himself, the petitioner has nonetheless spoken out strongly. . . . This activity, which once before resulted in his being charged with a serious crime (sedition, after helping a Negro buy a home in a white area), seems also to have been the primary reason for his being called before the Un-American Activities Committee. For the occasion . . . appears to have been the circulation of two letters, both in the nature of petitions to Congress. . . .One . . . signed by petitioner and his wife, asked those who read it to urge their representatives to vote against proposed legislation which would have empowered the States to enact antisedition statutes because . . . those statutes could too readily be used against citizens working for integration. The other petition, bearing the signatures of 200 Southern Negroes, was sent directly to the House of Representatives and requested that body not to allow the Un-American Activities Committee to conduct hearings in the South because, so the petition charged, 'all of its activities in recent years suggests that it is much more interested in harassing and labeling as subversive any citizen who is inclined to be liberal or an independent thinker' . . . .

The Indivisibility of Liberty

"The majority here affirms petitioner's conviction (for contempt in refusing on First amendment grounds to answer questions about his personal beliefs and associations) 'upon the reasoning and authority' of *Barenblatt v. U.S.* . . . the majority might well have, with equal justification, relied upon a much earlier decision of this Court, that in *Beauharnais v. Illinois.* . . . Ironically, the need there asserted by the State of Illinois and accepted by a majority of this Court as sufficiently compelling to warrant abridgement of the right of petition was the 610

need to protect Negroes against what was subsequently labelled 'libel
. . . of a racial group'. . . . Thus the decision in *Beauharnais* had all
the outward appearance of one which would aid the underprivileged
Negro. This decision, however, is a dramatic illustration of the short-
sightedness of such an interpretation of that case. For the very constitutional philosophy that gave birth to *Beauharnais* today gives birth
to a decision which may well strip the Negro of the aid of many of
the white people who have been willing to speak up in his behalf. If
the Un-American Activities Committee is to have the power to interrogate everyone who is called Communist, there is one thing certain
beyond the per-adventure of a doubt—no legislative committee, state
or federal, will have trouble finding cause to subpoena all persons
anywhere who take a public stand for or against segregation. The
lesson to be learned from these two cases is, to my mind, clear.
Liberty to be secure for any, must be secure for all—even for the
most miserable merchants of hatred and unpopular ideas.

"Both *Barenblatt* and *Beauharnais* are offspring of a constitutional
doctrine that is steadily sacrificing individual freedom of religion,
speech, press, assembly and petition to government control. . . . For
the presently prevailing constitutional doctrine, which treats the First
Amendment as a mere admonition, leaves the liberty-giving freedoms
which were intended to be protected by that Amendment completely
at the mercy of Congress and this Court whenever a majority of this
Court concludes, on the basis of any of the several judicially created
'tests' now in vogue, that abridgement of these freedoms is more desirable than freedom itself. . . . The very foundations of a true
democracy and the foundation upon which this Nation was built is
the fact that government is responsive to the views of its citizens, and
no nation can continue to exist on such a foundation unless its citizens are wholly free to speak out fearlessly for or against their officials
and their laws. When it begins to send its dissenters, such as Barenblatt, Uphaus, Wilkinson, and now Braden, to jail, the liberties indispensable to its existence must be fast disappearing. . . . Those
freedoms are being destroyed by sophistry and dialectics. . . .

"The majority's approach makes the First Amendment, not the rigid
protection of liberty its language imports, but a poor flexible imitation.
This weak substitute is, to my mind, totally unacceptable for I believe
that Amendment forbids, among other things, any agency of the federal
government—be it legislative, executive or judicial—to harass or punish
people for their beliefs, or for their speech about, or public criticism
of, laws and public officials. The Founders of this Nation were not
then willing to trust the definition of First Amendment freedoms to
Congress or this Court, nor am I now. History and the affairs of the
present world show that the Founders were right. There are grim
reminders all around this world that the distance between individual
liberty and firing squads is not always as far as it seems."

611

Martin Luther King, Jr.

Letter from Birmingham Jail

My Dear Fellow Clergymen:

While confined here in the Birmingham city jail I came across your recent statement calling my present activities "unwise and untimely." Seldom do I pause to answer criticism of my work and ideas. If I sought to answer all the criticisms that cross my desk, my secretaries would have little time for anything other than such correspondence in the course of the day, and I would have no time for constructive work. But since I feel that you are men of genuine good will and that your criticisms are sincerely set forth, I want to try to answer your statement in what I hope will be patient and reasonable terms.

I think I should indicate why I am here in Birmingham, since you have been influenced by the view which argues against "outsiders coming in." I have the honor of serving as president of the Southern Christian Leadership Conference, an organization operating in every southern state, with headquarters in Atlanta, Georgia. We have some 85 affiliate organizations across the south, and one of them is the Alabama Christian Movement for Human Rights. Frequently we share staff, educational and financial resources with our affiliates. Several months ago the affiliate here in Birmingham asked us to be on call to engage in a nonviolent direct action program if such were deemed necessary. We readily consented, and when the hour came we lived up to our promise. So I, along with several members of my staff, am here because I was invited here. I am here because I have organizational ties here.

Copyright 1963, Christian Century Foundation. Reprinted by permission of the author and publisher from the June 12, 1963 issue of *The Christian Century*. Martin Luther King, noted civil rights leader, is director of the Southern Christian Leadership Conference.

But more basically, I am in Birmingham because injustice exists here. Just as the prophets of the eighth century B.C. left their villages and carried their "thus saith the Lord" far afield and just as the Apostle Paul left his village of Tarsus and carried the gospel of Jesus Christ to the far corners of the Greco-Roman world, so am I compelled to carry the gospel of freedom beyond my own home town. Like Paul, I must constantly respond to the Macedonian call for aid.

Moreover, I am cognizant of the interrelatedness of all communities and states. I cannot sit idly by in Atlanta and not be concerned about what happens in Birmingham. Injustice anywhere is a threat to justice everywhere. We are caught in an inescapable network of mutuality, tied in a single garment of destiny. Whatever affects one directly affects all indirectly. Never again can we afford to live with the narrow, provincial "outside agitator" idea. Anyone who lives inside the United States can never be considered an outsider anywhere within its bounds.

You deplore the demonstrations taking place in Birmingham. But your statement, I am sorry to say, fails to express a similar concern for the conditions that brought about the demonstrations. I am sure that none of you would want to rest content with the superficial kind of social analysis that deals merely with effects and does not grapple with underlying causes. It is unfortunate that demonstrations are taking place in Birmingham, but it is even more unfortunate that the city's white power structure left the Negro community with no alternative.

In any nonviolent campaign there are four basic steps: collection of the facts to determine whether injustices exist, negotiation, self-purification and direct action. We have gone through all these steps in Birmingham. There can be no gainsaying the fact that racial injustice engulfs this community. Birmingham is probably the most thoroughly segregated city in the United States. Its ugly record of police brutality is widely known. Its unjust treatment of Negroes in the courts is a notorious reality. There have been more unsolved bombings of Negro homes and churches in Birmingham than in any other city in the nation. These are the hard, brutal facts of the case. On the basis of these conditions Negro leaders sought to negotiate with the city fathers. But the latter consistently refused to engage in good-faith negotiation.

Then last September came the opportunity to talk with leaders of Birmingham's economic community. In the course of the negotiations certain promises were made by the merchants—for example, the promise to remove the stores' humiliating racial signs. On the basis of these promises the Rev. Fred Shuttlesworth and the leaders of the Alabama Christian Movement for Human Rights agreed to a moratorium on all demonstrations. As the weeks and months went by we realized that we were the victims of a broken promise. The signs remained.

As in so many past experiences, our hopes had been blasted and our disappointment was keenly felt. We had no alternative except to prepare for direct action, whereby we would present our very bodies as a means of laying our case before the conscience of the local and the national community. Mindful of the difficulties involved, we decided to undertake a process of self-purification. We began a series of workshops on nonviolence, and we repeatedly asked ourselves: "Are you able to accept blows without retaliating?" "Are you able to endure the ordeal of jail?" We decided to schedule our direct action program for the Easter season, realizing that except for Christmas this is the main shopping period of the year. Knowing that a strong economic withdrawal program would be the by-product of direct action, we felt that this would be the best time to bring pressure to bear on the merchants.

But Birmingham's mayoral election was coming up in March, and when we discovered that Commissioner of Public Safety Eugene "Bull" Connor was to be in the run-off, we decided to postpone our demonstrations until the day after the run-off so that they could not be used to cloud the issues. It is evident, then, that we did not move irresponsibly into direct action. Like many others, we wanted to see Mr. Connor defeated, and to this end we endured postponement after postponement. Having aided in this community need, we felt that our direct action program could be delayed no longer.

III

You may well ask, "Why direct action? Why sit-ins, marches, etc.? Isn't negotiation a better path?" You are quite right in calling for negotiation. Indeed, this is the very purpose of direct action. Nonviolent direct action seeks to foster such a tension that a community which has constantly refused to negotiate is forced to confront the issue. It seeks so to dramatize the issue that it can no longer be ignored. My citing the creation of tension as part of the work of the nonviolent resister may sound rather shocking. But I readily acknowledge that I am not afraid of the word "tension." I have earnestly opposed violent tension, but there is a type of constructive, nonviolent tension which is necessary for growth. Just as Socrates felt that it was necessary to create a tension in the mind so that individuals could shake off the bondage of myths and half-truths and rise to the realm of creative analysis and objective appraisal, so must we see the need 614 for nonviolent gadflies to create the kind of tension in society that will help men rise from the dark depths of prejudice and racism to the majestic heights of understanding and brotherhood.

The purpose of our direct action program is to create a situation so crisis-packed that it will inevitably open the door to negotiation. I therefore concur with you in your call for negotiation. Too long has our beloved southland been bogged down in a tragic effort to live in monologue rather than dialogue.

One of the basic points in your statement is that the action that I and my associates have taken in Birmingham is untimely. Some have asked, "Why didn't you give the new city administration time to act?" The only answer that I can give to this query is that the new Birmingham administration must be prodded about as much as the outgoing one before it will act. We are sadly mistaken if we feel that the election of Albert Boutwell as mayor will bring the millennium to Birmingham. While Mr. Boutwell is a much more gentle person than Mr. Connor, they are both segregationists, dedicated to maintenance of the status quo. I have hope that Mr. Boutwell will be reasonable enough to see the futility of massive resistance to desegregation. But he will not see this without pressure from devotees of civil rights. My friends, I must say to you that we have not made a single gain in civil rights without determined legal and nonviolent pressure. Lamentably, it is a historical fact that privileged groups seldom give up their privileges voluntarily. Individuals may see the moral light and voluntarily give up their unjust posture; but, as Reinhold Niebuhr has reminded us, groups tend to be more immoral than individuals.

We know through painful experience that freedom is never voluntarily given by the oppressor; it must be demanded by the oppressed. Frankly, I have yet to engage in a direct action campaign that was "well timed" in the view of those who have not suffered unduly from the disease of segregation. For years now I have heard the word "Wait!" It rings in the ear of every Negro with piercing familiarity. This "Wait" has almost always meant "Never." As one of our distinguished jurists once said, "Justice too long delayed is justice denied."

IV

We have waited for more than 340 years for our constitutional and God-given rights. The nations of Asia and Africa are moving with jet-like speed toward gaining political independence, but we still creep at horse-and-buggy pace toward gaining a cup of coffee at a lunch counter. Perhaps it is easy for those who have never felt the stinging darts of segregation to say "Wait." But when you have seen vicious mobs lynch your mothers and fathers at will and drown your sisters and brothers at whim; when you have seen hate-filled policemen curse, kick and even kill your black brothers and sisters with im- 615 punity; when you see the vast majority of your 20 million Negro brothers smothering in an air-tight cage of poverty in the midst of an affluent society; when you suddenly find your tongue twisted as you seek to explain to your six-year-old daughter why she can't go to the public amusement park that has just been advertised on television, and see tears welling up when she is told that Funtown is closed to colored children, and see ominous clouds of inferiority beginning to form in her little mental sky, and see her beginning to distort her personality by unconsciously developing a bitterness toward white people; when you have to concoct an answer for a five-year-old son asking, "Daddy, why do white people treat colored people so mean?"; when you take a cross-country drive and find it necessary to sleep night after night in the uncomfortable corners of your automobile because no motel will accept you; when you are humiliated day in and day out by nagging signs reading "white" and "colored"; when your first name becomes "nigger," your middle name becomes "boy" (however old you are) and your last name becomes "John," and your wife and mother are never given the respected title "Mrs."; when you are harried by day and haunted by night by the fact that you are a Negro, never quite knowing what to expect next, and are plagued with inner fears and outer resentments; when you are forever fighting a degenerating sense of "nobodiness"—then you will understand why we find it difficult to wait. There comes a time when the cup of endurance runs over, and men are no longer willing to be plunged into an abyss of injustice where they experience the bleakness of corroding despair. I hope, sirs, you can understand our legitimate and unavoidable impatience.

V

You express a great deal of anxiety over our willingness to break laws. This is certainly a legitimate concern. Since we so diligently urge people to obey the Supreme Court's decision of 1954 outlawing segregation in the public schools, at first glance it may seem rather paradoxical for us consciously to break laws. One may well ask, "How can you advocate breaking some laws and obeying others?" The answer lies in the fact that there are two types of laws: just and unjust. I agree with St. Augustine that "an unjust law is no law at all."

Now what is the difference between the two? How does one determine whether a law is just or unjust? A just law is a man-made code that squares with the moral law or the law of God. An unjust law is a code that is out of harmony with the moral law. To put it in the terms of St. Thomas Aquinas, an unjust law is a human law that is not rooted in eternal law and natural law. Any law that uplifts human personality is just. Any law that degrades human personality is unjust. All segregation statutes are unjust because segregation distorts the 616 soul and damages the personality. It gives the segregator a false sense of superiority and the segregated a false sense of inferiority. Segregation, to use the terminology of the Jewish philosopher Martin Buber, substitutes an "I-it" relationship for an "I-thou" relationship and ends up relegating persons to the status of things. Hence segregation is not only politically, economically and sociologically unsound, it is sinful. Paul Tillich has said that sin is separation. Is not segregation an existential expression of man's tragic separation, his awful estrangement, his terrible sinfulness? Thus it is that I can urge men to disobey segregation ordinances, for such ordinances are morally wrong.

Let us consider some of the ways in which a law can be unjust. A law is unjust, for example, if the majority group compels a minority group to obey the statute but does not make it binding on itself. By the same token a law in all probability is just if the majority is itself willing to obey it. Also, a law is unjust if it is inflicted on a minority that, as a result of being denied the right to vote, had no part in enacting or devising the law. Who can say that the legislature of Alabama which set up that state's segregation laws was democratically elected? Throughout Alabama all sorts of devious methods are used to prevent Negroes from becoming registered voters, and there are some counties in which, even though Negroes constitute a majority of the population, not a single Negro is registered. Can any law enacted under such circumstances be considered democratically structured?

Sometimes a law is just on its face and unjust in its application. For instance, I have been arrested on a charge of parading without a permit. Now there is nothing wrong in having an ordinance which requires a permit for a parade. But such an ordinance becomes unjust when it is used to maintain segregation and to deny citizens the First-amendment privilege of peaceful assembly and protest.

I hope you are able to see the distinction I am trying to point out. In no sense do I advocate evading the law, as would the rabid segregationist. That would lead to anarchy. One who breaks an unjust law must do so *openly, lovingly,* and with a willingness to accept the penalty. I submit that an individual who breaks a law that conscience tells him is unjust and who willingly accepts the penalty of imprisonment in order to arouse the conscience of the community over its injustice is in reality expressing the highest respect for law.

Of course, there is nothing new about this kind of civil disobedience. It was evidenced sublimely in the refusal of Shadrach, Meshach and Abednego to obey the laws of Nebuchadnezzar, on the ground that a higher moral law was at stake. It was practiced superbly by the early Christians who were willing to face hungry lions rather than submit to certain unjust laws of the Roman empire. To a degree, academic freedom is a reality today because Socrates practiced civil disobedience. We should never forget that everything Adolf Hitler did in Germany was "legal" and everything the Hungarian freedom

617

fighters did in Hungary was "illegal." It was "illegal" to aid and comfort a Jew in Hitler's Germany. Even so, I am sure that had I lived in Germany at the time I would have aided and comforted my Jewish brothers. If today I lived in a communist country where certain principles dear to the Christian faith are suppressed, I would openly advocate disobeying that country's antireligious laws.

VI

I must make two honest confessions to you, my Christian and Jewish brothers. First, I must confess that over the past few years I have been gravely disappointed with the white moderate. I have almost reached the regrettable conclusion that the Negro's great stumbling block in his stride toward freedom is not the White Citizen's Counciler or the Ku Klux Klanner but the white moderate who is more devoted to "order" than to justice; who prefers a negative peace which is the absence of tension to a positive peace which is the presence of justice; who constantly says "I agree with you in the goal you seek, but I cannot agree with your methods"; who paternalistically believes he can set the timetable for another man's freedom; who lives by a mythical concept of time and who constantly advises the Negro to wait for a "more convenient season." Shallow understanding from people of good will is more frustrating than absolute misunderstanding from people of ill will. Lukewarm acceptance is much more bewildering than outright rejection.

I had hoped that the white moderate would understand that law and order exist for the purpose of establishing justice and that when they fail in this purpose they block social progress. I had hoped that the white moderate would understand that the present tension in the south is a necessary phase of the transition from an obnoxious negative peace, in which the Negro passively accepted his unjust plight, to a substantive and positive peace, in which all men will respect the dignity and worth of human personality. Actually, we who engage in nonviolent direct action are not the creators of tension. We merely bring to the surface the hidden tension that is already alive. We bring it out in the open where it can be seen and dealt with. Like a boil that can never be cured so long as it is covered up but must be opened with all its pus-flowing ugliness to the natural medicines of air and light, injustice must be exposed, with all the tension its exposure creates, to the light of human conscience and the air of national opinion before it can be cured.

In your statement you assert that our actions, even though peaceful, must be condemned because they precipitate violence. But is this a logical assertion? Isn't this like condemning a robbed man because his possession of money precipitated an act of robbery? Isn't this like 618 condemning Socrates because his unswerving commitment to truth and his philosophical inquiries precipitated the act by the misguided populace in which they made him drink hemlock? Isn't this like condemning Jesus because his unique God-consciousness and never-ceasing devotion to God's will precipitated the evil act of crucifixion? We must come to see that, as the federal courts have consistently affirmed, it is wrong to urge an individual to cease his efforts to gain his basic constitutional rights because the quest may precipitate violence. Society must protect the robbed and punish the robber.

I had also hoped that the white moderate would reject the myth concerning time in relation to the struggle for freedom. I have just received a letter from a white brother in Texas. He writes: "All Christians know that the colored people will receive equal rights eventually, but it is possible that you are in too great a religious hurry. It has taken Christianity almost 2,000 years to accomplish what it has. The teachings of Christ take time to come to earth." Such an attitude stems from a tragic misconception of time, from the strangely irrational notion that there is something in the very flow of time that will inevitably cure all ills. Actually, time itself is neutral; it can be used either destructively or constructively. More and more I feel that the people of ill will have used time much more effectively than have the people of good will. We will have to repent in this generation not merely for the hateful words and actions of the bad people but for the appalling silence of the good people. Human progress never rolls in on wheels of inevitability; it comes through the tireless efforts of men willing to be co-workers with God, and without this hard work time itself becomes an ally of the forces of social stagnation. We must use time creatively, in the knowledge that the time is always ripe to do right. Now is the time to make real the promise of democracy and transform our pending national elegy into a creative psalm of brotherhood. Now is the time to lift our national policy from the quicksand of racial injustice to the solid rock of human dignity.

VII

You speak of our activity in Birmingham as extreme. At first I was rather disappointed that fellow clergymen would see my nonviolent efforts as those of an extremist. I began thinking about the fact that I stand in the middle of two opposing forces in the Negro community. One is a force of complacency made up of Negroes who, as a result of long years of oppression, are so completely drained of self-respect and a sense of "somebodiness" that they have adjusted to segregation, and of a few middle class Negroes who, because of a degree of academic and economic security and because in some ways they profit

619

by segregation, have unconsciously become insensitive to the problems of the masses. The other force is one of bitterness and hatred, and it comes perilously close to advocating violence. It is expressed in the various black nationalist groups that are springing up across the nation, the largest and best-known being Elijah Muhammad's Muslim movement. Nourished by the Negro's frustration over the continued existence of racial discrimination, this movement is made up of people who have lost faith in America, who have absolutely repudiated Christianity, and who have concluded that the white man is an incorrigible "devil."

I have tried to stand between these two forces, saying that we need emulate neither the "do-nothingism" of the complacent nor the hatred of the black nationalist. For there is the more excellent way of love and nonviolent protest. I am grateful to God that, through the influence of the Negro church, the way of nonviolence became an integral part of our struggle.

If this philosophy had not emerged, by now many streets of the south would, I am convinced, be flowing with blood. And I am further convinced that if our white brothers dismiss as "rabble-rousers" and "outside agitators" those of us who employ nonviolent direct action and if they refuse to support our nonviolent efforts, millions of Negroes will, out of frustration and despair, seek solace and security in black nationalist ideologies—a development that would inevitably lead to a frightening racial nightmare.

VIII

Oppressed people cannot remain oppressed forever. The yearning for freedom eventually manifests itself, and that is what has happened to the American Negro. Something within has reminded him of his birthright of freedom, and something without has reminded him that it can be gained. Consciously or unconsciously, he has been caught up by the *Zeitgeist,* and with his black brothers of Africa and his brown and yellow brothers of Asia, South America and the Caribbean, the U.S. Negro is moving with a sense of great urgency toward the promised land of racial justice. If one recognizes this vital urge that has engulfed the Negro community, he should readily understand why public demonstrations are taking place. The Negro has many pent-up resentments and latent frustrations, and he must release them. So let him march; let him make prayer pilgrimages to the city hall; let him go on freedom rides—and try to understand why he must do so. If his repressed emotions are not released in nonviolent ways, they will seek expression through violence; this is not a threat but a fact of history. I have not said to my people, "Get rid of your discontent." Rather, I have tried to say that this normal and healthy discontent can be

620

channeled into the creative outlet of nonviolent direct action. And now this approach is being termed extremist.

But though I was initially disappointed as being categorized as an extremist, as I continued to think about the matter I gradually gained a measure of satisfaction from the label. Was not Jesus an extremist for love: "Love your enemies, bless them that curse you, do good to them that hate you, and pray for them which despitefully use you, and persecute you." Was not Amos an extremist for justice: "Let justice roll down like waters and righteousness like an everflowing stream." Was not Paul an extremist for the Christian gospel: "I bear in my body the marks of the Lord Jesus." Was not Martin Luther an extremist: "Here I stand; I can do no other so help me God." And John Bunyan: "I will stay in jail to the end of my days before I make a butchery of my conscience." And Abraham Lincoln: "This nation cannot survive half slave and half free." And Thomas Jefferson: "We hold these truths to be self-evident, that all men are created equal. . . ." So the question is not whether we will be extremists but what kind of extremists we will be. Will we be extremists for hate or for love? Will we be extremists for the preservation of injustice or for the extension of justice? Perhaps the south, the nation and the world are in dire need of creative extremists.

I had hoped that the white moderate would see this need. Perhaps I was too optimistic; perhaps I expected too much. I suppose I should have realized that few members of the oppressor race can understand the deep groans and passionate yearnings of the oppressed race, and still fewer have the vision to see that injustice must be rooted out by strong, persistent and determined action. I am thankful, however, that some of our white brothers have grasped the meaning of this social revolution and committed themselves to it. They are still all too few in quantity, but they are big in quality. Some—such as Ralph McGill, Lillian Smith, Harry Golden and James McBride Dabbs—have written about our struggle in eloquent and prophetic terms. Others have marched with us down nameless streets of the south. They have languished in filthy, roach-infested jails, suffering the abuse and brutality of policemen who view them as "dirty nigger lovers." Unlike so many of their moderate brothers and sisters, they have recognized the urgency of the moment and sensed the need for powerful "action" antidotes to combat the disease of segregation.

IX

Let me take note of my other major disappointment. Though there are some notable exceptions, I have also been disappointed with the white church and its leadership. I do not say this as one of those negative critics who can always find something wrong with the church. I say this as a minister of the gospel, who loves the church; who was nurtured in its bosom; who has been sustained by its spiritual blessings and who will remain true to it as long as the cord of life shall lengthen.

When I was suddenly catapulted into the leadership of the bus protest in Montgomery, Alabama, a few years ago I felt we would be supported by the white church. I felt that the white ministers, priests and rabbis of the south would be among our strongest allies. Instead, some have been outright opponents, refusing to understand the freedom movement and misrepresenting its leaders; all too many others have been more cautious than courageous and have remained silent and secure behind stained-glass windows.

In spite of my shattered dreams I came to Birmingham with the hope that the white religious leadership of this community would see the justice of our cause and with deep moral concern would serve as the channel through which our just grievances could reach the power structure. But again I have been disappointed.

I have heard numerous southern religious leaders admonish their worshipers to comply with a desegregation decision because it is the *law*, but I have longed to hear white ministers declare, "Follow this decree because integration is morally *right* and because the Negro is your brother." In the midst of blatant injustices inflicted upon the Negro I have watched white churchmen stand on the sideline and mouth pious irrelevancies and sanctimonious trivialities. In the midst of a mighty struggle to rid our nation of racial and economic injustice I have heard many ministers say, "Those are social issues with which the gospel has no real concern," and I have watched many churches commit themselves to a completely otherworldly religion which makes a strange, unbiblical distinction between body and soul, between the sacred and the secular.

We are moving toward the close of the 20th century with a religious community largely adjusted to the status quo—a taillight behind other community agencies rather than a headlight leading men to higher levels of justice.

X

I have traveled the length and breadth of Alabama, Mississippi and all the other southern states. On sweltering summer days and crisp autumn mornings I have looked at the south's beautiful churches with their lofty spires pointing heavenward, and at her impressive religious education buildings. Over and over I have found myself asking: "What kind of people worship here? Who is their God? Where were their voices when the lips of Governor Barnett dripped with words of interposition and nullification? Where were they when Governor Wallace gave a clarion call for defiance and hatred? Where were their voices of support when bruised and weary Negro men and women decided to rise from the dark dungeons of complacency to the bright hills of creative protest?"

Yes, these questions are still in my mind. In deep disappointment I have wept over the laxity of the church. But be assured that my tears have been tears of love. There can be no deep disappointment where there is not deep love. Yes, I love the church. How could I do otherwise? I am in the rather unique position of being the son, the grandson and the great-grandson of preachers. Yes, I see the church as the body of Christ. But, oh! How we have blemished and scarred that body through social neglect and through fear of being nonconformists.

There was a time when the church was very powerful—in the time when the early Christians rejoiced at being deemed worthy to suffer for what they believed. In those days the church was not merely a thermometer that recorded the ideas and principles of popular opinion; it was a thermostat that transformed the mores of society. Whenever the early Christians entered a town the power structure immediately sought to convict them for being "disturbers of the peace" and "outside agitators." But the Christians pressed on, in the conviction that they were "a colony of heaven," called to obey God rather than man. Small in number, they were big in commitment. By their effort and example they brought an end to such ancient evils as infanticide and gladiatorial contest.

Things are different now. So often the contemporary church is a weak, ineffectual voice with an uncertain sound. So often it is an archdefender of the status quo. Far from being disturbed by the presence of the church, the power structure of the average community is consoled by the church's silent—and often even vocal—sanction of things as they are.

But the judgment of God is upon the church as never before. If today's church does not recapture the sacrificial spirit of the early church, it will lose its authenticity, forfeit the loyalty of millions, and be dismissed as an irrelevant social club with no meaning for the 20th century. Every day I meet young people whose disappointment with the church has turned into outright disgust.

Perhaps I have once again been too optimistic. Is organized religion too inextricably bound to the status quo to save our nation and the world? Perhaps I must turn my faith to the inner spiritual church, the church within the church, as the true *ecclesia* and the hope of the world. But again I am thankful to God that some noble souls from 623 the ranks of organized religion have broken loose from the paralyzing chains of conformity and joined us as active partners in the struggle for freedom. They have left their secure congregations and walked the streets of Albany, Georgia, with us. They have gone down the highways of the south on torturous rides for freedom. Yes, they have gone to jail with us. Some have been kicked out of their churches, have lost the support of their bishops and fellow ministers. But they have acted in the faith that right defeated is stronger than evil triumphant. Their witness has been the spiritual salt that has preserved the true meaning of the gospel in these troubled times. They have carved a tunnel of hope through the dark mountain of disappointment.

I hope the church as a whole will meet the challenge of this decisive hour. But even if the church does not come to the aid of justice, I have no despair about the future. I have no fear about the outcome of our struggle in Birmingham, even if our motives are at present misunderstood. We will reach the goal of freedom in Birmingham and all over the nation, because the goal of America is freedom. Abused and scorned though we may be, our destiny is tied up with America's destiny. Before the pilgrims landed at Plymouth we were here. Before the pen of Jefferson etched across the pages of history the mighty words of the Declaration of Independence, we were here. For more than two centuries our forebears labored in this country without wages; they made cotton king; they built the homes of their masters while suffering gross injustice and shameful humiliation—and yet out of a bottomless vitality they continued to thrive and develop. If the inexpressible cruelties of slavery could not stop us, the opposition we now face will surely fail. We will win our freedom because the sacred heritage of our nation and the eternal will of God are embodied in our echoing demands.

XII

Before closing I feel impelled to mention one other point in your statement that has troubled me profoundly. You warmly commended the Birmingham police force for keeping "order" and "preventing violence." I doubt that you would have so warmly commended the police force if you had seen its angry dogs sinking their teeth into six unarmed, nonviolent Negroes. I doubt that you would so quickly commend the policemen if you were to observe their ugly and inhuman treatment of Negroes here in the city jail; if you were to watch them push and curse old Negro women and young Negro girls; if you were to see them slap and kick old Negro men and young boys; if you were to observe them, as they did on two occasions, refuse to give us food because we wanted to sing our grace together. I cannot join you in your praise of the Birmingham police department.

It is true that the police have exercised discipline in handling the demonstrators. In this sense they have conducted themselves rather "nonviolently" in public. But for what purpose? To preserve the evil system of segregation. Over the past few years I have consistently preached that nonviolence demands that the means we use must be as pure as the ends we seek. I have tried to make clear that it is wrong to use immoral means to attain moral ends. But now I must affirm that it is just as wrong, or perhaps even more so, to use moral means to preserve immoral ends. Perhaps Mr. Connor and his policemen have been rather nonviolent in public, as was Chief Pritchett in Albany, Georgia, but they have used the moral means of nonviolence to maintain the immoral end of racial injustice. As T. S. Eliot has said, there is no greater treason than to do the right deed for the wrong reason.

XIII

I wish you had commended the Negro sit-inners and demonstrators of Birmingham for their sublime courage, their willingness to suffer and their amazing discipline in the midst of great provocation. One day the south will recognize its real heroes. They will be the James Merediths, with a noble sense of purpose facing jeering and hostile mobs and the agonizing loneliness that characterizes the life of the pioneer. They will be old, oppressed, battered Negro women, symbolized in a 72-year-old woman in Montgomery, Alabama, who rose up with a sense of dignity and with her people decided not to ride segregated buses, and who responded with ungrammatical profundity to one who inquired about her: "My feet is tired, but my soul is rested." They will be the young high school and college students, the young ministers of the gospel and a host of their elders courageously and nonviolently sitting in at lunch counters and willingly going to jail for conscience' sake. One day the south will know that when these disinherited children of God sat down at lunch counters they were in reality standing up for what is best in the American dream and for the most sacred values in our Judeo-Christian heritage, thereby bringing our nation back to those great wells of democracy which were dug deep by the founding fathers in their formulation of the Constitution and the Declaration of Independence.

Never before have I written so long a letter. I can assure you that it would have been much shorter if I had been writing from a comfortable desk, but what else can one do when he is alone for days in a narrow jail cell, other than write long letters, think long thoughts and pray long prayers?

If I have said anything in this letter that overstates the truth and indicates an unreasonable impatience, I beg you to forgive me. If I have said anything that *under*states the truth and indicates my having a patience that allows me to settle for anything less than brotherhood, I beg God to forgive me.

I hope this letter finds you strong in the faith. I also hope that circumstances will soon make it possible for me to meet each of you, not as an integrationist or a civil rights leader but as a fellow clergyman and a Christian brother. Let us all hope that the dark clouds of racial prejudice will soon pass away and the deep fog of misunderstanding will be lifted from our fear-drenched communities and in some not too distant tomorrow the radiant stars of love and brotherhood will shine over our great nation with all their scintillating beauty.

L. D. Reddick

The Bus Boycott in Montgomery

Before last December, a visitor to Montgomery would have noticed Negroes standing up in the city buses, while there were empty seats right before them. Somebody could then explain that according to local practice, these unoccupied seats were reserved for "whites only." No matter how packed a bus might be with Negro passengers, they were prohibited from sitting in the first 4 seats (which hold about 10 persons). Theoretically, the last 3 back seats (holding about 10 persons) were similarly reserved for Negroes. In fact this was not so. Moreover, if white passengers were already occupying all of their reserved seats and additional white passengers boarded the bus, Negro passengers, sitting in the unreserved section immediately behind the whites, might be asked to get up and "move back" by the bus driver. At times this was done courteously; all-too-often it was an undisguised insult.

Race relations in Montgomery have traditionally been "good" in the sense that Negroes have seldom challenged their state of subordination. The structure of the society was more or less set. Opposition seemed futile. Personal difficulties might be adjusted through some prominent Negro, who would speak with an influential white person. This was the established pattern of paternalism; and it did not disturb the status quo.

But for some reason on Thursday afternoon, December 1, 1955, Mrs. Rosa Parks refused to "move back" when she was ordered to do so by the bus driver. She was *not* sitting in the section reserved for whites (as the *New York Times* mistakenly reported) but in the first seat of the unreserved section. At the time every seat in the bus was taken. So the command for her to "move back" meant that she would have to stand while a white male passenger, who had just taken the

Reprinted by permission from *Dissent*, March 1956.

627

bus, would sit. And so she was arrested and for a brief moment jailed. Mrs. Parks was ideally fitted for her role. She is attractive and quiet, a churchgoer who looks like the symbol of Mother's Day. Her trial was set for the following Monday, December 5. Out of nowhere, it seems, written and mimeographed appeals appeared in the Negro community, saying. ". . . This has to be stopped . . . if Negroes did not ride the buses they could not operate . . . every Negro stay off the buses Monday in protest of this arrest and trial. . . ."

Only a fraction of Negro bus riders saw these unsigned appeals but one of the notices did fall into the hands of the local paper, which put it on the front page. Negroes laugh when they tell about this. They say that the newspaper was mostly interested in letting the white folks know what the Negroes were up to. But through this story many Negroes got the news of the Monday plan for the first time. At the Sunday church service, Negro ministers hammered home their endorsement of the projected one-day "protest"— as they consistently called the boycott.

Physically, Montgomery is ideally fitted for a bus boycott. It is just 27.9 square miles in area. Its population, 130,000, is about 40 per cent Negro. Most residents *could* walk to most places in the city.

The judge who tried Mrs. Parks, had he looked into his crystal ball, would have probably dismissed the case. Instead, he found her guilty, fining her $14. She appealed.

All day long on December 5 Negroes stayed off the buses. They did so with such enthusiasm that there was a general feeling that "we ought to continue this."

The Negro ministers had hastily scheduled a mass meeting for Monday evening. Normally, the church holds about 1500 persons. Hours before meeting time, 7:00 p.m., people began filling up the place. By 7 o'clock every seat had been taken and some 3 or 4 thousand standees over-flowed into the street. Outdoor loudspeakers were set up.

Nobody expected such a response. The Negro ministers, rising to the occasion, improvised a declaration of principles. Amid the singing of hymns and some first class oratory—led by Rev. M. L. King Jr.— the audience unanimously adopted the following declaration as read by Rev. Ralph Abernathy: Negroes were not to resume riding the buses until (1) courteous treatment by bus operators was guaranteed; (2) passengers were seated on a first come first serve basis—Negroes seating from the back of the bus toward the front while white seat from the front toward the back; (3) Negro bus operators were employed on predominately Negro routes.

Then without the usual money-raising salesmanship, the crowd— inside and outside of the church—filed in and placed dimes, quarters and dollars on the collection table. This was altogether spontaneous. 628

Since the Negro ministers were cagey about revealing who was directing the movement, that seemed to whet the appetite of the reporters. As a matter of fact, at this point every thing was *ad hoc* and tentative. The emergence of King and Abernathy was almost by chance. No leader was calling the shots. As Abernathy said later, it was never "a one-man-show." The indignation and demands for action by the "common people" swept everyone along like a flood.

II

There had been a long history of abuse by the bus operators. Almost everybody could tell of some unfortunate personal experience that he himself had had or seen. Montgomery Negroes were fed up with the bus service in particular and, like Negroes throughout the South, with race relations in general. The outrage of the Emmett Till murder was alive in everybody's mind. The silence and inaction of the Federal Government, in the face of the daily abuse, beatings and killings of Negro citizens, was maddening. Negroes have no faith at all in Southern law-making and law-enforcing agencies, for these instruments of "justice" are all in the hands of "the brothers of the hoodlums who attack us."

Negroes themselves wanted to get into action. Here and elsewhere they were willing to fight it out—if the fighting was "fair." But Negroes knew on whose side the police and the lily-white militia would be when they came in to "put down disorder." And after that,—there would be the local judges and juries. To remain human, the Negroes could not stand by and do nothing. Under the circumstances, the channel into which the Negroes of Montgomery have poured their energies and resentments is the best answer thus far to the question of what to do. Here is organized struggle and group solidarity. It is legal, non-violent and effective.

And so the one-day boycott passed into an indefinite protest that, as of this writing, has run for fourteen weeks.

Both the press and the police expected violence. Early newspaper stories started off in this fashion: "Negro goon squads reportedly have been organized here to intimidate Negroes who ride . . . in violation of a Negro boycott . . . ." This was untrue.

The police were equally sure of the image in their minds. Accordingly, they arrested a college student, saying that he had pulled a Negro woman from a bus as she was attempting to get on it. In court it came out that the two were good friends and that they were merrily crossing the street, arm in arm, near a bus. She had told the cops this before the arrest was made but the police believed that there were goons— there had to be—so they saw what they were looking for: "believing is seeing."

The first reaction of the bus company officials was one of arrogance. They pretended that the Negroes were demanding that the company violate the law. This was absurd. The law required segregation, but did not specify the manner of seating so long as it was segregated. The bus company summarily rejected the proposal of the Negroes.

The city commission sided with the bus company, condemning the boycott and declaring that "first come, first serve" would be illegal. And so almost everybody—the bus company, the city commissioners and the white public—expected Negroes to be back on the buses in a few days.

This was only the first of a series of misjudgments on the part of the city fathers. All along they demonstrated that their conception of the Negro was the stereotype of the tired field hand or the witless house servant who could be cajoled or forced to do what the white folks wanted him to do. Even now, after 14 weeks of "education," the commissioners seem not to comprehend the intelligence, resourcefulness and resolve of the people with whom they are dealing.

III

The ex-bus riders soon found themselves face to face with a practical problem: since the buses were taboo, how were the Negroes to get about the city? At first, they called upon the taxis for cheap-rate jitney service. The police stopped this by warning the taxis that by law they must charge a minimum fare of 45 cents. Next, private cars began giving "friends" a lift, along the bus routes. The charge was 15 cents for "gasoline expense." The cops stopped this, too, by insisting that drivers had to have a taxi permit and license.

In reply, the Negroes organized a voluntary motor pool. Almost overnight Montgomery saw a network of private cars spread over the city, picking up and depositing passengers, from dawn until early evening. It was a marvel of quick organization. Even the local press had to concede that the pick-up system moved with "military precision." Some transportation problems that the bus company had grappled with for twenty years were, apparently, solved overnight.

The police searched the books for laws that would dry up the motor pool. One old rule forbade more than three persons to sit on the front seat of an automobile. Lights, brakes, even the position of license tags, were checked by the police frequently. Minor regulations that are seldom invoked in this normally easy-going town were resurrected and severely enforced. Negro taxi drivers really caught it!

The Negro community of Montgomery has neither its own radio station (as does Atlanta, Ga.) nor a widely-read local newspaper. Communication is by word of mouth and through churches mainly. This is probably why frequent mass meetings have proved a necessity. The

630

pattern was established during the first week of the boycott; mass meetings each Monday and Thursday evening. It has been adhered to ever since.

These twice-a-week get-togethers are the soul of the boycott; the Montgomery Improvement Association is the brains. The meetings are rotated from church to church. The speakers, in turn, represent the various denominations. Thus the ground is cut from under any institutional or sectarian jealousy. Rev. King and Rev. Abernathy make it plain by their words and by their sharing of the speakers' platform that they are not self-appointed "leaders" but only "spokesmen" of the movement. Incidentally, the people have "fallen in love" with King. a boyish-looking Ph.D. They look upon Abernathy, also young and an M.A., as a tower of strength. These two men symbolize the poise, the thoughtfulness and the ability of the independent ministers. They are the real and obvious leaders of this mass upsurge. The more vulnerable intellectuals stay discreetly in the background. Rufus Lewis, an ex-football coach and presently a civic-minded business man, is the cool-headed chairman of the motor pool committee.

People come hours ahead of time to get a seat at these mass meetings. A few read papers and books while waiting, but mostly the audiences sing. Hymns such as "Onward Christian Soldiers," "Abide With Me" and "Higher Ground" are moving but the really stirring songs are the lined, camp-meeting tunes, of low pitch and long meter. These seem to recapture the long history of the Negro's suffering and struggle.

IV

By 7 p.m., the time the meeting starts, virtually every inch of space is taken, including standing room. Often as many listeners are outside as inside. Many others do not come at all because they know they cannot get near the church. It is curious that meetings were never scheduled in different parts of the city at different hours on the same night or rotated to different parts of the city on different nights—in order to accommodate the crowds. This suggestion was made but the planning committee never got around to it or concluded that "the people prefer to be together," as several persons had said.

The mass meeting pattern is relatively simple: songs, prayer, latest news and plans, a "pep talk," collection. Often the pastor in whose church the meeting was held would preside or, after preliminary remarks, would turn the meeting over to some official of the Montgomery Improvement Association.

The meetings are serious but thoroughly relaxed. There are quips and jokes—a great deal of genial humor. All classes are present in the audiences but the bulk of the attendants are working class people. 631

It is here that morale is built and sustained. Unity is expressed in words and in the little kindnesses that the people show to each other. The automobile-owning folk, who never rode the buses, and the maids and day-laborers, who depended upon the buses, have come to know each other. The inter-denominational, inter-class integration of the Negro community has called forth much comment. Moreover, the mass meetings have given many persons some place to go; something to think about; something to absorb their energies. There is high purpose these days in the Negro community.

Few whites attend these meetings although they are open to all. Aside from a Lutheran minister who has a Negro congregation, no local white preacher has publicly identified himself with the Negro cause. Many, of course, give assurances privately. A few are in "hot water" for real or suspected sympathies with the boycotters.

But the main force that keeps the people and their leaders together is the idea of the movement itself. These people know that they are fighting a big battle and that it is a vital part of a larger war. Messages and money contributions from many parts of the nation as well as from remote parts of the world have confirmed this belief.

At first, the demands of the boycotters were limited—courtesy, fair play, fair employment. These were all within the segregation laws of the city and state. At one point, the Negroes would have called off the boycott for just the "first come, first serve" arrangement. That day, of course, has long since passed.

Apparently to impress the Negro community with what it could lose, the bus company abruptly stopped all service to Negro neighborhoods. This was supposed to bring Negroes to their knees, crying for the buses. But nobody was impressed. Instead, doubtful would-be bus riders were pushed into the motor pool. The water, they found, was just "fine." On second thought, the bus company decided to re-establish the discontinued lines. So the buses were put back on the routes in the Negro areas. They continued to roll empty.

For about a month negotiations were on and off. Neither side would yield. The boycott held its own. This meant that 75 per cent of the bus riding public was "out," and it cut some $3,000 from each day's revenue. Moreover, fewer whites—probably out of sympathy with the boycott—seem to be riding.

To counteract this economic squeeze, the mayor called on the white public to support the buses. The so-called White Citizens Council solicited contributions for the poor suffering bus company. No figures were ever given out but the general impression is that very few persons were willing to subsidize the National City Lines, an economic giant that is spread out over the cities and towns of the Middle West and South and has its main office in Chicago. A forced subsidy was made possible by raising the bus fare from 10 to 15 cents. At which point, additional whites stayed off the buses.

632

To break the impasse, the city commission pulled a fast one. On Sunday, January 22, the Negro community was astounded to read in the morning paper that a settlement had been reached. The article said: "The above agreement is concurred in by all three members of the City Commission, as well as by representatives of the bus company and the group representing the Negroes of Montgomery." The terms of the "agreement" were: (1) courtesy to all; (2) white reserve section at the front of the bus, Negro reserve section at rear of bus; (3) special, all-Negro buses during the rush hours. "First come, first serve" would obtain for the unreserved, middle section. The city commission stated that it had nothing to do with the question of employment. The declaration of courtesy carried no machinery for assuring its practice. In short, this latest "agreement" was merely a re-statement of the *status quo ante bellum*. Nevertheless, it sounded like a settlement and many persons who read the story felt that the boycott was over. Some whites were jubilant. Some Negroes were ill. "Why had the leaders given in?" they asked.

A very careful reading of the article raises the question whether it was just poor reporting or something much worse. For example, the names of the "prominent ministers" were not given. Other omissions were equally strange. If this was a release from the city commission, would any newspaper naively print such an important front-page story without first checking with the known Negro representatives, who had been negotiating with the bus company and city commission for weeks? Obviously, this announcement was a calculated maneuver to get the ex-bus riders back on the buses Sunday morning. Perhaps once the spell of not riding was broken, the boycott would dissolve.

The Negroes foiled this maneuver by a combination of luck and quick action. The story had been sent out Saturday evening by the Associated Press. As it came over the wires into the office of the *Minneapolis Tribune,* the reporter Carl T. Rowan, who had been down to Montgomery to cover the boycott, did what any good reporter would do: he called Rev. M. L. King Jr. to verify the story.

King was amazed. He knew absolutely nothing about any settlement. Rowan then contacted one of the Montgomery commissioners who confirmed the story but refused to give the names of the Negro ministers involved. Under prodding, the commissioner did reveal the denominations of the ministers. Rowan then called King again. This clue was enough. King and his colleagues by a process of checking soon identified the "three prominent Negro ministers." It turned out that they were neither prominent nor members of the negotiating committee.

It was now late Saturday night. Like minute men, the ministers of the Montgomery Improvement Association went themselves or sent 633 messages to all of the night clubs and taverns in the Negro community, informing the Saturday night revelers of the attempted hoax. Rev. King himself humorously stated that he got a chance to see the insides of many a night spot! Result: word got around so well that the next day the buses rolled empty as usual. At the Sunday morning services, the ministers excoriated the "fake settlement" and repeated that the "protest" was still on. The commissioners lost face. The Negroes were brought closer together.

By the next day, the "three prominent Negro ministers" had publicly repudiated the commission's press announcement. One of the three stated before an open meeting that he had been "tricked" into the conference on the basis of a telephone invitation, asking that he join in a discussion of group insurance for the city. This man said that neither he nor the other two ministers present agreed to any settlement, declaring that they were unauthorized to speak for the ex-bus-riders.

Few persons thought that these three Negro ministers would dare challenge the veracity of the city fathers; but they did. This, everybody was sure, would make front page news. But the local press reduced the sensational disclosure to a bare statement of denial that was buried near the end of a long story. When the local dailies did not print his statement, one of the ministers purchased space for a three-inch ad saying: "The rumor that is out that I agreed with the commissioners on the proposal that they issued is an untrue statement." These words have never been contradicted.

Things now took a turn for the worse. The mayor and the other commissioners embarked upon a "get tough" policy. With a show of anger the mayor denounced the boycott, declared that the white people did not care if another Negro ever rode the buses again, and called upon white employers to stop taking their Negro employees to and from work. He said that white businessmen informed him that they were discharging Negro workers who were participating in the boycott. All three commissioners let it be known that they had joined the White Citizens Council. Even the timid member of the trio mustered up enough bravado to go on television and join the "get tough with Negroes" act. All this, of course, was the traditional, Confederate, flag-waving appeal to white supremacy.

It was to be a field day. The police would "cut the legs off" the boycott by a campaign of arrests for real and imaginary traffic infractions. Negro drivers, who appeared to be in the motor pool, would be questioned about their employment, the balance due on the purchase of their automobiles and the firms with which they had their insurance.

VI

For a moment the protest movement seemed to be wavering. Again, Negroes saw that the very instruments of law and order were being used against them. Surely, a man had the right to give someone a ride in his own automobile. Persons who had not received a traffic ticket in years were booked. Some ex-bus riders, while waiting to be picked up, were told that there was a law against hitch-hiking; others were accused of "loud talking," walking on lawns and "congregating in white neighborhoods." The daily press printed next to nothing about the wholesale arrests and harassment.

Under such heavy blows the voluntary pick-up system began to weaken. Some drivers were already tired; others disliked "tangling with the law"; still others feared that they could not stand much more provocation without striking back.

The high point of the "get tough" operation was the arrest of Rev. King himself. But if this move was intended to frighten King, it fell flat. He calmly submitted to arrest and jailing. At first, he was not to be let out on bond. The news spread through the Negro community like wildfire. Negroes began rushing down to the jail in such numbers that King was released without having even to sign his own bond.

Meanwhile, a group of Negro business and professional men asked the city for permission to operate a jitney service. This was turned down on the grounds that sufficient transportation was already available. The mayor said, let them ride the buses now rolling empty through the streets. A strange stand for one who didn't care if another Negro rode a bus again!

But the city did care. It stood to lose part of the $20,000 in taxes it received from the bus company each year. Downtown merchants cared, too, for some of their businesses were off by as much as a third since the boycott had begun. Most of all, the bus company cared— each day it cared more and more. It let it be known that it would agree to any seating arrangement that the city commissioners would approve.

The worse was yet to come. The inflammatory appeals seemed to give the signal to the violent elements. A stick of dynamite was thrown on the porch of Rev. King's home. The job was amateurish; the damage slight; the intent vicious. Within minutes hundreds of Negroes flocked to King's home; also the police. It was at this moment that non-violent resistance almost faded. Many Negroes wanted to launch a counter-offensive. Rev. King, standing on the front porch of his "bombed" home, pleaded with the angry Negroes: "We are not harmed. Do not get your weapons. Let us not answer hate with hate, violence with violence. But we will continue to stay off the buses." Probably this saved the city from a race riot.

There had been other incidents. Some Negro and white high school students had clashed; one or more cars of white youths had made commando raids on the nearby Negro college, dashing through the campus with lights out, throwing out bags of water, eggs, rocks and a tiny flaming cross. One evening the commandos were ambushed and 635 bombarded with bricks. Another commando car was captured by special police. Another clumsy bomb-thrower hit the fence of E. D. Nixon, the president of the local NAACP chapter.

This flurry of violence had no noticeable effect on the boycott. The leaders were careful but nobody seemed to be at all afraid. On the other hand, it helped convince the patient hopefuls that an all-out fight was the only kind that made any sense.

For two months the Negroes had clung to the hope of a settlement on the basis of their limited demands. But failure of negotiations and the crude brutality of the "get tough" policy convinced the most conservative ex-bus riders that an attack had to be made upon bus segregation itself. Accordingly, on February 1 a suit was filed in the local federal courts, asking for the end of bus jim crow on the grounds that it is contrary to the 14th Amendment of the Constitution of the United States. Furthermore, the court was asked to stop the city commissioners from violating the civil rights of Negro motorists and pedestrians.

This was a sobering jolt for the city commissioners. The "get tough" policy evaporated overnight. The city fathers, who had been making speeches at the drop of the hat, lapsed into their usual quietude.

VII

Meanwhile, a fresh effort was made to re-open negotiations. This time a white business men's club intervened. Many of them had stores that had been hurt. It is estimated that the boycott had cost Montgomery $1,000,000. The business men's club met several times, separately, with the city commission and a committee from the Montgomery Improvement Association. Chicago Negroes had thrown a picket line around the offices of the parent bus company, so it was more willing than ever to come to terms. The city commissioners, however, remained adamant. They seem to feel that they can not afford to yield. So the best that the business men could offer was little more than the old "fake" settlement that had been palmed off on the "three prominent Negro ministers."

Some of the drivers in the motor pool were becoming exhausted. Twelve or thirteen weeks of free, voluntary service, four or five hours per day, is fatiguing. Most of these drivers have jobs and other obligations. Several of the leaders felt that maybe the boycott might as well be called off since in the end the courts would settle the issue. Understandably, people were becoming battle-weary. For over three months, life had been like a military operation for the Negro Improvement Association.

So the leaders, though reluctantly, submitted the proposals of the business men to the rank and file at one of the mass meetings. The answer was an almost total rejection. Out of approximately four thou-   636 sand persons present, *only two* voted in favor of calling off the boycott. The morale of the masses, once again, revived the morale of the leaders.

To date the latest move to break the boycott has been the indictment of the leaders of the Improvement Association. This was based on an old anti-labor law of doubtful constitutionality. And again nobody was frightened. Nobody tried to hide. Many inquired of the sheriff's office: "Is my name on that Grand Jury list?" If it was, the caller let it be known that he would come down immediately. Confident, orderly, loyal to each other, the Negroes again manifested their collective will and *esprit de corps*.

As for the future, nobody can be sure. The white people of Montgomery have been amazed by the group discipline of the Negro community and by the intelligence and organization with which the boycott has been maintained. "I didn't think they had it in them," is a frequent comment.

Many whites who would like to see the boycott ended and who feel that the demands of the Negroes are reasonable, are afraid to admit this. They fear that to "give in" on this means that "all" is lost. There are sincere apprehensions that desegregation at any one point will lead to general racial integration—and that means intermarriage! An absurd goblin hovers over every white household. The politicians and White Councils exploit these fears. The chief weakness of the movement for desegregation is that so little is done to remove the unfounded alarms of the thousands who in desperation are flocking to the hate organizations.

The fact is that desegregation has been magnified so greatly in the minds of so many Americans, both Negro and white, that they do not realize how ordinary and natural a non-segregated society is. Nonsegregation already prevails in many areas of Southern life—the super markets, for example—with scarcely passing notice. Negroes seem to feel that desegregation will work overnight miracles. Southern whites feel that it will precipitate disaster. They are both wrong. It is neither so glorious nor so dangerous as pictured, even in terms of the values of the opposing groups. A non-segregated society is merely a crude, basic, pre-condition for creating a social order in which the higher sensibilities can flourish.

We are all indebted to the Negroes of Montgomery. They say that they are confident of ultimate victory. In a sense, they have already won. They have given us a magnificent case study of the circumstances under which the philosophy of Thoreau and Gandhi can triumph. Moreover, the boycott movement has brought something new into the lives of the Negroes of Montgomery. They would be loath to give it up. Whenever the boycott ends, it will be missed. . 637

The Revolution in Expression

TWELVE

THE FOURTH REVOLUTION
AND ITS CRITICS

In the preceding sections we have tried to indicate that many of the social ills of contemporary American society could be understood as products of the coming together of three very general trends, each sufficiently different from its antecedents to be considered revolutionary. What will emerge from these sometimes conflicting and sometimes overlapping trends may be radically different from the society we have known until now. What is already somewhat distinct is the form of expression that the modern American protest movement is taking. We have called this departure in the expression of dissaffection with contemporary society the Fourth Revolution and have selected from the writings of three of its spokesmen, Paul Goodman, Carl Oglesby, and Stokley Carmichael, to convey its purposes *as seen by its leaders*.

The article by Paul Goodman was selected because it relates the goals of "the movement" to the major social problems brought on by the triple revolution. Goodman reacts particularly to the mindless manner in which technology creates the objectives for people to pursue, as in programmed education and the space race. The vitality of differences in individual purpose and style, once characteristic of American society as a whole, seems open now only to those who defect from the major directions of society.

The articles by Oglesby and Carmichael were selected to illustrate the reasons why the movement does not assume an existing good will on the part of society and why the mainstream white liberal who professes to favor change is not considered an ally. Carmichael's article was selected partly for the clarity of the argument presented. What the particular selection does not convey as well, perhaps, as other speeches by Carmichael, or the speeches of Malcolm X, or the writings of Negro poet LeRoi Jones, is the militancy, the sense of urgency, the desire to shake off oppressive authority and the de- 641 mand of the group to shape their own lives without accepting terms set by outsiders. Some of the emotional message is delivered by a theatre of protest which has grown through the efforts of such groups as the San Francisco Mime Troupe. In the arts, folk music also remains a traditional medium of expressing feelings about the waste and horror of war and the emptiness of modern life.

The techniques of the movement have been evolving, gradually bypassing the small discriminating barber shop or lunch counter, against which the sit-in or picket line may have been well suited. Marches for peace or civil rights are new occurrences in American society. Also new are the practices of leaving the country in preference to being drafted, individual cases of refusal to be inducted or, after induction, refusal to serve in Vietnam. "Teach-ins" which subjected American foreign policy to the guns of its academic critics, free universities and student protests for a voice in the administraton of their universities, rent strikes and consumer boycotts, third party politicking, tax withholding, and programs of assistance to the victims of American firepower, attempts to close down induction centers all reflect an amorphous groping for techniques for effective involvement.

The content of the expression is also different. Luis Valdez in his Tale of La Raza (1966) indicates how, in the aftermath of the organization of the grape picking braceros in the Delano Grape Strike, the crowd demanded that the platforms be used for poor grape pickers of their own race and regions and not for benevolent officials or outside helpers. Similarly, American Indians have spoken out against governmental failure to understand them or to allow them to preserve their sense of community against the arbitrary legal fictions of towns, cities, and states which are recognized by federal programs (Warrior, 1965).

The content of the new expression goes deeply into the latent feelings of individuals long forced to wear their color or their neighborhoods as a badge of inferiority. The topics of the new literature of protest deal with brutal frankness about amphetamines, addictive narcotics and psychedelic drugs, the problems of sex liberation, the meanings of inter-racial social and sexual ties to the self image of the Negro ghetto worker or of the civil rights reformer.

The new means of expression are not all associated with action directed to change the society. The communal hippie culture is an example of a quiet rejection of acquisitive material standards of American life. Sometimes one set of responses to frustrating conditions is substitutable for another set. Where civil rights activity was strong, the incidence of narcotic addiction has tended to subside. Some apparently fixated or habitual behaviors do change when more effective opportunities are present.

But what means of expression are suited to the existing needs of 642 society? Is protest activity in any form, whether moderate or radical, capable of inducing the desired changes? And is "the movement" in its present form an effective instrument, or a waste of time, or even a danger when held up to the task of social change which it has set for itself. This is the issue on which two critics of the movement, George Grant and Michael Harrington, express reservations. For Grant, the task of moving an empire seems headed for severe disillusionment. For Harrington, the movement, by shunning the establishment, has lost contact with the coalitions in society whose basic good will and effort are needed for improving the lot of the disadvantaged. It is entirely possible that the movement will splinter into isolated feuding factions which will dissipate what effectiveness it may have had. Racial antagonisms and anti-semitism have already appeared in groups originally designed to cure society of such practices.

There seems little doubt that extensive change is needed in American society and little doubt that some major changes are occurring and will continue. How much hard work will be required, how much zealous hatred will develop and how many people will be hurt by the changing conditions is not easily predicted. Revolutions started by humanitarian concerns are sometimes extremely violent in their execution. The question worthy of serious discussion is whether the demands of the movement and the resistances of the existing society can produce, without excessive violence, a set of institutions capable of control over the technological and bureaucratic forces which now restrict the current forms of individual and group expression of mankind's human needs.

REFERENCES AND ADDITIONAL READING

"Detroit: Violence on the Urban Frontier," Special Supplement, *Trans-action,* September, 1967, 6–32 (Articles by Irving L. Horowitz, Roger Montgomery, Tom Parmanter, and Lee Rainwater).

Bruce Detwiler, "A Time To Be Black," *The New Republic,* September 7, 1966, 19–22.

Ronald Hamowy, "Left and Right Meet," *The New Republic,* March 12, 1966, 14–16.

John R. Howard, "The Making of a Black Muslim," *Trans-action,* December, 1966, 15–21.

Paul Jacobs and Saul Landau, *The New Radicals,* New York: Vintage, 1966.

Jack Newfield, *A Prophetic Minority,* New York: New American Library, 1966.

Paul Seabury, "Gideon's Army and Moynihan's Pros," *The New Republic*, March 19, 1966, 23–25.

Sol Stern, "America's Black Guerrillas," *Ramparts,* September, 1967, 24–27.

Luis Valdez, "The Tale of La Raza," *Ramparts,* July, 1966, 40–43.

Clyde Warrior, "Poverty, Community and Power," *New University Thought*, 4, Summer, 1965, 5–10.

Arthur Waskow, "The New Student Movement," *Dissent*, 12, Autumn, 1965, 486–493.

Paul Goodman

The Empty Society

During Eisenhower's second administration, I wrote a book describing how hard it was for young people to grow up in the corporate institutions of American society. The statistics at that time indicated that most were content to be secure as personnel of big corporations; a few deviated in impractical, and certainly unpolitical, ways, like being Beat or delinquent. The system itself, like its President, operated with a cheerful and righteous self-satisfaction. There were no signs of its being vulnerable, though a loud chorus of intellectual critics, like myself, were sounding off against it. We were spoilsports.

Less than ten years later, the feeling is different; it turns out that the critics were not altogether unrealistic. The dominant system of institutions is even grander and more computerized, but it seems to have lost its morale. The baronial corporations are making immense amounts of money and are more openly and heavily subsidized by the monarch in Washington. The processing of the young is being extended for longer years and its tempo speeded up. More capital and management are being exported, interlocking with international capital, and more of the world is being brought under American control. When necessary, remarkable military technology is brought to bear to regularize the recalcitrant. At home, there is no political check, for no matter what the currents of opinion, by and large the dominant system wreaks its will, managing the parliamentary machinery to look like consensus.

Nevertheless, the feeling of justification is gone. Sometimes we seem to be bulling it through only in order to save face. Often enterprises seem to be expanding simply because the managers cannot think of any other use of energy and resources. The economy is turning into

645

a war economy. There are warnings of ecological disaster: pollution, congestion, poisoning, mental disease, anomie. We have discovered that there is hard-core poverty at home that is not easy to liquidate. And in contrast to the situation in Europe in the 40's, which we were able to deal with successfully through the Marshall Plan, it increasingly appears that poverty and unrest in Asia, Africa, and South America are not helped by our methods of assistance, but are perhaps made worse. There are flashes of suspicion, like flashes of lightning, that the entire system may be unviable. Influential senators refer to our foreign policy as "arrogant" and "lawless," but in my opinion, our foreign and domestic system is all of a piece and is more innocent and deadly than that; it is mindless and morally insensitive. Its pretended purposes are window-dressing for purposeless expansion and a panicky need to keep things under control.

And now very many young people no longer want to cooperate with such a system. Indeed, a large and rapidly growing number—already more than five per cent of college students—use language that is openly revolutionary or apocalyptic, as if in their generation they were going to make a French Revolution. More and more often, civil disobedience seems to make obvious sense.

We are exerting more power and feeling less right—what does that mean for the future? I have heard serious people argue for three plausible yet drastically incompatible predictions about America during the next generation, none of them happy:

(1) Some feel, with a kind of Virgilian despair, that the American empire will succeed and will impose for a long time, at home and abroad, its meaningless management and showy style of life. For instance, we will "win" in Vietnam, though such a victory of brute military technology will be a moral disaster. Clubbing together with the other nuclear powers, we will stave off the nuclear war and stop history with a new Congress of Vienna. American democracy will vanish into an establishment of promoters, mandarins, and technicians, though for a while maintaining an image of democracy as in the days of Augustus and Tiberius. And all this is probably the best possible outcome, given the complexities of high technology, urbanization, mass education, and overpopulation.

(2) Others believe, with dismay and horror, that our country is overreaching and is bound for doom; but nothing can be done because policy cannot be influenced. Controlling communications, creating incidents that it then mistakes for history, deceived by its own intelligence agents, our system is mesmerized. Like the Mikado, Washington is captive to its military-industrial complex. The way we manage the economy and technology must increase anomie and crime. Since the war economy eats up brains and capital, we will soon be a fifth-rate economic power. With a few setbacks abroad—for instance, when we 646

force a major South American country to become Communist—and with the increasing disorder on the streets that is inevitable because our cities are unworkable, there will be a police state. The atom bombs may then go off. Such being the forecast, the part of wisdom is escape, and those who cultivate LSD are on the right track.

(3) Still others hold that the Americans are too decent to succumb to Fascism, and too spirited to remain impotent clients of a managerial elite. Rather, the tide of protest will continue to rise. The excluded poor are already refusing to remain excluded and they cannot be included without salutary changes. With the worst will in the world, we cannot police the world. But the reality is that we are confused. We do not know how to cope with the new technology, the economy of surplus, the fact of One World that makes national boundaries obsolete, the unworkability of traditional democracy. We must invent new forms. Unfortunately, the present climate of emergency is bad for the social invention and experiment that are indispensable, and there is no doubt that our overcentralized and Establishment methods of organization make everybody stupid from top to bottom. But there is hope precisely in the young. They understand the problem in their bones. Of course, they don't know much and their disaffection both from tradition and from the adult world makes it hard for them to learn anything. Nevertheless, we will learn in the inevitable conflict, which will hopefully be mainly non-violent.

I myself hold this third view: American society is on a bad course, but there is hope for reconstruction through conflict. It is a wish. The evidence, so far, is stronger for either our empty success or for crack-up. But my feeling is the same as about the atom bombs. Rationally, I must judge that they are almost certain to go off in this generation; yet I cannot believe that they will go off, for I do not lead my life with that expectation.

(Since I have mentioned the bombs, I must stop a moment and make another comparison. Thirty years ago the Jews in Germany believed that Hitler did not mean to exterminate them; "nobody," they said, "can be that stupid." So they drifted to the gas chambers, and went finally even without resistance. Now the nuclear powers continue stockpiling bombs and pouring new billions into missiles, anti-missile missiles, and armed platforms in orbit. Afterward, survivors, if there are any, will ask, "How did we let it happen?")

II

To illustrate the current style of American enterprise, let me analyze a small actual incident. It is perfectly typical, banal; no one would raise his eyebrows at it.

Washington has allotted several billions of dollars to the schools. The schools are not teaching very well, but there is no chance that

647

anybody will upset the applecart and ask if so much doing of lessons is the right way to educate the young altogether. Rather, there is a demand for new "methods" and mechanical equipment, which will disturb nobody, and electronics is the latest thing that every forward-looking local school-board must be proud to buy. So to cut in on this melon, electronics corporations, IBM, Xerox, etc. have hastened to combine with, or take over, textbook houses. My own publisher, Random House, has been bought up by the Radio Corporation of America.

Just recently, General Electric and Time, Inc., which owns a text-book house, have put nearly forty million dollars into a joint subsidiary called General Learning. And an editor of *Life* has been relieved of his duties for five weeks, in order to prepare a prospectus on the broad educational needs of America and the world, to come up with exciting proposals, so that General Learning might move with purpose into this unaccustomed field. Boning up on the latest High Thought on education, the editor in due course invites me—as a severe critic of the school establishment—to lunch, to pick my brains for something new and radical. "The sky," he assures me, "is the limit." "Perhaps," he tells me at lunch, "there *is* no unique place for General Learning. They'll probably end up as prosaic makers of school hardware. But we ought to give it a try."

Consider the premises of this odd situation, where first they have the organization and the technology, and then they try to dream up a use for it. In the 18th century, Adam Smith thought that one started with the need and only then collected capital to satisfy it. In the 19th century, there was already a lot of capital to invest, but by and large the market served as a check, to guarantee utility, competence, and relevance. Now, however, the subsidy removes the check of the market and a promotion can expand like weeds in a well-manured field. The competence required is to have a big organization and sales force, and to be *in,* to have the prestige and connections plausibly to get the subsidy. Usually it is good to have some nominal relation to the ostensible function, e.g., a textbook subsidiary related to schooling or *Time-Life* related to, let us say, learning. But indeed, when an expanding corporation becomes *very* grand, it generates an expertise of its own called Systems Development, applicable to anything. For example, as an expert in Systems Development, North American Aviation is hired to reform the penal system of California; there is no longer the need to demonstrate acquaintance with any particular human function.

Naturally, along with the divorce of enterprise from utility and particular competence, there goes a heavy emphasis on rhetoric and public-relations to prove utility and competence. So an editor must be reassigned for five weeks to write a rationale. It is his task to add ideas or talking-points to the enterprise, like a wrapper. The personnel 648 of expanding corporations, of course, are busy people and have not had time to think of many concrete ideas; they can, however, phone writers and concerned professionals. Way-out radicals, especially, do a lot of thinking, since they have little practical employment. And since the enterprise is free-floating anyway, it is dandy to include, in the prospectus, something daring, or even meaningful.

In an affluent society that can afford it, there is something jolly about such an adventure of the electronics giant, the mighty publisher, the National Science Foundation that has made curriculum studies, and local school-boards that want to be in the swim. Somewhere down the line, however, this cabal of decision-makers is going to coerce the time of life of real children and control the activity of classroom teachers. These latter, who are directly engaged in the human function of learning and teaching, have no say in what goes on. This introduces a more sober note. Some of the product of the burst of corporate activity and technological virtuosity will be useful, some not—the pedagogical evidence is mixed and not extensive—but the brute fact is that the children are quite incidental to the massive intervention of the giant combinations.

I have chosen a wry example. But I could have chosen the leader of the American economy, the complex of cars, oil, and roads. This outgrew its proper size perhaps thirty years ago; now it is destroying both the cities and the countryside, and has been shown to be careless of even elementary safety.

Rather, let me turn abruptly to the Vietnam war. We notice the same family traits. Whatever made us embark on this adventure, by now we can define the Vietnam war as a commitment looking for a reason, or at least a rationalization. There has been no lack of policy-statements, rhetorical gestures, manufactured (it seems) incidents, and (certainly) plain lies; but as the war has dragged on and grown, all these have proved to be mere talking-points. Ringing true, however, has been the fanfare about the superb military technology that we have deployed. The theme is used as a chief morale-builder for the troops. In the absence of adequate political reasons, some have even said that the war is largely an occasion for testing new hardware and techniques. It is eerie to hear, on the TV, a pilot enthusiastically praise the split-second scheduling of his missions to devastate rice-fields. Such appreciation of know-how is part of the cheerful American disposition, but it does not do much credit to him as a grown man.

Yet what emerges most strikingly from our thinking about and prosecution of the Vietnam war is, again, the input-output accounting, the systems development, and the purely incidental significance of the human beings involved. The communiqués are concerned mainly with the body-count of V.C. in ratio to our own losses, since there is a theory that in wars of this kind one must attain a ratio of 5 to 1 or 10 to 1. According to various estimates, it costs $40,000 to $250,000 649 to kill 1 Vietnamese, hopefully an enemy. Similarly, the bombing of civilians and the destruction of their livelihood occur as if no human being were involved; they are officially spoken of as unfortunate but incidental. (Indemnity for a dead civilian averages $34.) We claim that we have no imperialist aims in Vietnam—though we are building air-bases of some very heavy concrete and steel—but evidently old-fashioned imperialism was preferable, since it tried to keep the subjugated population in existence, for taxes and labor.

At home, correspondingly, college students are deferred from the draft because they will be necessary to man the professions and scientific technology, while farm boys, Negroes, and Spanish-Americans are drafted because they are otherwise good for nothing. That is to say, war is not regarded as a dread emergency, in which each one does his bit, but as part of the ongoing business of society, in which fighting and dying are usual categories of the division of labor. But this is bound to be the case when 20 per cent of the Gross National Product is spent on war (using a multiplier of 2); when more than half of the gross new investment since 1945 has been in war industry; and when much of higher education and science is devoted to war technology.

The Americans are not a warlike or bloodthirsty people, though violent. The dehumanizing of war is part of a general style of enterprise and control in which human utility and even the existence of particular human beings are simply not paramount considerations. Great armaments manufacturers have said that they are willing and ready to convert their capital and skill to peaceful production when given the signal; this seems to mean that it is *indifferent* to them what they produce. Studies of American workmen have shown that they take their moral and aesthetic standards not from family, church, friends, or personal interests, but from the organization and style of work at the plant; and I think that this explains the present peculiar situation that other nations of the world regard our behavior in the Vietnam war with a kind of horror, whereas Americans sincerely talk as if it were a messy job to be done as efficiently as possible.

This brings us to a broader question. What do we mean by technical efficiency in our system?

III

Corporate and bureaucratic societies, whether ruled by priests, mandarins, generals, or business managers, have always tended to diminish the importance of personal needs and human feeling, in the interest of abstractions and systemic necessities. And where there has been no check by strong community ties, effective democracy, or a free market, it has not been rare for the business of society to be largely without 650 utility or common sense. Nevertheless, modern corporate societies that can wield a high technology are liable to a unique temptation: since they do not exploit common labor, they may tend to exclude the majority of human beings altogether, as useless for the needs of the system and therefore as not quite persons.

This has been the steady tendency in America. The aged are ruled out at an earlier age than before, the young until a later age. We have liquidated most small farmers. There is no place for the poor, e.g., more than twenty million Negroes and Latin Americans. A rapidly increasing number are certified as insane or otherwise incompetent. These groups already comprise more than a majority of the population. Some authorities say (though others deny) that with full automation most of the rest will also be useless.

There is nothing malevolent or heartless in the exclusion. The tone is not like that of the old exploitative society which threw people out of work during the lows of the business cycle. For humane and political reasons, efforts, even extraordinary ones, are made to shape the excluded into the dominant style, so that they can belong. Even though the system is going to need only a few per cent with elaborate academic training, all the young are subjected to twelve years of schooling and 40 per cent go to college. There is every kind of training and social service to upgrade the poor and to make the handicapped productive members of society. At a high cost in effort and suffering, mentally retarded children must be taught to read, if only "cat" and "rat."

But a frank look shows, I think, that, for most, the long schooling is a way of keeping the young on ice; the job training is busy-work; and the social services turn people into "community dependents" for generations. Much of the anxiety about the "handicapped" and the "underprivileged" is suburban squeamishness that cannot tolerate difference. What is *never* done, however, is to change the rules of the system, to redefine usefulness in terms of how people are, and to shape the dominant style to them. This cannot be done because it would be inefficient and, indeed, degrading, for there is only one right way to exist. Do it our way or else you are not quite a person.

Inevitably, such self-righteous inflexibility is self-mesmerizing and self-proving, for other methods and values are not allowed to breathe and prove themselves. Often it would be cheaper to help people to be, in their own way, or at least to let them be; but anything in a different or outmoded style has "deviant" or "underprivileged" written on it, and no expense is spared to root it out, in the name of efficiency. Thus, it would have been cheaper to pay the small farmers to stay put if they wished; and anyway it can even be shown that in many situations small farming and local distribution are not less efficient than the plantations and national chain-grocers that have supplanted them with the connivance of government policy. It would be far 651 cheaper to give money directly to the urban poor to design their own lives, rather than to try to make them shape up; it has been estimated that, in one area of poverty in New York City, the cost per family in special services is more than ten thousand dollars a year; and anyway, to a candid observer, the culture of poverty is not inferior to that of the middle class, if it were allowed to be decent. Very many of the young would get a better education and grow up usefully to themselves and society if we spent the school money on useful enterprises where they could learn something, or indeed if they were given the school money to follow their own interests, ambitions, and even fancies, rather than penning them for lengthening years in increasingly regimented institutions; and anyway, many young people could enter many professions without most of the schooling if we changed the rules for licensing and hiring. But none of these simpler and cheaper ways would be "efficient"; the clinching proof is that they would be hard to administer.

Are the people really useless? The concept of efficiency is largely, maybe mainly, systemic. It depends on the goals of the *system,* which may be too narrowly and inflexibly conceived; it depends on the ease of administration, which is considered as more important than economic or social costs; but it depends also on the method of calculating costs, which may create a false image of efficiency by ruling out "intangibles" that do not suit the method. This source of error becomes very important in advanced urban economies, where the provision of personal and social services grows rapidly in proportion to hardware and food production and distribution. In providing services—whether giving information, selling, teaching children, admitting to college, assigning jobs, serving food, or advising on welfare—standardization and punch-cards may seem to fulfill the functions, but they may do so at the expense of frayed nerves, waiting in line, bad mistakes, misfitting, and cold soup. In modern conditions, the tailormade improvisations of fallible but responsive human beings may be increasingly indispensable rather than useless. In the jargon of Frank Riessman, there is a need for "sub-professionals." Yet the mass-production and business-machine style, well-adapted to manufacturing hardware and calculating logistics, will decide that people are useless anyway, since they can mathematically be dispensed with. It is a curious experience to hear a gentleman from the Bureau of the Budget explain the budget of the War on Poverty according to cost-benefit computation. He can demonstrate that the participation of the poor in administering a program is disadvantageous; he can show you the flow chart; he cannot understand why poor people make a fuss on this point. It is impossible to explain to him that they do not trust the program (nor the director) but would like to get the money for their own purposes.

Abroad, the Americans still engage in plenty of old-fashioned exploitation of human labor, as in Latin America; yet the tendency is again to regard the underdeveloped peoples as not quite persons, and to try to shape them up by (sometimes) generous assistance in our own style. For example, one of the radical ideas of General Learning, the subsidiary of General Electric and Time, Inc., is to concentrate on electronic devices to teach literacy to the masses of children in poor countries; we must export our Great Society. Our enterprisers are eager to build highways and pipelines through the jungle, to multiply bases for our airplanes, and to provide other items of the American standard of living, for which the Western-trained native political leaders have "rising aspirations." Unfortunately, this largesse must often result in disrupting age-old cultures, fomenting tribal wars, inflating prices and wages, and reducing decent poverty to starvation, causing the abandonment of farms and disastrous instant urbanization, making dictatorships inevitable, and drawing simple peoples into Great Power conflicts. And woe if they do not then shape up, if they want to develop according to their local prejudices—for instance for land reform. They become an uncontrollable nuisance, surely therefore allied with our enemies, and better dead than Red. In his great speech in Montreal, Secretary McNamara informed us that since 1958, 87 per cent of the very poor nations and 69 per cent of the poor nations, but only 48 per cent of the middle income nations, have had serious violent disturbances. The cure for it, he said, was development, according to the criteria of our cash economy, and protection from subversion by our bombers. How to explain to this arithmetically astute man that he is not taking these people seriously as existing?

A startlingly literal corollary of the principle that our system excludes human beings rather than exploiting them is the agreement of all liberals and conservatives that there must be a check on population growth, more especially among backward peoples and the poor at home. We are definitely beyond the need for the labor of the "proletariat" (="producers of offspring") and the Iron Law of Wages to keep that labor cheap. Yet I am bemused by this unanimous recourse to a biological and mathematical etiology for our troubles. Probably there *is* a danger of world-overpopulation in the foreseeable future. Certainly with the likelihood of nuclear war there is a danger of world-underpopulation. However, until we institute more human ecological, economic, and political arrangements, I doubt that population control is the first order of business; nor would I trust the Americans to set the rules.

IV

I have singled-out two trends of the dominant organization of American society, its increasing tendency to expand, meaninglessly, for its own sake; and its tendency to exclude human beings as useless. It is

653

the Empty Society, the obverse face of the Affluent Society. When Adam Smith spoke of the Wealth of Nations, he did not mean anything like this.

The meaningless expansion and the excluding are different things, but in our society they are essentially related. Lack of meaning begins to occur when the immensely productive economy overmatures and lives by creating demand instead of meeting it; when the check of the free market gives way to monopolies, subsidies, and captive consumers; when the sense of community vanishes and public goods are neglected and resources despoiled; when there is made-work (or war) to reduce unemployment; and when the measure of economic health is not increasing well-being but abstractions like the Gross National Product and the rate of growth.

Human beings tend to be excluded when a logistic style becomes universally pervasive, so that values and data that cannot be standardized and programmed are disregarded; when function is adjusted to the technology rather than technology to function; when technology is treated as a good in itself, like science, rather than being regulated by political and moral prudence; when there develops an establishment of managers and experts who alone license and allot resources, and which deludes itself that it knows the only right method and is omnicompetent. Then common folk become docile clients, maintained by sufferance, or they are treated as deviant.

It is evident that, for us, these properties of the Empty Society are essentially related. If we did not exclude so many as not really persons, we would have to spend more of our substance on worthwhile goods, including subsistence goods, both at home and abroad; we would have to provide a more human environment for the children to grow up in; there would be more paths for growth and more ways of being a person. On the other hand, if we seriously and efficiently tackled the problems of anomie, alienation, riot, pollution, congestion, urban blight, degenerative and mental disease, etc., we would find ourselves paying more particular attention to persons and neighborhoods, rather than treating them as standard items; we would have a quite different engineering and social science; and we would need all the human resources available.

Certainly we would stop talking presumptuously about The Great Society and find ourselves struggling, in the confusing conditions of modern times, for a decent society.

The chief danger to American society at present, and to the world from American society, is our mindlessness, induced by empty institutions. It is a kind of mesmerism, a self-delusion of formal rightness, that affects both leaders and people. We have all the talking-points but less and less content. The Americans are decent folk, generous and fairly compassionate. They are not demented and fanatical, like some other imperial powers of the past and present, but on the con-   654 trary rather skeptical and with a sense of humor. They are not properly called arrogant, though perhaps presumptuous. But we have lost our horse sense, for which we were once noted. This kind of intelligence was grounded not in history or learning, nor in finesse of sensibility and analysis, but in the habit of making independent judgments and in democratically rubbing shoulders with all kinds and conditions. We have lost it by becoming personnel of a mechanical system and exclusive suburbanites, by getting out of contact with real jobs and real people. We suddenly have developed an Establishment, but our leaders do not have the tradition and self-restraint to come on like an establishment. Thus, we are likely to wreak havoc not because of greed, ideology, or arrogance, but because of a bright strategy of the theory of games and an impatient conviction that other people aren't quite human.

V

Opposing this strange doom-laden and (I fear) doom-bound social machine, there is only the tradition of America, populist, pluralist, and libertarian. To conclude this essay, let me make some remarks about the last of these, our peculiar libertarianism which is, I guess— along with our energy and enterprise—what most has impressed foreign peoples about us.

As a theme of history, the American kind of freedom has been traced to many things: the Americans were Englishmen, they were yeomen, they were Protestant refugees, they were other refugees, they had an open frontier—all these are relevant. But I am struck also by a constitutional aspect which I like, perhaps, to exaggerate.

Of all politically advanced peoples, the Americans are the only ones who started in a historical golden age of Anarchy. Having gotten rid of the king—and he was always far away, as well as being only an English king—they were in no hurry to reconstruct another sovereign, or even a concept of sovereignty. For more than thirty years after the outbreak of the Revolution, almost nobody bothered to vote in formal elections (often less than 2 per cent), and the national Constitution was the concern of only a few merchants and lawyers. Yet the Americans were not a primitive or unpolitical people; on the contrary, they had many kinds of civilized democratic and hierarchical structures; town meetings, congregational parishes, masters with apprentices and indentured servants, gentry with slaves, professionals and clients, provincial assemblies. The pluralism goes way back. But where was the sovereignty?

Theoretically, the sovereignty resided in the People. But except for sporadic waves of protest, like the riots, Tea Parties, and the Revolutionary War itself—the populism also goes way back—who were the People? One does not at all have the impression, in this congeries of 655 families, face-to-face communities, and pluralist social relations, that there was anything like a General Will, except maybe to be let alone.

Nevertheless, there *is*—it is clear from American behavior—a characteristic type of sovereignty. It is what is made up by political people as they go along, a continuous series of existential constitutional acts, just as they invented the Declaration, the Articles, and the Constitution, and obviously expected to keep rewriting the Constitution. The founding fathers were saddled with a Roman language, so they spoke of "unalienable rights"; but the American theory is idiomatically expressed by pragmatists like William James: I have certain rights and will act accordingly, including finally punching you in the nose if you don't concede them.

A few weeks ago, I was vividly reminded of the American idea of sovereignty when there were some sit-ins at the City Hall in Detroit and the Governor of Michigan said, in a voice that could only be called plaintive, "There is no Black Power, there is no White Power, there is no Mixed Power, the only power belongs to the government" —I presume that his textbook had said, "The only power belongs to the State." But there was no mystique in the Governor's textbook proposition; I doubt if anybody, but anybody, took it seriously as an assertion of moral authority, or as anything but a threat to call the cops. On the question of sovereignty, the unmistakable undertone in these incidents is, "Well, that remains to be seen."

VI

In the context of this pragmatic American attitude toward sovereignty, what is the meaning of the present wave of civil disobedience? Against direct actions like the civil-rights sit-ins, the student occupation of Sproul Hall at Berkeley, the draft-card burnings, it is always said that they foment disrespect for law and order and lead to a general breakdown of civil society. Although judicious people are willing to grant that due process and ordinary administration are not working well, because of prejudice, unconcern, doubletalk, arrogance, or perhaps just the cumbersomeness of overcentralized bureaucracy, nevertheless, they say, the recourse to civil disobedience entails even worse evils.

This is an apparently powerful argument. Even those who engage in civil disobedience tend to concede it, but, they say, in a crisis they cannot act otherwise; they are swept by indignation, or they are morally compelled to resist evil. Or they have an apocalyptic theory in which they are acting for a "higher" justice, and the present order is no longer legitimate.

In my opinion, all these views are exaggerations because they assign a status and finality to the sovereign which in America it does not have. If the State is not quite so determinate, then the insult to it does

656

not necessarily have such global consequences. Certainly the American genius, whether we cite Jefferson, or James and Dewey more than a century later, is that the State is in process, in a kind of regulated permanent revolution.

Empirically, is it the case that direct actions which are aimed at specific abuses lead to general lawlessness? Where is the evidence to prove the connection—e.g., statistics of correlative disorder in the community, or an increase of unspecific lawless acts among the direct activists? The flimsy evidence that we actually have tends to weigh in the opposite direction. Crime and delinquency seem to diminish where there has been political direct action by Negroes. The community and academic spirit at Berkeley has been better this year than it used to be. In 1944, the warden of Danbury prison assured me that the war-objectors penned up there were, in general, the finest type of citizens!

On sociological grounds, indeed, the probability is that a specific direct action, which cuts through frustrating due process, and especially if it is successful or partially successful, will tend to increase civil order rather than to destroy it, for it revives the belief that the community is one's own, that one has influence; whereas the inhibition of direct action against an intolerable abuse inevitably increases anomie and therefore *general* lawlessness. The enforcement of law and order at all costs aggravates the tensions that lead to explosions. But if place is allowed for "creative disorder," as Arthur Waskow calls it, there is less tension, less resignation, and more likelihood of finding social, economic, and political expedients to continue with.

Of course, this raises a nice legal question: how to distinguish between a rioting mob and citizens engaging in creative disorder? Theoretically, it is a rioting mob, according to the wisdom of LeBon and Freud, if it is in the grip of unconscious ideas of Father or the need to destroy Father, if it is after senseless power or to destroy senseless power. But it is a group of confused Americans if it is demanding to be paid attention to, and included. Perhaps it is petitioning for a redress of grievances, even if it has no writ of grievances to present, and even if there is no sovereign to petition. In actuality, in anomic conditions, the distinction is not easy to make. But in either case, the part of wisdom is to take people seriously and come up with a new idea that might make a difference to their problems. If the governors won't, or can't, do this, then we must do it. I am often asked by radical students what I am trying to do with all my utopian thinking and inventing of alternatives; perhaps the use of intellect is to help turn riot into creative disorder.

In brief, contrary to the conventional argument, anarchic incidents like civil disobedience are often essential parts of the democratic process as Americans understand it. So it was understood by Jefferson when, after Shay's rebellion was disarmed, he urged that nobody be punished, for that might discourage mutiny in the future, and then 657 what check would there be on government? So, in milder terms, it has been recently understood by the pragmatic Supreme Court, where many cases of apparently obvious trespass and violation have turned out to be legal after all, and only subsequently made legal by statute. This is not, I believe, because the Court has been terrorized or has blinked in order to avoid worse evils, but because in rapidly changing circumstances, there is often no other way to know what the Constitution is.

VII

Finally, I need hardly point out that in American rhetoric, American freedom—in an anarchic sense—has been held to be the philosopher's stone of our famous energy and enterprise. Mossback conservatives have always spoken for *laissez-faire* as the right climate for economic progress (though, to be sure, they then connive for tariffs and subsidies, hire strikebreakers, and form monopolies in restraint of trade). Radical liberals have cleaved to the Bill of Rights, for to be cowed by authority makes it impossible to think and experiment. Immigrants used to flock to the United States to avoid conscription, just as now some of our best young go to Canada and are welcomed. They came because there were no class barriers, and because there was open opportunity to make good in one's own way. By age nine, kids have learned to say, "It's a free country—you can't make me."

By and large, let me say, this rhetoric has been true. Anarchism is grounded in a rather definite social-psychological hypothesis: that forceful, graceful, and intelligent behavior occurs only when there is an uncoerced and direct response to the physical and social environment; that in most human affairs, more harm than good results from compulsion, top-down direction, bureaucratic planning, preordained curricula, jails, conscription, States. Sometimes it is necessary to limit freedom, as we keep a child from running across the highway, but this is usually done at the expense of force, grace, and learning; and in the long run it is usually wiser to remove the danger and simplify the rules than to hamper the activity. I think, I say, that this hypothesis is true, but whether or not it is, it would certainly be un-American to deny it. Everybody knows that America is great because America is free; and by freedom is not finally meant the juridical freedom of the European tradition, freedom under law, having the legal rights and duties of citizens; what is meant is the spontaneous freedom of anarchy, opportunity to do what you can, although hampered by necessary conventions, as few as possible.

Then, how profoundly alien is our present establishment, which has in one generation crept up on us and occupied all the positions of power. It has been largely the product of war, of the dislocations after World War I, the crash programs of World War II, and the chronic 658 low-grade emergency of the cold war which is fanning again into war. The cold war has lasted for twenty years. This is the period in which more than half of gross new investment has been in armaments. It has had consequences.

The term "establishment" itself is borrowed from the British—for snobbish and literary reasons, and usually with an edge of satire. But we have had no sovereign to establish such a thing, and there is no public psychology to accept it as legitimate. It operates like an establishment: it is the consensus of politics, the universities and science, big business, organized labor, public schooling, the media of communications; it sets the official language; it determines the right style and accredits its own members; it hires and excludes, subsidizes and neglects. But it has no warrant of legitimacy, it has no tradition, it cannot talk straight English, it neither has produced nor could produce any art, it does not lead by moral means but by a kind of social engineering, and it is held in contempt and detestation by the young. The American tradition—I think the *abiding* American tradtion—is pluralist, populist, and libertarian, while the establishment is monolithic, mandarin, and managed. And the evidence is that its own claim —that it is efficient—is false. It is fantastically wasteful of brains, money, the environment, and people. It is channeling our energy and enterprise to its own aggrandizement and power, and it will exhaust us.

I would almost say that my country is like a conquered province with foreign rulers, except that they are not foreigners and we are responsible for what they do.

VIII

The system at present dominant in America, then, will not do; it is too empty. On the other hand, it is possible that classical American democracy is necessarily a thing of the past; it may be too wild, too woolly, too mixed up—too anarchic, too populist, too pluralist—for the conditions of big population and high technology in a world that has become small. I hope this is not the case, for I love the American experiment; but I don't know. The American faces that used to be so beautiful, so resolute and yet poignantly open and innocent, are looking ugly these days, hard, thin-lipped, and like innocence spoiled without having become experienced.

We Americans have not suffered as most other peoples have, at least not since the Civil War a century ago. We have not been bombed, we have not been occupied. We have not been colonialized for two hundred years. We have not cringed under a real tyranny. Perhaps we would not ride so high today if we knew what it felt like to be badly hurt.

659

Carl Oglesby

Let Us Shape the Future

Seven months ago at the April March on Washington, Paul Potter, then President of Students for a Democratic Society, stood in approximately this spot and said that we must name the system that creates and sustains the war in Vietnam—name it, describe it, analyze it, understand it, and change it.

Today I will try to name it—to suggest an analysis which, to be quite frank, may disturb some of you—and to suggest what changing it may require of us.

We are here again to protest again a growing war. Since it is a very bad war, we acquire the habit of thinking that it must be caused by very bad men. But we only conceal reality, I think, to denounce on such grounds the menacing coalition of industrial and military power, or the brutality of the blitzkrieg we are waging against Vietnam, or the ominous signs around us that heresy may soon no longer be permitted. We must simply observe, and quite plainly say, that this coalition, this blitzkrieg, and this demand for acquiescence are creatures, all of them, of a government that since 1932 has considered itself to be fundamentally liberal.

The original commitment in Vietnam was made by President Truman, a main-stream liberal. It was seconded by President Eisenhower, a moderate liberal. It was intensified by the late President Kennedy, a flaming liberal. Think of the men who now engineer that war—those who study the maps, give the commands, push the buttons, and tally the dead: Bundy, McNamara, Rusk, Lodge, Goldberg, the President himself.

They are not moral monsters.

They are all honorable men.

They are all liberals.

Reprinted by permission of the author from *Liberation*, January 1966. Carl Oglesby is the former president of Students for a Democratic Society. 660

THE REVOLUTION IN EXPRESSION .

But so, I'm sure, are many of us who are here today in protest. To understand the war, then, it seems necessary to take a closer look at this American liberalism. Maybe we are in for some surprises. Maybe we have here two quite different liberalisms: one authentically humanist; the other not so human at all.

Not long ago, I considered myself a liberal. And if someone had asked me what I meant by that, I'd perhaps have quoted Thomas Jefferson or Thomas Paine, who first made plain our nation's unprovisional commitment to human rights. But what do you think would happen if these two heroes could sit down now for a chat with President Johnson and McGeorge Bundy?

They would surely talk of the Vietnam war. Our dead revolutionaries would soon wonder why their country was fighting against what appeared to be a revolution. The living liberals would hotly deny that it is one: there are troops coming in from outside, the rebels get arms from other countries, most of the people are not on their side, and they practice terror against their own. Therefore, not a revolution.

What would our dead revolutionaries answer? They might say: "What fools and bandits, sir, you make then of us. Outside help? Do you remember Lafayette? Or the 2,000 British freighters the French navy sunk for our side? Or the arms and men we got from France and Spain? And what's this about terror? Did you never hear what we did to our own loyalists? Or about the thousands of rich American Tories who fled for their lives to Canada? And as for popular support, do you not know that we had less than one-third of our people with us? That, in fact, the colony of New York recruited more troops for the British than for the revolution? Should we give it all back?"

Revolutions do not take place in velvet boxes. They never have. It is only the poets who make them lovely. What the National Liberation Front is fighting in Vietnam is a complex and vicious war. This war is also a revolution, as honest a revolution as you can find anywhere in history. And this is a fact which all our intricate denials will never change.

But it doesn't make any difference to our leaders anyway. Their aim in Vietnam is really much simpler than this implies. It is to safeguard what they take to be American interests around the world against revolution or revolutionary change, which they always call communism—as if it were that. In the case of Vietnam, this interest is, first, the principle that revolution shall not be tolerated anywhere, and second, that South Vietnam shall never sell its rice to China—or even to North Vietnam.

There is simply no such thing now, for us, as a just revolution—never mind that for two-thirds of the world's people the 20th century might as well be the Stone Age; never mind the melting poverty and hopelessness that are the basic facts of life for most of modern men; and never mind that for those millions there is now an increasingly perceptible relationship between their sorrow and our contentment.

Can we understand why the Negroes of Watts rebelled? Then why do we need a devil theory to explain the rebellion of the South Vietnamese? Can we understand the oppression in Mississippi, or the anguish that our Northern ghettoes makes epidemic? Then why can't we see that our proper human struggle is not with Communism or revolutionaries, but with the social desperation that drives good men to violence, both here and abroad?

To be sure, we have been most generous with our aid, and in Western Europe, a mature industrial society, that aid worked. But there are always political and financial strings. And we have never shown ourselves capable of allowing others to make those traumatic institutional changes that are often the prerequisites of progress in colonial societies. For all our official feeling for the millions who are enslaved to what we so self-righteously call the yoke of Communist tyranny, we make no real effort at all to crack through the much more vicious right-wing tyrannies that our businessmen traffic with and our nation profits from everyday. And for all our cries about the international Red conspiracy to take over the world, we take only pride in the fact of our 6,000 military bases on foreign soil.

We gave Rhodesia a grave look just now—but we keep on buying her chromium which is cheap because black slave labor mines it.

We deplore the racism of Verwoert's fascist South Africa—but our banks make big loans to that country and our private technology makes it a nuclear power.

We are saddened and puzzled by random back-page stories of revolt in this or that Latin American state—but are convinced by a few pretty photos in the Sunday supplement that things are getting better, that the world is coming our way, that change from disorder can be orderly, that our benevolence will pacify the distressed, that our might will intimidate the angry.

Optimists, may I suggest that these are quite unlikely fantasies. They are fantasies because we have lost that mysterious social desire for human equity that from time to time has given us genuine moral drive. We have become a nation of young bright-eyed, hard-hearted, slim-waisted, bullet-headed make-out artists. A nation—may I say it?—of beardless liberals.

You say I am being hard? Only think.

This country, with its thirty-some years of liberalism, can send 200,000 young men to Vietnam to kill and die in the most dubious of wars, but it cannot get 100 voter registrars to go into Mississippi.

What do you make of it?

The financial burden of the war obliges us to cut millions from an already pathetic War on Poverty budget. But in almost the same 662 breath, Congress appropriates $140 million for the Lockheed and Boeing companies to compete with each other on the supersonic transport project—that Disneyland creation will cost us all about $2 billion before it's done.

What do you make of it?

Many of us have been earnestly resisting for some years now the idea of putting atomic weapons into West German hands, an action that would perpetuate the division of Europe and thus the Cold War. Now just this week we find out that, with the meagerest of security systems, West Germany has had nuclear weapons in her hands for the past six years.

What do you make of it?

Some will make of it that I overdraw the matter. Many will ask: What about the other side? To be sure, there is the bitter ugliness of Czechoslovakia, Poland, those infamous Russian tanks in the streets of Budapest. But my anger only rises to hear some say that sorrow cancels sorrow, or that *this* one's shame deposits in *that* one's account the right to shamefulness.

And others will make of it that I sound mighty anti-American. To these, I say: Don't blame *me* for *that!* Blame those who mouthed my liberal values and broke my American heart.

Just who might they be, by the way? Let's take a brief factual inventory of the latter-day Cold War.

In 1953 our Central Intelligence Agency managed to overthrow Mossadegh in Iran; the complaint being his neutralism in the Cold War and his plans to nationalize the country's oil resources to improve his people's lives. Most evil aims, most evil man. In his place we put in General Zahedi, a World War II Nazi collaborator. New arrangements on Iran's oil gave 25 year leases on 40% of it to three US firms, one of which was Gulf Oil. The CIA's leader for this coup was Kermit Roosevelt. In 1960 Kermit Roosevelt became a vice president of Gulf Oil.

In 1954, the democratically elected Arbenz of Guatemala wanted to nationalize a portion of United Fruit Company's plantations in his country, land he badly needed for a modest program of agrarian reform. His government was overthrown by a CIA-supported right-wing coup. The following year, Gen. Walter Bedell Smith, director of the CIA when the Guatemala venture was being planned, joined the board of directors of the United Fruit Company.

Comes 1960 and Castro cries we are about to invade Cuba. The Administration sneers, "poppycock," and we Americans believe it. Comes 1961 and the invasion. Comes with it the awful realization that the United States Government had lied.

Comes 1962 and the missile crisis, and our Administration stands prepared to fight global atomic war on the curious principle that another state does not have the right to its own foreign policy.

663

Comes 1963 and British Guiana, where Cheddi Jagan wants independence from England and a labor law modelled on the Wagner Act. And Jay Lovestone, the AFL-CIO foreign policy chief, acting, as always, quite independently of labor's rank and file, arranges with our government to finance an eleven-week dock strike that brings Jagan down, ensuring that the state will remain *British* Guiana, and that any workingman who wants a wage better than 50 cents a day is a dupe of communism.

Comes 1964. Two weeks after Undersecretary Thomas Mann announces that we have abandoned the *Alianza's* principle of no aid to tyrants, Brazil's Goulart is overthrown by the vicious right-winger, Ademar Barros, supported by a show of American gunboats at Rio de Janeiro. Within 24 hours, the new head of state, Mazzilli, receives a congratulatory wire from our President.

Comes 1965. The Dominican Republic. Rebellion in the streets. We scurry to the spot with 20,000 neutral Marines and our neutral peacemakers—like Ellsworth Bunker, Jr., Ambassador to the Organization of American States. Most of us know that our neutral Marines fought openly on the side of the junta, a fact that the Administration still denies. But how many also know that what was at stake was our new Carribean Sugar Bowl? That this same neutral peacemaking Bunker is a board member and stock owner of the National Sugar Refining Company, a firm his father founded in the good old days, and one which has a major interest in maintaining the status quo in the Dominican Republic? Or that the President's close personal friend and advisor, our new Supreme Court Justice Abe Fortas, has sat for the past 19 years on the board of the Sucrest Company, which imports black-strap molasses from the Dominican Republic? Or that the rhetorician of corporate liberalism, and the late President Kennedy's close friend, Adolf Berle, was chairman of that same board? Or that our roving ambassador Averill Harriman's brother Roland is on the board of National Sugar? Or that our former ambassador to the Dominican Republic, Joseph Farland, is a board member of the South Puerto Rico Sugar Co., which owns 275,000 acres of rich land in the Dominican Republic and is the largest employer on the island —at about one dollar a day?

Neutralists! God save the hungry people of the world from such neutralists!

We do not say these men are evil. We say, rather, that good men can be divided from their compassion by the institutional system that inherits us all. Generation in and out, we are put to use. People become instruments. Generals do not hear the screams of the bombed; sugar executives do not see the misery of the cane cutters: for to do so is to be that much *less* the general, that much *less* the executive.

The foregoing facts of recent history describe one main aspect of the estate of Western liberalism. Where is our American humanism

664

hero? What went wrong? Let's stare our situation coldly in the face. All of us are born to the colossus of history, our American corporate system—in many ways, an awesome organism. There is one fact that describes it: with about 5% of the world's people, we consume about half the world's goods. We take a richness that is in good part not our own, and we put it in our pockets, our garages, our split-levels, our bellies, and our futures.

On the *face* of it, it is a crime that so few should have so much at the expense of so many. Where is the moral imagination so abused as to call this just? Perhaps many of us feel a bit uneasy in our sleep. We are not, after all, a cruel people. And perhaps we don't really need this super-dominance that deforms others. But what can we do? The investments are made. The financial ties are established. The plants abroad are built. Our system *exists*. One is swept up into it. How intolerable—to be born moral, but addicted to a stolen and maybe surplus luxury. Our goodness threatens to become counterfeit before our eyes—unless we change. But change threatens us with uncertainty —at least.

Our problem, then, is to justify this system and give its theft another name—to make kind and moral what is neither, to perform some alchemy with language that will make this injustice seem to be a most magnanimous gift:

A hard problem. But the Western democracies, in the heyday of their colonial expansionism, produced a hero worthy of the task.

Its name was free enterprise, and its partner was an *illiberal liberalism* that said to the poor and the dispossessed: What we acquire of your resources we repay in civilization. The white man's burden. But this was too poetic. So a much more hard-headed theory was produced. This theory said that colonial status is in fact a *boon* to the colonized. We give them technology and bring them into modern times.

But this deceived no one but ourselves. We were delighted with this new theory. The poor saw in it merely an admission that their claims were irrefutable. They stood up to us, without gratitude. We were shocked—but also confused, for the poor seemed again to be right. How long is it going to be the case, we wondered, that the poor will be right and the rich will be wrong?

Liberalism faced a crisis. In the face of the collapse of the European empires, how could it continue to hold together our twin need for richness and righteousness? How can we continue to sack the ports of Asia and still dream of Jesus?

The challenge was met with a most ingenious solution: the ideology of anti-Communism. This was the bind: we cannot call revolution bad, because we started that way ourselves, and because it is all too easy to see why the dispossessed should rebel. So we will call revolution *Communism*. And we will reserve the right to say what Communism means. We take note of revolution's enormities, wrenching them 665 where necessary from their historical context and often exaggerating them, and say: Behold, Communism is a bloodbath. We take note of those reactionaries who stole the revolution's need to consolidate itself, and say: Behold, Communism is a tyranny.

It has been all these things, and it will be these things again, and we will never be at a loss for those tales of atrocity that comfort us so in our self-righteousness. Nuns will be raped and bureaucrats will be disembowelled. Indeed, revolution is a *fury*. For it is a letting loose of outrages pent up sometimes over centuries. But the more brutal and longer-lasting the suppression of this energy, all the more ferocious will be its explosive release.

Far from helping Americans to deal with this truth, the anti-Communist ideology merely tries to disguise it so that things may stay the way they are. Thus, it depicts our presence in other lands not as a coercion, but a protection. It allows us even to say that napalm in Vietnam is only another aspect of our humanitarian love—like those exorcisms in the Middle Ages that so often killed the patient. So we say to the Vietnamese peasant, the Cuban intellectual, the Peruvian worker: You are better dead than Red. If it hurts or if you don't understand why—sorry about that.

This is the action of *corporate liberalism*. It performs for the corporate state a function quite like what the Church once performed for the feudal state. It seeks to justify its burdens and protect it from change. As the Church exaggerated this office in the Inquisition, so with liberalism in the McCarthy time—which, if it was a reactionary phenomenon, was still made possible by our anti-Communist corporate liberalism.

Let me then speak directly to humanist liberals. If my facts are wrong, I will soon be corrected. But if they are right, then you may face a crisis of conscience.

Corporatism or humanism: which? For it has come to that. Will you let your dreams be used? Will you be grudging apologists for the corporate state? Or will you help try to change it—not in the name of this or that blueprint ism, but in the name of simple human decency and democracy and the vision that wise and brave men saw in the time of our own Revolution?

And if your commitment to human value is unconditional, then disabuse yourselves of the notion that statements will bring change, if only the right statement can be written, or that interviews with the mighty will bring change if only the mighty can be reached, or that marches will bring change if only we can make them reasonable enough.

We are dealing now with a colossus that does not want to be changed. It will not change itself. It will not cooperate with those who want to change it. Those allies of ours in the government—are they really our allies? If they are, then they don't need advice, they need 666 constituencies; they don't need study groups, they need a movement. And if they are not, then all the more reason for building that movement with a most relentless conviction.

There are people in this country who are trying to build that movement, who aim at nothing less than a humanist reformation. And the humanist liberals must understand that it is this movement with which their own best hopes are most in tune. We radicals know the same history that you liberals know, and we can understand your occasional cynicism, exasperation, and even distrust. But we ask you to put these aside and help us risk a leap. Help us find enough time for the enormous work that needs doing here. Help us build. Help us shake the future in the name of plain human hope.

Stokely Carmichael

Toward Black Liberation

One of the most pointed illustrations of the need for Black Power, as a positive and redemptive force in a society degenerating into a form of totalitarianism, is to be made by examining the history of distortion that the concept has received in national media of publicity. In this "debate," as in everything else that affects our lives, Negroes are dependent on, and at the discretion of, forces and institutions within the white society which have little interest in representing us honestly. Our experience with the national press has been that where they have managed to escape a meretricious special interest in "Git Whitey" sensationalism and race-war mongering, individual reporters and commentators have been conditioned by the enveloping racism of the society to the point where they are incapable even of objective observation and reporting of racial *incidents,* much less the analysis of *ideas.* But this limitation of vision and perceptions is an inevitable consequence of the dictatorship of definition, interpretation and consciousness, along with the censorship of history that the society has inflicted upon the Negro—and itself.

Our concern for black power addresses itself directly to this problem, the necessity to reclaim our history and our identity from the cultural terrorism and depredation of self-justifying white guilt.

To do this we shall have to struggle for the right to create our own terms through which to define ourselves and our relationship to the society, and to have these terms recognized. This is the first necessity for a free people, and the first right that any oppressor must suspend. The white fathers of American racism knew this—instinctively it seems—as is indicated by the continuous record of the distor-

From *The Massachusetts Review*, Autumn 1966. Reprinted by permission of SNCC. Copyright © 1966 The Student Nonviolent Coordinating Committee. Stokely Carmichael, noted civil rights leader, is the former executive Secretary of the Student Nonviolent Coordinating Committee.

tion and omission in their dealings with the red and black men. In the same way that southern apologists for the "Jim Crow" society have so obscured, muddied and misrepresented the record of the reconstruction period, until it is almost impossible to tell what really happened, their contemporary counterparts are busy doing the same thing with the recent history of the civil rights movement.

In 1964, for example, the National Democratic Party, led by L. B. Johnson and Hubert H. Humphrey, cynically undermined the efforts of Mississippi's Black population to achieve some degree of political representation. Yet, whenever the events of that convention are recalled by the press, one sees only that version fabricated by the press agents of the Democratic Party. A year later the House of Representatives in an even more vulgar display of political racism made a mockery of the political rights of Mississippi's Negroes when it failed to unseat the Missisippi Delegation to the House which had been elected through a process which methodically and systematically excluded over 450,000 voting-age Negroes, almost one half of the total electorate of the state. Whenever this event is mentioned in print it is in terms which leaves one with the rather curious impression that somehow the oppressed Negro people of Mississippi are at fault for confronting the Congress with a situation in which they had no alternative but to endorse Mississippi's racist political practices.

I mention these two examples because, having been directly involved in them, I can see very clearly the discrepancies between what happened, and the versions that are finding their way into general acceptance as a kind of popular mythology. Thus the victimization of the Negro takes place in two phases—first it occurs in fact and deed, then, and this is equally sinister, in the official recording of those facts.

The "Black Power" program and concept which is being articulated by SNCC, CORE, and a host of community organizations in the ghettoes of the North and South has not escaped that process. The white press has been busy articulating their own analyses, their own interpretations, and criticisms of their own creations. For example, while the press had given wide and sensational dissemination to attacks made by figures in the Civil Rights movement—foremost among which are Roy Wilkins of the NAACP and Whitney Young of the Urban League —and to the hysterical ranting about black racism made by the political chameleon that now serves as Vice-President, it has generally failed to give accounts of the reasonable and productive dialogue which is taking place in the Negro community, and in certain important areas in the white religious and intellectual community. A national committee of influential Negro Churchmen affiliated with the National Council of Churches, despite their obvious respectability and responsibility, had to resort to a paid advertisement to articulate their position, while anyone shouting the hysterical yappings of "Black Racism" got ample space. Thus the American people have gotten at 669 best a superficial and misleading account of the very terms and tenor of this debate. I wish to quote briefly from the statement by the national committee of Churchmen which I suspect that the majority of Americans will not have seen. This statement appeared in the *New York Times* of July 31, 1966.

> We an informal group of Negro Churchmen in America are deeply disturbed about the crisis brought upon our country by historic distortions of important human realities in the controversy about "black power." What we see shining through the variety of rhetoric is not anything new but the same old problem of power and race which has faced our beloved country since 1619.
>
> ... The conscience of black men is corrupted because, having no power to implement the demands of conscience, the concern for justice in the absence of justice becomes a chaotic self-surrender. Powerlessness breeds a race of beggars. We are faced now with a situation where powerless conscience meets conscience-less power, threatening the very foundations of our Nation.
>
> ... We deplore the overviolence of riots, but we feel it is more important to focus on the real sources of these eruptions. These sources may be abetted inside the Ghetto, but their basic cause lies in the silent and covert violence which white middleclass America inflicts upon the victims of the inner city.
>
> ... In short; the failure of American leaders to use American power to create equal opportunity *in life* as well as *law,* this is the real problem and not the anguished cry for black power.
>
> ... Without the capacity to *participate with power, i.e.,* to have some organized political and economic strength to really influence people with whom one interacts—integration is not meaningful.
>
> ... America has asked its Negro citizens to fight for opportunity as *individuals,* whereas at certain points in our history what we have needed most has been opportunity for the *whole group,* not just for selected and approved *Negroes.*
>
> ... We must not apologize for the existence of this form of group power, for we have been oppressed as a group and not as individuals. We will not find our way out of that oppression until both we and America accept the need for Negro Americans, as well as for Jews, Italians, Poles, and white Anglosaxon Protestants, among others to have and to wield group power.

Traditionally, for each new ethnic group, the route to social and political integration into America's pluralistic society, has been through the organization of their own institutions with which to represent their communal needs within the larger society. This is simply stating what the advocates of black power are saying. The strident outcry, *particularly* from the liberal community, that has been evoked by this proposal can only be understood by examining the historic relationship between Negro and White power in this country.

670

Negroes are defined by two forces, their blackness and their power-lessness. There have been traditionally two communities in America. The White community, which controlled and defined the forms that all institutions with the society would take, and the Negro community which has been excluded from participation in the power decisions that shaped the society, and has traditionally been dependent upon, and subservient to the White community.

This has not been accidental. The history of every institution of this society indicates that a major concern in the ordering and structuring of the society has been the maintaining of the Negro community in its condition of dependence and oppression. This has not been on the level of individual acts of discrimination between individual whites against individual Negroes, but as total acts by the White community against the Negro community. This fact cannot be too strongly emphasized—that racist assumptions of white superiority have been so deeply ingrained in the structure of the society that it infuses its entire functioning, and is so much a part of the national subconscious that it is taken for granted and is frequently not even recognized.

Let me give an example of the difference between individual racism and institutionalized racism, and the society's response to both. When unidentified white terrorists bomb a Negro Church and kill five children, that is an act of individual racism, widely deplored by most segments of the society. But when in that same city, Birmingham, Alabama, not five but 500 Negro babies die each year because of a lack of proper food, shelter and medical facilities, and thousands more are destroyed and maimed physically, emotionally and intellectually because of conditions of poverty and deprivation in the ghetto, that is a function of institutionalized racism. But the society either pretends it doesn't know of this situation, or is incapable of doing anything meaningful about it. And this resistance to doing anything meaningful about conditions in that ghetto comes from the fact that the ghetto is itself a product of a combination of forces and special interests in the white community, and the groups that have access to the resources and power to change that situation benefit, politically and economically, from the existence of that ghetto.

It is more than a figure of speech to say that the Negro community in America is the victim of white imperialism and colonial exploitation. This is in practical economic and political terms true. There are over 20 million black people comprising ten percent of this nation. They for the most part live in well-defined areas of the country—in the shanty-towns and rural black belt areas of the South, and increasingly in the slums of northern and western industrial cities. If one goes into any Negro community, whether it be in Jackson, Miss., Cambridge, Md. or Harlem, N. Y., one will find that the same combination of political, economic, and social forces are at work. The   671 people in the Negro community do not control the resources of that community, its political decisions, its law enforcement, its housing standards; and even the physical ownership of the land, houses, and stores *lie outside that community.*

It is white power that makes the laws, and it is violent white power in the form of armed white cops that enforces those laws with guns and nightsticks. The vast majority of Negroes in this country live in these captive communities and must endure these conditions of oppression because, and only because, *they are black and powerless.* I do not suppose that at any point the men who control the power and resources of this country ever sat down and designed these black enclaves, and formally articulated the terms of their colonial and dependent status, as was done, for example, by the Apartheid government of South Africa. Yet, one can not distinguish between one ghetto and another. As one moves from city to city it is as though some malignant racist planning-unit had done precisely this—designed each one from the same master blueprint. And indeed, if the ghetto had been formally and deliberately planned, instead of growing spontaneously and inevitably from the racist functioning of the various institutions that combine to make the society, it would be somehow less frightening. The situation would be less frightening because, if these ghettoes were the result of design and conspiracy, one could understand their similarity as being artificial and consciously imposed, rather than the result of identical patterns of white racism which repeat themselves in cities as distant as Boston and Birmingham. Without bothering to list the historic factors which contribute to this pattern—economic exploitation, political impotence, discrimination in employment and education—one can see that to correct this pattern will require far-reaching changes in the basic power-relationships and the ingrained social patterns within the society. The question is, of course, what kinds of changes are necessary, and how is it possible to bring them about?

In recent years the answer to these questions which has been given by most articulate groups of Negroes and their white allies, the "liberals" of all stripes, has been in terms of something called "integration." According to the advocates of integration, social justice will be accomplished by "integrating the Negro into the mainstream institutions of the society from which he has been traditionally excluded." It is very significant that each time I have heard this formulation it has been in terms of "the Negro," the individual Negro, rather than in terms of the community.

This concept of integration had to be based on the assumption that there was nothing of value in the Negro community and that little of value could be created among Negroes, so the thing to do was to siphon off the "acceptable" Negroes into the surrounding middle-class white community. Thus the goal of the movement for integration was   672 simply to loosen up the restrictions barring the entry of Negroes into the white community. Goals around which the struggle took place, such as public accommodation, open housing, job opportunity on the executive level (which is easier to deal with than the problem of semi-skilled and blue collar jobs which involve more far-reaching economic adjustments), are quite simply middle-class goals, articulated by a tiny group of Negroes who had middle-class aspirations. It is true that the student demonstrations in the South during the early sixties, out of which SNCC came, had a similar orientation. But while it is hardly a concern of a black sharecropper, dishwasher, or welfare recipient whether a certain fifteen-dollar-a-day motel offers accommodations to Negroes, the overt symbols of white superiority and the imposed limitations on the Negro community had to be destroyed. Now, black people must look beyond these goals, to the issue of collective power.

Such a limited class orientation was reflected not only in the program and goals of the civil rights movement, but in its tactics and organization. It is very significant that the two oldest and most "respectable" civil rights organizations have constitutions which *specifically* prohibit partisan political activity. CORE once did, but changed that clause when it changed its orientation toward black power. But this is perfectly understandable in terms of the strategy and goals of the older organizations. The civil rights movement saw its role as a kind of liaison between the powerful white community and the dependent Negro one. The dependent status of the black community apparently was unimportant since—if the movement were successful —it was going to blend into the white community anyway. We made no pretense of organizing and developing institutions of community power in the Negro community, but appealed to the conscience of white institutions of power. The posture of the civil rights movement was that of the dependent, the suppliant. The theory was that without attempting to create any organized base of political strength itself, the civil rights movement could, by forming coalitions with various "liberal" pressure organizations in the white community—liberal reform clubs, labor unions, church groups, progressive civic groups— and at times one or other of the major political parties—influence national legislation and national social patterns.

I think we all have seen the limitations of this approach. We have repeatedly seen that political alliances based on appeals to conscience and decency are chancy things, simply because institutions and political organizations have no consciences outside their own special interests. The political and social rights of Negroes have been and always will be negotiable and expendable the moment they conflict with the interests of our "allies." If we do not learn from history, we are doomed to repeat it, and that is precisely the lesson of the Reconstruction. Black people were allowed to register, vote and participate in politics because it was to the advantage of powerful white 673 allies to promote this. But this was the result of white decision, and it was ended by other white men's decision before any political base powerful enough to challenge that decision could be established in the southern Negro community. (Thus at this point in the struggle Negroes have no assurance—save a kind of idiot optimism and faith in a society whose history is one of racism—that if it were to become necessary, even the painfully limited gains thrown to the civil rights movement by the Congress will not be revoked as soon as a shift in political sentiments should occur.)

The major limitation of this approach was that it tended to maintain the traditional dependence of Negroes, and of the movement. We depended upon the good-will and support of various groups within the white community whose interests were not always compatible with ours. To the extent that we depended on the financial support of other groups, we were vulnerable to their influence and domination.

Also the program that evolved out of this coalition was really limited and inadequate in the long term and one which affected only a small select group of Negroes. Its goal was to make the white community accessible to "qualified" Negroes and presumably each year a few more Negroes armed with their passport—a couple of university degrees—would escape into middle-class America and adopt the attitudes and life styles of that group; and one day the Harlems and the Watts would stand empty, a tribute to the success of integration. This is simply neither realistic nor particularly desirable. You can integrate communities, but you assimilate individuals. Even if such a program were possible its result would be, not to develop the black community as a functional and honorable segment of the total society, with its own cultural identity, life patterns, and institutions, but to abolish it—the final solution to the Negro problem. Marx said that the working class is the first class in history that ever wanted to abolish itself. If one listens to some of our "moderate" Negro leaders it appears that the American Negro is the first race that ever wished to abolish itself. The fact is that what must be abolished is not the black community, but the dependent colonial status that has been inflicted upon it. The racial and cultural personality of the black community must be preserved and the community must win its freedom while preserving its cultural integrity. This is the essential difference between integration as it is currently practised and the concept of black power.

What has the movement for integration accomplished to date? The Negro graduating from M.I.T. with a doctorate will have better job opportunities available to him than to Lynda Bird Johnson. But the rate of unemployment in the Negro community is steadily increasing, while that in the white community decreases. More educated Negroes hold executive jobs in major corporations and federal agencies than ever before, but the gap between white income and Negro income 674 has almost doubled in the last twenty years. More suburban housing is available to Negroes, but housing conditions in the ghetto are steadily declining. While the infant mortality rate of New York City is at its lowest rate ever in the city's history, the infant mortality rate of Harlem is steadily climbing. There has been an organized national resistance to the Supreme Court's order to integrate the schools, and the federal government has not acted to enforce that order. Less than fifteen percent of black children in the South attend integrated schools; and Negro schools, which the vast majority of black children still attend, are increasingly decrepit, overcrowded, under-staffed, inadequately equipped and funded.

This explains why the rate of school dropouts is increasing among Negro teenagers, who then express their bitterness, hopelessness, and alienation by the only means they have—rebellion. As long as people in the ghettoes of our large cities feel that they are victims of the misuse of white power without any way to have their needs represented—and these are frequently simple needs: to get the welfare inspectors to stop kicking down your doors in the middle of the night, the cops from beating your children, the landlord to exterminate the vermin in your home, the city to collect your garbage—we will continue to have riots. These are not the products of "black power," but of the absence of any organization capable of giving the community the power, the black power, to deal with its problems.

SNCC proposes that it is now time for the black freedom movement to stop pandering to the fears and anxieties of the white middle class in the attempt to earn its "good-will," and to return to the ghetto to organize these communities to control themselves. This organization must be attempted in northern and southern urban areas as well as in the rural black belt counties of the South. The chief antagonist to this organization is, in the South, the overtly racist Democratic party, and in the North the equally corrupt big city machines.

The standard argument presented against independent political organization is "But you are only 10%." I cannot see the relevance of this observation, since no one is talking about taking over the country, but taking control over our own communities.

The fact is that the Negro population, 10% or not, is very strategically placed because—ironically—of segregation. What is also true is that Negroes have never been able to utilize the full voting potential of our numbers. Where we could vote, the case has always been that the white political machine stacks and gerrymanders the political subdivisions in Negro neighborhoods so the true voting strength is never reflected in political strength. Would anyone looking at the distribution of political power in Manhattan, ever think that Negroes represented 60% of the population there?

Just as often the effective political organization in Negro communities is absorbed by tokenism and patronage—the time honored practice of "giving" certain offices to selected Negroes. The machine thus creates a "little machine," which is subordinate and responsive to it, in the Negro community. These Negro political "leaders" are really vote deliverers, more responsible to the white machine and the white power structure, than to the community they allegedly represent. Thus the white community is able to substitute patronage control for audacious black power in the Negro community. This is precisely what Johnson tried to do even before the Voting Rights Act of 1966 was passed. The National Democrats made it very clear that the measure was intended to register Democrats, not Negroes. The President and top officials of the Democratic Party called in almost 100 selected Negro "leaders" from the Deep South. Nothing was said about changing the policies of the racist state parties, nothing was said about repudiating such leadership figures as Eastland and Ross Barnett in Mississippi or George Wallace in Alabama. What was said was simply "Go home and organize your people into the local Democratic Party—*then* we'll see about poverty money and appointments." (Incidentally, for the most part the War on Poverty in the South is controlled by local Democratic ward heelers—and outspoken racists who have used the program to change the form of the Negroes' dependence. People who were afraid to register for fear of being thrown off the farm are now afraid to register for fear of losing their Head-Start jobs.)

We must organize black community power to end these abuses, and to give the Negro community a chance to have its needs expressed. A leadership which is truly "responsible"—not to the white press and power structure, but to the community—must be developed. Such leadership will recognize that its power lies in the unified and collective strength of that community. This will make it difficult for the white leadership group to conduct its dialogue with individuals in terms of patronage and prestige, and will force them to talk to the community's representatives in terms of real power.

The single aspect of the black power program that has encountered most criticism is this concept of independent organization. This is presented as third-partyism which has never worked, or a withdrawal into black nationalism and isolationism. If such a program is developed it will not have the effect of isolating the Negro community but the reverse. When the Negro community is able to control local office, and negotiate with other groups from a position of organized strength, the possibility of meaningful political alliances on specific issues will be increased. That is a rule of politics and there is no reason why it should not operate here. The only difference is that we will have the power to define the terms of these alliances.

The next question usually is, "So—can it work, can the ghettoes in fact be organized?" The answer is that this organization must be successful, because there are no viable alternatives—not the War on 676

Poverty, which was at its inception limited to dealing with effects rather than causes, and has become simply another source of machine patronage. And "Integration" is meaningful only to a small chosen class within the community.

The revolution in agricultural technology in the South is displacing the rural Negro community into northern urban areas. Both Washington, D. C. and Newark, N. J. have Negro majorities. One third of Philadelphia's population of two million people is black. "Inner city" in most major urban areas is already predominantly Negro, and with the white rush to suburbia, Negroes will in the next three decades control the heart of our great cities. These areas can become either concentration camps with a bitter and volatile population whose only power is the power to destroy, or organized and powerful communities able to make constructive contributions to the total society. Without the power to control their lives and their communities, without effective political institutions through which to relate to the total society, these communities will exist in a constant state of insurrection. This is a choice that the country will have to make.

677

George Grant

Realism in Political Protest

I speak as a Canadian nationalist and as a conservative. It is necessary to start here for the following reason. To speak of the moral responsibility of the citizen in general is impossible; the question entirely depends on the kind of regime in which one is a citizen. The United States is a world empire—the largest to date. Its life at home is controlled by mammoth corporations, private and public, and through these bureaucracies it reaches out to control a large proportion of the globe and soon beyond the globe. The nineteenth century idea of the democratic citizen making the society he inhabits by the vote and the support of political parties must have less and less meaning. In local matters, the citizen of an empire can achieve some minor goals. But he cannot shape the larger institutions or move the centres of power.

Democratic citizenship is not a notion compatible with technological empires. Now Canada moves more and more to being a satellite of that empire. And Canadians live much of their lives under the same imperial bureaucracies. The institutions of Toronto are much the same as those of Detroit. Yet despite this there is a sense in which we still have more citizenship here than in the U.S. because we have some political sovereignty, if we fight for it. Traditional democratic means—the vote and support for political parties—have more meaning in our smaller sphere. Political choice is both more real and more possible in Canada. This might be truly useful to the world, if we in Canada could use it to see that North American relations with Asia did not always simply follow Washington.

But to pass to the broader question of what it is to be a citizen in

Reprinted by permission of the author from *Christian Outlook*, November 1967, pp. 3–6. George Grant, D. Phil., F. R. S. C., is professor of religion at McMaster University, Hamilton, Ontario.

North America in this era, let me start from the position of the New Left, that is, the movement which has public significance because of what it did in the civil rights struggle. I find myself in agreement with the account the leaders of this movement give of the inhumanity of the institutions of North America. When I read Professor Lynd in *Liberation* speaking of what the institutions of his society do to human personality both at home and abroad, I agree with his account of those institutions. When I hear what Mr. Savio in Berkeley or Mr. Drushka in Toronto write about the inhumanity of our multiversities, by and large I agree with them. How can a conservative not feel sympathy with their outrage against the emptiness and dehumanization that this society produces?

But when the New Left speaks of overcoming these conditions by protest, I think they are indulging in dreams—dangerous dreams. The moral fervour that accompanies such dreams is too valuable to be wasted on anything but reality. When they speak as if it were possible by marching and sitting to turn North American society away from being an empire protecting its interests in the world, by violence, I just do not know how they can think this. When some of them speak as if the empires of the East were not moving in the same social direction as the United States, I think they are deluding themselves. When they propose that our modern universities can be overcome and turned into humane sources of enlightenment, I think they have not looked at our society closely enough.

Their politics of hope and of Utopia—indeed with some of them another outbreak of the traditional form of the politics of the apocalypse—seems to me a kind of dream from which analysis should awaken them. They seem to think that these massive institutions which stifle human excellence can be overcome, and I think this arises from a profound misinterpretation of modern history. For several centuries the chief energies of western society have been directed to the mastery of nature—at first non-human nature and now human nature. We now live in the era where that process moves quickly to its apotheosis. The motive of this pursuit was that by it men should be made free. Freedom was its rallying cry. And it is in the pursuit of this dream of freedom that we have built the mammoth institutions, international and national, in which we live. This pursuit of the mastery of nature has gained men great victories over natural necessity. Who can doubt that? But at the same time as it has produced these victories, it has subjected men to the forces of the artificial necessities of the technological society. "The further the technical mechanism develops which allows us to escape natural necessity, the more we are subjected to artificial technical necessities. The artificial necessity of technique is not less harsh and implacable for being much less obviously menacing than natural necessity." (J. Ellul, *The Technological Society*). This is the crucial question about citizenship in this era: what 679 is it to be a citizen in this new society ruled by its technical apparatus?

What I do not see is why anybody should believe that by some dialectical process of history there should suddenly spring out of this technological society a free and humane society. First western men and now men everywhere in the world are driving with enormous speed to the building of this technological strait jacket. This is a society which by its very mammoth nature must destroy the idea of the responsible citizen. What evidence is there for believing that this system can by protest be turned towards the ends of human excellence? What reason have we for believing that the vast imperial structures will act towards each other and towards their neighbours in a nobler way than empires have in the past? The Empires may restrain themselves from fright. But the small nations who are unfortunate enough to be caught between them will be ground between the millstones. And to speak about the institutions I know best—the universities—what reason is there to believe that they can be diverted from the very purpose for which they exist? The modern universities exist above all' to provide personnel to feed the vast technological apparatus. That technological apparatus is now autonomous and produces its own needs which are quite detached from human needs. Are such institutions which are of the very fabric of the modern quest to be diverted from this end?

TECHNOLOGICAL STRAIT JACKET

The supreme example of the autonomy of technique is surely the space programme. If it is possible for man to do something it must be done. Vast resources of brains, money, materials are poured out in the U.S. and U.S.S.R. to keep this fantastic programme proliferating. And it is accepted by the masses in both societies not only as necessary but as man's crowning glory. One leader of the U.S. space programme said that as we cannot change the environment of space, we will have to change man. So we are going to produce beings half flesh, half electronic organs. If it can be done, it must be done and it surely will be done. This is what I mean by the autonomy of technique. The question whether technique serves human good is no longer asked. It has become an end in itself.

There is a lot of talk among the New Left about the present system of society collapsing because of its internal contradictions. What signs are there of that collapse? The American system with its extension into western Europe seems to me supremely confident and to have the overwhelming majority of its citizens behind it—the same seems true of the Russian system and will be increasingly true of the Chinese system.

One immediate reason why I think the New Left is deluded about what is happening in North America is because it has misinterpreted 680 the events which took place in the southern United States. It says today: look at our triumphs in the south; we will now carry these triumphs of citizen action into new fields of social revolution. What has been forgotten is that the powerful among the people and institutions of North America were more than willing that the society of the white south should be broken. The civil rights movement had behind it all the powerful forces of the American empire. It marched protected by federal troops, it had the blessing of the leading government figures. It was encouraged night after night by N.B.C. and C.B.S. There was violence from the white south, but the white south is not an important part of the American power elite. It will surely be a different matter when the protests are against some position which is dear and close to the American liberal establishment. We have only to think of how much is immediately accomplished by protests about Vietnam, the Dominican Republic or nuclear policy. Anyway, dissent and protest are themselves bureaucratized in our society. They are taken into the system and trivialized. They are made to serve the interests of the system they are supposed to be attacking by showing that free speech is allowed.

I am not advocating inaction or cynicism. Nothing I have said denies for one moment the nobility of protest. Nothing I have said denies that justice is good and that injustice is evil and that it is required of human beings to know the difference between the two. To live with courage in the world is always better than retreat or disillusion. Human beings are less than themselves when they are cut off from being citizens. Indeed one of' the finest things about the present protest movements in North America is that they try to give meaning to citizenship in a society which by its enormity and impersonality cuts people off from the public world. Anybody who lives within a university must know that the students who care enough about the world to protest are much finer than those who are interested in public affairs simply because they want to climb within the system and use it to gain recognition for their egos. Indeed how much finer are those who protest than those who crawl through the university simply as a guarantee of the slow road to death in the suburbs. In our monolithic society, the pressures upon the individual to retreat from the public sphere are immense. The new politics of protest have tried to overcome those pressures and to give new meaning to citizenship. Nobody should attack them for that.

What I am arguing against is the politics based on easy hopes about the future human situation. The hope, for example, that some future transformation of power in North America is going to overcome the implicit difficulties of the technological apparatus. That North American society can in the future be radically changed in its direction. Hope in the future has been and is the chief opiate of modern life. Its danger is that it prevents men from looking clearly at their situa-   681 tion. It teaches them to dream dreams instead of coming to terms with facts. The most dangerous quality of the politics of Utopia is that it can easily turn into despair. If people have vast expectations of hope about a society such as ours, they are going to be disappointed and then their moral fervour can turn rancid and bitter. Moral fervour is too precious a commodity not to be put in the service of reality.

If protest is to be effective in this era, if we are to be successful in creating space for human spontaneity in the iron maiden of the technical apparatus we have created, then it is essential that those who are in the forefront of protest must combine with their action the deepest and most careful thought. Action without thought will be an impotent waste of time. In this ferocious era, if we are to keep ourselves human and to be effective citizens, then our first obligation is to be free. And by free I mean knowing the truth about things, to know what is so, without simplifications, without false hopes, without moral fervour divorced from moral clarity. The central Christian platitude still holds good: "The truth shall make you free." I use freedom here quite differently from those who believe that we are free when we have gained mastery over man and over nature. It is different even from the simple cry for political liberty: "Freedom now." For in the long pull, freedom without knowledge of reality is empty and vacuous. The greatest figure of our era, Gandhi, was interested in public action and in political liberty, but he knew that the right direction of that action had to be based on knowledge of reality—with all the discipline and order and study that that entailed.

Truth seeking is of course hard to accomplish in this society. Our universities have at many points retreated from it into fact gathering and technological mastery, what is now called the knowledge industry. Most of our social scientists have used the idea of a value free social science to opt out of the battle of what constitutes the good society, and spend their time discovering techniques for adjusting people to the system. The philosophers have often opted out to play clever professional games. Much of the religious tradition seems a worn out garment not able to help in the search for truth. Above all, what may hold people from the search for the truth is that the human situation in the totally realised mass world may be so unpalatable that we simply do not want to face it. If we do not face reality we may be able to avoid the great evils of despair and pessimism, but we also cut ourselves off from any chance of maturity and effectiveness.

I have concentrated on North America, because we in North America are inevitably in the forefront of the world. We are the society that has most completely realised the dominance of technique over every aspect of human life. Every year we are moving with prodigious speed to the greater and greater realisation of that system. All other societies move at various speeds to the same kind of society we are creating. 682

We are the first people who will have to learn what it is to be citizens in a society dominated by technique. Because that system is most fully realised with us, we are the first people who can look it in the face and we are called upon to see it for what it is and not fool ourselves about it. We must face the laws of its necessity—its potential to free men from natural necessity, its potential for inhumanity and tyranny. We must not delude ourselves and we must not throw up our hands. We must define our possible areas of influence with the most careful clarity. Where in this mammoth system can we use our intelligence and our love to open up spaces in which human excellence can exist? How can we use the most effective pressure to see that our empire uses moderation and restraint in its relations with the rest of the world? I end where I began, in agreement with the delegate from Cambodia, that our greatest obligation as Canadians is to work for a country which is not simply a satellite of any empire.

Michael Harrington

The Mystical Militants

The young radicals whose personal statements have appeared in *The New Republic* these past weeks are marvelously and problematically American. They are mystical militants, articulating the authentic miseries of the poor even while maintaining some of the attitudes of the middle class. They are also one of the most significant, hopeful developments in recent American life. I do not emphasize their importance as an uncritical compliment. They have already been subjected to quite enough journalistic flattery, and some of the mass media would probably like to package them as they did the Beats. Moreover, I have differences with the young radicals and have on occasion been puzzled, exasperated and even saddened by them. Yet the happy fact remains that the emergence of a personally committed generation seeking basic social change is momentous. They are a minority of their age group, to be sure, but a creative, activist minority who should place their stamp upon the times. Eventually, and it will probably try the anarchist spirit of some of them, they are going to lead adult movements and change this society. Whatever their shortcomings, the New Leftists hold out the hope for a renewal of American social criticism and action.

I do not intend to respond point by point to *The New Republic* series. Rather, what follows is an interpretive, discursive reaction to some of the themes the young radicals raise.

First, there is the Americanism of these rebels against American society.

When I became a radical in 1948 (the last year of the politics of

Reprinted by permission of the author and *The New Republic* from *The New Republic*, February 19, 1966, pp. 20–22. © 1966, Harrison-Blaine of New Jersey, Inc. Michael Harrington is Chairman of The Board of The League for Industrial Democracy.

the Thirties), it was taken for granted (on the Left) that the Fourth of July was really a front for the four hundred families. In part, this was a heritage of European socialist theory, in part a legacy of the American experience of a Depression which had demystified so many clichés. One did not get angry that the powers-that-be lied and cheated and manipulated. That, after all, was their function in life, just as is it was the task of the Left to create a society which would not need to corrupt its avowed values.

The young radicals of today, it seems to me. did not start with this inherited cynicism. They came to teenage during the American celebration of the Eisenhower years and were, for the most part, not really conscious until after both Korea and McCarthyism. They seemed to have believed what they were told about freedom, equality, justice, world peace and the like. They became activists in order to affirm these traditional values with regard to some ethical cause: defending civil liberties against HUAC, picketing for the life of Caryl Chessman, demanding an end to nuclear testing, fighting for civil rights. The shock generated by the society's duplicity in this or that single issue then opened their eyes to larger, and even more systematic, injustices.

It is, I suspect, this unique Fifties-Sixties experience which gives the New Left its distinctive flavor: a sense of outrage, of having been betrayed by all the father-figures, which derives from an original innocence. And it is also the source of the young radicals' insistence on sincerity and community. They begin, not with an image of the future which was received, in one way or another, from Europe and involves theory and history, but from a sense of the immediate contradiction between democratic posturing and the undemocratic reality. They descend from the Abolitionists and Wobblies, not from Marx.

This intense, even painful, consciousness of American hypocrisy has led the young radicals to people who do not, or cannot, play the national rhetorical game: the left-outs, the outcasts. And it has involved them in a contradiction between mysticism and militancy.

In the iconography of the Thirties, the proletarian was a figure of incipient power and a Puritan sense of duty. The *lumpen* proletarian was despised because he did not belong to a conscious class, because he floated; and he was feared as a potential shock trooper of fascism. By the Fifties, much of the old élan had left the labor movement and, with an overwhelming majority of the people satisfied with Eisenhower, there did not seem to be much of a political perspective for insurgency. At this point a cultural rebellion took place among young people. It was expressed among the Beats who contracted out of the system; it informed Norman Mailer's vision of the white man who aspired to the cool and the hip which white society provoked in the Negro.

685

As disestablishmentarians, the young radicals continue this tradition of the Fifties. They identify precisely with the *lumpen,* the powerless, the maimed, the poor, the criminal, the junkie. And there is a mystical element in this commitment which has nothing to do with politics. By going into the slum, they are doing penance for the sins of affluence; by sharing the life of those who are so impoverished that they are uncorrupted, values are affirmed. It is honest and moral and anti-hypocritical to be on the margin of society *whether the community organization works or not.* Indeed, there is a fear of "success," a suspicion that it would mean the integration of the oppressed into the corruption of the oppressors.

But, on the other hand, the New Leftists are not Fifties Beats (and, by the way, I do not use the term Beat pejoratively). They are angry militants who see the poor as a new force in America, perhaps even as a substitute for the proletariat that failed. So Stokely Carmichael, one of the best of the breed, insists that the Mississippi and Alabama sharecroppers can choose for themselves. He understands that ultimately, to paraphrase an old labor song, no one can abolish poverty for you, you've got to abolish it yourself. And from this point of view, it does make quite a bit of difference whether the community organizing campaign works or not.

An analogy from the Thirties might illuminate the political hope that is here asserted by the young radicals. In 1932 or 1933, many polite Americans believed that if you gave a worker a bathtub, he would put coal in it. And the skilled AFL members thought it preposterous that mass production machine operators could form *their own* union. On paper, the right to organize was proclaimed by the Wagner Act. In fact, it took at least five tumultuous years of picketing, striking and sitting-in before the CIO turned the brave words into something of a reality. Similarly in 1964, America declared war on poverty; and most of the well-bred citizenry did not intend by that to have field hands and janitors speaking up for themselves; and the young radicals, who have this knack of taking America's promises seriously, sought a surge from below to give meaning to the phrase-making on high. But, as I think the New Left realizes, this analogy is faulty in part. The mass production workers were, just as radical theory had said, forced by the conditions of their existence (thousands of men assembled at one miserable place with common problems and interests) into a solidarity which became the basis of union organization. The poor, as Tom Hayden noted in his *New Republic* contribution, are not grouped into incipient communities. A slum street fragments and atomizes people; the two largest groups of the poor, the young and the old, have little to do with one another; and even if they could get together, the poor are still a minority of the society. Therefore it is going to take even more creativity to help the outcasts into their own than it did to build industrial unionism.

686

For a number of reasons, the New Leftists shied away, until quite recently, from thinking through the problems posed by their own militancy. For one thing, they are indeed "American" in the empirical, activist, anti-theoretical sense of the word. For another, they rejected the scholasticism of some of the traditional Left formulae (as well as the genuine profundity of the Left's intellectual heritage) and they were imbued with the spirit of the civil rights movement of the early Sixties where the willingness to go to jail was more important than political abstractions. This winter there have been signs that the young radicals are moving into a phase of discussion and debate (at a Christmas vacation meeting at the University of Illinois, the SDS militants discussed political strategy, ideology, Communism, the role of women in the movement, etc.). And this is necessary if the conflict of mysticism and militancy is to be resolved. For if the poor are seen as Dostoevskian peasants whose beauty is their suffering, then politics and the inevitable alliances with others is a contamination; but if they are to be a social force, then coalition is a necessity.

The New Leftists regard the welfare state, rather than the economic royalists, as the incarnation of the status quo. This is an almost inevitable result of trying to look at America with the eyes of the poor. It is very right—and it is a dangerous half-truth.

The welfare state developed in the Thirties was created by, and for, the "middle third" of American society: the liberal middle class and the organized workers. The poor were, and still are, those who were left behind in the Depression because of bad geographical, occupational or political luck: migrants, farm workers, full-time laborers at poverty jobs, racial and ethnic minorities which came into the economic mainstream at the time of the computer rather than of the assembly line. In addition, the poor include all those who have suffered from a *relative deterioration* in various social insurance and income maintenance programs (social security, unemployment compensation, etc.).

The visible enemies of the poor are not the captains of industry but the landlords, shopkeepers and, often enough, the agents of the welfare state. For the welfare state is, of course, ill-financed and bureaucratic, and this distorts the good intentions of many of the fine people who work for it and it reinforces the vices of the bad. So for the poor the welfare state means a humiliating dependence and fear, and requires a constant, cunning, battle against authority. The young radicals attempt to articulate these fierce resentments which they discovered in the slums, and the experience does not leave them in a mood for sociological nicety. The welfare state is, they say, a fraud. And the liberals, who actually boast of having created this monster 687 in the name of humane values are therefore the worst hypocrites. In formulating this attitude, it is not simply that the New Leftists overlook some history, which youth always does, but that they ignore some *relevant* history. The welfare state did not come out of the Thirties as a result of a liberal plot to manipulate the dispossessed. It was created over the violent resistance of most men of property and wealth, and its creation required a major upheaval on the part of the workers, from the bottom up. Business did not begin its conversion to welfare statism until the World War II discovery that a federal agency staffed by corporation executives was not exactly a class enemy of the rich; and its final conversion to "tax cut" Keynesianism waited upon the persuasiveness of Lyndon B. Johnson. There was, and is, a very real element of buying off the restless natives in business acceptance of welfarism.

The relevance of this history is that the current welfare state consensus is not quite so homogeneous as the President and some New Leftists sometimes think. For the apparent agreement conceals the latent conflict between the sophisticated conservatives on the one hand, and the liberal-labor-civil rights forces on the other. One can rightly accuse the liberal welfarists of having been too nostalgically proud of *their* upheaval to understand the terrible urgency of more change now as seen from the bottom of society. But it is something else again to *equate* all present supporters of the welfare state with one another.

ACTING OUT A MORALITY PLAY

And here I think I come to my most serious criticism of the New Radicals: that they sometimes expect the poor to act out the moral values of the middle-class radical who has come to the slum.

I find, for instance, a genuine poignancy in Tom Hayden's realization that a coalition of the outcasts will not really be able to change the society and that radicalism can only give itself up to, and become part of, "the energy kept restless and active under the clamps of paralyzed imperial society. Radicalism then would go beyond the concepts of optimism and pessimism as guides to work, finding itself in working despite odds. Its realism and sanity would be grounded in nothing more than the ability to face whatever comes."

This attitude is a logical deduction from theory that all the welfare staters, from Henry Ford to Walter Reuther if you will, are the same kind of manipulative bureaucrats. For if everybody but the poor and outcast are "them," then "we" must inevitably lose, for by definition "we" are not strong enough to transform a fraud and scandal supported by 60 or 70 percent of the society.

The conscious and committed radical can find his solace in such a vision; most of the poor, I suspect, cannot. Indeed, one of the things that has made the poor so inarticulate, so unorganized, so hopeless, 688 is precisely the conviction that they can't win. Are they now to be told stoically to treasure their misery which, though permanent, is at least not corrupted by the hypocrisy of affluence? That will be cold comfort. And it will not move them to action, but rather reinforce them in their passivity.

The danger is that the poor will thus be assigned roles as abstractions in the morality plays of the disenchanted middle class. To fight this possibility, the New Leftists must come up with a strategy which offers real hope to the other America. And this means making a more sophisticated analysis of the coalition which supports the welfare state.

For the liberal wing of this consensus certainly did not start with the intention to build a manipulative bureaucracy, and it maintains values which *could* provide a basis for transforming the present structure. If the social-change movements of the previous generation must be shaken up by the poor, they must be shaken up in order to be made allies. To do this requires an intensification of the efforts to organize the slums and ghettos and backwoods as an independent political force. But if there is to be honest hope, that organization must be thought of as the catalyst of a new political majority in the United States, and not as a doomed last stand of noble savages.

There is reason to hope that these new directions will be taken. An incredibly American generation in our midst has become radical by taking the house platitudes seriously. Its hatred of hypocrisy and its identification with the outcasts are magnificent; its empiricism and its middle-class mysticism are sometimes troubling. Now that New Leftists are becoming more reflective, their anger and their activism should become even more effective, their radicalism that much deeper and more profound.